Lecture Notes in Computer Science   14054

The series Lecture Notes in Computer Science (LNCS), including its subseries Lecture Notes in Artificial Intelligence (LNAI) and Lecture Notes in Bioinformatics (LNBI), has established itself as a medium for the publication of new developments in computer science and information technology research, teaching, and education.

LNCS enjoys close cooperation with the computer science R & D community, the series counts many renowned academics among its volume editors and paper authors, and collaborates with prestigious societies. Its mission is to serve this international community by providing an invaluable service, mainly focused on the publication of conference and workshop proceedings and postproceedings. LNCS commenced publication in 1973.

Masaaki Kurosu · Ayako Hashizume ·
Aaron Marcus · Elizabeth Rosenzweig ·
Marcelo M. Soares · Don Harris · Wen-Chin Li ·
Dylan D. Schmorrow · Cali M. Fidopiastis ·
Pei-Luen Patrick Rau
Editors

HCI International 2023 – Late Breaking Papers

25th International Conference on Human-Computer Interaction
HCII 2023, Copenhagen, Denmark, July 23–28, 2023
Proceedings, Part I

 Springer

Editors
Masaaki Kurosu
The Open University of Japan
Chiba, Japan

Ayako Hashizume
Hosei University
Tokyo, Japan

Aaron Marcus
Aaron Marcus and Associates
Berkeley, CA, USA

Elizabeth Rosenzweig
World Usability Day and Bubble Mountain
Consulting
Newton Center, MA, USA

Marcelo M. Soares
Southern University of Science
and Technology
Shenzhen, China

Don Harris
Coventry University
Coventry, UK

Wen-Chin Li
Cranfield University
Cranfield, UK

Dylan D. Schmorrow
Soar Technology Inc.
Orlando, FL, USA

Cali M. Fidopiastis
Katmai Government Services
Orlando, FL, USA

Pei-Luen Patrick Rau
Tsinghua University
Beijing, China

ISSN 0302-9743   ISSN 1611-3349 (electronic)
Lecture Notes in Computer Science
ISBN 978-3-031-48037-9   ISBN 978-3-031-48038-6 (eBook)
https://doi.org/10.1007/978-3-031-48038-6

This Springer imprint is published by the registered company Springer Nature Switzerland AG
The registered company address is: Gewerbestrasse 11, 6330 Cham, Switzerland

Paper in this product is recyclable.

Foreword

Human-computer interaction (HCI) is acquiring an ever-increasing scientific and industrial importance, as well as having more impact on people's everyday lives, as an ever-growing number of human activities are progressively moving from the physical to the digital world. This process, which has been ongoing for some time now, was further accelerated during the acute period of the COVID-19 pandemic. The HCI International (HCII) conference series, held annually, aims to respond to the compelling need to advance the exchange of knowledge and research and development efforts on the human aspects of design and use of computing systems.

The 25th International Conference on Human-Computer Interaction, HCI International 2023 (HCII 2023), was held in the emerging post-pandemic era as a 'hybrid' event at the AC Bella Sky Hotel and Bella Center, Copenhagen, Denmark, during July 23–28, 2023. It incorporated the 21 thematic areas and affiliated conferences listed below.

A total of 7472 individuals from academia, research institutes, industry, and government agencies from 85 countries submitted contributions, and 1578 papers and 396 posters were included in the volumes of the proceedings that were published just before the start of the conference. Additionally, 267 papers and 133 posters were included in the volumes of the proceedings published after the conference, as "Late Breaking Work". The contributions thoroughly cover the entire field of human-computer interaction, addressing major advances in knowledge and effective use of computers in a variety of application areas. These papers provide academics, researchers, engineers, scientists, practitioners and students with state-of-the-art information on the most recent advances in HCI. The volumes constituting the full set of the HCII 2023 conference proceedings are listed on the following pages.

I would like to thank the Program Board Chairs and the members of the Program Boards of all thematic areas and affiliated conferences for their contribution towards the high scientific quality and overall success of the HCI International 2023 conference. Their manifold support in terms of paper reviewing (single-blind review process, with a minimum of two reviews per submission), session organization and their willingness to act as goodwill ambassadors for the conference is most highly appreciated.

This conference would not have been possible without the continuous and unwavering support and advice of Gavriel Salvendy, founder, General Chair Emeritus, and Scientific Advisor. For his outstanding efforts, I would like to express my sincere appreciation to Abbas Moallem, Communications Chair and Editor of HCI International News.

July 2023   Constantine Stephanidis

HCI International 2023 Thematic Areas and Affiliated Conferences

Thematic Areas

- HCI: Human-Computer Interaction
- HIMI: Human Interface and the Management of Information

Affiliated Conferences

- EPCE: 20th International Conference on Engineering Psychology and Cognitive Ergonomics
- AC: 17th International Conference on Augmented Cognition
- UAHCI: 17th International Conference on Universal Access in Human-Computer Interaction
- CCD: 15th International Conference on Cross-Cultural Design
- SCSM: 15th International Conference on Social Computing and Social Media
- VAMR: 15th International Conference on Virtual, Augmented and Mixed Reality
- DHM: 14th International Conference on Digital Human Modeling and Applications in Health, Safety, Ergonomics and Risk Management
- DUXU: 12th International Conference on Design, User Experience and Usability
- C&C: 11th International Conference on Culture and Computing
- DAPI: 11th International Conference on Distributed, Ambient and Pervasive Interactions
- HCIBGO: 10th International Conference on HCI in Business, Government and Organizations
- LCT: 10th International Conference on Learning and Collaboration Technologies
- ITAP: 9th International Conference on Human Aspects of IT for the Aged Population
- AIS: 5th International Conference on Adaptive Instructional Systems
- HCI-CPT: 5th International Conference on HCI for Cybersecurity, Privacy and Trust
- HCI-Games: 5th International Conference on HCI in Games
- MobiTAS: 5th International Conference on HCI in Mobility, Transport and Automotive Systems
- AI-HCI: 4th International Conference on Artificial Intelligence in HCI
- MOBILE: 4th International Conference on Design, Operation and Evaluation of Mobile Communications

Conference Proceedings – Full List of Volumes

1. LNCS 14011, Human-Computer Interaction: Part I, edited by Masaaki Kurosu and Ayako Hashizume
2. LNCS 14012, Human-Computer Interaction: Part II, edited by Masaaki Kurosu and Ayako Hashizume
3. LNCS 14013, Human-Computer Interaction: Part III, edited by Masaaki Kurosu and Ayako Hashizume
4. LNCS 14014, Human-Computer Interaction: Part IV, edited by Masaaki Kurosu and Ayako Hashizume
5. LNCS 14015, Human Interface and the Management of Information: Part I, edited by Hirohiko Mori and Yumi Asahi
6. LNCS 14016, Human Interface and the Management of Information: Part II, edited by Hirohiko Mori and Yumi Asahi
7. LNAI 14017, Engineering Psychology and Cognitive Ergonomics: Part I, edited by Don Harris and Wen-Chin Li
8. LNAI 14018, Engineering Psychology and Cognitive Ergonomics: Part II, edited by Don Harris and Wen-Chin Li
9. LNAI 14019, Augmented Cognition, edited by Dylan D. Schmorrow and Cali M. Fidopiastis
10. LNCS 14020, Universal Access in Human-Computer Interaction: Part I, edited by Margherita Antona and Constantine Stephanidis
11. LNCS 14021, Universal Access in Human-Computer Interaction: Part II, edited by Margherita Antona and Constantine Stephanidis
12. LNCS 14022, Cross-Cultural Design: Part I, edited by Pei-Luen Patrick Rau
13. LNCS 14023, Cross-Cultural Design: Part II, edited by Pei-Luen Patrick Rau
14. LNCS 14024, Cross-Cultural Design: Part III, edited by Pei-Luen Patrick Rau
15. LNCS 14025, Social Computing and Social Media: Part I, edited by Adela Coman and Simona Vasilache
16. LNCS 14026, Social Computing and Social Media: Part II, edited by Adela Coman and Simona Vasilache
17. LNCS 14027, Virtual, Augmented and Mixed Reality, edited by Jessie Y.C. Chen and Gino Fragomeni
18. LNCS 14028, Digital Human Modeling and Applications in Health, Safety, Ergonomics and Risk Management: Part I, edited by Vincent G. Duffy
19. LNCS 14029, Digital Human Modeling and Applications in Health, Safety, Ergonomics and Risk Management: Part II, edited by Vincent G. Duffy
20. LNCS 14030, Design, User Experience, and Usability: Part I, edited by Aaron Marcus, Elizabeth Rosenzweig and Marcelo Soares
21. LNCS 14031, Design, User Experience, and Usability: Part II, edited by Aaron Marcus, Elizabeth Rosenzweig and Marcelo Soares
22. LNCS 14032, Design, User Experience, and Usability: Part III, edited by Aaron Marcus, Elizabeth Rosenzweig and Marcelo Soares

23. LNCS 14033, Design, User Experience, and Usability: Part IV, edited by Aaron Marcus, Elizabeth Rosenzweig and Marcelo Soares
24. LNCS 14034, Design, User Experience, and Usability: Part V, edited by Aaron Marcus, Elizabeth Rosenzweig and Marcelo Soares
25. LNCS 14035, Culture and Computing, edited by Matthias Rauterberg
26. LNCS 14036, Distributed, Ambient and Pervasive Interactions: Part I, edited by Norbert Streitz and Shin'ichi Konomi
27. LNCS 14037, Distributed, Ambient and Pervasive Interactions: Part II, edited by Norbert Streitz and Shin'ichi Konomi
28. LNCS 14038, HCI in Business, Government and Organizations: Part I, edited by Fiona Fui-Hoon Nah and Keng Siau
29. LNCS 14039, HCI in Business, Government and Organizations: Part II, edited by Fiona Fui-Hoon Nah and Keng Siau
30. LNCS 14040, Learning and Collaboration Technologies: Part I, edited by Panayiotis Zaphiris and Andri Ioannou
31. LNCS 14041, Learning and Collaboration Technologies: Part II, edited by Panayiotis Zaphiris and Andri Ioannou
32. LNCS 14042, Human Aspects of IT for the Aged Population: Part I, edited by Qin Gao and Jia Zhou
33. LNCS 14043, Human Aspects of IT for the Aged Population: Part II, edited by Qin Gao and Jia Zhou
34. LNCS 14044, Adaptive Instructional Systems, edited by Robert A. Sottilare and Jessica Schwarz
35. LNCS 14045, HCI for Cybersecurity, Privacy and Trust, edited by Abbas Moallem
36. LNCS 14046, HCI in Games: Part I, edited by Xiaowen Fang
37. LNCS 14047, HCI in Games: Part II, edited by Xiaowen Fang
38. LNCS 14048, HCI in Mobility, Transport and Automotive Systems: Part I, edited by Heidi Krömker
39. LNCS 14049, HCI in Mobility, Transport and Automotive Systems: Part II, edited by Heidi Krömker
40. LNAI 14050, Artificial Intelligence in HCI: Part I, edited by Helmut Degen and Stavroula Ntoa
41. LNAI 14051, Artificial Intelligence in HCI: Part II, edited by Helmut Degen and Stavroula Ntoa
42. LNCS 14052, Design, Operation and Evaluation of Mobile Communications, edited by Gavriel Salvendy and June Wei
43. CCIS 1832, HCI International 2023 Posters: Part I, edited by Constantine Stephanidis, Margherita Antona, Stavroula Ntoa and Gavriel Salvendy
44. CCIS 1833, HCI International 2023 Posters: Part II, edited by Constantine Stephanidis, Margherita Antona, Stavroula Ntoa and Gavriel Salvendy
45. CCIS 1834, HCI International 2023 Posters: Part III, edited by Constantine Stephanidis, Margherita Antona, Stavroula Ntoa and Gavriel Salvendy
46. CCIS 1835, HCI International 2023 Posters: Part IV, edited by Constantine Stephanidis, Margherita Antona, Stavroula Ntoa and Gavriel Salvendy
47. CCIS 1836, HCI International 2023 Posters: Part V, edited by Constantine Stephanidis, Margherita Antona, Stavroula Ntoa and Gavriel Salvendy

48. LNCS 14054, HCI International 2023 - Late Breaking Papers: Part I, edited by Masaaki Kurosu, Ayako Hashizume, Aaron Marcus, Elizabeth Rosenzweig, Marcelo Soares, Don Harris, Wen-Chin Li, Dylan D. Schmorrow, Cali M. Fidopiastis, and Pei-Luen Patrick Rau
49. LNCS 14055, HCI International 2023 - Late Breaking Papers: Part II, edited by Qin Gao, Jia Zhou, Vincent G. Duffy, Margherita Antona, and Constantine Stephanidis
50. LNCS 14056, HCI International 2023 - Late Breaking Papers: Part III, edited by Hirohiko Mori, Yumi Asahi, Adela Coman, Simona Vasilache, and Matthias Rauterberg
51. LNCS 14057, HCI International 2023 - Late Breaking Papers: Part IV, edited by Vincent G. Duffy, Heidi Krömker, Norbert A. Streitz, and Shin'ichi Konomi
52. LNCS 14058, HCI International 2023 - Late Breaking Papers: Part V, edited by Jessie Y. C. Chen, Gino Fragomeni, and Xiaowen Fang
53. LNCS 14059, HCI International 2023 - Late Breaking Papers: Part VI, edited by Helmut Degen, Stavroula Ntoa, and Abbas Moallem
54. LNCS 14060, HCI International 2023 - Late Breaking Papers: Part VII, edited by Panayiotis Zaphiris, Andri Ioannou, Robert A. Sottilare, Jessica Schwarz, Fiona Fui-Hoon Nah, Keng Siau, June Wei, and Gavriel Salvendy
55. CCIS 1957, HCI International 2023 - Late Breaking Posters: Part I, edited by Constantine Stephanidis, Margherita Antona, Stavroula Ntoa, and Gavriel Salvendy
56. CCIS 1958, HCI International 2023 - Late Breaking Posters: Part II, edited by Constantine Stephanidis, Margherita Antona, Stavroula Ntoa, and Gavriel Salvendy

https://2023.hci.international/proceedings

25th International Conference on Human-Computer Interaction (HCII 2023)

The full list with the Program Board Chairs and the members of the Program Boards of all thematic areas and affiliated conferences of HCII2023 is available online at:

http://www.hci.international/board-members-2023.php

HCI International 2024 Conference

The 26th International Conference on Human-Computer Interaction, HCI International 2024, will be held jointly with the affiliated conferences at the Washington Hilton Hotel, Washington, DC, USA, June 29 – July 4, 2024. It will cover a broad spectrum of themes related to Human-Computer Interaction, including theoretical issues, methods, tools, processes, and case studies in HCI design, as well as novel interaction techniques, interfaces, and applications. The proceedings will be published by Springer. More information will be made available on the conference website: http://2024.hci.international/.

General Chair
Prof. Constantine Stephanidis
University of Crete and ICS-FORTH
Heraklion, Crete, Greece
Email: general_chair@2024.hci.international

https://2024.hci.international/

Contents – Part I

HCI Design and User Experience

Israel Railways App – From Research to Design 3
  Nitzan Avitouv

Literature Review on Human-Automation Interaction: Relation Between
Work from Home and Virtual Environments 16
  Min Ho Cho, Andrew Ravi Kamalraj, and Vincent G. Duffy

Gesture Hub Design: A Remote User Study Method for Evaluating
the Quality of Experience in Mobile Phone-Based Gesture Interaction 37
  Haoyu Dong, Jun Zhang, Wei Wang, Yijing Yang, Qi Chen, and Le Du

A Preliminary Study on the Kansei Evaluation of Physical and Virtual
Operation Interfaces 54
  Shih-Cheng Fann

Designing Multimodal User Interfaces for Hybrid Collaboration:
A User-Centered Approach 67
  Rongrong Gong and Min Hua

Enhancing the Natural Conversation Experience Through Conversation
Analysis – A Design Method 83
  Spencer Hazel and Adam Brandt

A Scoping Review of Mental Model Research in HCI from 2010 to 2021 101
  Xinhui Hu and Michael Twidale

Kinesiological Study of Wushu Performance: Toward Performer-Centered
Co-development of Wushu Taolu 126
  Yosuke Kinoe and Kana Ikeuchi

Negotiating Water Cooler Conversations Remotely: Perspectives from PhD
Students During COVID-19 142
  Xiaoyan Li and Susan R. Fussell

The Role of Audio in Visual Perception of Quality 155
  Maria Laura Mele, Damon Millar, and Silvia Colabrese

A Study on Variational Autoencoder to Extract Characteristic Patterns
from Electroencephalograms and Electrogastrograms   168
     Kohki Nakane, Rintaro Sugie, Meiho Nakayama, Yasuyuki Matsuura,
     Tomoki Shiozawa, and Hiroki Takada

Why Did the User Open the Email? - A Case Study in User Engagement   179
     Pankati Patel, Uko Ebreso, Alexander Fisher, and Patricia Morreale

Research on the Efficiency and Cognition of the Combination of Front
Color and Background Color and Color in the Interface of Express
Cabinets on the Operation of Human Machine Interface Tasks   194
     Yuying Pei, Linlin Wang, and Chengqi Xue

Episodic Future Thinking as Digital Micro-interventions   213
     Dan Roland Persson, Soojeong Yoo, Jakob E. Bardram,
     Timothy C. Skinner, and Per Bækgaard

Blink, Pull, Nudge or Tap? The Impact of Secondary Input Modalities
on Eye-Typing Performance   238
     Chris Porter and Gary Zammit

Research on Emotional Home Product Design Based on Five Senses
Experience   259
     Qianhang Qin, Yingyu Liao, Wenda Tian, Youtian Zhou, and Gengyi Wang

Exploration of Product Innovation Ideas Based on the Relationship
Between Science and Design   272
     Shuwen Qiu, Zixuan Huang, and Ying Cao

The Choice of a Persona: An Analysis of Why Stakeholders Choose
a Given Persona for a Design Task   288
     Joni Salminen, Sercan Şengün, João M. Santos, Soon-gyo Jung,
     Lene Nielsen, and Bernard Jansen

Machine Learning for Gaze-Based Selection: Performance Assessment
Without Explicit Labeling   311
     Yulia G. Shevtsova, Anatoly N. Vasilyev, and Sergei L. Shishkin

The Effect of Pseudo-Haptic Feedback on Weight Perception of Virtual
Objects on the Computer Side   323
     Yan Wang and Fan Qian

Gesture Mediated Timbre-Led Design based Music Interface
for Socio-musical Interaction   335
     Azeema Yaseen, Sutirtha Chakraborty, and Joseph Timoney

Cognitive Engineering and Augmented Cognition

A Helping Hand: Benefits of Primary Task Haptic Augmentation
on Secondary Visuospatial Task Performance 351
   Charlotte Collins, James Blundell, John Huddlestone, and Don Harris

Re-designing the Interaction of Day-to-Day Applications to Support
Sustained Attention Level 363
   Naile Hacioglu, Maria Chiara Leva, and Hyowon Lee

Research on Human Eye Fatigue Coefficient in Target Recognition Tasks 378
   Wanrong Han, Chengqi Xue, Shoupeng Li, and Xinyue Wang

Survey and Analysis on Experience Satisfaction of Remote ATC Tower
System User in China 389
   *Tingting Lu, Zhixuan An, Romano Pagliari, Haiming Shen, Zheng Yang,
   and Yiyang Zhang*

Resilience Strategies of Aviation During COVID-19 – A Bibliographical
Review 408
   Chien-Tsung Lu, Taoran Yin, and Haoruo Fu

Trends in Machine Learning and Electroencephalogram (EEG): A Review
for Undergraduate Researchers 426
   *Nathan Koome Murungi, Michael Vinh Pham, Xufeng Dai,
   and Xiaodong Qu*

A Study on Workload Assessment and Usability of Wind-Aware User
Interface for Small Unmanned Aircraft System Remote Operations 444
   Asma Tabassum, He Bai, and Nicoletta Fala

Influence of Movement Speed and Interaction Instructions on Subjective
Assessments, Performance and Psychophysiological Reactions During
Human-Robot Interaction 461
   *Verena Wagner-Hartl, Solveig Nakladal, Tobias Koch, Dzenan Babajic,
   Sergei Mazur, and Jonas Birkle*

Exploring the Challenges and Mitigations Associated with Operating
Multi-variant Aircraft 476
   Benjamin Whitworth and Rebecca Grant

Engineering Psychology in Job Design 491
   Anastasia Wood, Alexander Clark, and Vincent G. Duffy

Applying Touchscreen as Flight Control Inceptor: Investigating
the Perceived Workload of Interacting with Sidestick and Touchscreen
Inceptors 508
    Jingyi Zhang, Wen-Chin Li, and Wojciech Tomasz Korek

Cultural Issues in Design

Sustainability in Banana Tree Romanticism in the Economic Cycle
of Rural Community through Cultural Creative Design 523
    Erik Armayuda, Bayyinah Nurrul Haq, Damar Rangga Putra,
    and Ratih Mahardika

The Constraints of Global Design Systems on Local User Experience
Design 536
    Zhifang Du and Yong Xiao

From Useful Art to Service Design. Encouraging Migrants' Creative
Thinking Through Translocal Services for Social Innovation 552
    António Gorgel Pinto and Paula Reaes Pinto

Human Languages in HCI: Beyond User Interface Localization 564
    Diego Moreira da Rosa, Leandro Soares Guedes, Monica Landoni,
    and Milene Silveira

Technology Experience: Postsecondary Education Exploration
by Non-native English-Speaking Immigrant Parents 575
    Emmanuel K. Saka

Research on the Performance of Participatory Communication
on the Effectiveness of Attention Economy on SNS: Analysis Based
on the Case of "Xiaohongshu" 585
    Wenhao Shen, Zhiqin Zhao, and Helin Li

Designing a Pinyin-Based Keyboard Based on the Frequency of Pinyin
of Chinese Characters 604
    Chunyan Wang, Xiaojun Yuan, and Xiaoxin Xiao

Research on the Design and Consumption Intention of Chinese Urban
Subway Space Advertisement 619
    Yuxuan Xiao, Yi Liu, and Zhelu Xu

Research on the Current Situation of Yao Embroidery Based on Knowledge
Graph and the Aesthetic Characteristics of Its Decorative Patterns 635
    Yinjuan Xu and Shijun Liu

A Study of Interactive Design Based on Local Cultural Creativity
in the B&B Space 645
    Chunlan Zeng and Ganyi Yu

The Influence of Design Aesthetics on the Purchase Intention
of AI-Generated Products: Taking Cultural and Creative Products
as an Example 657
    Xinrui Zhang and Luo Wang

Combining Offline with Online: A User Experience Study of Recruitment
Platforms for Migrant Workers in China 670
    Hangyu Zhou, Fanghao Song, Yulin Wang, and Min Hua

Author Index 685

HCI Design and User Experience

Israel Railways App – From Research to Design

Nitzan Avitouv[✉]

UXPERT Ltd., Petah Tiqwa, Israel
nitzan@uxpert.com
http://www.uxpert.com

Abstract. This industry white paper includes a case study demonstrating how research insights were translated to design decisions in the Israel Railways app and made the app stand out and double its usage despite good transportation app alternatives such as Google Maps, Moovit etc. It will describe how the design approach, which was different from similar apps in this field, proved to be successful.

Keywords: Usability · User-centered Design · User Experience · World Usability Day · Design Challenge · UXPERT · Israel Railways app · Research · Design · UX · UI · Interaction Design · Motion Design

1 Introduction

The Israel Railways company initiated a redesign process of their app, which was outdated and lacked important features.

The goals were to design a simple, easy to use and fun train ride planning app, improve the Israel Railways company's public image through an innovative app, and most importantly - show differentiation and added value over other transportation apps.

An interesting question was raised – is there a real need today for a specialized train app when there are good transportation app alternatives such as Google Maps, Moovit etc.? The main challenge was to design an effective train app that brings real value beyond other apps and will be largely used by the rail passengers despite the alternatives.

Following comprehensive research, a straightforward train ride planning process was designed with new features and improved processes to meet users' needs.

This document details how the research insights led to design decisions, to differentiate this app from similar apps in this field[1], leading to a successful product launch. The app downloads and usage were doubled.

2 Research

Research was conducted at each phase of the project (before starting the design, during the design phase, prior to app launch and after launch), using UCD (User Centered Design) methodology, enabling us to plan and validate the solution (Abras et al. 2004).

---

[1] See project page: https://www.uxpert.com/work/apps/isr-app

M. Kurosu et al. (Eds.): HCII 2023, LNCS 14054, pp. 3–15, 2023.
https://doi.org/10.1007/978-3-031-48038-6_1

2.1 Research at the Beginning of the Design Process

The process began with **stakeholder interviews**. These interviews helped understand the organization's strategy, goals, and objectives, and also to gather insights and directions. These interviews were conducted as round table conversations and free form discussions with all involved parties – Marketing, Operations and Development.

Following the interview insights, a **user survey** was created using Google Forms, and a link to it published on social media. 160 responses were analyzed. About 94% of the respondents had previously used the original Israel Railways app or website. This qualitative input helped learn about user travel and app usage patterns and understand users' needs. A combination of closed and open-ended questions was used. The open-ended questions helped gather user thoughts and find out issues that might have been missed.

Download and usage data from the previous app and website was analyzed. In this specific case it provided information about the popular features, which was relatively trivial (mainly travel planning) and a bit about the days and times with high traffic. It did, however, help when comparing usage data after the change.

An **expert review** of the existing app was conducted. This helped learning what's good about it and what should be improved. (Harley 2018). And finally – **market research**. Other apps in this field were reviewed – train apps, transportation apps (such as Google Maps, Moovit, Waze). Garnering ideas about features and UX/UI solutions implemented by others in this field and other fields. All reviewed apps used a standard search form for train ride planning. Thus, the design team offered a different approach that is described later.

The entire research phase, at the beginning of the process, helped understand the user journey and needs, to come up with proper design. The user survey and interviews helped identify the key points to focus on for the features and design process.

2.2 Research During the Design Process

During the design process, usability testing was conducted numerous times, to find out what works and what does not work for the users. These started with guerilla tests and then formal lab tests. Users were given full control over the app and asked to perform tasks while thinking aloud so we could learn what they saw, thought, and wanted to do.

First usability testing phase with 12 users was done using a **UX Prototype** (Wireframes) during the **UX Design Phase**. The test's goal was to assess the effectiveness and efficiency of the design solution and make sure that the design approach, which was different than other train apps was clear to the users. This resulted in a few improvements.

On the **visual design phase**, more accurate usability testing sessions were conducted using **a fully designed prototype**[2] tested with a combination of the previous and new users. This helped validate the fixes, test the actual design as well as show the developers exactly how the app should look and behave.

---

[2] See the designed, fully interactive prototype here:https://l8ee8b.axshare.com/#id=obdnr9&p=start_-_isr_app&sc=2&c=1

2.3 Pilot Before Launch

Since lab testing is often different than field testing, we conducted a pilot phase prior to launching the app (Kaikkonen et al. 2005).

After developing the app, about 50 users were selected and given the app to use for their daily train rides. These users provided feedback and completed surveys. Conclusions & fixes were made before the official launch.

This phase helped validate the design in field conditions and create a final version ready for launch.

2.4 Research After Launch

Work did not end after launching the app. App usage data is being analyzed and user feedback collected continuously (from app stores, social media, direct feedback and more). Version updates are launched as needed, with gradual improvements.

3 Results and Analysis

3.1 Sample User Survey Insights

Here are just a few examples of the questions asked to learn about users' usage patterns:

Figure 1 shows that most respondents travel very often. This means that most of the users are repeat users and the interface should support this.

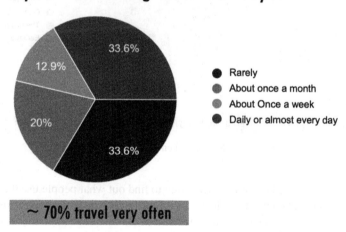

Fig. 1. Frequency of Travel

Figure 2 shows that most respondents traveled the same routes. For instance, from home to work and back. This means that our focus should be on the travel history and preferred rides rather than forcing users to search from scratch each time.

Are you traveling in similar or different routes?

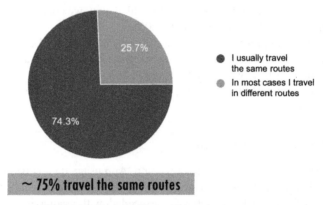

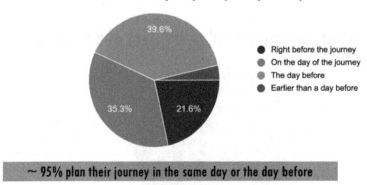

Fig. 2. Similar or Different Routes

Figure 3 shows that the vast majority of respondents plan their journey very close to the ride. On the same day or the day before. This means that "Today" and "Tomorrow" must be very accessible and only rarely will they need a calendar to pick another date.

In most cases — when do you plan your journey?

Fig. 3. When do users plan their journey

Open-ended questions were used to find out what people use the app for, what they like about it and what is missing. As shown in Figure 4, the comments were **grouped** by categories and then **sorted** by the number of times each of them was raised. This helped identify the features perceived by the users as most important.

What's missing in current app?

Before the ride	During the ride
• Save favorite routes • Reminders • Notifications for changes • Load. Available seats • Parking information • Buses to origin station	• Reminder when to get off • Train location • Info on current ride • Trains schedule • Buses from destination
Technical	*Tickets*
• Make it really updated • Short process. Less clicks • Make it easy to use • High performance • Less popups	• Digital tickets • Load my Smart Card • Ticket recommendations
Information	*Additional Features*
• Station information • Food and drinks	• Personal area • Complaints form • Refund request • Customer service / chat

Fig. 4. Comment categorizing and sorting

What do you mainly use the app for?

- Ride planning, swaps, train schedule
- Getting updates on delays or changes

4   The Solution

The design directives following the research were both on the strategic level (the features and the flow) as well as on the tactical level (specific interface solutions on each screen).

On the **strategic level** - we noticed a few points that were perceived by users as the Israel Railways app's most valuable features, and that made it stand out and be different than other apps, thus making users want to use it even though there were alternatives such as Google Maps, Moovit, etc.: The Israel Railways app is perceived as the one that can provide the most **complete and reliable information, accompany the users throughout their entire journey** (Before and during the trip) and provide real-time **updates, reminders and notifications**.

With this in mind, the design focused on these as main features.

On the **tactical level** – we identified the information and actions that users needed on each screen and designed accordingly. Details are explained in the "Solution" section.

The app design took a unique approach. Rather than using a standard travel planning form (From-to-Time) for route planning, it contains a simple and fast guided process for **new route planning**, and a shorter process for **frequent travelers** using travel history and preferred routes that help the passengers throughout their **entire journey.** In addition to the improved route planning process, **new features** were implemented according to research conclusions.

Following are highlights of the design decisions that were derived from the research conclusions.

4.1   Quick Guided Process for <u>New Route Planning</u>

Since users must specify origin, destination, and time anyway, a guided step-by-step process was created for new route planning, using the entire screen real-estate. (Chaudhuri, n.d.) This included the following sequential steps/screens: From – to – when.

Thus, creating a simple "5-click" process on average, rather than 10 in standard form approach. Each having a simple user decision point for the users and a very low cognitive load.

Research showed that users usually travel from the nearest station and in most cases use similar routes, so, as shown in Fig. 5, the origin selection screen displays nearby stations at the top of the list, and the destination selection screen highlights the recently selected destinations.

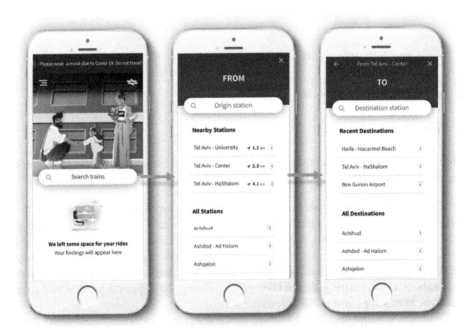

Fig. 5. Guided process for new ride planning

4.2 Faster, Efficient Process for <u>Frequent Travelers</u>

Research showed that users wanted to save and use their favorite rides, so frequent travelers (which are the majority) can easily find their previous and favorite rides right on the main page and do not need to search every single time. After selecting one of their favorite or frequent trips, they just need to specify the time to find trains. A simple "2-clicks" process. See Fig. 6.

As for time selection – it was found that users usually plan their travel right before or the day before, so the design hierarchy supports that: The default date is "Today" focused on the current time, and they can simply select time, or switch to tomorrow, and only rarely will they need to select a different date (only then – a calendar appears).

Fig. 6. Faster process for frequent travelers

4.3 Train and Route Info

The train app is perceived as the one that has the most complete and reliable sources for train travel information. All required information that the users need is displayed for each ride (time, duration, platforms, delays, swaps, route, accessibility, etc.), helping them make the most educated travel decision. As shown in Fig. 7.

Important updates for routes or specific train are shown if relevant.

Fig. 7. - Full, reliable travel information

4.4 Notifications and Updates

Research showed that users require some features throughout their entire journey and that they would appreciate updates in case of changes and notifications to help them during their travel, Fig. 8 shows how when tapping the Bell icon on any journey card, a few actions are available: Ask to be reminded when to get off the train, add the ride to calendar to get alert when it's time to go, sign up for Push Notifications in case of changes, and share the ride with friends.

Fig. 8. Notifications and Updates

4.5   Flexible Search

Observations showed that people are not always searching by exact station names, so we asked the developers to use flexible search that would find a station by various names or synonyms. See Fig. 9.

For example, the airport station will be found when typing "Ben Gurion" or "Terminal" or "Airport" or "Lod".

Fig. 9. Flexible search

4.6 Visual and Motion Design

In addition to the improved processes and features, illustration, animation, and motion are used to create a sophisticated, innovative, clear and enjoyable experience and serve the organization's goal to improve public image. For example, loading animation of illustrative turning train wheels that turn into success or failure icons.

Lively hand drawn illustrations make the app more appealing and convey the desired brand messages: Service, connecting people, enjoying the ride. Figure 10 shows some of the animation and illustrations.

Fig. 10. Illustration and Animation

Smart motion design and screen transitions helps users notice the important elements and/or understand what to do next.

For example, when entering the time selection screen, the toggle element moves from right to left to the "Today" state, thus making users understand that they are in "Today" and that they can select other days by tapping them and the toggle will move.

Another example is demonstrated in Fig. 11 - the transitions of the capsule element: It transforms from a button to origin-destination fields, to date toggle, to date/time drop down. In addition to drawing user's attention to the main element that requires their input, it also makes the app seem sophisticated and innovative.

▷ **Button**   ▷ **Field**   ▷ **Toggle**   ▷ **Dropdown**

Fig. 11. Smart Transitions

5   The Results

Despite the alternatives, the app is very popular. Downloads and searches doubled from the previous app version: increasing to 1.8 million downloads and about 400K searches per month. Israel adult (over 17 years old) population is about 6 million, so these numbers are relatively high.

User feedback received following the launch of the new app included:

"Wow, I used the new Israel Railways app this morning and it was amazing! So easy to use, it feels like every single detail was designed through the passenger's eyes.

Chapeau! I had to find out who did the UX design. found out that was you and wanted to thank you for a wonderful work!"

The app won three awards in 2022 and positive professional reviews.[3]

6   Lessons Learned

This process led to new learning outcomes, including:

---

[3] **Sample review:** https://www.designrush.com/best-designs/apps/israel-railways-app-design

Focus on added value. The most important thing is to try to figure out the real added value and differentiation – the features that can make the app stand out and provide capabilities that the users really need.

Guided step-by-step processes, especially on mobile, are more efficient than standard forms as they ease the cognitive load and focus the users on a simple task each time. Studies and other projects showed that step-by-step processes increase conversion rate. For **frequently used tasks** (ride planning in our case), use shortcuts ("accelerators") such as history and favorites to make the process more efficient.

Prototyping is an essential tool in the design process. It helps make sure that designs make sense, introduce new ideas to the designer, serve to demonstrate the design, and most importantly, are used to validate the new concepts and solutions through usability testing in various project phases.

Visual design, motion, animation and microcopy are very important for a holistic and positive user experience and contribute to the overall organization image.

Sometimes, the obvious and standard solutions are not what users really need. **Prior to market research, try creating your own concept**. A concept that meets user needs and the organization goals, and if possible, also unique. After seeing what others are doing, we might be biased and locked into a solution.

References

Abras, C., Maloney-Krichmar, D., Preece, J., Bainbridge, W.: User-Centered Design. Encyclopedia of Human-Computer Interaction, vol. 37, pp. 445–456. Sage Publications, Thousand Oaks (2004). https://www.academia.edu/1012299/User_centered_design

Chaudhuri, M. (n.d.). Single-Step Forms vs Multi-step Forms: What to Choose? Giosg. https://www.giosg.com/blog/single-step-forms-vs-multi-step-forms. Accessed 2 Jul 2023

Harley, A.: UX Expert Reviews (2018). https://www.nngroup.com/articles/ux-expert-reviews

Kaikkonen, A., Kekäläinen, A., Cankar, M., Kallio, T., Kankainen, A.: Usability testing of mobile applications: a comparison between laboratory and field testing. J. Usability Stud. 1(1), 4–16 (2005)

Siuhi, S., Mwakalonge, J.: Opportunities and challenges of smart mobile applications in transportation. J. Traffic Transp. Eng. 3(6) (2016). https://www.sciencedirect.com/science/article/pii/S2095756416302690

Strenitzerova, M., Stalmachova, K.: Customer requirements for urban public transport mobile application. Transp. Res. Procedia **55**, 95–102 (2021). https://www.sciencedirect.com/science/article/pii/S2352146521003562

Literature Review on Human-Automation Interaction: Relation Between Work from Home and Virtual Environments

Min Ho Cho[✉], Andrew Ravi Kamalraj[✉], and Vincent G. Duffy[✉]

Purdue University, West Lafayette, IN 47906, USA
{cho486,aravikam,duffy}@purdue.edu

Abstract. As the world faced the COVID-19 pandemic, numerous companies in different industries started to develop technologies or virtual environments and adopted the practice of working from home. With the increasing preferences for remote work, the main purpose of this study is to analyze and find the relationship between two topics, "Work from Home" and "Virtual Environments" by performing a systematic literature review on the two topics. Metadata of the topics are gathered from various sources including Google Scholar, Scopus, Web of Science, and Dimension with the keywords, 'virtual environment', 'virtual reality', 'automation', 'virtual work', 'home office', and 'digital communication'. Based on the metadata gathered from different sources, VOSViewer, Vicinitas, Mendeley, MaxQDA, and Google Ngram were used to perform different analyses such as engagement measure, trend analysis, co-citation analysis, content analysis, and cluster analysis to find the relationship between the topics and future projection of studies, identify the patterns and trends in terms of literature. This report discusses the listed keywords and other related terms, including different ways of generating relationships between the content. The report additionally shows the various ways to perform this analysis which can generate relationships between authors, citations, and content. Based on the review and the identified relationships, potential future work connecting the two topics is suggested and analyzed.

Keywords: Virtual Environment · Virtual Reality · Automation · Virtual Work · Home Office · Digital Communication

1 Introduction and Background

Due to the COVID pandemic, remote work has become increasingly common across various industries, such as technology, supply chain, and office jobs. Many organizations have opted for a virtual work environment, enabling employees to work from home. Despite its advantages like improved work-life balance, lower commuting costs, and increased productivity, remote work has introduced some ergonomic challenges, which can cause both physical and mental strain on workers, including musculoskeletal disorders, eye strain, and mental health problems (Delanoeije & Verbruggen 2019). Therefore, it is crucial to comprehend the ergonomic implications of remote work and virtual environments to minimize negative outcomes. In this literature review, we will examine

M. Kurosu et al. (Eds.): HCII 2023, LNCS 14054, pp. 16–36, 2023.
https://doi.org/10.1007/978-3-031-48038-6_2

different factors linked to remote work and virtual environments such as workspace design, equipment selection, and psychological factors, and see the occurrence of these two keywords among the ergonomic discipline. We will also examine the top countries contributing to research in this field, providing a better understanding of the current state and future direction of remote work and virtual environment research (Dikkers 2007).

Work From Home: refers to a work arrangement where employees perform their job duties remotely from their homes, utilizing various communication technologies such as email, video conferencing, and instant messaging. This practice has become increasingly popular due to the COVID-19 pandemic, as it reduces the risk of infection transmission and provides flexibility for employees (Innstrand 2023).

Virtual Environment: A virtual environment refers to a simulated environment created by computer software that allows individuals to interact with a computer-generated world in a way that mimics the real world (Hafner 2013).

Virtual work: Refers to work that is done in a virtual or remote environment, often using digital technology to communicate and collaborate with colleagues and client (Innstrand 2023).

The following graphics in Fig. 1 represents the number of articles that are published about "Work From Home" and "Virtual Environments" in the aspect of ergonomics and safety engineering. This data was gathered through the Scopus software for analysis. For the keyword, "Work From Home", the top five countries for publications include the United States, United Kingdom, Sweden, Japan, and Australia. For the keyword, "Virtual Environment", United States, France, Italy, Germany, and China. These results can indicate that the listed countries are continuously developing research based on these topics.

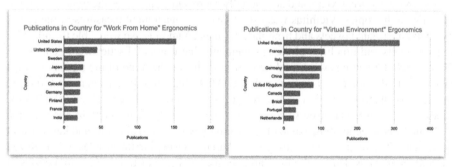

Fig. 1. Publications by Country for the Keywords, "Work from Home" ergonomics and "Virtual Environment" ergonomics.

Through the introductory analysis, we can find the relationship between articles on these topics. We also see the similarities in countries investigating these topics and perhaps also an insight into the countries most affected by the work-from-home and virtual environment phenomena in terms of the workplace (NGram Viewer).

2 Purpose of Study

The primary objective and purpose of this study is to utilize three different databases, Google Scholar, Dimensions, and Scopus, to justify the different relationships between the articles, databases, and keywords by performing various systematic literature reviews. The data that was collected and derived from these database sources were then analyzed. The data collected from these databases were analyzed through content analysis, co-citation analysis, cluster analysis, and other analytical methods to validate the relationship between the topics and perform a comprehensive systematic literature review. It is crucial for society to acknowledge the gravity of the matter as it affects a substantial number of individuals in today's workforce. To effectively address this issue, society should allocate funds toward researching and developing ergonomic technologies, tools, and strategies that promote comfortable and secure work practices in virtual environments. This could involve creating specialized ergonomic equipment, software that prompts individuals to take breaks regularly, and virtual reality tools that replicate a healthy work setting. Additionally, comprehensive training should be provided to educate individuals on how to be productive in work-from-home scenarios (Delanoeije & Verbruggen 2019).

3 Procedure

Figure 2 represents the sequential steps of the systematic literature review and analysis to identify the relationship between the topics, "Work from Home" and "Virtual Environments". The study derived metadata for both keywords from various databases including Web of Science, Dimensions, Scopus, and Google Scholar. This metadata was generated for the entire historical years and additionally for recent years to see the trend lines associated with the topics. Vicinitas was used to gather engagement measures of the topics by analyzing related tweets and timelines. By using Vicinitas, we were able to gather the related tweets and timelines of the engagements that users of Twitter were generating. Google Scholar settings were modified and used to see the trend of the topics in recent years due to the apparent rise in popularity. After analyzing the engagement and trend measures of the topics, various software was used to perform different kinds of analysis. Firstly, VOSviewer was used to conduct co-citation analysis and content analysis in a CSV file format, generating a map of connectivity with shared citations and keywords in the articles. The map of connectivity with shared keywords in the articles was analyzed by content analysis. Due to the high number usage of prepositions and conjunctions, it was important to eliminate unrelated words to get an accurate result. Cluster analysis was performed with Citespace which showed the relationship and patterns of keywords shared between articles. MaxQDA was used to generate the Wordcloud images to visualize the keywords on the articles and associate other key terms with them. Like the map generated by VOSviewer, irrelevant words were eliminated to generate accurate depictions of the word cloud analysis. Based on the results from the different analysis tools, we were able to find the relationships, dissimilarities, and attributes of the topics, articles, authors, citations, and keywords. Combining these results, we were able to conclude the report by providing the significance of the topics in the future by providing the synergy of the two topics (Sodhi, Darpan & Duffy 2019).

Steps	Activities
1	Select Two Topics for the Literature Review
1.1	Find the Partner for the Project
1.2	Practice Different Analysis Tools/Databases for the Review
1.3	Finalize which Analysis is going to be used
2	Write the Draft of Introduction / Abstract
3	Collect the Data from Different Databases
3.1	Utilize Scopus, Google Scholar, and Dimensions
3.2	Use Google Ngram to Perform Trend Analysis
3.3	Create Wordcloud
3.4	Utilize Vicinitas for Engagement Metrics
4	Analyze with the Initial Results
4.1	Perform Additional Analysis and Revise if Needed
5	Perform Alternate Analysis
5.1	VOSviewer: Co-citation/Content Analysis & Pivot Table
5.2	Citespace: Cluster Analysis
6	Write Discussion / Conclusion
7	Future Work / Appendix
8	Edit References and Add In Text Citation
9	Review / Revise Formatting of the Paper
10	Submit the Finalized Systematic Literature Review

Fig. 2. Sequential Steps depicting the Procedure for this Literature Review

4 Research Methodology

4.1 Data Collection

The two areas of interest, "Work from Home" and "Virtual Environments" were analyzed throughout the systematic literature review. The data on each topic was collected from three different databases, Google Scholar, Scopus, and Dimensions. With three databases, the number of articles for the entire number years available in the database and the number of articles after 2018 was collected for comparison.

Database	Keywords Used	Number of Results
Google Scholar (Entire Year)	Work From Home	6,990,000
Google Scholar (After 2018)	Work From Home	29,900
Scopus (Entire Year)	Work From Home	91,597
Scopus (After 2018)	Work From Home	33,883
Dimensions (Entire Year)	Work From Home	9,553,903
Dimensions (After 2018)	Work From Home	2,983,723

Fig. 3. "Work From Home" data collected from the three databases for all historical years vs after 2018

The Fig. 3 above represents the number of articles for the topic "Work from Home" collected from three different databases, Google Scholar, Scopus, and Dimension. These data were collected for the entire historical years and after 2018 for comparison. Google Scholar had the highest number of results at 6,990,000 across entire historical years with 29,900 results after 2018. Scopus has the least with 91,597 results in historical years and 33,883 after 2018. Despite the different range of results, the high percent of articles after 2018 indicates the growing popularity of this key word study.

Database	Keywords Used	Number of Results
Google Scholar (Entire Year)	Virtual Environments	4,180,000
Google Scholar (After 2018)	Virtual Environments	23,800
Scopus (Entire Year)	Virtual Environments	130,524
Scopus (After 2018)	Virtual Environments	46,111
Dimensions (Entire Year)	Virtual Environments	2,820,295
Dimensions (After 2018)	Virtual Environments	1,152,674

Fig. 4. "Virtual Environments" data collected from the three databases for all historical years vs after 2018

The Fig. 4 above shows the number of articles for the topic "Virtual Environments" collected from three different databases. This data was also collected for the entire historical years and after 2018 for comparison. We can identify from the results that Dimensions just had slightly a smaller number of total articles historically in comparison to Google Scholar, at 2,820,295 results and 1,152,574 of those coming after the year, 2018. Scopus, like for the previous keyword search, came up with the least number of articles, resulting in 130,524 and 46,111 of the totals were after 2018.

Fig. 5. Graphical Representation of the Number of Articles Per Topic Acorss 3 Databases

The Fig. 5 above represents the overall number of articles for the two topics, "Work from Home" and "Virtual Environments", from the metadata in three different databases. For the topic "Work from Home", Dimensions had the greatest number of articles whereas Scopus had the least. For the topic "Virtual Environments", Google Scholar had the greatest number of articles and Scopus had the least. From the figure above, Scopus database has the least number of articles between the three. Dimensions has the greatest number of recent articles and Google Scholar has the greatest number of articles for entire historical years.

4.2 Engagement Measure

Vicinitas is a social media analytics tool that searches through social media databases including Twitter to identify engagement measures. Not only does it let the users track engagement measures for certain words and topics they are interested in, but also further delves deeper into identifying word cloud patterns and sentiment analysis. Engagement measure was tracked for the terms, "Work From Home" and "Virtual Environments" and the Vicinitas tool tracks this by identifying the number of likes, comments, shares, and other factors.

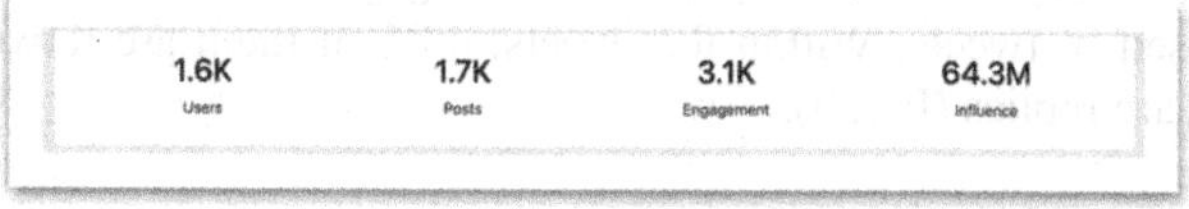

1.6K	1.7K	3.1K	64.3M
Users	Posts	Engagement	Influence

Fig. 6. Vicinitas results for the keyword, "Work From Home"

From Fig. 6 above, we can see that the term, "Work From Home" has an influence of 64.3M, with approximately 1.6K number of users utilizing that term with around 1.7K posts. Each one of those posts' ranges with an engagement of likes, shares, and comments of around 3.1K.

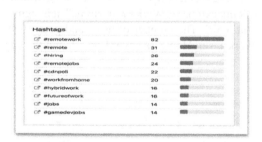

Fig. 7. Hashtag correlation of words associated with "Work From Home" ergonomics

From Fig. 7 above, we can see the approximate hashtags being used in these posts for the key term and in this case, a lot of interchangeability and similar posts are being shared with other terms including "Hybrid Work", "Future of Work" and "Remote Work". An indicator for the future of this term is that there is a lot of emphasis on remote work being possibly growing in different job sectors and will continue to grow in the future (Boukerche et al., 2010).

Types of Posts
36.9%
42.7%
20.4%
Retweets
Tweets
Replies

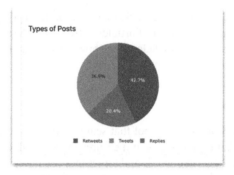

Fig. 8. Percent of Posts Associated with the Type including Retweets, Tweets and Replies for "Work From Home"

By observing Fig. 8, it can be noted that the engagement measure for the key term is divided into three categories. The majority of the engagement metrics, which is around 37%, is composed of tweets. Within the tweets, 43% of them are retweets while the remaining 20% are replies (Fig. 9).

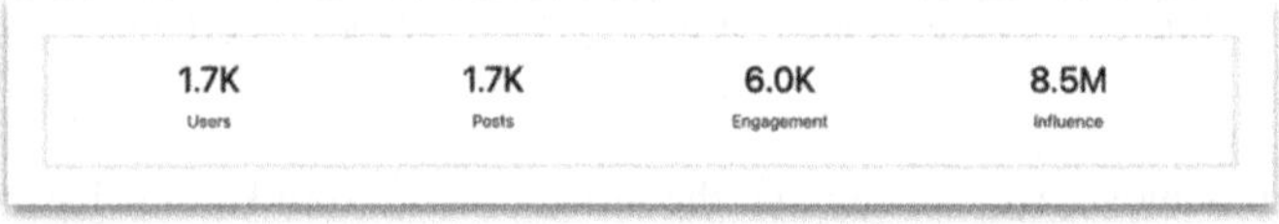

1.7K
Users
1.7K
Posts
6.0K
Engagement
8.5M
Influence

Fig. 9. Vicinitas results for the keyword, "Virtual Environment"

When analyzing the engagement measure for virtual environments, Vicinitas lists the breakdown and in comparison, to "Work From Home", it is significantly less in terms of influence, ranking at 8.5M. The number of users and posts, both at 1.7K, are both comparable to the "Work From Home" keyword search and the engagement stands at 6K.

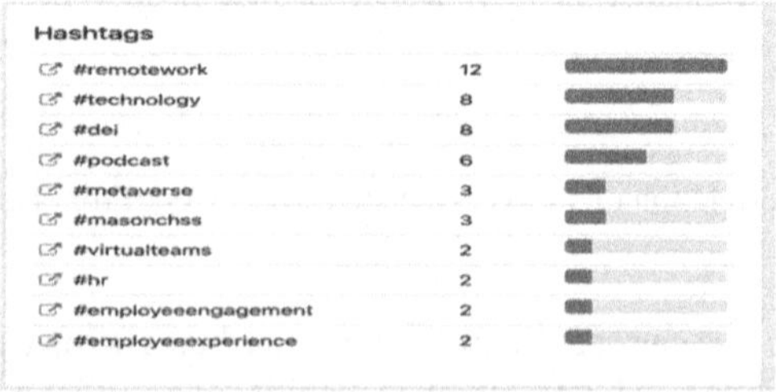

Hashtags
#remotework 12
#technology 8
#dei 8
#podcast 6
#metaverse 3
#masonchss 3
#virtualteams 2
#hr 2
#employeeengagement 2
#employeeexperience 2

Fig. 10. Hashtag correlation of words associated with "Virtual Environment" ergonomics

The data presented in Fig. 10 indicates the different hashtags being used in social media posts related to the key term "Virtual Environments". It is observed that there is a significant amount of interchangeability between the hashtags used in these posts, including "Remote Work", "Metaverse", and "Technology". The posts also suggest that virtual environments are closely associated with remote work, and that virtual teams and roles are becoming increasingly common. Specifically, the hashtag for "Virtual Team" is linked to the key term "Virtual Environments".

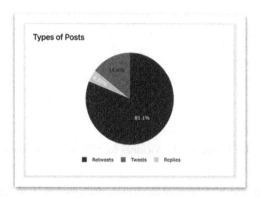

Fig. 11. Percent of Posts Associated with the Type including Retweets, Tweets and Replies for "Virtual Environments"

The above Fig. 11 illustrates the distribution of engagement metrics for the key term. It can be observed that tweets account for about 14.4% of the total engagement, while retweets and replies make up 81.1% and 4.52%, respectively. This is a significant difference from the engagement distribution from the "Work From Home" search where we see a massive increase in the number of retweets for "Virtual Environments".

Word clouds provide a graphical representation of textual information where the size of a word corresponds to its occurrence or significance within the text. They enable the identification of frequently occurring words in extensive textual data, allowing for straightforward visualization of patterns and trends. The utilization of word clouds helps to summarize the content of a document, analyze customer feedback, or recognize key phrases in social media posts (Fig. 12).

Fig. 12. Word Cloud generated by Vicinitas for "Work From Home" ergonomics

For the keyword search of "Work From Home" we see that the most commonly occurring words are "remote", "office" and "employee. Analyzing the context in which these words appear provide insights into the ergonomics of remote work. Especially for employees that work from home, ergonomics plays a factor into how their workspace is set up and how ergonomics affects their work habits.

Fig. 13. Word Cloud Generated by Vicinitas for "Virtual Environment" ergonomics

For the keyword search of "Virtual Environments", we see from Fig. 13 that the most commonly occurring words are "stand", "virtual" and "style. All these words could be related to work styles in home offices and how there is an emphasis on standing, being virtually involved in work.

4.3   Trend Analysis

Google Ngram Viewer is a tool where the user can search the different keywords to see how those keywords were used in a different corpus. It represents the change of frequencies over the year. From the topic, "Work from Home" and "Virtual Environments", the keywords "Virtual Environment", "Virtual Reality", "Automation", "Virtual Work", "Home Office", and "Digital Communication", were used for the trend analysis after the 1980s to visualize the change over the number of years (Fig. 14).

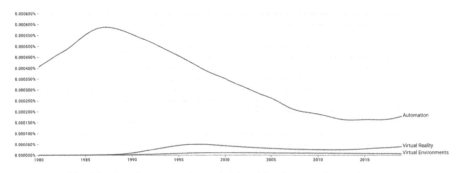

Fig. 14. Google Ngram visual of "Virtual Environment" over the years

The topic "Virtual Environments" was searched on Google Ngram Viewer. However, there were not any results reported as there were no matches with exact key word. Due to this gap, two different subtopics and keywords, "Automation" and "Virtual Reality", were searched to see the appearance and the trend of those keywords as they both closely relate to "Virtual Environments". "Virtual Reality" started to increase after the 1990s where the term "Automation" peaks around the 1980s and decreases throughout the year (Fig. 15).

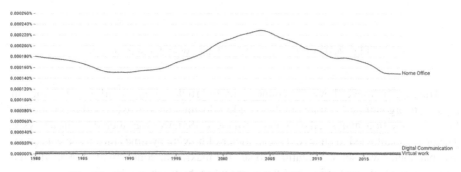

Fig. 15. Google Ngram visual of "Work From Home" over the years

The topic "Work from Home" was searched on Google Ngram Viewer with three different keywords, "Home Office", "Digital Communication", and "Virtual Work". "Digital Communication" and "Virtual Work" did not show any results. However, "Home Office" shows significant trend movements throughout the search. The search slightly decreases around the 1990s and increases again around the 2000s. There is a relationship between the keyword, "Home Office" and "Virtual Reality" where both keywords' searches increased around the 1990s and slightly decreased after the 2000s.

5   Result

5.1   Co-citation Analysis

Co-citation analysis aims to identify the interrelationships between various articles related to the same topic by analyzing the citations among them. With the help of VOSviewer, it is possible to visualize the connections between different articles based on their citations in other publications. For topics, "Work From Home", and "Virtual Environments", each data was generated in a "CSV" file since the VOSviewer did not allow other formats of data.

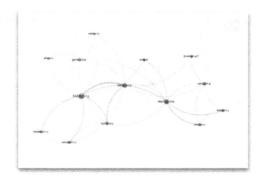

Fig. 16. Co-Citation Analysis about "Work From Home"

The Fig. 16 above shows the connectivity of articles about "Work From Home" in relation to ergonomics. A total number of 1137 documents were extracted from Scopus. During co-citation analysis, the parameter of the VOSviewer was altered for the analysis. The program allowed to change the parameter of how many times the article was cited. The parameter was set to 5 citations to see the maximum connectivity. Since with the larger citations, it was hard to find the connectivity between articles.

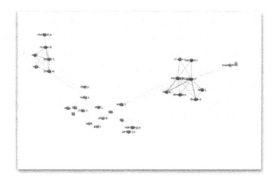

Fig. 17. Co-Citation Analysis about "Virtual Environments"

The Fig. 17 above shows the connectivity of articles about "Virtual Environments" in relation to ergonomics. A total number of 788 documents were extracted from Scopus. 129 articles met the parameter, and we can see the connectivity of the citations between these authors. There are three major sub clusters from the list of citations provided and from this we can see how referenced this topic is and from the total number, we see these strong clusters.

5.2   Content Analysis

VOSviewer is a tool that can generate different maps with connectivity from network data, bibliographic data, and text data. The "CSV" files were generated from Scopus searching the topics, "Work from Home" and "Virtual Environments". The main purpose of the content analysis generated from VOSviewer is to analyze the connectivity and the relationship of shared keywords from different articles.

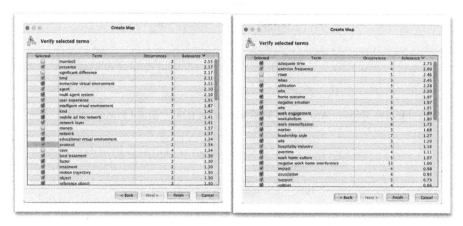

Fig. 18. Vos Viewer Keyword Search identifying Occurrence and Relevance

Figure 18 above represents the different shared keywords from the topic "Work from Home" and "Virtual Environments". These figures show lists of terms, occurrences, and relevance throughout the articles. The user is allowed to select the keywords for the analysis since there are numerous conjunctions and prepositions and those are unrelated to the topics. By selecting and deselecting those keywords, the user can increase the accuracy of the analysis which will impact on the relationship and connectivity between the keywords. We can see that some common terms with high relevance include 'adequate time', 'presence' and 'immersive virtual environment'.

Figure 19 represents the content analysis created by VOSviewer of the topic, "Virtual Environments". The size of the nodes represents the occurrence of the keywords. If the size of the node is bigger, it represents that it has higher occurrence and vice versa. Also, differently colored connections represent the connectivity and relationship between keywords and the articles. From the content analysis, keywords, Virtual Environment, Intelligent Virtual Environment, and User Experience, are some of most influenced keywords from the articles of "Virtual Environments".

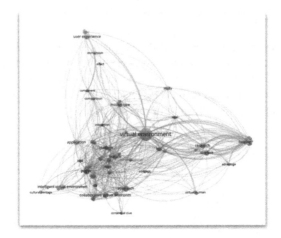

Fig. 19. Content Analysis of VOS Viewer for term, "Virtual Environment"

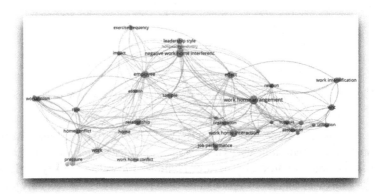

Fig. 20. Content Analysis of VOS Viewer for term, "Work From Home"

Figure 20 represents the content analysis created by VOSviwer of the topic, "Work from Home". From the content analysis, keywords, Job Performance, Work Home Interaction, Negative Work Home Interference, and Work Home Conflict, are emphasized and most influence keywords from the articles. By analyzing the connectives and nodes for the content analysis, the reader can easily define the main point of the different articles and evaluate the articles within the topics.

5.3 Industry Identification with Dimensions

Dimensions.ai is a research and discovery platform that offers access to scholarly literature, research data, and funding opportunities. It is designed to assist researchers, institutions, and organizations to make informed decisions by providing them with a broad collection of scientific publications, patents, clinical trials, and research outputs. We leverage this software into indicating the categories of research of publications that

"Work From Home" and "Virtual Engineering" publications are made in. As much of the information and computer systems industries have converted full-time on-site jobs into remote work, it is no surprise to see the bulk of the research for both keywords in this field, from Fig. 21. Additionally, we see the importance of the health sciences industry being a close second in terms of the "Work From Home" keyword search.

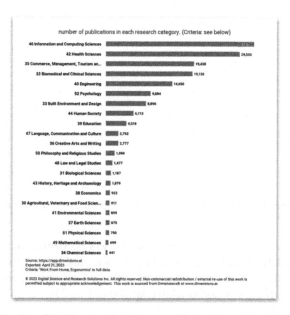

Fig. 21. Number of Publications in Category of Industries – "Work From Home"

For the "Virtual Environment" keyword search, we see that from Fig. 22 other than the Information and Computing Sciences category, Engineering, Commerce and Biomedical all place into the topmost categories of industry research. Biomedical industry is involved with the research into virtual environments and working from home due to the impact of the COVID 19 pandemic. Forcing everyone to work from home during those years of the pandemic and the lockdown created more research into this field and could have caused this spike (Clark 2013).

5.4 Cluster Analysis Word Cloud

Citespace analysis tool is a software that can generate cluster analysis of different articles from the metadata. It not only provides the cluster analysis of the keywords, but it also generates citation bursts and the information of different citations. Before the analysis, the metadata of the topic, "Work from Home" and "Virtual Environments", were derived from Web of Science in a text format. After analyzing the text files, Citespace allowed the user to the connectivity of the terms per each topic. Also, it allowed the user to generate the main point of the articles, citations, and researchers. For the "Virtual Environments",

Fig. 22. Number of Publications in Category of Industries – "Virtual Environment"

some of the clusters were generated with the keywords, virtual embodiment, virtual reality sickness, spatial awareness, and social presence. Furthermore, for the "Work from Home", some of the clusters were generated with the keywords, work-home conflict, teleworking, job satisfaction, and GitHub (Dai 2009) (Fig. 23).

Fig. 23. Cluster Analysis from CiteSpace for Keywords, Virtual Environment (bottom) and Work From Home (top)

5.5 Pivot Table

Using VOSviewer and BibExcel, a pivot table can be created by importing a "CSV" file from Scopus. The pivot table serves the purpose of displaying the number of times articles have been cited in other articles. It not only presents the citation count but also the degree of association between articles that share a similar topic. The pivot table provides valuable insights into authors and articles that contribute to the topic, along with numerical values related to the topic. The Fig. 24 below displays the pivot tables for the topics "Work From Home" and "Virtual Environments" respectively, arranged in descending order of the number of citations. We see this on the columns, with the pivot table for "Work From Home" keyword search indicating that the most cited author is Wilson J.R. with 722 citations, and Garg A, for Virtual environments with 352 citations.

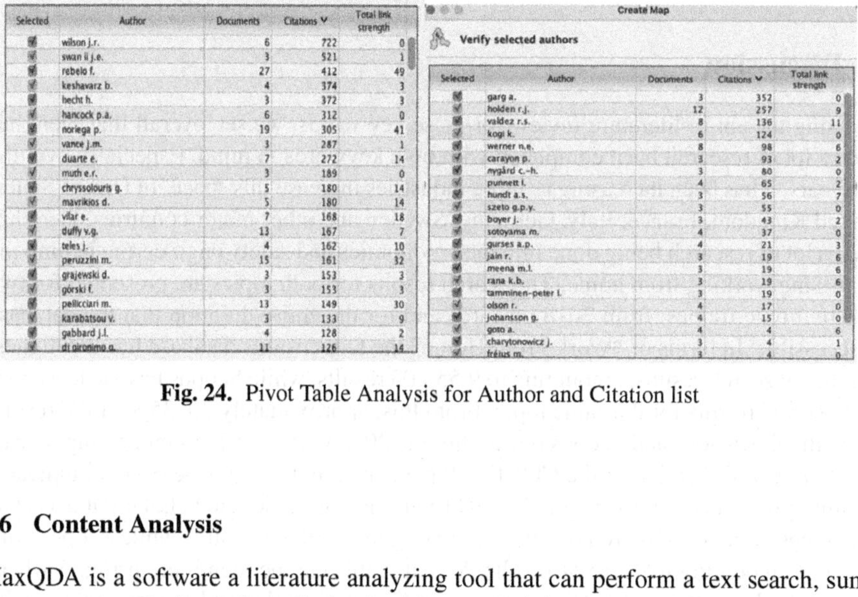

Selected	Author	Documents	Citations	Total link strength
	wilson j.r.	6	722	0
	swan ii j.e.	3	521	1
	rebelo f.	27	412	49
	keshavarz b.	4	374	3
	hecht h.	3	372	3
	hancock p.a.	6	312	0
	noriega p.	19	305	41
	vance j.m.	3	287	1
	duarte e.	7	272	14
	muth e.r.	3	189	0
	chryssolouris g.	5	180	14
	mavrikios d.	5	180	14
	vilar e.	7	168	18
	duffy v.g.	13	167	7
	teles j.	4	162	10
	peruzzini m.	15	161	32
	grajewski d.	3	153	3
	górski f.	3	153	3
	pellicciari m.	13	149	30
	karabatsou v.	3	133	9
	gabbard j.l.	4	128	2
	di gironimo g.	11	126	14

Selected	Author	Documents	Citations	Total link strength
	garg a.	3	352	0
	holden r.j.	12	257	9
	valdez r.s.	8	136	11
	kogi k.	6	124	0
	werner n.e.	8	98	6
	carayon p.	3	93	2
	nygård c.-h.	3	80	0
	punnett l.	4	65	2
	hundt a.s.	3	56	7
	szeto g.p.y.	3	55	0
	boyer j.	3	43	2
	sotoyama m.	4	37	0
	gurses a.p.	4	21	3
	jain r.	3	19	6
	meena m.l.	3	19	6
	rana k.b.	3	19	6
	tamminen-peter l.	3	19	0
	olson r.	4	17	0
	johansson g.	4	15	0
	goto a.	4	4	6
	charytonowicz j.	3	4	1
	fréius m.	3	4	0

Fig. 24. Pivot Table Analysis for Author and Citation list

5.6 Content Analysis

MaxQDA is a software a literature analyzing tool that can perform a text search, summary, tweet analysis, and word cloud with imported documents. Web of Science was used to gather the metadata of topics, "Work from Home" and "Virtual Environments". From Web of Science, the highest cited publications and articles were downloaded and uploaded on the MaxQDA for the analysis. After uploading articles for each topic, Word Clouds were generated under the visual tools. since there were a lot of irrelevant shared keywords throughout the articles, the frequency of word occurrences was increased to 30. After increasing the limitation, the irrelevant keywords were moved to "Stop Word List" to reduce the numbers, conjunctions, and prepositions. Figure 25 below represents the resulting Word Clouds of two topics. For "Work from Home, some of the associated keywords are productivity, organizations, impacts physical, and workaholism. For "Virtual Environments", some of the associated keywords are collaborative, environment, environments construction, and visual significant.

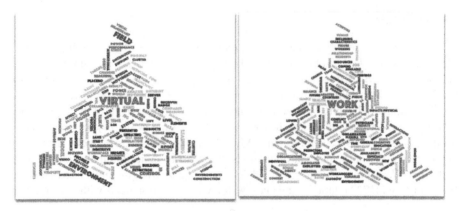

Fig. 25. Word Clouds of "Virtual Environment" (top) and "Work From Home" (bottom)

6   Discussion

Revising the entire literature review for these key words, we see overall that there has been a lot of research been completed with both keywords in mind. Especially over the last years, it has been increasing as more industries increase this space. In United States, United Kingdom, France, Italy, Germany, Sweden and other major countries, there has been a lot of research being done into the ergonomics and safety engineering behind the increasing working from home. The search results for both topics are presented for two different time frames: from 2018 onwards and for the entire duration that the database is accessible. In terms of "Work From Home" the Dimensions database has the highest number of search results, amounting to 9,553,03 results, while Scopus has the least with only 91,597 results for the same topic. From this, approximately 30–35% of the results for both Dimensions and Scopus occur after the 2018 year. This is an interesting note as this is around the period of the COVID-19 pandemic and could have been an indicator for this spike. In comparison, for "Virtual Environments", Google Scholar database has the highest number of search results, amounting to 4,180,000 results while Scopus with the least amounting to 130,524 results. Visually, this can be identified in Fig. 5 where we see the high results for Dimensions and Google Scholar and the minimal results provided by Scopus (Kiourt 2017).

According to the Vicinitas report, which utilizes Twitter analytics, "Work From Home" has influenced 64.3M tweets, while "Virtual Environments influencing 8.5M tweets. Additionally, the number of users and posts for both keywords are seemingly comparable with approximately 1.6K but there is a significant increase in engagement for "Virtual Environments", where the engagement metrics stands at 3.1K for "Work From Home, and it is 6.0K for "Virtual Environments". The associated keywords are also listed as per the Vicintas search report with remote work, technology and metaverse relating to the "Virtual Environments" and the terms remote work, hiring and hybrid work being related to "Work From Home". WordCloud generated for "Work From Home" highlights keywords such as 'remote', office, and job, which are associated with this topic. Conversely, the WordCloud for "Virtual Environments" includes other keywords such as virtual, machine, and future (Kiourt 2017).

The trend analysis was conducted using Google Ngram, and the results show a significant increase in the topic of "Work From Home" was broken down into Home Office", "Digital Communication", and "Virtual Work". The term "Home Office" showed a significant difference in comparison to the other two keywords and had a consistent range in publications from the year 2000 and beyond, depicted on the y-axis in an exponential manner. The term "Virtual Environments" was broken down into the keywords, "Automation" and "Virtual Reality", which were searched to see the appearance and the trend of those keywords. After the 1990s, there was an upward trend in the topic of "Virtual Reality," while "Automation" peaked in the 1980s and gradually declined over time.

The co-citation analysis aims to illustrate the relationships between articles for each of the two identified topics. By setting a parameter of 5 citations for "Work From Home", we can determine the number of citations that are most closely associated with the relevant works. Out of the 1137 articles that resulted, only 127 met the citation analysis parameter. In contrast, "Virtual Environment" had a pool of 788 articles, with 129 articles meeting the parameter. Despite the difference in total articles, we see that there is a higher ratio of articles that fit the parameter for "Virtual Environments". This is further supported by Figs. 16 and 17, by the depiction of the connectivity of articles and citations shown. We see that for "Virtual Environment", the connectivity appears to be stronger due to the stronger lines and density in the visuals in comparison to the other keyword (Marianne & Blomme 2014).

According to the analysis performed using VOS Viewer, some of the most frequently occurring and relevant words for "Work From Home" include the terms, Job Performance, Work Home Interaction, Negative Work Home Interference, and Work Home Conflict. On the other hand, for "Virtual Environments," some of the strongest words with high occurrence and relevance are Virtual Environment, Intelligent Virtual Environment, and User Experience. This information not only sheds light on the current research in these fields but also on prospects. For "Work From Home", research is focused on navigating the work-from-home environment addressing the negative interface, and how to deal with conflicts in terms of interaction. On the other hand, "Virtual Environments" research revolves around user experience and the optimal ways to optimize your virtual work environment. The pivot table in the VOS Viewer analysis identifies Dr. Wilson J.R. as one of the most cited authors in the field of "Work From Home" while Garg A. has 352 co-citations in"Virtual Environments".

The Figs. 16 and 17 illustrate the results of uploading the text file of published articles from Web of Science into Citespace. These figures show the common cluster words for these topics, such as virtual environment and work from home, and the number of articles clustered together based on these words. It also showcases the major cluster words for "Work From Home" which include work-home conflict, teleworking, job satisfaction, and GitHub, as well as the corresponding articles listed in this analysis. For the keyword, "Virtual Environments", some of the major cluster words include virtual reality sickness, spatial awareness, and social presence.

There has been an increase in research in the areas of safety engineering and ergonomics related to working from home and virtual environments. The COVID-19 pandemic seems to have played a role in this increase in research in both areas. The use of different databases such as Dimensions, Scopus, and Google Scholar to search for articles related to the two keywords shows variations in the number of search results. It is important to continue studying these areas to optimize virtual work environments and minimize negative work-home interactions, ultimately ensuring a safe and productive workforce (Innstrand 2023).

7 Conclusion

The field of work-from-home ergonomics is distinct from traditional ergonomics due to its unique challenges that are not found in traditional office or industrial settings. In her article "Prediction of Work from Home and Musculoskeletal Discomfort: An Investigation of Ergonomic Factors in Work Arrangements and Home Workstation Setups Using the COVID-19 Experience," Justine Chim stresses the importance of researching this topic to address the associated risks, such as Musculoskeletal Disorders. Through the optimization of workspace for comfort and safety, workers can alleviate fatigue and stress levels, leading to improved mental health and overall well-being. Work-from-home ergonomics is crucial in ensuring that the home office is safe, comfortable, and efficient for workers. By preventing injuries, increasing productivity, and enhancing workers' overall well-being, ergonomics plays a crucial role in work-from-home settings (Chim 2023). A systematic literature review was conducted on the two topics of, "Work from Home" and "Virtual Environments", using metadata gathered from different data sources based on the content, citations, authors, and keywords. The analysis indicates that the relationships between two topics exist and can be incorporated in different fields. Due to the COVID-19 pandemic, remote work from home is becoming common in numerous industries and companies, while virtual environments comprise more recent articles and trends in comparison (Moen 2013). It indicates that virtual environments are currently getting developed and researched with more emphasis of studies being placed especially in the countries identified earlier. It is important to see the relationship between the two topics continue to develop and research various technologies and environments which can promote students, researchers, and employees in the future (Innstrand 2023).

8 Future Work

The COVID-19 pandemic has driven the growth of remote work, with many companies acknowledging the advantages of flexibility and reduced expenses. This trend is anticipated to continue, as more workers opt for work from home and virtual environments. Consequently, companies are anticipated to invest more in virtual collaboration tools and platforms to support remote work. In terms of ergonomics, smart technologies may be integrated into the future of work to monitor and enhance worker health and safety. Wearable devices may be used to track movement and posture, provide real-time feedback to workers, and warn them about possible ergonomic problems (Tromp & Blomme 2014). Moreover, virtual environments can simulate real-world workspaces and test ergonomic designs before they are put into practice, which can increase safety and reduce the likelihood of injury (Kumari 2020).

The research titled "Working and Teaching from Home in New York State amidst the COVID-19 Pandemic" by addresses the difficulties faced by employees and teachers who had to transition to remote work during the pandemic. The study identifies the lack of appropriate ergonomics in-home workspaces as a major challenge, which can cause physical strain and discomfort (Innstrand 2023). Traditionally, ergonomics research has focused on physical workspaces, but the shift towards remote work has emphasized the need for further research on ergonomics in virtual environments. The research emphasizes the significance of considering ergonomics in remote work environments and suggests that further research in this area is crucial to gain a better understanding of the challenges and potential solutions to creating more ergonomic workspaces in virtual environments (Kumari 2020).

References

Afrooz, A., Ding, L., Pettit, C.: An immersive 3D virtual environment to support collaborative learning and teaching. In: Geertman, S., Zhan, Q., Allan, A., Pettit, C. (eds.) CUPUM 2019. LNGC, pp. 267–282. Springer, Cham (2019). https://doi.org/10.1007/978-3-030-19424-6_15

Bouras, Ch., Tsiatsos, Th.: Architectures and protocols for educational virtual environments. In: IEEE International Conference on Multimedia and Expo. ICME 2001 (2001). https://doi.org/10.1109/icme.2001.1237920

Boukerche, A., Zarrad, A., Araujo, R.B.: A cross-layer approach-based Gnutella for collaborative virtual environments over mobile ad hoc networks. IEEE Trans. Parallel Distrib. Syst. 21(7), 911–924 (2010). https://doi.org/10.1109/tpds.2009.91

Chellali, A., Milleville-Pennel, I., Dumas, C.: Elaboration of a common frame of reference in collaborative virtual environments. In: Proceedings of the 15th European Conference on Cognitive Ergonomics: The Ergonomics of Cool Interaction (2008). https://doi.org/10.1145/1473018.1473045

Lin, C.-Y., Wang, L.-C., Hung, P.-H., Lin, C.-C.: Reducing cognitive load through virtual environments among hearing-impaired students. In: 2010 Second Pacific-Asia Conference on Circuits, Communications and System (2010). https://doi.org/10.1109/paccs.2010.5627061

Chim, J.M.Y., Chen, T.L.: Prediction of work from home and musculoskeletal discomfort: an investigation of ergonomic factors in work arrangements and home workstation setups using the COVID-19 experience. Int. J. Environ. Res. Public Health 20(4), 3050 (2023). https://doi.org/10.3390/ijerph20043050.PMID:36833747;PMCID:PMC9967171

"CiteSpace." n.d. http://cluster.cis.drexel.edu/~cchen/citespace/

Clark, M.A., Michel, J.S., Stevens, G.W., Howell, J.W., Scruggs, R.S.: Workaholism, work engagement and work-home outcomes: exploring the mediating role of positive and negative emotions. Stress. Health 30(4), 287–300 (2013). https://doi.org/10.1002/smi.2511

Dai, K., Lu, S., Liu, G., Sun, Y.: Research on path planning of intelligent virtual human in distributed virtual environment. In: 2009 IEEE International Conference on Intelligent Computing and Intelligent Systems (2009). https://doi.org/10.1109/icicisys.2009.5358053

Delanoeije, J., Verbruggen, M.: The use of work-home practices and work-home conflict: examining the role of volition and perceived pressure in a multi-method study. Front. Psychol. 10 (2019). https://doi.org/10.3389/fpsyg.2019.02362

Dikkers, J.S., Geurts, S.A., Den Dulk, L., Peper, B., Taris, T.W., Kompier, M.A.: Dimensions of work–home culture and their relations with the use of work–home arrangements and work–home interaction. Work Stress 21(2), 155–172 (2007). https://doi.org/10.1080/02678370701442190

Dikkers, J., Geurts, S., den Dulk, L., Peper, B., Kompier, M.: Relations among work-home culture, the utilization of work-home arrangements, and work-home interference. Int. J. Stress Manag. **11**(4), 323–345 (2004). https://doi.org/10.1037/1072-5245.11.4.323

"Dimensions." n.d. https://www.dimensions.ai/

Geurts, S.A., Taris, T.W., Kompier, M.A., Dikkers, J.S., Van Hooff, M.L., Kinnunen, U.M.: Work-home interaction from a work psychological perspective: development and validation of a new questionnaire, the Swing. Work Stress **19**(4), 319–339 (2005). https://doi.org/10.1080/026783 70500410208

"Google Books NGram Viewer" n.d. https://books.google.com/ngrams/

Hafner, P., Vinke, C., Hafner, V., Ovtcharova, J., Schotte, W.: The impact of motion in virtual environments on memorization performance. In: 2013 IEEE International Conference on Computational Intelligence and Virtual Environments for Measurement Systems and Applications (CIVEMSA) (2013). https://doi.org/10.1109/civemsa.2013.6617404

Innstrand, S.T., Langballe, E.M., Espnes, G.A., Aasland, O.G., Falkum, E.: Personal vulnerability and work-home interaction: the effect of job performance-based self-esteem on work/home conflict and facilitation. Scandinavian journal of psychology. U.S. National Library of Medicine. https://pubmed.ncbi.nlm.nih.gov/20338010/. Accessed 18 Apr 2023

Kiourt, C., Pavlidis, G., Koutsoudis, A., Kalles, D.: Multi-agents based virtual environments for cultural heritage. In: 2017 XXVI International Conference on Information, Communication and Automation Technologies (ICAT) (2017). https://doi.org/10.1109/icat.2017.8171602

Konstantinidis, A., Tsiatsos, T.: Selecting a networked virtual environment platform and the design of a collaborative e-learning environment. In: 22nd International Conference on Advanced Information Networking and Applications - Workshops (aina workshops 2008) (2008). https://doi.org/10.1109/waina.2008.59

Kubicek, B., Tement, S.: Work Intensification and the Work-Home Interface. J. Pers. Psychol. **15**(2), 76–89 (2016). https://doi.org/10.1027/1866-5888/a000158

Kumari, V., Rai, A.: Ergonomic challenges and opportunities for remote workers during COVID-19 pandemic. Work **67**(2), 275–280 (2020). https://doi.org/10.3233/WOR-203206

Marianne Tromp, D., Blomme, R.J.: Leadership style and negative work-home interference in the hospitality industry. Int. J. Contemp. Hospitality Manag. **26**(1), 85–106 (2014). https://doi.org/10.1108/ijchm-04-2012-0058

"MAXQDA." n.d. https://www.maxqda.com/

Moen, P., Fan, W., Kelly, E.L.: Team-level flexibility, work-home spillover, and health behavior. Soc. Sci. Med. **84**, 69–79 (2013). https://doi.org/10.1016/j.socscimed.2013.02.011

National Science Foundation. "NSF Award Search: Award#2028055 - RUI: Collaborative Research: Electrochemical Insights into the Structure-Property Relationships of Multimetallic Nanoparticles." NSF Award Search (2020). www.nsf.gov/awardsearch/showAward?AWD_ ID=2028055&HistoricalAwards=false

"Scopus." n.d. https://www.scopus.com/

Sodhi, D., Duffy, V.: A systematic review of ergonomics training and working from home. In: Duffy, V.G., Ziefle, M., Rau, P.-L.P., Tseng, M.M. (eds.) Human-Automation Interaction: Mobile Computing. Springer, Cham (2022). https://doi.org/10.1007/978-3-031-10788-7_29

Tcha-Tokey, K., Emilie Loup-Escande, O.C., Richir, S.: Effects on user experience in an edutainment virtual environment. In; Proceedings of the European Conference on Cognitive Ergonomics 2017 (2017). https://doi.org/10.1145/3121283.3121284

Tromp, D.M., Blomme, R.J.: The Effect of Effort Expenditure, Job Control and Work-Home Arrangements on Negative Work-Home Interference in the Hospitality Industry. Int. J. Hosp. Manag. **31**(4), 1213–1221 (2012). https://doi.org/10.1016/j.ijhm.2012.02.011

"Vicinitas" n.d. https://www.vicinitas.io/

"VOSviewer." n.d. https://www.vosviewer.com/

Gesture Hub Design: A Remote User Study Method for Evaluating the Quality of Experience in Mobile Phone-Based Gesture Interaction

Haoyu Dong[1], Jun Zhang[1](✉), Wei Wang[1], Yijing Yang[1], Qi Chen[2], and Le Du[3]

[1] School of Design, Hunan University, Changsha, China
zhangjun@hnu.edu.cn
[2] User Experience and Solution Department,
Guangdong OPPO Mobile Telecommunications Corp., Ltd., Shenzhen, China
[3] User Experience and Solution Department,
Guangdong OPPO Mobile Telecommunications Corp., Ltd., Nanjing, China

Abstract. As a key facet of the mobile user experience, mobile phone-based gesture design has established its importance in the competitive landscape of leading manufacturers. Mobile phone-based gestures, distinguished by high cognitive load and metaphorical nature, contribute to a continuing divergence between the user's subjective perceptions and the designer's official definitions in the scope of gesture design and experience evaluation. Furthermore, the obstacles presented by the COVID-19 pandemic's isolation measures have curtailed short-term user involvement in gesture experience appraisals. Online user testing platforms, while providing basic research tools, fall short of adequate integration with gesture operation experience knowledge and lack sufficient validation of tool usage procedures for gesture studies. In light of a potentially prolonged COVID-19 period, our research endeavors to refine and authenticate user research techniques for gesture experience, advancing the flexibility of gesture Quality of Experience evaluations and circumventing irrelevant or detrimental research results. Informed by the literature review, the study constructed the 'Gesture Hub' - a user evaluation framework specifically designed for gesture experiences. Applied in a remote user testing project, this framework's efficacy was corroborated, with ensuing analysis highlighting its merits and demerits. The study broadens the user QoE evaluation methodologies in the gesture interaction arena, providing crucial direction for remote user-expert collaborations and enhancing the accuracy of user gesture experience evaluations and requirements.

Keywords: Mobile Phone-based Gesture Interaction Design · Quality of Experience · User Study · Evaluation Method · Remote Testing Tools

1 Introduction

As smartphone performance and gesture recognition technologies have advanced (Heo & Lee 2011; Ikematsu et al., 2020; Jiang, 2017), novel opportunities have arisen for enhancing satisfaction in user experience (UX) with mobile phone-based gesture interaction. It must also be recognized that smartphones have ascended as the most prevalent mobile devices, with their global usage exceeding 80% in 2022 and projected to increase further

© The Author(s), under exclusive license to Springer Nature Switzerland AG 2023
M. Kurosu et al. (Eds.): HCII 2023, LNCS 14054, pp. 37–53, 2023.
https://doi.org/10.1007/978-3-031-48038-6_3

(Statista, 2022). Hence, concentrating on studies on gesture interaction experiences on smartphones constitutes a significant research direction.

Within existing literature, Quality of Experience (QoE) is an evaluation criterion in the quality management process of mobile phone-based gesture interaction (Juran, 2021; Qi & Li, 2021), and various variants of its definition can be found. In this study, the QoE of the gesture interaction is defined as the subjective feelings of users when performing gestures on mobile devices (Prates et al., 2000), starting from the research perspective of user emotion evaluation methods and metric indicators, evaluating usability and UX to enhance the sense of design experience (Brdnik et al., 2022; Hu et al., 2019). Therefore, the QoE of the gesture assessment is particularly important in user-centered design, especially against the current backdrop of widespread smartphone usage, demonstrating prominent value in enhancing UX.

User testing within design evaluation not only facilitates user learning but also manifests as a collaborative design process, generally prompting designers to orchestrate the experiment and steer users in articulating their experiences throughout the process. Regrettably, imposed isolation measures triggered by the pandemic have hindered the co-location of designers and users for in-person gesture assessment tests, necessitating their unavoidable separation (Giroux et al., 2021).

The complex challenge associated with gesture QoE assessment stems from the inherently metaphorical, cognitive, and abstract nature of gestures. Aspects such as temporal sampling, directional offsets, and other performance parameters, along with aesthetic, practical, emotional, and cognitive design factors (Hesenius & Gruhn, 2019; Vyas & van der Veer, 2005; Xia et al., 2022) call for a comprehensive user evaluation that encompasses subjective appraisal, cognitive processing, and emotional perspectives. However, existing assessment methodologies are predominantly tailored towards conventional software or GUI evaluations and fail to fully consider the distinctive aspects of gesture interactions, such as the composite assessment of usability and UX in QoE (Brdnik et al., 2022; Paz & Pow-Sang, 2015). Despite user research tools offered by platforms like UXTesting facilitating user testing, these tools often struggle to establish a close connection with specific research subjects due to variations in application domains (Giroux et al., 2021). Furthermore, communicating through appropriate gesture vocabulary in diverse testing environments remains a challenging task (Xia et al., 2022). The lack of clear guidelines and validation from Human-Computer Interaction (HCI) literature compounds these issues. Therefore, under the protracted influence of the COVID-19 pandemic, and to ensure the flexibility of the gesture QoE user assessment process, it is incumbent on professionals to redefine user research content about gesture QoE, adjust testing methodologies, and validate their effectiveness.

To address this research shortfall, the objective of the study is to devise an online user assessment approach tailored to mobile phone-based gesture experiences, thus facilitating remote user participation in the design process and enabling identification of their requirements. The research structure of the paper unfolds as follows: Initially, the study delineates the user testing elements for gesture experiences by scrutinizing QoE, remote user testing methodologies, task operation processes, and tools. Subsequently, leveraging design insights, it is introduced an online approach dubbed 'Gesture Hub' (GH), encompassing card tools and user operation guidelines, while offering a structured user assessment process within the experiment. Finally, The proposed method undergoes validation across diverse mobile operating systems (OS), including iOS, HarmonyOS, and

ColorOS, and the strengths and weaknesses of this approach are discussed. The research found that the GH method can effectively provide strategies and tools for the subjects, suitable for preliminary screening and in-depth exploration of experience problems. The online GH method formed in this study can enrich the user QoE evaluation methods in the gesture interaction field, help to understand gesture experience issues and guide the design process to achieve a better UX.

2   Method Development

2.1   QoE Elements and Models

During the process of assessing the QoE related to mobile phone-based gestures, it's crucial to inspect the systems and models pertinent to the QoE, aiming to compile a list that characterizes this quality. The assessment terminology spans a variety of dimensions including situational, cognitive, physical, and system properties (Pu et al., 2015; Wei & Gong, 2011; Xia et al., 2022), encompassing specifics such as discoverability, complexity, ergonomic obstruction, learnability, and utility. Furthermore, Whitney Quesenbery proposed the 5Es of product experience evaluation: Ease of Learning, Effectiveness, Engagement, Error Tolerance, and Efficiency (Quesenbery, 2004). Building upon the foundation of usability, this principle introduces the dimension of UX. It provides a more nuanced approach than traditional usability models, assisting in uncovering and detailing various facets of UX, and has been broadly adopted within the realm of interactive experience (Habib et al., 2022; Qi & Li, 2021).

Currently, the indicators for the QoE in gesture interactions are still a topic of discussion. Basic dimensions like "Error Tolerance" lack a direct correlation to specific metrics, complicating the quantification of users' subjective evaluations and leading to a dearth of implementable details for this process. Furthermore, the selection of precise measurement methods and indices necessitates additional exploration and study, tailored to specific contexts (Meng & Zhu, 2021). In pursuit of a more accurate reflection of the UX in gesture interactions, this study redefines each foundational dimension based on a combination of the 5Es model and literature review (refer to the following Table 1). The objective is to transform these redefined dimensions into questions that stimulate user evaluations in subsequent research.

2.2   Remote User Testing Methods

Mutual communication plays an indispensable role in user research (Pahk et al., 2018). Amid the COVID-19 pandemic, despite the restrictions on physical spaces, digital domains have opened up avenues for user research. This approach's advantages lie in its cost-effective and rapid remote testing capabilities, which furnish viable channels for examining context-dependent interface settings (Bolt & Tulathimutte, 2010; Liu & Kim, 2021). Contemporary research employs a variety of online tools such as UserTesting, Userlytics, and even Zoom and VR Chat. These tools enable users to participate in the design process and express their perspectives. In gesture experience studies, such user feedback becomes a treasured resource (Xia et al., 2022). For instance, the utilization of

Table 1. Definition of 5Es versus GH's gestural experience metric.

Basic dimensions	Original definition of 5Es	Redefinition of GH
Easy to learn	Focus on the extent to which the product supports initial orientation and deeper learning	1. The degree of guidance in the first learning of the gestures 2. The difficulty of mastery over time in terms of memory and reuse
Effective	Whether the software is useful and helps users to achieve their goals accurately	1. The ergonomic nature of the interaction process 2. The degree of the intended action or function achievement
Engaging	The degree to which the interface is pleasant, satisfying to use or interesting to use	1. Instant and fluid interaction 2. Easy to understand and master the meaning and use of gestures 3. Free and rich interaction 4. Emotional empathy and fun
Error tolerant	This includes the ability of the product to prevent errors and help users recover from errors that occur	1. Tolerance of possible gesture malfunctions or inaccurate gesture execution 2. Fault-tolerant handling and support for undo operations
Efficient	The speed with which work is completed	1. The time required to complete a given task 2. Effectiveness of task completion 3. Speed and precision of gestures

think-aloud protocols is instrumental in eliciting user reflections and evaluations (Fan et al., 2022; Nielsen et al., 2002).

However, the existing problem is that most gesture user tests only consider user-led (Brudy et al., 2019) or expert-led (Rodda et al., 2022; Truong et al., 2006)approaches. If research is conducted solely from the user-led perspective, due to subjectivity and individual differences, there might be a low degree of consensus. Overreliance on expert-led approaches may lead to excessive or insufficient optimization work, thus hindering the understanding of the learnability or discoverability of gestures (Xia et al., 2022). In gesture experience research, user testing is not just data collection; more importantly, it is about obtaining the quality of communication and qualitative insights related to the gesture experience. For example, semi-structured interviews are researchers helping users express their opinions, with results tending towards fine-grained data (DeJonckheere & Vaughn, 2019).

Therefore, inspired by participatory design, this study emphasizes considering both user and expert leadership in the process of gesture QoE assessment. This approach can compensate for the shortcomings of a single perspective. Meanwhile, given that in the post-epidemic era, it needs to consider the feasibility of developing remote experiments to adapt to changes in user activity and experimental environments. In this collaboration, users need to complete gesture operation tasks and provide insights and experimenters need to have the ability to remotely collect related data along with the ability to moderate the user testing process online.

2.3   Task Operation Process and Tools

Focusing on gesture interaction testing, task situation is an important aspect (Sun, 2014; Zhang et al., 2019). According to Dey's definition, a situation describes all information that characterizes the circumstances under which the gesture will be performed (i.e., people, places, and devices) (Dey, 2001). Literature review studies show that the term situation is rarely used, while terms like user, environment, or task are more common (Xia et al., 2022). Hesenius created a gesture card tool of hybrid graphics and text symbols through the synergistic interaction of gesture interaction and some symbols, providing a basis for understanding and recording gesture situations (Hesenius & Gruhn, 2019; Hesenius et al., 2017). It can be seen that the process of gesture interaction is embedded in the subjective feelings and experiences of operating system service providers and also on individual users. In this process, card tools and dialogues are the core of cooperation between designers and users, which can promote participation and understanding. Hence, the fulfillment of gesture tasks ought to comply with situation requirements and reestablish the symbolic guidance of user operation tasks. The following are examples of situational research content that inspires gesture evaluation.

Gesture Task Forms

The arena of touch gesture research can adopt individual tasks and task groups as experimental approaches. Typically, tasks are designed as independent entities, aiding efficient data cleansing. For example, Joachim Normann Larsen et al., in their investigation of the correlation between hand size and touch precision, tasked participants with completing five independent activities (Larsen et al., 2019). On the other hand, task groups involve creating a sequence of tasks mimicking ongoing operations in real-life situations, thereby presenting a holistic image of user behavioral patterns. Task groups support users in comprehending and adapting to specific operation process requisites, enhancing accuracy and efficiency during remote testing, and offering systematic viewpoints. Consequently, the GH method, acknowledging the advantages and shortcomings of both task formats, utilizes a blend of the two in experimenting.

Competitive Comparison

Competitive comparative research can be seen as a cognitive constraint expression of situation setting and personal experience, that is, the situation in which gestures are performed (Xia et al., 2022). The code package that supports gesture operation is highly dependent on the target OS (Brdnik et al., 2022), such as iOS, HarmonyOS, and ColorOS. When researching users and potential users of a certain OS, competitive comparisons can obtain different user preferences and expectations for gesture interaction in different OS. Therefore, in the GH method, to improve and optimize gesture design according to user preferences and comparative feedback, the evaluation process considers task setting in representative OS and obtains comparative evaluation.

Autonomous User Data Collection

Autonomous user data collection is commonly employed in online HCI research and intends to gather comprehensive experimental data in scenarios where researchers cannot be physically present. Users are responsible for setting up their camera stations to record experiments. The objective is to procure data on users' gesture operational processes, and overall experimental procedures during online experiments. However, the self-collection of data imposes a substantial burden on users, requiring them to manage equipment and environmental setups. Practical operations may encounter inadequacies in camera placement, with data collection being influenced by the user's testing environment and equipment possession. Moreover, guidelines in the HCI domain remain somewhat scant (Giroux et al., 2021). Thus, providing explicit instructions for equipment setup within the method execution's user guide is of paramount importance.

3   Gesture Hub Method and Process

To ensure task completion by users and maximize data quality during remote testing, a comprehensive set of Gesture Experience Evaluation cards (GEE cards), complemented by a User Operation Guide, was devised for this study. Utilizing these tools, UX was conducted, which encompassed the accumulation of user questionnaire scoring, interview evaluations, and operational videos. Ultimately, these collected data served as the foundation for an in-depth analysis of issues and requirements related to the experience of gesture interactions.

3.1   Gesture Experience Evaluation Cards

Cards represent a beneficial tool capable of not only enabling users outside the design field to engage in the evaluation process but also sparking a variety of expression methods (Flórez-Aristizábal et al., 2022; Pahk et al., 2018). The card format assists in consolidating gesture task instructions and obtaining organized user feedback, leading to the development of basic GEE cards (see Fig. 1). Unlike standard questionnaires, this represents a specialized tool card for online gesture-based experimental tasks. The basic GEE cards, designed to accumulate user input, are bifurcated into a Task Guidance area and an Evaluation Fill-in area, both of which are easily comprehendible and fillable by the users. The Task Guidance area includes a unique task code and name, imagery for task instruction, and textual operation guidance. The Evaluation Fill-in area encompasses a textual experience evaluation scale and an open-ended evaluation description.

Furthermore, engaging in competitive comparison enables researchers and designers to comprehend the disparities inherent in the gesture experiences across different OS. To this end, the competitive comparison adaptation of the GEE cards augments the original two foundational areas with an additional Comparison Evaluation area. This area, too, contains scales and open-ended evaluations (see Fig. 2). For example, if a user has previously interacted with HarmonyOS in the last 1–2 years and is now asked

Fig. 1. A basic GEE cards.

to appraise the gesture QoE of ColorOS, the question proposed in the Comparison Evaluation area would be, "In comparison to a Huawei mobile phone furnished with HarmonyOS, does the experience of ColorOS improve upon a given index?" Moreover, the gestures corresponding to the same function often diverge among various OS, a fact that can be simultaneously pointed out in the text description of the task operation guidance portion to facilitate swift user comparison.

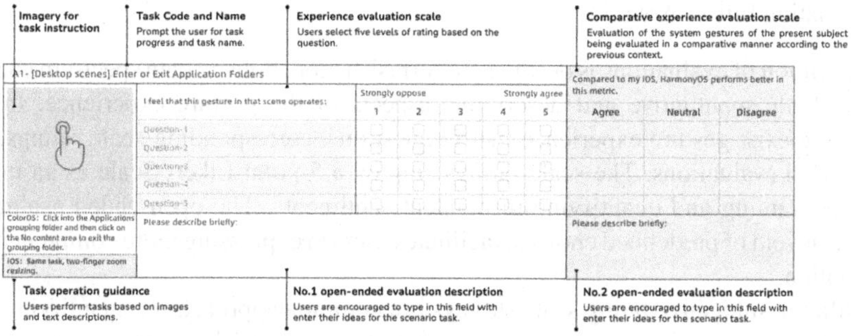

Fig. 2. A GEE cards for comparative evaluation.

- Task Guidance Area

Task guidance is developed to accurately and efficiently convey task operations to users. At the outset, researchers assign tasks a unique code and name. The specific task instruction that follows consists of screenshots from the task scenario, gesture graphical symbols, and text operation guidance (see Fig. 3). Text operation guidance can describe various gesture operations and real-world operating contexts (Hesenius et al., 2017). Visual aids like images and graphical symbols assist users in understanding the text while also alleviating potential reading monotony. The style of the task's textual description needs to be chosen based on the specific use scenarios, generally involving combinations of tasks and independent tasks. For example, Fig. 3(a) depicts a task combination: a single-finger tap to access the application group folder, followed by another tap in an empty area to exit the group folder. Conveying these two steps as separate tasks during remote testing would be challenging for users to understand. However, the task combination allows users to seamlessly transition between different operational tasks in a specific order. Figure 3 (b) presents an independent task, such as a three-finger vertical swipe applicable in any context for capturing a screenshot. The rationale behind using an independent task description in this context is that executing a screenshot is a common, brisk operation for users, thereby eliminating the need for extraneous content prompts.

Fig. 3. Task Guidance Area.

- Evaluation Fill-in Area

The execution of evaluations is designed to furnish a more holistic data spectrum encompassing both quantitative and descriptive aspects of the gesture experience. In this area, there exist gesture experience metric questions, corresponding scale ratings, and open-ended evaluations. The scale ratings employ a 5-point Likert Scale as an instrument for framing and quantifying respondent sentiments. The open-ended evaluation section, devoid of predefined choices, facilitates users in expressing more comprehensive information.

Utilizing subjective rating scale surveys is a common approach for quantifying data when assessing users' personal experiences and operational burdens associated with various gestures (Meng & Zhu, 2021). The questionnaire can be customized to suit specific research subjects. As the majority of experimental participants may lack professional backgrounds, it is vital to present the evaluation model's components in a language easily understood by users. Therefore, this study translated gesture experience metrics into user-friendly questions, converting the five key indicators— effectiveness, learnability, error tolerance, attractiveness, and efficiency—into five succinct questions (see Fig. 4). This forms a 5-point scale questionnaire. "Efficient" is expressed as, "I can complete tasks accurately and swiftly," "Effective" as, "I believe the entire gesture operation accurately achieves the intended goal," "Easy to learn" as, "I find this gesture easy to understand, remember, and execute," "Engaging" as, "I enjoy using this gesture and would do so frequently," and "Error tolerant" as, "I can easily recognize or interrupt incorrect gesture operations."

- Comparison Evaluation Area

Within the Comparative Evaluation area, a transition has been effected from a five-tier rating to a more streamlined three-tier rating (Guan et al., 2020): agree, neutral, and disagree (see Fig. 4). This adjustment primarily takes into account the indistinct past experiences and the multiplicity of operational tasks. Minimizing the scoring tiers, to some extent, alleviates the cognitive load on users and enhances the efficiency of the evaluation process.

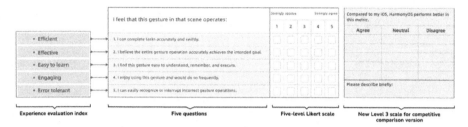

Fig. 4. Questions on the Gesture Experience Evaluation Scale.

3.2 User Operation Guide

The User Operation Guide (OG) dispenses explicit directives to users engaged in the evaluation process. In this research, a pre-experiment was implemented utilizing various remote testing devices and tools. Two users, devoid of previous participation in gesture-related experiments, were enlisted. During the pre-experiment, these participants exhibited comprehension of the experimental protocol, independently arranged the recording devices, and fulfilled the evaluation questionnaire. However, frequent communication with the research team via chat software was necessitated to dispel their uncertainties. Feedback from the pre-experiment participants prompted further adjustments by the researchers to diminish the comprehension difficulties for users. For instance, the portrayal of gesture experience evaluation cards was modified to "unit tables". Subsequently, the study advanced the following four facets of the OG.

- OG 1: Introduction to Questionnaire Sections and Module Forms

The total number of tasks in this questionnaire is specified, divided into four chapters with each task corresponding to a unit table. Participants are required to fill out and record the entire testing process as instructed. For instance, the first chapter includes a single-finger tap and single-finger double-tap gestures, along with 24 specific unit scenario tasks. It is recommended that users fill in the questionnaire in the order of the sections during the testing process. The estimated completion time for the questionnaire is around 1.5 to 2 h, and users are advised to allocate sufficient time in advance to complete it in one session.

- OG 2: Criteria for Completing Unit Forms

In this section, examples of both correct and incorrect responses are provided (see Fig. 5). If any omissions or errors occur in the completion of the questionnaire, the researchers will contact the users for clarification or revisions.

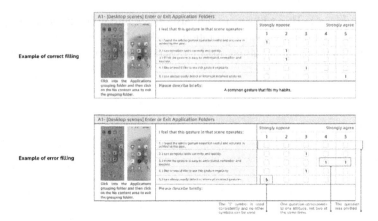

Fig. 5. Example of correct and incorrect completion.

- OG 3: Unit Form Completion Tool

The questionnaire's contents are distributed to users via a PDF file, with a computer or tablet recommended for completion. It is advised that users download an app such as WPS, which was frequently used in this study, featuring a text annotation function. In addition, the use of the tablet's handwriting capability is suggested.

- OG 4: Filmed Recordings while Completing the Questionnaire

First, users set up recording positions according to the requirement, and the researchers will provide remote guidance if necessary (see Fig. 6). In cases where users have limited equipment, they can prioritize capturing hand movements by using a phone holder or seek assistance from family or friends for recording. Second, before starting the actual tasks, the experimenter needs to ensure that the frame meets the requirements, with the hands fully visible and screen information displayed (see Fig. 6). Furthermore, it is crucial to confirm that the recording device has functional audio output (e.g., speakers) and input (e.g., microphone) capabilities. Finally, during the formal experiment, users are advised to segment their recordings based on the chapters. Additionally, they are encouraged to provide verbal cues about the corresponding task code. For example, when switching to the next task, users can state, "Now moving on to A1 bar 14." After recording, researchers collect the recorded videos and assign them standardized names.

3.3 Application Process

The tools and guidelines mentioned above consist of a "Subjective Evaluation Questionnaire for Gesture Experience." This questionnaire was used in a remote user testing of a research project, aiming to assess the current state of gesture QoE in commonly used OS. The questionnaire comprised 85 tasks identified through desktop research. ColorOS was elected as the experimental group for this experiment, with iOS and HarmonyOS functioning as the control groups. The study recruited 15 participants, varying in educational backgrounds and ages spanning 18 to 55 years, distributed evenly across

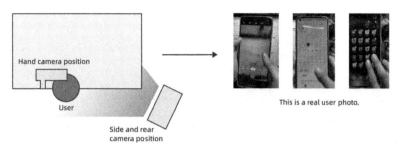

Fig. 6. Instructions for setting up image capture location: environmental requirements and image capture requirements.

the three OS (ColorOS: iOS: HarmonyOS = 1:1:1). Participants were grouped based on their existing mobile OS and were tasked with identical assignments sourced from ColorOS. All participants were required to follow the provided guidelines to complete the tasks, fill in the questionnaire, and record the process. It is worth mentioning that the composition of the questionnaires differed among the groups (see Fig. 7–8). Participants in the iOS and HarmonyOS groups were asked to compare their experience with the respective OS and provide descriptions and ratings on a 3-point scale.

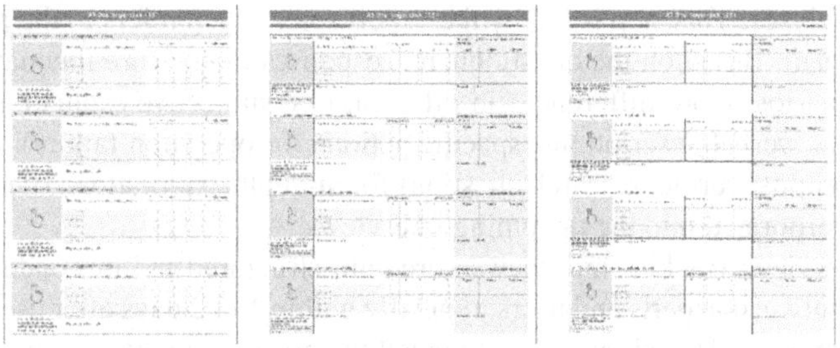

Fig. 7. Questionnaires used in the 3 sets of tests.

The process of GH firstly resembles assigning the experimental tasks as "homework" to participants, who are expected to autonomously complete the evaluation questionnaires and follow the OG. And the whole evaluation process involves the participation of both users and experts, which is divided into four steps (see Fig. 9).

- Step 1-Probes: The probe phase is user-driven, with the researchers responsible for distributing and gathering the "homework". In this step, the experimental devices are sent to the users via courier services. Users autonomously establish the experimental context, comprehend and carry out the tasks, and fill out the questionnaire as directed. The questionnaire's results, along with the recordings of users' actions and verbal feedback, build the foundation for the database used in later analysis. For the convenience of data organization and assessment by the experimenters at later stages, users' actions are captured through audio and video methods.

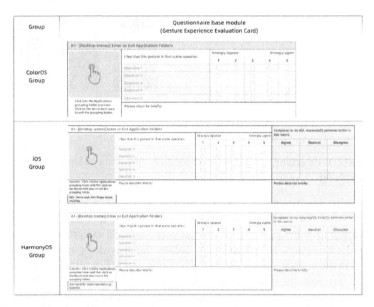

Fig. 8. Differences in the CEE cards used in the 3 sets of tests.

- Step 2-Analyses: This step is led by the expert role, which refers to the professional research team. Based on the questionnaire responses (e.g., score fluctuations in different scenarios, score differences in different OS, subjective evaluations), and the videos (e.g., verbal descriptions, specific actions for operation failure), experts discuss and propose further research questions for in-depth exploration. These questions can be incorporated into the upcoming interviews.

- Step 3-Interview: Tracking interviews were semi-structured and are conducted collaboratively between experts and users, typically within 1 to 2 days after users complete the questionnaire. This allows users to recall the process of performing the tasks and provide more detailed insights. As the interviews are conducted remotely, an online conferencing platform is necessary. The experimenter can demonstrate gesture operations and communicate with the users. The interview started with basic questions, such as demographic information and gesture operation habits, to confirm user details and help users adapt to the interview. The following questions are generally related to the research questions proposed in the previous stage, such as users' preferred gestures and inner reasons, and the experience issues linked to the low ratings. The expert should collect participants' descriptions in written or audio form.

- Step 4-Re-analyses: The researchers utilized thematic analysis (Braun & Clarke, 2006) to organize the content of the interview outcome, and integrate the information provided by participants during the probe step. Specifically, this information was encoded and categorized into key themes to summarize user tendencies in gesture experience. Additionally, the researchers may derive quantitative subjective data based on the questionnaires to further analyze problematic gesture scenarios and compare user satisfaction among different OS.

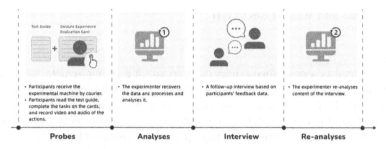

Fig. 9. The process of GH method.

4 Result and Discussion

4.1 Perceived Effectiveness of GH

A total of 15 questionnaires were distributed in the applied research, with 15 questionnaires collected and 11 questionnaires completed with all tasks answered, resulting in a completion rate of 73.3%. After the applied research, 15 participants' feedback on the evaluation tool, namely the GEE cards, was collected. This survey validated the effectiveness of the GH method in evaluating gesture experiences. All 15 users responded (n = 15), stating that the cards helped them understand and perform tasks. However, four of them did not complete the rating or answering of the GEE cards, and these incomplete responses were mainly due to unfamiliarity or inability to perform the task, such as doubts about functional necessity and finger size issues. Besides, 15 users also expressed that the cards helped generate ideas and express their viewpoints in different ways. Generally, the users' ratings in the questionnaires provide initial and overall evaluations of specific gesture task operations, which serve as a quick and concise reflection of personal preferences. But they are also relatively rough. The subsequent completion of open-ended responses helps users further organize their thoughts and provide descriptive feedback based on their personal experiences. The open-ended responses may be influenced by not only the current task operation but also a comparison between tasks. The latter situations often lead to modifications in rating or inspiration in open-ended responses. Additionally, participants using the competitive comparison version can also reflect on potential experience issues by comparing the two OS.

In detailed interviews, researchers amalgamated similar and differing ratings, prompting users to revisit and compare them, thereby fostering the identification of relationships among tasks. By encouraging focused reflection, issues about the abstract nature of gesture experiences became tangible, resulting in a more profound comprehension of these experiences.

In summary, through the online tools, participants were guided to independently complete the tasks, offering evaluations and corresponding justifications. They also had the opportunity to further explore and delve into their thoughts during the interviews with design experts. These discussions aimed to attribute problematic experiences to specific factors, such as oversized or undersized hotspots.

4.2   Strengths and Weaknesses of GH

Strengths

The GH method is a preliminary, integrated approach enabling remote user involvement in the evaluation of gesture QoE. Confronted with the high cognitive load and the metaphorical nature of gestures, non-expert users find it difficult to provide multi-dimensional descriptions. Further, the currently available online tools are ill-equipped for user-friendly gesture experience evaluation, showing a noticeable absence of efficient guidance and integration. Thus, the creation of the GH method is directed at surmounting these impediments.

It overcomes the differences between online and offline experimental environments by creating tools and procedures that are tailored to the characteristics of gesture research, resulting in feasible solutions in the current context. Specifically, it combines gesture task prompts, Likert scale evaluations, and open-ended language descriptions into an online questionnaire that users can autonomously operate. The purpose is to provide users with task guidance and capture subjective experiences and perceptions synchronized with the task stimuli. In terms of task setup and expression, individual tasks and task groups are employed based on the situation, allowing users to smoothly transition between tasks. Furthermore, during the questionnaire response process, users can rate the five aspects of gesture experience, namely Efficient, Effective, Easy to learn, Easy to learn, Engaging, and Error tolerant, using a Likert scale. They can also provide detailed descriptions in the open-ended evaluation area. And during the competitive comparison of OS, users are encouraged to provide quantitative score-based justifications and insights for their evaluations.

Another significant contribution of this research is to improve the gesture experience through a joint evaluation between users and experts. Firstly, during the user task operations, a combination of the think-aloud method was employed to capture users' spontaneous viewpoints (Fan et al., 2022; Nielsen et al., 2002). This provides an informational basis for understanding the psychological processes underlying user gesture execution to experts (Marques Correa et al., 2022). Secondly, the use of subjective evaluation questionnaires allows experts to further explore issues or points of interest based on the information provided by users, combined with their professional knowledge. Thirdly, when researchers have doubts about user evaluations, they can develop specific questions for follow-up interviews instead of subjectively speculating about user thoughts. Semi-structured interviews, a prevalent method for probing users' cognitive processes, facilitate the revelation of contextual information and expose users' underlying thoughts, problems, and opportunities for design enhancements (George, 2022). Lastly, designers can analyze comprehensive user data, such as changes in user gesture behavior within a specific OS, user psychological needs, and interests, to better identify gaps and improve existing mobile OS.

Weaknesses

Validation of this technique unveiled certain limitations. During the probing step, some participants voiced difficulties with specified tasks and insensitivity to rating scales. For instance, a participant aged over 40, due to infrequent use of multi-finger gestures and a series of unsuccessful attempts, exhibited increasing impatience. It was observed by the researchers that this participant assigned a "1" rating to all five elements. However, upon further investigation, it was found that the primary reasons for its negative experience were a lack of learning ability and a low tolerance for frequent errors. This discrepancy between the ratings and the participant's subjective impressions underscores the necessity for researchers to seek multiple confirmations. Thus, experimenters should provide remote online guidance during instances of repeated task execution failures, ensuring participants complete the tasks within a stable emotional state, thereby yielding more dependable data.

During the analysis and interview stage, researchers identified a methodological gap between outlier scores on rating scales and the interpretation of these outliers. More rigorous steps are required to provide explanations for score variations that correspond to subjective evaluations. Score variations may be caused by environmental factors or individual physiological factors (such as hand size), which are difficult to observe and challenging for participants to recall during the retrospective interviews. The research team may need to employ video analysis techniques, such as frame extraction observation and digital image processing, to quickly obtain materials that aid participants' recall or provide the basis for researchers' analysis and summarization.

5 Conclusion and Future Work

The GH method was developed in this study to support online user research in the field of mobile phone-based gesture experience. The application process of the GH method in projects was described, highlighting how UX evaluations can be transformed into insights that contribute to enhancing gesture experiences. This research enriches the evaluation methods for QoE in the field of gesture interaction, providing theoretical and practical support for understanding and evaluating gesture experience issues. GH extends the collaborative identification of design value and innovation to the joint insights of users and experts. The reciprocal enhancement of evaluation perception also contributes to the maintenance and improvement of gesture interaction-related features and services (Pahk et al., 2018). Moreover, the introduction of the GH method opens up new opportunities for research that previously faced challenges in conducting laboratory-based user testing, as remote data collection methods can now be leveraged (Giroux et al., 2021).

However, the method has limitations in terms of sample size and environmental validation, relying on participants' perceptions and the design team's observations of the tool. Future research is expected to focus on building new online platforms, providing rigorous means of data observation, and validating its effectiveness with larger and more diverse samples, thus further advancing the method.

References

Bolt, N., Tulathimutte, T.: Remote Research: Real Users, Real Time, Real Research. Rosenfeld Media (2010)

Braun, V., Clarke, V.: Using thematic analysis in psychology. Qual. Res. Psychol. 3(2), 77–101 (2006)

Brdnik, S., Heričko, T., Šumak, B.: Intelligent user interfaces and their evaluation: a systematic mapping study. Sensors (Basel) **22**(15) (2022). https://doi.org/10.3390/s22155830

Brudy, F., et al.: Cross-device taxonomy: survey, opportunities and challenges of interactions spanning across multiple devices. In: Proceedings of the 2019 CHI Conference on Human Factors in Computing Systems, pp. 1–28 (2019)

DeJonckheere, M., Vaughn, L.M.: Semistructured interviewing in primary care research: a balance of relationship and rigour. Family Medicine Community Health **7**(2) (2019)

Dey, A.K.: Understanding and using context. Pers. Ubiquit. Comput. **5**, 4–7 (2001)

Fan, M., Wang, Y., Xie, Y., Li, F.M., Chen, C.: Understanding how older adults comprehend COVID-19 interactive visualizations via think-aloud protocol. Int. J. Hum.–Comput. Interact. 1–17 (2022)

Flórez-Aristizábal, L., Collazos, C.A., Cano, S., Solano, A.: CollabABILITY cards: supporting researchers and educators to co-design computer-supported collaborative learning activities for deaf children. Sustainability **14**(22), 14703 (2022)

George, T.: Semi-Structured Interview | Definition, Guide & Examples (2022). https://www.scribbr.com/methodology/semi-structured-interview/

Giroux, F., et al.: Guidelines for collecting automatic facial expression detection data synchronized with a dynamic stimulus in remote moderated user tests. In: Human-Computer Interaction. Theory, Methods and Tools: Thematic Area, HCI 2021, Held as Part of the 23rd HCI International Conference, HCII 2021, Virtual Event, July 24–29, 2021, Proceedings, Part I 23 (2021)

Guan, L.L., Zhu, Z.M., Zhang, L., Wang, S.L.: Research on the functions and services of scientific research crowdsourcing platform in the perspective of open science: a case study of Daemo. Res. Lib. Sci. (05), 59–66 (2020). https://doi.org/10.15941/j.cnki.issn1001-0424.2020.05.009

Habib, H., Li, M., Young, E., Cranor, L.: "Okay, whatever": an evaluation of cookie consent interfaces. In: Proceedings of the 2022 CHI Conference on Human Factors in Computing Systems, pp. 1–27 (2022)

Heo, S., Lee, G.: ForceTap: extending the input vocabulary of mobile touch screens by adding tap gestures. In: Proceedings of the 13th International Conference on Human Computer Interaction with Mobile Devices and Services, pp. 113–122 (2011)

Hesenius, M., Gruhn, V.: GestureCards: a hybrid gesture notation. In: Proceedings of the ACM on Human-Computer Interaction, **3**(EICS), 1–35 (2019)

Hesenius, M., Sternal, S., Gruhn, V.: A multi-touch-recognizer for gesturecards. In: Proceedings of the ACM SIGCHI Symposium on Engineering Interactive Computing Systems, pp. 75–80 (2017)

Hu, Y., Du, X., Bryan-Kinns, N., Guo, Y.: Identifying divergent design thinking through the observable behavior of service design novices. Int. J. Technol. Des. Educ. **29**, 1179–1191 (2019)

Ikematsu, K., Tsubouchi, K., Yamanaka, S.: PredicTaps: latency reduction technique for single-taps based on recognition for single-tap or double-tap. In: Extended Abstracts of the 2020 CHI Conference on Human Factors in Computing Systems, pp. 1–9 (2020)

Jiang, L.: Interactive Data Exploration using Gestures [Doctoral dissertation, The Ohio State University] (2017)

Juran, J.: Quality 4.0: the future of quality? Web blog. In (2021)

Larsen, J.N., Jacobsen, T.H., Boring, S., Bergström, J., Pohl, H.: The influence of hand size on touch accuracy. In: Proceedings of the 21st International Conference on Human-Computer Interaction with Mobile Devices and Services, pp. 1–11 (2019)

Liu, J., Kim, S.: Space design guide for public areas in a multicultural environment: based on the theory of social atomism. Arch. Des. Res. **34**(2), 21–31 (2021)

Marques Correa, C., Diniz Junqueira Barbosa, G., Diniz Junqueira Barbosa, S., Selbach Silveira, M.: HCI research experiences during the pandemic: lessons learned for the road ahead. Interact. Comput., iwac036 (2022)

Meng, M., Zhu, Q.H.: A review of research on user experience at home and abroad. Res. Lib. Sci. (09), 9–19 (2021). https://doi.org/10.15941/j.cnki.issn1001-0424.2021.09.002

Nielsen, J., Clemmensen, T., Yssing, C.: Getting access to what goes on in people's heads? Reflections on the think-aloud technique. In: Proceedings of the Second Nordic Conference on Human-Computer Interaction, pp. 101–110 (2002)

Pahk, Y., Self, J., Baek, J.S.: COVALENT, a method for co-designing value exchange in community-centred design. CoDesign **14**(4), 275–292 (2018)

Paz, F., Pow-Sang, J.A.: Usability evaluation methods for software development: a systematic mapping review. In: 2015 8th International Conference on Advanced Software Engineering & Its Applications (ASEA), pp. 1–4. IEEE (2015)

Prates, R.O., De Souza, C.S., Barbosa, S.D.: Methods and tools: a method for evaluating the communicability of user interfaces. Interactions **7**(1), 31–38 (2000)

Pu, Y.-H., Chiu, P.-S., Chen, T.-S., Huang, Y.-M.: The design and implementation of a mobile library app system. Library Hi Tech **33**(1), 15–31 (2015)

Qi, W., Li, D.: A user experience study on short video social apps based on content recommendation algorithm of artificial intelligence. Int. J. Pattern Recognit Artif Intell. **35**(02), 2159008 (2021)

Quesenbery, W.: Balancing the 5Es of usability. Cutter IT Journal **17**(2), 4–11 (2004)

Rodda, J., Ranscombe, C., Kuys, B.: A method to explore strategies to communicate user experience through storyboards: an automotive design case study. AI EDAM **36**, e16 (2022)

Statista: Mobile network subscriptions worldwide 2028 (2022). https://www.statista.com/statistics/330695/number-of-smartphone-users-worldwide/

Sun, P.: The gesture-based context user interface. Pack. Eng. **35**(08), 96–100 (2014). https://doi.org/10.19554/j.cnki.1001-3563.2014.08.024

Truong, K.N., Hayes, G.R., Abowd, G.D.: Storyboarding: an empirical determination of best practices and effective guidelines. In: Proceedings of the 6th Conference on Designing Interactive Systems, pp. 12–21 (2006)

Vyas, D., van der Veer, G.C.: APEC: a framework for designing experience. Spaces, Places & Experience in HCI, pp. 1–4 (2005)

Wei, W., Gong, X.D.: HCI develop trend based on user-experience. J. Beijing Univ. Aeronaut. Astronaut. **37**(07), 868–871 (2011). https://doi.org/10.13700/j.bh.1001-5965.2011.07.009

Xia, H., Glueck, M., Annett, M., Wang, M., Wigdor, D.: Iteratively designing gesture vocabularies: a survey and analysis of best practices in the HCI literature. ACM Trans. Comput.-Hum. Interact. (TOCHI) **29**(4), 1–54 (2022)

Zhang, J., Liu, Y., Chen, K.J.: Gesture interaction design for wearable devices based on scenario model. Pack. Eng. **40**(12), 140–146 (2019). https://doi.org/10.19554/j.cnki.1001-3563.2019.12.025

A Preliminary Study on the Kansei Evaluation of Physical and Virtual Operation Interfaces

Shih-Cheng Fann[✉]

Bachelor Program in Interdisciplinary Integrated Design, National Yunlin University of Science and Technology, Douliu, Taiwan
fann72515@gmail.com

Abstract. The rapid advancement of technology has prompted significant changes in the design of high-tech products, transitioning from physical operation interfaces to virtual interfaces, such as touch screens. This study focuses on the operation interface of automotive control panels and investigates the differences in kansei evaluation and user preferences between physical and virtual interfaces. Through kansei evaluations and eye-tracking experiments, participants' subjective evaluations and visual attention patterns towards both interface types are analyzed. The findings indicate that participants' attention is primarily directed towards the control panel interface and the steering wheel, highlighting the considerable impact of these designs on kansei evaluations. Furthermore, the control panel interface receives a greater number of visual fixations compared to the steering wheel, indicating users' heightened visual focus on this area. Additionally, the position and size of the screen significantly influence the distribution of participants' visual attention, with vertical or large screens attracting more gaze. This research contributes to a comprehensive understanding of the kansei differences during the transition from physical to virtual interfaces. The findings provide valuable insights for interface design research and offer practical design recommendations for automotive control panel interfaces.

Keywords: Kansei Engineering · Eye tracking · Car design

1 Introduction

In recent years, with the maturity of virtual and touch technologies, replacing physical interfaces with virtual interfaces has become a pre-vailing design trend. However, the tangible kansei (aesthetic) feel of a product is crucial, as the actual tactile and psychological sensations may differ. Many designers focus primarily on the visual aspects of design, neglecting the importance of touch and feel in our behavioral evaluations of products, particularly in the realm of operating inter-faces. This design trend has even impacted automotive control panels and dashboards, where drivers are unable to intuitively achieve their operational goals through touch sensations like pressing and rotating in a short period of time. The sense of tangibility is of great importance to humans, as physical objects possess weight, materiality, and appearance, making them "tangible."

© The Author(s), under exclusive license to Springer Nature Switzerland AG 2023
M. Kurosu et al. (Eds.): HCII 2023, LNCS 14054, pp. 54–66, 2023.
https://doi.org/10.1007/978-3-031-48038-6_4

Kansei systems constitute a significant part of the human brain, and through continuous exploration and interaction with the environment, products should fully utilize such interactions involving touch, smell, hearing, etc. (Norman 2004). This study aims to investigate the kansei evaluations and preferences of participants regarding physical and virtual interfaces through eye-tracking experiments. It seeks to understand the differences in kansei evaluations and preference between the two interfaces and the key morphological features that influence participants' evaluations of control panel designs for different operating interfaces.

Subsequent paragraphs, however, are indented.

2 Literature Review

2.1 Definition and Applications of Virtual Interfaces/Virtual Reality

Virtual interfaces/virtual reality, as proposed by Burdea & Coiffet (2003), refer to computer-generated simulated interfaces/spaces that resemble the real world. Users can interact with and immerse themselves in these artificial interfaces/environments. The three main characteristics of virtual interfaces/reality are interactivity, imagination, and immersion (Sheridan 2000; Stanney & Zyda 2002). The development of virtual interfaces/reality focuses on achieving high realism through lifelike visuals and high resolution, as well as high interactivity with an emphasis on feedback and real-time responsiveness. The experience of virtual interfaces/reality is an illusion that provides users with a mentally imaginative space (Heim 1993), and it can be categorized into seven types:

1. Interactivity: The ability to communicate and respond to system-generated messages.
2. Artificiality: All scenes and characters in the virtual world are created by humans.
3. Immersion: The illusion of being immersed in a virtual world created through hardware and software interfaces.
4. Networked communication: Virtual reality establishes channels for mutual communication, creating an environment for information sharing.
5. Full-body immersion: Users can freely move within the virtual world without the need for heavy equipment.
6. Simulation: Highly realistic images of characters and scenes blur the distinction between reality and virtuality.
7. Telepresence: The illusion of being in a different location due to the inability to distinguish between real and virtual in the virtual world.

Virtual interfaces/reality utilize computer simulation to provide users with a Kansei experience that simulates the real world. It exists between the virtual, the real, and the user, and is characterized by immersion, interactivity, and imagination.

2.2 Kansei Engineering

Kansei engineering has become an important discipline in the design field over the past thirty years. Kansei research is divided into three areas: KE (kansei engineering), KS (kansei science), and KD (kansei design). KE represents the intersection between sensibility and engineering (Levy 2013) and is a technique that "transforms consumers' feelings and images of products into design elements" (Nagamachi 1995). By identifying important visual elements and arranging or adding/removing them within a certain parameter of element combinations, viewers can easily feel the sensibility set by the designer (Chan 2000). In studies on the impact of human factors on product development and design, the most important influencing factors when people decide to purchase products are "product customization," "kansei value," and "design." Therefore, understanding the sensibility that arises from using a product is crucial for designers during product development (Schmitt et al. 2015).

According to Desmet (2003), it is difficult to provide a single definition of sensibility. There are many different perspectives on how to define, study, and explain sensibility in psychology. The most common definition is to view sensibility as a multifaceted phenomenon composed of four elements: 1. Behavioral responses, 2. Expressed responses, 3. Psychological responses, and 4. Kansei. By measuring these elements, one can understand how people respond sensibly. There are many different methods for measuring sensibility, ranging from paper-and-pencil scales to high-tech instruments, and can be mainly divided into kansei and objective physiological measures.

2.3 Method of Semantic Differential

The Method of Semantic Differential (SD), also known as the "cross-modality matching" method, is a research technique that explores the relationship between different kansei experiences. When one sense is stimulated, it evokes a sensation that is associated with another sense. According to Osgood's (1961) research, the purpose of using the SD method is to help researchers understand perceptual images, which involves three components: the concept stimulus, a set of opposing adjectives on a scale, and the subject, who evaluates the degree of sensation on the adjective scale. Through various introductions and analyses, the subject's perceptual cognition can be quantified by data and obtained as established information. Regarding level selection on the scale, Zhang and Xu (2001) conducted an image assessment of the formation style using five scales ranging from 3 to 11 levels for subjects, investigating the differences in product style perception among subjects at different scale levels. They found that using a 7 or 9-level scale could avoid excessive mental burden on the subjects. Therefore, this study will use a 7-level scale as the research measurement scale. In kansei engineering research, kansei descriptions of products are often used to discuss the kansei response that products elicit in individuals through the SD method. After further analysis of the obtained data, a kansei database or expert system can be established and applied to different types of design (Bouchard 2003).

2.4   Eye Tracking and Kansei Evaluation

Observing eye movements provides valuable insights into the areas of interest and visual preferences of individuals towards objects. Many researchers have utilized eye-tracking technology to investigate human eye movements when viewing images found that when viewing line drawings, the fixation time of the human eye is not evenly distributed across the image; instead, it is primarily concentrated on several important visual features. Moreover, individuals can quickly identify interesting and significant areas within the picture. In a study on the impact of mobile phone packaging on consumer purchasing decisions, Hendrickson & Ailawadi (2014) also found that consumers can locate desired products on store shelves within a short period, and packaging designs that are easy for consumers to read can increase their willingness to purchase. The eye movement trajectory of participants when viewing visual stimuli is not smooth lines or curves but rather composed of numerous pauses and fixations. Buswell (1935) conducted eye movement research on human perception of pictures and identified two perceptual stages. The first stage is the general survey mode, where individuals make brief fixations on several parts of the picture. The second stage is the quality metric mode, characterized by longer fixations that are typically focused on a small area of the image, indicating the detailed examination of specific details within the picture. When individuals have limited time to observe an image, the general survey mode is predominantly observed. This suggests that initially, individuals focus on the overall structure of the visual stimuli, and if given sufficient time, they proceed to examine the finer details (such as elements and features) of the stimuli. Based on the above, it can be concluded that participants' visual attention not only focuses on the key areas of the overall visual stimuli but also exhibits consistent visual observation patterns towards the stimuli. By utilizing heat maps, information regarding the distribution of visual attention and the concentration of fixations can be obtained. Therefore, analyzing heat maps allows us to grasp the visual patterns of participants when evaluating the Kansei aspects of visual stimuli, enabling us to understand the key features that influence participants' judgments of visual aesthetics.

3   Research Methods

3.1   Collection and Extraction of Samples and Adjectives

In this study, the SD evaluation was combined with an eye-tracking experiment for the current market car center console design research. It is expected to be able to combine kansei engineering with eye tracking experiment to understand how the subjects feel when more and more automobile central control interface designs are designed from physical interfaces to virtual interface, and analyze how does it affect the subjects' visual attention when evaluate the kansei of the center console design. To screen for representative samples and adjective pairs, this study used a semantic differential pre-test screening by expert panels. The pre-test SD survey used a Likert seven-point scale for the kansei scale ranging from 1 to 7, as shown in Table 1. Experts trained in industrial design were invited to conduct the SD pre-test evaluation (five males and five females, all with a master's degree in industrial design). First, a hierarchical analysis of the adjective pairs was performed, and the pairs were selected from the clusters. Items with high similarity and unclear subject perceptions were deleted from the clusters. The following pairs of adjectives were finally selected: 1. Simple-Complex, 2. Plain-Luxurious, 3. Common-Unique, 4. Traditional-Futuristic, 5. Rational- Emotional, 6. Calm-Exciting, 7. Uncomfortable-Comfortable. As there were 7 pairs of adjectives, the 44 central console samples were also clustered into 7 groups using the data obtained from the SD pre-test through the K-means clustering method. The two samples closest to the cluster center were selected from each group, resulting in 14 central console samples for use in subsequent experiments, as shown in Table 2. The eye movement behavior of the subjects was measured when they were conducting kansei evaluation of the car central control samples. The Eyefollower 2.0 eye tracking system was planned to be used, with a sampling rate of 120 Hz, and the matched monitor was a 24-in. standard LCD screen.

Table 1. A7 pairs of adjectives (This study organizes).

1. Concise – complex	2. Plain – luxurious	3. Ordinary – unique	4. Traditional – future
5. Rational – sensual	6.calm – heartwarming	7. uncomfortable – comfortable	

Table 2. List of experimental samples (This study organizes)

DS1	DS2	DS3	DS4

DS5	DS6	DS7	DS8

DS9	DS10	DS11	DS12

DS13	DS14		

3.2 Factor Analysis and Cluster Analysis

In this study, after extracting the adjective pairs from the pretest and selecting the effective samples, a formal SD survey was conducted with 20 participants, consisting of 10 males and 10 females, with an average age range of 23 years and corrected visual acuity within the normal range. After the experiment, factor analysis using the principal component analysis method was used to extract factors from the SD scores, with the criterion for factor extraction being eigenvalues greater than 1. Seven groups of Kansei factors were condensed into two factors, and a factor rotation was performed using the maximum variance method, as shown in Table 3. As can be seen from the above, the adjectives included in Factor 1, such as "ordinary-unique", "calm-exciting", "traditional-futuristic", "plain-luxurious", all represent the strength of arousal that the sample elicited in the participants. Therefore, it was named the "Arousal factor". The adjectives included in Factor 2, such as "uncomfortable-comfortable", "simple-complex", "rational- emotional", clearly indicate the kansei evaluation that the participants made of the sample. Therefore, it was named the "Valence factor". The scoring data obtained from the SD method was clustered using hierarchical cluster analysis to understand which central console samples the participants would group together in their Kansei judgments. The hierarchical cluster analysis resulted in six clusters containing a total of 14 samples, as shown in Fig. 1.

Table 3. The result of factor analysis of experiment

Adjectives	Factor 1	Factor 2	Commonality
Common-Unique	0.920	-0.043	0.809
Calm-Exciting	0.881	0.283	0.815
Traditional-Futuristic	0.836	0.219	0.849
Plain-Luxurious	0.765	-0.361	`0.756
Uncomfortable-Comfortable	0.705	0.802	0.388
Simple-Complex	-0.004	-0.798	0.857
Rational-Emotional	-0.619	0.611	0.677
Eigenvalues	3.237	1.914	
Variation %	46.245	27.337	
Cumulative Variation %	46.245	73.582	

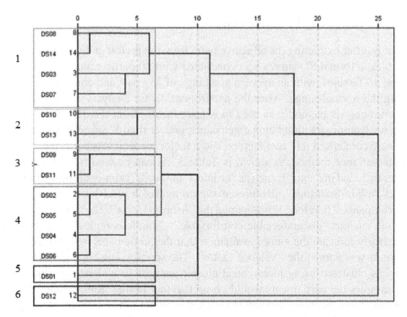

Fig. 1. Cluster analysis

4 Research Result

The present study aimed to explore the relationship between different design elements and kansei evaluations in a sample. Kansei evaluation was conducted using the SD method, followed by factor analysis and cluster analysis to understand the Kansei factors that influenced the participants' kansei evaluations and the kansei adjectives represented by each cluster. The following are the research findings.

4.1 Cluster 1, the "Complex, Unique, Future" Sample Group

Cluster 1, the "complex, unique, future" sample group, contains samples DS08, DS14, DS03, and DS07, as shown in Table 4 and the heat map shown in Fig. 2. It can be seen that the participants' attention is primarily focused on the control panel interface and the steering wheel and the samples in this group share a common preference for "complex", "unique", and "future" feelings, with all samples in the group scoring above or close to 5 points on the common sensibility scale (ranging from 1 to 7). In terms of "rational- emotional " and "calm-exciting" evaluations, there is no clear preference within the group. However, among the "uncomfortable-comfortable" evaluations, the design of sample DS08 received the highest "comfortable" rating (5.20) among the four samples, while sample DS03's design was clearly perceived as "uncomfortable" (3.20) by users.

Table 4. SD survey score and kansei bias of Cluster 1 samples.

Adjectives	DS08	DS14	DS03	DS07
Simple-Complex	5.35	6.00	5.65	4.60
Plain-Luxurious	5.50	5.95	4.35	4.65
Common-Unique	4.80	5.10	4.90	5.30
Traditional-Futuristic	4.85	4.95	4.80	4.80
Rational-Emotional	3.35	3.15	2.80	4.10
Calm-Exciting	4.45	4.50	4.30	4.15
Uncomfortable-Comfortable	5.20	4.95	3.20	4.10

Fig. 2. Samples of cluster 1.

4.2 Cluster 2, the "Luxurious, Unique, Futuristic, Exciting, and Comfortable" Sample Group

Cluster 2, the "luxurious, unique, futuristic, exciting, and comfortable" sample group, contains samples DS10 and DS13, as shown in Table 5 and the heat map shown in Fig. 3. It can be seen that the participants' attention is primarily focused on the control panel interface and the steering wheel and the samples in this cluster share a common inclination towards "luxurious", "unique", "futuristic", "exciting", and "comfortable" sensations. From the kansei ratings, it is evident that the kansei preferences of the participants for samples DS10 and DS13 are very prominent. Sample DS10 received a rating of over 5 for "complex" (5.55), "luxurious" (6.45), "unique" (6.50), "futuristic" (6.45), "exciting" (5.45), and "comfortable" (5.25), while sample DS13 received a rating of over 5 for "luxurious" (5.80), "unique" (6.00), "futuristic" (5.95), "exciting" (5.05), and "comfortable" (5.40) (kansei scale ranging from 1 to 7).

4.3 Cluster 3, the "Rational" Sample Group

This group includes samples DS09 and DS11, as shown in Table 6 and the heat map shown in Fig. 4. It can be seen that the participants' attention is primarily focused on the control panel interface and the steering wheel and the samples in this group have a common preference for "rational" feelings, and their kansei ratings are all below or close to 3 (DS09: 3.15, DS11: 2.80). There are no other common kansei preferences in this group (kansei scale ranges from 1 to 7).

Table 5. SD survey score and kansei bias of Cluster 2 samples

Adjectives	DS10	DS13
Simple-Complex	5.55	3.70
Plain-Luxurious	6.45	5.80
Common-Unique	6.50	6.00
Traditional-Futuristic	6.45	5.95
Rational-Emotional	3.40	3.25
Calm-Exciting	5.45	5.05
Uncomfortable-Comfortable	5.25	5.40

DS10   DS13

Fig. 3. Samples of cluster 2.

Table 6. SD survey score and kansei bias of Cluster 3 samples.

Adjectives	DS09	DS11
Simple-Complex	4.05	4.70
Plain-Luxurious	4.05	4.60
Common-Unique	3.55	3.85
Traditional-Futuristic	3.60	3.90
Rational-Emotional	3.15	2.80
Calm-Exciting	3.75	3.25
Uncomfortable-Comfortable	4.50	4.00

DS09   DS11

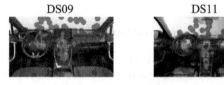

Fig. 4. Samples of cluster 3.

4.4   Cluster 4, "Comfortable" Sample Group

This group includes samples DS02, DS05, DS04, and DS06, as shown in Table 7 and the heat map shown in Fig. 5. It can be seen that the participants' attention is primarily focused on the control panel interface and the steering wheel and the samples in this group share a common preference for "comfortable" feelings, with all samples in the group scoring above 5 on the "comfortable" dimension (on a kansei scale from 1 to 7). There is no common kansei preference among the group for other dimensions.

Table 7. SD survey score and kansei bias of Cluster 4 samples.

Adjectives	DS02	DS05	DS04	DS06
Simple-Complex	2.80	2.50	4.00	3.65
Plain-Luxurious	3.95	4.30	4.17	4.65
Common-Unique	3.60	4.05	3.50	4.25
Traditional-Futuristic	4.70	4.35	4.17	4.20
Rational-Emotional	3.65	3.20	4.83	4.25
Calm-Exciting	4.10	4.70	4.67	4.65
Uncomfortable-Comfortable	5.35	5.20	5.17	5.15

DS02	DS05	DS04	DS06

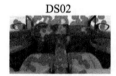  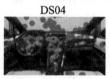 

Fig. 5. Samples of cluster 4.

4.5   Cluster 5 Consists of Sample DS01, and Cluster 6 Consists of Sample Group DS12

Cluster 5 consists of sample DS01, and Cluster 6 consists of sample group DS12, as shown in Table 8 and the heat map shown in Fig. 6. It can be seen that the participants' attention is primarily focused on the control panel interface and the steering wheel. The kansei tendencies of sample DS01 are "simple," "plain," "ordinary," "rational," "calm," and "comfortable." The kansei tendencies of sample DS12 are "simple," "plain," "unique," "future," and "comfortable." Although both have kansei tendencies of "simple," "plain," and "comfortable," the kansei ratings show that sample DS01 gives a significant "ordinary" feeling to participants (2.50), while sample DS12 gives a significant "unique" feeling to participants (5.50). While sample DS01 cannot give participants a significant bias in "traditional-future" (4.05), sample DS12 gives participants a significant "future" feeling (5.80). Although the two have three similar kansei tendencies, there are greater differences in "ordinary-unique" and "traditional-future," suggesting that they were classified into two separate clusters for this reason (the kansei scale ranges from 1 to 7).

Table 8. SD survey score and kansei bias of Cluster 5 & Cluster 6 samples.

Adjectives	DS01	DS12
Simple-Complex	3.05	1.15
Plain-Luxurious	2.70	2.80
Common-Unique	2.50	5.50
Traditional-Futuristic	4.05	5.80
Rational-Emotional	2.90	3.70
Calm-Exciting	2.85	4.40
Uncomfortable-Comfortable	5.25	5.35

DS01   DS12

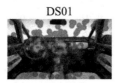   

Fig. 6. Samples of cluster 5 & cluster 6

5   Conclusion and Recommendations

This study used SD and eye-tracking experiments to investigate the design of central consoles in cars. It aimed to explore the kansei aspects and identify influential features. Results showed participants' kansei evaluations were influenced by arousal and evaluative factors. Conclusions from six sample clusters are:

1. Screen size and configuration impact kansei evaluations. Regardless of orientation, participants judged consoles as "luxurious," especially in clusters 1 and 2.
2. Screen size affects the perception of "uniqueness" in console design, especially in clusters 1, 2, and 6 with large screens.
3. Symmetrical designs elicit "rational" perception, as seen in cluster 3, regardless of screen size or orientation.
4. "Complex" console designs tend to evoke "luxurious" evaluations. Samples rated as "complex" were mostly seen as "luxurious," e.g., DS08, DS14, DS07, DS10, and DS11. Incorporating more design elements is necessary for a "luxurious" perception.
5. Participants primarily focus on the console interface and steering wheel, influencing their kansei evaluations.

6. More gaze fixations occur on the console interface than the steering wheel, indicating higher visual attention to console design.
7. Screen position and size significantly affect participants' visual attention. Vertical or large-area screens attract more gaze.

The results of this study indicate the key features and corresponding kansei evaluations that participants focus on when observing the design of car central consoles. It was found that the design of the central console screen influences participants' "luxurious" and "unique" kansei evaluations, while the overall form of the central console affects "unique" and "rational" kansei evaluations. The focal observation features are the console interface and the steering wheel. These findings provide valuable reference for designers in contemporary car central console design and serve as a basis for kansei research in contemporary car design and next-generation central console design. It is important to note that the use of images as experimental stimuli in this study may differ from the observation of physical objects. Future researchers are recommended to combine relevant recording equipment and conduct experiments with physical samples to obtain more comprehensive results.

References

Burdea, G.C., Coiffet, P.: Virtual Reality Technology. Wiley, New York (2003)

Norman, D.A.: Emotional Design: Why We Love (or Hate) Everyday Things. Basic Civitas Books (2004)

Parasuraman, R., Sheridan, T.B., Wickens, C.D.: A model for types and levels of human interaction with automation. IEEE Trans. Syst. Man Cybern.-Part A: Syst. Hum. **30**(3), 286–297 (2000)

Stanney, K.M., Zyda, M.: Virtual environments in the 21st century. In: Handbook of Virtual Environments, pp. 41–54. CRC Press (2000)

Heim, M.: The essence of VR. Ideal. Stud. **23**(1), 49–62 (1993)

Levy, P.: Beyond kansei engineering: The emancipation of kansei design. Int. J. Des. **7**(2), 83–94 (2013)

Nagamachi, M.: Kansei engineering: a new ergonomic consumer-oriented technology for product development. Int. J. Ind. Ergon. **15**(1), 3–11 (1995)

Chan, C.-S.: Can style be measured? Des. Stud. **21**(3), 277–291 (2000)

Schmitt, R., Falk, B., Stiller, S., Heinrichs, V.: Human Factors in Product Development and Design Advances in Production Technology, pp. 201–211. Springer, New York (2015)

Desmet, P.: Measuring emotion: development and application of an instrument to measure emotional responses to products. In: Blythe, M., Monk, A. (eds.) Funology 2. HIS, pp. 391–404. Springer, Cham (2018). https://doi.org/10.1007/978-3-319-68213-6_25

Osgood, C.E.: Psycholinguistic relativity and universality. Acta Physiol. (Oxf) **19**, 673–678 (1961)

Zhang, J., Xu, W.: A study of semantic differential analysis scale. In: Proceedings of the 2nd Workshop on Industrial Design, Science and Art, Huafan University. Taipei, Taiwan (2001)

Bouchard, C., Lim, D., Aoussat: Development of a Kansei Engineering system for industrial design: identification of input data for Kansei Engineering Systems. J. Asian Des. Int. Conf. **1**(12) (2003)

Hendrickson, K., Ailawadi, K.L.: Six lessons for in-store marketing from six years of mobile eye-tracking research. In: Shopper Marketing and the Role of In-Store Marketing. Emerald Group Publishing Limited (2014)

Buswell, G.T.: How People Look at Pictures: A Study of the Psychology and Perception in Art, pp. 142–144. University of Chicago Press, Chicago (1935)

Designing Multimodal User Interfaces for Hybrid Collaboration: A User-Centered Approach

Rongrong Gong[1] and Min Hua[2(✉)]

[1] Product Group, Vibe Inc., Shanghai 201210, China
[2] USC-SJTU Institute of Cultural and Creative Industry, Shanghai Jiao Tong University,
Shanghai 200241, China
huamin@sjtu.edu.cn

Abstract. Hybrid collaboration has gained significant popularity in recent years due to globalization and international collaboration, which has been further accelerated by the COVID-19 pandemic. Although some studies have investigated the features of hybrid collaboration, there is still a lack of understanding regarding efficient and effective human-computer interactions that can facilitate this mode of collaboration. Research has shown that humans process information faster and better when it is presented in multiple modalities. Therefore, this study aims to develop a user-centered approach that integrates multimodal user interfaces (MUIs) to better support hybrid collaboration. User research was conducted to gather insights into the needs and preferences of both co-located teams and remote members. The study also investigated the benefits of multimodal interactions. Building upon the understanding of user requirements and MUIs, the research explored the most effective MUIs for two typical activities in hybrid collaboration. Subsequently, a high-fidelity prototype was developed and evaluated to validate the research hypothesis. The findings identified the advantages of MUIs and formulated design principles for MUIs in a hybrid collaboration environment. This research could contribute to the growing body of knowledge on MUI design, and practical implications were presented and tested for enhancing hybrid collaboration.

Keywords: Multimodal User Interfaces · Hybrid Collaboration · User-Centered Design

1 Introduction

Hybrid collaboration, characterized by the integration of co-located teams and remote members, has gained significant popularity in recent years due to globalization and the rapid advancement of digital technologies [1]. It has gained significant attention since it combines the strengths of both face-to-face and remote collaboration, which has the potential to bridge the gap between these two modes [2]. Recognizing the benefits, organizations, including Microsoft, have shown interest in hybrid work, as it offers

M. Kurosu et al. (Eds.): HCII 2023, LNCS 14054, pp. 67–82, 2023.
https://doi.org/10.1007/978-3-031-48038-6_5

flexibility to individuals, allowing them to work in a manner that suits their preferences and maximizes their productivity. Moreover, technology plays a vital role in facilitating hybrid collaboration, assisting in building interpersonal trust, providing visibility into team members' contributions and whereabouts, and enabling spontaneous engagement throughout the workday [3].

Despite its advantages, hybrid collaboration presents challenges for both co-located teams and remote members. These challenges encompass various aspects. First, the physical separation of team members and the increased reliance on digital communication tools can lead to issues such as misunderstandings, delays, and reduced information sharing [4]. Second, building trust and cohesion among team members becomes more difficult due to limited face-to-face interactions [5]. Third, maintaining a healthy work-life balance becomes increasingly difficult as the boundaries between work and personal life blur, potentially resulting in overwork and difficulty in disconnecting from work [6].

To address these challenges, an increasing array of communication technologies have been developed to engage both co-located teams and remote members, such as video conferencing tools, desktop video and audio conferencing, and chat rooms for text interactions [7]. While these technologies bring benefits to hybrid collaboration, such as providing location flexibility, facilitating idea-sharing and problem-solving among distributed team members, and speeding up the collaboration process, they often focus on improving efficiency and pay less attention to psychological aspects like team cohesion and engagement, not to mention work-life balance. Consequently, there remain several challenges in hybrid collaboration that require further exploration.

Multimodal user interfaces (MUIs), which integrate various input and output modalities such as speech, touch, and gesture, have emerged as a promising solution to enhance user experience and improve collaboration efficiency in hybrid environments [8]. In this study, we propose a user-centered approach to explore the optimal MUIs that better support hybrid collaboration.

The goal of this study is to explore the needs and preferences of co-located teams and remote members engaged in hybrid collaboration. Specifically, we aim to improve communication, increase engagement and participation, and build stronger team cohesion. To achieve these goals, we address the following research questions:

RQ1. What are the main barriers and challenges to effective hybrid collaboration related to communication technologies and devices?

RQ2. What are the best practices for designing and implementing MUIs to enhance hybrid collaboration?

By addressing these questions, we seek to expand understanding of hybrid collaboration and provide insights into developing effective MUIs for these environments.

2 Literature Review

2.1 Hybrid Collaboration

Hybrid collaboration, characterized by the integration of remote and co-located team members, has gained significant prominence in today's dynamic work environments. It includes a wide range of collaboration practices involving synchronous and asynchronous interactions, cross-device and cross-application collaboration, and co-located and remote team members [9]. This mode of collaboration offers numerous benefits, including enhanced flexibility, access to diverse talent, and reduced costs. However, it also presents several challenges that can impede effective communication and collaboration. These challenges encompass the lack of social presence and awareness, difficulties in coordinating and synchronizing activities, and variations in communication preferences and styles.

The concept of social presence, as defined by Dourish and Bellotti [10], refers to an individual's perception of being present in a mediated communication environment. In the context of hybrid collaboration, remote team members often experience a sense of disconnection from the co-located team, missing out on crucial social cues and nonverbal communication. This can lead to misunderstandings, reduced trust, and decreased team cohesion [4]. Additionally, coordinating and synchronizing activities pose a significant challenge in hybrid collaboration. Olson and Olson describe coordination as the process of managing task dependencies, while synchronization refers to aligning activities in time. Given that team members in hybrid collaboration may have disparate schedules, work styles, and communication preferences, effectively coordinating and synchronizing their activities becomes challenging [7].

Despite these challenges, hybrid collaboration also presents opportunities for innovation and creativity. Paulus and Nijstad suggest that diverse team compositions can foster increased creativity and better problem-solving outcomes [11]. By leveraging the strengths and perspectives of both remote and co-located team members, hybrid collaboration enables teams to generate more innovative solutions and make better decisions [12].

By understanding the benefits and challenges associated with hybrid collaboration, organizations can develop strategies and deploy technologies that effectively address the challenges while capitalizing on the potential for enhanced collaboration and creativity. The following sections of this paper will further explore the specific barriers and facilitators of hybrid collaboration and propose strategies for effective implementation and management in today's work environments.

2.2 Multimodal User Interfaces

The interaction between humans and the world encompasses multiple sensory modalities, as humans utilize all available senses to comprehend and navigate their environment [13]. Multimodal User Interfaces (MUIs) capitalize on this inherent human ability by integrating various input and output modalities, such as speech, touch, and gesture, to enhance user experience and improve the efficiency of interactions [14]. A pioneering demonstration that highlighted the value and potential of multimodal interfaces is the "Put That There" system developed by Richard Bolt, which is widely recognized as a groundbreaking milestone in this field [15].

Researchers Jaimes and Sebe conducted a comprehensive survey on multimodal human-computer interaction, exploring the challenges and opportunities involved in designing and implementing multimodal systems. Their work provides valuable insights into the complexities of creating effective multimodal interfaces [16].

Multimodal user interfaces have been proven to offer numerous advantages, including error prevention, interface robustness, facilitating error recovery, increasing communication bandwidth, and providing alternative communication methods for different situations and environments [17]. Moreover, humans often process information faster and more effectively when it is presented in multiple modalities [18].

MUIs also hold potential for supporting remote collaboration, enabling users to collaborate effectively across different geographical locations and time zones [19]. However, there is a lack of standardization in multimodal interaction design. Additionally, widely accepted guidelines or best practices for designing MUIs specifically tailored to hybrid collaboration are currently unavailable. User needs vary significantly depending on the type of collaboration, the physical environment, and the available technology, making it challenging to determine the most effective approach for a given context (Table 1).

Table 1. Human sensory modalities relevant to human–computer interaction [20].

Modality	Examples
Visual Modality	Graphical User Interfaces (GUI) Gesture-based interfaces Virtual Reality (VR) Augmented Reality (AR)
Auditory Modality	Speech recognition Voice-based assistants Sound effects and notifications Background music or ambient sound
Tactile Modality	Haptic feedback in touchscreens or touch-enabled devices Force feedback (vibration, haptic responses) Braille displays for visually impaired users Vibration alerts on smartphones or wearable devices
Olfactory Modality	Scent-enabled systems Ambient scent diffusers Smell-based alarms for safety or accessibility purposes Olfactory feedback systems for medical simulations or training
Gustatory Modality	Taste-based interfaces for food-related applications Flavor-enhanced experiences in VR or AR Taste simulation devices Artificial sweeteners or flavorings

While visual modalities are the most commonly used in user interfaces, auditory input plays a central role in any multimodal system that incorporates it [14]. Recent advances in hardware sensors have made it possible to incorporate the tactile modality, significantly enriching the user experience. The olfactory and gustatory modalities are not commonly utilized in hybrid collaboration environments and will not be the focus of this study. Although the indirect sensing of neural activity, such as through brain-computer interfaces (BCIs), holds promise for future multimodal interaction systems, the current limitations of sensor configurations in commonly used devices necessitate a focus on the first three modalities in this research [21].

In summary, MUIs support natural and intuitive interaction, facilitating both synchronous and asynchronous communication and enabling users to exchange information and feedback in real time or at their own pace. However, the lack of standardization and widely accepted guidelines for designing MUIs in the context of hybrid collaboration highlights the need for further research and development in this area. The present study aims to address this gap by exploring the design and implementation of MUIs that effectively support hybrid collaboration.

2.3 User-Centered Design Approaches

User-centered design (UCD) has emerged as a critical approach in the design of interactive systems, prioritizing the needs and preferences of users throughout the design process. This approach ensures that the resulting systems are usable and effective [22]. The International Organization for Standardization (ISO) established the ISO 9241-210:2010 standard, which provides principles and guidelines for human-centered design of interactive systems [23]. By adopting UCD methods such as contextual inquiry, personas, and usability testing, designers can gain valuable insights into user needs, preferences, and behaviors [24].

Norman introduces the concept of mental models, which refers to the internal representations that individuals form of the external world [25]. Understanding how users perceive and interact with the world enables designers to create products that are more user-friendly and effective [25]. Notably, the mental models of co-located team members and remote members have been found to exhibit significant differences. Therefore, it is crucial to incorporate multiple cycles of design, prototyping, and testing, with each iteration incorporating user feedback and insights [26]. This iterative approach ensures that the developed products meet the requirements and expectations of both co-located teams and remote members.

Adhering to UCD principles and utilizing appropriate methods throughout the design process enables designers to gain a deep understanding of the users and their needs. This user-centric approach contributes to the development of hybrid collaboration systems that are tailored to the specific requirements and preferences of both co-located and remote team members. By incorporating user feedback at each stage of the design process, designers can create solutions that effectively bridge the gap between remote and co-located collaboration, leading to improved usability, productivity, and overall user satisfaction.

3 User-Centered Approach

This study employed a UCD approach, comprising three distinct stages: 1) User research 2) Ideation and Prototyping 3) Testing and Evaluation.

3.1 User Research

Participants. The study included 16 participants who possessed hybrid collaboration experience in China, distributed across eight distinct groups. Each group was composed of two participants, one of whom had prior experience working in a co-located setting, while the other had prior experience working remotely, and participants in each group knew each other. The age of participants ranged between 26 and 45 years (Mean(M) = 35.06 years; Standard Deviation (SD) = 5.78). Nine participants were females and seven were male. The work experience of participants in hybrid environment ranged from 1 to 5 years (M = 3.5 years; SD = 1.06). Each participant possessed a touch device, either a smartphone or a tablet, and all of them had prior experience in conducting meetings through video conferencing.

Interviews Design. The goal of the interview is to answer RQ1 regarding primary barriers and challenges with communication technologies and devices. And the insights from the interviews will help to explore ideal practices of MUIs in RQ2. The interview questions focus on three perspectives: 1) Current tools and technologies as well as the challenges and limitations. 2) Challenges during hybrid collaboration. 3) Ideal hybrid experience. Although all interviews were conducted remotely, participants were asked to join the interviews in their real working environment, which help to gather the most real and intuitive feelings during their daily work.

Data Collection and Analysis. Interview transcripts and observation notes were analyzed using thematic analysis to identify recurring themes and patterns related to user needs and preferences [27].

Commonly Used Devices. In terms of personal working devices, the study participants predominantly utilized laptops for their work-related tasks, with smartphones serving as a supplementary tool for quick text or audio communication while on the go. A minority of participants (three individuals) employed touchscreen devices for their work. Additionally, two participants who had prior experience working in a co-located setting reported using interactive whiteboards in the office, while the remaining participants relied on projectors and large displays for their collaborative work.

Commonly Used Tools. Various communication tools are available for geographically distributed teams, including instant messaging tools like Slack, Microsoft Teams, WeChat Work, and Ding Talk. Video conferencing tools like Zoom, Microsoft Teams, and Tencent Meeting are also popular. Project management tools like Trello, Jira, and Teambition, and documentation tools like Evernote, Notion, and Microsoft OneNote are also useful. Our study revealed that teams with remote members tend to use digital tools over conventional communication methods such as email and phone calls. This is primarily because of language barriers and the need for efficient communication.

Challenges and Limitations. Some key challenges and limitations include:

- Technical issues. Despite technological progress, hybrid collaboration still faces problems with connectivity, audio/video quality, and software compatibility. These issues can increase tension and frustration. For example:

  "Sometimes I even don't know I got lost in the video conference." (Participant 1b)
- Communication obstacles. Differences in work styles, communication norms, and language between remote and co-located members can hinder shared understanding. For example, remote members may struggle to interpret non-verbal cues or fully engage in discussions. For example:

  "I feel like I'm left out of casual chats with my team in the same location." (Participant 2b)
- Engagement and Participation. Remote teams often struggle to fully engage and involve all members due to lack of in-person interaction. This can lead to communication gaps, difficulty building relationships, and delays sharing information. Limited opportunities for informal interaction and face- to-face communication make it hard to build and sustain trust in remote teams. As a result, some members may feel disconnected, excluded, or isolated. For example:

  "It's sad when you can't join team building or hang out with your coworkers because you're not present." (Participant 3b)
- Task coordination and management. Coordinating tasks and managing workloads is complicated when team members are in different time zones, locations, and use different communication channels. Geographic dispersion makes task coordination and oversight more difficult. For example:

  "It can be tough to schedule meetings or coordinate tasks when everyone is in different time zones." (Participant 2a)
- Difficulty in managing work-life balance. The line between work and personal life can blur, leading to information overload, burnout, reduced creativity, and feeling overwhelmed by constant messages and notifications. For example:

  "I have to check messages from time to time to make sure I look unreliable." (Participant 2b)

In summary, hybrid work environments combining remote and co-located members face complex challenges that can undermine communication, inclusion, engagement, coordination, trust, team cohesion, and performance. Organizations must proactively address these challenges to enable successful hybrid collaboration.

3.2 Ideation and Prototyping

Ideal Hybrid Collaboration Experience. To achieve an optimal hybrid work experience, it is necessary to address the key challenges and limitations outlined in Sect. 3.1. In addition to technology infrastructure and enterprise culture and management, here are some crucial factors to consider:

- Inclusive communication practices: All team members should be actively involved, regardless of their location.
- High engagement and participation: Regular social interactions should be fostered between co-located and remote team members.
- Adequate communication for decision-making: Tools should be established to enable thorough discussions on intricate interdependence matters.

Devices Settings. In the context of co-located teams, the technological devices utilized include interactive smartboards, styluses, cameras, and personal laptops. Conversely, remote team members rely on personal desktops and touch screen devices (see Fig. 1 and Fig. 2).

Fig. 1. Co-located team and remote member

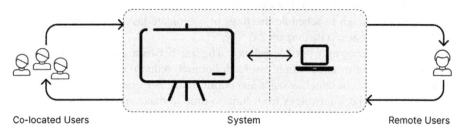

Co-located Users   System   Remote Users

Fig. 2. Device settings for hybrid collaboration

Use Cases. We categorize hybrid collaboration activities into four quadrants based on two factors:

- Collaboration time: Synchronous (real-time) or Asynchronous (non-real time)
- Decision complexity: High cooperation (complex, interdependent decisions) or Low cooperation (simple, independent decisions) (Table 2)

Table 2. Activities in hybrid collaboration.

Category	Example
Synchronous, High cooperation	Ideate and brainstorm for a design solution
Synchronous, Low cooperation	Co-work, virtual team-building activities
Asynchronous, High cooperation	Design Review and Feedback
Asynchronous, Low cooperation	Announcements and Broadcasts

Our approach focuses on the synchronous collaboration quadrants that require effective communication, engagement, and team cohesion to address the challenges identified in Sect. 3.1. While we will discuss ways to improve the user experience regarding technical issues, task coordination, and work-life balance, these are not the primary focus of our research. We define two use cases:

- Co-located teams and remote members working together online.
- Co-located teams and remote members ideating and brainstorming to develop a design solution.

Module and Features. To achieve a productive hybrid work environment, co-located team members should balance in-person and virtual interactions to ensure inclusion and engagement for remote participants. Remote team members must actively participate in discussions and contribute to the team's work to maintain visibility and engagement. By promoting informal interactions and virtual face-to-face communication, co-located and remote team members can establish trust and cohesion. In this research, we will focus on the module and features that are relevant to this topic (Table 3).

Table 3. Module and main features

Modules	Features
Virtual spaces	Real-time chat Background music Space status
Digital whiteboarding	Write Sticky notes and idea capture Real-time feedback
Meeting & Social Interaction	Audio and video conferencing Virtual team-building activities Customizable environments

Multimodal Interactions Experience. We will incorporate multimodal interactions based on insights gained in user research. These interactions are outlined in Table 4, which utilize the traditional graphical user interface (GUI).

Table 4. Multimodal interactions

Multimodal Interactions	Examples
Voice input	Start, join, or end meetings using voice commands Music or ambient sound for interaction
Touch input	Draw, write, and collaborate on a shared digital whiteboard Vote on and prioritize ideas or tasks with touch gestures Navigate through virtual environments
Gesture recognition	Control presentation slides
Haptic feedback	Get haptic alerts for new messages or reactions Immersive experiences for user engagement

Ideate and Prototype. This study proposes an approach that utilizes various modes of interaction to facilitate idea contribution among team members in both local and remote settings. A hybrid collaboration tool prototype was developed through iterative design processes, starting with basic prototypes, and advancing to a high-fidelity prototype for user evaluation and testing.

Use Case 1: Working Together Online. It aims to bridge the gap of team engagement between co-located teams and remote members. Users can configure the virtual workspace based on their needs. For example, users can set it as Focus on work mode, where team members share the same online space. The Audio modality is always available. When they need it, they can talk or ask for help. They can also use visual modality to have more team activities, like online coffee time, online yoga, etc. (Figs. 3, 4 and 5).

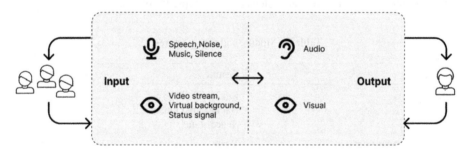

Fig. 3. Multimodal interaction for working together online.

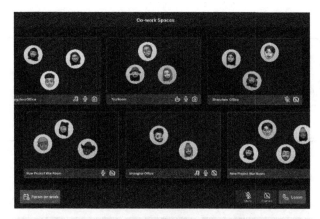

Fig. 4. High-fidelity prototype for virtual workspaces overview

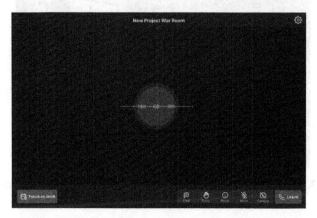

Fig. 5. High-fidelity prototype for working together online.

Use Case 2: Ideating and Brainstorming to Develop a Design Solution. This task requires frequent discussion throughout the process. Furthermore, the incorporation of visual aids is essential in facilitating effective communication and enabling the comprehensive exchange of innovative concepts (Figs. 6, 7 and 8).

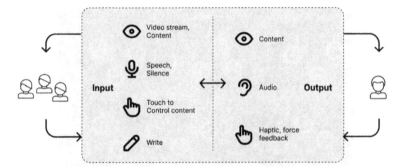

Fig. 6. Multimodal interaction for ideation and brainstorming

Fig. 7. High-fidelity prototype for video conferencing with less interaction

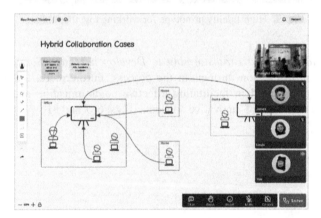

Fig. 8. High-fidelity prototype with digital whiteboarding for ideating and brainstorming.

3.3 Testing and Evaluation

After several iterations in the Ideation and Prototyping stage, a high-fidelity prototype with fully functioning features was developed. In this stage, we conducted user testing to evaluate the prototype. Chang and Bourguet provide a usability framework for the design and evaluation of multimodal interaction systems [28], while limited by the real interaction of the high-fidelity prototype, the test was focusing on feedbacks about effectiveness, efficiency and satisfaction.

Participants and Tasks. The user testing was conducted with participants involved in the user research before. Participants were asked to complete two tasks, a) Work together with team online, b) Conduct a brainstorming or project planning. Participants were asked to give a rating for three criteria after completing the required tasks. The scoring was done on a 5-point Likert scale (1 = strongly disagree to 5 = strongly agree).

Testing Result. 16 participants gave ratings, the results are as shown in Table 5.

Table 5. Rating summary ton the effectiveness, efficiency, and satisfaction

Criteria	M (SD)
Effectiveness	4.375 (0.60)
Efficiency	3.875 (0.78)
Satisfaction	4.25 (0.66)

The findings of this study suggest that participants were highly satisfied with the effectiveness of the application. Specifically, participants expressed a strong affinity for the virtual workspace feature, which allowed for seamless audio and visual communication between co-located and remote team members, thereby reducing communication barriers. However, the application's efficiency received lower scores, with some participants expressing concerns about balancing engagement with team members and deep concentration work. Overall, the satisfaction results indicate that the platform was perceived as a valuable tool for facilitating work in a hybrid environment.

3.4 Design Principles

Oviatt identified ten myths for multimodal interaction [14], including the belief that speech and pointing are the dominant multimodal integration pattern. Additionally, when designing MUIs for hybrid collaboration, it is important to consider fundamental principles as below:

- Leveraging the strengths of different modalities, such as voice and touch, to create MUIs that are more efficient and natural, motivating users to initiate spontaneous communication.
- Leveraging the capabilities of commonly used devices to increase adoption of the MUIs.

- Taking into account the needs of different types of users, such as those who are co-located and those who are remote. These users have different mental models and requirements, such as communication efficiency, engagement, and participation.
- Designing for different scenarios, such as synchronous and asynchronous activities, and activities that require high or low cooperation.

4   Discussion

The results of our study provide important insights into the challenges and requirements of hybrid collaboration. Our findings indicate that both co-located teams and remote members encounter various challenges and limitations, including technical issues, communication barriers, difficulties in engagement and participation, task coordination and management challenges, and work-life balance issues. These findings align with previous research and emphasize the need for effective solutions to address these challenges.

To address the challenges identified in hybrid collaboration, we developed a prototype that underwent iterative refinement and user testing. The outcomes of the testing demonstrated the potential of the prototype in addressing these challenges and enhancing engagement in hybrid collaboration. The prototype incorporated valuable features such as digital whiteboarding and a configurable virtual workspace, which were well-received by participants for promoting team engagement and communication.

However, there're areas that could be improved, such as finding a balance between engagement and immersive working time, as well as the need for better support in different scenarios. Additionally, the technical feasibility of certain features necessitates further validation, particularly when integrating multimodal interactions.

5   Conclusion

This paper presents a user-centered approach to designing multimodal interfaces for hybrid collaboration. By incorporating various input and output modalities, we can create more flexible and adaptable interfaces that cater to individual user preferences and accommodate different collaboration activities. Engaging users in an iterative design process ensures that resulting interfaces meet real-world needs and expectations.

This study advances the field of hybrid collaboration by developing a prototype that addresses the challenges faced by co-located teams and remote members. The results from evaluations demonstrate the prototype's potential in improving hybrid collaboration. Participants appreciated the multimodal interactions and configurable virtual workspace, recognizing the value they bring to team engagement and communication.

Future research should focus on refining the prototype based on feedback received and conducting more extensive user evaluations to ensure its effectiveness in real-world hybrid collaboration scenarios. Additionally, investigating the long-term effects of using such tools on team performance, satisfaction, and overall collaboration dynamics would provide valuable insights for organizations adopting hybrid work models.

In conclusion, this study establishes the foundation for user-centered tools that improve hybrid collaboration. Incorporating user insights and iterative design processes can lead to effective solutions that enhance hybrid collaboration, ultimately improving teamwork, communication, and overall productivity.

References

1. Bosch-Sijtsema, P.M., Ruohomäki, V., Vartiainen, M.: Knowledge work productivity in distributed teams. J. Knowl. Manag. **13**(6), 533–546 (2009). https://doi.org/10.1108/136732709 10997178
2. Schubert, C.: Working Together Apart: Collaboration Over the Internet by Judith S Olson and Gary M. Olson. Taylor & Francis, San Rafael (2015)
3. Teevan, J., et al.: Microsoft New Future of Work Report 2022. Microsoft, MSR-TR-2022-3, May 2022. https://www.microsoft.com/en-us/research/publication/microsoft-new-future-of-work-report-2022/
4. Hinds, P.J., Mortensen, M.: Understanding conflict in geographically distributed teams: the moderating effects of shared identity, shared context, and spontaneous communication. Organ. Sci. **16**(3), 290–307 (2005). https://doi.org/10.1287/orsc.1050.0122
5. Mortensen, M., Hinds, P.J.: Conflict and shared identity in geographically distributed teams. Int. J. Confl. Manag. **12**(3), 212–238 (2001). https://doi.org/10.1108/eb022856
6. Kossek, E.E., Thompson, R.J.: Workplace Flexibility, vol. 1. Oxford University Press (2015). https://doi.org/10.1093/oxfordhb/9780199337538.013.19
7. Olson, G.M., Olson, J.S.: Distance matters. Hum.–Comput. Interact. **15**(2–3), 139–178 (2000). https://doi.org/10.1207/S15327051HCI1523_4
8. Oviatt, S.: Multimodal interfaces. In: The Human-Computer Interaction Handbook, pp. 439–458 (2007)
9. Neumayr, T., Jetter, H.-C., Augstein, M., Friedl, J., Luger, T.: Domino: a descriptive framework for hybrid collaboration and coupling styles in partially distributed teams. In: Proceedings of the ACM on Human Computer Interaction, vol. 2, no. CSCW, pp. 1–24, November 2018. https://doi.org/10.1145/3274397
10. Dourish, P., Bellotti, V.: Awareness and coordination in shared workspaces. In: Proceedings of the 1992 ACM Conference on Computer-Supported Cooperative Work - CSCW 1992, Toronto, Ontario, Canada, pp. 107–114. ACM Press (1992). https://doi.org/10.1145/143457.143468
11. Paulus, P.B., Nijstad, B.A.: Group Creativity: Innovation Through Collaboration. Oxford University Press, New York (2003)
12. Majchrzak, A., Rice, R.E., Malhotra, A., King, N., Ba, S.: Technology adaptation: the case of a computer-supported inter-organizational virtual team. MIS Q. **24**(4), 569 (2000). https://doi.org/10.2307/3250948
13. Quek, F., et al.: Multimodal human discourse: gesture and speech. ACM Trans Comput.-Hum. Interact. **9**(3), 171–193 (2002). https://doi.org/10.1145/568513.568514
14. Oviatt, S.: Ten myths of multimodal interaction. Commun. ACM **42**(11), 74–81 (1999). https://doi.org/10.1145/319382.319398
15. Bolt, R.A.: Put-that-there' Voice and gesture at the graphics interface. In: Proceedings of the 7th Annual Conference on Computer Graphics and Interactive Techniques, pp. 262–270 (1980)
16. Jaimes, A., Sebe, N.: Multimodal human–computer interaction: a survey. Comput. Vis. Image Underst. **108**(1–2), 116–134 (2007). https://doi.org/10.1016/j.cviu.2006.10.019
17. Cohen, P.R., McGee, D.R.: Tangible multimodal interfaces for safety-critical applications. Commun. ACM **47**(1), 41–46 (2004). https://doi.org/10.1145/962081.962103
18. Van Wassenhove, V., Grant, K.W., Poeppel, D.: Visual speech speeds up the neural processing of auditory speech. Proc. Natl. Acad. Sci. U.S.A. **102**(4), 1181–1186 (2005). https://doi.org/10.1073/pnas.0408949102
19. Munteanu, C., Molyneaux, H., Moncur, W., Romero, M., O'Donnell, S., Vines, J.: Situational ethics: re-thinking approaches to formal ethics requirements for human-computer interaction.

In: Proceedings of the 33rd Annual ACM Conference on Human Factors in Computing Systems, Seoul Republic of Korea, pp. 105–114. ACM, April 2015. https://doi.org/10.1145/270 2123.2702481

20. Turk, M.: Multimodal interaction: a review. Pattern Recogn. Lett. **36**, 189–195 (2014). https://doi.org/10.1016/j.patrec.2013.07.003

21. Nicolas-Alonso, L.F., Gomez-Gil, J.: Brain computer interfaces, a review. Sensors **12**(2), 1211–1279 (2012). https://doi.org/10.3390/s120201211

22. Pea, R.D.: User centered system design: new perspectives on human-computer interaction. J. Educ. Comput. Res. **3**(1), 129–134 (1987)

23. 14:00-17:00: ISO 9241-210:2010. ISO. https://www.iso.org/standard/52075.html. Accessed 22 May 2023

24. Pruitt, J., Adlin, T.: The Persona Lifecycle: Keeping People in Mind Throughout Product Design. Elsevier, Amsterdam (2010)

25. Norman, D.A.: The Psychology of Everyday Things. Basic Books, New York (1988)

26. Nielsen, J., Molich, R.: Heuristic evaluation of user interfaces. In: Proceedings of the SIGCHI Conference on Human Factors in Computing Systems Empowering People - CHI 1990, pp. 249–256. ACM Press, Seattle (1990). https://doi.org/10.1145/97243.97281

27. Braun, V., Clarke, V.: Using thematic analysis in psychology. Qual. Res. Psychol. **3**(2), 77–101 (2006)

28. Chang, J., Bourguet, M.-L.: Usability framework for the design and evaluation of multimodal interaction. Presented at the People and Computers XXII Culture, Creativity, Interaction, September 2008. https://doi.org/10.14236/ewic/HCI2008.48

Enhancing the Natural Conversation Experience Through Conversation Analysis – A Design Method

Spencer Hazel and Adam Brandt(✉)

Newcastle University, Newcastle upon Tyne, UK
{spencer.hazel,adam.brandt}@newcastle.ac.uk

Abstract. As Voice User Interfaces (VUIs) become increasingly embedded in a wide range of activities in our everyday life, it falls to the conversation designer to ensure that the user experience is a satisfactory one. Embedding qualities of natural speech in the design output is considered one way to achieve this. Conversation Analysis (CA), the study of naturally-occurring talk and interaction, has been proposed as a useful tool in developing VUIs. However, little practical advice is currently available for how conversation designers can leverage CA for improving the VUI user experience. Drawing on a collaboration between Conversation Analysts and conversation designers, this paper outlines a step-by-step workflow of conversation design procedures that allow designers greater opportunities to link the study of natural talk with the conversational design output. This enables designers to build on general insights from CA as well as specific instances of human-human interactional data, modelling the VUI design on naturally-occurring patterns for carrying out equivalent interactional activities. In the examples, we highlight such features as word choice, intonation contouring, stress, and pitch, to show how naturally-occurring interactional data can provide a platform on which to develop the design of a conversational agent.

Keywords: Voice User Interfaces · Conversation Design · User Experience · Conversation Analysis

1 Introduction

With the ongoing expansion of Voice User Interfaces (VUIs) into many areas of our social life, the need for conversation design that caters to the everyday user is as great as ever. However, it is broadly accepted that the resources available to conversation designers (such as training support, usability heuristics or design patterns) are currently limited in number and scope [1, 2]. Similarly, it has been argued that there is a need for more consistent and informed guidelines for VUI design [1, 3]. Because of the importance of 'naturalness' to conversation designers, central to this need is guidance on how to embed qualities of natural speech in conversation design.

© The Author(s), under exclusive license to Springer Nature Switzerland AG 2023
M. Kurosu et al. (Eds.): HCII 2023, LNCS 14054, pp. 83–100, 2023.
https://doi.org/10.1007/978-3-031-48038-6_6

'Naturalness' is reported to be at the centre of design principles for VUIs (such that they are). Despite this, making interaction which is natural is reported by professional conversation designers as one of their major challenges [4]. Relatedly, it is suggested that there are insufficient guidelines on 'designing for naturalness' [5]. Among over 100 conversation designers surveyed, none reported examining natural conversation at the design stage [4]. Instead, common approaches include checking similar existing VUIs, accessing online resources, and discussing with colleagues. While these are valuable approaches, they do not enable designers to draw upon natural speech to inform their design work. Even though materials produced by leading tech companies such as Google and Amazon promise to help designers (for example) "craft conversations that are natural and intuitive for users" [6], they do not suggest examining natural conversation to inform design, let alone provide a framework for doing so.

To supplement existing conversation design practices, Conversation Analysis (CA) has been suggested as a field of study that can add value by contributing additional empirical observations on which to model VUIs [e.g. 7–10]. In this paper, we provide a model for how this can be done, by introducing a set of procedures through which conversation designers can mobilise insights from CA to improve the user experience for VUIs. The paper reports on a collaboration between Conversation Analysts and AI Conversation Engineers, and the resulting design method that merges a CA understanding of interaction with the design of talk for VUIs. It expands upon our previous collaborative exploration of, and proposal for, the use of CA for conversation design [11].

The CADENCE (Conversation Analytic Design for Enhanced Natural Conversation Experience) method offers designers a step-by-step workflow for developing a conversational model and improving the functionality and user experience of VUIs. The method builds on CA's procedures for studying natural talk-in-interaction, and on the body of knowledge that this field has generated over decades of close scrutiny of social interaction. Most importantly, however, it affords designers practical procedures for applying this approach to the development of their interfaces.

2 Background

2.1 Conversation Analysis – The Study of Natural Talk-in-Interaction

Conversation Analysis has emerged over the past 50 years as the scientific method *par excellence* for studying natural language use in social interaction, more recently also including in its remit the nonverbal and non-vocal features of face-to-face interaction. Among social science approaches to the study of language in use, CA is unique in its insistence on working exclusively on recordings of naturally occurring interaction, rather than using hypothetical and/or imagined dialogue analysis, or by relying on accounts elicited from people describing what might happen in interaction. In adopting this principle, Conversation Analysis is more closely aligned with natural observational sciences found elsewhere, with subjects studied in their natural environment. Schegloff & Sacks [12] propose that in approaching the study of humans in this way, the approach offers us a "naturalistic observational discipline that could deal with the details of social action rigorously, empirically and formally" (p289).

One main reason behind this insistence is the observation that there are levels of formatting in how people design their turns at talk that are so ingrained, they are built into speech subconsciously, and as such these are the features the most difficult to articulate. Such formatting features make up what on the surface might appear to be inconsequential micro-details, and overlooked by our recollections or imaginings of interactional events, replaced by often false assumptions of how talk works. Take for example the intonation contours that are assumed to accompany a question. Ask someone to describe the systematicities of such formatting, and a common response will be that a question is formatted with turn-final rising intonation, a formatting marker that sets it aside from non-question utterances [e.g. 13]. This may well be the case for many questions, but even the most cursory of glances at empirical data would show that this is most definitely not the case for many others. And likewise, many non-question utterances are formatted with turn-final rising intonation. Examples of these are provided in the transcribed segments shown in Figs. 1 and 2. Each of these transcripts are representations of segments of audio/video recordings of authentic interactions from a range of real-world settings (arrows indicate whether turn-final intonation is falling, rising, or flat)

```
DOCtor speaking to patient in telephone consultation
71 DOC:  okay and have you had any flashing lights or floaters↘

DOCtor speaking to patient in telephone consultation
95 DOC:  and is that the right eye↘

SHEelagh speaking to a colleague in a Danish workplace
61 SHE:  hej→
         skal du også spille guitar↘
%tra:    hi are you also playing guitar↘
```

Fig. 1. Examples of turn-final falling intonation

```
DOCtor speaking to patient in telephone consultation
13 DOC:  um: so my name is doctor grey
14       (one of) X just doing u:h follow up calls today↗

DOCtor speaking to patient in telephone consultation
42 DOC:  I think we can do that↗

GUIde speaking to visitors in an art gallery
01 GUI:  all these pictures on the wall are people-
02       different people's mothers↗
```

Fig. 2. Examples of turn-final rising intonation

So whereas there is a commonly held assumption that rising intonation is indexical of a question, and falling intonation indicates a statement, we actually find both intonation trajectories in use across the respective types of utterance. Indeed, in certain English speech communities, turn final rising intonation is a widely used sociolinguistic feature that permeates talk throughout, for example in certain dialectal variation [e.g. 14], or in identity marking such as the phenomenon of uptalk in what has been termed Valley Girl English [e.g. 15].

Turn formatting of course goes beyond pitch and intonation contouring; it involves such resources as variations in lexical choice, syntactic structure, timing of onset and of completion of a turn, pauses within a turn, non-lexical vocalisations, voice timbre, volume and speed. Moreover, these are strands that are woven together to produce not only the complexity we identify when we look more closely at turn design. Importantly, such features, and their complex interplay, also index additional levels of meaning: however inconsequential such elements might appear on first reflection, they are quite the opposite. As Sacks [16] argues, "the detailed study of small phenomena may give an enormous understanding of the ways humans do things and the kinds of objects they use to construct and order their affairs" (p24). These objects are the building blocks through which we construct our talk and through which we perceive meaning in that of others'.

Beyond turn design, formatting features relating to how these turns-at-talk are sequentially organised in relation one another is crucial for how a turn is understood. A turn at talk is constructed to fit what has preceded it and what possible types of turn are required in response. Such sequential organisational formatting involves issues of timing, for example what a micro-delay in response can signify, or an early onset of a response. It also involves the overall organisation of actions within a given conversation – what things are interactants normatively expected to do in this kind of interaction, and in what particular order (as we will consider when examining the opening of telephone calls in Sect. 3.2)? Where people have visual or tactile access to one another, additional multimodal patterns are also in play, for example in the areas of gaze conduct, facial-, gestural- and postural configurations, the use of the material surround, or interpersonal touching.

Although people are not consciously aware of such micro-details of our conversational conduct, 50+ years of Conversation Analytic research has demonstrated that these features do have an impact; elements such as a stressed syllable, a small micro-pause, a hesitation marker, or a shift in pitch can affect how a turn at talk is understood, and accordingly how it is responded to. As such, they are central, and essential, to the naturalness of human conversation. And, as we argue, they can and should be mobilised when designing systems with which humans will engage in conversation.

2.2 Voice User Interfaces and the Natural User Experience

'Naturalness' is at the centre of existing VUI design guidelines (such that they are), and aspirations. However, 'natural' is a concept with varied interpretations in the literature [5]. Indeed, not all VUIs are designed to emulate a natural interaction experience. At the very least, there may be aspects of natural human-human interaction that the designer may choose to exclude. The design of an agent may on the one hand emulate organisational features characteristic of turn-taking in everyday interaction; but may for example avoid those features of everyday interaction where sentience is implied, or empathy, or cognition. There may then be legitimate arguments not to pursue such a natural conversation experience.

However, there are many ways in which conversation designers may find it desirable to approximate the talk found in everyday interaction. Similar to how some naturalistic art, such as that found in some theatre, literature or film, is structured to evoke in an audience some semblance of interaction as found in the life-worlds of the audience members, so too might conversation designers model their conversational AI to mirror similar interactional episodes in human-human interaction. In the naturalistic arts, it is an aesthetic practice, modelling but never fully replicating the everyday details of human sociality, and subject to genre constraints for dramatic representation. On the surface, aspects of the social world are presented in what appear to be an authentic representational form, for example character dialogue to parallel episodes of talk-in-interaction. However, these dramatic representations never fully replicate the complexity and perceived messiness of actual interaction, for to do so would transgress the genre conventions. Also, even the most social realist of writers, actors and directors draw on imagination to populate their naturalistic scenes, rather than base their work on empirical data of similar settings or episodes[1].

In building conversational AI models that do seek to emulate features of natural conversation, we contend that it is not sufficient to generate text and code on the basis of imaginings, even those informed by research on talk. Like the naturalism described above, these conversation designs tend to be only partially successful in accounting for the details of the comprehensive toolkit speakers themselves draw on. Rather, to be able to design conversational output that approximates the particular conversation patterns into which human users are culturally socialised, designers need to be able to look in detail at the complex, fine-grained sets of systematic resources speakers mobilise in their interactions with one another. Furthermore, we must then have a method through which knowledge of these details can be incorporated into the design of the agent. The CADENCE method offers this: a method that marries the study of natural talk with procedures for emulating such natural talk in voice user interfaces.

Before outlining the procedures of the method, we will consider VUI in the context of a wider body of human endeavour that seeks to represent social interaction in naturalistic cultural products.

2.3 A Tradition for Developing a Naturalistic Effect in Text for Speech

Representations of social interaction can be found in a wide range of artistic output, from novels and drama to film and painting. Within this body of work can be found a strand that strives to approximate the everyday social world more closely than others, namely naturalism.

Naturalism as an aesthetic movement emerged in the West in the 19th century. It seeks to represent real life on stage, with believable characters, narrative action and plot [17]. The premise is that art should hold up a mirror to nature, exposing in the artistic product the minutiae of human social life. The narrative action represented in the output must be designed also to resemble the outside world. In theatre for example, actors appear in dramatic scenarios designed to compare with similar interactional events in the real world. They dress in recognizable costume for the period and place, use objects from the equivalent settings, and speak in ways that correspond with speech in the world being depicted. Although literary and dramatic dialogue differs from everyday speech [18], there are levels of interdependence between them [19]. By using the social

---

[1] There are other genres, for example verbatim theatre and post-dramatic theatre, which do draw more closely on the features of actual social interaction.

organization of everyday language, the artists (novelist, playwright, director, actors) create a 'commonality' of ground between them and their audience [20].

In order to achieve this sense of commonality, dramatists deploy what Burns [21] has termed *authenticating conventions*, design features which:

> "'model' social conventions in use at a specific time and in a specific place and milieu. The modes of speech, demeanour and action… have to imply a connection to the world of human action of which the theatre is only a part. These conventions suggest a total and external code of values and norms of conduct from which the speech and action of the play is drawn. Their function is, therefore, to *authenticate* the play" (p. 32, emphasis in the original)

In naturalistic theatre and film production, we find members drawing on shared pools of knowledge pertaining to how equivalent scenes of social interaction in naturally occurring mundane or institutional interaction are occasioned [e.g. 22, 23]. Scripts are presented in dialogue form, with characters taking turns to speak, and modelling the speech patterns of everyday social interaction. In converting this written script to its embodied form, members of the creative team (e.g., actors, script-writer, director, dramaturg) subsequently work together in an iterative process of rehearsal to discover how to present the written script as embodied performance. In doing so, we find them orienting to such knowledge domains as everyday routinized features of turn-taking [e.g. 24, 25], sociolinguistic features of speech [e.g. 26, 27], social identity marking [e.g. 28], and the overall performance features that suggest a close correspondence with equivalent scene in the real world.

To achieve the naturalistic effect in these performances, the creative team engages in an iterative process of trialling a particular sequence, analysing the output, and suggesting modifications, and implementing these in a next round. In the diagnostic step between takes, members orient to everyday equivalent interaction, and how the formatting of the performed actions in the dramatic sequence would mirror equivalent real-world interaction, and would shape the dynamic of the scene and characters therein. In carrying out this development work, the creative team draw on their knowledge of how interaction works. Speaking of the script-writer, Herman [19] proposes:

> "Aspects of the turn-taking system, like the mechanics of speech transition, are thus a useful resource for the dramatist, since the different options available can, when used, color our assessment of character behavior and the nature of the unfolding situation itself as it is being enacted."

Although the above focuses on how turn-taking practices form the basis for naturalistic dramatic art, it can equally be applied to conversational AI. In the same way that theatre creators draw on their knowledge of the social conventions pertaining to talk-in-interaction, we also find conversation designers drawing on their knowledge of normative conventions for performing mundane everyday and institutional social interaction in how they design their products.

In this, the work of the conversation designer for VUI is not so far removed from that of the dramatist working within the naturalistic tradition. Both draw on their understandings of how talk works in order to design dialogic output that finds some correspondence with the properties of everyday talk-in-interaction. Both aim to afford the audience an experience of some degree of naturalism in their engagement with the product.

The iterative process of the rehearsal, however, where text is turned into embodied speech, with actors working with director, dramaturg, and any other contributor to find the most appropriate – in this case naturalistic - format of the speech production, is less prominent in conversation design. Closest to this would be where the conversation design team employ voice actors rather than automated text-to-speech for voicing the agent's spoken output. In such cases, the artist would be able to draw on their own experience and understanding for how particular types of turns at talk are produced in human-human interaction, while also being able to trial different formats. Where available, members of the conversation design team may assume the role of director, prompting the voice actor to modify the speech formats until an acceptable version has been achieved.

Working with text-to-speech synthesis, however, does not afford conversation designers these opportunities for rehearsing and developing the output with the easy adaptability of working with a human voice. Rather, to mould and manipulate the speech output so it maps onto patterns of human voice production, a different set of design procedures need to be adopted. This is where the CADENCE model is proposed.

3 Design Procedures to Enhance the Naturalistic Effect in VUIs

3.1 Introducing CADENCE

The CADENCE model (Conversation Analytic Design for Enhanced Natural Conversation Experience) describes a set of procedures adopted by the authors in how they assisted the further development of an AI-enabled conversational agent, Dora. While the model was first conceived and implemented through this particular project, it can be applied to the design of any voice-based conversational agent (and also, potentially with some adaptation, text-based chatbots).

Dora is an autonomous clinical assistant developed by Ufonia for use in various National Health Service Trusts in the UK. The automated system is used to carry out a range of routine phone-based consultations with patients, calls that would conventionally be carried out by clinicians themselves or other clinical staff within the hospital trusts. The system operates as a conversational agent by means of a range of technologies, including automated speech recognition (ASR), Natural Language Understand (NLU), Natural Language Generation (NLG) and Speech Synthesis (Text to Speech, TTS).

The authors were engaged by Ufonia to help analyse test-user and trial data. The aim was to involve Conversation Analysts in the further development of Dora's conversation design and ultimately the overall user experience. As Conversation Analysts, our focus was not on the technical aspects of the system, but rather drawing on our understanding of human interaction to inform the development of the system's spoken output as part of the engagement with users. As will be shown, this ultimately involved suggestions of changes to the TTS process (for example), although this was not our primary focus at the outset. Figure 3 shows a transcribed extract of an early test call.

```
01  Call placed
02  PAT answers phone
03  PAT:    hello⤴
04          (3.0)
05  DOR:    good morning⤵
06          I'm calling back from the Ufonia Testing Team→
07          to follow-up after your cataract surgery⤵
08          (0.7)
09  DOR:    is this ms purple speaking⤴
10          (1.3)
11  PAT:    yes ?it is?⤵
12          (3.1)
13  DOR:    okay⤵ (0.3) great⤵
            I'm dora⤵ (.) an automated assistant⤵
            calling to follow-up after your ⸢cataract surgery⤵
```

Fig. 3. Example from user testing call between Ufonia's agent (DORa) and tester (PATient)

Accessing both the recordings from the early test calls and the scripts generated for these, the team worked together to identify areas for potential development. These included for example, moments in the calls where there were apparent 'communication breakdowns' between the agent and the user. They also included aspects of Dora's spoken output which did not match how a human might perform the same activity (as informed by decades of empirical conversation analytic research on telephone call interactions, healthcare interactions, and institutional interactions more broadly). In particular, we were interested in aspects of sequential organisation (for example, what actions – such as greetings, self-introductions, disclosure of the purpose of the call, etc.- are produced in what order) or turn formatting (such as lexical choice and intonation contouring, for example) which appeared to be having a negative impact on how the patient engaged in the interaction, such as displaying uncertainty in how or when to respond appropriately.

In summary form, the CADENCE model follows many of the same procedures used by conversation design more generally. However, it adds an additional component into the iterative process. Rather than designing script on the basis of recollected or imagined models for talk-in-interaction, the script is designed (where available using Speech Synthesis Markup Language (SSML)) to encode in the automated speech output, turn-design patterning found across similar interactional episodes in natural data. Where on comparison there are observable differences in formatting between the natural language (T1) and the automated speech output (T3), the designer modifies the script code and mark-up (T2) for subsequent trial. This is done repeatedly until some level of acceptable approximation is achieved between T3 and T1 (Fig. 4).

In what follows, we present a brief explainer that sets out in more detail what each of the procedural steps requires of the designer. We have designed this for the conversational design team rather for any particular research-focused academic audience. Being aware that many VUI designers and moderators do not have a background in Conversation Analysis, we seek to avoid any requirement for designers to engage in the actual methodological procedures for carrying out a conversation analysis, although we would advise that there is much to be gained from either learning how to do this, or by engaging a Conversation Analyst as part of the design team.

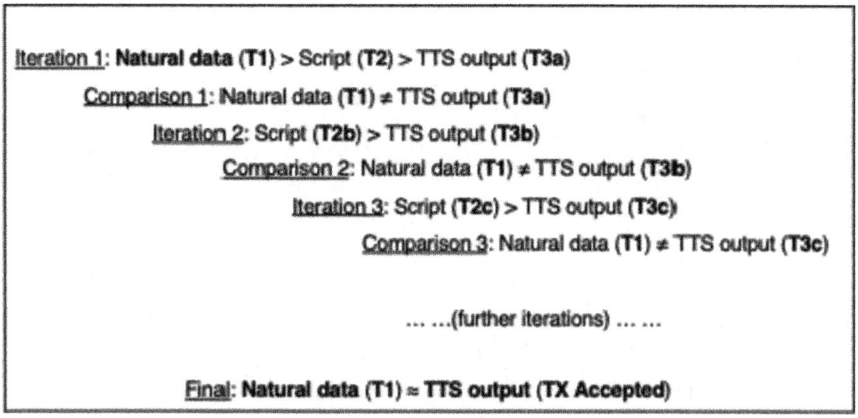

Iteration 1: **Natural data (T1) > Script (T2) > TTS output (T3a)**

  Comparison 1: Natural data (T1) ≠ TTS output (T3a)

    Iteration 2: Script (T2b) > TTS output (T3b)

      Comparison 2: Natural data (T1) ≠ TTS output (T3b)

        Iteration 3: Script (T2c) > TTS output (T3c)

          Comparison 3: Natural data (T1) ≠ TTS output (T3c)

          ... ...(further iterations) ... ...

    Final: **Natural data (T1) ≈ TTS output (TX Accepted)**

Fig. 4. Flowchart of CADENCE design procedure

The overall set of procedures are organised into two broad stages: a preparatory stage and a design implementation stage. We describe these over the following two sub-sections.

3.2 Stage 1: Preparatory Work

Sourcing Data. In order to be able to base our Text-to-Speech (TTS) transcoding on natural interaction patterns, access to data recordings from equivalent types of interactional events would be optimal. Many of the conversations developed by conversation design teams build on equivalent human-human interactions, and indeed may be designed to eventually replace those human-human interactions. Having access to the human-human interactions and being able to generate recorded data from those settings would make for a rich data set of interactional data on which to build the conversation design.

For example, where healthcare resources are stretched, a call from clinician to a patient may be replaced by a call from an automated agent. A point of departure would be to analyse the clinician call for particular patterns, which then could be designed into the automated call, as shown in Fig. 5 (note that this transcript has been anonymized, and the content of the patient's talk has been removed).

This transcript shows an extract from a follow-up call to a UK patient following a cataract operation, and it follows a canonical pattern for opening such calls. This means that regardless of each interaction being unique and different from all others, there still are particular patterns in evidence that we find across call openings of this type, regardless of the persons conducting the call. There should not be anything here that strikes a reader as odd at least.

As source material, such data provide a conversation analyst and conversation designer with an incredibly rich resource, one which evidences a range of turn-formatting features which could subsequently be used in the design of an automated agent. We can use this for example as a basis for understanding the order of actions that are routine in such interactional episodes: the presence or absence of a greeting sequence, of identification/recognition sequences, or a business disclosure, or howareyou sequences [29].

```
PAT answers phone
01        (0.6)
02 DOC:  ↑hi:.→
03        good afternoo:n→
04        it's ↓doctor grey calling from the trentwood u:h ↑cataract
05        clinic↗
06        ·h [i'm looking for:]=
07 PAT:      [responds in overlap]
08 DOC:  =missus green→
09        (0.4)
10 PAT:  [responds]
11        (0.2)
12 DOC:  oh hi missus green→
13        thanks for picking up
14        um: so my name is doctor grey
15        (one of) X just doing u:h follow up calls today↗
```

Fig. 5. Clinician-patient telephone call (human-human)

What are the lexical choices ('hey' or 'hi', or 'good afternoon', or 'greetings')? What the syntactic features ("It's doctor Grey" or "Doctor Grey here", or "I am" or "I'm")? What means of identification are used, as well as issues of recognisability ("It's Dr Grey calling from the Trentwood Cataract Clinic")? What intonation contouring is in evidence, and what this does in terms of inflecting the turn ("It's Dr Grey calling from the Trentwood Cataract Clinic." or "It's Dr Grey calling from the Trentwood Cataract Clinic?")? How is the institutionality of the call worked up in interaction ("Dr Grey" versus "Marjorie Grey"; "thanks for picking up")?

What is more, we can compare an opening such as this with other types of call openings, to identify further specificities to the patterns produced here. How does this differ from calls from a patient to a clinic, rather than the other way around [e.g. 30]? How might it differ from call openings between friends and acquaintances [e.g. 29]? How are these calls carried out differently in different cultural groups [e.g. 31]? How do technological developments impact interactional features of call-openings [e.g. 32]?

Where recordings of equivalent activities are not available, then finding either data or research output on the types of interactional sequences involved in the episode being designed would be important. If the conversation design output involves a cold-call, then explore publicly available data banks (for example Talkbank) for data of similar activities, or seek out conversation analytic literature on cold-calling [e.g. 33] and use the data extracts and findings from these to feed into the conversation design. But even at the level of turn-design and turn-taking within any interaction, there may be additional literature to draw on. If for example the automated agent needs to produce a number of items as a list in a multi-unit turn, then knowing how this is made recognisable as a list and not simply a number of items, and making it recognisable when the 'listing' has been completed, is important in the design of the sequence in question. Identifying empirical studies on these matters - see, for example Jefferson [34] on list production – provides insights into the particular systematic practices through which people make sense to each other and of each other.

Transcribing Source Data. Where recordings of naturally-occurring interaction are generated, a subsequent step involves transcribing it at a relatively detailed degree of granularity. This includes at the most basic level the transcribing of the words and the order in which they are produced. Beyond that, however, there are a range of other elements found in any interaction, which can also be added to the transcription. These pertain to such features as gaps, silences and pauses (both inside turns at talk and between them); non-lexical vocalisations such as tuts and hesitation markers; intonation contouring; noticeable pitch shifts in the turn production; vocal stress; sound-stretches and cut-offs; and where appropriate particular vocal qualities such as smiley-voice or strained voice. Convention for Conversation Analysis transcripts of telephone calls is to use the Jeffersonian system, developed by Gail Jefferson in the 1970s [35], which captures such fine-grained detail of participants' vocal conduct.

Transcripts of such equivalent naturally-occurring interactions offer a tool through which to structure our observations of the recorded data. They may also serve as a springboard for designing the target script for the TTS output.

3.3 Stage 2: Design and Development Work

Select a Module. Any conversation design dialog will be made up of different 'modules', or broader structural sub-activities that together make up the whole of the call flow. For an example pertinent to this case, see Khavandi et al. [36] for a breakdown of the modules which make up Dora's cataract calls. These episodes might be for example the call opening (such as in Fig. 5), the business disclosure, an information gathering phase, a wrapping up and closing of the interaction. These modules themselves are normatively made up of different sequences, recognisable patterns or structures in conversation. We saw how in the call opening example above, it included a greeting component, an identification component, a business disclosure component. These are produced together in a particular order that establishes the grounds for this interaction. They work as a set, but they each do different work. They can be analysed as part of a larger sequence, but also separately in terms of formatting and what the sequence needs to achieve.

Select a Sequence. From the larger module, we select a particular sequence that we want to develop. In doing so, we may already be comparing how well the overall structure of the module design maps onto the regularised structures found in the natural data. Where particular types of action are ordered differently in the natural data compared with the proposed or previously developed conversational design, we may need to look at a. how regular each pattern is in the source data, and b. whether we can reorganise the components embedded in the conversational design to more closely align with the sequence organisation found in the natural data (and by implication more aligned with the normative expectations of the human participant in these interactions).

Once a sequence has been selected for development, we move on to designing or improving the VUI input.

Identify Natural Source Data (T1). Once a particular module and sequence has been selected for development, its equivalent is identified in the source data (we will refer to this as T1, or Text 1, an example for which is given as Fig. 6). If this segment of source data has not yet been transcribed, then we do so, paying attention to turn design, including the types of lexical choices that are being used, the syntactic formatting in the turn-at-talk, any pauses (or lack thereof), hesitation markers, intonation contouring, pitch-shifts, word-lengthening, and changes in volume and speed of delivery.

Important also is to pay attention to how this is oriented to by the recipient. How do they format their response to the target turn at talk? In doing so, we are able to see how the co-participant understands the previous turn, and judge whether they produce the kind of action required of the human participant in the human-machine interaction. Where we find evidence of a co-participant either initiating repair, or misunderstanding the previous turn, we can look at other data of similar sequences to identify whether there is something particular about how the turn is formatted that may lead to trouble.

```
02 DOC:   ↑hi:.→
03         good afternoo:n→
04         it's ↓doctor grey calling from the trentwood u:h ↑cataract
05         clinic↗
```

Fig. 6. T1 source data from clinician-patient telephone call

Produce the Line of Transcode (T2). Once the transcription is available, we can turn to designing or improving the equivalent line of script in the conversational design (what we will call Text 2, T2). Here, we model the equivalent section of script on the source data. By doing so, we design an initial line of transcode – i.e. a particular line of script that is used for processing through Text-to-Speech (TTS) synthesis (Fig. 7).

```
hi. good afternoon, it's dora, calling from the trentwood cataract
clinic.
```

Fig. 7. T2 script produced for TTS, based on source data

Trial Through TTS. Here starts the iterative process, where the transcode is used for generating the automated speech through TTS. We will refer to this output as T3. Once available, this output is used as a basis for checking how the speech synthesiser behaves with the particular formatting of the transcode (T2). Figure 8 shows a transcript representation of how our example T2 is converted into spoken output through TTS.

```
01 DOR:   hi↘ (0.3) good afternoon↘ (0.3)
02         it's dora↘ (0.3)
03         calling from the trentwood cataract clinic↘
```

Fig. 8. T3 agent spoken output produced through TTS

Compare T3 with T1. Here we can test for 'naturalness', by comparing the automated speech output (T3) with the segment of source data that this is modelled on (T1). At this stage, we can note any particular differences in how the initial data is formatted and how the speech synthesiser behaves. Readers are invited to examine the transcripts from Fig. 6 and Fig. 8 for differences. Figure 9 below provides a comparison of the volume and intonation contour patterns of these two speech samples.

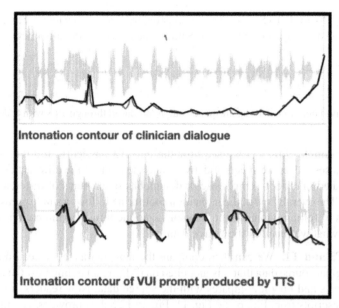

Fig. 9. Comparison of T1 and T3 speech samples

Modify the T2. On the basis of the diagnostic work carried out in comparing T3 with T1, we return to the line of transcoding (T2) and add in modifications to the script. It may be sufficient to simply change the elements already present in the transcode, for example removing punctuation marking where it inadvertently introduces pauses in speech output. We may also include an additional level of coding, namely by manipulating the speech synthesiser by enhancing the script with Speech Synthesis Markup Language (SSML) markup. This allows the conversation designer an additional level of control over the automated speech output, with opportunities to direct such formatting features as intonation contouring, variations of speed of various parsed segments within the sequence, volume and pitch modulations within the output. Figure 10 provides an example of SSML markup used to produce a T3 which more closely resembles the T1 source data.

```
SSML. English (United States) - Neural Voice 2 - en-US-Neural2- H (Speed 1.0; Pitch 0.0)
https://cloud.google.com/text-to-speech#section-2

<speak>
<prosody rate="90\%" pitch="+4st" > hai </prosody>
<prosody rate="98\%" pitch="+2st" > good afternoon </prosody> <prosody rate="105\%" pitch="+4st" >
this </prosody> <prosody rate="105\%" pitch="+8st" > is </prosody>
<prosody pitch="+3st">DORA</prosody>
<prosody rate="120\%">the clinical assistant from </prosody> <prosody rate="110\%"> trentwood cataract
clinic? </prosody> </speak>
```

Fig. 10. SSML markup used to produce a new T3

Trial Again Through TTS. The new augmented transcode is again processed through TTS, this time drawing upon SSML markup as necessary, producing a new T3.

```
01 DOR:   thi good afternoon→
02        this is dora→
03        Δthe clinical assistantΔ from trentwood cataract clinic↗
```

Fig. 11. Revised iteration of T3 agent spoken output produced through TTS with SSML markup

In this example (Fig. 11) we see how the new T3 has led to the removal of the intra-turn pauses. Also, the speed of delivery and the pitch of the different components are manipulated in order to emphasise or de-emphasise elements of different levels of importance. The overall flow of the intonation contouring follows a single phrasing rather than a series of falling intonation components, and the turn-final intonation is upward, in line with what we found in the source data.

Compare T3 and T1. We can then compare the new automated speech output (T3) with the original source data that it is modelled on (T1), again noting how the automated speech behaves and how it compares with the source data. Now readers are invited to compare transcripts from Fig. 6 and Fig. 11. Figure 12 below provides a comparison of the volume and intonation contour patterns of these two speech samples.

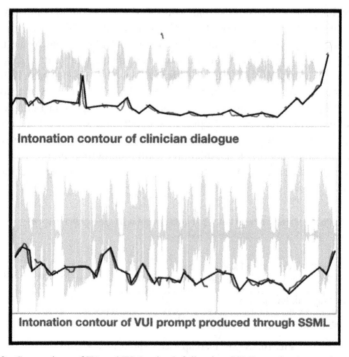

Intonation contour of clinician dialogue

Intonation contour of VUI prompt produced through SSML

Fig. 12. Comparison of T1 and T3 (revised, following SSML markup) speech samples

Repeat the Cycle Until Satisfied. The designer works through a number of cycles of modifying the transcode (T2) and then comparing the automated speech output (T3) with the source data (T1). On each pass, the goal is to manipulate the speech synthesiser to generate a format that is recognisable as being modelled on the source data.

Once satisfied with the output, T3 is provisionally ratified.

Trial with Human Participants. The T3 can be finally trialled with human participants, with a view to identifying how they treat the automated speech. This would ideally be as part of a full interaction, with all agent output modelled on human equivalent. Where areas of further development are deemed necessary, the designer returns to modify further, as per the above steps.

Summary. The set of design procedures proposed here allows conversation designers to leverage previous Conversation Analytic research as well as recordings of naturally occurring interaction in how they approximate the conventions of natural language use. Rather than by hypothesising how speech events may play out, the conversation designer models the script on recurrent patterns found in equivalent human-human interactions, including regularities in how talk is formatted. Rather than the script writing stage marking the left-boundary of the design activity, here it occupies a coordinating position between previously generated knowledge and data on the one hand, and its subsequent transformation into usable script (transcode) for speech synthesis.

4 Conclusion

In a recent 'state of the art' literature review paper on speech in Human-Computer Interaction [1], the authors proposed a number of challenges to the field of HCI. Among these were two challenges which the CADENCE method contributes to addressing, particularly in relational to conversation design for VUIs: (1) improving theories of speech-based interaction, and (2) increasing guidelines for carrying out conversation design. It addresses the former by providing a framework through which to draw upon a long-established body of research on language and social interaction. In doing so, it builds on previous work championing the case of CA for conversation design [7–11]. It also addresses the latter by providing a step-by-step set of procedures which conversation designers can follow in their design process.

By drawing upon real-world human-human interactions as source data, and informed by the decades of insights into the fine-grained details of human conversational conduct that CA has provided, the CADENCE model could provide conversation designers with the potential to unlock greater authenticity and 'naturalness' of their VUIs. It supports the design of VUIs which more closely resemble human spoken conduct in the rele-vant settings (such as healthcare consultations, customer service, etc.) or, where that is not possible, in the production of sequences of actions (such as greetings and self-introductions, information-seeking questions, offers, suggestions, requests, and so on) from similar settings.

This is not an aesthetic endeavour, with the aim of developing an agent that can pass as a human. In the case of most VUIs, one would anticipate that this would not be desirable. Indeed, in our collaborative development of Dora, changes have been made to remove elements of the system's talk which may inadvertently imply some level of sentience, or empathy, or agency. The development of an agent which produces talk more closely resembling human conduct is solely with the aim of developing a more effective system, and a more positive user experience.

When users engage with a system which draws upon the same norms and conventions of conversation with which they are accustomed (and into which they have been socialised throughout their lives), those users are more likely to interact without the need to consciously consider what the system is attempting to do, and how they might be expected to respond, at every given moment. Instead, they will interact more unconsciously, more intuitively and more spontaneously. One can anticipate that this will remove some of the frustrations currently reported by users engaging with VUIs, and the general sense of VUIs not currently living up to the hype or expectations with which they are promoted [37].

As mentioned, this model was developed, and has been tested, through collaboration with a team of conversation designers, working on one system, in the specific context of automated clinical consultations. Future work could test this model across a broader range of VUIs, such as customer services, where possible. Such work will provide a far broader base upon which to test the efficacy of the model, and for greater potential to examine how user conduct, and user experience, differs across VUI systems which resemble human conversational conduct to varying degrees.

Acknowledgements. This project was supported by a British Academy Innovation Fellowship (IF2223/230141).

References

1. Clark, L., et al.: The state of speech in HCI: trends, themes and challenges. Interact. Comput. **31**(4), 349–371 (2020). https://doi.org/10.1093/iwc/iwz016
2. Murad, C., et al.: Let's talk about CUIs: putting conversational user interface design into practice. In: Extended Abstracts of the 2021 CHI Conference on Human Factors in Computing Systems (CHI EA 2021), Article 98, pp. 1–6 (2021). https://doi.org/10.1145/3411763.3441336
3. Murad, C., Munteanu, C.: "I don't know what you're talking about, HALexa": the case for voice user interface guidelines. In: Proceedings of the 1st International Conference on Conversational User Interfaces (CUI 2019), Article 9, pp. 1–3 (2019). https://doi.org/10.1145/3342775.3342795
4. Murad, C., Munteanu, C.: "Voice-first interfaces in a GUI-first design world": barriers and opportunities to supporting VUI designers on-the-job. In: 4th Conference on Conversational User Interfaces (2022). https://doi.org/10.1145/3543829.3543842
5. Kim, Y., Reza, M., Mcgrenere, J., Yoon, D.: Designers characterize naturalness in voice user interfaces: their goals, practices, and challenges. In: Proceedings of the 2021 CHI Conference on Human Factors in Computing Systems (CHI 2021), Article 242, pp. 1–13 (2021). https://doi.org/10.1145/3411764.3445579
6. Google: Conversation Design. https://developers.google.com/assistant/conversation-design/welcome. Accessed 20 June 2023

7. Housley, W., Albert, S., Stokoe, E.: Natural action processing. In: Proceedings of the Halfway to the Future Symposium 2019 (HTTF 2019). Article 34, pp. 1–4 (2019). https://doi.org/10.1145/3363384.3363478

8. Moore, R.J., An, S., Ren, G.: The IBM natural conversation framework: a new paradigm for conversational UX design. Hum.-Comput. Interact. **3**(3–4), 168–193 (2023). https://doi.org/10.1080/07370024.2022.2081571

9. Moore, R.J., Arar, R.: Conversational UX Design: A Practitioner's Guide to the Natural Conversation Framework. Association for Computing Machinery, New York (2019)

10. Stokoe, E., Albert, S, Parslow, S., Pearl, C.: Conversation Design and Conversation Analysis: Where the Moonshots Are. Medium (2021). https://elizabeth-stokoe.medium.com/conversation-design-and-conversation-analysis-c2a2836cb042

11. Brandt, A., Hazel, S., McKinnon, R., Sideridou, K., Tindale, J., Ventoura, N.: From writing dialogue to designing conversation: considering the potential of conversation analysis for voice user interfaces. In: ACM Conference on Conversational User Interfaces (2023). https://doi.org/10.1145/3571884.3603758

12. Schegloff, E.A., Sacks, H.: Opening up closings. Semiotica **8**, 289–327 (1973). https://doi.org/10.1515/semi.1973.8.4.289

13. McCulloch, B.: Conversation Design: Paralanguage. Medium (2019). https://medium.com/voice-tech-podcast/conversation-design-paralanguage-73ef042c0117

14. Bradford, B.: Upspeak in British English. English Today **13**(3), 29–36 (1997). https://doi.org/10.1017/S0266078400009810

15. Nycum, R.: In defense of valley girl English. Compass **1**(5), 23–29 (2018). https://scholarworks.arcadia.edu/thecompass/vol1/iss5/4

16. Sacks, H.: Notes on methodology. In: Atkinson, J.M., Heritage, J. (eds.) Structures of Social Action: Studies in Conversation Analysis, pp. 21–27. Cambridge University Press, Cambridge (1984)

17. Allain, P., Harvie, J.: The Routledge Companion to Theatre and Performance. Routledge, Abingdon (2006)

18. Culpeper, J., Short, M., Verdonk, P.: Exploring the Language of Drama: From Text to Context. Routledge, London (1998)

19. Herman, V.: Dramatic Dialogue and the Systematics of Turn-Taking. Semiotica **83**(1–2), 97–121 (1991)

20. Herman, V.: Dramatic Discourse: Dialogue as Interaction in Plays. Routledge, Abingdon (1995). https://doi.org/10.1515/semi.1991.83.1-2.97

21. Burns, E.: Theatricality: A Study of Convention in the Theatre and in Social Life. Longman, London (1972)

22. Hazel, S.: Acting, interacting, enacting. Akademisk Kvarter **12**, 44–64 (2015). https://doi.org/10.5278/ojs.academicquarter.v0i12.2727

23. Lefebvre, A.: Reading and embodying the script during the theatrical rehearsal. Lang. Dialog. **8**(2), 261–288 (2018). https://doi.org/10.1075/ld.00015.lef

24. Crow, B.K.: Conversational performance and the performance of conversation. TDR (Drama Rev.) **32**(3), 23–54 (1988). https://doi.org/10.2307/1145905

25. Norrthon, S.: To stage an overlap: the longitudinal, collaborative and embodied process of staging eight lines in a professional theatre rehearsal process. J. Pragmat. **142**, 171–184 (2019). https://doi.org/10.1016/j.pragma.2019.01.015

26. Bell, A., Gibson, A.: Staging language: an introduction to the sociolinguistics of performance. J. Socioling. **15**, 555–572 (2011). https://doi.org/10.1111/j.1467-9841.2011.00517.x

27. Johnstone, B.: Dialect enregisterment in performance. J. Socioling. **15**, 657–679 (2011). https://doi.org/10.1111/j.1467-9841.2011.00512.x

28. Lemon, A.M.: "Form" and "Function" in Soviet Stage Romani: modeling metapragmatics through performance institutions. Lang. Soc. **31**(1), 29–64 (2002). https://doi.org/10.1017/S0047404502001021

29. Schegloff, E.A.: The routine as achievement. Hum. Stud. **9**(2), 111–151 (1986). https://doi.org/10.1007/BF00148124

30. Sikveland, R., Stokoe, E., Symonds, J.: Patient burden during appointment-making telephone calls to GP practices. Patient Educ. Couns. **99**(8), 1310–1318 (2016). https://doi.org/10.1016/j.pec.2016.03.025

31. Houtkoop-Steenstra, H.: Opening sequences in Dutch telephone conversations. In: Boden, D., Zimmerman, D.H. (eds.) Talk and Social Structure: Studies in Ethnomethodology and Conversation Analysis, pp. 232–50. Polity, Cambridge (1991)

32. Laurier, E.: Why people say where they are during mobile phone calls. Environ. Plan. D Soc. Space **19**(4), 485–504 (2001). https://doi.org/10.1068/d228t

33. Humă, B., Stokoe, E.: The anatomy of first-time and subsequent business-to-business "Cold" calls. Res. Lang. Soc. Interact. **53**(2), 271–294 (2020). https://doi.org/10.1080/08351813.2020.1739432

34. Jefferson, G.: List-construction as a Task and a Resource. In: Psathas, G. (ed.) Interaction Competence, pp. 63–92. University Press of America (1990)

35. Jefferson, G.: Glossary of transcript symbols with an introduction. In: Lerner, G.H. (ed.) Conversation Analysis: Studies from the First Generation, pp. 13–31. Benjamins, Amsterdam (2004)

36. Khavandi, S., et al.: User-acceptability of an automated telephone call for post-operative follow-up after uncomplicated cataract surgery. Eye (2022). https://doi.org/10.1038/s41433-022-02289-8

37. Clark, L., et al.: What makes a good conversation? Challenges in designing truly conversational agents. In: Proceedings of the 2019 CHI Conference on Human Factors in Computing Systems (CHI 2019), Paper 475, pp. 1–12 (2019). https://doi.org/10.1145/3290605.3300705

A Scoping Review of Mental Model Research in HCI from 2010 to 2021

Xinhui Hu and Michael Twidale[✉]

School of Information Sciences, University of Illinois at Urbana-Champaign,
Urbana-Champaign, IL 61820, USA
twidale@illinois.edu

Abstract. Research on mental models has been ongoing in Human-Computer Interaction (HCI) since the 1980s. A mental model derives from humans' perception, memories, knowledge, and causal beliefs about the external reality, mediating how they describe, explain, and predict the world surrounding them. By understanding users' mental models of a target system, designers can improve the learnability and usability of a system via a better interface. Although understanding mental models is important for interface design, unfortunately understanding what is meant by the term 'mental model' can be a challenge. The field has historically been plagued by inconsistent usage of the term, as pointed out by prior researchers. It has been some time since the last comprehensive evaluation of HCI-related mental model research. This scoping review provides a comprehensive overview of the current literature on mental model research in HCI from 2010 to 2021, exploring aspects such as where research has been conducted, by whom, on what, using which methods, and for which purposes. The findings suggest a growing diversity in approach, with new perspectives and methodologies being introduced. Our review was initiated by a desire to understand the state of the art of mental models research, and sustained by a sense of confusion about the different ways that different researchers used the term. We hope that it will help people new to the field to make sense of the rich, diverse, but at times rather confusing ways that the term 'mental model' is used in HCI research.

Keywords: Mental model · HCI · Scoping review

1 Introduction

The black-box nature of the human mind has been a persistent challenge for Human-Computer Interaction (HCI) researchers. A sufficient understanding of users' perceptions and expectations for a target system is critical for successful HCI designs. However, the opaqueness and elusiveness of the human mind have posed tremendous challenges. Directly taking the users' answers to need assessment questions is risky, as what the users need, what they think they need, and what they have stated as their needs can all be very different. In this case, with its potential to reveal what underlies human thinking and reasoning, the concept of a mental model has shed new light and been widely used in HCI research and practice.

© The Author(s), under exclusive license to Springer Nature Switzerland AG 2023
M. Kurosu et al. (Eds.): HCII 2023, LNCS 14054, pp. 101–125, 2023.
https://doi.org/10.1007/978-3-031-48038-6_7

Mental models, in the broadest sense, refer to humans' internal representations of the external world that derive from their perception, memories, knowledge, and causal beliefs [1, 2]. From a functional perspective, in the HCI design context, mental models can be conceived of as a synthesis of users' past experiences, current observations, and anticipated future interactions with a target system that mediates how humans describe, explain, and predict the behaviors of that system [3–5]. Therefore, for decades, the promising future of mental model research has brought cross-disciplinary attention to this field, leading to the publication of numerous significant research findings.

However, HCI-related mental model research has grown more diverse, which raises doubts about whether researchers are studying the same phenomenon when using the term 'mental model'. Inconsistent perspectives regarding the nature of mental models have repeatedly been identified from conflicting descriptions of this concept on very basic features [4, 6]. For example, there has been a lack of consensus regarding whether mental models should be descriptive or analytic, static or dynamic, generic or instantiated, accurate or inaccurate, subjective or objective, and in a variety of other dimensions [7]. Indeed some studies have adopted misaligned definitions and methodologies, such as citing a definition that describes 'mental model' as a dynamic concept but then in the study measuring it with static methods. These issues have been identified and observed multiple times in the past few decades, and each time they are brought back into the scope, the gaps reappear. In the last comprehensive review of HCI-related mental model research in 2003, it was pointed out that "even a casual inspection of the HCI and cognitive-science literature reveals that the term is used in so many different ways as to be almost void of any force beyond the general idea of users' knowledge about the system they use" [8]. Since then, it became unclear how this field has developed.

Despite the continued research in this field, there has been little discussion over whether the previously identified issues have been resolved or persisted as the field evolves. Even identifying which disciplines are active in this research area and tracking their progress has become a challenging task. Therefore, we believe it is a good time to revisit some essential questions: in the current mental model research field, what exactly is a mental model, and what do HCI researchers mean when they use the term? We might even ask what are HCI researchers' mental models of the concept they call 'mental model'. To bridge this gap, this study has conducted a scoping review of mental model research in HCI from 2010 to 2021 with the following objectives: (1) determining the current scope and volume of this research field; (2) itemizing the research methods used; and (3) identifying the major concerns and gaps in this research theme.

2   Research Background: A Brief History of Mental Model Research

When studying the concept of a mental model, it is essential to be aware of its multifaceted nature, especially its historical development. Mental model research did not emerge from a single theory but rather was built on findings from several research disciplines. The first mental model is often attributed to Craik's small-scale models: "If the organism carries a "small-scale model" of external reality and of its own possible actions within its head, it is able to try out various alternatives, conclude which is the best of them, react to future situations before they arise, utilize the knowledge of past events in dealing with the present and future, and in every way to react in a much fuller, safer, and more competent manner to the emergencies which face it" [9, p. 61]. Craik's theory was strikingly similar to the modern definition and application of a mental model and has hence been credited with establishing this field.

However, recognizing Craik as the originator of this research theme does not necessarily indicate that current research on mental models is entirely founded on this theory. Several signs suggest that multiple disciplines have independently developed a mental model-like concept within their theoretical framework, as shown in Fig. 1. For example, in 1948, Tolman independently proposed a similar concept termed cognitive map, which suggested that the brain structurally learns a representation of the environment, akin to a map [2]. Moreover, prior to Craik and Tolman, a number of 19th-century theorists predicted the rise of mental model theories [2] on the premise that individuals would need to extract their mental constructions to make their thoughts more transparent and comprehensible. In the embryonic stage, 'mental model' referred to a nebulous concept that encompassed all kinds of mental representations that exhibit relatively obvious patterns and a certain level of predictability.

From the 1960s to the mid-1970s, at least three fields made independent contributions to mental model research. The education, cognitive psychology, and supervisory domains each developed their own theoretical framework and methodologies for mental model research [6]. Education researchers generally applied the term 'mental model' in studying how learners construct their knowledge, where this concept was usually interpreted as humans' subjective understanding of real-world phenomena [10]. Cognitive psychologists, on the other hand, tend to use the term 'mental model' to refer to the mental mechanisms with which humans encode and comprehend information. The supervisory control researchers perceived a mental model as a model in the mind that embodies knowledge and skill in directing an operation toward optimal outcomes. Technical developments in the late 1970s brought them together with a converging focus on understanding humans' mental models in their interaction with systems and transferring this knowledge to improve design, which set the stage for the flourishing of mental model research in the following decade.

The 1980s were by far the most productive decade for mental model research, during which the phrase 'mental model' was ubiquitous in the literature [4]. In 1983, several influential publications on mental model research collectively brought this research theme to the general public, among which Johnson-Laird's *Mental Models: Towards a Cognitive Science of Language, Inference, and Consciousness*[11], Gentner and Stevens' *Mental Models* [10], Norman's *Some Observations on Mental Models* [7], and Card et al.'s [12] Goal, Operator Method, and Selection rule (GOMS) model were the most renowned.

Johnson-Laird's book was often cited for providing the most commonly referenced definition of mental model and attributing the first mental model theory to Craik. However, its theoretical significance resides in its integration of the psychology of meaning and the psychology of reasoning [13], which set the base for the analytic reasoning aspect of mental model research. In this book, Johnson-Laird mainly represented mental models in the format of formal rules of deductive inferences that are similar to those in

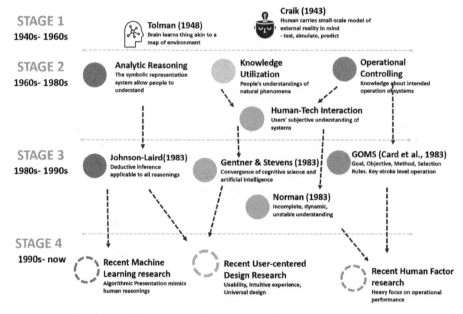

Fig. 1. A brief outline of different mental model research approaches

logical calculus, such as "all A are B, all B are C, hence all A are C". [11, p. 75]. With these deductive representations, humans could encode, assimilate, and process information, functioning as the brain's "machine code" that supports the execution of the mental model. While Johnson-Laird's early chapters in the book were insightful from an interaction standpoint, it is important to note that his approach was based on an analytic reasoning perspective.

Genter and Stevens' book was a collection of articles that offered a vivid illustration of how educational mental model research fused into the HCI context. The initial few chapters of this book were clearly HCI-focused, whereas the later chapters preserved many features of instructional education mental model research. The selection of these mix-themed contents appeared to be purposeful, as Gentner and Stevens predicted that the future mental model would be "a confluence of two major lines of research: one being cognitive psychology and related disciplines of linguistics, anthropology, and philosophy while the other being artificial intelligence" [10]. Having envisioned the two fundamental pillars of mental model research in human-computer interaction (HCI), Gentner and Stevens also envisaged a list of naturalistic methodologies that have since become widely adopted.

As a core chapter in Gentner and Stevens' book, Norman's [7] observation on mental models was also frequently cited separately from the book for its unique theoretical contributions. In this chapter, Norman made two significant observations. With a deep understanding of its multifaceted nature, Norman's first observation was the need to distinguish three distinct concepts: the users' mental model, the designers' conceptual model, and the scientists' conceptualization of the users' models on the meta-level. The other observation addressed the characteristics of a normal mental model, with Norman noting that people's mental models are typically incomplete, unstable, effort-intensive to operate in the mind, and without firm boundaries. These models are unscientific and may contain unneeded behavior patterns, with people doing extra physical operations as a trade-off for reduced mental complexity.

The book by Card, Morgan, and Newell [12] was considered the cornerstone of the operational supervisory approach of mental model research [14]. This approach assumed that users construct models of the task and the system in mind, which could be inferred from their behavior. According to this model, for each given task, four components should be specified: (1) interaction Goals, (2) Operators, (3) Methods to achieve the goals, and (4) Selection rules for prioritizing the competing methods. The GOMS model as it was known focused on breaking down complex tasks into simpler subtasks or operations and then mapping out the mental processes required to perform those subtasks. By specifying these metrics, the model can uncover redundant operations that can be eliminated for improved performance, efficiency, and error prevention. As a result, the concept of mental model in GOMS often appears to be more task-specific and precise compared to the other approaches.

Throughout the 1980s, the promise depicted in these publications attracted interdisciplinary attention to this rapidly evolving field and encouraged researchers to apply the concept of mental model in describing, explaining, and predicting users' interaction with technologies [4]. Interaction scenarios between humans and technologies expanded from industrial settings to everyday contexts, and user groups studied grew from trained operators to the general public. The diverse knowledge and skills of different user groups required designers and user researchers to understand users' mental models of the products in order to determine what to enhance for better user experiences, system performance, and system logic. However, with the rapid expansion of activity in diverse settings, mental model researchers from different backgrounds did not seem to communicate sufficiently [4], particularly with regard to their divergences in interpreting the core concepts and selecting methodologies. Since the mid-1980s, confusion caused by inconsistent and at times incoherent mental model definitions has been repeatedly identified. While some researchers advocated for bringing order back to this field with explicit definitions and taxonomies [4, 6], the pace of growth of mental model research has outpaced their efforts.

In the 1990s, theoretical and empirical HCI-related mental model research ceased to develop in a balanced way. As new technologies were constantly introduced into daily life, each of their mental models warranted investigation, which led to another wave of application-oriented mental model research. Studies at that time had a strong focus on measuring, evaluating, and implementing mental models [15, 16]. Meanwhile, theoretical research on mental models appeared to come to a standstill. During this time, efforts were directed towards integrating the diverse theoretical perspectives of mental models into a comprehensive and coherent framework [17, 18], as well as developing taxonomies to effectively classify the various dimensions of mental models [18, 19]. However, despite the valuable insights provided by these studies, their contributions appear to have been largely overlooked in subsequent decades.

In the 2000s, the gap between practical and theoretical studies of mental models in the HCI domain continued to widen. More researchers joined the field seemingly fully connecting their usage of the term to the existing body of literature on mental models, so that distinguishing the different understandings of this concept became even more challenging. Indeed Payne [8] argued that "even a casual inspection of the HCI and cognitive-science literature reveals that the term is used in so many different ways as to be almost void of any force beyond the general idea of users' knowledge about the system they use". Since then, developments of the field have been even less clear. Without a recent comprehensive review, it is hard to answer many basic questions. For instance, it is unclear whether the previously detected confusion and mismatching understandings have been alleviated or if they persist as the area evolves. Moreover, how do the recent mental model researchers study this concept? Which domains do they come from? And where do they publish their progress? How do they define, represent, measure, and evaluate the mental models? The absence of concrete answers to these basic questions is exactly the problem that this study seeks to address.

3   Method

The procedures and frameworks were developed based on Preferred Reporting Items for Systematic Reviews and Meta-analysis Protocols (PRISMA), with reference to previous studies on scoping review methodologies [20, 21]. This scoping review includes the following key phases: (1) identifying the research questions, (2) searching the relevant studies, (3) screening and selecting the retrieved studies, (4) synthesizing the data, and (5) comparing the results to the baseline knowledge in this field.

3.1   Research Questions

This review was guided by the question "How have HCI researchers studied mental models in the most recent decade?" In exploring the answers, this review specifically addressed the following aspects:

1. Between 2010 to 2021, who has contributed to HCI-related mental model research?
2. What were the motivations for studying mental models?
3. How has the concept of mental model been defined and interpreted in this decade?
4. Which methods have been used to represent, measure, and evaluate mental models?
5. What are the current challenges in this research domain?
6. In what ways do the HCI-related mental model studies conducted in this decade differ from those conducted in earlier decades?

3.2   Search Strategy

The literature search was implemented on February 19, 2022, in three mainstream databases: Ebsco, Scopus, and Web of Science using the keyword combination "TITLE-ABS-KEY ("mental model" AND hci)" and limiting the time span between 2010 to 2021. The reason for choosing these databases is their comprehensive coverage of literature across a wide spectrum of disciplines. The search term was tested using multiple variants to confirm that this relatively simply query could retrieve an appropriate body of literature.

3.3 Eligibility Criteria

Studies were eligible for initial inclusion if they were published in books, peer-reviewed journals, or conference proceedings, or if they had undergone a rigorous investigation process similar to that of a dissertation, during the period from 2010 to 2021. Moreover, eligible studies must fulfill at least one of the following criteria:

1. Provide a definition of mental model in the context of HCI and appropriately elaborate on the definition.
2. Compare and/or contrast the concept of mental model with other HCI concepts.
3. Measure the mental model in the HCI context.
4. Evaluate a measured mental model in the HCI context.

Examples of the application of the exclusion criteria were studies that misapplied the mental model concept to refer to other concepts, explored mental models outside the realm of HCI, or centered on topics not relevant to mental models.

3.4 Data Characterization and Extraction

Given that the search keywords ensured relevance in the titles and abstracts, all retrieved records have undergone full-text selection to determine their eligibility. In this process, the following research characteristics have been extracted for further analysis: title, authors, publication year, affiliated disciplines, publishing sector, the definition of mental model, reported background of mental model, concepts associated with mental model, concepts distinguished from mental model, the rationale for investigating mental model, representation methods of mental model, measuring methods of mental model, and evaluation methods of mental model.

4 Results

4.1 Literature Search Results

The literature search yielded 196 potentially relevant records. After deleting duplicates and filtering for peer-reviewed publications, 169 records remained for full-text selection. Following this strategy, 70 retrieved publications eventually met the inclusion criteria for further analysis, as shown in Fig. 2.

4.2 Scope of the selected publications

Scope by Year. The analysis of the publication years (Fig. 3.) indicates a slight increasing trend in the HCI-related mental model domain between 2010 and 2019. Further investigation is required to determine whether the lower publication count in 2020 and 2021 represents an actual decrease or is due to incomplete database coverage.

Scope by Field. In determining which fields have an active interest in investigating mental models in the HCI context, only the affiliation of the first author is analyzed. As shown in Fig. 4, the first authors of the selected publications represented a wide range

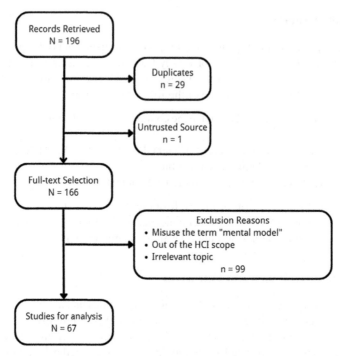

Fig. 2. Flowchart of publication selection process

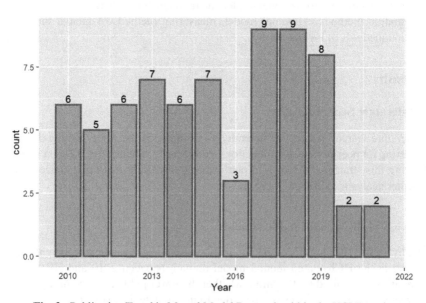

Fig. 3. Publication Trend in Mental Model Research within the HCI Domain

of academic disciplines, which can be coded into eight broad categories: engineering (18), computer science (13), design (10), psychology (7), information/informatics (7), communication (1), business (1), and those without clear affiliation information (12).

Over the past ten years, traditional HCI domains like engineering, computer science, design, psychology, usability studies, and information sciences have continued to make the majority of contributions to this field, with scholars in communication and business bringing an increase in diversity. On a more granular level, there has been a convergence among these fields. For example, subdisciplines in engineering, design, and psychology, such as industrial design, industrial design engineering, ergonomics, usability, user experience, and user interface, have converged on the interests of the mental model in the interaction context. Similarly, while studying the analytical reasoning aspect of mental models, the areas of psychology, computer science, and information studies were observed to fuse. In addition, the subdivisions like system engineering, engineering and management, and integrative systems within the engineering domain exhibit a clear tendency towards the operational control fields. On the other hand, the 12 publications without affiliated departments were mostly from non-academic organizations and companies, which suggested that mental model research is now of interest to researchers outside traditional academic fields.

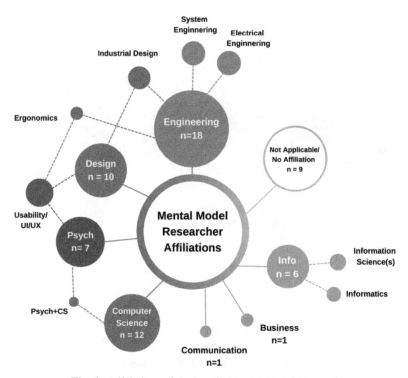

Fig. 4. Affiliations of Authors in Mental Model Research

Scope by Venue. The venues of selected publications are determined by the titles, themes, and keywords of the journals and conferences where they were published. Not surprisingly, the majority of the papers were found in HCI and related fields, such as computer science, information sciences, engineering design, and psychology (Fig. 5.). Outside the traditional HCI field, some publications were in fields such as security and privacy, humanities, education, business, and ecology. This suggests a growing trend towards interdisciplinary research in the field, in line with the observations made in the analysis of affiliated fields.

Scope by Research Target. The analysis indicates that the targets of selected publications have covered a broad range of technology systems, including graphical user interfaces [22], gesture control systems [23–25], voice interfaces [26], encryption algorithms [27], cybersecurity systems [28], virtual reality [29], augmented reality [30], railway control interface [31], explainable artificial intelligence [32], as well as other advanced technology systems. The broad range of technology systems studied in the selected publications underscores the importance of interdisciplinary collaboration and the consideration of diverse user groups and contexts in mental model research. These factors are critical to ensuring that the resulting insights are transferable and applicable across various settings.

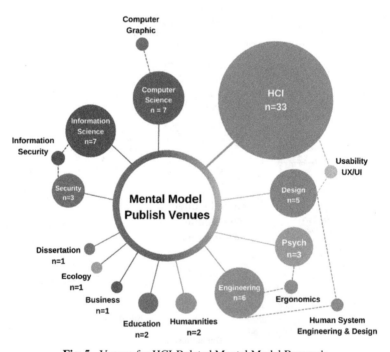

Fig. 5. Venues for HCI-Related Mental Model Research

4.3   Motivations for Mental Model in HCI

Approximately 60% (41 out of 70) of the selected publications explained their motivations and purposes for studying mental models within the context of HCI, which mainly centered around the need to understand, predict, and enhance interaction between users, designers, and the target systems.

Table 1. Motivations and themes in HCI-related mental model research

Motivation	Specific purposes	Examples
Understanding	Helping designers better understand users	- Behaviors: "Mental models are valuable because they are the lenses through which individuals see and interact with the world" [50] - User's conceptualization: "…gain a better understanding of how users conceptualize the cause-and-effect relationships between their actions and the responses of the various devices in the smart home" [30] -User's mental process: "Using mental models to better understand user state of mind" [34] - Problem-solving strategy: "While people are given a particular task, they also construct a mental model to solve that task" [35] - Extract implicit knowledge [36]
	Aiding users to better understand the system	- "Mental models make it easier for us to understand our environment" [51] - "Mental models help users better understand and predict system behavior" [33]
	Enhance mutual understandings	- "In HCI, Mental Model can help designers better understand the user, and also can help users better understand the product" [37] - "Since mental models vary from person to person, it is necessary to keep same mental models in each mind for good communication"[38]
Prediction	Predict user behaviors	- "Mental models enable users to predict and explain the operation of a target system" [50] - "mental model framework helps to identify and predict a user's behaviors" [3]
	Predict system performance	- "Mental models are consciously or unconsciously used to predict situations or to make decisions in relation to product usage" [42]
	Predict potential error	- "…highlighting situations where the user's mental model is in conflict with the actual behavior of the system" [43]

(continued)

Table 1. (*continued*)

Motivation	Specific purposes	Examples
Interaction	Guide interaction	- "Mental models still have high guiding significance in the interaction design…" [24] - "… gaining attention by breaking the mental model" [34] - "A mental model is functional in the sense that it helps the agent to determine and tune its behavior and to develop an approach for solving a problem" [44]
	Improve interactive design	- "Address design gaps by match the user interface and mental model of the user" [47] - "help designer produced reasonable design schemes to meet the physiological, psychological needs and context characteristics of the users" [46] - "Looking for ways to help our students overcome their difficulties in defining functional system requirements" [45]
Combination of above		- "Every learner exploits his/her mental model to reason about the system, to anticipate its behavior and to comprehend why it reacts as it does" [41] - "Mental models are valuable for allowing prediction and understanding of how things should behave" [40] - "…provides both explanatory and predictive power and determines the users performance"[48] - "1. prediction 2. assessing the probability of specified events 3. assenting conditioned probabilities 4. counterfactual assessment 5. assessment of causality" [49]

As summarized in Table 1, in the cases where mental models were studied to facilitate understanding of interaction, the following subthemes were identified: (1) helping designers in gaining a better understanding of users' behaviors [33], causal beliefs [30], mental processes [34], problem-solving strategies [35], and knowledge during their interactions [36]; (2) aiding users in gaining a better understanding of the target system; (3) enhancing mutual understanding between designers, users, and systems [37, 38].

Upon understanding the mental models of the users, mental models were also used to predict (1) the users' potential interaction behaviors [3, 39], (2) the system's performance [40–42], and (3) the potential errors [43]. In addition, with an anticipation of the interaction, these insights were utilized to optimize the interaction, with the aims of (1) providing better user guidance [24, 34, 44] and (2) enhancing system design [45–47]. Given the interdependence of these three themes, many studies reported a fusion of them [40, 48, 49].

4.4 Theorizing Mental Models

Contextualizing Current Work in Prior Discussions of Mental Models. In spite of the mental model's complex history and many facets, analysis of the literature search shows that a majority of them do not sufficiently investigate these contexts. Only 23 (33%) of the selected publications explored the evolution of the concept of mental model. In the publications that investigated the historical development of the concept of mental model, Craik (1943, n = 15; 1952, n = 1), Johnson-Laird (1983, n = 9), Norman (1983, n = 4), and Gentner & Stevens (1983, n = 3) were the most frequently cited sources. Other scholars and their works, such as Indi Young (2008, n = 1), Lakoff and Johnson (1980, n = 1), Veldhuyzen and Stassen (1977, n = 1), Wickens (1984, n = 1), and Piaget, were also mentioned, albeit less frequently.

On the other hand, 31 (44%) of the selected publications acknowledged its multi-faceted nature in their discussion. In particular, 12 papers explicitly pointed out the lack of coherent understanding of mental models in the HCI domain [3, 52, 53]. Meanwhile, 13 publications aimed to clarify the terminology, such as differentiating between related concepts like mental models and conceptual models [23, 39, 48, 49], as well as discerning hierarchical differences between mental models in general and specific subtypes like security mental models [54] and shared mental models [5]. Another 6 publications attempted to identify taxonomies of mental models, such as categorizing them based on dimensions like deductive versus inductive [33], static versus dynamic [42], functional versus structural [55, 56], and expert versus non-expert [28]. The majority of them did not adhere to the existing taxonomies but instead developed their own ones.

Defining a Mental Model. Analysis of how 'mental model' is defined in the selected publications reveals that the field is still plagued with confusion since Payne's critique of 2003. Among the 70 selected publications, 44 (62%) of them provided definitions of mental models, while the remaining 26 (38%) publications used this term on an intuitive basis without defining it. Within the 44 publications that provided definitions of mental models, the following defining strategies were observed: (1) adhering to the simplest definition (n = 16), (2) elaborating on the basic definition (n = 12), (3) integrating multiple classic definitions (n = 10), (4) adopting domain-specific definitions (n = 2), and (5) creating an extended definition (n = 4), as summarized in Table 2.

Studies that opted for the simplest definition strategy often offered no further explanation beyond the extremely vague "internal representations of the external world by humans," or they merely cited the names of the seminal publications to imply that they had acquired the notions from them. Given the complexity of the mental model, this strategy is regarded by some as ineffective [4, 6, 8]. Studies with the simplest definitions, along with those without definitions, tend to use this term to refer to any arbitrary mental constructs in the mind, irrespective of their properties.

Studies that used elaborated definitions, on the other hand, added more details to the simple definition based on other research. For example, they said whether mental models in their studies were considered subjective or objective [5, 57], specific or general [58], causal, intentional, or spatial [58]. This research was better able to illustrate which aspects of the mental model they are investigating, thereby reducing confusion and uncertainty. Publications with this type of definition usually describe mental models as a subjective and hypothetical mental representation that integrates an individual's memory, knowledge, perception, and assumptions of the target system. This interpretation shares similarities with Norman's concept of the "user's mental model" and is most often observed among publications from the HCI, design, usability, and information science fields.

Moreover, the integrative definition strategies brought together the classic definitions that stemmed from different angles for a more comprehensive and accurate description of this concept. Studies with this strategy frequently refer to works by Craik [9], Johnson-Laird [11], Gentner and Stevens [10], Norman [7], and Rouse and Morris [4]. Within the scope of this review, the publications adopting this strategy typically aimed to address the incoherent understanding of this concept [48] or attempt to bring order back to the field with a new framework [49].

In this review, the strategy of using domain-specific definitions of mental models was primarily observed in publications from the engineering domain. These publications were heavily influenced by the GOMS model [12], which employs the term mental model' to denote the model based on which the system was designed [14, 43], similar to Norman's notion of the designer's conceptual model.

Furthermore, studies were classified as employing the extended definition strategy if their conceptualizations of mental models contained nuanced details or novel elements that went beyond the common knowledge in this field. For instance, the extended definitions describe mental models as being exact, stable, and steady, while the mainstream description of mental models tends to depict this concept as imprecise, unstable, and dynamic. Neither of these descriptions is necessarily inaccurate, as they may simply reflect different perspectives on this complex concept. However, it is important to recognize these distinctions before employing them.

Table 2. Strategies for defining mental models

Strategy	Features	Examples
No definition (n = 26)	- Use the term without defining it	
Simple definition (n = 16)	- Adopt a simple version of definition or only cite the cornerstone paper without specifying features of this concept	- "Mental models are internal representations of the external world." [33, 36, 59, 60]
Elaborated definition (n = 12)	- Elaborate on the simple version with additional features	- "…the types of hypothesized knowledge structures humans build in order to make sense of their world, to make inference based on the available information and to make predictions about future states" [5] - "Overall, the conceptualization of mental models represents a summary of users' previous experience, current observation, and subsequent behaviors of interactions with a system and the knowledge accumulated during the interactions" [3]
Integrative definition (n = 10)	- Integrating several classic definitions to enrich the definition	- "Mental models are thought to be representations of the physical world (Johnson-Laird, 1983; Rasmussen, 1983; Veldhuyzen & Stassen, 1977), constructs that can explain human behaviour (Wickens 1984, Kempton 1986) and internal mechanisms allowing users to understand, explain, operate and predict the states of systems (Craik 1943, Gentner and Stevens 1983, Kieras and Bovair 1984, Rouse and Morris 1986, Hanisch et al. 1991)" [49]

(continued)

Table 2. (*continued*)

Strategy	Features	Examples
Domain-specific definition (n = 2)	- Citing the definitions that are prevalent to the authors' domain	- "In this context, a mental model is not meant to capture a human cognitive model; rather, it is meant to capture the implicit and intended model of operation according to which the system developer designs the system" [14] - "Rasmussen's work highlights that the user must represent the internal structure of a system with a "mental model" which may help drive goal-oriented action" [43]
Extended definition (n = 4)		- Mental models describe what exactly users think about a specific topic or problem [27] - "It implies that there is a thing existing between interface consistency and usability, which determines whether it is a positive correlation between them or not. It is the mental model" [61] - "Mental models are individually created stabile structures of knowledge regarding a segment of reality…They are based on heuristic analogies, and hence are incomplete, robust, and steady…mental models emerge from visual perception" [62]

4.5 Methodological Analysis

Measuring Methods. From 2010 to 2021, researchers studying mental models in HCI introduced or employed a diverse array of measurement techniques, which can be broadly classified into four categories: naturalistic methods, usability methods, experimental methods, and a few special cases, as summarized in Table 3.

The naturalistic methods employed in recent decades were rather standard, including focus groups, observation, interviews, questionnaires/surveys, behavior coding, and think-aloud protocols. On the other hand, the usability methods included a combination of common and less common measurements. The former includes path diagramming, card sorting, analogies and metaphors, concept mapping, and drawing/sketching, while the latter encompasses a storyboard, modeling/prototyping, cognitive walkthrough, and the teaching-back protocol. Experimental methods mainly measured performances for given tasks, mostly operational and searching tasks, while one study measured the psychophysiological signals of participants to infer their mental processes. Notably, algorithmic modeling and statistical learning methods are increasingly employed alongside these prevalent methods. Additionally, there were two special cases, where one study utilized an "interaction-related mental models method" unique to those researchers [63] and another established a Users' Inherent Mental Model framework [37] to measure mental models.

Table 3. Methods used to measure mental model.

Type	Methods	Examples
Naturalistic	Focus group	[64]
	Observation	[65, 66]
	Interviews	[3, 24, 27, 28, 30, 36, 37, 48, 64, 66–68]
	Questionnaire/Survey	[25, 54, 56, 58, 59, 69, 70]
	Behavior coding	[43]
	Think-aloud protocol	[24, 25, 48, 50, 71]
Usability	Path diagramming	[66, 72]
	Card sorting -Open -Closed	[36, 48, 56, 65, 66, 71]
	Analogies and metaphors	[23, 33]
	Concept mapping	[33, 66]
	Drawing/Sketching	[23, 30, 48, 65, 67, 72–74]
	Storyboard	[23]
	Modeling/Prototyping	- Algorithmic modeling [75] - Physical modeling [23]
	Cognitive walkthrough	[59]
	Teaching-back protocol	[30, 71]
Experimental	Experiment	[35, 43]
	Task performance	- Operational task [22, 25, 56, 61, 71] - Searching task [5, 69] - Error [43]
	Physiological measures	[3]
Special cases		- interaction-related mental models method [63] - Users' Inherent Mental Model [37]

Representation Methods. The methods used to represent mental models were comparatively less diverse than the methods used to measure them. All the selected methods involved externalizing the mental model in human minds. On a continuum from abstract to concrete (as shown in Table 4), the selected literature has demonstrated mental models in the following formats: mathematical expressions [5], algorithmic models [14, 76], logical deduction [77], metaphors [51], network/path diagrams [48, 60, 66, 78], knowledge structures/cognitive maps [74], drawings [30], and physical models [23].

Table 4. Methods for representing mental model.

Level of Abstraction	Methods	Examples
Abstract	Mathematical expression	[5]
	Algorithmic model	[14], [76]
	Logical deduction	[77]
	Network/Path diagram	[48], [66], [78], [79]
	Knowledge structure/ Cognitive map	[74]
	Metaphor	[51]
	Drawing	[30]
Concrete	Physical model	[23]

Evaluation Methods. The evaluation methods adopted in the selected literature were highly dependent on the specific context, with many of them tailored to align with the corresponding measurement techniques. Comparing task performance before and after integrating the new mental model was one method for determining the effectiveness of the assessed mental model. Spero et al. [59], for example, evaluated the quality of the updated mental model by comparing users' task success rate and usability rating before and after its implementation. An alternative comparison-based method for evaluating the mental models utilized statistical metrics. Doi et al. [56] and Dou and Qin [46] calculated the interdependence and correlation of different dimensions, aiming to uncover the relationship and causal structure among different aspects of the data. Similarly, Mlilo and Thatcher [69] and Goodrich and Yi [76] evaluated the quality of the mental model using statistical approaches, specifically employing the Chi-square test and Bayesian statistics, respectively.

Meanwhile, some studies evaluated mental models based on their inherent characteristics. For instance, Vlist et al. [30] assigned scores to the measured mental model based on its completeness, explanation of concepts, and structural accuracy. Chen and Su [73] evaluated the drawn mental models based on their level of detail, categorizing strategy, reliability, validity, and several other criteria. Lei et al. [37] assessed the consistency of a spatial mental model by scoring its effectiveness, efficiency, satisfaction, learnability, and memorability. Shirehjini et al. [71] conducted an evaluation of the accuracy of the mental model by comparing it to the conceptual model that was used to design the target system. Van Kerckhoven et al. [31] assessed the effectiveness of a mental model by its level of abstraction, complexity, and value added.

5 Discussion

In reviewing the 70 selected publications that closely addressed mental model research in HCI contexts between 2010 and 2021, we found a steadily expanding trend. With the practical application of the HCI-related mental model achieving significant progress, this research theme has attracted cross-domain attention. The major contributions to this domain still came from traditional HCI domains like engineering, psychology, computer science, design, and information studies, while scholars from communication, business, and non-academic organizations have also joined this research theme. The increasing diversity in this domain has introduced a wider range of approaches for measuring, representing, and evaluating mental models, especially algorithmic and statistical methods. In addition, the targets for mental model research expanded from the early focus on simple operational systems such as word processors and calculators to a broad category of advanced technology entities, including graphical user interfaces, gesture control, voice interfaces, encryption, social media platforms, extended reality, and artificial intelligence.

On the other hand, theoretical research on the HCI-related mental model appeared to stall, as evidenced by a lack of a strong theoretical explanation and an increase in the confusion surrounding the interpretation of the concept of mental model. Understanding, anticipating, and smoothing interaction patterns between users and target systems remained the driving forces behind HCI-related mental model research conducted during the past decade. However, when it comes to defining the concept of mental model, less than half of the reviewed literature acknowledged the multidimensional nature of the term, and many papers seemed to use it in an intuitive way. Even among studies that recognized the need to define what they mean by 'mental model', the vast majority merely used a broad statement like "humans' internal representation of the external reality" that neither distinguished it from other concepts nor facilitated system development. Moreover, there were multiple instances of intra-study inconsistency, where the studies cited but failed to address conflicting definitions and methods. Retrieving historical literature on mental models raises additional concerns. The current theoretical discussion almost exclusively relies on milestone research from the 1980s, which exposes two problems: (1) recent studies still depend on theoretical frameworks that have not evolved with this field's growth, and (2) recent studies fail to retrieve more recent theoretical studies, leading to duplications in efforts to reinvent existing concepts. The result suggests that further attention should be given to bridging the theoretical gaps across domains.

While the present study adhered closely to the scoping review methodology, it was limited by time and scope constraints. Our search was confined to the title, abstract, and keywords, which may have resulted in the unintentional exclusion of publications that address mental models but do not use the term mental model in their title, abstract, or keywords. In addition, we did not include synonyms in the search, which may have caused us to omit publications that properly discussed this concept but did not include it in their title, abstract, or keyword area. Although our findings already provide an abundance of information, it would be beneficial to address these limitations in future research.

6 Conclusion

The scoping review provides a comprehensive overview of the current literature on mental model research in HCI contexts, exploring aspects such as where research has been conducted, by whom, on what, in when, using which methods, and for what purposes. From our database search, 70 studies published between 2010 and 2021 met our inclusion criteria and were selected for analysis. Our findings suggest a growing diversity in this field, with new perspectives and methodologies being introduced to enrich the research theme. However, we also note a concerning trend of a widening gap between the thriving empirical research and the limited amount of theoretical research. To address this issue, there is a need for a cohesive theoretical framework that can accommodate the various perspectives on HCI-related mental models and reconcile the disparities in the field. Our review was initiated by a desire to understand the state of the art of mental models research, and sustained by a sense of confusion about the different ways that different researchers used the term. We hope that this review will help people new to the field to make sense of the rich, diverse, but at times rather confusing ways that the term 'mental model' is used in HCI research.

References

1. Holtrop, J.S., Scherer, L.D., Matlock, D.D., Glasgow, R.E., Green, L.A.: The importance of mental models in implementation science. Front. Publ. Health **9** (2021). https://www.frontiersin.org/article/10.3389/fpubh.2021.680316. Accessed 16 May 2022
2. Johnson-Laird, P.N.: The history of mental models. In: Psychology of Reasoning. Psychology Press (2004)
3. Lee, Y.-C., Malcein, L.A.: Users' mental models for computer-mediated communication: theorizing emerging technology and behavior in eHealth applications. Hum. Behav. Emerg. Technol. **2**(4), Article no. 4 (2020). https://doi.org/10.1002/hbe2.212
4. Rouse, W.B., Morris, N.M.: On looking into the black box: prospects and limits in the search for mental models. Psychol. Bull. **100**(3), 349–363 (1986). https://doi.org/10.1037/0033-2909.100.3.349
5. Scheutz, M.: Computational mechanisms for mental models in human-robot interaction. In: Shumaker, R. (ed.) VAMR 2013. LNCS, vol. 8021, pp. 304–312. Springer, Heidelberg (2013). https://doi.org/10.1007/978-3-642-39405-8_34
6. Wilson, J.R., Rutherford, A.: Mental models: theory and application in human factors. Hum. Factors **31**(6), 617–634 (1989). https://doi.org/10.1177/001872088903100601
7. Norman, D.A.: Some observations on mental models. In: Mental Models. Psychology Press (1983)
8. Payne, S.J.: Users' Mental Models: The Very Ideas. Elsevier Inc., Amsterdam (2003). https://doi.org/10.1016/B978-155860808-5/50006-X
9. Craik, K.J.W.: The Nature of Explanation, pp. viii, 123. University Press, Macmillan, Oxford (1943)
10. Gentner, D., Stevens, A.L.: Mental Models. Psychology Press (1983)

11. Johnson-Laird, P.N.: Mental Models: Towards a Cognitive Science of Language, Inference, and Consciousness. Harvard University Press (1983)
12. Card, S.K., Moran, T.P., Newell, A.: The Psychology of Human-Computer Interaction I Guide Books (1983). https://dl.acm.org/doi/abs/10.5555/578027. Accessed 13 Apr 2022
13. Ahmed, F.: Profile of Philip N. Johnson-Laird. Proc. . Acad. Sci. USA **108**(50), 19862–19864 (2011). https://doi.org/10.1073/pnas.1117174108
14. Combefis, S., Giannakopoulou, D., Pecheur, C., Feary, M.: A formal framework for design and analysis of human-machine interaction. In: 2011 IEEE International Conference on 2011 IEEE International Conference on Systems, Man, and Cybernetics, Systems, Man, and Cybernetics (SMC), pp. 1801–1808, October 2011. https://doi.org/10.1109/ICSMC.2011.6083933
15. Rowe, A.L., Cooke, N.J., Neville, K.J., Schacherer, C.W.: Mental models of metal models: a comparison of mental model measurement techniques. In: Proceedings of the Human Factors Society Annual Meeting, vol. 36, no. 16, pp. 1195–1199, October 1992. https://doi.org/10.1177/154193129203601603
16. Cooke, N.J., Rowe, A.L.: Evaluating mental model elicitation methods. In: Proceedings of the Human Factors and Ergonomics Society Annual Meeting, vol. 38, no. 4, Art. no. 4, October 1994. https://doi.org/10.1177/154193129403800416
17. Paivio, A.: Mental Representations: A Dual Coding Approach. Oxford University Press, Oxford (1990)
18. Sasse, M.A.: Eliciting and describing users' models of computer systems. Electronic thesis or dissertation (1997). [Online]
19. Nielsen, J.: A meta-model for interacting with computers. Interact. Comput.Comput. **2**(2), 147–160 (1990). https://doi.org/10.1016/0953-5438(90)90020-I
20. Arksey, H., O'Malley, L.: Scoping Studies: Towards a Methodological Framework. vol. 8, no. 1, pp. 19–32, February 2005. https://doi.org/10.1080/1364557032000119616
21. Pham, M.T., Rajić, A., Greig, J.D., Sargeant, J.M., Papadopoulos, A., McEwen, S.A.: A scoping review of scoping reviews: advancing the approach and enhancing the consistency. Res. Synth. Methods **5**(4), 371–385 (2014). https://doi.org/10.1002/jrsm.1123
22. Long, R., Zhang, J.: Research on information architecture based on graphic reasoning and mental model. In: Stephanidis, C. (ed.) HCI 2018. CCIS, vol. 850, pp. 85–92. Springer, Cham (2018). https://doi.org/10.1007/978-3-319-92270-6_12
23. Khairuddin, I.E., Sas, C., Speed, C.: BlocKit: a physical kit for materializing and designing for blockchain infrastructure. In: DIS – Proceedings of ACM Designing Interactive Systems Conference, pp. 1449–1462 (2019). https://doi.org/10.1145/3322276.3322370
24. Long, R., Liu, X., Lei, T., Chen, X., Jin, Z.: The impact of chinese traditional cultural on the gesture and user experience in mobile interaction design. In: Rau, P.-L.P. (ed.) CCD 2017. LNCS, vol. 10281, pp. 49–58. Springer, Cham (2017). https://doi.org/10.1007/978-3-319-57931-3_5
25. Renzi, A.B., Freitas, S.: Affordances and gestural interaction on multi-touch interface systems: building new mental models. In: Marcus, A. (ed.) DUXU 2014. LNCS, vol. 8518, pp. 615–623. Springer, Cham (2014). https://doi.org/10.1007/978-3-319-07626-3_58
26. Du, Y., Qin, J., Zhang, S., Cao, S., Dou, J.: Voice user interface interaction design research based on user mental model in autonomous vehicle. In: Kurosu, M. (ed.) HCI 2018. LNCS, vol. 10903, pp. 117–132. Springer, Cham (2018). https://doi.org/10.1007/978-3-319-91250-9_10
27. Dechand, S., Naiakshina, A., Danilova, A., Smith, M.: In encryption we don't trust: the effect of end-to-end encryption to the masses on user perception. In: Proceedings - IEEE European Symposium on Security and Privacy, EURO S P, pp. 401–415 (2019). https://doi.org/10.1109/EuroSP.2019.00037

28. Prettyman, S.S., Furman, S., Theofanos, M., Stanton, B.: Privacy and security in the brave new world: the use of multiple mental models. In: Tryfonas, T., Askoxylakis, I. (eds.) HAS 2015. LNCS, vol. 9190, pp. 260–270. Springer, Cham (2015). https://doi.org/10.1007/978-3-319-20376-8_24

29. Bertrand, P., Guegan, J., Robieux, L., McCall, C.A., Zenasni, F.: Learning empathy through virtual reality: multiple strategies for training empathy-related abilities using body ownership illusions in embodied virtual reality. Front. Robot. AI **5** (2018). https://doi.org/10.3389/frobt.2018.00026

30. Vlist, B., Niezen, G., Rapp, S., Hu, J., Feijs, L.: Configuring and controlling ubiquitous computing infrastructure with semantic connections: a tangible and an AR approach. Pers. Ubiquit. Comput.Ubiquit. Comput. **17**(4), 783–799 (2013)

31. Van Kerckhoven, J., Geldof, S., Vermeersch, B.: Contextual inquiry in signal boxes of a railway organization. In: Palanque, P., Vanderdonckt, J., Winckler, M. (eds.) HESSD 2009. LNCS, vol. 5962, pp. 96–106. Springer, Heidelberg (2010). https://doi.org/10.1007/978-3-642-11750-3_8

32. Rutjes, H., Willemsen, M., IJsselsteijn, W.: "Considerations on explainable AI and users' mental models. In: Where is the Human? Bridging the Gap Between AI and HCI: Workshop at CHI'19, 4–9 May 2019, Glasgow, Scotland UK, May 2019. https://research.tue.nl/en/publications/considerations-on-explainable-ai-and-users-mental-models. Accessed 10 Jan 2022

33. Coopamootoo, K.P.L., Groß, T.: Mental models for usable privacy: a position paper. In: Tryfonas, T., Askoxylakis, I. (eds.) HAS 2014. LNCS, vol. 8533, pp. 410–421. Springer, Cham (2014). https://doi.org/10.1007/978-3-319-07620-1_36

34. Johns, J.D.: Strategic design: breaking mental models initiates learning in video games. In: Zaphiris, P., Ioannou, A. (eds.) LCT 2017. LNCS, vol. 10295, pp. 443–461. Springer, Cham (2017). https://doi.org/10.1007/978-3-319-58509-3_35

35. Chunpir, H.I., Ludwig, T.: A software to capture mental models. In: Antona, M., Stephanidis, C. (eds.) UAHCI 2017. LNCS, vol. 10279, pp. 393–409. Springer, Cham (2017). https://doi.org/10.1007/978-3-319-58700-4_32

36. Pantförder, D., Schaupp, J., Vogel-Heuser, B.: Making implicit knowledge explicit – acquisition of plant staff's mental models as a basis for developing a decision support system. In: Stephanidis, C. (ed.) HCI 2017. CCIS, vol. 713, pp. 358–365. Springer, Cham (2017). https://doi.org/10.1007/978-3-319-58750-9_50

37. Lei, T., Liu, X., Wu, L., Jin, Z., Wang, Y., Wei, S.: The influence of matching degree of the user's inherent mental model and the product's embedded mental model on the mobile user experience. In: Kurosu, M. (ed.) HCI 2016. LNCS, vol. 9732, pp. 320–329. Springer, Cham (2016). https://doi.org/10.1007/978-3-319-39516-6_31

38. Nishimoto, H., Koyanagi, T., Sarata, M., Kinoshita, A., Okuda, M.: "Memes" UX-design methodology based on cognitive science regarding instrumental activities of daily living. In: Duffy, V.G. (ed.) HCII 2019. LNCS, vol. 11582, pp. 264–273. Springer, Cham (2019). https://doi.org/10.1007/978-3-030-22219-2_20

39. Phillips, R., Lockton, D., Baurley, S., Silve, S.: Making instructions for others: exploring mental models through a simple exercise. In: Interactions **20**(5), Article no. 5 (2013). https://doi.org/10.1145/2505290

40. Chammas, A., Quaresma, M., Mont'Alvão, C.R.: Children's mental model as a tool to provide innovation in digital products. In: Marcus, A. (ed.) DUXU 2015. LNCS, vol. 9187, pp. 23–33. Springer, Cham (2015). https://doi.org/10.1007/978-3-319-20898-5_3

41. Hvorecký, J., Drlík, M., Munk, M.: Enhancing database querying skills by choosing a more appropriate interface. In: IEEE EDUCON 2010 Conference, Education Engineering (EDUCON), April 2010, pp. 1897–1905. IEEE (2010). https://doi.org/10.1109/EDUCON.2010.5492434

42. Varga, E., Pattynama, P., Freudenthal, A.: Manipulation of mental models of anatomy in interventional radiology and its consequences for design of human-computer interaction. Cogn. Technol. Work **15**(4), Article no. 4 (2013)

43. Yarosh, S., Zave, P.: Locked or not? Mental models of IoT feature interaction. In: Conference on Human Factors in Computing Systems and Processing, vol. 2017-May, pp. 2993–2997 (2017). https://doi.org/10.1145/3025453.3025617

44. van den Bosch, K., Schoonderwoerd, T., Blankendaal, R., Neerincx, M.: Six challenges for human-AI co-learning. In: Sottilare, R.A., Schwarz, J. (eds.) HCII 2019. LNCS, vol. 11597, pp. 572–589. Springer, Cham (2019). https://doi.org/10.1007/978-3-030-22341-0_45

45. Beimel, D., Kedmi-Shahar, E.: Improving the identification of functional system requirements when novice analysts create use case diagrams: the benefits of applying conceptual mental models. Requir. Eng. **24**(4), Article no. 4 (2019). https://doi.org/10.1007/s00766-018-0296-z

46. Dou, J., Qin, J.: Research on user mental model acquisition based on multidimensional data collaborative analysis in product service system innovation process. In: Harris, D. (ed.) EPCE 2017. LNCS (LNAI), vol. 10276, pp. 35–44. Springer, Cham (2017). https://doi.org/10.1007/978-3-319-58475-1_3

47. Loeffler, D., Hurtienne, J., Hess, A., Maier, A., Schmitt, H.: Developing intuitive user interfaces by integrating users' mental models into requirements engineering. In: HCI 2013 - 27th International British Computer Society Human Computer Interaction Conference: The Internet of Things (2013). https://doi.org/10.14236/ewic/hci2013.14

48. Qian, X., Yang, Y., Gong, Y.: The art of metaphor: a method for interface design based on mental models. In: Proceedings of VRCAI: ACM SIGGRAPH Conference on Virtual Reality and Continuum Its Applications Industry, Hong Kong, pp. 171–178 (2011). https://doi.org/10.1145/2087756.2087780

49. Revell, K.M.A., Stanton, N.A.: Models of models: filtering and bias rings in depiction of knowledge structures and their implications for design. Ergonomics **55**(9), Article no. 9, Sep. 2012

50. Coopamootoo, K.P.L., Groß, T.: Mental models of online privacy: structural properties with cognitive maps. In: Proceedings of the 28th International BCS Human Computer Interaction Conference: Sand, Sea and Sky - Holiday HCI, HCI 2014, pp. 287–292 (2014). https://doi.org/10.14236/ewic/hci2014.46

51. Gondomar, R., Mor, E.: Understanding agency in human-computer interaction design. In: Kurosu, M. (ed.) HCII 2021. LNCS, vol. 12762, pp. 137–149. Springer, Cham (2021). https://doi.org/10.1007/978-3-030-78462-1_10

52. Payne, S.J.: Mental models in human-computer interaction. In: The Human-Computer Interaction Handbook: Fundamentals, Evolving Technologies, and Emerging Applications, 3rd edn, pp. 41–54. CRC Press, Boca Raton (2012). https://doi.org/10.1201/b11963-ch-3

53. Heuer, T., Stein, J.: From HCI to HRI: about users, acceptance and emotions. In: Ahram, T., Karwowski, W., Pickl, S., Taiar, R. (eds.) IHSED 2019. AISC, vol. 1026, pp. 149–153. Springer, Cham (2020). https://doi.org/10.1007/978-3-030-27928-8_23

54. Albalawi, T.F.: Quantifying the effect of cognitive biases on security decision-making (2018)

55. Kulesza, T., Burnett, M., Kwan, I., Stumpf, S.: Tell me more? The effects of mental model soundness on personalizing an intelligent agent. I:n Conference on Human Factors in Computing Systems - Proceedings, January 2012, pp. 1–10 (2012). https://doi.org/10.1145/2207676.2207678

56. Doi, T., Ishihara, K., Yamaoka, T.: Verification of the questionnaire for the level of mental models building. In: Stephanidis, C. (ed.) HCI 2013. CCIS, vol. 373, pp. 105–108. Springer, Heidelberg (2013). https://doi.org/10.1007/978-3-642-39473-7_22

57. Jones, N., Ross, H., Lynam, T., Perez, P., Leitch, A.: Mental models: an interdisciplinary synthesis of theory and methods. Ecol. Soc. **16**(1), Article no. 1 (2011). https://doi.org/10.5751/ES-03802-160146

58. Zhang, L., Zhang, X., Duan, Y., Fu, Z., Wang, Y.: Evaluation of learning performance of e-learning in China: a methodology based on change of internal mental model of learners. Turk. Online J. Educ. Technol. - TOJET **9**(1), 70–82 (2010)

59. Spero, E., Stojmenović, M., Biddle, R.: Helping users secure their data by supporting mental models of VeraCrypt. In: Stephanidis, C. (ed.) HCII 2019. CCIS, vol. 1032, pp. 211–218. Springer, Cham (2019). https://doi.org/10.1007/978-3-030-23522-2_27

60. Valdez, A.C., Ziefle, M., Sedlmair, M.: Priming and anchoring effects in visualization. IEEE Trans. Vis. Comput. Graph.Comput. Graph. **24**(1), 584–594 (2018). https://doi.org/10.1109/TVCG.2017.2744138

61. Lei, T., et al.: Gestures: the reformer of the user's mental model in mobile HCI. In: Design, User Experience & Usability. User Experience Design for Diverse Interaction Platforms & Environments, pp. 586–597, January 2014

62. Nelles, J., Kuz, S., Schlick, C.M.: Ergonomic visualization of logistical control parameters for flexible production planning and control in future manufacturing systems. In: Stephanidis, C. (ed.) HCI 2015. CCIS, vol. 529, pp. 684–689. Springer, Cham (2015). https://doi.org/10.1007/978-3-319-21383-5_116

63. Filippi, S., Barattin, D.: Considering users' different knowledge about products to improve a UX evaluation method based on mental models. In: Marcus, A., Wang, W. (eds.) DUXU 2018. LNCS, vol. 10918, pp. 367–378. Springer, Cham (2018). https://doi.org/10.1007/978-3-319-91797-9_26

64. Jenness, J., Lenneman, J., Benedick, A., Huey, R., Jaffe, J., Singer, J., Yahoodik, S.: Spaceship, guardian, coach: drivers' mental models of advanced vehicle technology. In: Stephanidis, C. (ed.) HCII 2019. CCIS, vol. 1034, pp. 351–356. Springer, Cham (2019). https://doi.org/10.1007/978-3-030-23525-3_46

65. Di Mascio, T., Gennari, R., Tarantino, L., Vittorini, P.: Designing visualizations of temporal relations for children: action research meets HCI. Multimedia Tools Appl. **76**(4), Article no. 4 (2017). https://doi.org/10.1007/s11042-016-3609-6

66. Xie, B., Zhou, J.: The influence of mental model similarity on user performance: comparing older and younger adults. In: Zhou, J., Salvendy, G. (eds.) ITAP 2017. LNCS, vol. 10298, pp. 569–579. Springer, Cham (2017). https://doi.org/10.1007/978-3-319-58536-9_45

67. Acemyan, C.Z., Kortum, P., Byrne, M.D., Wallach, D.S.: Users' mental models for three end-to-end voting systems: Helios, Prêt à voter, and scantegrity II. In: Tryfonas, T., Askoxylakis, I. (eds.) HAS 2015. LNCS, vol. 9190, pp. 463–474. Springer, Cham (2015). https://doi.org/10.1007/978-3-319-20376-8_41

68. Zheng, Y., Zhao, G.: Natural interaction in video image investigation and its evaluation. In: Harris, D. (ed.) EPCE 2018. LNCS (LNAI), vol. 10906, pp. 520–532. Springer, Cham (2018). https://doi.org/10.1007/978-3-319-91122-9_42

69. Mlilo, S., Thatcher, A.: Mental models: have users' mental models of web search engines improved in the last ten years? In: Harris, D. (ed.) EPCE 2011. LNCS (LNAI), vol. 6781, pp. 243–253. Springer, Heidelberg (2011). https://doi.org/10.1007/978-3-642-21741-8_27

70. Nourani, M., et al.: Anchoring bias affects mental model formation and user reliance in explainable AI systems. In: International Conference on Intelligent User Interfaces Proceedings, IUI, pp. 340–350 (2021). https://doi.org/10.1145/3397481.3450639

71. NazariShirehjini, A.A., SoltaniNejad, F., Saniee-Monfared, G., Semsar, A., Shirmohammadi, S.: Mental model development using collaborative 3D virtual environments. In: Streitz, N., Markopoulos, P. (eds.) DAPI 2016. LNCS, vol. 9749, pp. 279–290. Springer, Cham (2016). https://doi.org/10.1007/978-3-319-39862-4_26

72. Lai, L.-L.: How do they tag? Senior adults' tagging behavior in cultural heritage information. In: Nah, F.F.-H., Xiao, B.S. (eds.) HCIBGO 2018. LNCS, vol. 10923, pp. 475–484. Springer, Cham (2018). https://doi.org/10.1007/978-3-319-91716-0_38

73. Chen, Z., Su, Z.: Using participatory design methods to study users' emotional experiences. In: Proceedings of International Conference on E-Business E-Goverence, ICEE, Guangzhou, pp. 425–428 (2010). https://doi.org/10.1109/ICEE.2010.115
74. González, V.M., Juárez, R.: How do you understand Twitter?: Analyzing mental models, understanding and learning about complex interactive systems. In: Collazos, C., Liborio, A., Rusu, C. (eds.) CLIHC 2013. LNCS, vol. 8278, pp. 103–110. Springer, Cham (2013). https://doi.org/10.1007/978-3-319-03068-5_18
75. Wohler, M., Loy, F., Schulte, A.: Mental models as common ground for human-agent interaction in cognitive assistant systems. In: HCI-Aero 2014 - Proceedings of the International Conference on Human-Computer Interaction in Aerospace, vol. 30 (2014). https://doi.org/10.1145/2669592.2669686
76. Goodrich, M.A., Yi, D.: Toward task-based mental models of human-robot teaming: a Bayesian approach. In: Shumaker, R. (ed.) VAMR 2013. LNCS, vol. 8021, pp. 267–279. Springer, Heidelberg (2013). https://doi.org/10.1007/978-3-642-39405-8_30. http://www.library.illinois.edu/proxy/go.php?url=https://search.ebscohost.com/login.aspx?direct=true&db=edselc&AN=edselc.2-52.0-84884829119&site=eds-live&scope=site
77. Johnson-Laird, P.N.: Mental models and human reasoning. PNAS **107**(43), Article no. 43 (2010). https://doi.org/10.1073/pnas.1012933107
78. Kramer, J., Noronha, S.: Designing with the user in mind a cognitive category based design methodology. In: Marcus, A. (ed.) DUXU 2014. LNCS, vol. 8520, pp. 152–163. Springer, Cham (2014). https://doi.org/10.1007/978-3-319-07638-6_16
79. Calero Valdez, A., Ziefle, M., Alagöz, F., Holzinger, A.: Mental models of menu structures in diabetes assistants. In: Miesenberger, K., Klaus, J., Zagler, W., Karshmer, A. (eds.) ICCHP 2010. LNCS, vol. 6180, pp. 584–591. Springer, Heidelberg (2010). https://doi.org/10.1007/978-3-642-14100-3_87

Kinesiological Study of Wushu Performance

Toward Performer-Centered Co-development of Wushu Taolu

Yosuke Kinoe[1](✉) and Kana Ikeuchi[1,2]

[1] Hosei University, 2-17-1, Fujimi, Chiyoda City 102-8160, Tokyo, Japan
kinoe@hosei.ac.jp
[2] Japan WUSHU TAIJIQUAN Federation, 1-9-15, Matsue, Edogawa City, Tokyo, Japan

Abstract. This paper describes a kinesiological study of Wushu performance, in which Japanese leading Wushu players participated. Precise full-body 3D performance data while the players performed five Wushu routines were captured and analyzed by applying the kinetics and kinematic analysis. This paper focused on a comparison of Wushu performance by a top player and an intermediate player.

First, it can be considered that the results based on kinesiological analysis provided players and teachers with a helpful communication tool at least for examining the accuracy and the conformance of external characteristics of basic Wushu movements such as a stance and a stroke.

Second, as for evaluation of the overall quality of performance, it was important to provide players with the analysis results of multiple levels. For example, velocities of segments such as hands and legs were effective in evaluating rhythm and speed of Wushu movements; the trajectories of anatomical landmarks such as fingertips were helpful for evaluating connection between individual basic movement. Especially, movement of the CoM was helpful for grasping the smoothness and stability of the movement in Wushu performance.

On the other hand, to develop a set of concrete indexes which relate to evaluation of overall quality of performance and to enhance method for integrating those multiple evaluation viewpoints should be our important future works.

We proposed performer-centered co-development model of Wushu Communication (CMWC) that consisted of five essential components of co-creations by players, teachers/coaches, judges/audiences as well as past masters.

Keywords: Kinesiology · Sport Wushu · Wushu Taolu · Top athletes · Performer-centered Design

1 Introduction

Wushu is an international sport based on traditional Chinese martial arts which has a long history [e.g. 1, 12]. This paper describes a kinesiological study of Wushu performance, in which Japanese leading players of Wushu participated.

© The Author(s), under exclusive license to Springer Nature Switzerland AG 2023
M. Kurosu et al. (Eds.): HCII 2023, LNCS 14054, pp. 126–141, 2023.
https://doi.org/10.1007/978-3-031-48038-6_8

1.1   Wushu as a Combination of Wu(武) and Shu(术)

Wushu is a combination of performance elements and martial arts [8]. Sport Wushu has developed from traditional Wushu and is presented to the world in the form of a modern Olympic-level sport with a combination of ancient practices and modern sports principles [5].

Wushu Taolu refers to the set routine practice component of Wushu. Individual routine of Wushu Taolu ("套路") comprises of a continuously connected set of pre-determined techniques choreographed according to certain principles and philosophies to incorporate stylistic principles of attack and defense [5]. It focuses on basic movements that involve stances, strikes, kicks, throws, jumps as well as elements of grappling, quickness, balances, explosive power, and relaxed movement [8].

Figure 1 illustrates an example of a basic element of Wushu Taolu, "Gongbu Chongquan" (GCQ; "弓步冲拳"). It consists of four phases. GCQ features several basic techniques, for example, a punch with left fist in *horse-riding step* (Fig. 1, 2 and 3) and a punch with right fist *in bow step* (Fig. 1, 2, 3 and 4). GCQ was adopted as one of five tasks used in our experiment described in next chapter.

| 1.Ready position | 2. Hold fist with feet together | 3. Punch with *left* fist in *horse-riding step* | 4. Punch with *right* fist in *bow step* |

Fig. 1. The phases and forms of "Gongbu Chongquan (GCQ: 弓步冲拳)".

1.2   Co-development Model of Wushu Taolu Through Performance

To clarify our research framework, we proposed the "Co-development Model of Wushu Communication" (CMWC). Based on our previous discussion on Dance communication [6], components of co-development of Wushu performance were defined.

Two different models of Wushu Taolu communication are shown in Fig. 2. The first one is SMCR (source, message, channel, receiver) based model, a conventional sequential model of communication (Fig. 2-b).

On the other hand, the CMWC model emphasizes five components of co-creation (Fig. 2-a): (i) co-creation by a choreographer, teachers/coaches and players (e.g. at lessons and tutorials), (ii) co-creation by players, (iii) co-creation by players and audiences (especially at exhibitions and competitions), (iv) co-creation among audiences including critiques, and (v) co-creation by past masters, teachers/coaches, audiences and players. The audiences involve judges, critics, other choreographers and other players. Especially we focused on an essential aspect of various interactions with Wushu predecessors' contributions and added this aspect to our model.

The CMWC model doesn't assume a player's completed Wushu performance in advance, like an improvisation by Jazz players. Wushu performance develops and evolves via autopoietic processes [9] of co-creation I, II, III, IV and V.

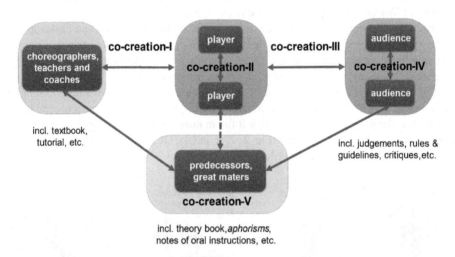

(a)   Co-development Model of Wushu Communication through Performance

(b) conventional SMCR-based model

Fig. 2. Co-development Model of Wushu Communication (CMWC). Revised from Kinoe & Sato (2022) [6].

"Performer-Centered Co-development". This model emphasizes an essential role of performers in every component of "co-creation". It implies a *"performer-centered" co-development*. It sheds light on the potential of leading *players' creative performances and inspirations* toward continuous evolution of Wushu Taolu, beyond a conventional relationship between performers vs. judges or teachers.

1.3   Enhancing Common Ground and Vocabulary of Wushu Communication

Wushu has long history. Wushu players, in particular top players well understand the profoundness for becoming proficient in artistic skills of Wushu. Many great masters of Chinese Martial Arts consistently insisted that the art and techniques of Wushu ("功夫") needed to be cultivated through life [8, 12, 13]. On the other hand, Sport Wushu emphasizes modernization as an international sport [5].

Enriching Wushu Communication. It is important to expand common ground of Wushu Communication so that Sport Wushu further develops in the form of a modern international sport that integrates with its ancient practices. However, for example, players and teachers/coaches as well as judges sometimes have several difficulties that relate to Wushu Communication.

For example, in daily reinforcement training, technical instructions and feedback are often expressed in sensuous or abstract words between teachers/coaches and players. To improve Co-creation I, they need more interpretable communication with adequate terminology.

On the other hand, for example, clear common understanding of grading criteria is one of an important basis for facilitating Co-creation III. Wushu players, especially top athletes are naturally familiar with the "Rules of International Wushu Competition" released by International Wushu Federation [4]. Table 1 excerpts descriptions of a part of "Criteria for Grading and Evaluating Overall Performance" extracted from the current rule book. The description of guideline seem still ambiguous or abstract in distinguishing between "superior", "average" or "inferior".

Table 1. "Criteria "for Grading and Evaluating Overall Performance" extracted from "Rules of International Wushu Competition" published by IWUF [4].

Level	Points	Criteria
Superior	3.00–2.51	"Superior" for correct movements and techniques, full power flowing smoothly to the right points, for good harmony between hands and eyes, between body and steps, and between body and apparatus; for distinct rhythm and conspicuous style; and for accord between movements and accompanying music
Average	2.50–1.91	"Average" for above-mentioned elements to a fairly good degree
Inferior	1.91–1.01	"Inferior" for lack of above-mentioned elements

Bridging Gulfs of Communication. There exist gulfs of communication. To enrich common ground and vocabulary of Wushu Communication are effective, for instance for the co-creations of useful reinforcement menu for players as well as a clear grading guideline for judges, players and teachers/coaches. To enhance visual representations may be one possible compliment to current communication.

This paper emphasizes players' viewpoints. We aimed to provide players and their teachers/coaches with a set of charts based on kinesiological analysis of Wushu performance, which were expected helpful for co-creating their concrete reinforcement plans. This paper describes our first attempt toward it.

2 Experiment

The purpose of the experiment was to obtain precise 3D performance data of full body while the leading Wushu players performed several Wushu routines including International Competition Routines. We conducted kinetics and kinematic analysis [7, 10] based on the obtained performance data of Wushu routines by applying human musculoskeletal model [2, 3]. This study has been approved by the institutional Research Ethics Committee (reference no. 11120001).

2.1 Participants

Nine leading Wushu players and skilled players participated (males and females). The participants included strengthening designated players of JWTF (Japan Wushu Taijiquan Federation) and a former winner of International Wushu Games. The participants declared that they were free of orthopedic injuries and illness. After explaining about the experiment, a written informed consent was signed to agree to participate in this study, prior to the experiment.

In this paper, two players (females, ave. Age: 24.5 yrs; ave. 163.5 cm tall; ave. Weight: 53.5 kg) were focused on. The player O is a JWTF's strengthening designated player for International Games. The player X is an intermediate player who plans to debut at domestic level. The performances by two Wushu players were compared.

2.2 Materials and Methods

Task. The participants were asked to perform five different routines including International Wushu Competition Routines and an one minute's quiet-standing. Especially, this paper featured two Wushu routines: Gongbu Chongquan (GCQ, "弓步冲拳") and the first set of the International Competition Routine (BZH, "国际第一套路").

The GCQ is a basic element that features a punch with left fist in *horse-riding step* and a punch with right fist in *bow step*. It consists of four phases (see Fig. 1).

The BZH is one of the most popular routine adopted as the international competition routine of Wushu Taolu. The BZH consist of six phases. Figure 2 shows the phases and forms of BZH. The detailed description of whole body movements are explained in Table 2.

Procedure. Each participant individually stood on floor (3.5 M × 5 M) and was asked to perform five sets of five Wushu routines that included GCQ and BZH and an one minute's quiet-standing. Therefore, each participant sequentially performed thirty attempts. The participants were allowed to proceed at their preferred paces and to take a break.

| 1.Ready position | 2.Press palms with feet together | 3. Uppercut palm with feet together | 4. Raise palm with arm straight in resting step | 5. Step forward and slap kick | 6. Bow step and push palm |

Fig. 3. The phases and forms of the first set of International Wushu Competition Routine (BZH: "国际第一套路").

Table 2. The phases and movements of the first set of International Wushu Competition Routine (BZH).

#	Phase	Description of whole body movements
1	预备势	Ready position
2	并步按掌	Press palms with feet together
3	并步撩掌	Uppercut palm with feet together
4	歇步挑掌	Raise palm with arm straight in resting step
5	上步拍脚	Step forward and slap kick
6	弓步推掌	Bow step push palm

2.3 Data Collection

3D motion data of whole-body performances of Wushu players were captured with 71 anatomical landmarks (see Fig. 4) at one-300th seconds accuracy, by using Qualisys motion capture system, Sweden. According to the calibration, standard deviation of marker tracking error was 0.35 mm.

The data collection was performed between December 2022 and January 2023, in Tokyo.

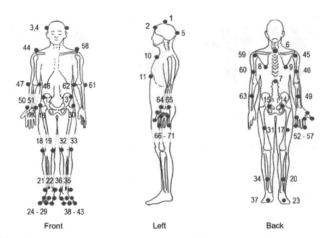

Fig. 4. Marker set of Wushu performances that consists of 71 anatomical landmarks.

2.4 Data Analysis

3D full-body motions of all the participants' performances were tracked with 71 markers predefined for human full body, by using Qualisys track manager (QTM). Kinetics and kinematic analysis were performed on all the participants' performance data based on human musculoskeletal model, by using Visual3D software. The CoM (the center of mass) was calculated based on 3D full-body motion data.

We focused on two Wushu players: player O (top level) and player X (intermediate level). The performances by those two players were compared in the analyses.

3 Results

3.1 Analysis 1: External Characteristics of Basic Movement

The analysis 1 emphasized the most fundamental aspect, that is, external characteristics and the accuracy of individual basic Wushu movement. The players' performance data obtained from the experiment were analyzed according to the standards of Wushu basic movements [4]. In this section, we focused on punches and stances as examples of elements of the basic Wushu movements.

Punch with Fist ("冲拳"). GCQ includes punches with left and right fists in the phases 3 and 4. Punching is an element of the basic movement of Wushu.

Trajectories of Right Fist During a Punch in GCQ. Figure 5 shows a comparison of the trajectories of the landmark at the participant's right fist (R-MCP2): (a) player O (top-level) vs. (b) player X (intermediate level).

The swing width in lateral direction of the punch by player O (0.14 M) was much smaller than that by player X (0.25 M) although vertical fluctuation of each player was almost the same (approximately 0.37 ± 0.02 M (Fig. 5).

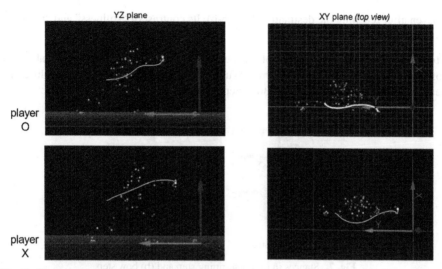

Fig. 5. The trajectories of right fist (R-MCP2) while punching in the phase 4 of GCQ: player O (upper line) vs. the player X.

Velocity of Punch with Fist in GCQ. Figure 6 shows a comparison of the velocity of right punch in the phase 4 of GCQ. The maximum velocities of the punch were 6.16 (M/s) by player O and 4.22 (M/s) by player X. The result indicated the punch with right fist by player O was 46% faster as well as quicker than player X.

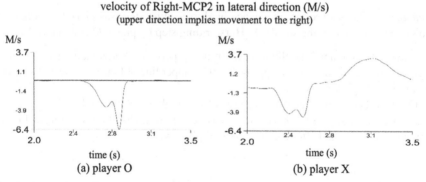

Fig. 6. Comparison of the velocity of right fist during the phase 4 of GCQ: player O vs. player X. In player O, the contrast of state "stillness" and state of "motion" was distinct.

Contrast of "Stillness" and "Motion". Furthermore, meaningful difference was observed before and after punching. Figure 6-a clearly indicated that player O's right fist movement had entirely stopped (approx. 0 M/s) except for the moment of punching. In player O, the contrast of state "stillness" and state of "motion" was distinct (Fig. 6-a). Conversely, player X's right hand fluctuated before initiating a punch (2.0–2.3 s) as well as even after reaching the destination (Fig. 6-b). Its contrast of "stillness" and "motion" was ambiguous.

Steps. Steps are the basic element of Wushu, which are essential for building a stable and solid foundation for performing correct Wushu movement. GCQ contains two different basic steps, Horse-riding step and Bow-step.

a. Horse-riding step   b. Bow step

Fig. 7. Stances in (a) horse-riding step and (b) bow step.

Horse-Riding Step (Manbu, "馬步"). In this step, it's important to confirm (a) the thigh of the front leg is level and (b) the joint-angle of its knee maintains around 90° (c) the CoM sustains low and stable (see Fig. 7-a).

Bow Step (Gonbu "弓步"). In this step, it's important to confirm (a) the thigh of the front leg is level and (b) the joint-angle of its knee maintains around 90° (c) the heel of the rear foot should not leave the floor (see Fig. 7-b).

Comparison. In this section, the stance in Horse-riding step was picked up. Figure 8 shows a comparison of the stances in Horse-riding step by player O and player X.

Player O maintained the thigh of the front leg perfectly horizontally and the joint-angle of left knee maintained at approx. 87–92° (upper line of Fig. 8) during 0.4 s before and after the beginning of phase 4.

On the other hand, Player X's hip was placed higher and the thigh of front leg was tilted. The joint-angle of left knee varied between approx. 25–73° (lower line of Fig. 8) during 0.2 s before and after the beginning of phase 4.

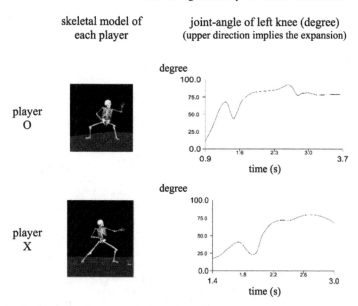

skeletal model of   joint-angle of left knee (degree)
each player   (upper direction implies the expansion)

Fig. 8. Comparison of stance in Horse-riding step: player O (upper line) vs. player X

3.2 Analysis 2. Overall Performance of Wushu Routine

The analysis 2 emphasized the overall quality of individual Wushu routine. A set of analysis viewpoints were established based on various sources which included theory books [e.g. 8] and old notes of the great masters' oral instructions [1, 12, 13] as well as the IWUF's rule book (the panel B) [4].

Stability of the Center of Mass (CoM). To pay attention on breathing and to continuously consider the movements of their own Center-of-Mass are the basic principles of Wushu [8].

Movement of the CoM During a Punch in Horse-Riding Step. Figure 9 shows movements of the CoM of player O (upper line) and player X while they made a left punch in Horse-riding step (phase 3) and a right punch in Bow step (phase 4) in GCQ.

In this chart, the CoM of player O quickly descended to reach objective point at 1.85 s and quickly ascended in returning to the previous level at 4.63 s. At 2.33 s, the phase changed to next phase of punching with right fist. Importantly in that duration from 1.85 to 3.66 s, the CoM of player O stably maintained 0.56–0.61 M high, except that it ascended 0.06 M when initiating next movement of punching with right fist (2.89 s) (Fig. 9-a), while the CoM moved slightly very slowly to the front (Fig. 9-b). It is considered that the stability of the movement of the CoM, especially of vertical movement, contributed in realizing the smoothness of transition between the phases of GCQ.

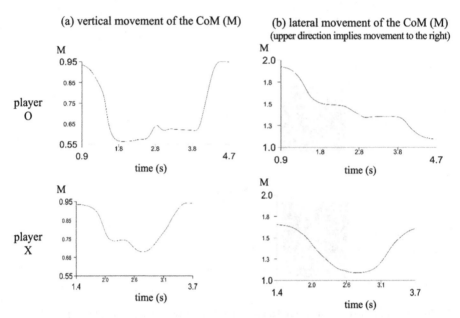

Fig. 9. Comparison of vertical movement (left) and lateral movement (right) of the CoM during a punch in Horse-riding step in GCQ: by player O (upper line) vs. player X.

On the other hand, the vertical movement of the CoM of player X was slower while descending to objective point (around 2.14 s) and while ascending to previous position (around 3.61 s). Duration that the CoM of player X stayed in low level was much shorter period of time. Except for that period, it *continuously moved* slowly in those phases of GCQ. The lowest of the CoM of player X was 0.68 M high during the above period. The lowest level of the CoM of player X was 0.12 M higher than that of player O despite player X was 0.03 M shorter than player O.

Speed and Rhythm of Wushu Performance. In this section, we investigated the change of speed and rhythm of Wushu movement. We picked up the phase 4 of BZH, in which the movement changes its speed and rhythm.

Movement of Right Hand During the Phase 3–5 of BZH. Figure 10 shows a comparison of vertical and anteroposterior movements of right wrist (medial) of player O and player X during the phases 3, 4 and 5 of BZH.

The chart indicated that in player O, there were two different types of movements: a prompt movement (e.g. 9.3 s) and a longer gentle movement (e.g. 9.7–12.5 s). On the other hand, in player X, the distinction of those two types of movement was unclear. In player X, the velocity of a prompt movement was slower (e.g. during 4.8–5.4 s) and the duration of a gentle movement was very short (e.g. 5.6–5.8 s).

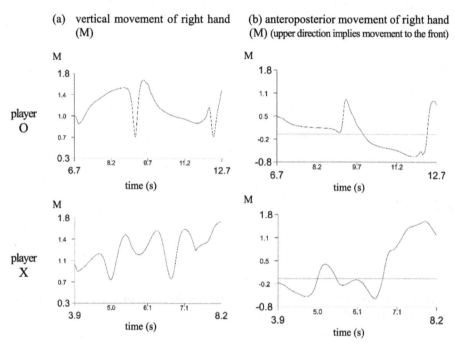

Fig. 10. Comparison of the movement of right wrist (medial) during the phase 3, 4 and 5 of BZH: player O (upper line) vs. player X.

Movement of CoM during the phase 3–5 of BZH. Figure 11 shows a comparison of vertical and anteroposterior movements of the CoM of player O and player X during the phases 3, 4 and 5 of BZH.

The chart revealed two different movements of the CoM of player O. There were a pair of prompt back-and-forth movements (e.g. 9.4 s and 11.7 s) and a longer gentle movement (e.g. 9.8–11.5 s). On the other hand, in the CoM of player X, the chart showed that the distinction of two types of movement was unclear. There was a pair of slower back-and-forth vertical movements (e.g. 5.3 s and 5.8 s) and a very short gentle movement (e.g. 5.7–5.8 s).

Interestingly, the results revealed that the movement of player O explicitly divided into state of "stillness" and state of "motion". Importantly, it's considered that those contrast of the pace of movements played an important role in creating the unique distinct rhythm of individual player's Wushu performance. On the other hand, in player X, the contrast between a quick motion and slow motion was not distinct. State of "stillness" of the movements were apparently shorter.

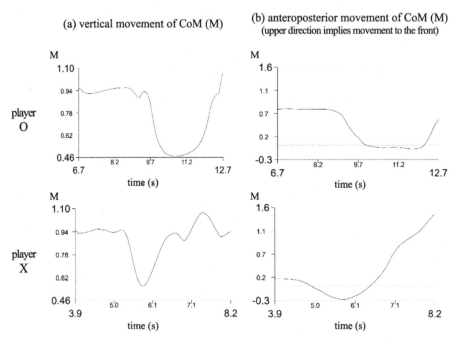

Fig. 11. Comparison of the movement of the CoM during the phase 3,4 and 5 of BZH: player O (upper line) vs. player X.

Smoothness of Wushu Movement. In Wushu performance, the smoothness of movement ("運転円滑") is one of the important aspects of cultivation of the art and techniques of Wushu [1, 12, 13]. For example, in the BZH routine, the movement of hands and feet in the form of a large arc is effectively used for connecting the current movement smoothly to next Wushu movement [8].

Drawing Large Arc with the Movement of Left and Right Fingertips. Figure 12 shows a comparison of the trajectories of left and right fingertips of player O and player X during the phases 4 and 5 of BZH.

The result revealed that the shape and size of the trajectories of fingertips were different in player O and player X. The trajectory of player O's fingertips drawn arcs and both radius of the trajectories of left and right fingertips were large. On the other hand, in player X, the trajectories of left and right fingertips drawn only a part of arcs and either radius was smaller.

This difference in shape and size affected in the transition of the Wushu movements, for example, between phase 4 to phase 5 of BZH. The movements of upper limbs which move in an arc shape in large radius contributed to establish more smooth continuity of Wushu performance between phases of BZH as well as within the current phase.

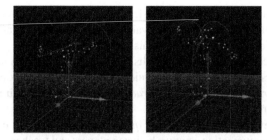

Fig. 12. Comparison of the trajectories of left and right fingertips (L/R-TIP2) during the phase 4 and 5 of BZH routine: player O (left) vs. player X (right).

4 Discussion

Further studies will be needed to evaluate our methodology conducted in this study, but our initial results described above indicated the potential of this methodology.

Evaluation of the Accuracy of Basic Wushu Movements. As for the first component mentioned in the Sect. 3.1, (a) to define expected adequate movements of basic Wushu techniques and (b) to translate them into external characteristics of human movements using kinesiological terminology will be the key elements. Therefore, the concreteness of the definition as well as the adequate translation are essential. Our approach of this part goes along those of recent advanced smart support system for some sports such as golf and baseball [11].

Overall Quality of Wushu Performance. To approach to the second component, that is, the evaluation of "overall quality of Wushu performance" mentioned in the Sect. 3.2 is more challenging. In the evaluation of overall quality of performance, for instance evaluation of some limited aspect of the smooth elegant connection between movements can probably be characterized using kinesiological terminologies. However, to expand the aspects of evaluation should be important for providing more effective basis of communication with players and teachers. The CMWC model (Fig. 2) indicates that the Co-creation V by teachers/coaches, past masters, judges as well as leading players, is expected to advance the clarification of a set of viewpoints for evaluating the overall quality of Wushu performance.

Final objective of this study is to develop a methodology that activates performer-centered co-creation processes, as well as the development of kinesiological vocabulary of basic Wushu movements which provides the basis for communicating. This paper described our first step toward it.

5 Conclusion

This paper describes a kinesiological study of Wushu performance, in which Japanese leading athletes of Wushu participated. Precise full-body 3D performance data by the leading Wushu players were obtained. In this paper, we especially focused on two players: a top player of Wushu Taolu of international level and an intermediate player. The obtained performance data were analyzed from two different viewpoints based on the kinetics and kinematic model. Detailed evaluation is ongoing, but at least the results obtained so far indicated the potential of this methodology.

First, it can be considered that the results based on kinesiological analysis provided players and teachers with a helpful communication tool at least for examining *the accuracy and the conformance of external characteristics* of basic Wushu movements such as a stance and a stroke.

Second, as for evaluation of the *overall quality of performance,* it can be considered important that a communication-support between players and teachers/coaches required the feedback information of multiple levels. For example, the velocity of the movement of hands and legs (i.e. segment level) were effective in evaluating rhythm and speed control of fast/slow movements in Wushu performance; the trajectories of fingertips (i.e. anatomical landmarks) were helpful for evaluating smooth connection of individual basic movement in between different phases of the Wushu routine. The movement of CoM (i.e. whole-body level) was particularly helpful for grasping the smoothness and stability of the movement in overall Wushu performance.

Our future works include expansion of the coverage of tasks and participants. The above results also revealed issues as well as potential of our current approach based on specific individual analysis viewpoint. Development of a new set of concrete viewpoints and indexes which relate to overall quality of performance and enhancement of integrated analysis method according to multiple evaluation viewpoints should be effective future works.

Acknowledgement. The authors thank all the Wushu players who participated to our experiment. We thank Hana M., Asuka T. and our lab members2022, and Ryoji Hayakawa. They devotedly supported conducting our experiment.

References

1. Bu, U.: Understanding how to practice the Thirteen Dynamics with commentary and songs. handwritten in Chinese (19c)
2. Fitt, S.S.: Dance Kinesiology, 2nd edn. Schirmer/Thomson Learning (1996)
3. Haas, J.G.: Dance Anatomy, 2nd edn. Human Kinetics (2018)
4. International Wushu Federation: Rules for International Wushu Taolu Competition (2005)
5. International Wushu Federation (IWUF) homepage. http://www.iwuf.org/sport-wushu/. Accessed 24 Dec 2022
6. Kinoe, Y., Sato, M.: Analysis of nonverbal interaction among competitive ballroom dance couple: kinesiology and time-frequency analysis. In: Springer Lecture Notes in Computer Science (LNCS), vol. 13306, pp. 247–266, Springer, Switzerland (2022). https://doi.org/10.1007/978-3-031-06509-5_18
7. Kinoe, Y., Akimori, Y.: Appeal of inconspicuous body movements during spatial invasion. In: Yamamoto, S., Mori, H. (eds.) HCII 2020. LNCS, vol. 12185, pp. 175–193. Springer, Cham (2020). https://doi.org/10.1007/978-3-030-50017-7_12
8. Li,T.: Guide to Chinese Martial Arts. New Phoenix Intl Llc. (1995)
9. Maturana, H.R., Varela, F.J.: The Tree of Knowledge: The Biological Roots of Human Understanding, Revised. Shambhala, Boston (1992)

10. Neumann, D.A.: Kinesiology of the Musculoskeletal System, 3rd edn. Elsevier, Amsterdam (2016)
11. Rapsodo Pitching homepage. https://rapsodo.com/pages/baseball-pitching. Accessed 26 Jan 2023
12. Wang, Z.: The TAIJI boxing treatise. Handwritten in Chinese. Handwritten (18c)
13. Wang, Z.: Thirteen Dynamics Song. Handwritten in Chinese. Handwritten (18c)

Negotiating Water Cooler Conversations Remotely: Perspectives from PhD Students During COVID-19

Xiaoyan Li[✉] and Susan R. Fussell

Cornell University, Ithaca 14850, USA
xl656@cornell.edu

Abstract. Brief, spontaneous and informal interactions (also called water cooler conversations) are essential for achieving both productive and social goals but are often poorly supported by common computer-mediated communication technologies. During the unexpected, widespread move to remote work due to the COVID-19 pandemic, people were suddenly forced to rely more, if not entirely, on technologies to meet their communication needs. To further explore how people engaged in informal communication during COVID-19 and the challenges they faced, we conducted semi-structured, in-depth interviews with 16 PhD students. Results revealed challenges in maintaining remote informal conversations (such as lack of availability information and opportunities for interactions before, during and after activities), which sometimes led participants to refrain from communicating online, and intensified their mental health issues such as those around social isolation. Experiences of remote informal communication shaped by novel challenges pointed to important design implications.

Keywords: Communication · Remote Communication · Zoom · Computer-mediated Communication · PhD Students

1 Introduction

Computer-mediated communication (CMC) technologies have made it possible for people in geographically separated places to collaborate remotely [29][31]. The onset of COVID-19 led to an unexpected transition to remote work at a large, global scale [47][30]. This has created challenges, reflections [25][26], as well as an increased scale of remote work for many organizations even after the mandatory lockdown phase [2][34]. Working remotely comes with challenges including issues around communication [26], collaboration [30] and wellbeing [34]. Among them, a major challenge is the significantly reduced opportunities for informal communication.

Informal communication (also called "water cooler" conversation [15][30]) refers to spontaneous, unscheduled and lightweight talk (e.g., small talks in the office or the hallway) [16][22][32], and is a dominant activity in organizations [10][22]. People work in their offices and ask quick questions to those sitting next to them; they walk in the hallway, run

M. Kurosu et al. (Eds.): HCII 2023, LNCS 14054, pp. 142–154, 2023.
https://doi.org/10.1007/978-3-031-48038-6_9

into someone and engage in spontaneous conversations. Through these processes, both work-related and social goals can be flexibly, efficiently and effectively accomplished 1416.

When people work remotely, however, opportunities for informal interactions are significantly reduced and poorly supported by current technology. Previous tools aimed at facilitating remote informal communication were unsatisfactory: e.g., they largely failed to provide a subtle mechanism to gracefully initiate and terminate conversations 162832. Meanwhile, novel contexts created by COVID-19, wherein remote work is much more large-scale, raise new research questions about how well technology can support informal communication 263034.

In this study, we conducted in-depth interviews (n = 16) to explore the processes of conducting informal interactions remotely, identify changes to them after the unexpected transition to remote work, as well as people's efforts and challenges in addressing these changes. We focus on PhD students, because they faced unique challenges intensified by COVID-19, such as social isolation, delayed research progress and escalated mental health issues 121920. As informal communication is essential for providing social support, reducing stress, forming good work relationships and coordinating work 91617, it is important to see how PhD students experienced challenges of reduced informal interactions when they worked from home during COVID-19.

Interview results showed that the abrupt transition to remote work brought both challenges and opportunities. For example, participants often refrained from initiating conversations online with colleagues due to lack of availability information and the need to be more "intentional"; they also shared examples where technology failed to support spontaneous small-group, semi-private conversations, which indicated important insights with respect to future designs. PhD students struggled with mental health issues and social isolation worsened by lack of effective information transfer and lack of opportunities to ask quick, work-related questions, or overhear office conversations with crucial information about people, relationships and activities. Our findings contribute to the overall understanding of informal communication in remote work.

2   Related Work

In this section, we review literature on the characteristics and roles of informal communication (2.1), the challenges faced by PhD students (2.2), as well as an overview of current popular technology and the present study (2.3).

2.1   Informal Communication in Organizations

Informal communication is frequent, brief, spontaneous, unscheduled, rich, interactive and flexible 1622; its timing, participants and content are often unplanned in advance 16. Informal communication is a dominant activity in organizations, and plays a fundamental role in achieving both productive and social goals 1022.

A primary role of informal communication is to coordinate work-related activities, because formal communication channels do not work well for unplanned, unexpected activities and spontaneous conversations 16. Informal communication is also essential for achieving social goals, such as connecting with others, building relationships and getting social support 22, which could lead to more effective cooperation and higher cohesion in the workplace 9. Even when not actively participating in conversations, people learn important information about work environment, relationships, alliances and crises by overhearing others in conversations 16.

2.2 PhD Students, Mental Health and Informal Communication

Research on PhD students has highlighted concerns about their mental health caused by their unique research and working conditions in universities 18192033. Stress levels and mental health issues are high among this group due to factors such as financial uncertainty, high academic demands, job insecurity, and social isolation 121920. In addition, PhD students often need to work as part of larger project teams, which rely extensively on informal interactions for coordinating work-related matters 1620.

As informal communication is essential for providing social support, reducing stress, forming good work relationships and coordinating work 9161722, it is important to see how PhD students perceived and addressed challenges of reduced informal interactions during COVID-19. The unexpected shutdown of campus resources (e.g., laboratories) and transition to remote work led to additional academic disruptions, uncertainty and stress, changed traditional ways of collaborating and created further obstacles for them to combat social isolation and meet high academic demands 812. Meanwhile, experiences of this group could enhance our overall understanding of informal communication, as they represent a wider population who experienced social isolation, work disruptions and reduced opportunities for informal interactions due to the transition to remote work.

2.3 Current Popular Technology and the Present Study

When people work remotely, opportunities for informal interactions are limited due to factors including lack of physical proximity 1632 and high cost of initiating and terminating conversations 28. Previous tools specifically devoted to fostering these conversations (e.g., 2124) have been unsatisfactory: for example, they failed to provide a subtle mechanism to gracefully coordinate initiation and rejection of conversations. For instance, in an early desktop system Cruiser, which allows glancing into offices through video connections, blinds are bluntly closed when interruption is unwanted, as opposed to more subtle ways of ending conversations in-person (see more in 2832).

In addition to these efforts, popular CMC technologies such as IM (Instant Messaging) have been widely used to support certain types of informal interactions, including negotiating availability, asking quick clarification questions, coordinating work-related matters, scheduling meetings, and maintaining social connections 523. Although IM and other text-based team collaborations tools such as Slack are able to provide recipients more flexibility in terms of their response time, and message initiators have the ability to text others without interrupting too much 5, they still largely rely on the initiator to intentionally start the interactions 162328. Therefore, we believe they play a better role supporting *planned* (A and B mutually scheduled conversations, although the content might be unscheduled) and *intended* conversations (A set out to visit B for a conversation) than *opportunistic* (A intended to talk to B, but the intention was temporarily placed on hold until A ran into B) and *spontaneous* conversations (neither party had prior plans to talk) (see detailed definitions in 16).

Since COVID-19, popular video conferencing technologies such as Zoom and Microsoft Teams have received unprecedented widespread acceptance and creative use (e.g., "meet my pet" virtual social meetings) 52627. However, we do not know if/how well they supported informal interactions, especially those that are opportunistic or spontaneous. Some recent work explored how work patterns and time management have changed after COVID-19; however, they focused on statistical trends 47, collaboration patterns 2634, or organizational outcomes (36). While a few studies mentioned that people miss informal water cooler conversations 3034, further research is needed to explore processes and challenges of negotiating informal interactions when remote work is much more common. We ask the following research questions:

RQ1: What were some challenges PhD students faced in conducting informal interactions after the unexpected transition to remote work?

RQ2: How did PhD students respond to challenges brought by the change of informal interactions?

RQ3: What new insights can we provide to improve technologies that support remote informal interactions?

3   Method

We used semi-structured, in-depth interviews to uncover detailed processes and examples embedded in conducting remote informal conversations. Prior to data collection, the study was approved by the Institutional Review Board in our institution. All interviews were conducted in August 2021 by the first author, either via Zoom (n = 15) or in-person (n = 1) based on the participants' preference. Participants gave us their verbal consent before being interviewed. In this section, we elaborate on the participants, the interview protocol and the process of data analysis.

3.1   Participants

We recruited 16 PhD students by posting recruitment messages on social media and sending emails through institutional email lists. Among them, six identified as female and 10 as male. The mean age of the participants was 29 (range 25–37) years old. Seven participants identified as White, eight as Asian and one as mixed-race. The participants were from a variety of fields, including communication, psychology, human development, information science, and engineering. They received 10 USD as compensation for a 45-min interview.

3.2   Interview Materials

We conducted in-depth interviews to investigate how people interacted with close friends and colleagues remotely through technology. During the interviews, we first explored processes and instances of initiating and maintaining informal conversations in detail. Following that, we investigated people's efforts in staying in touch with others, as well as challenges experienced in the process. Among the 16 participants, four started their PhD journeys entirely remotely, so we invited them to share experiences of those special journeys. The interviews were conducted over Zoom (n = 15) or in-person (n = 1) and lasted for approximately 45 min each.

3.3 Data Analysis

The interviews were audio-recorded and then transcribed into text. We used a grounded theory approach 11 to guide data collection and analysis. Emerging themes from early interviews were followed up in future interviews, and we stopped recruiting after reaching data saturation. Interview transcripts were coded using the software ATLAS.ti 1. The first author open-coded the interview transcripts to create the initial codes, assigning them to significant instances and quotations. They then discussed the codes and excerpts with the last author to discover emerging categories, and critically re-arranged them to identify higher-level themes and relationships between the themes. We provide a detailed report of these themes in the next Sect. (4).

4 Results

Our analysis indicated that the unexpected transition to remote work brought both challenges and opportunities. Extensive experiences of attending online activities provided novel insights pointing to important limitations of current technology. In this section, we report the challenges of conducting remote informal communication (4.1), the negative impacts of reduced informal interactions (4.2), as well as the opportunities of remote work (4.3).

4.1 Challenges of Conducting Informal Communication Remotely

The most prevalent theme from the data revealed challenges in engaging in informal conversations online.

Lack of Information about Others' Situation and Availability. One of the major challenges people experienced in initiating conversations online was caused by a lack of information about others' situation and availability. Participants' reflection on this challenge identified two aspects: not knowing what has been going on in general (e.g., P2 & P3) and not knowing if someone is available for an interaction at a specific time (e.g., P7 & P8).

When people worked collocated together, it was easier to know what was happening in others' lives and build on that in following conversations. However, when they shifted to working remotely and could not see each other regularly, they lost track of each other's whereabouts. Therefore, it became more difficult to initiate conversations:

We didn't know what was really going on in each other's lives. So when you reach out, it kind of feels like, if you reach out of the blue, those conversations are awkward... (P2).

A second aspect of this challenge is that it is hard to determine if someone might be available for or interested in having an informal conversation. Participants talked about difficulty of determining if someone's available for a chat after a Zoom meeting.

When in-person, you can judge from their expression to see if they are busy or want to talk. When online, we just shut down our video and leave the Zoom meeting immediately. So we're not sure if others are busy (P8).

The same thing happens to the breaks during online activities where people usually shut down their video, as opposed to face-to-face breaks, where it is easy to see that someone is "doing nothing now too" (P7). When availability information is unclear, people are more likely to refrain from starting conversations.

I don't want to bother someone, because I'm sure they're busy. I just assumed that. (Whereas when face-to-face), you know when you can take a few minutes of their time (P7).

The Need to be More Intentional Starting Conversations Online. Reflecting on reasons of reduced informal interactions when working remotely, participants consistently emphasized that they needed to be more intentional initiating conversations online, as opposed to, for example, asking a quick question in the office because "it's just easier to talk to someone who's right next to you about something work related (P5)".

Even during online activities, people felt that they need to have "a clear intention" if they want to chat with someone attending the same activity. For example, Participant 2 talked about how it was natural to catch someone after an in-person church event and start a casual conversation that could last for 30 s before naturally moving on to talking to someone else. However, this was harder to achieve when they had the church activity over Zoom, because current functions on Zoom, i.e., messaging someone or inviting them to chat in a breakout room require a clear, expressed "purpose".

I think you have to be a lot more purposeful about it on Zoom. You'd have to message them and say, hey, let's go on a breakout room… it just feels a lot more formal. With anyone who's not a close friend, it feels like you have to have a reason for wanting to talk to them on Zoom. Whereas if it's just like, after church, you just catch someone's eye and be like, hey, and just start a casual conversation. But then it can last for two minutes, it can last for 30 seconds, and then you just kind of move on and talk to someone else, you know? (P2).

Participants also uniformly emphasized the ease of asking questions to colleagues working in the same office, and challenges of doing so when working remotely. For example, participants 11 and 4 experienced additional challenges when preparing for their PhD candidacy exams because they didn't easily have access to more experienced colleagues like they did in a physical office, and therefore could not "run some ideas past a colleague (P4)". In response to this challenge, some tried to answer those questions on their own by exploring more options.

Sometimes when I write out the question, I will think about it and be like, before I send this, let me try one more thing. And a lot of times the one more thing will work. So that I don't have my question anymore (P5).

Less Opportunities for Interactions Before, During and After Activities. Another important challenge was that there are less opportunities for interactions before, during and after activities. Although this is intertwined with the first two challenges, we further elaborate on this theme due to its rich insights on the limitations of current technology.

Different from in-person meetings/activities, when people meet online, they turn on or shut down their camera to join and leave a meeting, and the natural processes of transitioning into and out of meetings/activities, as well as the informal conversations embedded in these processes are missing. For example, Participant 1 talked about social norms around informal communication after in-person events:

Sometimes the conversation starts just because you have to have the conversation. Otherwise, it will be awkward walking silently together to the office, right? However, you don't have a reason to still talk if the meeting has already been over online (P1).

During breaks or after in person events, people often have the opportunity to hang out and talk to each other, potentially developing friendships (P2). However, when an activity breaks or ends online, participants commented that it would be awkward to still hang out and "stare at each other" afterward.

For an in-person church, after the more structured section you just hang out, talk, and develop friendships. Like, hey, let's go get ice cream later this week. That wasn't as possible online. Like we couldn't hang out in the group chat afterwards. It was just weird when everyone's staring at each other, because normally you break off in small groups and have individual conversations, but you can't really do that on Zoom (P2).

These comments pointed to an important limitation of popular video conferencing technologies such as Zoom, i.e., they are unable to support spontaneous small group or individual conversations before, after or during the break of a group activity. Participant 6 described in detail the process of talking to a group of people in Zoom gatherings.

On Zoom, if you're talking, you're always talking to all 20 people, instead of like, an actual in-person gathering of that amount of people, you would be talking to the person next to you and the few people around you and not all 20 people about whatever stupid thing you want to talk about (P6).

In addition to lack of opportunities for smaller group conversations, there was also the pressure to keep talking to the same group of people, instead of being able to switch between different groups as one might do during in-person gatherings. Therefore, Participant 12 felt frustrated about "sitting in front of a computer" and talking to the same group of people "for a whole 20 min" while trying hard to think about topics that they "may not share". This was different from in-person events (e.g., a party), where they could casually "through in a few comments" and have a pleasant conversation without having the pressure to continue that conversation.

Although Zoom has the breakout room feature that allows people to split into smaller groups, the way it works is significantly different from how small groups are formed in in-person gatherings or events. Participant 10 elaborated more on these differences.

When in person, you can have different groups, which are spatially separated, right? So there are these multiple conversations, and you can quietly go from one to another, or you can participate in any of those. But with online, if you're all in one breakout room, it's one conversation at a time and everybody has to listen on it. And it's not like you can (spontaneously) break out into four smaller breakout rooms (P10).

In addition to video-conferencing technologies, other current technologies (e.g., emails, messaging features embedded in video conferencing platforms) also largely failed to support the spontaneous conversations. This is especially true for meeting strangers. For example, Participant 9 talked about the difficulty of initiating private conversations with a job talk candidate after her presentation. Instead of pulling her aside and giving her suggestions privately as he wished to, he had to give his feedback "in a performative way" while everyone else was listening at the same time when the job talk happened online. When the interviewer brought up the option of using email, text messages or the messaging feature in the video conferencing platform, the participant commented on the closeness between communicators and the formality of communication. He considered it as more natural and informal to chat with a complete stranger after their job talk while inviting them to a quick visit to their office, as opposed to sending a message or email to set up an official time to meet.

If you get an email or text message from somebody you don't know super well, like hey do you have a quick moment to chat, it's like, I gotta sit down and get ready, so I think the informality (is important) (P9).

4.2   Negative Impacts of Reduced Informal Interactions

Although the interview focused more on experiences of conducting informal interactions during the mandatory remote work period between March 2020 to August of 2021, some negative impacts of reduced informal interactions emerged from the data.

Some participants struggled with mental health issues around social isolation related to lack of informal interactions, especially those that were socially oriented. This was particularly evident among those who started their PhD journeys during the mandatory remote work period. For example, when asked to describe their first year as a PhD student, Participant 15 commented:

Crazy? Shitty? I had to get therapy last year. That was horrible (P15).

He then further explained that he had to go to therapy due to mental health issues, which was caused by starting his PhD journey in an entirely new country and not being able to have a social circle with regular social interactions or get social support when needed. At the same time, "the Zoom thing just doesn't substitute it" for him.

Others also mentioned different types of challenges related to social isolation worsened by reduced opportunities of informal interactions. For example, Participant 4 had to prepare his PhD candidacy exam in "total isolation" due to lack of opportunities to get support from colleagues by asking quick questions and getting immediate responses.

It's hard to ask random questions (online), you have to set it up. I think that's part of what made for me, like doing my PhD candidacy exam, really challenging. It was just total isolation. It was just hard to run some ideas past a colleague; but setting it up and finding a time that works for everyone, at that time felt like more frustration than what's worth (P4).

Participant 3, who also started her PhD journey remotely, elaborated on the social isolation issue caused by not knowing "what's going on". She further reflected that this is the kind of information that she could only get "passively" because she simply did not know what to ask, or as she put it "I don't know what I don't know". She expected to get this information by overhearing people talk and casually asking follow-up questions if they worked in the same physical office.

I think one thing that has been tricky is… an abstract challenge. I don't know who the professors are, what their laboratory research is. Or are there talks or activities happening, or even like politics in the department, a lot of the topics I'm not familiar with or don't have opinions on because I don't know what's going on (P3).

This was also shared by Participant 6, who brought up the issue of inter-cohort cohesion, and pointed out the lack of "information transfer" that they "usually get from older grad students" because working remotely deprived them of an effective channel to connect with those more senior graduate students.

4.3   Opportunities and Perceptions of Remote Work

An important opportunity brought by the unexpected transition to remote work was the unprecedented widespread acceptance and use of Zoom. Inspired by the new possibilities, participants made creative efforts to stay in touch using Zoom and other online technology, including holding online movie nights (P7, P16), game nights (P8, P13), church activities (P2), Zoom study rooms (P3, P14), and attending online concerts together with friends (P2).

Participant 13, for example, realized that because "suddenly everyone was using Zoom", it provided a great opportunity for him and his friends to discover new ways of communicating and connecting with each other.

I think it's been such a great thing during the pandemic that we discovered this new (way of communicating). I don't think we ever played video games together before. During the pandemic, it was like oh let's do this because it was a way of us connecting. I think it's made me feel a little more present with my friend (P13).

People also saw advantages of working remotely in general. For example, when attending conferences online, there's less pressure for people to ask and respond to questions on the spot, because they could take their time to "think through" (P5) and "figure out exactly" what they wanted to say (P4). Other benefits of remote work included more flexibility of time arrangement and outfit choices (P1, P3, P6, P7, P8, P11, P13, P14, P16), saving commute time (P2, P3, P5, P11, P16), necessary family care (P4), more focus time and less forced conversations (P14), more convenient and a higher variety of lunch options (P3, P4, P5), etc.

However, when asked if they were happy to go back to in-person work, 15 out of 16 participants gave affirmative answers. Many factors attracted the respondents to work in the office, including better workplace set up (P5), clear work-life boundaries (P2, P4, P5, P11), access to research facilities (P5), meetings in-person (P4, P13), getting to know new colleagues (P5, P6), more engaging classes (P6), spontaneous social interactions with colleagues (P1, P3, P4, P8, P14), and ease of asking quick questions (P4, P7, P11) in the office.

5   Discussion

This study showed that while participants were able to navigate the unexpected transition to remote work through creative efforts, they still experienced a variety of challenges keeping in touch with others for both work-related and social purposes. The challenges fall under three sub-categories: lack of information about others' situation and availability, the need to be more intentional starting conversations online, and less opportunities for interactions before, during and after activities. Our data provides unique perspectives from participants who are unexpectedly put into a natural environment of large-scale remote work. Insights based on their extensive experiences of attending online activities suggest important limitations of current popular technology (see 5.1).

Lack of information about others' situation and availability, once only applying to the isolated teleworkers 9 who usually constitute just a small portion of the workforce in organizations 30, escalated into a challenge that the majority of office workers faced during the mandatory lockdown phase 34. Our data showed that not knowing what was going on in general, was particularly detrimental for PhD students who started their academic journeys remotely. They struggled with mental health issues and social isolation caused by problematic inter-cohort cohesion, lack of effective information transfer and lack of opportunities to overhear office conversations that could provide crucial information about people, relationships and activities in their organization.

A sizeable benefit brought by the unexpected transition to remote work was that it had facilitated an unprecedented widespread acceptance and creative use of Zoom. That had made it possible for people to do a wide range of activities they never considered doing online before, including holding online movie nights, game nights, church activities, Zoom study rooms and attending online concerts, etc..

5.1   Design Implications

Although we did not specifically probe into participants' perceptions of Zoom, insights emerged from their extensive experiences using this interface pointed to promising improvement to current features offered by Zoom. As suggested by insights elaborated in 4.1, a major limitation of Zoom is that they do not support the opportunity to spontaneously break up into and switch between smaller groups before, during and after Zoom gatherings/events. Although it has the breakout room feature that allows people to split into smaller groups, the way it works is significantly different from how small groups are formed in in-person gatherings/events. They are often formally assigned by the host instead of voluntarily formed. In addition, once in a breakout room, 1) participants are expected to talk to the same small group for a specific amount of time; 2) there is usually no way for participants to monitor what's happening in the main room or in another breakout room unless they leave their current room.

Inspired by these limitations, we believe the current breakout room feature on Zoom could be improved by making it easier for people to hang out after Zoom activities, e.g., by creating permeable spaces 13 where people could monitor multiple small group conversations and switch between them when they wish to. We are also currently building a prototype that would further facilitate these conversations.

5.2 Limitations and Future Directions

In this study, we only recruited a specific group of participants, i.e., PhD students from universities. Office workers from different types of organizations might offer different insights. We used interviews to explore the specific processes and instances embedded in initiating informal interactions online. Additional work is needed to include other research methods to complement results from our study, for example, surveys that could cover a larger sample, or observation that could explore participant behaviors in a natural environment.

6 Conclusion

We conducted in-depth interviews to explore processes of negotiating informal interactions and challenges experienced under the impact of the unexpected large-scale transition to remote work. Results showed that the sudden transition to remote work brought novel insights and unique challenges to PhD students. Experiences shaped by the new context suggested important limitations of current popular technology and contributed to the general perception of informal communication over technology, which is meaningful to the current context considering that the increased scale of remote work lasted after the mandatory lockdown phase 234. We provided design implications based on the results.

Bibliography

1. ATLAS.ti: The qualitative data analysis research software. http://atlasti.com
2. Balogová, K.: Looking at yourself on zoom. Doctoral dissertation, Master's thesis. University College London, London, UK (2021). https://uclic.ucl.ac.uk/content/2-study/4-current-taught-course/1-distinction-projects/15–21/balogova_karolina_2021.pdf

3. Bao, L., Li, T., Xia, X., Zhu, K., Li, H., Yang, X.: How does working from home affect developer productivity? – A Case Study of Baidu During COVID-19 Pandemic. arXiv preprint arXiv:2005.13167 (2020)
4. Beland, L.-P., Brodeur, A., Wright, T.: COVID-19, stay-at-home orders and employment: evidence from CPS data (2020)
5. Bleakley, A., et al.: Bridging social distance during social distancing: exploring social talk and remote collegiality in video conferencing. Hum.-Comput. Interact. **37**(5), 404–432 (2022). https://doi.org/10.1080/07370024.2021.1994859
6. Bloom, N., Liang, J., Roberts, J., Ying, Z.J.: Does working from home work? Evidence from a Chinese experiment. Quart. J. Econ. **130**, 165–218 (2015)
7. Brynjolfsson, E., Horton, J.J., Ozimek, A., Rock, D., Sharma, G., TuYe, H.-Y.: Covid-19 and remote work: an early look at us data. Technical Report (2020). https://www.nber.org/papers/w27344
8. Chan, C., Oey, N.E., Tan, E.-K.: Mental health of scientists in the time of COVID-19. Brain Behav. Immun. **88**, 956 (2020)
9. Fay, M.J., Kline, S.L.: Coworker relationships and informal communication in high-intensity telecommuting. J. Appl. Commun. Res. **39**(2), 144–163 (2011)
10. Fish, R.S., Kraut, R.E., Chalfonte, B.L.: The VideoWindow system in informal communications. In: Proceedings of Conference on Computer Supported Cooperative Work, pp. 1–12. New York: ACM Press (1990)
11. Glaser, B.G., Strauss, A.L.: The discovery of grounded theory: strategies for qualitative research. Aldine Publishing Co, Chicago, IL (1967)
12. Guest, E., et al.: Being a PhD student in the age of COVID-19. Canad. J. New Scholars Educ./Revue canadienne des jeunes chercheures et chercheurs en éducation **12**(1), 30–38 (2021)
13. Hu, E., Azim, M.A.R., Heo, S.: FluidMeet: enabling frictionless transitions between in-group, betweengroup, and private conversations during virtual breakout meetings. In: CHI Conference on Human Factors in Computing Systems (CHI 2022), 29 April - 5 May 2022, New Orleans, LA, USA. ACM, New York, NY, USA, p. 17 (2022). https://doi.org/10.1145/3491102.3517558
14. Kiesler, S., Cummings, J.N.: What do we know about proximity and distance in work groups? A legacy of research. Distrib. Work **1**, 57–80 (2002)
15. Koch, T., Denner, N.: Informal communication in organizations: work time wasted at the water-cooler or crucial exchange among co-workers? Corporate Commun. Int. J. **27**, 494–508 (2022)
16. Kraut, R.E., Fish, R.S., Root, R.W., Chalfonte, B.L.: Informal communication in organizations: form, function, and technology. In: Human Reactions to Technology: Claremont Symposium on Applied Social Psychology, pp. 145–199 (1990)
17. Kraut, R.E., Streeter, L.A., L. A.: Coordination in software development. Commun. ACM **38**(3), 69–82 (1995)
18. Kurtz-Costes, B., Helmke, L.A., Ülkü-Steiner, B.: Gender and doctoral studies: the perceptions of Ph. D. students in an American university. Gender Educ. **18**(2), 137–155 (2006)
19. Kusurkar, R.A., Isik, U., van der Burgt, S.M.E., Wouters, A., van der Vossen, M.M.: What stressors and energizers do Ph. D. students in medicine identify for their work: a qualitative inquiry. Med. Teach. **44**(5), 559–563 (2022)
20. Levecque, K., Anseel, F., De Beuckelaer, A., Van der Heyden, J., Gisle, L.: Work organization and mental health problems in Ph. D. students. Res. Policy **46**(4), 868–879 (2017)
21. Luo, A., Olson, J.S.: Informal communication in collaboratories. In: CHI2006 Extended Abstracts on Human Factors in Computing Systems, pp. 1043–1048 (2006)

22. Mintzberg, H.: The nature of managerial work (1973)
23. Nardi, B.A., Whittaker, S., Bradner, E.: Interaction and outeraction: instant messaging in action. In: Proceedings of the 2000 ACM Conference on Computer Supported Cooperative Work, pp. 79–88 (2000)
24. Nardi, B.A., Whittaker, S.: The place of face-to-face communication in distributed work. Distrib. Work **83**(112), 10–7551 (2002)
25. Ralph, P., Baltes, S., Adisaputri, G., et al.: Pandemic programming: how COVID-19 affects software developers and how their organizations can help. Empir. Softw. Eng. **25**, 4927–4961 (2020). https://doi.org/10.1007/s10664-020-09875-y
26. Singer-Velush, N., Sherman, K., Anderson, E.: Microsoft analyzed data on its newly remote workforce. Harvard Business Review. https://hbr.org/2020/07/microsoft-analyzed-data-on-its-newly-remoteworkforce (2020)
27. Spataro, J.: A pulse on employees' wellbeing, six months into the pandemic (2020). Accessed from Microsoft Work Trend Index. https://www.microsoft.com/en
28. Tang, J,C.: Approaching and leave-taking: negotiating contact in computer-mediated communication. ACM Trans. Comput.-Hum. Interact. (TOCHI) **14**(1), 5-es (2007)
29. Tang, J.C., Isaacs, E.A., Rua, M.: Supporting distributed groups with a montage of lightweight interactions. In: Proceedings of the 1994 ACM Conference on Computer Supported Cooperative Work, pp. 23–34 (1994)
30. Wang, Y., et al.: Returning to the office during the COVID-19 pandemic recovery: early indicators from China. In: Extended Abstracts of the 2021 CHI Conference on Human Factors in Computing Systems, pp. 1–6 (2021)
31. Walther, J.B.: Computer-mediated communication: Impersonal, interpersonal, and hyperpersonal interaction. Commun. Res. **23**(1), 3–43 (1996)
32. Whittaker, S., Frohlich, D., Daly-Jones, O.: Informal workplace communication: what is it like and how might we support it? In: Proceedings of the SIGCHI Conference on Human Factors in Computing Systems, pp. 131–137 (1994)
33. Woolston, C.: PhDs: the tortuous truth. Nature **575**(7782), 403–407 (2019)
34. Yang, L., et al.: How work from home affects collaboration: a large-scale study of information workers in a natural experiment during COVID-19. arXiv preprint arXiv:2007.15584 (2020)

The Role of Audio in Visual Perception of Quality

Maria Laura Mele[1]([⊠]), Damon Millar[2], and Silvia Colabrese[1]

[1] Intel Corporation, Rome, Italy
{maria.laura.mele,silvia.colabrese}@intel.com
[2] Intel Corporation, London, UK
damon.millar@intel.com

Abstract. Subjective Video Quality Assessment (VQA) is typically based on video stimuli without sound, for studying pure visual quality perception. This silent approach to VQA does not accurately represent the typical multisensory everyday use of video content. Previous studies have highlighted that audio plays a role in shaping subjective video quality because audio provides cues for viewers to interpret the visual content. The literature on subjective VQA agrees that not only the presence, but also the quality of audio influences perceived video quality, particularly in scenes with high visual complexity. Studies of the visual saliency of multimodal stimuli show that audio influences attention allocation through semantic and spatial cues, or semantic congruency. This study combines traditional subjective VQA methodology with psychophysics measures of perception such as eye-tracking and facial expression recognition. Its aim is to investigate how audio affects both video quality scores and the unconscious components of viewers' perception during the assessment task. Findings show (i) lower levels of visual quality scores and engagement for silent video, (ii) the influence of audio impairment on quality scores and visual attention spatial allocation, (iii) the influence of audio characteristic on visual attention, emotions, and engagement, but not on quality scores.

Keywords: Video Quality Assessment · Visual Saliency · Multimodal Perception

1 Introduction

Standard Video Quality Assessment (VQA) methodologies are typically based on soundless video stimuli, with the intention to isolate and analyze only the factors of a video that affect visual quality, with no influence from audio-related artifacts or discrepancies [1]. Removing audio from multimedia clips allows for a more focused analysis of pure visual features such as compression artifacts or color accuracy, without additional factors related to audio perception that would increase complexity in the assessment process [2]. However, video content is usually accompanied by audio when it is consumed. To know whether the absence of audio affects the perception of video quality, studying the human perception of multimedia complexity is therefore needed to account for everyday scenarios of use [3].

© The Author(s), under exclusive license to Springer Nature Switzerland AG 2023
M. Kurosu et al. (Eds.): HCII 2023, LNCS 14054, pp. 155–167, 2023.
https://doi.org/10.1007/978-3-031-48038-6_10

Visual Attention of Audio-Video. The human visual system is one of the most important sensory channels sighted humans rely on for perceiving the environment. However human attention involves multimodal information processing - when sensory signals reach the brain, they congregate in the same area of the superior colliculus, and most neurons exiting the superior colliculus are multisensory [4].

From an evolutional perspective, perceptual multimodality might have a facilitatory effect. In visual attention, a multimodal attentional process can benefit auditory stimuli to facilitate location of visual targets in terms of both accuracy and speed [5]. Neuroscience works on multisensory attention suggest that contextual auditory signals enhance the neural response to a synchronized visual event, thus increasing the chances that a viewer selects the target in a multiple object environment [6]. Eye tracking studies confirm that coherent audio information (e.g., the sound of a car engine on a video showing a car) offers key cues for improving the feature-specific response to the target object [7]. Viewers seem also to be better able to detect visual targets shown in a fast-changing sequence of visual distractors when an abrupt sound is presented nearly simultaneously with the visual target. The impact of sound on visual perception is not restricted to contextual audio, noise lowers the recognition threshold for visual stimuli [8]. Salient auditory stimuli such as unexpected sounds can generate cross-modal correspondence with visual attention by unintentionally driving gaze to the direction of the sound, even when the viewers are asked to ignore audio stimuli [9].

Previous research on the influence of audio in VQA has focused on the various aspects of audio that could affect video quality, including quality level, source location, semantic components, and genre. The VQA affecting conditions listed below come from studies of audio-video VQA conducted over the last two decades [2].

Audio Impairment and Video Quality. Several studies of audio-video quality showed that visual quality has significantly higher impact than audio quality on the overall perception of audio-video stimuli [10]. However, when the video quality is high, audio quality level has a stronger impact on the audio-visual quality [11]. Audio distortions negatively affect the ability to discriminate among different levels of visual quality [10].

Audio Characteristic and Video Quality. Four main characteristics of audio could affect video quality. (1) *Audio source location.* The location of an audio source attracts visual attention and may influence visual quality perception. Visual distortions could be less perceptible in areas far from the sound source than in areas where the sound originates [9]. (2) *Audio-video semantic consistency.* Audio information that is consistent with the video content could be an important cue for improving feature-specific responses to targets. Conversely, inconsistent audio information could have little effect on visual attention [12]. (3) *Audio tone.* Audio frequency and pitch seem to act as a spatial cue and could also modify the viewers' attention of visual quality. For example, tones respectively rising or falling in frequency seem to improve response to respectively pointing up or down displayed arrows [2]. (4) *Audio genre.* Audio such as scene music, sound effects, and narration can add realism to visual information, and give viewers a more engaging experience [13].

The investigated literature on audio-video visual quality provides an overview of the main factors that may influence visual perception in VQA of multimedia content. However, their findings are based on separate studies, each focusing on different audio conditions and with different video quality impairment levels, display resolutions, monitor screens, and experimental setting conditions.

This paper presents a study that uses three experimental tests to comprehensively investigate how the main factors of audio perception affect video quality perception, under identical controlled conditions. The study aims to answer the following questions: (i) Does audio influence viewers' engagement and opinion of visual quality compared to soundless video? (ii) How does audio compression and audio characteristic affect visual quality perception? The findings of this study provide insights into how the VQA methodological choice affects video quality opinion scores, visual attention, emotional states, and engagement of viewers.

2   Method

Three tests were conducted to investigate: (Test 1) how does audio affect opinion of visual quality compared to soundless video; (Test 2) how does audio compression and (Test 3) audio characteristics affect video quality perception in audio-video clips.

A Single Stimulus Continuous Quality Scale (SSCQS) method [1] was used for the three tests. The SSCQS method presents one video at a time to the viewer. Video quality was the same across all the stimuli, only audio quality or characteristic varied. At the end of each trial video, observers were asked to evaluate the visual quality using a grading scale of integers in the range 1–100 (1 = Bad, 100 = Excellent) on a slider. The position of the slider was automatically reset to mid-scale after each evaluation.

A first test (Test 1) was conducted online to investigate the influence of audio presence in video, in the uncontrolled home condition. Two further tests (Test 2 and 3) were conducted in controlled laboratory conditions to investigate the role of audio quality degradation at different levels, and the impact of audio characteristics on VQA.

The tests were created and administered using a biometric research platform called iMotions (www.imotions.com). During the test, gaze (Test 2 and 3) and facial expression (Test 1, 2 and 3) were collected together with VQA subjective scores. Fixations (here defined as the maintaining of the gaze on a single location for more than 60 ms), saccades (i.e., rapid movement of the eye between fixation points), and both horizontal and vertical coordinates of participants' gaze were measured using a Tobii X3-120 Hz eye tracker and processed by the iMotions platform.

Participants were asked to wear headphones during the test. Online participants were asked to set the audio level of their headphones to 90%. Laboratory participants were provided with noise-cancelling headphones which audio level was set to 90% loudness percentage (100.8 dB). Before each testing session, participants were asked to turn off their personal devices to avoid any distraction. The tests were conducted in a soundproof laboratory built for psychophysics experiments, with controlled light and temperature for all participants. The laboratory tests were conducted on a desk-and-chair experimental setting. A 32 inches monitor screen with a 3840 × 2160 pixel resolution was used. The monitor was 140 cm distant from the viewer's position.

2.1 Material

Eight videos that were recorded for this experiment were used as experimental stimuli. The video content equally showed outdoor/indoor and dynamic/static scenes, with animal, humans, landscapes, and urban contexts. All the video clips were in the UltraHD 4K resolution, 30 fps, h.264, 4:2:0, 8 bits. Each video had duration of approximately 10 s.

Stereophonic audio tracks with two channels in Advanced Audio Coding (AAC) format were used. All audio tracks had a 32 bit-depth and a 48 kHz sampling rate. The audio content included music, nature sounds, machine sounds and human crowd scene speech. The original audio was encoded with AAC at four bitrate levels (64 kbps, 128 kbps, 320 kbps, 800 kbps), which range from very poor audio quality to high audio quality, consistent with the common practice in the consumer audio market, where the threshold for acceptable audio quality is 192 kbps for AAC codecs [14]. Table 1 shows the conditions and characteristic of content used in each test.

Table 1. Conditions under analysis in the Video Quality Assessment tests.

Test 1 Soundless Video vs Audio-video	Test 2 Audio Compression	Test 3 Audio Characteristics
Condition: audio presence	*Condition: audio quality level*	*Condition: audio characteristics*
No audio	Reference audio quality	reference scene sound
Video with reference scene sound	800 kbps audio	sound & music: *scene sound with additional sound music*
	320 kbps audio	music: *sound music audio only (no scene sound)*
	128 kbps audio	inconsistent audio: *scene sound audio that is not consistent with the content of the video*
	64 kbps audio	high pitch: *scene sound edited to + 10 pitch audio*
		low pitch: *scene sound edited to −10 pitch audio*

Subjective opinion scores of video quality, gaze, emotional states, attention, and engagement were measured. Emotional states measures were computed by Affectiva software (https://www.affectiva.com) following The Facial Action Coding System (FACS), which refers to a set of facial muscle micromovements which universally correspond to emotions and affective valence [15].

2.2 Participants

Test 1. Visual Quality of Soundless Video vs Audio-Video. Overall, 60 participants (68% male, mean age = 39) completed the subjective test on 17 March 2023 between

3 p.m. and 5 p.m., Central European Time (CET). The pre-screening of the subjective test scores consisted of determining if the participants met the following preliminary requirements: no uncorrected vision impairments, no color blindness, English language as a first language. All participants were in the same country (United Kingdom) so it was possible to conduct the test with the same range of daylight conditions. Participants were recruited and rewarded £11.16/hr through an online platform called Prolific.co (www. prolific.co). The mean time of the testing session and questions was about 10 min.

Test 2–3. Visual Quality of Audio-Video: Audio Compression and Audio Characteristic. 15 participants per test (Test 2: 60% male, mean age = 29; Test 3: 66% male, mean age = 27) completed the subjective test in April 2023 under controlled laboratory conditions. The pre-screening of the subjective test scores consisted of determining if the participants met the preliminary requirements (no uncorrected vision impairments, no uncorrected hearing impairments, no color blindness). Participants were recruited and rewarded €40/hr through Amazon gift codes. The mean time of sessions was about 30 min, including the time required for the signature of the pre-testing informed consent, instructions, and eye tracking calibration.

3 Results

3.1 Test 1. Visual Quality of Soundless Video vs Audio-Video

Mean Opinion Scores (MOS). Mean, standard deviation and standard error of video quality opinion scores were computed for soundless video clips (MOS = 61.584, SD = 10.485, SE = 7.041) and audio-video stimuli (MOS = 74.597, SD = 11.6082, SE = 6.182).

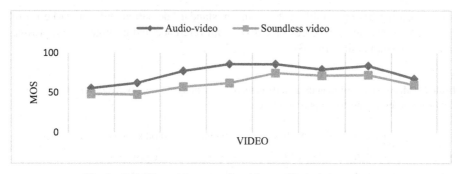

Fig. 1. Soundless video vs audio-video quality opinion scores.

A highly significant positive correlation was found between audio-video MOS and soundless video MOS ($r = 0.850$, $p = 0.007$) (Fig. 1).

The independent-samples nonparametric analysis (Mann-Whitney $U = 12$, $p = 0.038$) showed a significant difference between the MOS assigned to soundless video/clips and MOS assigned to audio-video.

Engagement and Emotions. The mean values of engagement and basic emotions per video clip and condition were analyzed using Affectiva (Fig. 2).

Higher levels of engagement ($Z = -2.380$, $p = 0.017$) were found in audio-video stimuli compared to soundless video clips.

The non-parametric Related-Samples Wilcoxon Signed Rank Test highlighted significant differences between the soundless video and audio-video clips for all the measures. Overall, higher levels of basic emotions were found for audio-video clips compared to no-audio clips ($Z = -2.521$, $p = 0.012$), except for Surprise ($Z = 0.140$, $p > 0.05$), Joy ($Z = -1.400$, $p > 0.05$), and fear ($Z = -0.560$, $p > 0.05$).

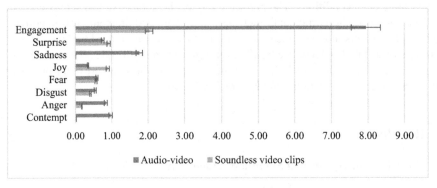

Fig. 2. Emotions and engagement in soundless video vs audio-video clips.

3.2 Test 2. Visual Quality of Audio-Video: Audio Compression

Mean Opinion Scores. Table 2 shows mean, standard deviation and standard error of the video quality opinion scores of videos, with reference and a range of compressed audio scene sound clips (Fig. 3).

Table 2. Mean, standard deviation and standard error of video quality MOS assigned to video clips with different audio compression levels.

	64 kbps	128 kbps	320 kbps	800 kbps	Reference
MEAN	68.966	69.022	69.868	70.001	**70.842**
S.D.	**7.124**	6.064	7.061	6.209	5.426
S.E.	**2.057**	1.751	2.038	1.792	1.566

A highly significant positive correlation has been found between the MOS assigned to video with compressed audio and the MOS assigned to reference sound video (mean $r = 0.834$, $p < 0.01$).

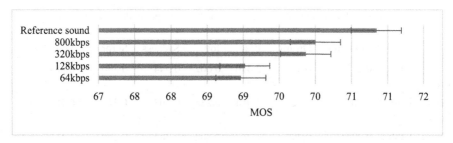

Fig. 3. MOS of video quality per compression level.

A paired-samples parametric T-test analyzed statistical differences among the MOS of video quality. The analysis showed no significant difference among the MOS assigned to video clips with different audio compression levels. However, there is a trend of increasing subjective visual quality MOS with increasing audio quality.

Gaze Coordinates, Fixations and Saccades. Comparisons among horizontal (x) and vertical (y) coordinates of gaze on all video stimuli showed that, overall, gaze positions across video clips with different audio quality levels significantly differ from each other (Gaze x – Wilks' Lambda $F(4, 4375) = 43.415$, $p = 0.000$; Gaze y – Wilks' Lambda $F(4, 4375) = 202.112$, $p = 0.000$). There were no differences found between the vertical coordinates on reference videos compared to videos with 128 kbps audio. Difference in the horizontal coordinates on reference videos compared to videos with 128 kbps audio have been found (Gaze x $- t = -11,711$, $p = 0.000$). Furthermore, no difference between the horizontal coordinates of gaze between reference videos and 320 kbps and 800 kbps have been found. Difference between the vertical coordinates of gaze between reference videos and 320 kbps (Gaze y $- t = -16.651$, $p = 0.000$) and 800 kbps have been found (Gaze y $- t = -10.567$, $p = 0.000$).

Mean fixation and saccades per video have been analyzed. No statistical differences were found for both fixation and saccade number and duration among the videos with different audio compression. No significant correlation has been found for fixations and saccades number and duration among the videos with different audio compression.

Engagement and Emotions. Table 3 shows the mean values of engagement and basic emotions per compression level. The parametric repeated measures ANOVA on emotional values among the audio compression levels did not indicate any significant differences. The affective data showed no significant difference between reference videos and videos with compressed audio.

Table 3. Mean values of emotions and engagement levels per audio compression level.

	Anger	Contempt	Disgust	Fear	Joy	Sadness	Surprise	Engagement
64 kbps	0.093	0.214	0.423	2.476	0.002	0.344	0.300	0.884
128 kbps	0.101	0.205	0.421	3.054	**0.225**	0.303	**0.346**	0.786
320 kbps	**0.280**	0.221	0.490	2.783	0.002	0.385	0.290	1.168
800 kbps	0.083	0.211	0.421	2.640	0.002	0.375	0.276	0.678
Ref	0.164	**0.268**	**0.581**	**3.212**	0.002	**0.581**	0.281	**1.423**

3.3   Test 3. Visual Quality of Audio-Video: Audio Characteristics

Mean Opinion Scores. Table 4 shows mean, standard deviation and standard error of the video quality MOS of videos with the analyzed audio characteristics (Fig. 4).

Table 4. Mean, Standard deviation and Standard error of MOS assigned to video quality of clips with different audio characteristics.

	scene sound reference	sound & music	music	inconsistent audio	high pitch	low pitch	right audio	left audio
MEAN	66.95	**68.22**	66.79	62.32	63.20	67.18	66.22	67.70
S.D.	7.17	8.48	9.29	**14.65**	11.67	9.51	10.66	9.20
S.E.	1.92	2.27	2.48	**3.92**	3.12	2.54	2.85	2.46

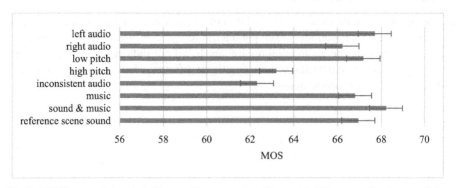

Fig. 4. MOS per participant of video quality across the videos with different audio characteristics.

Gaze Coordinates, Fixations and Saccades. Comparisons among horizontal (x) and vertical (y) coordinates of gaze on all video stimuli showed that, overall, gaze positions across video clips with different audio quality levels significantly differ from each other (Gaze x – Wilks' Lambda $F(7, 774) = 30.723$, p = 0.000), Gaze y – Wilks' Lambda $F(7, 757) = 30.002$, p = 0.000).

The following audio characteristics seem to affect gaze, compared to the reference scene audio:

- scene sound & music (gaze x – t = -9.196, p = 0.000; gaze y – t = -16.164, p = 0.000)
- music (only y axis is affected, gaze y – t = 2.068, p = 0.039)
- high pitch (gaze x – t = -7.864, p = 0.000);
- gaze y – t = -20.088, p = 0.000),
- low pitch (only y axis is affected, gaze y – t = -5.798, p = 0.000),
- right audio channel only (gaze x – t = -3.240, p = 0.001; gaze y – t = -10.187, p = 0.000),
- left audio channel only (gaze x – t = -13.943, p = 0.000; gaze y – t = -17.022, p = 0.000).

Only the sound of characteristic "semantically inconsistent" did not show any statistical difference for either axis.

The audio characteristics significantly affect the number and duration of both fixations and saccades, specifically for the following comparisons: higher fixation number in low pitch audio compared to reference scene audio (t = -2.486, p = 0.042), higher saccades number in low pitch audio than in scene sound reference audio (t = -2.94, p = 0.021).

Engagement and Emotions. Table 5 shows the mean values of engagement and basic emotions per audio condition.

Table 5. Mean affective states per audio characteristic.

	scene reference	sound & music	music	inconsistent audio	high pitch	low pitch	right audio	left audio
Anger	0.03	**0.26**	0.08	0.04	0.04	0.02	0.07	0.02
Contempt	0.2	**0.3**	0.2	0.2	0.19	0.28	0.19	0.19
Disgust	0.44	0.42	0.42	**0.5**	0.43	0.45	0.48	0.44
Fear	**2.91**	2.45	2.33	2.82	2.7	2.44	2.74	2.22
Joy	0.34	**2.45**	1.99	0.43	0.16	0	0.34	0.05
Sadness	0.27	0.18	**0.69**	0.48	0.25	0.1	0.34	0.16
Surprise	0.3	0.33	**0.36**	0.31	0.32	0.31	0.3	0.3
Engagement	1.59	**4.66**	3.68	1.73	2.21	0.63	1.95	1.42

The parametric repeated measures ANOVA on emotional values among the audio compression levels did not highlight any overall significant difference on engagement and emotions among the audio characteristics except for surprise in the inconsistent audio condition versus the sound music condition (t = −0.028, p = 0.018), and engagement in the high pitch audio condition versus the low pitch condition (t = 1.579, p = 0.02).

4 Discussion

This section analyzes the results of the comprehensive VQA study focusing on three conditions: the presence/absence of audio in testing video stimuli (Test 1), the level of audio compression (Test 2) or the audio characteristic (Test 3) in audio-video testing stimuli. The study aims to provide insights into the implications on visual perception of adding audio to video in VQA by answering two main questions: (i) Does audio influence viewers' engagement and opinion of visual quality compared to soundless video? (ii) How do audio compression and audio characteristic affect visual quality perception?

(i) Does audio influence viewers' engagement and opinion on visual quality compared to soundless video? Results of Test 1 support previous findings showing that the presence of audio influences how viewers rate the quality [2]. In this study, soundless video receives video quality scores significantly lower than video-clips streamed with scene sound. A highly positive correlation between the quality scores of sound vs soundless suggests that audio does not affect the trend of scores assigned to visual quality, which decrease with lower bitrates, but only the magnitude of visual quality.

Interestingly, compared to soundless video, audio-video clips are related to higher levels of viewers' engagement and negative emotions such as sadness, disgust, anger, or contempt, but not positive emotions such as joy, or surprise, which levels are the same in both conditions. Previous studies highlighted that emotions induced by video content seem to be directly related to video quality scores (the higher the positive emotions, the better the subjective video quality score) [16, 17]. The results found in this study highlight that emotions induced by audio quality seem to follow a reverse trend than emotions induced by video quality. Further studies on the impact of audio induced emotions on VQA are needed.

(ii) How do audio compression and audio characteristic affect video quality assessment, visual perception, and engagement? Audio compression and audio characteristics were analyzed.

Audio Compression. Test 2 assesses visual quality with five audio quality degradation levels. Results show no statistical difference among the subjective scores, but a positive trend line of video quality scores on audio quality level can be observed. Audio quality level seems to affect the magnitude of visual quality opinion scores.

Test 2 also analyzes how audio compression affects visual perception in terms of gaze positions, fixations, and saccades. Audio quality seems to significantly affect the spatial components of gaze (horizontal and vertical coordinates), especially when the audio quality is strongly impaired (64 kbps). The dynamic components of gaze (duration and number of fixations and saccades) don not significantly change among videos with different quality levels. This result suggests that audio quality affects visual saliency in terms of where to allocate visual attention, not how to visually process it, which seems strictly guided by the video content independently from audio quality.

Engagement and emotions seem to have similar levels independently of the audio impairment level. This result is in line with a previous study on video-gaming, where audio encoding bitrate do not have any effect on viewers' quality of experience even at low bitrates (32 kbps) [18].

Audio Characteristic. Test 3 assesses how eight main audio characteristics affect visual quality perception. Results highlighted that no audio characteristics affects video quality opinion scores. Opinion scores of videos are statistically similar regardless the characteristic of sound (scene sound or music), the location of the audio source (left or right), the audio tone (high or low pitch), and the semantic consistency between audio content and video content.

As for audio compression, audio characteristic seems to affect the spatial components of visual attention. Compared to the gaze measured in videos with their reference scene audio, there are significant differences in gaze positions on all the experimental conditions except for videos with semantically inconsistent audio. Low pitch seems to also affect the dynamic components of gaze, with higher numbers of both fixations and saccades compared to scene audio. This result seems to be in line with previous studies finding that low pitch could increase perceptual processing load [19, 20].

Audio characteristic do not affect engagement and emotion levels. Two exceptions were (a) the semantically inconsistent audio, which had significantly lower levels of surprise than videos with music sound, and (b) the high pitch audio, which received higher levels of engagement than videos with low pitch audio.

5 Conclusion

Subjective video quality assessment plays a central role in understanding and enhancing the viewer experience in today's multimedia. VQA methodologies traditionally use soundless video, thus not accounting for the everyday use of multimedia content. This study aimed to investigate the role of audio in subjective perception of visual quality. Three tests combined standard VQA methodology with eye-tracking and facial expression recognition techniques for studying visual saliency, engagement, and basic emotions during perception of visual quality with different audio compression levels and characteristics. Test 1 investigated the influence of audio presence in video. Test 2 investigated the role of audio quality degradation at different levels, and Test 3 investigated the impact of audio characteristics on VQA.

The findings in Test 1 of this study confirmed previous studies showing that soundless video has lower levels of video quality MOS and engagement. The results obtained through Test 2 and Test 3 provide new insights on multimedia video quality assessment: (1) Soundless video has lower levels of visual quality perception and engagement than videos with their own scene sound; (2) When video is accompanied by its scene sound, audio quality improves video scores and causes us to look in different places, but does not affect engagement and emotions; (3) Changing audio characteristic affects where we look at in a video and how we look. This may affect emotions and engagement but does not affect quality scores.

As video content keeps growing in importance for technological research and development, VQA plays a key role in ensuring high-quality video experiences in domains such as video encoding, video streaming, video conferencing, virtual and augmented reality, video analytics and content analysis. The major finding of this study is the common practice of using silent video to obtain subjective video scores is inaccurate and may lead to misleading quality.

The study reinforces the need for ongoing research and development in multimedia video quality assessment, including the exploration of novel subjective evaluation methodologies that would adopt not only traditional scores of visual quality, but also psychophysics measures of visual attention such as gaze and facial expressions.

Future research is needed to study the influence of audio on visual perception when the level of visual impairment changes. This study focused only the impact of audio quality/audio characteristic changes on the VQA of one unique high-quality video condition. Future studies will investigate subjective quality and attention when both audio and video compression levels are combined.

References

1. ITU-R BT: Methodologies for the subjective assessment of the quality of television images, document recommendation ITU-R BT. 500-14 (10/2019). ITU, Geneva (2020)
2. Akhtar, Z., Falk, T.H.: Audio-visual multimedia quality assessment: a comprehensive survey. IEEE Access **5**, 21090–21117 (2017)
3. Cisco, U.: Cisco annual internet report (2018–2023) white paper **10**(1), 1–35 (2020). Cisco, San Jose
4. Klein, R.M.: Perceptual-motor expectancies interact with covert visual orienting under conditions of endogenous but not exogenous control. Can. J. Exp. Psychol./Revue Canadienne de psychologie expérimentale **48**(2), 167 (1994)
5. Driver, J., Spence, C.: Attention and the crossmodal construction of space. Trends Cogn. Sci. **2**(7), 254–262 (1998)
6. Van der Burg, E., Talsma, D., Olivers, C.N., Hickey, C., Theeuwes, J.: Early multisensory interactions affect the competition among multiple visual objects. Neuroimage **55**(3), 1208–1218 (2011)
7. Chen, Y., Nguyen, T.V., Kankanhalli, M., Yuan, J., Yan, S., Wang, M.: Audio matters in visual attention. IEEE Trans. Circ. Syst. Video Technol. **24**(11), 1992–2003 (2014)
8. Vroomen, J., Gelder, B.D.: Sound enhances visual perception: cross-modal effects of auditory organization on vision. J. Exp. Psychol. Hum. Percept. Perform. **26**(5), 1583 (2000)
9. Lee, J.S., De Simone, F., Ebrahimi, T.: Influence of audio-visual attention on perceived quality of standard definition multimedia content. In: 2009 International Workshop on Quality of Multimedia Experience, pp. 13–18. IEEE (2009)
10. Becerra Martinez, H., Hines, A., Farias, M.C.: Perceptual quality of audio-visual content with common video and audio degradations. Appl. Sci. **11**(13), 5813 (2021)
11. Beerends, J.G., De Caluwe, F.E.: The influence of video quality on perceived audio quality and vice versa. J. Audio Eng. Soc. **47**(5), 355–362 (1999)
12. Min, X., Zhai, G., Gao, Z., Hu, C., Yang, X.: Sound influences visual attention discriminately in videos. In: 2014 Sixth International Workshop on Quality of Multimedia Experience (QoMEX), pp. 153–158. IEEE (2014)
13. Ansani, A., Marini, M., D'Errico, F., Poggi, I.: How soundtracks shape what we see: analyzing the influence of music on visual scenes through self-assessment, eye tracking, and pupillometry. Front. Psychol. **11**, 2242 (2020)

14. Cunningham, S., McGregor, I.: Subjective evaluation of music compressed with the ACER codec compared to AAC, MP3, and uncompressed PCM. Int. J. Digit. Multimed. Broadcast. **2019**, 1–17 (2019)
15. Ekman, P., Friesen, W.: Facial Action Coding System: A Technique for the Measurement of Facial Movement. Consulting Psychologists Press, Palo Alto (1978), pp. 1125–1134
16. Mirkovic, M., Vrgovic, P., Culibrk, D., Stefanovic, D., Anderla, A.: Evaluating the role of content in subjective video quality assessment. Sci. World J. **2014**, 1–9 (2014)
17. Msakni, H.G., Youssef, H.: Impact of user emotion and video content on video Quality of Experience. In: Proceedings 5th ISCA/DEGA Workshop on Perceptual Quality of Systems (PQS 2016), pp. 97–101 (2016)
18. Schmidt, S., Zadtootaghaj, S., Wang, S., Möller, S.: Towards the influence of audio quality on gaming quality of experience. In: 2021 13th International Conference on Quality of Multimedia Experience (QoMEX), pp. 169–174. IEEE (2021)
19. Cheek, J.M., Smith, L.R.: Music training and mathematics achievement. Adolescence **34**(136), 759–761 (1999). https://doi.org/10.1177/105971239900700311
20. Zhang, G., Wang, W., Qu, J., Li, H., Song, X., Wang, Q.: Perceptual influence of auditory pitch on motion speed. J. Vis. **21**(10), 11 (2021)

A Study on Variational Autoencoder to Extract Characteristic Patterns from Electroencephalograms and Electrogastrograms

Kohki Nakane[1], Rintaro Sugie[1($\boxtimes$)], Meiho Nakayama[2], Yasuyuki Matsuura[3], Tomoki Shiozawa[4], and Hiroki Takada[1]

[1] Graduate School of Engineering, University of Fukui, Fukui 910-8507, Japan
Rinta1903@gmail.com, takada@u-fukui.ac.jp
[2] Hospital Good Sleep Center, Nagoya City University, Nagoya 467-8602, Japan
[3] Education and Research Center for Data-Driven Science, Gifu City Women's College, Gifu 501-0192, Japan
[4] School of Business, Aoyama Gakuin University, Tokyo 150-8366, Japan

Abstract. Autoencoder (AE) is known as an artificial intelligence (AI), which is considered to be useful to analyze the bio-signal (BS) and/or conduct simulations of the BS. We can show examples to study Electrogastrograms (EGGs) and Electroencephalograms (EEGs) as a BS. In previous study, we have analyzed the EGGs by using the AE and have compared mathematical models of EGGs in the seated posture with those in the supine. The EEGs of normal subjects and patients with Meniere's disease were herein converted to lower dimensions using Variational AE (VAE). The existence of characteristic differences was verified.

Keywords: Electroencephalograms (EEGs) · Electrogastrograms (EGGs) · Variational Autoencoder(VAE) · Recurrent Neural Network · Polysomnography · Meniere's disease

1 Introduction

Meniere's disease, a type of inner ear disease, is thought to be caused by ischemic lesions in the inner ear, especially endolymphatic hydrops [1]. However, it has been reported that Meniere's disease is accompanied by sleep disorders such as sleep apnea [2]. Despite the existence of such cases and the highlighting of this association, there has been little research on it. One of the symptoms of Meniere's disease is dizziness. Benzodiazepines may be administered to patients with dizziness for anxiety and depression. However, some of these intermediate to long-acting benzodiazepines have a half-life of 10 h or more, and consequently, they cause circadian rhythm disorders, or unnoticeably exacerbate sleep apnea syndrome due to muscle relaxation [3]. Therefore, it has been reported in recent years that improvements have been observed in Meniere's disease symptoms when drug therapies including benzodiazepines and other medications

M. Kurosu et al. (Eds.): HCII 2023, LNCS 14054, pp. 168–178, 2023.
https://doi.org/10.1007/978-3-031-48038-6_11

that may affect sleep have been discontinued or restricted to improve the sleeping state of Meniere's patients [4, 5]. Moreover, when sleep electroencephalograms of Meniere's disease patients were measured by polysomnography (PSG), a significant difference was observed between them and healthy subjects [4]. This suggests that Meniere's disease is closely related to sleep.

Moreover, in recent years, the field of machine learning has made remarkable progress [6–8], and it is now possible to detect minute differences imperceptible to humans.

Therefore, in this study, we assumed that sleep electroencephalograms of Meniere's disease patients have a characteristic low-dimensional pattern that is not observed in healthy subjects. Sleep electroencephalograms of healthy subjects and Meniere's disease patients were converted to lower dimensions using a variational autoencoder (VAE) [9] x_t , which is a type of statistical machine learning, and latent variables were extracted. This verified whether there was a characteristic difference in the latent variables of sleep electroencephalograms extracted between healthy subjects and Meniere's disease patients.

2   Classical Neural Network

In practical matters, it is sometimes difficult to make a clean dichotomy between two different states. We believe that the state of the body falls into this category. Therefore, we wondered if it would be possible to express the degree of a certain state, rather than simply dividing it into two.

In our previous research, we have been working on classifying biological signals using a method that incorporates metric learning so that classification can be performed while maintaining interpretability, rather than simple binary classification. In this chapter, we present our efforts to classify the presence or absence of caloric intake from EGG using Autoencoder (AE) [10].

2.1   Autoencoder

AE is one of the deep-learning models that excels in information compression, consisting of two types of networks: Encoder and Decoder. Since the Encoder compresses some information x so that it can be reconstructed by the Decoder, the compressed information retains the main features that make up x. It is thought that the main features of the information are preserved in the compressed information. Geoffrey Hinton, a researcher in computer science and cognitive psychology at the University of Toronto, and his colleagues proposed AE. They argued that dimensional compression using AE preserves more information than the compression using principal component analysis [11]. AE can also be used as a generative model. For example, assume that we can compress some data, say A and B, into the latent space, and then restore it to the original A and B again. In this case, by inputting a value that is the midpoint of A and B in the latent space as a point where the original compressed data does not actually exist into the Decoder and restoring it, data with intermediate characteristics between A and B can be generated. Most neural network models, which are widely used in tasks such as classification and prediction, require teacher labels to be paired with the input data. AE, on the other hand, does not require teacher labels because it learns to compress and reconstruct the input data so that it can output the input data again. The prepared data can be compressed into a latent space, and tasks such as classification and prediction can be performed by clustering the compressed data.

2.2   Proposed Model and Classification Method

We partially modified the structure of AE, an unsupervised learning model, and modified it into a semi-supervised learning model that performs restoration and class classification for Decoder. This is expected to reflect class information when embedding into latent variables by Encoder, since reducing Decoder's learning error requires appropriate embedding that takes into account the label information by Encoder. In other words, the presence or absence of caloric intake can be expressed as a distance when embedding the EGG on the latent space. With sufficient training of AEs with such modifications, we can obtain an Encoder that can perform embedding while estimating label information.

We measured 11 channels of seated posture EGG at 1 kHz for 90 min each in 8 healthy subjects (8 females) aged 19 to 24 years after caloric intake and as controls in a calorie uninoculated state. Informed consent was obtained from each subject prior to the recording experiment. Approval was also obtained from the Ethics Committee of the Graduate School of Natural Science and Technology, Nagoya City University. The details of this experiment are described in [10].

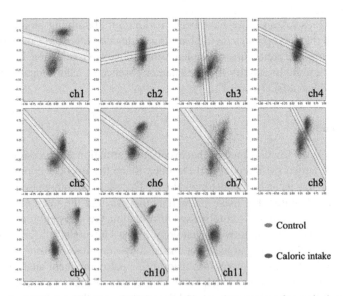

Fig. 1. SVM classification of EGGs embedded on latent space for each channel.

A 0.15 Hz low-pass filter was applied to the measured data as data preprocessing, and then the data were downsampled to 1 Hz. The data were then cropped to 32 samples per channel (32 s) and embedded in a two-dimensional latent space using Encoder to determine the presence or absence of caloric intake. However, since it is necessary to make each class label binary in order to evaluate the classification accuracy, binary classification was performed for each channel by linear SVM (Fig. 1). The class that accounted for more than 5 of the 11 channels was then used as the final class classification result.

2.3 Example

We evaluated the classification accuracy of the presence or absence of caloric intake using the F1 score, which is calculated as the harmonic mean of Precision and Recall, as described in Sect. 3.2. To confirm the relationship between the number of data embedded in the latent variable and classification accuracy, the F1 score was calculated each time the length of the time series of embedded EGG was increased by 32 s. As a result, the F1 score exceeded 0.9 from 96 s onward, indicating that classification could be performed with high accuracy (Fig. 2).

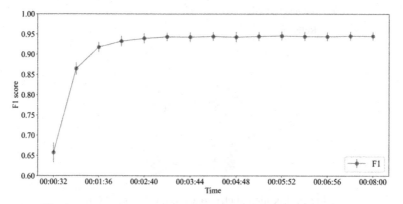

Fig. 2. EGG series length used for class classification and F1 score.

3   Method

3.1   Experimental Method

The data set used in this experiment was from the Good Sleep Center of Nagoya City University Hospital. It was extracted from 20 cases in a test results system for polysomnography (PSG) conducted on 10 men and women with Meniere's disease (average ± standard deviation: 67.8 ± 13.00 years), and 10 healthy men and women (average standard deviation: 66 ± 12.70 years) with a series length of 2048. This experiment is a study approved by the Ethical Review Committee of Nagoya City University Medical School (No. 60-21-0136). Additionally, the following preprocessing was performed with the value x_t for time.

$$x_t = \begin{cases} \log(x_t + 1) & as \ x_t \geq 0 \\ -\log(-x_t + 1) & as \ x_t < 0 \end{cases} \tag{1}$$

Subsequently, the following standardization was performed to adjust the domain of the hyperbolic tangent function to $[-1, 1]$, which is an input of the activation function of our neural network.

$$\hat{x} = \frac{2(x_t - \min x_t)}{\max x_t - \min x_t} - 1, \tag{2}$$

where is modified from the min-max normalization.

Here, PSG refers to overnight polysomnography. In PSG, a subject's sleep dynamics, mainly biological phenomena such as brain waves, eye movements, electromyogram, electrocardiogram, and body position, are recorded simultaneously throughout the night. Based on these records, physiological phenomena can be evaluated comprehensively and objectively [12]. Moreover, electroencephalogram measurement during PSG was performed by attaching the center left (C3), center right (C4), occipital left (O1), and occipital right (O2) electrodes, according to the standard method (10/20 method) [13] stipulated by the International Electroencephalography Society (Fig. 3).

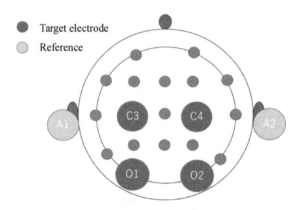

Fig. 3. Location of electrodes (O1, O2, C3 and C4).

3.2 Evaluation Method

In this study, we acquired the latent space of brain waves during sleep using VAE, divided it in two using a Support Vector Machine (SVM) [14], and evaluated it based on the results obtained here. The evaluation was mainly based on the correct answer rate according to the SVM and F1 scores obtained from a mixing matrix. A mixing matrix is a tabular evaluation index used to evaluate the performance of a classifier. Prediction data that was truly positive for the training data was the true positive (TP), falsely positive was false positive (FP), truly negative was true negative (TN), and falsely negative was false negative (FN).

F1-score were calculated from the precision and recall obtained from these scores. Precision was calculated with the following.

$$Precision = \frac{TP}{TP + FP} \tag{3}$$

This shows the percentage of true positives among the judged positive. Recall was calculated with the following.

$$recall = \frac{TP}{TP + FN} \tag{4}$$

This shows the percentage judged positive among the truly positive. Thus, from the harmonic mean of these scores.

$$F_1 = \frac{2}{\frac{1}{Precision} + \frac{1}{recall}} \tag{5}$$

is calculated, which is the F1 score; the F1 score ranges from 0 to 1, with the closer to 1, the better the performance.

4 New Deep Learning Analysis

We extracted latent variables from sleep electroencephalograms using VAE, a type of statistical machine learning. Moreover, the loss function was defined as follows.

$$loss = \frac{1}{n} \sum (x - \hat{x})^2 + D_{KL} \tag{6}$$

Here, D_{KL} refers to Kullback-Leibler information content [15]. The Kullback-Leibler information content is a distance measurement between the distribution of latent variables and standard normal distribution. In other words, this model is expressed by the sum of the mean square error between the input and reconstructed sleep electroencephalogram, and the Kullback-Leibler information content in latent space.

In addition, the internal structure of VAE consists of the Gated Recurrent Unit (GRU) [16], which is the gate mechanism of a recurrent neural network for extracting temporal information, a Convolutional Neural Network (CNN) [17] for extracting spatial information, and a Skip Connection [18] to prevent gradient vanishing. Table 1 lists the detailed structure and number of filters. Additionally, the generalization ability of the model was validated using group 5-fold cross-validation [19, 20]. Table 2 lists the number of data in each fold.

4.1 Sleep Analysis

The electroencephalogram was cut at 2048 points in each channel, and 10 epochs were learned for each channel and all channels. The channels used were C3, C4, O1, and O2 channels. The generalization ability of the model was also validated using group 5-fold cross-validation [19, 20].

The obtained latent variables were subjected to binary classification using SVM, and the correct answer rate and F1 score here were examined. The RBF kernel was used as a kernel function.

Table 1. Kernel size of CNN layer and the number of filters

Layers	Section	Kernel size	Filters
1	Encoder	4 × 1	36
2	Encoder	4 × 1	72
3	Encoder	4 × 1	144
4	Encoder	4 × 1	288
5	Encoder	4 × 1	576
6	Decoder	4 × 1	576
7	Decoder	4 × 1	288
8	Decoder	4 × 1	144
9	Decoder	4 × 1	72
10	Decoder	4 × 1	36

Table 2. The number of train data and valid data for each fold.

Fold	Train Data		Valid Data	
	Ménière	Other	Ménière	Other
1	34922	25719	6257	6081
2	29541	25174	11638	6626
3	30179	25713	11000	6087
4	35216	25789	5963	6011
5	34858	24805	6321	6995

5   Results

5.1   Correct Answer Rate

The results of learning VAE models for each channel and performing binary classification using SVM are shown. The SVM correct answer rates for the O1, O2, C3, and C4 channels were $88.28 \pm 8.97\%$, $87.90 \pm 6.18\%$, $73.05 \pm 10.35\%$, and $82.62 \pm 6.37\%$, respectively. Consequently, the O1 channel had the highest correct answer rate, followed by the O2 channel, thus, the highest correct answer rate was obtained for the channel located in the occipital region. Thus, the C3 channel, which had the lowest correct answer rate, also had the largest standard error.

5.2   F1 Scores

The F1 scores for the O1, O2, C3, and C4 channels were $74.12 \pm 10.51\%$, $75.31 \pm 9.20\%$, $57.22 \pm 11.29\%$, and $73.40 \pm 9.46\%$, respectively. As with the correct answer rate, the value was highest in the channel located in the occipital region. Furthermore, the C3 channel, which had the lowest F1 score, had the largest standard error. Additionally, Fig. 3 shows a typical example of the spatial plot of the latent variables in fold 1 extracted from the data of each channel.

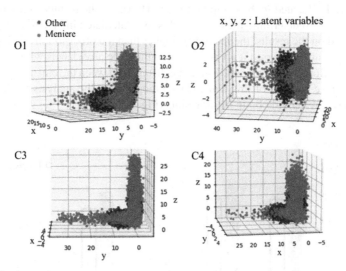

Fig. 4. Typical example of the distribution of latent variables in each channel.

6 Discussion

This paper was written based on the papers cited [10] and [21].

6.1 Correct Answer Rate for Each Channel

From the SVM correct answer rate for each channel, we deduced that the O1 and O2 channels located in the occipital region had the highest correct answer rate. In the occipital region, we observed the predominate generation of 9 to 11 Hz alpha waves at approximately 30 to 60 μV [22]. Based on the analysis results of this study and this fact, it is conceivable that the alpha waves of the sleep electroencephalograms of Meniere's disease patients are the most characteristic. The fact that the correct answer rate of the centrally located C3 channel was particularly low is thought to be a phenomenon caused by sleep electroencephalograms. The standard errors also increased compared to other channels, suggesting the inclusion of particular patient-specific characteristics with or without Meniere's disease. In other words, if we classify this using a label other than the presence or absence of Meniere's disease, the correct answer rate may be improved.

6.2 F1 Scores for Each Channel

Similar to the correct answer rate, we obtained particularly high scores for the O2 channel. Considering this result and the results of the correct answer rate mentioned above, it is reasonable to think that the characteristics of Meniere's disease were captured by the electrodes located in the occipital region. However, the results were below 80% for all channels. To determine the cause of this, we calculated the recall and precision (Fig. 4). Based on the results, the recall was higher than the precision in all channels. In other words, it can be inferred it is easy to discriminate positive labels without omission in this model. Moreover, it is possible that the distance between the clusters of the latent variables is close because of this, thus, if we proceed with the analysis so that this F1 score improves, we could obtain better results (Fig. 5).

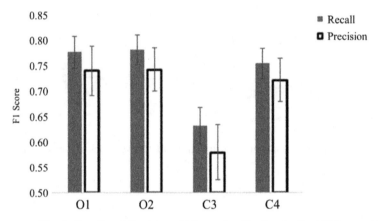

Fig. 5. Recall and Precision of binary classification by the SVM.

7 Conclusion

In this study, it was proposed that VAE could be used to extract the characteristic patterns contained in sleep electroencephalograms of Meniere's disease patients. Particularly, it was suggested that sleep brain waves emitted from the occipital region contain these characteristics. From this result, it is conceivable that the alpha wave contains particular characteristics. Based on these results, future analysis should be performed from all angles, including deep learning analysis as well as nonlinear analysis, to identify the relationship between Meniere's disease and sleep electroencephalograms. This will make it possible to extract severity and other low-dimensional information; not only dichotomize healthy subjects.

Acknowledgments. *This work was supported in part by the Japan Society for the Promotion of Science, Grant-in-Aid for Scientific Research (C) Number 20K12528, 22K12141 and 23H03678.*

References

1. Lopez-Escamez, J.A., et al.: Diagnostic criteria for Menière's disease. J. Vestib. Res. **25**(1), 1–7 (2015)
2. Takahashi, M., Odagiri, K., Sato, R., Wada, R., Onuki, J.: The systemic application of diazepam facilitates the reacquisition of a well-balanced vestibular function in a unilateral vestibular re-input model with intracochlear tetrodotoxin infusion using an osmotic pump. ORL J. Otorhinol. Relat Spec. **67**, 300–304 (2005)
3. Takeno, K., Shimogori, H., Takemoto, T., Tanaka, K.: Diagnostic criteria for Menière's disease. Brain Reserch **1096**(1), 113–119 (2006)
4. Nakayama, M., Sato, S., Fukui, A., Arima, S.: How do sleep affect balance system?, O.R.L.Tokyo, Vol.60, No.1, pp. 10–16 (2017) (in Japanese)
5. Nakayama, M., Hamajima, Y.: A new therapy for Meniere's disease from the perspective of sleep medicine, Stomato-pharyngol, Vol.25, 1, pp. 35–39 (2012) (in Japanese)
6. Ronneberger, O., Fischer, P., Brox, T.: U-Net: convolutional networks for biomedical image segmentation. In: MICCAI2015, pp. 234–241 (2015)
7. Radford, A., et al.: Learning transferable visual models from natural language supervision. PMLR **139**, 8748–8763 (2021)
8. Rombach, R., Blattmann, A., Lorenz, D., Esser, P., Omme, B.: High-resolution image synthesis with latent diffusion models. In: CVPR2022, pp. 10684–10695 (2022)
9. Kingma, D.P., Welling, M.: Auto-encoding variational bayes. In: Proceedings of ICLR 2014 (2014)
10. Nakane, K., Ichikawa, K., Ono, R., Matsuura, Y., Takada, H.: A study of classification for electrogastrograms before/after caloric intake using autoencoder. In: Antona, M., Stephanidis, C. (eds) Universal Access in Human-Computer Interaction. Design Methods and User Experience. HCII 2021. Lecture Notes in Computer Science, vol 12768. Springer, Cham (2021). https://doi.org/10.1007/978-3-030-78092-0_41
11. Hinton, G.E., Salakhutdinov, R.R.: Reducing the dimensionality of data with neural net-works. Science **313**(5786), 504–507 (2006)
12. Noda, A., Koike, Y.: Polysomnography, JSMBE, Vol.46, No.2, pp. 134–143 (2008) (in Japanese)
13. Yanagisawa, N., Shibasaki, H.: Clinical Neurophysiology, pp. 15–37. Igakushoin, Tokyo (2008) (in Japanese)
14. Boser, B.E., Guyon, I.M., Vapnik, V.N.: A training algorithm for optimal margin classifiers. In: Proceeding of COLT 1992, pp. 144–152 (1992)
15. Kullback, S., Leibler, A.: On information and sufficiency. Ann. Math. Statist **22**(1), 79–86 (1951)
16. Kyunghyun, C., et al.: Learning phrase representations using RNN Encoder-Decoder for statistical machine translation. In: EMNLP, pp. 1724–1734 (2014)
17. Fukushima, K.: Neocognitron: a self-organizing neural network model for a mechanism of pattern recognition unaffected by shift in position. Compet. Coop. Neural Nets **45**, 267–285 (1982)
18. He, K., Zhang, X., Ren, S., Sun, J.: Deep Residual Learning for Image Recognition. In: 2016 IEEE Conference on Computer Vision and Pattern Recognition (CVPR), Las Vegas, NV, USA, pp. 770–778 (2016)
19. Kohavi, R.: A study of cross-validation and bootstrap for accuracy estimation and model selection. In: IJCAI'95, Vol.2, No.12, pp. 1137–1143 (1995)
20. Chang, J., Luo, Y., Su, K.: GPSM: A Generalized Probabilistic Semantic Model for ambiguity resolution, ACL'92, pp. 177–184 (1992)

21. Sugie, R., Takada, H., Nakayama, M., Okazaki, R.: A study on variational autoencoder to extract characteristic patterns from electroencephalograms during sleep. IEEJ Trans. Electron. Inform. Syst. **143**(4), 510–514 (2023). https://doi.org/10.1541/ieejeiss.143.510

22. Berger, H.: Über das Elektrenkephalogramm des Menschen Archiv f. Psychiatrie **87**, 527–570 (1929)

Why Did the User Open the Email? - A Case Study in User Engagement

Pankati Patel[✉] , Uko Ebreso, Alexander Fisher, and Patricia Morreale

Department of Computer Science and Technology, Kean University, Union, NJ 07083, USA
{patpanka,ebresou,fisheral,pmorreal}@kean.edu

Abstract. This case study investigates methods to increase user engagement within an organization. An academic department at a university encourages students to participate in career and academic development opportunities, which are regularly distributed by email. Students have a low engagement with the emails as approximately 30% students view emails and less than 5% of the students interact with hyperlinks embedded within the text. Students are missing valuable opportunities, crucial to their professional and academic development. In this research, a methodology for broadcast communication to a community of students has been developed. First, a pre-survey was given to a wide demographic of students. Utilizing the responses, the same information, drafted using different techniques, was broadcasted to various categories of students. Data was collected on student engagement and compared to answer the research questions on why student engagement is low: (1) Does the presence of an incentive have an impact on a student's engagement? (2) Will broadcasting to a targeted demographic impact student engagement? (3) Does the composition of the information delivered impact student engagement? Interviews, focus groups, and a post-survey were used to gather and triangulate data. Results showed that user engagement doubled with more than 50% of the users opening the engineered email communication. Recommendations include generalizing the subject line, including portable incentives, and considering organizational origination.

Keywords: Human computer interaction · User Engagement · Broadcast Communication

1 Introduction

Career and academic development opportunities are an important aspect for individuals in higher education. These opportunities help a student ascertain what career path they would like to pursue. There are many fields within computer science (CS) and information technology (IT) hence, it is important that these different fields are introduced to students through career and academic development opportunities. An academic department at a public university is used in this case study to investigate methods that will increase student engagement. With over 700 students, career and academic opportunities such as alumni talks, company visits, job opportunities, or club events are broadcasted to students regularly through their university emails. Student engagement with

M. Kurosu et al. (Eds.): HCII 2023, LNCS 14054, pp. 179–193, 2023.
https://doi.org/10.1007/978-3-031-48038-6_12

these emails is low, resulting in missed opportunities. A comprehensive evaluation of the present methodologies employed in disseminating educational content to students were evaluated to determine the effectiveness and shortcomings of these methods. From the results gathered, an automated system was developed that allows the department to broadcast emails to students within a given category. Filters can be applied to create a custom classification of students to broadcast information. This approach allows for career and academic opportunities to be more personalized to the individual, and reduce the abundance of emails students accumulate daily. This system also generates statistics on the total number of students that have engaged with the email being broadcasted by either opening, or clicking on the hyperlinks embedded within the text. A pre-survey was given to a wide demographic of students, pertaining to questions that assessed their engagement and what characteristics influence their decision on opening an email. Utilizing the responses, the same information, drafted in different ways were broadcasted to different categories of students to assess if composition of the information being delivered had an impact on student engagement. Their engagement was assessed through the system to see if broadcasting to a targeted demographic increases the likelihood of students engagement. Emails with incentive were also broadcasting to students to determine if incentive has an impact on student engagement.

2   Related Work

Interactions and responses from students through communication is a vital metric in understanding their perception of potential opportunities and events made possible by Universities. Schemas revolving around engagement can be abridged into three main categories: Behavioral Engagement, Emotional Engagement and Cognitive Engagement [1, 2]. The two main approaches to student engagement can be defined as physical engagement in the form of posters, papers, or verbal communication and digital engagement, in the form of online correspondence, social media, or automated text messaging. It is imperative that academic departments understand the inner mechanisms of student engagement and what specific traits influence.

2.1   Categories of Engagement

Engagement can be defined as a "multi-dimensional" aspect that involves behavioral, emotional, and cognitive properties [1, 2].

Behavioral Engagement. Behavioral engagement comprises primarily student involvement with academic and social activities. Schools are encouraged to invoke attentive, persistent, hardworking, inquisitive and participatory natures within students. Standard ways of doing this is cultivating student interaction with school related activities such as special interest clubs, school government, or athletic clubs/teams.

Emotional Engagement. A Students' attitude, interests, and values in relation to their positive or negative interactions with faculty, students, academics, or the institution make up their emotional engagement. Institutions can increase students' emotional well-being and encourage involvement by giving them a sense of belonging.

Cognitive Engagement. Cognitive engagement combines cognitive and psychological components. The psychological factors that influence whether students are motivated to learn or participate are the inner principles, goals, and values of a student. This influences the decision, whether the activity for engagement is consistent with their values. Whether a student will be involved with career or academic opportunities, and internalize its value depends on cognitive factors (Table 1).

Table 1. Behavioral, emotional, and cognitive engagement categories and components

Category	Behavioral Engagement	Emotional Engagement	Cognitive Engagement
Components	• Positive Conduct • Learning Involvement • Participation in school related activities	• Affective Student Reactions • Emotional Reactions • School Identification	• Self regulated learning • Metacognition • Application of Learning Strategies

2.2 Print vs Digital Advertising Efficacy

Within advertising, the main forms of communication are Print Advertising and Digital Advertising [3]. Print Advertising entails newspaper ads, posters, billboards, flyers, signage, mail or any physical printed/created piece of advertisement. In comparison, Digital Advertising relates to engagement in the form of online ads, website articles, and emails. Regardless of the methodology, both mediums have the shared goal of increasing user engagement and sustaining a loyal audience.

When reaching out to the intended audience, those pitching an idea or an event must be able to convince the audience that their involvement is in their best interest and to present offers of noteworthy value. Part of what distinguishes digital advertising over other methods is that currently, the world is becoming technologically integrated and can encompass aspects from other avenues like sound, images, and/or visual tools [3].

Results of numerous studies [3] contrasting the two media have been ambiguous, with evidence supporting either side or claiming equal efficacy. Important points were made, though, such as the fact that producers had more control over consumers' exposure to online advertising compared to print advertising. 50 male and 50 female students were included in the sample size of 100, and they each completed a survey to help the researchers better understand their tendencies. According to the survey [3], because they spend more time online, students are more likely to be aware of online forms of communication and prefer advertisements with multimedia elements. As a result, students were found to be more interactive with marketers who made use of these features.

3   Background

User engagement with communication in organizations is challenging. An academic department at a public university is used in this case study as an example. With over 700 students, opportunities such as alumni talks, company visits, or research opportunities are regularly announced to students. Job postings are shared with students weekly in the form of an electronic career bulletin. These emails are for students using two tools, the Handshake product and Google's Gmail tool, which manages the university's email system with the Google Workspace tool. The opportunities shared with students are often time-critical and necessary for professional skills development and alignment with internship and graduate opportunities.

3.1   Handshake

Handshake [4] is currently one form of communication being utilized to broadcast emails to students and gather data on their engagement. Handshake is an online recruiting platform widely used in the United States that partners with universities to streamline and simplify the recruiting process. This system allows an academic department at a university to broadcast emails to users who have an active account on Handshake. Emails can be delivered to students within defined categories by choosing filters like major, class standing, or degree program. Employers work with Handshake to distribute internship and job openings nationwide. Statistics on the percentage of students who open an email message, and the percentage of students who click on the hyperlinks embedded within the text of the email can be gathered for every email broadcasted. Analysis gathered from Handshake for this case study showed that student engagement with the broadcast emails was low, as only 30% of targeted students opened the email, and less than 5% of the students clicked on a hyperlink in the email. Broadbase email communication as a method is only successful if all students within the department have an account on Handshake, and if the account is actively updated by the students as they move up class levels. Handshake does not detect if a student has completed a requirement for credits to categorize them within a class level. Hence, if a student fails to update their account they will be distinguished within a misleading category of students.

3.2   Google's Gmail

Another form of communication being utilized to broadcast information is Gmail. Students' university emails are used to broadcast information to all students enrolled in Computer Science (CS) and Information Technology (IT) programs. Although Gmail does offer a way to apply filters on the recipients, it is not automated. Each filter needs to be manually created and the recipients need to be manually entered. Consequently, students start accumulating many emails that may not pertain to their demographic, as some opportunities are beneficial for a particular category of students. Gmail also does not give statistics on the student engagement with emails, if they viewed the email, or if they clicked on embedded hyperlinks. In order to gain these statistics the sender can request read receipts on Google Workspace accounts [5]. This method comes with limitations, as the recipient has the authority to enable and disable their read receipts, this can skew the statistics.

Both approaches used by the department were ineffective in reaching the majority of students. This was clear as student awareness and attendance at events was low. Conversation with other groups, including academic departments, industry employers, and other organizations identified low user engagement in communication as a shared problem.

4 Methodology

The research questions investigated to provide information as to why student engagement is low were:

(1) Does the presence of an incentive have an impact on a student's engagement?
(2) Will broadcasting to a targeted demographic impact student engagement?
(3) Does the composition of the information delivered impact student engagement?

Using the concepts from Handshake, an email broadcasting system was developed that gathers statistics on the percentage of students that open each email and the percentage of students that click on the hyperlinks within each email's body. This system also allows for emails to be personalized, filters can be applied to broadcast to a specific category of students. A pre-survey was given to a wide demographic of students to gather data on how engaged they are within the department, and what characteristics of an email initiate them to open. Using the responses from the pre-survey emails containing the same information were drafted and broadcasted to different categories of students. Using the system, statistics on student engagement was gathered and analyzed.

4.1 Design of Broadcast System

To provide insight and granular control of emails, the Daily Roar, an email broadcasting system, was developed. This system reduces the number of overall student emails sent by allowing emails to be broadcasted based on a given student classification. These classifications include class level (freshman, sophomore, junior, senior), major (CS,IT), and degree program (undergraduate, graduate). By allowing information to be broadcasted based on a specific set of categories, students will receive opportunities that are personalized to them as an audience. Figure 1 highlights the flow of filter selection within the system, where FR denotes freshman, SO denotes sophomore, JR denotes junior, SR denotes senior, and GR denotes graduate.

This system is automated which allows for student information to be uploaded at the beginning of each semester in the form of a CSV file. The information is extracted from the university registrar to ensure that student records are up to date. The system also implements functions that gather statistics on the percentage of students that view the email, and the percentage of students that click on the embedded hyperlinks.

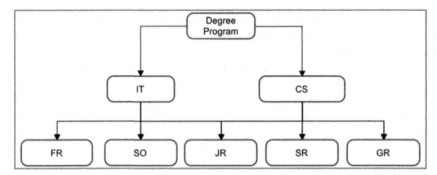

Fig. 1. Filter selection flow chart used in the Daily Roar

Email Viewing Status. The function which indicates if the recipient has viewed the email was implemented by inserting an "img" HTML tag within the body of each sent email, as shown in Fig. 2, a segment of the Daily Roar's source code. As the system sends out emails to each student that falls within the selected filters, the "img" HTML tag's source property is set to the URL of a PHP file called "tracking.php", hosted on the Daily Roar website, rather than to a URL of an actual image. The system embeds query parameters within the tracking URL, signifying which email and which student the embedded URL is for. When the recipient clicks on the email, the "img" tag loads the source URL, essentially executing the PHP file that marks down which student opened which email.

```
$final_body = $new_link_body. '<img src="'.$base_url.'tracking.php?
             email_id='.$email_id .'&student_id='.$ID.'&tracking_type=open"
             width="1" height="1" />';
```

Fig. 2. Code snippet of email viewing status

Hyperlink Click Status. The function which indicates if the recipient has clicked on the hyperlinks embedded within the email body was implemented by using methods similar to that of the email viewing status. To track hyperlinks, before the system sends out emails to each student that falls within the selected filters, the email body's HTML is scanned for any hyperlink, which are known in HTML as "a" tags. For those "a" HTML tags found, the hyperlink property is modified by replacing the hyperlink with the same PHP file used for the email viewing status, "tracking.php". The difference here is that the original hyperlink for each "a" tag is URI encoded and sent through to the PHP file as a query parameter, along with parameters signifying which student opened a hyperlink in which email. Once a student clicks on a link in an email, they will first be redirected to the PHP file that tracks them clicking the link, and then redirects them to the original page the hyperlink was for (Fig. 3).

```
$newUrl = $url.'tracking.php?redirect_url=' . urlencode($url) .
          '&email_id='. $email_id .'&student_id='.$recipient_id .
          "&tracking_type=click";;
```

Fig. 3. Code snippet of hyperlink clicking status

4.2 Pre-survey

Student opinions were gathered through a pre-deployment survey, to learn about their email behavioral patterns, preferences, and potential circumstances that might enhance their interaction with department offered opportunities. Students were presented with questions regarding their preference in email subject lines, what characteristics determined if an email was to be viewed, or how often they were involved in career and academic opportunities. This survey was broadcasted to a wide demographic (n = ~100) of which 35 students responded. The range of class levels in which the respondents belonged to were evenly distributed: 18% Freshman (0–29 credits), 21% Sophomore (30–59 credits), 21% Junior (60–89 credits), 21% Senior (90+ credits), 21% Graduate Students. From the survey it was concluded that the majority (67.6%) of students gain knowledge of academic and career development opportunities through email communication, but 52.9% of the students still are not engaged with these opportunities.

It is important to note that emails being broadcasted through Handshake are directed to students with the name *The School of Computer Science and Technology*. Emails being broadcasted through Gamil are directed to students with the faculties name. Students were asked how often they viewed emails broadcasted within these categories. According to the analysis, students' engagement was significantly greater with communication from one entity that is associated with prevalent content than they did with communication that was dispersed and distributed from a specific individual (Figs. 4 and 5).

Further questions were asked to the students about what characteristics determined if they opened an email. They were provided with six email subject lines, which were used in previous emails, and asked to pick which prompt would likely lead to engagement. The subject line is as follows:

(1) Reminder: Java Review Happening Today & More
(2) Need an Internship? Or a Job? UNITED HEALTH GROUP, L3Harris Technologies & More
(3) Mid-Summer Check-In + Opportunities
(4) *Urgent* Thursday @ 3pm - Mini Research Presentation Availability
(5) Research Opportunity for Undergraduates in Computing Sciences
(6) CAHSI Local REU Program is Summer REU | Deadline April 14th

The results from the survey show that 58.8% of students consider the subject line before they open an email. For the preference in subject lines there was a combination of selections. Students preferred a combination of buzz words (urgent, reminder, important), creativeness, or date of the event in the subject line (Fig. 7).

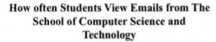

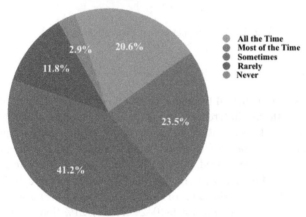

Fig. 4. Survey results from how often students view emails from The School of Computer Science and Technology

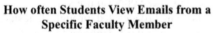

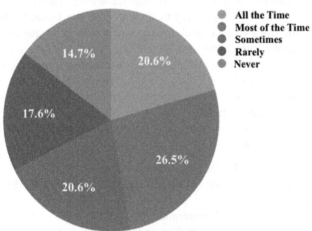

Fig. 5. Survey results from how often students view emails from a specific faculty member

**Aspect of an Email a Student Considers
Before Engaging**

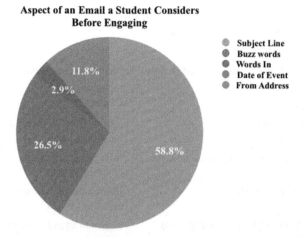

Fig. 6. Survey Results from aspects of an email a students notices before engaging

Subject Lines That Intrigue Students

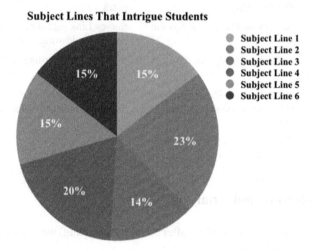

Fig. 7. Survey response from the subject lines that intrigued students

4.3 Drafting Emails

After analyzing the data that was gathered from the pre-survey emails were drafted and broadcasted to different categories of students. Figure 6 outlines the importance of an email subject line. Utilizing this finding, different subject lines were drafted incorporating buzz words, incentive, and date of events. The email body was crafted with both extensive and short text with embedded hyperlinks at the end of the message. The subject line and content of the emails are highlighted in Table 3. The first three emails were broadcasted to test the system. After successful testing, the system was given to a faculty member to send regular academic and career development opportunity broadcasts. In total eight emails were broadcasted, and using the Daily Roar System engagement was monitored (Table 2).

Table 2. Broadcasted Emails with Content Description

Email	Subject Line	Content
1	The Daily Roar is here!	Informational message about the new emailing system
2	[Important] Notice For Research Days	Informational message about the new emailing system
3	The Daily Roar is Here!	Informational message about the new emailing system
4	[TOMORROW] RSVP For Pizza and Senior Showcase	Notice to attend event and RSVP for pizza
5	[TOMORROW] RSVP FOR PIZZA AND SENIOR SHOWCASE	Notice to attend event and RSVP for pizza
6	Student Feedback on Daily Roar System [Survey]	Survey Link regarding feedback on the email broadcasting system
7	Student Feedback on Daily Roar System [Survey]	Survey Link regarding feedback on the email broadcasting system
8	Today's the Day! Senior Showcase, Grad Cords and Resume Reviews! Oh Yeah, did we mention Pizza!	Final notice for event occurring on that date with monetary value of pizza

5   Data Collection and Analysis

Interviews, focus groups, and surveys (after email broadcasting) were used to gather and triangulate data for analysis.

5.1   Email Data

The Email Broadcasting system was used to send emails, and the platform was used to monitor student engagement. To help determine what factors affect metrics like email opening rate and link click-through rate, eight emails with different aspects were sent. The data pool was split into two categories, Freshman/Sophomores (Group 1) and Junior/Senior/Graduates (Group 2), similar to the survey mentioned earlier. 8 emails were sent over the course of 3 days with characteristics and results to all students within the Department of Computer Science and Technology highlighted in Table 3.

Table 3. Statistics of Emails Broadcasted

Email	Total Recipients	Recipient Categories	Open Rate (Percentage)	Click Rate (Percentage)
1	395	Freshmen, Sophomores	55.19%	1.01%
2	366	Junior, Senior and Graduates	3.83%	1.09%
3	366	Junior, Senior and Graduates	56.01%	1.64%
4	17	Graduates	82.35%	35.39%
5	744	Freshmen, Sophomore, Junior, Senior	58.87%	3.63%
6	395	Freshman, Sophomore	72.91%	3.80%
7	366	Junior, Senior, Graduate	65.85%	4.64%
8	761	Freshmen, Sophomore, Junior, Senior, Graduate	68.99%	3.02%

In comparison to Group 1, Group 2 members generally had a lower open rate. It's crucial to recognize the variations between emails 1 through 3. Both emails—Email 1 to Group 1 and Email 2 to Group 2—contained the same information. Other than target audience, the subject line of the email was the primary distinction between these two. Email 2's subject line contained more keywords related to the mail's subject, while Email 1's was more broadly worded. As a result, Email 1 had an open rate of 55.19% and Email 2 had an open rate of 3.83%. Students told researchers that certain subject line keywords immediately discouraged them from opening the email, which was covered in more detail in the interview section. Email 3 was identical to Email 2, with the exception that it had the same subject as Email 1. Following this modification, Email 3 generated a 56.01% open rate. The open rates for emails 4 through 8 ranged from 58% to 82%. These emails were used to inform students about events while avoiding any particularly technical terminology. With email 4 being the only one with the smallest recipient pool, link click rates were almost always under 5%.

5.2 Post Survey

A post-deployment survey was distributed to students following the deployment of the email broadcasting system. Freshman/Sophomores (Group 1) and Junior/Senior/Graduates (Group 2) comprised the two groups that made up the sample pool for this study. The same 7 questions were posed to both groups:

1. What prompted you to open the email sent by the Daily Roar System?
2. For those who clicked the link in the email, please tell us why you clicked the link
3. Did you read the full contents of the email?

4. What does your current inbox look like?
5. How do you currently receive information regarding job opportunities and/or campus events?
6. Would you interact and engage with more department emails and events if there was a potential reward attached to it for having the most engagement?
7. Which of these Email headers are you more likely to engage with?

62.5% and 58.3% of Groups 1 and 2 respectively indicated that the main reason they opened the email was to learn more about the new system. Between the two groups, there was a significant difference in link click through rates. 25% of Group 1 either felt like clicking the link or didn't click the link at all, while 25% of Group 1 wanted to know where the link redirected. 25% of members of Group 2 clicked the link simply because they felt like it or because they were curious to see where it led, respectively, while 37.5% did not click the link at all. Only 62.5% of the participants from Group 1 read the email in its entirety, compared to 83.3% of participants from Group 2. In Group 1, 50% of respondents said their inboxes were cluttered and disorganized, compared to 75% in Group 2 who said they had finished reading all of their emails. Emails accounted for 87.5% of Group 1's and 100% of Group 2's communication regarding job openings and campus events, respectively. Their second-highest selections are interestingly different, with Group 1 choosing "word of mouth" at 75% and Group 2 choosing posters at 66.7%. At 87.5% and 75%, correspondingly, Groups 1 and 2 expressed interest in potential rewards for greater engagement. Headers with monetary values, like "Free Pizza", produced the highest percentages for both groups, 50% each.

After examining the post-survey data, it can be inferred that having a single source of information is more likely to engage students than having the same information sent through faculty-specific emails. Comparatively to participants in Group 1, participants from Group 2 were less likely to open the email to start the engagement. Early findings suggest that Group 1 participants are more engaged as they adjust to higher institution environments, whereas Group 2 participants have behavioral engagement habits that have been ingrained since earlier in their education. Compared to Group 1, Group 2 had a 50% higher likelihood of reading most of their emails. As a result, it can be assumed that Freshmen and Sophomores are not thinking about organizing and keeping track of their email as they adjust to their new institution. Seniors, Juniors, and Graduates can monitor the status of their emails, most likely after developing organizational and time-management skills. Because 87.5% and 100% of the members of Groups 1 and 2 respectively are aware that there are currently job opportunities available by means of email, there is still some level of engagement with emails. Participants appear to be drawn to the idea of receiving rewards in the form of money for showing noteworthy engagement with institutions' emails and events, with Group 1 aligning more closely with this than Group 2. Because Group 2 has been at the institution longer and has a preconceived idea of what potential incentives may be, early analysis is pointing to the possibility that behavioral and cognitive engagement plays a role in this difference. More supporting evidence is evident by Email Subject lines containing an incentive generated a more positive response.

5.3 Interviews and Focus Groups

Students who received emails were asked to participate in focus groups and individual interviews to provide feedback on the Daily Roar Email and to learn more about the current characteristics of student engagement. 15 students were interviewed for this section. "How do you feel about the previous system used to send emails regarding school events and opportunities?" was the question posed to student A. Student A who was a senior and an Army Reserve responded that they thought the previous system of various staff members sending out various opportunities and events was cumbersome and disorganized. In the experiment, two emails with the same bodies but different headers were sent (Emails 2 and 3). "Why did they open one of the emails but not the other?" was the next question posed to Student A. In response, they said that because of their busy schedules, the header's discussion of any research discouraged them from engaging, but the email's discussion of a new campus system encouraged it because they approached it unbiasedly. This information indicates that specific keywords in email subject lines and headers have an impact on students' behavioral and cognitive engagement with an institution's emails because of the hectic and varied schedules that students have. Even if the email's contents apply to them, students won't be engaged if the keywords are in conflict with their internal values.

Junior in college Student B agreed that the new broadcast system's ability to deliver emails to them quickly and succinctly made the previous method of communication ineffective. Student B added that the length of emails affected whether or not they were read. They found that compared to brief, concise emails, a sea of text was challenging to follow. For longer emails, they requested a table of contents so they could quickly determine whether an email was relevant to them or not.

Email data hinted that there was a correlation between class level and engagement was supported by interviews with the students. While juniors, seniors, and graduates were less engaged because they were accustomed to previous forms of communication and instead looked to outside sources for job opportunities and events, freshmen and sophomores were more open to the idea of communication for events and job opportunities.

The next step was to create and interview focus groups of students who had received emails to get their feedback on email engagement and potential improvement areas. 40 students from the Department of Computer Science and Technology were divided into groups of five to form focus groups. Students were free to express their opinions about the new communication channel in these groups. The requirement for a table of contents for lengthy emails was a topic that was frequently brought up. As they believe it is unreasonable to expect recipients to read every email sent to them, they claimed that if a large email was sent, having a table of contents for large emails will help them decide whether an email is worthwhile to them or not. The possibility of incentives to boost student responses was a further topic of discussion [6]. Students are encouraged to engage with emails frequently, take advantage of job opportunities, and attend institution events by giving them a monetary value. The potential monetary value was a crucial factor. Because they saw no use for certain incentives, some students displayed less interest in them. The focus groups received less positive responses to concepts like pizza parties and campus clothing that is already in widespread use. New school supplies like laptops, cash prizes in the form of gift cards, and campus money, if available, were among the many responses that produced positive feedback. All of these had one thing in common: they were items that helped both campus lifestyle and their own individual endeavors. This relates to the earlier idea of cognitive and emotional engagement because students would respond favorably to emails about the advantages of interaction if the incentive for participating improved their lives and if they could use the incentive.

6 Results

In this study there were three main questions that served as objectives:

1. Does the presence of an incentive have an impact on a student's engagement?
2. Will broadcasting to a targeted demographic impact student engagement?
3. Does the composition of the information delivered impact student engagement?

The study revealed that incentives would increase students' interest in email communication in response to research question 1. Focus groups and email data revealed that students would be more likely to participate if an incentive were offered to them. When compared to their counterparts, emails that mentioned pizza at events had higher open rates and link click-through rates.

Regarding research question 2, email data is consistent with the notion that emails sent to specific demographics will elicit different responses. Less engagement was displayed by recipients in their junior and higher years than by sophomores and freshmen. According to analysis thus far, freshmen and sophomores are more engaged because they are unfamiliar with campus life and want to stay on top of any new information as soon as possible. Due to the fact that they are already accustomed to the institution's communication standards, juniors, seniors, and graduates most likely have a lower engagement rate.

Finally, it is reasonable to assume that the content of emails influences students' engagement. Interviews and focus groups revealed that longer emails received fewer responses, and subject lines, headers, and the use of keywords all affected how well recipients were engaged. In order to draw students in, keywords must reflect their personal values.

The results from the usage of the Daily Roar system showed that with the new system on average user engagement doubled with more than 50% of the users opening the engineered email communication. The Daily Roar's open email rate was 60.13% which was a 100.43% increase from the previous methodologies of communication utilized by the university. The email click rate was 6.77% which was a 35.4% increase from the aforementioned methodology.

7 Future Work

In the future, here are some concepts, ideas and research questions that could be investigated after conducting this study.

– What types of incentives have the greatest impact on student interaction?

- Do demographics such as gender, ethnicity, home city, major, campus presence have an impact on student interaction?
- Is there a correlation between the time emails are broadcasted and interaction?
- Does adding multimedia to emails increase student engagement?

Each of these could serve to bolster or expand upon the findings of this study.

References

1. Lester, D.: A review of the student engagement literature. Natl. Forum J. **7**(1), 1–3 (2013)
2. Fredericks, J.A., Blumenfeld, P.C., Paris, A.H.: School engagement: potential of the concept, state of the evidence. Rev. Educ. Res. **74**(1), 59–109 (2004)
3. Vinaya Kumar, C.M., Mehrotra, S.: Print vs. online advertising: impact on buying behavior of youth. Glob. Media J. **16**(31), 1 (2018)
4. Handshake Homepage. https://joinhandshake.com. Accessed 2 Apr 2023
5. Sachin: Gmail email tracking: how to track email opens and clicks in Gmail. Mass Email & Mail Merge for Gmail. Gmass Blog (2022). https://www.gmass.co/blog/gmail-email-tracking-track-opens-clicks/#:~:text=You%20can%20track%20Gmail%20email,link%20tracking%20in%20Google%20Analytics
6. Levitt, S.D., List, J.A., Sadoff, S.: The effect of performance-based incentives on educational achievement: evidence from a randomized experiment. Nber Working Paper Series (2016)

Research on the Efficiency and Cognition of the Combination of Front Color and Background Color and Color in the Interface of Express Cabinets on the Operation of Human Machine Interface Tasks

Yuying Pei, Linlin Wang, and Chengqi Xue[✉]

School of Mechanical Engineering, Southeast University, Nanjing 211189, Jiangsu, China
ipd_xcq@seu.edu.c

Abstract. With the development of Internet technology, a large number of interfaces are needed to assist people in their daily life. Therefore, the design of the interface has an important impact on the efficiency of users' task completion and user experience. Among the interface elements, color is one of the main factors that directly impact the user's vision. Therefore, In this paper, we will focus on designing color matching schemes of different foreground colors and background colors, and study the effect of the matching of lightness and saturation in colors on the efficiency of users to complete tasks with the help of eye tracker. Through comparative analysis, we can get the most efficient color lightness and saturation matching scheme, which provides a reference for the matching of foreground colors and background colors in the future interface color design. In this paper, based on the design of the Nearby Express Cabinet interface, we changed the brightness and saturation of the foreground and background colors of the interface, combined 21 different brightness and saturation combination interfaces, and conducted experimental research to study the impact of different interface color states on user cognitive efficiency. Through the comparative analysis of the experimental data, the law of the influence of the change of the color of the interactive interface on the picking task is obtained.

Keywords: Express interface · Color · saturation · Lightness · Operation Efficiency · Eye Movement Experiment

1 Research Background

Anlu [1] and others started from color psychology, through the application of Smarteye5.4 eye tracker equipment, combined with the questionnaire survey. Point scale was used for evaluation, and 15 college students were taken as subjects to record their reading of PPT with different color backgrounds and analyze. The influence of background color on learners. It is found that white is the most suitable background color for PPT,

M. Kurosu et al. (Eds.): HCII 2023, LNCS 14054, pp. 194–212, 2023.
https://doi.org/10.1007/978-3-031-48038-6_13

followed by yellow, and blue is the least. Suitable as background color. To provide reference for designers from a scientific perspective, and to design and open the multimedia courseware competition in China. Development has an important enlightening effect. Wang Qiuhui [2] and others explored the visual perception of service robot design color to the elderly in the context of the wide application of intelligent elderly care Impact of performance. 24 elderly subjects were selected for eye movement experiment, and their eye movements were obtained when they observed 8 groups of experimental pictures Indicators. First of all, objective analysis was conducted on the two eye movement data of total fixation times and first fixation time, using univariate variance. Analyze and verify the significance of data; Secondly, the data of the elderly and young subjects were analyzed by t-test to study different years. Whether there are differences in visual cognitive performance of service robot color design among users of different ages; Finally, use correlation analysis method Verify whether color weakness will affect the visual cognitive performance of the elderly. It is concluded that the elderly are sensitive to black and are very easy to ignore white, There is no significant difference between warm and cold colors; Users of different age groups pay different attention to color; Weak color will slightly affect aging. The visual cognitive performance of young people will not affect their choice of color. Sun Bowen [3] and others explored the color design in the context of the wide application of information technology and digital technology in the field of vehicle human-computer interaction. Consider ways to improve vehicle human-computer interface and improve user driving experience. From the relationship level, classification level and use level of color. Analyze the color elements of the human-computer interface of the vehicle, invite the subjects to have a simulation experience, and measure the number of experiences through eye movement experiment. According to the objective analysis and subjective evaluation, evaluate the color design in the vehicle human-computer interface. Cui Yu [4] pointed out the saturation range value of the background color icon color in the interface color analysis and experimental study of the eye control system, so the data selection will be based on the relevant conclusions given in this experiment. LIU Tiru [5] By studying the interface design of the in-vehicle system, the Tobii Pro Glasses2 wearable eye tracker is used to test the color of the in-vehicle HMI interface sample, including the output of eye tracking data such as eye tracking map, heat map and AOI area of interest fixation duration, and analyze and verify the accuracy of the eye tracking data [6].

2   Research Hypothesis

There are three basic ways of eye movement: fixation, saccades and Pursuit Movement 1. The effect of color on the express cabinet interface. All hypotheses are divided into three groups of experimental data: background color saturation change correlation experiment, color brightness [7].

Degree change related experiment, different saturation background and different brightness foreground change related experiment [8].

Hypothesis 1: The foreground and background colors with different lightness and saturation have a significant impact on the efficiency of college students' information acquisition.

Hypothesis 2: The foreground and background colors with different lightness and saturation have a significant impact on the difficulty of obtaining information for college students.

Hypothesis 3: The foreground and background colors with different lightness and saturation have significant differences in the eye-catching degree of the keyboard in the interface.

Hypothesis 4: The foreground and background colors with different lightness and saturation have a significant impact on the concentration of information obtained by college students.

3   Research Methods

Based on the literature review, this paper mainly adopts the empirical research methods and qualitative research methods advocated by management science. Root theory and structural equation are used for empirical analysis. The research methods can be summarized as follows: literature research method, experimental method, etc. [9].

3.1   Literature Research Method

A large number of documents related to team communication and team cohesion have been retrieved through databases such as China Journals Network and China Knowledge Network Information. Through the sorting and analysis of the literature, we can learn about team communication, team performance, team cohesion and The current situation of team performance research has laid a solid theoretical foundation for the construction of this theoretical framework [10].

3.2   Experimental Research Method

The data obtained according to the implementation of specific experiments provide strong data support for this study. It is a method to control certain conditions and conduct research with the help of special experimental instruments. Explore independent variables and causes A method of the relationship between variables [11].

3.3   Paired Sample t-Test

The subjects were paired according to the principle of similar important characteristics, and two individuals in each pair were randomly given two treatments [12].

It is called random paired design.

3.4   Independent Sample t-Test

Independent sample t-test (there is no correlation between the experimental treatment groups, that is, independent sample) is used to test the two groups. The difference of data obtained by relevant sample subjects [13].

3.5 Analysis of Repeated Measurement Variance

Analysis of variance of repeated measurement data is an experimental design technique for repeated measurement of the same dependent variable. In giving one Observation of indicators obtained by repeated measurement of the same subject at different time points after one or more treatments. Value, or the observed value of the index obtained by repeatedly measuring different parts (or tissues) of the same individual [14].

4 Experimental Design

4.1 Experimental Preparation

1. Selection of subjects for the experiment: 24 undergraduate students majoring in industrial design were selected, including 12 boys and 12 girls, with an average age of 20 years old. The subjects had an eye degree between 300 hyperopia and 600 nearsightedness or normal vision, and had no symptoms of color blindness or color weakness. Before the test, the subjects were asked to avoid stimulating or numbing food such as coffee and alcohol. Divide 24 participants into three groups, each consisting of 8 individuals, with half male and half female.

Experimental instruments: computer, TOBII eye tracker, mobile phone.

4.2 Experiment

1. Experimental Title: Research on the Impact of Color Design on the Pickup Screen of Express Cabinets on User Access to Information
2. Experimental Purpose
   (1) In the case of main tone color matching design, experimental tests are conducted to compare the brightness and saturation to test the changes in visual comfort. Explore the relationship between visual comfort and the brightness and saturation of colors in the same background.
   (2) Analyze whether there is a comfort matching pattern in color design based on experimental data, and find the best combination of comfort in color design.
3. Experimental hypothesis:
4. Experimental explanation: A brief analysis was conducted on the color design principles of the experimental interface category (express cabinet interface), in order to determine the experimental object.
5. Experimental materials

Divide the saturation of colors into three gradients: high saturation, original saturation, and low saturation; Similarly, brightness is divided into three stages: original brightness, medium brightness, and low brightness for experiments. In the background color, saturation is set at 12%, 36%, and 60% as low, medium, and high values. Brightness values of 22%, 44%, and 66% are used as low, raw, and high values. In the foreground color (text), the brightness is set at 33%, 66%, and 100% (original) as the low, medium, and original values. There are a total of 18 test interfaces arranged and combined (Figs. 1 and 2).

Fig. 1. Background color change

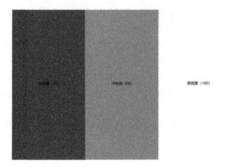

Fig. 2. Foreground color change

(1) Color saturation related experiments

In this summary experiment, the saturation of the background color was changed while maintaining brightness in the same color phase, to explore the impact of interface saturation on the efficiency of user information acquisition (Table 1 and Fig. 3).

Table 1. Color Matching Table

Background color	Low saturation	Original saturation	High Saturation
Foreground color	Original saturation	Original saturation	Original saturation

(2) Experiments related to changes in color brightness

This summary experiment changes the brightness of the foreground and background colors while maintaining saturation, and explores the impact of interface brightness on the efficiency of user information acquisition. The specific experimental sample color matching is shown in the table below (Table 2 and Fig. 4):

(3) Experiment on the Changes of Different Saturation Background and Brightness Foreground (Table 3)

Fig. 3. Interface color matching (Color figure online)

Table 2. Color Matching Table

Background color	Low brightness	Original brightness	High Brightness
Foreground color	Low brightness	Low brightness	Low brightness
	Medium brightness	Medium brightness	Medium brightness
	Original brightness	original brightness	original brightness

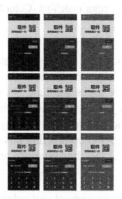

Fig. 4. Interface color matching (Color figure online)

Table 3. Color Matching Table

Background color	Low saturation	Original saturation	High Saturation
Foreground color	Low brightness	Low brightness	Low brightness
	Medium brightness	Medium brightness	Medium brightness
	Original brightness	Original brightness	Original brightness

This summary mainly focuses on the experimental research of color matching in the same color phase, with background changing saturation and foreground changing brightness. Use the original color of the express cabinet interface as the main color tone to change the above color attributes, and the specific combinations are shown in the table below (Fig. 5).

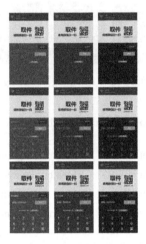

Fig. 5. Interface color matching (Color figure online)

6. Subject arrangement: 24 participants will conduct the experiment. The experiment will play 17 sets of images in sequence. Before viewing each interface, participants will first watch a string of three digits and have 5 s to remember these three digits. After 5 s, the participants will jump to the courier pickup page. They need to search for these three numbers on the pickup page and say the numbers that repeat these three numbers in the interface. After completing this action, click the mouse to jump to the next set of images. Repeat the above steps to browse through the 17 interfaces.
7. Experimental process

(1) Observation of the display equipment and color model used in the experiment: This study used the HSB color mode to perform attribute changes. The experimental samples used a courier cabinet interface, with a size of 4.7 in. and a font size of 28px for the experimental text. The experiment was conducted in a quiet natural light environment, with images displayed on an Apple AIR laptop screen. The screen size was 13.3 in., the resolution was 1440 × 900, and the screen brightness was 315lx.

This article preliminarily selects the original interface of the express delivery cabinet for experiments, with the aim of testing whether the combination of foreground and background colors has an impact on users' information acquisition under the changes in the basic properties of saturation and brightness colors. Provide participants with a rough description of the design plan to be tested, allowing them to complete tasks according to the process.

5   Data Analysis

5.1   Data Collection Indicators

Eye movement technology extracts data such as gaze point, gaze time, gaze frequency, saccade distance, pupil size, etc. from the recording of eye movement trajectories, in order to study individuals' internal cognitive processes. The structure of modern eye trackers generally includes four systems, namely optical system, pupil center coordinate extraction system, scene and pupil coordinate superposition system, and image and data recording and analysis system. There are three basic ways of eye movement: fixation, saccades, and Pursuit Movement.

1. Gazing refers to aligning the central fovea of the eye with an object. When the eye is fixed on an object, even a stationary object, it is not motionless, but accompanied by three types of eye movement effects: Drift, Tremor, and small involuntary saccades.
2. Eye twitching was discovered by Professor Javal from the University of Paris. Usually, we don't easily notice that our eyes are beating, but rather feel that they are moving smoothly. For example, when people are reading or observing objects, they always believe that their eyes smoothly follow the expected line of sight trajectory. In fact, the eye stays on the object being gazed at, and then continues to stay at the next point of gaze. Because the dwell speed is extremely short, it cannot be distinguished by the naked eye, and the trajectory of eye movements on eye tracking devices is very clear.
3. When people observe a line of text, in order to keep their heads straight, their eyes must follow the object for movement, which leads to following motion.

When analyzing the user's pickup process, the following main parameters can be considered:

(1) Gazing time refers to the time spent focusing on a fixation point. Gazing time reflects the participant's level of attention to material processing, and is also influenced by factors such as the length, difficulty, and layout of the material.
(2) The number of fixations refers to the number of fixations. The number of fixations reflects the familiarity and difficulty of the subject with the interface, which is closely related to the duration of the fixation.
(3) The first glance time represents the time it takes the subject to observe the area of interest for the first time, which is used to reflect the attraction of the area of interest to people ability, which is an important indicator of how eye-catching an interface is.
(4) The average fixation time represents the ratio of total fixation time to total fixation points in the region of interest, which is used to reflect the distinguishability of information.
(5) The number of fixation points represents the number of points that the subject focuses on in the area of interest, which reflects search efficiency and degree of interest. The average fixation time represents the ratio of total fixation time to total fixation points in the area of interest, which reflects the distinguishability of information.
(6) The percentage of fixation time in the area of interest to the total fixation time refers to the percentage of time the subject spends browsing the entire interface while

focusing on the target area. The larger the proportion, the more attention resources the target area occupies.

A hot spot map is a visual form that displays visual behavioral features by overlaying eye movement data from multiple subjects, reflecting the distribution of line of sight trajectories and intuitively displaying the key areas of visual attention on the interface. It not only represents the central tendency and dwell time of multiple subjects' gaze on the same page, but also represents the eye movement patterns superimposed by multiple subjects on the same interface. The colored areas on the hotspot map represent the areas that were observed during the observation process, the red areas indicate long fixation time, the yellow areas indicate average fixation time, and the green areas indicate less fixation time.

(1) Fixation time
Gazing time refers to the efficiency of the subject's acquisition of the target.

Background color saturation related experiments (Table 4)
The significance of the lower limit Mochilai sphericity test was <0.05, and the significance of the Billet trajectory in the multivariate test was <0.05, indicating a significant difference in the search time of participants under different brightness background colors and foreground colors. Through pairwise comparison, it was found that the search time under the condition of low saturation of the background color and the original brightness of the foreground color was significantly shorter than that under other different brightness conditions.

Experiments related to changes in color brightness (Table 5):
The significance of the Mochilai sphericity test was <0.05, and the significance of the Billet trajectory in the multivariate test was <0.05, indicating a significant difference in the search time of participants under different brightness background colors and foreground colors. Through pairwise comparison, it was found that the search time under brightness conditions in high brightness foreground colors was significantly shorter than that under other different brightness conditions.

Experiment on the Changes of Different Saturation Background and Brightness Foreground
Obtained using the same analysis method as above
The significance of the Mochilai sphericity test was <0.05, and the significance of the Billet trajectory in the multivariate test was <0.05, indicating a significant difference in the search time of participants under different brightness background colors and foreground colors. Through pairwise comparison, it was found that the search time under the condition of low saturation of the background color and the original brightness of the foreground color was significantly shorter than that under other different brightness conditions.

Minimum time comparison

After three sets of multiple analyses, it was found that the search time under the conditions of low saturation of the background color, original brightness, and high brightness of the background color, medium brightness, was the smallest within the group. Paired sample testing was conducted to obtain the optimal combination with the smallest search time (Table 6).

Table 4. Data Analysis Table

Mochilai sphericity test [a]							
Intrasubjective effects	Mochilai W	Approximate card square	freedom	significance	Epsilon [b]		
Background color saturation	.66	7.61	2.00	.02	.74	.79	.50
Multivariate Test [a]							
		Value	F	Error degree of freedom	significance		
Backgroundcolor saturation	Billet trajectory	.67	.67	.67	.67		
	Wilk Lambda	.33	18.397	18.00	.00		
	Hotelling trajectory	2.04	18.397	18.00	.00		
	Roy's largest root	2.04	18.397	18.00	.00		

paired comparison

					95% confidence interval b of the difference	
(I) Background color saturation		Mean difference (I-J)	error	Significance b	lower limit	
1	2	-1.719[*]	.35	.00	(2.46)	
	3	-.965[*]	.22	.00	(1.42)	
2	1	1.719[*]	.35	.00	.98	
	3	.75	.40	.07	(0.08)	
3	1	.965[*]	.22	.00	.51	
	2	(0.75)	.40	.07	(1.58)	

Table 5. Data Analysis Table

Mochilai sphericity test [a]

Intrasubjective effects	Mauchly W	Approximate chi square	freedom	significance	Significance Greenhouse Gessler	Feidete	lower limit
						Epsilon[b]	
color value	.01	77.07	35.00	.00	.46	.58	.13

Multivariate test [a]

effect		Value	F	Assuming degrees of freedom	Error degree of freedom	significance
color value	Billet trajectory	.95	30.041b	8.00	12.00	.00
	Wilk Lambda	.05	30.041b	8.00	12.00	.00
	Hotelling trajectory	20.03	30.041b	8.00	12.00	.00
	Roy's largest root	20.03	30.041b	8.00	12.00	.00

Paired comparison

(I) Color brightness	(J) color value	Mean difference (I-J)	error	significance[b]	95% confidence interval b of the difference	
					Lower	upper
1	2	1.467*	.20	.00	1.05	1.89
	3	1.601*	.33	.00	.92	2.28
	4	2.002*	.23	.00	1.51	2.49
	5	1.357*	.35	.00	.62	2.10
	6	2.401*	.32	.00	1.73	3.07
	7	1.163*	.30	.00	.53	1.79
	8	.930*	.36	.02	.19	1.67
	9	1.575*	.36	.00	.82	2.33

(*continued*)

Table 5. (*continued*)

2	3	.13	.19	.50	-.27	.54
	4	.535*	.16	.00	.21	.86
	5	-.11	.26	.67	-.64	.42
	6	.934*	.17	.00	.59	1.28
	7	-.31	.16	.07	-.64	.03
	8	-.538*	.23	.03	-1.02	-.06
	9	.11	.20	.60	-.32	.53
3	4	.40	.20	.06	-.01	.82
	5	-.24	.33	.46	-.93	.44
	6	.800*	.18	.00	.42	1.18
	7	-.438*	.20	.04	-.85	-.02
	8	-.671*	.22	.01	-1.12	-.22
	9	-.03	.17	.88	-.38	.33
4	5	-.645*	.26	.02	-1.19	-.10
	6	.399*	.18	.04	.03	.77
	7	-.840*	.16	.00	-1.18	-.50
	8	-1.073*	.23	.00	-1.56	-.58
	9	-.43	.22	.07	-.89	.03
5	6	1.044*	.23	.00	.56	1.53
	7	-.20	.20	.35	-.62	.23
	8	-.43	.22	.07	-.88	.03
	9	.22	.28	.44	-.36	.80
6	7	-1.238*	.16	.00	-1.56	-.91
	8	-1.471*	.18	.00	-1.85	-1.10
	9	-.826*	.14	.00	-1.12	-.53
7	8	-.23	.20	.26	-.65	.19
	9	.41	.21	.06	-.03	.85
8	9	.645*	.21	.01	.20	1.09

In paired sample testing, sig <0.05, indicating a significant difference in time between the two. Through paired sample statistics, it can be concluded that low saturation of background color and original brightness of foreground color have the best effect on the efficiency of subjects in obtaining information.

Table 6. Data Analysis Table

Paired sample correlation				
		Number of cases	correlation	significance
Pairing 1	278 & 120	20	.76	.00

(2) Number of fixation points

The number of fixations reflects the difficulty of the retrieval interface.

Related experiments on background color saturation

The significance of Mochilai sphericity test was <0.05, and the significance of Billet trajectory in multivariate test was <0.05, indicating a significant difference in the number of fixation points in the interface area of interest under different brightness background colors and foreground colors. Through pairwise comparison, it was found that the number of fixation points under the original brightness condition of the low saturation foreground color was significantly smaller than that under other different brightness conditions.

Experiments related to changes in color brightness:

The significance of Mochilai sphericity test was <0.05, and the significance of Billet trajectory in multivariate test was <0.05, indicating a significant difference in the number of fixation points in the region of interest under different brightness background colors and foreground colors. Through pairwise comparison, it was found that the number of fixation points under brightness conditions in the high brightness foreground of the background color was significantly smaller than that under other different brightness conditions.

Experiment on the Changes of Different Saturation Background and Brightness Foreground

The significance of Mochilai sphericity test was less than 0.05, and the significance of Billet trajectory in multivariate test was less than 0.05, indicating a significant difference in the number of fixation points in the area of interest of the interface under different background colors and foreground colors. Through pairwise comparison, it was found that the number of fixation points under the original brightness condition of the low saturation foreground color was significantly smaller than that under other different brightness conditions.

Minimum fixation point comparison

After three sets of multiple analyses, it was found that the number of fixation points under the original brightness conditions of low saturation foreground colors and high brightness foreground colors was the least within the group. Paired sample testing was conducted to obtain the best combination with the least fixation points and the easiest to obtain information.

In paired sample testing, sig >0.05, therefore the difference in time between the two is not significant, and it is not possible to determine the optimal combination with the least fixation points between the two.

(3) First time entering the interest zone

Divide the keyboard into areas of interest, indicating the eye-catching level of the keyboard under different colors.

Related experiments on background color saturation.

The significance of the Mochilai sphericity test was <0.05, and the significance of the Billet trajectory in the multivariate test was <0.05, indicating a significant difference in the eye-catching degree of the keyboard under different brightness background colors and foreground colors. Through pairwise comparison, it was found that the first entry time into the region of interest under the original brightness condition of the low saturation foreground color was significantly shorter than that under other different brightness conditions.

Experiments related to changes in color brightness:

The significance of the Mochilai sphericity test was <0.05, and the significance of the Billet trajectory in the multivariate test was <0.05, indicating a significant difference in the eye-catching degree of the keyboard under different brightness background colors and foreground colors. Through pairwise comparison, it was found that the first entry time into the region of interest under high brightness background colors and low brightness foreground colors was significantly shorter than under other different brightness conditions.

Experiment on the Changes of Different Saturation Background and Brightness Foreground

he significance of the Mochilai sphericity test was <0.05, and the significance of the Billet trajectory in the multivariate test was <0.05, indicating a significant difference in the eye-catching degree of the keyboard under different brightness background colors and foreground colors. Through pairwise comparison, it was found that the first entry time into the region of interest under the original brightness condition of the low saturation foreground color was significantly shorter than that under other different brightness conditions.

(4) Minimum First Entry Time Comparison

After three sets of multiple analyses, it was found that the first entry time into the region of interest under the conditions of high brightness of the background color, low brightness of the foreground color, and medium brightness of the background color, was the smallest within the group. Now, paired sample testing is conducted to obtain the optimal combination with the smallest first entry time into the region of interest.

In paired sample testing, sig >0.05, therefore there is no significant difference in the time of first entry into the region of interest between the two, making it impossible to determine the optimal combination with the smallest first entry time between the two.

(5) Hotspot map analysis

The eye tracker can display the line of sight trajectory in different colors, known as a hotspot map. The area with the densest fixation points is represented in red. As the fixation points decrease, the color changes from red to yellow, and finally filters to green. The reading hotspots for background images are as follows (Table 7 and Fig. 6):

Table 7. Color Matching Table

Background color	Low saturation	Original saturation	High Saturation
Foreground color	Original saturation	Original saturation	Original saturation

Fig. 6. Interface color matching hotspot map (Color figure online)

From these three images, it can be seen that the interface of foreground color saturation and background color saturation is relatively concentrated, while the line of sight of high saturation original saturation is the most dispersed. This indicates that when performing the button retrieval operation, the background color saturation and foreground color saturation are more focused, while the attention is more dispersed during the other two gaze operations (Table 8 and Fig. 7).

Table 8. Color Matching Table

Background color	Low brightness	Original brightness	High Brightness
Foreground color	Low brightness	Low brightness	Low brightness
	Medium brightness	Medium brightness	Medium brightness
	Original brightness	original brightness	original brightness

From these nine pictures, it can be seen that when the background color is low brightness and the foreground color is medium brightness, attention is most concentrated. When the background color is original brightness, the foreground color is original brightness, and attention is most concentrated. When the background color is high brightness, the foreground color is medium brightness, and attention is most concentrated. In summary, when the background color changes, the foreground color is medium brightness, and attention is highest. When the current color is low brightness, the background color is high brightness, the level of attention concentration is highest. When the current scenery is medium brightness, the background color is high brightness, and the level of attention concentration is highest. When the current scenery is original brightness, the background color is original brightness, and the level of attention concentration is

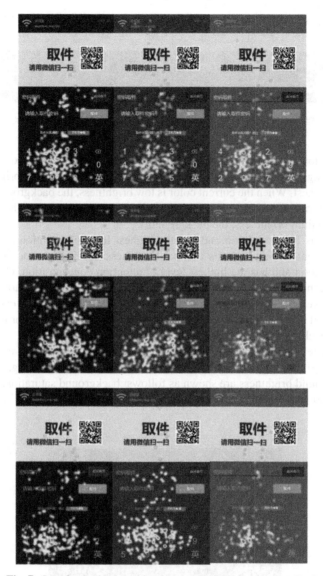

Fig. 7. Interface color matching hotspot map (Color figure online)

highest. Overall, when the current scenery changes, the background color is high brightness, and the level of attention concentration is highest. So, the background color is high brightness, the foreground color is medium brightness, and the level of attention concentration is the highest (Fig. 8).

From these nine pictures, it can be seen that when the background color is low saturation and the foreground color is medium brightness, attention is most concentrated. When the background color is original saturation, the foreground color is low brightness, and attention is most concentrated. When the background color is high saturation, the

Fig. 8. Interface color matching hotspot map (Color figure online)

foreground color is medium brightness, and attention is most concentrated. In summary, when the background color changes, the foreground color is medium brightness, and attention is highest. When the current color is low brightness, the background color is at its original saturation, with the highest level of attention concentration. When the current scene is at medium brightness, the background.

The color is low saturation and has the highest level of attention concentration. When the current scenery is at its original brightness, the background color is at its original saturation and has the highest level of attention concentration. Overall, when the current scenery changes, the background color is at its original saturation and has the highest level of attention concentration. However, considering the overall image, the background color is at its original saturation and the foreground color is at medium brightness, resulting in the highest level of attention concentration.

Finally, after comparison, the hotspots of background saturation, foreground saturation, background high brightness, foreground brightness, and background saturation in foreground brightness are shown as follows: background saturation, foreground saturation, and foreground saturation have the highest level of attention concentration (Fig. 9).

Fig. 9. Interface color matching hotspot map (Color figure online)

6 Conclusion

(1) The foreground and background colors with different brightness and saturation have a significant impact on the efficiency of information acquisition for college students. And the low saturation of the background color and the original brightness of the

foreground color have the best effect on the efficiency of obtaining information for participants.

(2) The foreground and background colors with different brightness and saturation have a significant impact on the difficulty of obtaining information for college students. The number of fixation points under low saturation background color and high brightness background color foreground brightness conditions is the lowest and the difficulty is the lowest within the group, respectively.

(3) The foreground and background colors with different brightness and saturation have a significant impact on the eye-catching level of the keyboard in the interface. The first entry time into the region of interest under the conditions of high brightness of the background color, low brightness of the foreground color, and medium brightness of the background color, is the smallest within the group, and the keyboard part is the most eye-catching.

The foreground and background colors with different brightness and saturation have a significant impact on the concentration of information obtained by college students. And the saturation of background and foreground color is the highest level of attention concentration.

7 Discussion

Selection of Interface Colors for Express Cabinets

(1) Analysis of gaze time reveals that low saturation backgrounds take the shortest time, while high saturation backgrounds take longer,

When operating the express cabinet interface, a low saturation background takes longer than a high saturation background. Low saturation background is not acceptable

May cause fatigue.

(2) By analyzing the fixation time, it can be found that compared to foreground colors with different intensities under the same background color, the fixation

The short duration indicates that when operating the express cabinet interface, the medium brightness foreground is not easy to cause fatigue.

(3) Analyzing the number of fixations, it can be found that the number of high brightness fixations in the foreground is relatively small, while the number of low brightness fixations is relatively small. For many, it indicates that high brightness foreground scenes under the same background are more easily accepted by people. High brightness when designing the pick-up interface with a dark background

Degree fonts can make it easier for users to quickly find the target number.

(4) Analyzing the number of fixations, it can be found that there are relatively fewer fixations for low saturation background colors, while fixations for high saturation backgrounds. The relatively high frequency indicates that the low saturation background color under the same foreground color is easier to distinguish and the difficulty of finding the target is lower. In the Designing a low saturation background can make it easier for users to quickly find the target number.

(5) Analyzing the heat zone map, it was found that the original interface was the best and the ineffective fixation was the least. It can be seen that for attention In terms of concentration, the color matching of the original interface is the best.

(6) In order to make the user experience more comfortable, the pick-up interface should be beautiful and elegant, simple and easy to understand, and highlight the expressed content Rong can enable users to obtain more information in the shortest possible time and pick up items more quickly and comfortably. Based on the above conclusions

Considering this, it is recommended to use a combination of low saturation background color and original brightness foreground color when designing the pickup interface.

References

1. An, L., Ziyun, L.: Experimental study on eye movement of background color in teaching PPT. Res. Electron. Educ. **33**(01), 75–80 (2012)
2. Wang, Q., Chen, W.: Research on visual cognitive performance of color design for elderly service robots. Packag. Work. Cheng, 1–9 (2020)
3. Sun, B., Yang, J., Sun, Y., Yan, H., Li, S.: Research on color design of vehicle human-machine interface based on eye movement experiments. Packag. Eng. **40**(02), 23–30 (2019)
4. Cui, J.: Interfacial Color Analysis and Experimental Research of Eye Control System. Southeast University (2020). https://doi.org/10.27014/d.cnki.gdnau.2020.004141
5. Liu, T.: Research on Color Perception of Vehicle HMI Interface. Jilin University (2021). https://doi.org/10.27162/d.cnki.gjlin.2021.002691
6. Sun, B.: Research on Interface Hierarchy Design of Vehicle Information System for Complex Interaction Scenarios. Beijing Institute of Technology (2018). https://doi.org/10.26948/d.cnki.gbjlu.2018.000222
7. Bailing: Research on Digital Interface Color Coding Evaluation Based on Eye Tracking Technology. Southeast University (2019). https://doi.org/10.27014/d.cnki.gdnau.2019.003030
8. Cheng, H.: Research on the Design of Vehicle Information Interaction Interface From the Perspective of Emotion. China University of Mining and Technology (2020). https://doi.org/10.27623/d.cnki.gzkyu.2020.002532 、
9. Lu, Y.: Research on Interface Visualization of Complex Information System Based on Visual Attention Capture. Nanjing University of Aeronautics and Astronautics (2020). https://doi.org/10.27239/d.cnki.gnhhu.2020.001362
10. Shen, Z.: Research on Interface Aided Design Software Architecture and Core Functional Modules Based on Complex Information System. Southeast University (2018)
11. Jiang, M.: Research and Application of Color Semantics of College Students' Smartphone Interface. Harbin University of Science and Technology (2015)
12. Han, P.: Optimization Design of Shenyang Forbidden City Website Based on Eye Tracking Analysis. Shenyang University of Aeronautics and Astronautics (2019). https://doi.org/10.27324/d.cnki.gshkc.2019.000617
13. Wang, L.: Research on Interactive Interface Design of Urban Life Mobile Platform Based on User Cognitive Psychology. Xi'an Polytechnic University (2018)
14. Ma, Y.: Research and application of commercial WIFI APP usability of interactive interface. Jiangsu University (2016)

Episodic Future Thinking as Digital Micro-interventions

Dan Roland Persson[1]([⊠]) [ID], Soojeong Yoo[2] [ID], Jakob E. Bardram[3] [ID],
Timothy C. Skinner[4] [ID], and Per Bækgaard[1] [ID]

[1] Department of Applied Mathematics and Computer Science,
Technical University of Denmark, Kongens Lyngby, Denmark
{danrp,pgba}@dtu.dk

[2] University College London, Interaction Centre, London, UK

[3] Department of Health Technology, Technical University of Denmark,
Kongens Lyngby, Denmark
jakba@dtu.dk

[4] Institute of Psychology, University of Copenhagen, Copenhagen, Denmark

Abstract. Micro-interventions are quick focused behavioural interventions aimed at matching users' current capacity for engagement. Mobile devices are powerful, interactive, and sensor-rich platforms for delivering micro-interventions and for determining when and where to do so. This paper presents a novel smart-phone based approach to micro-interventions based on established 'Episodic Future Thinking (EFT)' research. The paper both presents the background for EFT-based micro-interventions and the design of an 'EFT' smartphone application implementing this. The approach and technology were evaluated in a feasibility study including 14 participants using the system for 14 days. Results demonstrate the feasibility of implementing EFT as micro-interventions, with participants willing to use the application, providing positive feedback and constructive suggestions. The paper concludes with a thorough discussion of the implications for smartphone-based EFT delivered as micro-interventions and how these can be used as part of a larger behaviour change and health improvement initiatives.

Keywords: Micro-interventions · mHealth · Delay Discounting · Episodic Future Thinking

1 Introduction

Self-management of a chronic illness is for many a long, arduous journey spanning decades of uncertain health outcomes and worries, where faraway consequences of smaller repeated gratifying behaviours seem less relevant. However, forgoing such seemingly minor gratifying behaviours, like being less sedentary, can have a large impact on long term health [26]. This underlying discounting of future outcomes has therefore been suggested as a therapeutic target for preventing transition from pre-diabetes to type 2 diabetes [18]. Despite the transition being largely

© The Author(s), under exclusive license to Springer Nature Switzerland AG 2023
M. Kurosu et al. (Eds.): HCII 2023, LNCS 14054, pp. 213–237, 2023.
https://doi.org/10.1007/978-3-031-48038-6_14

avoidable through lifestyle changes and weight loss, the uptake in prevention programs remains low [27]. Similar discounting of the future has been shown to correlate with poorer self-management outcomes in type 2 diabetes [11].

The human tendency of discounting the future can be assessed via the method of 'delay discounting', a behavioural economic trans-disease process measuring the extent to which people prefer smaller immediate rewards over larger delayed ones [19]. One intervention shown to be effective at reducing delay discounting is Episodic Future Thinking (EFT) [60]. In EFT a person mentally projects him/herself into the future though a personal vivid and sufficiently detailed episodic future event [51]. This can be facilitated by first asking the person to imagine one or more attractive future events, for instance "*I am playing football with the grandchildren on a summer day*", and associate these with a created audio cue, that can then afterwards be used to recall the future event.

Recent research has shown EFT to be effective in reducing delay discounting in relation to multiple areas like the risk of type 2 diabetes [51], overeating [47] and cigarette smoking [54]. A potential way of increasing the accessibility of EFT is through scalable and cost effective digital means. Mobile health (mHealth) applications present one such technology [44], and individual components of EFT have previously been demonstrated in a digital setting.

Such components of EFT delivered as a digital intervention can be broken into 3 primary tasks 1) a *generation task* [51] creating a cue representing an episodic future 2) a *projection (or review) task* where a person pre-experiences the episodic future and 3) an *assessment tasks* where the delay discounting is measured. It can be argued that the first two of these tasks are *micro-interventions*, given their short duration and positive impact on in-moment behaviours [8,47] whereas the third task simply acts as an assessment component. Micro-interventions are defined as resources that can be quickly consumed, intended to have an immediate positive effect on targeted symptoms [24], and can include both just-in-time (JIT) [43] and ecological momentary interventions (EMI) [6].

However, despite the increased accessibility of self-guided real world digital health interventions, research suggests uptake in real world settings remains low [9,23,42]: A recent meta-analysis looking at attrition and dropouts rates across app-interventions found these to be as high as 43% across studies [42]. Another recent study related to popular mental health apps found user retention as low as 3.9% after just 15 days [9]. This could indicate a lack of acceptance by users or a failure to address the specific, and often evolving, user needs [21]. Alternatively, it could be that patients' experiences and needs might not always align with clinical judgement [59] used to create the interventions, or it could be that users might not want to invest much effort into these, despite being interested in their effects [8]. This highlights a need to consider the larger context for delivery of mHealth applications like EFT, taking into account intervention timing, differences in population [22] and personal preference [50], which in turn implies tackling *personal context* and larger *therapeutic perspectives* while meeting peoples' capacity to engage with the interventions. The idea of leveraging several different micro-interventions in combination through a larger narrative that aims to achieve an overall outcome has been coined *micro-intervention care* [8].

This paper presents an approach to embed EFT-based micro-interventions into a mHealth application, aiming to support micro-interventions both stand-alone and as part of a larger narrative. The EFT-based micro-intervention approach is based on a theoretical engagement into the theory behind EFT combined with a thorough design process, involving a wide range of chronic patients engaged in focus groups, formative usability testing, and an initial feasibility study of the mHealth application.

We therefore explore how EFT might be implemented as micro-interventions. We further look at users' experiences with EFT as micro-interventions i.e., the facilitators and barriers and we discuss the potential areas and use-cases where EFT may be used as part of micro-intervention narratives. We designed an application to deliver EFT as a number of micro-interventions in a human-centred design process and implemented the design in Flutter for Android and iOS using a pre-existing mobile sensing framework for mHealth applications, and ran a 2 week single-arm feasibility study involving 14 participants. The users overall gave positive feedback, although engagement varied with less than half completing the full 2 week period. In this paper, we include the design and the results from the study, and discuss their implications for future design considerations.

2   Theoretical Background and Related Work

Both delay discounting and EFT are areas with significant contemporary research, and micro-interventions are an emerging field of research with increasing interest in recent years. The following sections provide background knowledge on the core concepts of delay discounting, EFT and micro-interventions.

2.1   Delay Discounting

Delay discounting is a measure of the perceived difference in value of an immediate reward when postponed to the future. As humans, we often prefer gratifying behaviours or rewards now rather than later, and to have more rewards rather than less [46]. From a health perspective this might translate to preferring pleasurable behaviours here and now, rather than taking in-moment actions for a larger reward impacting long term health. Delay discounting stems from behavioural economics and describes the extent to which we prefer immediate gratification against future larger gratifications or rewards [35]. Mazur suggests delay discounting to be described by a hyperbolic mathematical model:

$$V = A/(1 + kD)$$

where V represents the perceived present subjective value, A is the actual value, D is the delay and k is the delay discounting coefficient [19,39]. Persons with higher values of k therefore perceive the subjective value of a reward to drop significantly when delayed, resulting in distant outcomes being considered of lesser value. Persons with higher values of k thus prefer smaller rewards soon, and may e.g., be inclined to consume high caloric food rather than foregoing this with a benefit of a better long term health [58]. High delay discounting has been associated with obesity and the inability to delay gratification [14]. This also translates to other behavioural areas related to health, such as smoking [54], engaging in lifestyle changes halting the transition to type 2 diabetes [51] and engagement in diabetes self-management [11], and in other behaviours such as different forms of addiction [2]. Epstein et al. further suggests delay discounting as a potential target for prevention of prediabetes to type 2 [18] while showing a relationship between high discounting and multiple health related behaviours such as lower adherence to medication, diet quality, physical activity and HbA1c[1] [19].

Delay discounting can be assessed through a series of choices usually presented in the form of money, i.e., "Would you prefer $20 now or $200 in 6 months". Depending on the exact method either the less immediate or the greater delayed reward is adjusted according to the user's reply. Alternatively, the delays or both amounts are adjusted. Eventually a tipping point is reached where a subject changes opinion between rewards, also known as the indifference point [38], which can be used to calculate the overall discounting rate, expressed through the discounting coefficient, k.

Several methods are used in common practice, such as the adjusting amounts task [19] or the Kirby Delay-Discounting Questionnaire [32] although several variations of delay discounting measures exist [38]. The Kirby Delay-Discounting Questionnaire e.g., consists of 27 questions that present immediate values, fixed delays and uses shorter time periods (7–186 days) whereas the adjusting amounts task deals with longer periods of time (1 day - 25 years) and can be based on either $100 or $1000. The adjusting amounts task e.g., starts with $50 now versus $100 later for a given time period, and for each choice the subject takes, the amount now is adjusted by 50% depending on that choice e.g., if $50 is chosen over $100, the amount now is adjusted to $25. Similarly the amount may be adjusted to $75 if the delayed amount is chosen, with these choices being repeated another 4 times until indifference is reached, and it then repeated across 6 time periods.

2.2   Episodic Future Thinking

Episodic Future Thinking (EFT), which is a growing area of research in both cognitive neuroscience and psychology [49], refers to the ability to imagine one's personal future.

In EFT, one projects oneself forward into the future in order to pre-experience an event [4], e.g., "I am sitting outside enjoying the warm spring weather, in a few moments I will be going on a walk to enjoy the park". EFT is a type of prospective thinking and is thought to reduce impulsiveness by increasing the perceived

---

[1] Average blood glucose over 2–3 months, also known as the Hemoglobin A1 test.

value of delayed outcomes, thereby encouraging decisions with long-term benefits [56]. A recent meta-analysis supports EFT's effects on delay discounting across studies, noting positive EFT events are more effective than neutral or negatively toned future events [60]. EFT's ability to reduce delay discounting and impulsiveness has been shown in a number of contexts [10,14,15,47,51,54]. Dassen et al. for example showed EFT to be effective in reducing discounting rate and snacking, suggesting it as effective also in reducing the need for immediate gratification [15]. Similarly, O'Neill et al. found that EFT significantly reduces energy intake when carried out in a public food court [47], indicating effectiveness of EFT as ecological momentary interventions. This is further backed by Hollis et al. showing EFT to impact in-moment ecological decisions made in grocery shopping [28]. Additionally, Sze et al. shows that online-administered EFT can reliably reduce delay discounting and demands for fast foods [56]. In studies related to chronic disease [17] and substance abuse [3] EFT has shown equally effective in reducing delay discounting. Stein et al. found EFT reduced delay discounting to directly affect self-administration of cigarettes [53,54] and reduce delay discounting in persons at risk of type 2 diabetes [51].

The use of smartphones in EFT has often been limited and mainly focused on the delivery of audio cues. The study by Sze et al. makes use of an online web-based system compatible with desktops, tablets and mobile devices allowing participants to access their cues on smartphones [55]. Generation of cues was handled with a case manager at an introductory session using separate open-source software and a laptop to facilitate recording [55]. In a later study Sze et al. further showed the feasibility of using an online self-guided generation task for audio cue creation [56]. Similarly, O'Neill et al. leverages participants own smartphones to deliver the studies audio cues, with none-compatible phones replaced by an iPod where cue generation is handled through a moderated EFT cue-development interview and is recorded using a recorder [47].

2.3   Micro-interventions

Fuller et al. defines micro-interventions as quick resources that can be easily consumed and should have an immediate positive impact on targeted symptoms. Micro-interventions can be both just-in-time (and just-in-time adaptive interventions) [20] or ecological momentary interventions EMI [41] by nature [24]. These micro-interventions can consist of a single event [25], repetitions [16], variations [20] and sequences of events [24].

One convenient way to look at micro-interventions can be found in the conceptualization by Baumel et al. describing the core components of micro-interventions [8]. An important distinction presented in this work is that of the micro-interventions themselves and the micro-intervention care. Micro-intervention care consists of individual micro-interventions as steps in a therapeutic process linked together in a coherent therapeutic narrative maintained by a "hub" [8]. A hub refers to an entity (or multiple entities including systems in combination) that recognises an individual's state and context, recommending relevant interventions and creating and maintaining a therapeutic narrative [8].

This narrative is driven by conceptual models, determining how/when a digital micro-intervention should be used in the therapeutic process. The delivery, timing and context for events are determined by decision rules. Proximal assessments may be carried out to determine the outcome of events, with the outcome of the micro-intervention possibly also being a proxy for an overall clinical goal [8].

Current implementations of micro-interventions have mostly revolved around the interventions themselves rather than micro-intervention care. Micro-interventions have for example been used to promote physical activity [13], positive body image [25] and improve mood [16]. Meanwhile, Meinlschmidt et al. allowed users a daily choice of one of four ecological momentary interventions micro-interventions aiming to improve mood [40]: vicesensory attention (shifting attention from sensations), emotional imagery (imaging emotional situations), facial expression (simulating emotional facial expressions), and contemplative repetition (repeating short sentences) [40]. Micro-interventions events can be triggered in response to context and with resources adapted based on user preference [16] with Everitt et al. using JIT micro-interventions to decrease depressive symptoms [20].

3   System Design

The EFT mobile health application was designed to facilitate the creation and delivery of EFT as micro-interventions on a smartphone platform. As outlined above, the smartphone presents a good platform for understanding the context and behaviour of a person and for delivering an intervention through e.g., the notification system. The "EFT" application was designed for a generic audience in order to investigate the technology and user experience of EFT implemented on a smartphone platform. A selection of the applications screens can be found in Fig. 1.

3.1   Design Process

We considered prior work on EFT, delay discounting, and micro-interventions (Sect. 2) to design our initial prototype, and adopted a human-centred design process to evolve the prototype: The initial design was refined and validated based on feedback from 3 focus groups with in total 11 participants with Type 2 Diabetes Mellitus (T2DM), and further by formative usability sessions where 6 potential users tested core elements of EFT when performing different tasks with the prototype. The aim of the focus groups was to discuss key topics, problems, and opportunities for the design with a target user group that may benefit from EFT (see Sects. 1 and 2.1). The formative usability tests focused on key elements of the design, specifically the self-guided self-generation of cues and initial perceptions of generating and listening to audio cues.

3.2   Design Considerations

In order to deliver a minimal implementation of EFT we aimed for at least three distinct micro-interventions (MIs) and one method for assessment (A): 1. **MI1** – A self-guided generation task for creating cues. 2. **MI2** – Audio-based projection (or review) session where audio cues are experienced. 3. **MI3** – Image-based projection micro-intervention where the image represents one of the episodic futures. 4. **A1** – An adjusting amounts task to assess delay discounting.

Fig. 1. Design of the EFT mobile application. The leftmost picture shows part of the integrated study consent form. At the centre are the main menu showing different uncompleted sessions and a reflection session playing audio cues. Rightmost is an example of an image based projection delivered through a notification.

Self-guided Generation Task. Generation of episodic futures was facilitated through a series of steps presented to the participants and is based on the self-guided generation task [51]. Positive episodic futures are emphasised as these have been shown more effective at reducing delay discounting [60]. Once a vividly imagined future has been created, the participants record it as an audio cue for future review. Based on the created episodic future, the participants are asked to give the cue a name and to add an image representing the created future event. Each self-guided generation task consists of creating a single episodic future, as it reduces the effort required at any one given time and meets peoples' capacity for smaller investments of time [8], in line with the idea of micro-interventions.

Initially, users complete the first micro-intervention creating a single episodic future, set approximately a month into the future. Following Stein et al.'s suggestion that EFT's effects depend on the number of generated futures and the time frames of those futures [52], we designed additional self-guided generation tasks with different time frames. The initial period of 1 month was chosen based on formative usability testing, as most users could easily imagine events in that time frame. To address any learning curve subsequent self-guided generation tasks were set at increasing time periods i.e., 3 months, 6 months 1 year etc in the future. As suggested in focus groups examples of cues were also added for the different time frames. The most distant future considered for cue generation was 10 years based on formative usability testing with participants expressing doubts they could effectively generate cues in a 25-year time frame and suggesting it might be inappropriate for older persons. As a final step of the self-guided generation task users are asked to add an image representation of their created episodic future, which is used for image-based projection. Users are periodically notified to generate at least 7 cues [17]. The overall design of the cue-creation can be seen in Fig. 2.

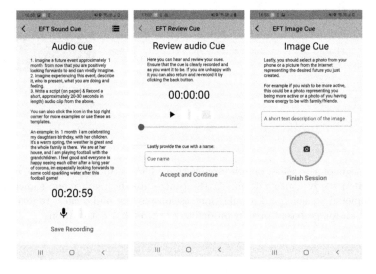

Fig. 2. Design of the app's self-guided generation task. The leftmost picture shows instructions and an initial example as well as the recorder. In the middle users can give their cue a name and review the quality of the recording. The rightmost screenshot shows the tab for creating image cues.

Audio-Based Future Projection. Projection sessions are scheduled twice a day and timed before the first meal and the last meal of the day, respectively [55]. Should participants not complete them, reminders will be sent after a while. Each session consists of pre-experiencing a number of self-generated episodic futures per session by listening to the episodic futures in audio format, thus allowing multiple events to be pre-experienced.

Image-Based Future Projection. Given that it is not always feasible to listen to audio cues an image-only notification representing the episodic future may be useful to remind persons of their episodic future in those contexts. This is reminiscent of the work by Chan & Cameron on mental imaging wherein mental imagery was used to promote active behaviour [12]. In line with micro-interventions these images could be delivered in contexts different to traditional EFT aiming to affect in moment decision making.

Assessing Delay Discounting. The app measures delay discounting through an adjusting-amount task [19]. The task itself is designed as described in Sect. 2.1 and the delay discounting coefficient is calculated based on Mazur's hyperbolic model [39]. The measurement was initially based on the $100 task modified to the local currency (Danish krone) and rounded to the nearest meaningful amount in kroner, resulting in a 1000 kr adjusting amount task. Formative usability tests revealed users generally perceived this amount as inconsequential, requesting higher amounts to be used to make more meaningful decisions, in line with Epstein et al.'s suggestion, that: "Perhaps if a reward is too small, most people discount it [...]" – Epstein [18]. As a consequence, the adjusting amount task was updated to reflect a larger amount, 10.000kr or $1000.

3.3 Implementation

The application was implemented in Flutter and thereby available for both Android and iOS smartphones. The software architecture is shown in Fig. 3 and is based on the CACHET Research Platform (CARP), which is an open source research platform for digital phenotyping[2]. The application makes use of the CARP Mobile Sensing framework [7] for mobile data collection, the CARP Research Package for collection of informed consent from the user and uses the CARP Web Services infrastructure for secure data upload and management. CARP was chosen as the basis for the application as it allows for collection of a wide variety of data automatically and does so securely and in compliance with the General Data Protection Regulation (GDPR). The real-time collection of contextual and behavioural data is especially relevant for this EFT application, as it can be used for just-in-time or ecologically relevant triggers in the application. These automatic triggers are, however, outside the scope of this initial feasibility study. Data collected on the participants smartphone is sent to the CARP Web Service backend, where it is made accessible to the project researchers.

In addition to handling data collection CARP mobile sensing also controls the timing of new sessions, scheduling of notifications and delivery of image reminders through the Study protocol.

4 Feasibility Study

Following the best practices in early mHealth technology research, a single-arm feasibility study was carried out with the aim of gaining a deep understanding

---

[2] http://carp.cachet.dk/.

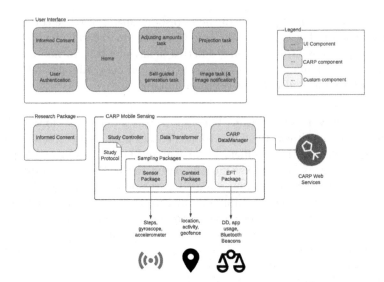

Fig. 3. Architecture of the EFT mobile health application. The application-specific components are shown in red and resemble the UI components such as the ones shown in Figs. 1 and 2. Data collection is handled by the CARP Mobile Sensing framework components (green), which include a custom sampling package for recording usage statistics, beacons and delay discounting (yellow). (Color figure online)

of how and why the system used or is not by its users [33]. Our aim is thus to obtain a comprehensive understanding of use, usability, perceived usefulness and feasibility of EFT as digital micro-interventions in the real world. Given our aim of broadly looking at the usefulness of the micro-interventions, both as self-contained digital micro-interventions and as part of other narratives, we did not impose any restrictions on recruitment. Due to the study's technical and non-clinical objectives, the feasibility study was exempted from ethical approval by the Danish Ethical Committee (journal no. 21066249). The Institutional Review Board at the Department of Applied Mathematics and Computer Science at the Technical University of Denmark (DTU) have approved the study. (DTU-COMP-IRB-2021-02).

4.1 Recruitment

Due to the early nature of this study and the aim of making EFT as micro-interventions generally applicable, participants were recruited more broadly through announcements, board messages, and email lists at (DTU) and through word of mouth externally and not specifically targeting persons with T2DM. Interested subjects were presented with a subject information letter and a link for a sign-up. Upon signing up, participants were invited to the study via email.

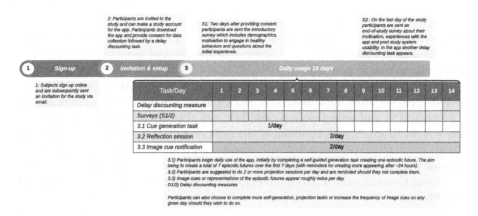

Fig. 4. Overall study structure, showing the major phases of the study from sign-up till completion.

4.2 Procedure

The study timeline can be seen in Fig. 4. Upon signing up for the study, participants were invited to the study through the CARP platform via an email invitation, prompting them to create a study account for the app. When participants had created this account they could download the app and sign-in. Once signed-in participants were presented with the full subject information letter again and asked to provide signed consent for participation via the app.

Once signed consent was obtained, participants were asked to do an initial delay discounting assessment, and once finished the participants can use the app. Initially the main menu presents participants with an introduction to the app and its different features and urge the participant to complete the first self-guided generation task which can be found in a card view of available sessions. A day after setting up the app, participants receive an introductory questionnaire via email exploring the initial experience with cue creation and an assessment of motivation to engage in healthy behaviours through the Treatment Self-Regulation Questionnaire (TSRQ) [36] and some exploratory questions about the initial experience of cue generation/projection. The TSRQ questionnaire specifically assesses the degree of which one's motivation is self-determined or autonomous. In the present case, as the focus revolves around delay discounting in regard to lifestyle changes, we use the versions of TSRQ that focuses on diet and exercise motivation.

Participants were urged to engage with the application two or more times daily in the form of review sessions where they pre-experience their recorded episodic futures. These sessions automatically pop up in the app in the early morning and afternoon, with notification reminders some hours afterwards. Participants may additionally receive notifications containing their image representations of the futures at some points throughout the day. After 2 weeks, the participants were presented with another delay discounting adjusting amount task and an end-of-study questionnaire. This end of study questionnaire consists of the same TSRQ questionnaire on motivation, a Post-Study System Usability Questionnaire (PSSUQ) [37], and additional specific and more general questions about the overall experience.

The specific exploratory questions were inspired by experience sampling and included participants approach, difficulties and experiences with completing the cue generation and reflection sessions. The end of study questionnaire additionally sought to explore perceptions of the interventions focused more broadly on the accumulated experiences with the micro-interventions. The general questions allowed the participants to tell if they liked, disliked or were indifferent towards aspects of the system or micro-intervention events and an opportunity to suggest improvements.

5   Results

In total 24 participants signed up for the study, with 14 accepting the study invitation and downloading the app. Twelve participants answered the introductory questionnaire and 9 the end-of-study questionnaire. 83% of the participants were between 20 and 30 years of age; half were female. 3 participants (25%) were from a minority group.

The CARP Mobile Sensing framework collected a total of 262,223 data points, including location, activity, pedometer, battery, and device information. A total of 1,632 app interactions were recorded. These include opening the app, interacting with the app, and completing sessions, with 2 participants sporadically continuing to use the app after the 14-day study period. Participant engagement over all sessions can be seen in Fig. 5. We were not able to detect any meaningful difference in the measured delay discounting comparing the beginning and end of the study due to the small sample size and low completion rate of the final delay discounting assessment task. Accumulated attrition was 21.4% (day 3), 43% (day 7) and 78.6% (day 14).

We carried out a within-subjects statistical analysis (using python 3.7.0, scipy 1.7.3) of TSRQ score between the study start and end surveys for both diet and physical activity. We did not observe any statistically meaningful differences in TSRQ score for participants between the beginning and end of the study. However, we did observe a noticeable positive mean difference in score of 1.65 (likert scale, p = 0.31 relative to baseline) for question 14: "Because I want others to see I can do it" (Physical Activity).

The usability of the application was assessed using PSSUQ and supporting questions, gauging the experience of completing key tasks. The PSSUQ results can be seen in Fig. 6, showing that a majority of the participants were satisfied with the usability of the system, with some adding suggestions for improvements to the UI. However, two exceptions can be found in relation to question 6 and 8 namely "I felt comfortable using this system" and "I believe I could become productive quickly using this system", where participants seem to rate the solution less favourable. The exploratory experience questions added some nuance

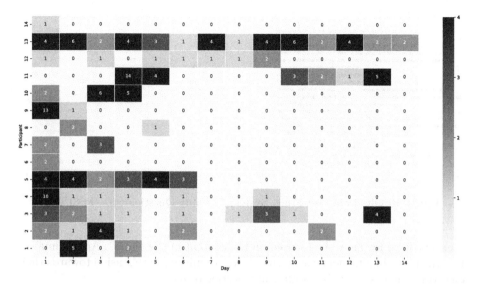

Fig. 5. Number of engagements with self-guided generation tasks, audio or image-based projections, for each user over the 14 day study period.

to these ratings: In terms of feeling comfortable, roughly half the participants commented on the experience of listening to their own voice, to varying degrees describing it as uncomfortable or annoying. Regarding the productivity of using the system, some participants felt that it was unclear how exactly EFT would help them e.g., become healthier, perceiving a disconnect between futures and specific outcomes.

5.1   Qualitative Results

A total of 5 recurring themes were identified through a thematic analysis of participants experiences. These were related to 1) Listening to one's own voice, 2) contextual appropriateness, 3) imagining the future, 4) perceived value, and 5) the facilitating system. In the following paragraphs we have these synthesised insights, highlighting both barriers, facilitators and participants own suggestions for improvement.

Listening to One's Own Voice. Generally, participants reported very different experiences when it came to listening to their voice. Some participants were mostly indifferent or positive towards the experience: "I'm not a fan of my voice so, it was a little odd hearing myself speak", "It was strange hearing my voice" and "I think hearing what I had to say was kinda nice – it was like getting a mail from future me". However, others reported more mild or severe unease/discomfort from listening to their own voice: "I have slight difficulties listening to the recordings of my voice" and "I don't like the sound of my voice so it

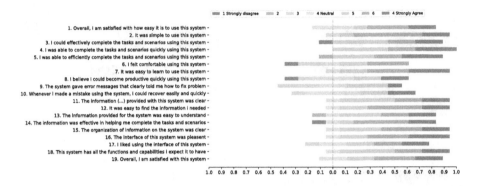

Fig. 6. Results from Post-Study System Usability Questionnaire (PSSUQ).

was very hard for me to be focused on the content of the audio". Approximately half the participants mentioned some degree of initial apprehension towards their own voice suggesting it is a significant barrier to use.

Participants themselves suggested various ways to mitigate this issue; one suggestion was to keep a textual representation of the episodic future used in the self-generation task simply reading it themselves during projection rather than listening to a recording. Another participant suggested that another person could record the audio cue. However, given the personal nature of some futures this may not always be appropriate.

Contextual Appropriateness. Participants commented on the ability to complete projection sessions, stating that it could be difficult to find a quiet place to concentrate in between everyday activities. Some participants also found it was difficult to find time for engaging in the planned projection sessions due to other events or sudden occurrences, suggesting an option to have more sessions on certain days and less at other times.

Comparing audio and image cues, some participants had a preference for image cues, citing the aforementioned issue with one's own voice adding that the image cues suited them better in-moment while others citing a personal preference for image-based intervention formats. One participant commented "I prefer the photo part", with yet another participant adding that the image cue was often enough to remember the episodic future. Participants suggested using different types of media, including text, to deliver the episodic futures: "I would prefer writing something instead of talking to my phone". Participants also touched upon the situational appropriateness of different resources noting: "[It is] a bit annoying that I have to find a place without people to do this. I would prefer text".

Imagining Futures. Some participants noted it could be difficult to imagine events in certain time frames due to uncertainty and that the time period was outside of what they usually think about. Moreover, initial experiences with the projection task indicate that while the examples provided were useful, their limited numbers and variation were not necessarily enough for all participants.

Imagining distant futures was more difficult than those more present, with comments that not everyone considers long-term future events (~5–10 years). One participant comment from the first survey in particular seems to support the idea of a learning curve effect in cue generation: "Perhaps in the next sessions [cue generation] I would have liked to imagine something bigger like a fitness goal".

Perceived Value. Participants generally found the experience of thinking about the future pleasant in itself, describing it as encouraging to remind one-self about things to look forward to. Some participants found that it provided hope for a bright future: "It gave me a sense of hope, and it felt like something to look forward to" and others commented "It [reflecting on the future] was encouraging", "It is nice to be reminded that there is something to look forward to". However, not all were equally positive and found it difficult to see how EFT or rather future thinking in general would actively help them achieve more tangible health related goals: "It did not particularly motivate me but it did remind of where I want to be" and "I don't think I understand the actual purpose of the task [reflection]".

The System. The system facilitating EFT through micro-interventions was also mentioned as both a facilitator and occasional barrier.

In terms of positive perceptions participants found the system easy to learn and to use, and found information such as task descriptions sufficient to quickly complete micro-interventions. Several participants especially liked the image cues delivered as notifications with their association to the future.

On the contrary, barriers included the design of certain interactions such as manually having to click "next recording" in projection sessions as participants seemingly preferred audio cues automatically playing one after the other. Other negative technical aspects included battery drain (from mobile sensing), some general technical issues, and the stability of certain background processes.

6   Discussion

6.1   Design of the Micro-intervention Events

In this study we designed 3 micro-intervention events and adapted one type of assessment that can also be used as part of a larger therapeutic narrative addressing delay discounting. Results from our feasibility study including suggestions from the participants highlight multiple opportunities for improvements and variations to these micro-interventions. These ranges from the content, i.e., micro-intervention resource, to their timing and intensity based on context. We note, however, that more work is necessary to explore appropriate decision rules for triggering these in relation to context, and whether these *end-user* developed variations are effective. Formative usability tests indicates that *self-guided gener-ation tasks and review sessions can be directly translated to unmoderated micro-interventions*. However, *the tasks must be performed chronologically in sequence*, as a self-guided generation task is needed before a projection of episodic futures can take place.

Based on our qualitative usability data we believe perceived usefulness to be the primary contributor to the observed low usage and thus also the lack of mean-ingful differences in delay discounting. This is in line with previous research show-ing that perceived usefulness of a micro-interventions can be linked to usage [24], similar to results from traditional mHealth interventions [57]. This indicates the paramount importance of ensuring perceived value is clear for users in unmod-erated micro-interventions if these are to be effective in the real world. Partic-ipants' own ideas to solve this perceived gap suggests *goal-oriented EFT* [45] *may be better suited for micro-intervention use* as it bridges the perceived gap between purpose and intervention, which could increase perceived value. Goal-oriented EFT was originally created to explicitly leverage an observed tendency for future thinking to lean towards future goals [45]. In this variation goals are directly and explicitly tied into the future events e.g., "In 2 weeks I am pur-chasing a new computer" - O'Donnell et al. [45]. Focus group participants even discussed (unprompted) the idea of cues to being tied to specific health goals in diabetes, without prior introduction to goal-oriented EFT by researchers. A recent study similarly expanded on this concept by modifying the financial incen-tive to health goals i.e., health goal-oriented EFT [5]. While this form of health goal-oriented EFT was not found to be more effective than traditional EFT it was found to have additional behavioural benefits [5]. Prior research therefore indicates that goal-oriented EFT may be more effective compared to traditional EFT [5,45]. Our findings add to this by suggesting goal-oriented EFT has the additional benefit of increasing perceived usefulness.

While it could be argued that the self-guided generation task should not be considered a micro-intervention but rather as required setup for EFT as it is not designed to have a positive effect on target symptoms itself. Our findings indicate that *the task of creating a cue in itself can provide a positive outlook on the future, and therefore has an immediate positive effect* in line with the definition of micro-interventions. Coupled with goal-oriented EFT, this could indeed provide a good starting point for the micro-interventions, highlighting their value and promoting engagement. We therefore argue that the self-generation task is to be seen as a micro-intervention providing a direct impact, in line with Fuller et al's definition of micro-interventions [24]. While the projection task, i.e., listening to audio cues and seeing image representations of future events, attempt an in-the-moment change, our study did not implement a proximal assessment for judging the effect of isolated events. We further note that using a standard adjusting amounts task to judge the effect of individual events may not be feasible for use in the "wild", as this would effectively double task duration. Therefore, further work is required to explore the impact of each events' effect, possibly through micro-randomized trials [34].

Research in EFT has previously shown the ability to reframe temporal decision-making during discrete moments of time [47]. Data collection from the feasibility study indicates that *we may be able to expand the system to include simple just-in-time delivery of EFT, thereby adjusting or entirely avoiding delivery of components when they are not necessary or not preferred* by users [43]. Utilizing the mobile sensing platform, the application successfully collected several kinds of contextual data in near real-time that could allow for delivering EFT micro-interventions in response to the user's context and situation. Examples from our data collection include activity, sedentary behaviour, location based events and beacon proximity, which individually or in combination could be used to identify opportune moments to trigger EFT events. E.g., Alexander et al. has already demonstrated the feasibility of leveraging sensor data from smartphones, smartwatches and Bluetooth beacon proximity to identify contexts where users are having meals [1].

6.2   User Experience

While participants reported some bugs, as well as usability issues specifically related to background processes on iOS, the overall feedback was positive; the participants appreciated the simple design, ease of interaction and the task instructions. We note however, that more work is needed to fully communicate the value of the system, especially if EFT micro-interventions are to be part of a larger narrative. Participants' own suggestion for goal-oriented EFT indicates it may be preferential and a facilitator for value perception. Comments from the formative usability testing implicitly supports this may be accomplished by more directly coupling health goals to episodic futures and the overall condition.

Contextualization: Looking at users' experience we see several potential facilitators and barriers to EFT as micro-interventions. While participants could simply engage with the micro-interventions daily, such as before the first meal and the last, real-world usage may vary depending on the context. *Contextual image based futures may be more appropriate than audio cues situationally.* Participant comments specifically highlight this is the case for both projection tasks and self-guided generation tasks, suggesting engagement is subject to contextual task acceptance. Especially the self-guided generation task was difficult to complete in part due as it was inherently more difficult, requiring relatively quiet and sometimes private spaces for recording of audio cues; it is necessary both to concentrate on cue generation and to ensure recording quality while not inadvertently sharing cues when recording in public, as also noted by some users.

One's Own Voice: Another significant barrier was plainly listening to one's own voice which several participants described as "cringe" inducing, with participants comments indicating this feeling gradually lessened over time. However, even at the 14-day mark, some participants still commented that *listening to one's own voice was distracting*, which could indicate it is a significant barrier to a large group of users and may hinder uptake of the micro-interventions. Given micro-interventions relatively short duration compared to traditional care [24], being unable to overcome barriers related to listening to one's own voice may limit the micro-intervention's effectiveness and perceived usefulness outside traditional psychological uses. Another alternative is to consider an AI voice system to play back cues so they are not in the user's own voice.

Audio vs Visual Cues: The perceived in-moment acceptance of the resource, i.e., the audio, image or text, may impact effectiveness of the intervention in the wild. Users may simply not be able to engage with the resource or may perceive the resource as inappropriate given the surrounding context. Accordingly, comments by participants indicate that this is further complicated by resource preference, where *some users preferred the image based resources whereas others instead suggested textual representations of their episodic futures* that they can read in the moment.

Long vs Short Term: Meeting users capacity for engagement, context and preference may be key to implement EFT in different narratives. In line with observations by Howe et al. we see some indications that suggest *users perceive low effort interventions as more helpful despite results indicating higher effectiveness from high effort ones* [29]. User comments for example suggest the shorter mental imagery delivered was enough to make them think about the future, with some participants preferring this type of projection. Adapting intervention resources to better suit users' preferences may therefore facilitate improved engagement but possibly at the cost of effectiveness requiring further research. Focus group discussions with persons with diabetes further suggests that *"it may be beneficial to provide direct links to the disease or health picture over time"*. These discussions also highlight that while people are interested in the longer-term goal of the micro-interventions i.e., increased engagement in diabetes self-management behaviours through a reduction in delay discounting they may not necessarily be that interested in the in-moment effects. However, this could be due to the in-moment effects of EFT not being clearly perceived by users. This observation may be especially important given previous micro-intervention research couples perceived usefulness micro-intervention with user retention [24].

Despite the positive usability feedback received we nevertheless note the resulting engagement was lower than expected. Indications from participants are that the primary contributors were: i) the perceived gap between micro-intervention aims and health outcomes (the perceived value), ii) lack of contextualisation and adaptation to individual preferences, in line with Eyles et al. [21] reporting a potential relation between high attrition and a lack of acceptance and iii) failure to address users' specific needs. As our aim was not to adapt to individual user needs, we note that our participants may not have had a specific *need* or preference for EFT micro-interventions; i.e., we did not specifically recruit from groups with risk of high delay discounting or groups with a particular interest in health goals. Decreased engagement generally occurred within the first few days or after the first week of use. Our attrition rate resembles Baumel et al., looking at app uptake in the wild with the majority of retention loss occurring in the first week [9]. Perceived usefulness and acceptance is apparently judged either immediately or within a relatively short period of time and may determine continued use before any longer term benefits may have reached the user [31]. This time frame may thus be indicative of the window of opportunity where suggesting other micro-interventions could retain longer term engagement.

6.3 Potential Use Cases

Interviews with participants with T2DM indicates they themselves perceive EFT as an interesting intervention shortly after diagnosis representing one concrete narrative use. This is further supported by a recent project [48], where in an open co-creation process participants identified discounting of the future in diabetes as an issue. While the participants themselves did not refer to this as delay discounting, they found the inactivity problematic in avoiding future comorbidities.

Looking at other possible narrative use cases for smartphone delivered EFT as micro-interventions we may get inspiration from previous suggested targets for EFT which has shown effects in a multitude of contexts [10,14,15,47,51, 54]. EFT as micro-interventions may thus be relevant to systems working with changing behaviours related to: prediabetes, overeating, cigarette smoking, or more generally where discount of the future may have an adverse effect on future outcomes.

Based on the usage-data made available by the CARP platform, we stipulate that it would be possible to leverage mobile sensing to identify poor adherence, such as not listening to cues, and in turn as an opportunity to suggest other interventions to enrich the narrative [8].

We found the implemented EFT micro-interventions to be subject to user preference, with certain individual barriers to the use of EFT, negatively affecting adherence. This suggests the need for conceptual models of use for determining which users are susceptible to EFT, alternative EFT micro-interventions or if users should be provided other micro-interventions.

6.4 Overall Feasibility

The design of our application and the resulting feasibility study hint that it may be feasible to implement EFT as digital micro-interventions, potentially opening the doors for EFT to become part of a larger micro-intervention care narrative that could provide value in different clinical and therapeutic processes involving behaviour change. Furthermore, the implementation of simple just-in-time and ecological momentary interventions using CARP mobile sensing seems feasible and potentially enable targeting specific in-moment behaviours with EFT, which has previously been shown as effective in both laboratory and simulated real world settings [47]. However, future work is needed to determine the acceptability of receiving EFT in different contextual real world settings and what format of resource can best engage users in these different contexts.

7   Limitations

Although our study shows promising initial results, supporting the application of EFT as part of micro-intervention care narratives and the potential feasibility of delivering simple just-in-time events aiming to affect in-moment decision making, our study did not explore the effectiveness of these. Furthermore, while our study included testing in-the-wild, our relatively small sample size and limited time frame for use limit the generalizability of our results. In the presented exploratory study, our focus has been on discussing findings in-depth with perspectives from existing literature. Future research is required to explore the effectiveness of micro-intervention based EFT delivered with simple just-in-time events, both in order to explore the effect of the different types of events and the overall effect as part of a larger micro-intervention care narrative. Given the technical and usability focus of the study, diversity in recruitment was also limited and does not necessarily include a high delay discounting group, nor were persons with T2DM or other chronic diseases targeted.

8   Conclusion

In this paper we presented the design of an mHealth application for delivering EFT as a series of three micro-interventions and we explore the users' experience of these interventions, their facilitators and barriers. The technological design of the mHealth application was based on a general-purpose mobile sensing framework, which in future applications will allow for flexible collection of contextual data and enable the use hereof to trigger just-in-time events. The system was subject to a single-arm feasibility study involving 14 participants to explore the experience of EFT as micro-interventions, their design, and the implications for use as part of larger micro-intervention narratives.

User's themselves rated usability positively, however engagement was relatively low with identified causes including intervention context, user traits, and perceived value. Based on their experiences, participants themselves suggested various new micro-interventions for different contexts, situations, and preferences. Participant feedback indicates goal-oriented EFT may be preferably compared to traditional EFT due to the direct relation between health and episodic futures. Initial analysis of collected data further suggests the feasibility of leveraging mobile sensing to target simple contexts where EFT may positively affect in-moment decision making.

Acknowledgements. This research is part of the iPDM-GO project [30] that has received funding from EIT Health. EIT Health is supported by the European Institute of Innovation and Technology (EIT), a body of the European Union that receives support from the European Union's Horizon Europe research and innovation programme.

References

1. Alexander, B., et al.: A behavioral sensing system that promotes positive lifestyle changes and improves metabolic control among adults with type 2 diabetes. In: 2017 Systems and Information Engineering Design Symposium (SIEDS), pp. 283–288. IEEE (2017). https://doi.org/10.1109/SIEDS.2017.7937732
2. Amlung, M., Vedelago, L., Acker, J., Balodis, I., MacKillop, J.: Steep delay discounting and addictive behavior: a meta-analysis of continuous associations. Addiction **112**(1), 51–62 (2017). https://doi.org/10.1111/add.13535
3. Aonso-Diego, G., González-Roz, A., Martínez-Loredo, V., Krotter, A., Secades-Villa, R.: Episodic future thinking for smoking cessation in individuals with substance use disorder: treatment feasibility and acceptability. J. Subst. Abuse Treat. **123**, 108259 (2021). https://doi.org/10.1016/j.jsat.2020.108259
4. Atance, C.M., O'Neill, D.K.: Episodic future thinking. Trends Cogn. Sci. **5**(12), 533–539 (2001). https://doi.org/10.1016/S1364-6613(00)01804-0
5. Athamneh, L.N., et al.: Setting a goal could help you control: comparing the effect of health goal versus general episodic future thinking on health behaviors among cigarette smokers and obese individuals. Exp. Clin. Psychopharmacol. **29**(1), 59 (2021). https://doi.org/10.1037/pha0000351
6. Balaskas, A., Schueller, S.M., Cox, A.L., Doherty, G.: Ecological momentary interventions for mental health: a scoping review. PLoS ONE **16**(3), e0248152 (2021). https://doi.org/10.1371/journal.pone.0248152
7. Bardram, J.E.: The carp mobile sensing framework-a cross-platform, reactive, programming framework and runtime environment for digital phenotyping. arXiv preprint arXiv:2006.11904 (2020). https://doi.org/10.48550/arXiv.2006.11904
8. Baumel, A., Fleming, T., Schueller, S.M., et al.: Digital micro interventions for behavioral and mental health gains: core components and conceptualization of digital micro intervention care. J. Med. Internet Res. **22**(10), e20631 (2020). https://doi.org/10.2196/20631
9. Baumel, A., Muench, F., Edan, S., Kane, J.M., et al.: Objective user engagement with mental health apps: systematic search and panel-based usage analysis. J. Med. Internet Res. **21**(9), e14567 (2019). https://doi.org/10.2196/14567
10. Bromberg, U., Lobatcheva, M., Peters, J.: Episodic future thinking reduces temporal discounting in healthy adolescents. PLoS ONE **12**(11), e0188079 (2017). https://doi.org/10.1371/journal.pone.0188079
11. Campbell, J.A., Williams, J.S., Egede, L.E.: Examining the relationship between delay discounting, delay aversion, diabetes self-care behaviors, and diabetes outcomes in us adults with type 2 diabetes. Diabetes Care **44**(4), 893–900 (2021). https://doi.org/10.2337/dc20-2620
12. Chan, C.K., Cameron, L.D.: Promoting physical activity with goal-oriented mental imagery: a randomized controlled trial. J. Behav. Med. **35**(3), 347–363 (2012). https://doi.org/10.1007/s10865-011-9360-6
13. Conroy, D.E., Hojjatinia, S., Lagoa, C.M., Yang, C.H., Lanza, S.T., Smyth, J.M.: Personalized models of physical activity responses to text message micro-interventions: a proof-of-concept application of control systems engineering

methods. Psychol. Sport Exerc. **41**, 172–180 (2019). https://doi.org/10.1016/j. psychsport.2018.06.011

14. Daniel, T.O., Stanton, C.M., Epstein, L.H.: The future is now: comparing the effect of episodic future thinking on impulsivity in lean and obese individuals. Appetite **71**, 120–125 (2013). https://doi.org/10.1016/j.appet.2013.07.010

15. Dassen, F.C., Jansen, A., Nederkoorn, C., Houben, K.: Focus on the future: episodic future thinking reduces discount rate and snacking. Appetite **96**, 327–332 (2016). https://doi.org/10.1016/j.appet.2015.09.032

16. Elefant, A.B., Contreras, O., Muñoz, R.F., Bunge, E.L., Leykin, Y.: Microinterventions produce immediate but not lasting benefits in mood and distress. Internet Interv. **10**, 17–22 (2017). https://doi.org/10.1016/j.invent.2017.08.004

17. Epstein, L.H., et al.: Effects of 6-month episodic future thinking training on delay discounting, weight loss and HbA1c changes in individuals with prediabetes. J. Behav. Med. **45**(2), 227–239 (2022). https://doi.org/10.1007/s10865-021-00278-y

18. Epstein, L.H., et al.: Role of delay discounting in predicting change in HBA1c for individuals with prediabetes. J. Behav. Med. **42**(5), 851–859 (2019). https://doi. org/10.1007/s10865-019-00026-3

19. Epstein, L.H., et al.: Delay discounting, glycemic regulation and health behaviors in adults with prediabetes. Behav. Med. **47**(3), 194–204 (2021). https://doi.org/ 10.1080/08964289.2020.1712581

20. Everitt, N., et al.: Exploring the features of an app-based just-in-time intervention for depression. J. Affect. Disord. **291**, 279–287 (2021). https://doi.org/10.1016/j. jad.2021.05.021

21. Eyles, H., et al.: Co-design of mHealth delivered interventions: a systematic review to assess key methods and processes. Curr. Nutr. Rep. **5**(3), 160–167 (2016). https://doi.org/10.1007/s13668-016-0165-7

22. Fleming, G.A., Petrie, J.R., Bergenstal, R.M., Holl, R.W., Peters, A.L., Heinemann, L.: Diabetes digital app technology: benefits, challenges, and recommendations. a consensus report by the European association for the study of diabetes (EASD) and the American diabetes association (ADA) diabetes technology working group. Diabetes Care **43**(1), 250–260 (2020). https://doi.org/10.2337/dci19-0062

23. Fleming, T., Bavin, L., Lucassen, M., Stasiak, K., Hopkins, S., Merry, S., et al.: Beyond the trial: systematic review of real-world uptake and engagement with digital self-help interventions for depression, low mood, or anxiety. J. Med. Internet Res. **20**(6), e9275 (2018). https://doi.org/10.2196/jmir.9275

24. Fuller-Tyszkiewicz, M., et al.: A randomized trial exploring mindfulness and gratitude exercises as ehealth-based micro-interventions for improving body satisfaction. Comput. Hum. Behav. **95**, 58–65 (2019). https://doi.org/10.1016/j.chb.2019. 01.028

25. Gobin, K.C., McComb, S.E., Mills, J.S.: Testing a self-compassion microintervention before appearance-based social media use: implications for body image. Body Image **40**, 200–206 (2022). https://doi.org/10.1016/j.bodyim.2021. 12.011

26. Golay, A., et al.: Taking small steps towards targets-perspectives for clinical practice in diabetes, cardiometabolic disorders and beyond. Int. J. Clin. Pract. **67**(4), 322–332 (2013). https://doi.org/10.1111/ijcp.12114

27. Griauzde, D., et al.: A mobile phone-based program to promote healthy behaviors among adults with prediabetes who declined participation in free diabetes prevention programs: mixed-methods pilot randomized controlled trial. JMIR Mhealth Uhealth **7**(1), e11267 (2019). https://doi.org/10.2196/11267

28. Hollis-Hansen, K., Seidman, J., O'Donnell, S., Epstein, L.H.: Episodic future thinking and grocery shopping online. Appetite **133**, 1–9 (2019). https://doi.org/10.1016/j.appet.2018.10.019

29. Howe, E., et al.: Design of digital workplace stress-reduction intervention systems: effects of intervention type and timing. In: CHI Conference on Human Factors in Computing Systems, pp. 1–16 (2022). https://doi.org/10.1145/3491102.3502027

30. Jones, A., et al.: Integrated personalized diabetes management goes Europe: a multi-disciplinary approach to innovating type 2 diabetes care in Europe. Prim. Care Diabetes **15**(2), 360–364 (2021). https://doi.org/10.1016/j.pcd.2020.10.008

31. Karapanos, E., Zimmerman, J., Forlizzi, J., Martens, J.B.: User experience over time: an initial framework. In: Proceedings of the SIGCHI Conference on Human Factors in Computing Systems, pp. 729–738 (2009). https://doi.org/10.1145/1518701.1518814

32. Kirby, K.N., Petry, N.M., Bickel, W.K.: Heroin addicts have higher discount rates for delayed rewards than non-drug-using controls. J. Exp. Psychol. Gen. **128**(1), 78 (1999). https://doi.org/10.1037/0096-3445.128.1.78

33. Klasnja, P., Consolvo, S., Pratt, W.: How to evaluate technologies for health behavior change in HCI research. In: Proceedings of the SIGCHI Conference on Human Factors in Computing Systems, pp. 3063–3072 (2011). https://doi.org/10.1145/1978942.1979396

34. Klasnja, P., et al.: Microrandomized trials: an experimental design for developing just-in-time adaptive interventions. Health Psychol. **34**(S), 1220 (2015). https://doi.org/10.1037/hea0000305

35. Lebeau, G., et al.: Delay discounting of gains and losses, glycemic control and therapeutic adherence in type 2 diabetes. Behav. Proc. **132**, 42–48 (2016). https://doi.org/10.1016/j.beproc.2016.09.006

36. Levesque, C.S., Williams, G.C., Elliot, D., Pickering, M.A., Bodenhamer, B., Finley, P.J.: Validating the theoretical structure of the treatment self-regulation questionnaire (TSRQ) across three different health behaviors. Health Educ. Res. **22**(5), 691–702 (2007). https://doi.org/10.1093/her/cyl148

37. Lewis, J.R.: Psychometric evaluation of the PSSUQ using data from five years of usability studies. Int. J. Hum.-Comput. Interact. **14**(3–4), 463–488 (2002). https://doi.org/10.1080/10447318.2002.9669130

38. Matta, A.D., Gonçalves, F.L., Bizarro, L.: Delay discounting: concepts and measures. Psychol. Neurosci. **5**(2), 135–146 (2012). https://doi.org/10.3922/j.psns.2012.2.03

39. Mazur, J.E.: An adjusting procedure for studying delayed reinforcement. Quant. Anal. Behav. **5**, 55–73 (1987)

40. Meinlschmidt, G., et al.: Smartphone-based psychotherapeutic micro-interventions to improve mood in a real-world setting. Front. Psychol. **7**, 1112 (2016). https://doi.org/10.3389/fpsyg.2016.01112

41. Meinlschmidt, G., et al.: Personalized prediction of smartphone-based psychotherapeutic micro-intervention success using machine learning. J. Affect. Disord. **264**, 430–437 (2020). https://doi.org/10.1016/j.jad.2019.11.071

42. Meyerowitz-Katz, G., Ravi, S., Arnolda, L., Feng, X., Maberly, G., Astell-Burt, T., et al.: Rates of attrition and dropout in app-based interventions for chronic disease: systematic review and meta-analysis. J. Med. Internet Res. **22**(9), e20283 (2020). https://doi.org/10.2196/20283

43. Miller, C.K.: Adaptive intervention designs to promote behavioral change in adults: what is the evidence? Curr. Diab.Rep. **19**(2), 1–9 (2019). https://doi.org/10.1007/s11892-019-1127-4

44. Mönninghoff, A., et al.: Long-term effectiveness of mhealth physical activity interventions: systematic review and meta-analysis of randomized controlled trials. J. Med. Internet Res. **23**(4), e26699 (2021). https://doi.org/10.2196/26699

45. O'Donnell, S., Daniel, T.O., Epstein, L.H.: Does goal relevant episodic future thinking amplify the effect on delay discounting? Conscious. Cogn. **51**, 10–16 (2017). https://doi.org/10.1016/j.concog.2017.02.014

46. Odum, A.L.: Delay discounting: i'm ak, you're ak. J. Exp. Anal. Behav. **96**(3), 427–439 (2011). https://doi.org/10.1901/jeab.2011.96-423

47. O'Neill, J., Daniel, T.O., Epstein, L.H.: Episodic future thinking reduces eating in a food court. Eat. Behav. **20**, 9–13 (2016). https://doi.org/10.1016/j.eatbeh.2015.10.002

48. Persson, D.R., Zhukouskaya, K., Wegener, A.M.K., Jørgensen, L.K., Bardram, J.E., Bækgaard, P.: Exploring patient needs and solutions in type 2 diabetes: a cocreation study. Publication in preparation (2023)

49. Schacter, D.L., Benoit, R.G., Szpunar, K.K.: Episodic future thinking: mechanisms and functions. Curr. Opin. Behav. Sci. **17**, 41–50 (2017). https://doi.org/10.1016/j.cobeha.2017.06.002

50. Skinner, T., Joensen, L., Parkin, T.: Twenty-five years of diabetes distress research. Diabet. Med. **37**(3), 393–400 (2020). https://doi.org/10.1111/dme.14157

51. Stein, J.S., et al.: Bleak present, bright future: II. Combined effects of episodic future thinking and scarcity on delay discounting in adults at risk for type 2 diabetes. J. Behav. Med. **44**(2), 222–230 (2020). https://doi.org/10.1007/s10865-020-00178-7

52. Stein, J.S., Sze, Y.Y., Athamneh, L., Koffarnus, M.N., Epstein, L.H., Bickel, W.K.: Think fast: rapid assessment of the effects of episodic future thinking on delay discounting in overweight/obese participants. J. Behav. Med. **40**(5), 832–838 (2017). https://doi.org/10.1007/s10865-017-9857-8

53. Stein, J.S., Tegge, A.N., Turner, J.K., Bickel, W.K.: Episodic future thinking reduces delay discounting and cigarette demand: an investigation of the good-subject effect. J. Behav. Med. **41**(2), 269–276 (2017). https://doi.org/10.1007/s10865-017-9908-1

54. Stein, J.S., Wilson, A.G., Koffarnus, M.N., Daniel, T.O., Epstein, L.H., Bickel, W.K.: Unstuck in time: episodic future thinking reduces delay discounting and cigarette smoking. Psychopharmacology **233**(21), 3771–3778 (2016). https://doi.org/10.1007/s00213-016-4410-y

55. Sze, Y.Y., Daniel, T.O., Kilanowski, C.K., Collins, R.L., Epstein, L.H.: Web-based and mobile delivery of an episodic future thinking intervention for overweight and obese families: a feasibility study. JMIR Mhealth Uhealth **3**(4), e4603 (2015). https://doi.org/10.2196/mhealth.4603

56. Sze, Y.Y., Stein, J.S., Bickel, W.K., Paluch, R.A., Epstein, L.H.: Bleak present, bright future: online episodic future thinking, scarcity, delay discounting, and food demand. Clin. Psychol. Sci. **5**(4), 683–697 (2017). https://doi.org/10.1177/2167702617696511

57. Tatara, N., Årsand, E., Bratteteig, T., Hartvigsen, G.: Usage and perceptions of a mobile self-management application for people with type 2 diabetes: qualitative study of a five-month trial (2013). https://doi.org/10.3233/978-1-61499-289-9-127

58. Weller, R.E., Cook, E.W., III., Avsar, K.B., Cox, J.E.: Obese women show greater delay discounting than healthy-weight women. Appetite **51**(3), 563–569 (2008). https://doi.org/10.1016/j.appet.2008.04.010

59. Xu, X., et al.: Creating a smartphone app for caregivers of children with atopic dermatitis with caregivers, health care professionals, and digital health experts: participatory co-design. JMIR Mhealth Uhealth **8**(10), e16898 (2020). https://doi.org/10.2196/16898

60. Ye, J.Y., et al.: A meta-analysis of the effects of episodic future thinking on delay discounting. Q. J. Exp. Psychol. 1876–1891 (2021). https://doi.org/10.1177/17470218211066282

Blink, Pull, Nudge or Tap? The Impact of Secondary Input Modalities on Eye-Typing Performance

Chris Porter[(✉)] and Gary Zammit

Faculty of Information and Communication Technology, University of Malta, Msida, Malta
{chris.porter,gary.zammit.14}@um.edu.mt

Abstract. Eye trackers (ET) are used in various domains, from assistive technology to virtual reality and gaming. Typing with one's eyes using on-screen soft keyboards is one activity common to all these domains. Using ET technology is liberating but can also be frustrating due to inherent issues such as Midas-Touch - where unintentional actions are not distinguished from intentional ones. To mitigate this, dwell times are typically introduced to distinguish between intentional selections and scanning, however, this has a negative effect on typing speed as well as the perception of workload. Secondary input modalities, such as switches, introduce an explicit way to make on-screen selections, bypassing the need for dwelling. With this in mind, we sought to investigate the impact of various secondary input modalities within a controlled lab study. We recruited 15 individuals who were asked to perform a series of eye-typing tasks using both the dwell-based approach as the baseline, as well as a series of multi-modal configurations. Along with five different input modalities, two different keyboard layouts were also included as independent variables. Results show that, with some exceptions, secondary input modalities generally have a positive impact on eye-typing performance with lower perceived workload scores.

Keywords: Eye-typing · Multi-modal interaction · Performance

1 Introduction

Determining the user's action intents based solely on eye movements is not trivial. Unlike traditional pointing devices such as mice, eye trackers (ET) do not afford a natural way to activate on-screen targets, such as links or buttons. Techniques exist to interpret between scanning and selection using an eye-tracker, and the use of dwelling is one such technique that helps distinguish between glances and fixations on specific areas of interest. Secondary input modalities, such as mechanical switches, have also been adopted to help ET users confirm selections [22,24,31]. Dwell-based typing necessitates that a person holds the gaze on a target for a pre-specified period of time until a selection is confirmed. This dwell time varies depending on the person, however, it typically starts from just under a second (e.g., 900 ms) for more advanced users, but could also be set to 1.5 s or more [9]. The downside of using this approach is that it reduces interaction speed as well as throughput while potentially increasing fatigue - since it takes longer to type. Techniques have been suggested to dynamically calculate the dwell-time based on usage patterns over time [25] and by changing the dwell time for each specific target depending on the probability of it being selected next [11,13]. Using a second input modality instead of, or along with, dwell-time may improve performance and throughput since selections can be confirmed without unnecessary delays (e.g., by pressing a switch). This, however, depends on the person's ability to interact with the second device (e.g., fine motor control and range of motion), along with the choice of hardware (e.g., JellyBean, String switch, Wobble switch) and its affordances (e.g., push, pull, touch). To the best of our knowledge, there are no studies that assess the impact of different commercially available secondary input modalities on eye-typing activities. With this in mind, this study aims to provide performance and perceived workload-related data for a number of secondary input modalities in a controlled environment. Eye-typing was adopted as the core activity since we believe (a) it is a central human activity to communicate and work, (b) it is a highly laborious activity, and (c) it is highly prone to human error due to the proximity and density of on-screen keyboard targets.

The rest of this document is organised as follows. The following section provides some background for this study, along with a review of related work. This is then followed by an outline of the methodology adopted, along with the presentation of results and a discussion thereon. We then conclude this paper with insights and potential avenues for future work.

This paper is based on postgraduate research carried out at the Human-Computer Interaction lab at the University of Malta [29].

2   Background and Related Work

Dwelling is typically used in eye-tracking applications; however, researchers have been investigating alternative and configurable dwell times to, as much as possible, reduce fatigue and increase performance [11,13,16,25]. As expected, setting it too high reduces input throughput, while setting it too low could lead to increased error rates - and neither is desirable. A number of researchers have turned their attention to the use of second modalities in conjunction with eye trackers [10,17,22,24,31] ranging from soft switches to foot switches and blink-based switches, with generally promising results. To our knowledge, most studies revolved around a single device, with no comparative data for different second modality configurations targeting different parts of the body.

2.1   Eye-Typing – To Dwell or Not to Dwell

Eye movements are significantly faster than movements performed by any other limb [20]. For instance, a saccade - a shift in fixation from one point to another -

takes between 30 ms to 120 ms [18]. This makes the eyes, in conjunction with an eye tracker, the fastest pointing device; however, unlike other pointing devices such as mice, eye-gaze control does not have explicit in-built mechanisms to indicate selection intent (e.g., left mouse button). In eye-tracking interaction, the eyes are used for both perception and control, and therefore an explicit way to distinguish the two (e.g., casual viewing vs intentional control) is needed to avoid problems such as the 'Midas-Touch'. Dwell-based interaction requires eye-tracker users to fixate on a target for a short period of time to purposefully activate a selection. This is the simplest approach to tackle the 'Midas-Touch' problem and is entirely based on a trade-off between interaction speed and error rates [13]. Higher dwell times will typically result in fewer typing errors at the expense of text entry speed. Conversely, lower dwell times will afford faster text entry, but at the risk of making more mistakes. This is because users will have less time to shift their gaze before a selection is made. Dwell-based interaction has been on the map for a number of years, with Ware and Mikaelian [28] presenting results on this technique back in 1986 for making on-screen selections using an eye tracker. Along with dwelling the authors also considered physical buttons as well as an on-screen select button [28]. This dwelling time is typically set upwards of 300 ms, with the lower and upper limits informed by the person's preferences and experience levels with the technology. In [8,16] authors have shown that with practice users are able to perform reasonably well with lower dwell times. As observed in [12], the Midas-Touch problem will become less likely with more experience, and in certain situations, experienced users may also be able to interact reasonably well using dwell times ranging from around 400 ms to 500 ms. Some researchers have explored the notion of a variable dwell time based on observation of the user's interaction patterns. Spakov et al. [25] managed to observe a typing speed of 12 words per minute (WPM) when dynamically calculating the dwell time based on the exit time from the target area following a selection. Other authors [13] studied probabilistic dwell-time adjustments, whereby shorter times are assigned to more likely characters and vice versa, based on the probability of each character being selected next. Irrespective of the users' skill and experience, this dwell time presents a "permanent barrier against a substantial speed-up" [28] over time. This is because the time required to register a fixation and in turn activate a target cannot be bypassed or even lowered beyond a minimum level before usability and error rates are impacted. Dwell-free eye typing partially removes this barrier by letting ET users glance at a series of characters making up specific words without pauses (referred to as the gaze plot or input trace), after which algorithms are put in place to determine the intended words. Although a very valid approach, this technique is considered to be out of scope for this particular study.

2.2   Using a Second Modality with Eye Typing

An alternative approach to tackle the Midas-Touch problem and to counteract the unavoidable performance hit associated with a fixed dwell-time is to adopt a second input modality in conjunction with an eye tracker. This second modality allows users to indicate their selection intent without having to also use their gaze. Back in 1985, the authors in [28] empirically observed that people who have a disability and who are able to "make a button press", opting for a physical switch "may be the selection technique of choice" to distinguish between gazing and selection intent using an eye tracker. Furthermore, physical buttons, the authors argue, afford performance gains over time since, with extended practice, users may learn to "synchronise button presses and eye movements", which would, in turn, further improve interaction speed. This is contrasted to the dwell-based technique, which typically presents a permanent time barrier before any action is registered. In [30], it was also noted that dwell-based approaches have the effect of overloading the visual perceptual channel with both vision and control tasks, which is described as unnatural. Zhai et al. [30] present MAGIC (Manual and Gaze Input Cascaded), which adopts gaze input in conjunction with a traditional pointing device to minimise fatigue and workload. MAGIC reduces the need for coarse pointing actions, using gaze to move the cursor to different areas on the screen, while still relying on traditional pointing devices for selection and control. Gaze interaction is largely used to reduce the travel distance, otherwise required using traditional pointing devices.

Secondary input modalities are generally selected according to a person's abilities and available range of motion and could include a wide variety of hardware, from off the shelf plug and play assistive technologies such as soft switches, which could be mounted for use through any limb, to more advanced technology such as Electromyography (EMG) activated switches [3] which can react to a person's muscular activity. This in turn frees up eye interaction from control-related activities. Multi-modal eye interaction is understood to increase accuracy as well as tolerance for errors, which typically characterise single-modal approaches [22]. One reason for this is that multi-modal eye-tracking interaction builds on a person's motor capabilities, whichever these may be, to make explicit on-screen selections, without having to carry out precise holding patterns required in dwell-based approaches. If a person is able to carry out coarse motor actions such as blinking or even moving a finger, then a second input device could be designed around those capabilities to bypass the need for dwelling which requires precision and consistency.

Various authors have looked at second modalities when it comes to eye typing. Singh et al. [22] observed that adopting a soft-switch as a second modality dramatically reduced the Midas-Touch problem while at the same time significantly increased the average typing speed (13.36 $\pm$ 1.22 characters per minute (CPM)) using a novel keyboard layout). Error rates also dropped significantly. Meena et al. [10] studied several non-invasive input devices as second modalities, including a soft switch and surface EMG. Using soft switches, the authors observed better performance over other modalities, with the least number of errors and the highest text-entry rate (21.83 $\pm$ 6.58 CPM) using a novel keyboard layout. Zhao et al. [31] considered a tooth clicker as a second input modality. The on-ear sensor, which detects subtle jaw clenches, was adopted for text entry tasks with considerably higher CPM rates over a dwell-based approach. However, the authors also noted that error rates increased using this second modality. This was attributed to a steeper learning curve and a lack of experience with this type of technology that depends on eye-jaw coordination. Furthermore, participants observed that a tooth clicker is not convenient for use in a typing context, however, it might be better suited for reading or interacting with screen elements. While a short dwell time (e.g. 490 ms) was considered to be more efficient for participants, all of them also noted that the second modality gives them a greater degree of control over dwell-based interaction, eliminating "their concerns about generating unintended activations", and therefore reducing the Midas-Touch problem. Similarly, mouth switches operated with one's tongue were also adopted in multi-modal eye typing activities. Soundarajan and Cecotti [24] adopted this technology with an unambiguous soft keyboard (one key is associated with one character) and reported significantly higher typing speeds (36.6 ± 8.4 CPM using an alphabetical keyboard layout) when compared with dwell-time based approaches.

Other second modalities have been adopted in research studies, including the use of voice [2,27] and voluntary blinking [1,15,21]. Voice commands and utterances were adopted to toggle selections or to perform typing-related actions such as corrections or word formatting. Mixed results are reported, particularly in terms of error rates. Furthermore, the use of speech recognition can be very limiting both in terms of contextual appropriateness but also for people who find it difficult to speak clearly or at all. On the other hand, utterances, clicks or throat vibrations may be more applicable to a wider range of people as a second modality, however still limited with contextual appropriateness (e.g., use in quiet public spaces). The use of blinking is available to a wider range of people, including non-verbal people and people with severe motor restrictions [6]. A challenge associated with blink-based interaction is to effectively differentiate between reflexive blinks (e.g., to keep the eye lubricated) and voluntary blinks. For this reason, techniques such as blink patterns [7] and blink duration [1,15] are used to be able to distinguish between the two, and are used in conjunction with gaze and head tracking to trigger actions.

3   Methodology

This study consisted of the following steps. First, a shortlisting exercise was carried out to determine which second modalities, and on-screen keyboard layouts, are to be included in this study. This phase included a review of related literature, a review of commercially available hardware, along with in-depth discussions with domain experts. For all shortlisted second modalities a comparative study was then carried out in a controlled environment. This study was designed to collect performance data under best-case scenario conditions for various eye-typing configurations, which include the use of an eye-tracker only and an eye-tracker along with a series of second modalities, in both cases using two keyboard layouts - Grid and Grouped. To study the influence of the second modality on performance, the study controlled for variances in both the participants' range of motion and also in environmental conditions. A purpose-built multi-modal on-screen keyboard, code-named ModaliKey, was developed for this study and was used in the data collection exercise.

3.1 Shortlisting of Second Modalities and Keyboard Layouts

This study considered devices that are operable using as many different parts of the body with varying ranges of motion, which could all be adopted as second input modalities in activities such as eye-typing. A review of related literature was carried out to determine the state of the art in multi-modal eye typing, including keyboard layouts, while commercial and readily available input technologies, primarily used in ATs, were also taken into account. Further to the review, domain experts were consulted to sanity check and augment this shortlist, and these included occupational therapists working with assistive technologies as well as the Open Assistive online community of AT developers. The scope of these discussions was to shed light on past experiences with modalities that are commonly used for eye-typing tasks. The following devices were identified as options for a second input modality:

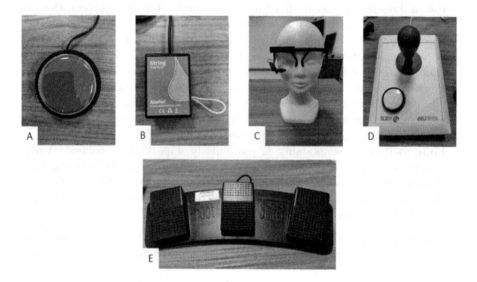

Fig. 1. (A) JellyBean (B) String switch (C) Blink switch (D) Joystick switch (E) Foot switch

1. **JellyBean**: As observed in related literature [4,5,19], switches such AbleNet's JellyBean are regularly adopted as input modalities in Augmentative and Alternative Communication (AAC) systems. These are inexpensive and highly sensitive mechanical devices requiring minimal motor movement that could be configured to emulate several computer commands through a switch interface (e.g. Hitch 2). Practitioners also noted that this switch is typically

highly adaptable, and can be mounted to be operated in various ways, including using one's hand, elbows, head movement and so forth - depending on contextual and motor-related factors. See Fig. 1 (A).

2. **String switch**: This switch is operated by pulling a string loop with very minimal force and with very little travel distance. This makes it ideal for people who have little finger or hand movement abilities, or in contexts where movement is highly restricted, such as wearing a cast. For this reason, we opted for an AbleNet 100SS String switch. See Fig. 1 (B).

3. **Blink switch**: Blink detection is often used with gaze-only approaches since most users with sufficient eye control have the ability to also blink voluntarily [1,7,15,21]. PupilCore, a wearable eye-tracker from PupilLabs was adapted to detect blinks using its infrared camera located within proximity of the user's eye. Custom software was required to (a) detect voluntary blinks and (b) send selection commands to the on-screen keyboard. See Fig. 1 (C).

4. **Joystick + switch**: A senior occupational therapist suggested this device as a typical device used to control hardware and software in various domains and contexts, from gaming to wheelchair control. It was therefore deemed to be a suitable candidate, particularly since along with its activation button, a Joystick may also afford a way to correct for gaze inaccuracies. To our knowledge, this modality was not investigated in the context of multimodal eye typing. In [23], a JoyStick was adopted to assist people with motor impairments in text entry activities with word prediction, however, this was adopted as the sole input device rather than as a second modality. Further investigation was deemed to be appropriate, and a BJoy Stick-C Lite, which is also equipped with a sensitive switch, was adopted for this purpose. Custom software was required to integrate BJoy's x-y axis movements and selection commands with the on-screen keyboard. See Fig. 1 (D).

5. **Foot switch**: This modality is particularly important in contexts where upper body limitations exist, either due to situational limitations (e.g. handling machinery using one's hands) or due to limited motor abilities. An Accuratus X3P Foot Switch was adopted to understand the impact of using one's feet as a second input modality. See Fig. 1 (E).

Furthermore, from discussion with domain experts along with a review of commercial AAC systems, the most commonly adopted layouts were also shortlisted:

1. **Grid layout**: the Grid layout provides all characters on a Grid with equal spacing between all characters. This layout is typically offered in both QWERTY format and also in an Alphabetical format. In this study, it was decided to allow participants to select either QWERTY (see Fig. 2 (A - top) or Alphabetical (see Fig. 2 (A - bottom) ahead of time, according to what they are most familiar with. This was done to control for unfamiliarity which might have a negative impact on performance (e.g. participants wasting time scanning for letters).

2. **Grouped layout**: the Grouped layout offers larger targets consisting of groups of characters. To select a character, users would first need to activate the group in which that character is found (e.g. 'ABCDE' - see Fig. 2

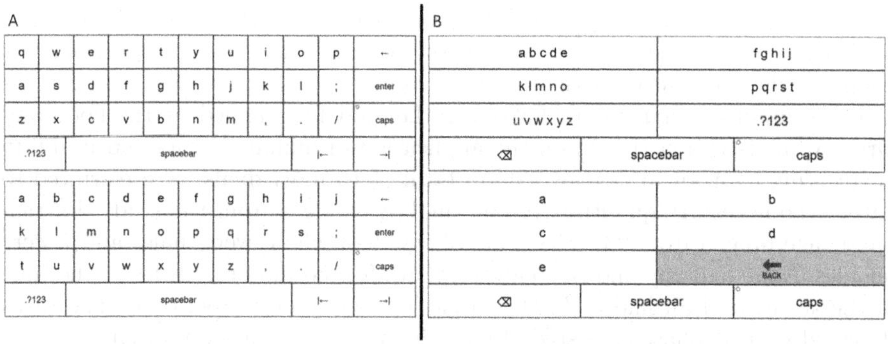

A

q	w	e	r	t	y	u	i	o	p	←
a	s	d	f	g	h	j	k	l	;	enter
z	x	c	v	b	n	m	,	.	/	caps
.?123			spacebar						←	→

a	b	c	d	e	f	g	h	i	j	←
k	l	m	n	o	p	q	r	s	;	enter
t	u	v	w	x	y	z	,	.	/	caps
.?123			spacebar						←	→

B

a b c d e	f g h i j
k l m n o	p q r s t
u v w x y z	.?123
⊗	spacebar	caps

a	b
c	d
e	←BACK
⊗	spacebar	caps

Fig. 2. (A) Grid layout QWERTY (top) and Alphabetical (bottom) (B) Grouped layout top level (top) and second level (bottom)

(B - top)), and then select the desired character (e.g. 'D' - see Fig. 2 (B - bottom)). This approach allows for larger targets and font sizes, potentially reducing the number of errors when using an eye-tracker, but at the expense of additional steps in the typing process.

3.2 Controlled Study

Informed by insights obtained from the preliminary investigation, this study is centred around a cross-platform purpose-built soft keyboard affording native integration with various input modalities, ranging from basic switches to blink-detection devices. This arising technology, code-named ModaliKey, served as both a data collection tool and was also meant to lend itself as a purpose-built multi-modal soft keyboard for eye-typing. The scope of this study was to shed light on the potential impact of second modalities on typing performance as well as perceived workload when compared to dwell-based gaze-only typing (the Baseline) using either keyboard layout. This investigation was carried out in best-case scenario conditions, controlling for varying motor conditions. During each session, a number of metrics were recorded as outlined in Table 2. The study design, along with the selection of dependent and independent variables, was carried out with the aim of producing reliable results that clearly outline the extent of impact from the adoption of various second modalities and keyboard layouts. Other potential independent variables, such as motor abilities, hardware layout as well as ET accuracy, were controlled for by adopting a consistent setup and associated study protocol for each session. Before each session, participants were required to go through a calibration process to ensure that a level of ET precision was obtained. Also, their preference between the QWERTY and Alphabetical format was established based on experience, which format was then adopted for all tasks for that participant whenever the Grid keyboard layout was used. Since this study focused on the performance of input modalities rather than individuals making use of them, it was important to control for motor-related variances in results. Consequently, all the participants in this phase did not have any known motor impairments. Furthermore, a within-subjects approach was adopted whereby every participant was observed performing a series of tasks using all input configurations. Following the guidelines issued by the Food and Drug Administration (FDA) on the application of human factors and usability engineering to medical devices, [26], a total of 15 individuals were recruited to gather the necessary quantitative and qualitative data from the study. Participants' age ranged from 23 to 58 years of age, 8 of whom were males and 7 were females. None had any known condition that affected motor abilities at the time of the study, and all had at least a basic level of typing experience. The tasks designed for this phase consisted of participants copying a series of pangrams of similar length using each and every interaction configuration (i.e. all keyboard layouts and input modalities along with a gaze-only approach). Pangrams contain every letter of the English alphabet, reducing bias towards more popular characters and spreading interaction across the entire soft keyboard. Some examples include '*The bizarre guy quickly waves and jumps off a number of boxes*', '*Tex balked at my request of anchovy pizza and a jug of wine*' and '*Just wear pants every day to excel in the biz of quilt making*'.

Prior to each task, participants were given some time to familiarise themselves with the setup, to ensure that technical difficulties were tackled ahead of data collection. For a task to be considered completed, participants had to type in the pangram as provided, including case sensitivity. If selection errors were made, participants were given the chance to correct them. To minimise bias on treatments due to the order in which they were administered during the study, modality and keyboard layout configurations were randomised, along with the choice of pangram for each task. Short breaks were given in between tasks to minimise the impact of fatigue. For each input modality, participants had to carry out two tasks, one for each keyboard layout. Each participant session took around 90 min to complete with 12 input configurations (see Table 1).

Table 1. Task input/layout configuration

Input Modalities	Keyboard Layouts
Gaze (Baseline)	Grid and Grouped
Gaze + JellyBean	Grid and Grouped
Gaze + String	Grid and Grouped
Gaze + Blink	Grid and Grouped
Gaze + Joystick	Grid and Grouped
Gaze + Foot	Grid and Grouped

ModaliKey was built in a way to guide participants while performing the tasks - whereby a pangram was displayed along with the characters being typed simultaneously. This approach was adopted to avoid participants moving their gaze away from the monitor, risking shifts in position and overall ET calibration accuracy. Furthermore, ModaliKey was designed to also record selection errors, the time on task (marked at the time when the entire pangram is copied correctly), as well as typing speed in words per minute (WPM). Visual and auditory feedback was provided while participants typed and also when mistakes were made. Also, the tool allowed users to correct mistakes by deleting incorrect characters; however, correct characters could not be deleted to avoid accidental deletions and unnecessary delays. Auto-completion and text prediction were disabled. For the gaze-only interaction tasks, considered as the Baseline measurements, it was decided to use a dwell-based approach which is the most common gaze-interaction technique. A dwell-time of 1000 ms was set according to typical configurations informed by both literature and domain experts as well as through observations during pilot studies. During the tasks, a number of task-level metrics were recorded (see Table 2), while after using each input configuration, participants were asked a few questions about the modality adopted. Quantitative measures were eventually evaluated using statistical tests to analyse and compare means across modalities and keyboard layouts against the Baseline. The setup displayed in Fig. 3 consisted of a PC equipped with a Tobii 4C ET (used to control the mouse cursor) along with the shortlisted input modalities.

Table 2. Dependent variables adopted for this study

Dependent variable	Observation source	Description
TOT	Data collection tool	Time on Task
Completion rate	Direct observation	Tasks completed successfully
WPM	Data collection tool	Words per minute
Errors	Data collection tool	Number of incorrect selections
SEQ	Post-task questionnaire	Single Ease Question
RTLX	Post-task questionnaire	Raw NASA-TLX computation
Perceived Satisfaction	Post-modality questionnaire	Likert scale (7-point)
User Experience	Post-modality questionnaire	Qualitative

The specifications of the hardware used consisted of a Dell laptop with Windows-10 Pro (64-bit), Intel Core i7-9200 CPU with 32-bit RAM, and a 24" LED monitor with a resolution of 1920 by 1080 pixels. Moreover, an emulator was required to convert the switch actions into a computer command. The Jelly Bean and String switch required routing through a Hitch 2.0 computer switch interface to emulate a mouse click when toggled. Custom code was developed for the PupilLabs eye tracker to detect and convert blinks into mouse clicks. Similarly, custom code was developed to allow users to correct selections using a Joystick. The foot switch came with software that allowed for custom action mapping. Every participant performed the experiment using the same setup under the same lighting conditions, position, and distance from the ET at the HCI Lab within the Faculty of ICT at the University of Malta (see Fig. 3).

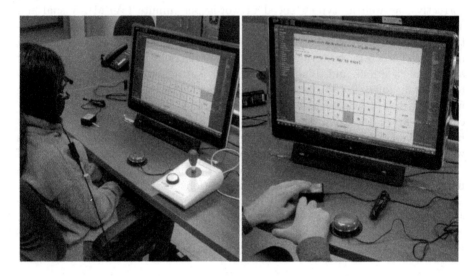

Fig. 3. The experimental setup design, including several modalities

This research is in conformity with the University of Malta's Research Code of Practice and Research Ethics Review Procedures.

4   Results

The following sections outline recorded results for the various metrics collected throughout participant sessions, including errors made, task time (ToT), typing speed (WPM), perceived difficulty (SEQ), perceived workload (RTLX) and overall experience. The Baseline configuration refers to participants using an eye tracker without a second modality, with a 1000 ms dwell-time. It is important to point out that results for Errors, ToT and WPM are all based on data obtained from 14 participants. One of the participants was consistently unable to obtain reasonably good calibration levels with the eye-tracker, making ET-only interaction significantly ineffective, despite several attempts through different lighting conditions and positioning. Having said that, the same participant was able to complete all tasks when using secondary input modalities since selections could be made without the need to precisely hold the gaze on the target. This was an interesting result, highlighting a clear benefit of second input modalities for ET interaction. Data from this participant is, however, reported for the SEQ, RTLX and overall experience scores.

Table 3. Errors made per modality for both keyboard layouts (N = 14)

	Baseline		JellyBean		String		Blink switch		Joystick		Foot	
	Grid	Grpd	Grid	Grpd	Grid	Grpd	Grid	Grpd	Grid	Grpd	Grid	Grpd
Mean	3.71	3.50	1.50	1.21	1.14	1.29	15.86	12.07	2.07	1.36	1.64	2.86
St. Dev.	3.049	2.47	1.18	1.21	1.10	1.10	9.914	5.68	2.94	1.11	1.17	0.64

4.1 Errors

Table 3 shows the mean number of errors made per modality for both the Grid and Grouped keyboard layouts. On the other hand, Table 4 outlines Tukey's Honest Significant Difference (HSD) post hoc test results for errors made by modality against the Baseline for both keyboard layouts. This determines statistically significant mean differences between errors made using any of the modalities under evaluation with errors made when using the Baseline. Mean errors in the Baseline were found to be 3.71 (N = 14, SD = 3.05) for the Grid layout and 3.50 (N = 14, SD = 2.47) for the Grouped layout. Except for the Blink switch, all modalities resulted in lower mean error counts overall. In both Grid and Grouped layouts, the Blink switch resulted in the largest amount of errors with a mean of 15.86 (N = 14, SD = 9.91) and 12.07 (N = 14, SD = 5.68), respectively. Both values are significantly different to the Baseline results. Some issues observed when using the Blink switch include the main eye tracker losing the participants' gaze position as the blink was being performed. At times, while blinking, the gaze position shifted downwards, in turn making incorrect selections. In certain cases, blinks were incorrectly detected, particularly when the participant was gazing at

Table 4. Tukey HSD test for Errors made by modality for both keyboard layouts (N = 14)

	Modality (I)	Modality (J)	Mean Diff (I-J)	Std. Error	Sig.
Grid	Baseline	Jellybean	2.21429	1.69676	0.781
		String	2.57143	1.69676	0.655
		Footswitch	2.07143	1.69676	0.825
		Joystick	1.64286	1.69676	0.927
		Blinking	**−12.14286***	1.69676	**0.000**
Grouped	Baseline	Jellybean	2.28571	1.04529	0.256
		String	2.21429	1.04529	0.289
		Footswitch	0.64286	1.04529	0.990
		Joystick	2.14286	1.04529	0.324
		Blinking	**−8.57143***	1.04529	**0.000**

*. The mean difference is significant at the 0.05 level.

keys further down the screen and the eyelid would already be partially lowered. Overall, it can be argued that every participant performed better when a second modality was available to activate a selection.

4.2   Time on Task

Table 5 shows the mean task duration in seconds per modality for both the Grid and Grouped keyboard layouts. On the other hand, Table 6 shows Tukey's Honest Significant Difference (HSD) post hoc test results for task duration by modality against the Baseline for both keyboard layouts. This determines statistically significant mean differences between ToT values using any of the modalities under evaluation with ToT obtained with the Baseline.

Table 5. Time on Task (seconds - rounded) per modality for both layouts (N = 14)

	Baseline		JellyBean		String		Blink switch		Joystick		Foot	
	Grid	Grpd	Grid	Grpd	Grid	Grpd	Grid	Grpd	Grid	Grpd	Grid	Grpd
Mean	139	255	78	149	79	152	219	304	78	142	89	194
St. Dev.	39.97	46.64	25.56	40.98	18.13	28.46	120.38	143.67	17.49	30.68	19.53	38.71

Mean ToT in the Baseline was 139.32 (N = 14, SD = 39.97) for the Grid layout and 254.60 (N = 14, SD = 46.64) for the Grouped layout. Except for the Blink switch, all modalities afforded demonstrably better performance in terms of mean task completion times compared to the Baseline. On the other hand, in both Grid and Grouped layouts, with the Blink switch, participants took the longest to complete tasks, with a mean of 218.60 (N = 14, SD = 120.38) and 303.79 (N = 14, SD = 143.67), respectively. For the Grid layout, the Blink switch performed significantly worse than the Baseline. It is evidently clear that a second modality significantly improves performance in both keyboard layouts. The JellyBean, Joystick and String switch resulted in the lowest ToT values in both Grid and Grouped layouts, while the difference from the Baseline was statistically significant in the Grouped keyboard layout. Having a second modality to confirm selections affords a bypass mechanism to the dwell-time that was necessary in the Baseline. With respect to keyboard layouts, it was expected that the Grouped layout would result in larger ToT values since participants were required to perform multiple selections before reaching the target character.

Table 6. Tukey HSD test for Time on Task by modality for both keyboard layouts (N = 14)

	Modality (I)	Modality (J)	Mean Diff (I-J)	Std. Error	Sig.
Grid	Baseline	Jellybean	61.49657	21.33802	0.055
		String	60.50093	21.33802	0.062
		Footswitch	50.70821	21.33802	0.177
		Joystick	61.17971	21.33802	0.058
		Blinking	**−79.28050***	21.33802	**0.005**
Grouped	Baseline	Jellybean	**105.43621***	26.67236	**0.002**
		String	**102.39429***	26.67236	**0.003**
		Footswitch	60.45414	26.67236	0.220
		Joystick	**112.18643***	26.67236	**0.001**
		Blinking	−49.19129	26.67236	0.444

*. The mean difference is significant at the 0.05 level.

4.3 Words per Minute

Table 7 shows the text-entry rate in WMP per modality for both the Grid and Grouped keyboard layouts. On the other hand, Table 8 outlines Tukey's Honest Significant Difference (HSD) post hoc test results for WPM by modality against the Baseline for both keyboard layouts. This determines statistically significant mean differences between WPM values using any of the modalities under evaluation with WPM obtained with the Baseline. Other than the Blink switch, all modalities achieved a higher text-entry rate than the Baseline.

Table 7. WPM per modality for both keyboard layouts (N = 14)

	Baseline		JellyBean		String		Blink switch		Joystick		Foot	
	Grid	Grpd	Grid	Grpd	Grid	Grpd	Grid	Grpd	Grid	Grpd	Grid	Grpd
Mean	5.61	2.91	10.20	5.06	9.42	4.50	4.25	2.49	9.45	5.19	8.37	3.94
St. Dev.	1.48	0.59	2.89	1.61	2.21	0.83	1.80	0.83	1.99	0.63	2.12	0.74

The JellyBean, String switch, Footswitch and Joystick achieved statistically significantly better results than the Baseline for the Grid layout. In contrast, in the Grouped layout, the JellyBean, String and Joystick obtained statistically significantly better results in terms of text entry rates (WPM).

Table 8. Tukey HSD test for WPM by modality for both keyboard layouts (N = 14)

	Modality (I)	Modality (J)	Mean Diff (I-J)	Std. Error	Sig.
Grid	Baseline	Jellybean	−4.58732*	0.83416	**0.000**
		String	−3.81278*	0.83416	**0.000**
		Footswitch	−2.75435*	0.83416	**0.018**
		Joystick	−3.84013*	0.83416	**0.000**
		Blinking	1.35779	0.83416	0.583
Grouped	Baseline	Jellybean	−2.15150*	0.36650	**0.000**
		String	−1.56520*	0.36650	**0.001**
		Footswitch	−1.02956	0.36650	0.067
		Joystick	−2.27783*	0.36650	**0.000**
		Blinking	0.42358	0.36650	0.856

*. The mean difference is significant at the 0.05 level.

4.4   SEQ and RTLX

Following each task, participants were asked to submit an SEQ score. This single-question instrument measures the perceived level of difficulty from the users' perspective, with values ranging between one to seven, with one implying a high level of perceived difficulty ('very difficult') and seven denoting the lowest level of perceived difficulty ('very easy') [130]. Table 9 lists mean SEQ scores for every modality and keyboard layout across all tasks. Due to calibration issues, one participant was not able to carry out any actions using either the ET only (Baseline) or the Blink switch modalities in the Grid layout - and has therefore not provided an SEQ score in these two instances. In all other configurations, the participant was still able to perform tasks, with limitations. Further to this, NASA-TLX, a multi-dimensional subjective workload assessment tool was used to measure perceived workload after each task - across six dimensions, namely: (a) mental demand, (b) physical demand, (c) temporal demand, (d) overall performance, (e) effort and (f) frustration. It was decided to report the Raw TLX (RTLX) values as opposed to the Mean Weighted Workload (MWW). To obtain the MWW, a pair-wise comparison of the six subscales would be required with a total of 15 combinations. This process would significantly lengthen the duration of the post-task evaluation. Research shows that RTLX is sufficient to highlight workload-related concerns [14] due to the high level of correlation between Raw TLX and MWW values. Following the completion of each task, participants were asked to score each of the six dimensions. The raw workload (RTLX) for every participant is computed by dividing the sum of the participants' dimension scores by the number of dimensions [14]. Table 11 provides mean RTLX scores by modality for the Grid and Grouped layouts.

Table 9. Overall task-level SEQ scores.

		Baseline	JellyBean	String	Blink switch	Joystick	Foot
Grid	Mean	5.79	6.67	6.87	3.64	6.27	6.2
	St. Dev.	1.0127	0.4714	0.3399	1.3420	0.6799	0.9092
Grouped	Mean	4.8	6.33	6.6	3.13	6.6	5.73
	St. Dev	1.0456	0.5963	0.6110	0.9568	0.4899	0.5735

Overall, all modalities achieved a lower level of perceived workload with respect to the Baseline, except for the Blink switch which recorded the highest level of perceived workload, almost double that of the Baseline for both Grid and Grouped layouts. It is clear that introducing a second input modality resulted in less perceived workload, reflecting lower WPM, ToT and Error-values demonstrated in the previous sections. Furthermore, participants generally experienced lower levels across the various NASA-TLX subscales as shown in Table 10.

Table 10. Mean workload scores for individual NASA-TLX subscales for both layouts, contrasted with the baseline value (n.b. for Performance, lower values are better)

		Baseline	JellyBean	String	Blink	Joystick	Foot
Grid	Mental Demand	35.93	17.21 ↓	15.07 ↓	63.21 ↑	19.36 ↓	26.71 ↓
	Physical Demand	24.43	17.21 ↓	16.07 ↓	51.14 ↑	23.50 ↓	31.79 ↑
	Temporal Demand	33.93	27.57 ↓	22.29 ↓	52.07 ↑	23.43 ↓	28.71 ↓
	Performance	32.86	19.36 ↓	17.21 ↓	55.07 ↑	20.36 ↓	31.79 ↓
	Effort	25.64	19.36 ↓	17.21 ↓	67.36 ↑	20.29 ↓	28.79 ↑
	Frustration	25.64	16.14 ↓	14 ↓	62.29 ↑	18.29 ↓	23.57 ↓
Grouped	Mental Demand	42.07	18.29 ↓	22.50 ↓	69.21 ↑	25.64 ↓	35.86 ↓
	Physical Demand	27.64	21.50 ↓	20.29 ↓	62.21 ↑	27.71 ↑	38.79 ↑
	Temporal Demand	46.00	25.50 ↓	23.36 ↓	62.21 ↑	27.57 ↓	30.71 ↓
	Performance	35.93	20.43 ↓	19.36 ↓	51 ↑	21.50 ↓	26.79 ↓
	Effort	39.86	21.36 ↓	18.29 ↓	74.36 ↑	19.36 ↓	33.86 ↓
	Frustration	32.64	18.21 ↓	19.29 ↓	70.21 ↑	21.50 ↓	31.79 ↓

Table 11. Overall perceived workload (Raw TLX) for different modalities across tasks and keyboard layouts (N = 15)

		Baseline	JellyBean	String	Blink switch	Joystick	Foot
Grid	Mean RTLX	29.74	19.48	16.98	58.52	20.87	28.56
	St. Dev.	7.16	5.72	4.41	20.77	8.53	7.59
Grouped	Raw TLX	37.36	20.88	20.51	64.87	23.88	32.96
	St. Dev.	10.16	6.55	6.92	10.72	6.43	9.34

4.5   Modality-Level User Experience

For each modality, and after completing all related tasks using both keyboard layouts, participants were asked to rate their overall experience with the last modality used, using a 7-point Likert scale question, ranging from a 'bad experience' to a 'very good experience'. Moreover, every participant was asked whether there were any useful or frustrating aspects about the modality under investigation. It is important to point out at this point that each participant was introduced to different modalities in a random order to reduce learning effects and bias arising from fatigue. Quantitative results are outlined in Table 12, and show that except for the Blink switch, most modalities exceeded (or were close to) the Baseline in terms of perceived experience, with 1 being bad to 7 being very good. The Blink switch received the lowest score overall of 3.64 (N = 15, SD = 1.44) while the String switch received the highest score at 6.64 (N = 15, SD = 0.61), followed closely by the Joystick and JellyBean switch. Once all tasks were performed, using all modalities, participants were asked to indicate which second input modality they found most usable, except for the Baseline. It was clear that the String switch was the most preferred input modality (46%), followed closely by the JellyBean switch (27%) and the Joystick (27%).

Table 12. Overall scores for experience on a 7-point Likert scale ranging from bad (1) to very good (7) (N = 15)

	Baseline	JellyBean	String	Blink switch	Joystick	Foot
Mean Experience Score	5.86	6.29	6.64	3.64	6.43	5.64
St. Dev.	0.74	0.70	0.61	1.44	0.62	0.97

4.6   Qualitative Perspectives

Several participants considered the notion of a bi-modal interaction as more intuitive when compared to gaze-only interaction. This was due to a feeling of "more control". Objectively, the String switch was deemed to be the least difficult modality to use (see Table 9), with the least level of perceived workload (see Table 11) and the highest experience score (see Table 12). From a qualitative point of view, this was backed up with statements such as being "very sensitive" and "feeling natural" while using it. Similarly, the JellyBean switch was described as being very "easy to use", and this could also be reflected in the scores this modality obtained. On the other hand, the Blink switch was described as "cumbersome" and "difficult" to use, particularly when wearing glasses. This is due to several reasons, including the form factor adopted, the setup process required and errors made while using the technology. Having said that, participants observed that it is a more "universal" modality since it relies on the same muscles and actions used for ET interaction - and could therefore be suitable for more individuals. The Joystick modality was perceived as "useful" as it "allows correction" while other modalities could not, and therefore reduced frustration levels associated with corrections, despite the modality being more complex when compared to simpler switches. Furthermore, using the Joystick and particularly in the Grouped keyboard layout, on average, participants spent less time on each task when compared to other modalities, even if the number of errors made was similar to other modalities, such as the JellyBean and String switch. This is because such errors could be corrected before committing to a target and therefore minimising the amount of time spent undoing mistakes. As discussed earlier on, one of the participants was not able to obtain good calibration with the eye tracker and therefore was not able to interact effectively. However, this participant found the Joystick to be highly useful, as it allowed for ET inaccuracies to be corrected on the fly, in turn reducing the amount of perceived workload associated with gaze interaction and at the same time, increasing text-entry rates in such a specific scenario. Finally, the Foot switch was deemed to be less sensitive than the other modalities, while it was also reported to cause high levels of fatigue after some minutes of use due to the fact that the foot had to be raised repeatedly from the heel when making selections.

5   Discussion

Considering the results obtained, it is evident that adopting a second modality in ET interaction impacts both measured and perceived performance across most shortlisted modalities. Similarly, in most cases, the perceived workload is also positively affected when adopting a second modality. Specifically, the String switch and JellyBean switch introduced drastic improvements in terms of WPM while also reducing the number of errors and ToT for both keyboard layouts. Furthermore, these two modalities also produced the lowest perceived workload (RTLX) scores. For the Grouped keyboard layout, the perceived workload was reduced from a mean value obtained by the Baseline of 37.36 ($N = 14$, $SD = 10.16$) down to 20.51 ($N = 14$, $SD = 6.92$) for the String switch and 20.88 ($N = 14$, $SD = 6.55$) for the JellyBean switch. On the other hand, for the Grid keyboard layout, the perceived workload was reduced from a mean value of 29.74 ($N = 14$, $SD = 7.16$) down to 16.98 ($N = 14$, $SD = 4.41$) for the String switch and 19.48 ($N = 14$, $SD = 5.72$) for the JellyBean. It turns out that most participants opted for the String switch when asked for their preferred modality (46%). Introducing a second modality reduces perceived workload and increases typing efficiency. Results show increased text-entry rates, fewer errors and faster task completion times when compared to the Baseline for almost all modalities. Although the Blink switch obtained the lowest scores, even when compared to the Baseline, it still was a better alternative for the participant who experienced issues with the eye tracker. This was because the participant had the option to select a target without having to dwell on it and, in turn, involuntarily moving away from it due to ET accuracy issues. Furthermore, people who cannot use any of the other switches due to mobility issues can still opt for this modality.

The selection of modalities ultimately is a personal preference unless limitations dictate otherwise.

6 Conclusion

This paper outlines a study which investigates the impact of a second input modality on eye typing performance. Informed by literature and through discussions with practitioners, five secondary input modalities, along with two keyboard layouts, were shortlisted. A lab-based study with 15 individuals was carried out, and a number of quantitative metrics were recorded, including the time on task, words per minute, errors, perceived ease (SEQ) and perceived workload (RTLX). Qualitative techniques were also adopted to understand the usability properties of the shortlisted modalities. A purpose-built cross-platform multi-modal soft keyboard was developed and used as a data collection tool (ModaliKey).

In general, using a second input modality has a positive impact on performance while at the same time reducing the impact on perceived workload over gaze-only eye typing. The Blink switch produced the worst performance figures, compared to dwell-based interaction (Baseline), while the String switch consistently outperformed all other second input modalities in most metrics. Having said that, the results presented here are by no means a measure of utility for specific individuals. This is because different people will have different capabilities and attitudes towards technology, and it is ultimately up to each individual to select the best technology that works best for them in specific contexts of use.

This work lends itself to various avenues of investigation, including the adoption of different categories of switches (e.g. Electromyography-based switches), the inclusion of other groups to study the effect of previous experience with technology (e.g. children) as well as the inclusion of specific contexts of use (e.g. assistive technology, automotive industry).

References

1. Ashtiani, B., MacKenzie, I.S.: Blinkwrite2: an improved text entry method using eye blinks. In: Proceedings of the 2010 Symposium on Eye-Tracking Research & Applications, ETRA 2010, pp. 339–345. Association for Computing Machinery, New York (2010). https://doi.org/10.1145/1743666.1743742
2. Beelders, T.R., Blignaut, P.J.: Measuring the performance of gaze and speech for text input. In: Proceedings of the Symposium on Eye Tracking Research and Applications, ETRA 2012, pp. 337–340. Association for Computing Machinery, New York (2012). https://doi.org/10.1145/2168556.2168631
3. Cecotti, H., Meena, Y.K., Prasad, G.: A multimodal virtual keyboard using eye-tracking and hand gesture detection. In: 2018 40th Annual International Conference of the IEEE Engineering in Medicine and Biology Society (EMBC), pp. 3330–3333. IEEE (2018)

4. Elsahar, Y., Hu, S., Bouazza-Marouf, K., Kerr, D., Mansor, A.: Augmentative and alternative communication (AAC) advances: a review of configurations for individuals with a speech disability. Sensors **19**(8) (2019). https://doi.org/10.3390/s19081911

5. Gibbons, C., Beneteau, E.: Functional performance using eye control and single switch scanning by people with ALS. Perspect. Augmentative Altern. Commun. **19**(3), 64–69 (2010)

6. Grauman, K., Betke, M., Lombardi, J., Gips, J., Bradski, G.R.: Communication via eye blinks and eyebrow raises: video-based human-computer interfaces. Univ. Access Inf. Soc. **2**(4), 359–373 (2003). https://doi.org/10.1007/s10209-003-0062-x

7. Krapic, L., Lenac, K., Ljubic, S.: Integrating *Blink Click* interaction into a head tracking system: implementation and usability issues. Univ. Access Inf. Soc. **14**(2), 247–264 (2013). https://doi.org/10.1007/s10209-013-0343-y

8. Majaranta, P.: Text entry by eye gaze. Ph.D. thesis, University of Tampere (2009)

9. Majaranta, P., Bulling, A.: Eye tracking and eye-based human–computer interaction. In: Fairclough, S.H., Gilleade, K. (eds.) Advances in Physiological Computing. HIS, pp. 39–65. Springer, London (2014). https://doi.org/10.1007/978-1-4471-6392-3_3

10. Meena, Y.K., Cecotti, H., Wong-Lin, K.F., Prasad, G.: Design and evaluation of a time adaptive multimodal virtual keyboard. J. Multimodal User Interfaces **13**(4), 343–361 (2019). https://doi.org/10.1007/s12193-019-00293-z

11. Mott, M.E., Williams, S., Wobbrock, J.O., Morris, M.R.: Improving dwell-based gaze typing with dynamic, cascading dwell times. In: Proceedings of the 2017 CHI Conference on Human Factors in Computing Systems, pp. 2558–2570 (2017)

12. Paulus, Y.T., Remijn, G.B.: Usability of various dwell times for eye-gaze-based object selection with eye tracking. Displays **67**, 101997 (2021). https://doi.org/10.1016/j.displa.2021.101997

13. Pi, J., Shi, B.E.: Probabilistic adjustment of dwell time for eye typing. In: 2017 10th International Conference on Human System Interactions (HSI), pp. 251–257. IEEE (2017)

14. Porter, C.: From aircraft to e-government-using NASA-TLX to study the digital native's enrolment experience for a compulsory e-service. In: Proceedings of the Human Factors and Ergonomics Society Europe Chapter 2016 Annual Conference. HFES Europe (2016). http://hfes-europe.org

15. Purwanto, D., Mardiyanto, R., Arai, K.: Electric wheelchair control with gaze direction and eye blinking. Artif. Life Robot. **14**(3), 397–400 (2009)

16. Räihä, K.J., Ovaska, S.: An exploratory study of eye typing fundamentals: dwell time, text entry rate, errors, and workload. In: Proceedings of the SIGCHI Conference on Human Factors in Computing Systems, pp. 3001–3010 (2012)

17. Rajanna, V., Russel, M., Zhao, J., Hammond, T.: Presstapflick: exploring a gaze and foot-based multimodal approach to gaze typing. Int. J. Hum. Comput. Stud. **161**, 102787 (2022). https://doi.org/10.1016/j.ijhcs.2022.102787

18. Raupp, S.: Keyboard layout in eye gaze communication access: typical vs. ALS. Ph.D. thesis, East Carolina University (2013)

19. Roark, B., De Villiers, J., Gibbons, C., Fried-Oken, M.: Scanning methods and language modeling for binary switch typing. In: Proceedings of the NAACL HLT 2010 Workshop on Speech and Language Processing for Assistive Technologies, pp. 28–36 (2010)

20. Sibert, L.E., Jacob, R.J.: Evaluation of eye gaze interaction. In: Proceedings of the SIGCHI Conference on Human Factors in Computing Systems, pp. 281–288 (2000)

21. Singh, H., Singh, J.: Real-time eye blink and wink detection for object selection in HCI systems. J. Multimodal User Interfaces **12**(1), 55–65 (2018)
22. Singh, J.V., Prasad, G.: Enhancing an eye-tracker based human-computer interface with multi-modal accessibility applied for text entry. Int. J. Comput. Appl. **130**(16), 16–22 (2015)
23. Song, Y.C.: Joystick text entry with word prediction for people with motor impairments. In: ASSETS 2010, pp. 321–322. Association for Computing Machinery, New York (2010). https://doi.org/10.1145/1878803.1878892
24. Soundarajan, S., Cecotti, H.: A gaze-based virtual keyboard using a mouth switch for command selection. In: 2018 40th Annual International Conference of the IEEE Engineering in Medicine and Biology Society (EMBC), pp. 3334–3337. IEEE (2018)
25. Špakov, O., Miniotas, D.: On-line adjustment of dwell time for target selection by gaze. In: Proceedings of the Third Nordic Conference on Human-Computer Interaction, pp. 203–206 (2004)
26. U.S. Food and Drug Administration: Human factors and usability engineering to medical devices (2016). https://www.fda.gov/regulatory-information/search-fda-guidance-documents/applying-human-factors-and-usability-engineering-medical-devices. Accessed 06 Dec 2022
27. Vertanen, K., MacKay, D.J.: Speech dasher: fast writing using speech and gaze. In: Proceedings of the SIGCHI Conference on Human Factors in Computing Systems, CHI 2010, pp. 595–598. Association for Computing Machinery, New York (2010). https://doi.org/10.1145/1753326.1753415
28. Ware, C., Mikaelian, H.H.: An evaluation of an eye tracker as a device for computer input2. In: Proceedings of the SIGCHI/GI Conference on Human Factors in Computing Systems and Graphics Interface, CHI 1987, pp. 183–188. Association for Computing Machinery, New York (1986). https://doi.org/10.1145/29933.275627
29. Zammit, G.: Optimising performance in multi-modal virtual typing for users with limited range of movement. Master's thesis, University Of Malta (2021)
30. Zhai, S., Morimoto, C., Ihde, S.: Manual and gaze input cascaded (MAGIC) pointing. In: Proceedings of the SIGCHI Conference on Human Factors in Computing Systems, CHI 1999, pp. 246–253. Association for Computing Machinery, New York (1999). https://doi.org/10.1145/302979.303053
31. Zhao, X., Guestrin, E.D., Sayenko, D., Simpson, T., Gauthier, M., Popovic, M.R.: Typing with eye-gaze and tooth-clicks. In: Proceedings of the Symposium on Eye Tracking Research and Applications, pp. 341–344 (2012)

Research on Emotional Home Product Design Based on Five Senses Experience

Qianhang Qin[✉], Yingyu Liao[✉], Wenda Tian, Youtian Zhou, and Gengyi Wang

School of Design, Guangxi Normal University, Guilin 541006, China
20190128@mailbox.gxnu.edu.cn, 565747245@qq.com

Abstract. The application and innovative development of the five senses experience are explored in home product design. In order to enhance the user experience and the emotional design features of products, the team starts from the close connection between the five senses experience and people's daily life. The characteristics and expressions of emotional design of home products are analyzed, and then design practiced is carried out by combining the current needs of people for emotional regulation and management in different situations. This product design research is based on the five senses experience, with the aim of bringing a more three-dimensional sensory experience to the public's life through emotional products. Users in the use of the process to achieve product-user-environment interoperability and mutual integration, so that they can better create a home atmosphere and assist in the benign regulation of emotions.

Keywords: sensory experience · emotional regulation · emotional interaction · interactive

1 Introduction

In today's fast-paced society, people have positive or negative emotions when facing work, life and study. However, some of these emotions need to be soothed, relieved, regulated or transformed. The pressure of fast-paced life and high-intensity work brings people emotional changes cannot be underestimated. Therefore, modern people's mental health issues such as emotional regulation is very worthy of the attention and consideration of designers and researchers. This is also an important topic that design researchers are willing to design to solve. When we feel different good and bad emotions of our self, we need to manage and regulate our emotions. In addition to the two ways of suppressing emotions or self-elimination of emotions, we can also choose to make adjustments to the way we express our emotions. People can use emotionally designed products to assist in the regulation of emotions. This can be used to reduce negative emotions or amplify positive emotions. There is a trend in the market today for products designed to assist with emotional regulation. Therefore, to address and meet the emotional regulation needs of people, and to meet the specificity of human emotions, products with the function of emotional regulation are gradually entering our lives.

M. Kurosu et al. (Eds.): HCII 2023, LNCS 14054, pp. 259–271, 2023.
https://doi.org/10.1007/978-3-031-48038-6_16

How can people feel at ease in their own private living area space? How can people effectively regulate their emotions in a positive way? This is the main question of this study. We take the five senses of human experience as the key to design products that assist in emotion regulation. The designer uses this design approach to solve the problem of emotional regulation at the level of people's perceptual needs, based on the process of using the product with the five senses experience. Design products that create atmosphere and assist in emotion regulation for individuals and spaces, so that users can achieve emotion regulation when interacting with the product. For example, reducing negative emotions and enhancing positive ones. The user uses the product in a self-approved space, and the interaction process conveys and regulates emotions through the product in an appropriate manner. Thus, the user's self-awareness of emotions is increased, while gaining a new emotional experience and psychological satisfaction.

2   Five Senses Experience and Product Design

2.1   Five Senses Experience

People's feelings, impressions, and thoughts about something are basically generated through behavioral experiences such as watching, touching, and listening. This is a direct, realistic emotional experience that enables people to generate new views or emotions. The five senses experience generally refers to the sensations generated by the stimulation of the external environment and things through the sensory organs such as eyes, mouth, ears, nose and skin. These are mainly the senses of sight, taste, hearing, smell and touch. The "five senses" in a broad sense are richer and are mainly at the level of consciousness. It can be understood as people consciously observe, perceive, analyze and process their surroundings through the five senses. Then, based on this, a series of information synthesis and processing is carried out, and finally a higher level of rational construction is achieved [1].

Therefore, under the five senses experience, designers can guide the specific product design based on the senses' perception of things. This allows users to gain the most realistic personal experience through the interaction process of using the product, so as to strengthen the "five senses" and "interactivity" of users. In the product design, more consideration is given to the user's perceptions, psychological changes and emotions in the process of use, and the product will transform the user's "perceptions" into "emotions" in the process of use. Users will get a good and positive emotional feeling in the use of the product, which is a kind of beauty enjoyment. By using the product to form this special emotional experience effect, the product will be more humane. It will give the product strong emotional characteristics, highlight the theme to be expressed, and increase the satisfaction and comfort of the user experience [2]. A typical example of this is a CD player designed by Naoto Fukasawa for MUJI. The CD player is shaped like an exhaust fan in daily life, and the switch is controlled by a corded design with a vertical entrance door. Based on the user's ritualistic behavior and visual appreciation during use (the CD player runs with the disc rotating like the fan blades of an exhaust fan), the product's dynamic approach fits with the changing and jumping nature of music. The product can well guide the user's senses and awaken the user to feel the mood and emotion of different music. Thus, the user gets an emotionally charged and systematic product experience.

2.2   Five Senses Experience to Enhance the User Experience in Product Design

In the process of using products to experience human-computer interaction, people pay more attention to the optimization of the sensory experience of the product. At the same time, they also have innovative expectations for the basic functions of the product. The five senses experience can make users communicate more effectively with the things around them from different perspectives. Traditional product design can go to improve the performance of the product while improving its appearance. These innovations all contribute to the optimization of its function, structure and form upgrades. And as the use of products continues to be enriched, a good sense of product use and sensory pleasure becomes the new face of attracting users. This sensory experience in the application of product design, can be faster and more effective delivery of product-specific information to make its communication with the user more in-depth, to meet the needs of users while feeling a diverse experience. However, in the design, the principle of simplicity of human-computer interface operation should be followed, so as to avoid overly complex use of the user's expectations contrary to perception (Table 1).

Table 1.   Five senses experience design tools.

Five senses experience design tools	
Synesthesia	Associative perception is a design technique that utilizes the interaction between different senses. Its most common application is "color and auditory" synesthesia. The application of synesthesia in product design can enhance the interaction between the senses and deepen the design [3]
Augmented Reality Technology	A technology that "seamlessly" integrates information from the real world and the virtual world, such as computer science and technology, simulation and overlay, etc. It enables people to perceive physical information that they would otherwise experience in the real world, including visual information, sound, taste, touch and other sensory experiences beyond reality. In the specific design of the five senses experience, the use of augmented reality technology can enhance the user sensory experience
Human-computer interaction	The process of using the product is the process of communication and interaction between people and the product. Good interaction experience combined with excellent interface design, which can improve the continuity of user operation and make the operation more comfortable to enhance the user experience
Ergonomic	The relationship between human-machine-environment is studied from a system perspective. Using the knowledge of physiology, psychology and other related disciplines, the designer cuts from the perspective of the environment, the user and the characteristics and conditions of the machine to reasonably allocate the operating functions of the machine. Through the design of the three to adapt to each other, so as to create a safe and comfortable working environment, so that the efficiency and effectiveness of the optimal

3 Classification of Emotional Design Products Related to the Five Senses Experience

(1) Classification by the Type of Product. Currently on the market for the relevant existing product types, can be divided into two categories: online products and offline products. Online products are mainly based on application APPs, experience websites, etc. Offline products are divided into physical products and physical research projects. Physical products are mostly home appliances, toys, ornaments, etc. Physical research projects include relaxation and stress reduction rooms, mood rooms, scream and shout rooms, etc.

(2) Classification by Applicable Population. The applicable population refers to the corresponding users who use the product, and the population can be widely divided into: youth, middle-aged and elderly. From other directions, such as social level restrictions, geographical area restrictions, etc., corresponding to the use of different groups, the use of the product needs vary.

(3) Classification by Regulation Mode. At present, the existing products are mainly through the interaction with the product to form a five-sense experience to achieve the purpose of emotional regulation, through the use of different interaction methods to match different five-sense experience to the user to present and feel. For example, by changing the product material to let users feel from the sense of touch, using visual and auditory to attract users and so on.

(4) Classification by Environment. Emotion regulation products can be classified into two types: household and public. In the design process, it can be combined with the specific design requirements and use of the environment (context), different categories can go to the free combination, and continue to refine to achieve the user's experience to enhance and alleviate the problem [4].

With the continuous development of society, the issue of emotion regulation has been more continuously concerned, and various products have emerged and iterated. In the research, we know that at this stage, most of the products related to emotion regulation, only a small number of products are better integrated into the five senses experience products. Among them, products that combine the use of products with the five senses experience belong to the products that are more targeted to emotion regulation. At present, there are problems that the relevant products are not yet able to solve and meet the needs of users. At the same time, it can be seen that products that integrate the five senses experience can better attract users and influence their emotions to change, and we can also try a variety of human-computer interaction design forms in the design to enhance the user's experience and emotional feelings.

4 User Analysis of Emotional Home Product Design Based on Five Senses Experience

4.1 Categorized Population Characteristics

The target users of this study are mainly for the adult group for research and analysis. The adult group, especially the post-90s, has become the leading group of the new era. Between different age stages, users of each age stage are actually different and varied.

(1) Struggling Youth. This type of youth is generally in the age group of 20–30 years old, this stage of youth is growing into the backbone of society, mostly for the first time in the workplace, work, life pressure is relatively high. In the entertainment mode, focus on interaction and expression, the pursuit of freedom, high demand for music playback and environmental feedback. In terms of consumption needs and consumption habits, the obvious personality stands out. In the context of the era of constant new things, they have a jumpy way of thinking and the ability to accept new things quickly. They also pay more attention to the feeling and experience of consumption and use process, and the products that can stimulate sensory experience in life are more attractive.

(2) Responsible Youth. These young people generally have already established families and have a certain degree of independent thinking, judgment and strong adaptability to the environment. Their purchasing behavior and ability are relatively independent, and they can clearly define their needs for products. They pay more attention to taste and grade, mostly pursue spiritual satisfaction, and have their own preferences and needs for design and function.

Young people's ideas and personality gradually become one of the mainstream of the development of society, the demand for emotional management driven by young people began to be constantly personalized. This change also makes more audience groups recognize and pay attention to the importance of managing emotions, emotional regulation and other mental health issues. This is conducive to promoting the gradual development of related product design. The middle-aged group is not only focused on the satisfaction of material needs, but also on the satisfaction of spiritual needs. They hope that the products can effectively improve their quality of life. Therefore, in the process of product design, we should not only continue to explore the user's emotional needs, which is more important to understand and respect the user [5].

4.2 Categorized Population Characteristics

Through research on the general behavior of users' home life, we can find that the adult population in urban China is generally "short" in the morning and "long" at night. Compared to daytime, people generally spend their time at night freely and leisurely (Fig. 1).

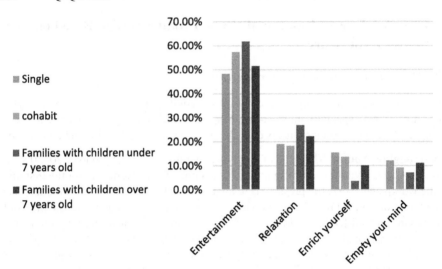

Fig. 1. Analysis of common user behavior at home.

According to the analysis, 57% of home behaviors and time are almost consumed in personal entertainment activities. People spend most of their time at home in the evening, and their specific behavioral activities include watching TV, playing electronic products, etc. In addition to personal entertainment activities, 22.8% of the respondents' activities in the bedroom are mainly relaxing, such as listening to songs and exercising. Most of their behaviors at home are relaxing recreational activities, and most of them will be assisted by out-of-body products (Table 2).

Throughout the behavioral journey from work to home, the main behavioral activities of the target users are relaxation activities that regulate the body and mind. The emotional state of the interviewees varies from one area to another. Therefore, the behavioral activities presented by users in the home zone and the emotional states affected are very important. It is analyzed in detail and the functions of the home products using the space are subdivided differently. We can find that the product is positioned in the appropriate context, more able to bring the user a good feeling of use. The design gives the product more emotional regulation and guidance of the function to affect the user's emotions, the user has a sense of satisfaction and comfort to be able to recognize the product (Table 3).

Table 2. Respondent's home behavior/emotional state.

Task/Sequence	User behavior	User Emotional State
1. Arrival at home	Changing shoes, disinfection, hand washing	Urgency, uneasiness/reassurance, relaxation
2. **Bathroom Washing**	Bathing, dressing, storage, **playing music**	Compression, compactness, **soothing**, comfort
3. Kitchen cooking	Cooking, cleaning, playing music/video	Cumbersome, pleasurable, satisfying
4. **Living room activities**	Seating, dining, watching and listening to theater and **games**	**Exhaustion**, pleasure, enjoyment
5. **Study Activities**	**Adjust the desktop light source**, office, reading and studying	Anxious, **focused**, calm
6. **Resting in the bedroom**	Adjust the sleep light source, **charging**, sleeping, **sleep aid products use**	Restful, peaceful, **relaxed,** tired

Table 3. Respondents' needs for different spaces.

The Space	User requirements	Demand classification
Living room	Changing shoes, disinfection, hand washing	Urgency, uneasiness/reassurance, relaxation
Study Room	Bathing, dressing, storage, playing music	Compression, compactness, soothing, comfort
Bedroom	Cooking, cleaning, playing music/video	Cumbersome, pleasurable, satisfying
Bathroom	Seating, dining, watching and listening to theater and games	Exhaustion, pleasure, enjoyment

Bathroom, living room, study and bedroom are the high frequency areas where users perform behavioral activities. Bedroom and bathroom are the two spaces that respondents cannot live without in performing their behaviors. They use more functional things in these two spaces, and their emotional state is mostly comfortable and relaxed. While in the living room and study, people need to meet the basic functions of the products used. At the same time, they want to create a living space with strong atmosphere or personal style.

We grouped and classified the needs of the target users and analyzed the user states under the needs. Respondents in the process of using the product in the form of transmission of emotions and the five senses feedback, we summarize the results as shown in Table 4. In the feedback mode, product design can be based on the user's original pleasant emotions in the process of using the product, through the product human-computer interaction in the visual feedback, tactile feedback, auditory feedback, etc. to provide users with positive emotional feedback. In the user is in a negative emotional state to use the product, it is for the user to reduce the output of negative emotions, the product to promote the formation of effective coordination and cooperation between the different senses of the user.

Table 4. Respondents' key needs extraction.

Demand classification	User's status	Feedback method
Entertainment and Leisure	Generally more focused and at rest/in motion	Sound feedback, vibration feedback, visual feedback
Home Security Class	None	Visual feedback
Home life category	Focused and at rest	Sound feedback, haptic feedback, visual feedback, olfactory feedback

5   The Application and Presentation of the Five Senses Experience in the Product

(1) Material Path. When users touch different material texture, they will have different physical experience and psychological feeling. Materials achieve sensory experience by transmitting their texture, characteristics, temperature, etc. The careful design of the product material can make the user get a good first feeling from the visual aspect. The user is superimposed by the touch experience of the material, which enhances the feeling of use.

(2) Color Path. Color is essential in product design. Different colors and shapes make the use of the product will have a different sensory experience for the user. In the five senses experience design to choose the right color scheme, can obviously enhance the product's infectious power. Aided by the emotional regulation of product design is to focus on product form and color matching. The product gives the user a pleasant visual psychological feedback and with the coordination of the use of the scene, which can avoid the use of abrupt sense [6].

(3) Formal Path. In product design, different use function selection and matching can result in different functions and different shapes of products. Designers in the design time can try multiple combinations, different functional forms to express the design goals. For example, designers can create the same element of the series of products, through the design of more multi-faceted use of the experience to bring the user a three-dimensional five-sense experience [4].

6 Five Senses Emotional Experience of Home Product Design Practice

Through the interview research, we understand people's behavior of expressing emotions, user needs, feedback and the role of the five senses experience. We analyzed and summarized the different emotions expressed by people in different situations and the way people behave to express their emotions. The product design can be designed for different emotions in people's life, work and study, combined with the five senses experience. Through the use of home products that assist in regulating emotions, users can achieve positive effects of emotion regulation in the process of human-computer interaction. Such products help to improve the user's conscious awareness of emotions, get satisfaction and comfort, thus improving the quality of life [7] (Table 5).

Table 5. Product Design Positioning.

Demand classification	User orientation	Five Senses Extraction	Five senses experience design direction
Emotion regulation products	Young people group	Vision	1. The design of the collocation between the associative sense. The use of geometric figures. Enhance the product aesthetics 2. The application and matching of colors to make users feel happy 3. Designing product interaction actions and fun. When users interact with the product, add new ways to use daily life products, and play a slight role in regulating and influencing users' emotions 4. Create atmosphere in the environment of the area where the product is used
Home use products	Texture needs	Aural	
Emotional design	Atmosphere creation needs	Haptics	

We are gaining insight into the different emotions that people express in different situations. At the same time, we studied and analyzed the emotions that people generally produce. We try to integrate the five senses experience into the design of home products, and design products with five senses experience for desk lamps, electronic products chargers and stereos in home products. The target users are young people living in the city, who pursue the quality of life and want to create a niche and high-quality home life.

Product one is an ambient light. Its main function is to illuminate and create atmosphere. The lighting part is hemispherical, with soft silicone material and bumpy texture. The user interacts with the product by toggling. The user gently toggles the articulating surface of the light body with a finger, and then starts the ambient light. The lower part of the ambient light has a light source adjustment button, which adjusts the brightness intensity of the light by changing the number of touches (Fig. 2).

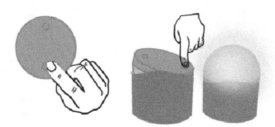

Fig. 2. Product One: Ambient light use chart.

Product two is a wireless charger. Its main function is to charge electronic products for use. Put cell phones and other electronic products into the charging compartment, the wireless charger's colorful fan will be in the form of dynamic slow up and down shaking. Give the user to form an ornamental colorful dynamic sculpture, increasing visual enjoyment. When the product automatically senses that the electronic product is fully charged, the fan will shake and stop, reminding the user that charging is complete. The product can give users a better focus and visual atmosphere during use, effectively reducing the user's dependence on the phone (Fig. 3).

Fig. 3. Product Two: Wireless charger use chart.

Product three is a Bluetooth audio. It has the basic function of playing, but also for the user in the bath to play the role of the atmosphere, create a good mood. This product by changing the single nature of traditional audio, giving the audio lighting to create the function. Its soft light with the leaping notes, allowing users to enjoy the visual and auditory stimulation of the senses (Fig. 4).

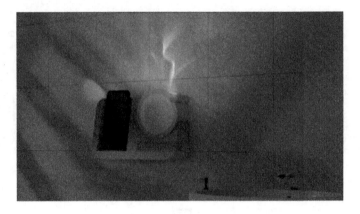

Fig. 4. Product Three: Bluetooth speaker use chart.

7   Conclusion

The five-sensory experience-based home product design is centered on the user's emotional experience. This approach uses multi-sensory participatory design to evoke the user's emotional experience. It not only satisfies the user's need for the basic functions of the product, but also accumulates and increases positive emotions as the user interacts with and perceives the product. Ultimately, users get sensory pleasure and emotional satisfaction. This achieves the purpose of product-assisted emotion regulation. In the product design, we integrate the five senses experience that is to solve the problem, but also to highlight the characteristics of the work through three-dimensional sensory feelings. With emotional design to awaken the user's emotions, to relieve and guide the user's benign emotions, to bring them a "happy feeling experience".

Acknowledgements. This research has been partially supported by the 2023 Guangxi University Young and middle-aged Teachers' Basic Research Ability Improvement Project (2023KY0040), Guangxi Normal University Innovation and Entrepreneurship Education Fund (No. CXCYSZ2021007), Research topics of philosophy and social science planning of Guangxi Zhuang Autonomous Region (21FMZ036).

References

1. Qian, L., Ye, C.: Research on modern art design based on "five senses" experience. Packag. Eng. **37**(20), 220–223 (2016). (in Chinese)

2. Wang, X.: Research on experiential product design based on multisensory participation. Art Des. (Theory) **2**(09), 109–111 (2017). (in Chinese)
3. Li, Y., Wu, W., Mu, J.: Fluency and association in all-suitability design. Packag. Eng. **39**(06), 29–33 (2018). (in Chinese)
4. Liu, Y.: Research on the Application of Five Senses in the Functional Expression of Products. Central Academy of Fine Arts, Beijing (2017). (in Chinese)
5. Gong, L.: Research on the Design of Intelligent Stress-Reducing Products Based on the Emotional Needs of Adults. Qingdao University, Qingdao (2020). (in Chinese)
6. Li, F.: Research on color of product design based on emotional orientation. Ind. Des. **12**, 32–33 (2017). (in Chinese)
7. Zheng, W.: Research on the Application of Five Senses in Product Form Design. Jiangnan University, Jiangsu (2015). (in Chinese)

Exploration of Product Innovation Ideas Based on the Relationship Between Science and Design

Shuwen Qiu[✉], Zixuan Huang, and Ying Cao

School of Mechanical Science and Engineering, Huazhong University of Science and Technology, Wuhan, People's Republic of China
1941583637@qq.com

Abstract. As society progresses and people's quality of life improves, China is transforming and upgrading from product manufacturing to product creation. The two aspects that have a great impact on modern life are science and design. They play an important role in the transformation and upgrading of product creation. In this paper, the definitions of science and design are summarized. An overview is given about the development and application of science and design in China and globally. Through the analysis of the interrelationship between science and design, the impact of modern science and technology on design is identified – the application of modern science and technology can improve human-computer interaction and enhance the user experience of product design. By combining the six design dimensions of "5W1H", we propose the idea of product innovation based on science and design. Through the innovation of product design from the perspective of science and technology, it not only improves the quality and value of the product, but also provides new inspirations for designers. In addition, the design methodology proposed in this study is applied to express and embody the theories through design cases. The research results show that science and design as a special element of human-computer interaction design. It has a positive value to the breakthrough of product creation and can further promote the mutual integration and common progress of science and design.

Keywords: science and design · product innovation · human-computer interaction · product design

1 Introduction

As history progresses, it can be understood that there is a relationship between science and design. The issue of the relationship between science and design has always been a hot topic of conversation. Science is the intellectual activity of human beings to understand the world, nature, society and self. Design is the creative activity of human emotion expression, aesthetic appreciation and communication. Different people have different opinions about the definition of science and design, and there is no definite answer. The breakthrough and development of science will promote the development of design. At the same time, the development of design will also require higher-end science, thus promoting the development of science. There is a complex relationship between science and design that promotes, facilitates and develops each other.

© The Author(s), under exclusive license to Springer Nature Switzerland AG 2023
M. Kurosu et al. (Eds.): HCII 2023, LNCS 14054, pp. 272–287, 2023.
https://doi.org/10.1007/978-3-031-48038-6_17

The relationship between the two is complex due to the wide range of disciplines involved. And the related research lacks practicality and relevance. Therefore, it is difficult for junior designers to grasp and utilize the role of science in design. The purpose of this paper is to summarize the interrelationship between science and design, and propose product innovation ideas based on the relationship between science and design to achieve a better human-computer interaction experience. The theory will guide the practice and provide more design inspiration for designers.

For junior designers, it seems that design is always limited to the appearance of the design. As people enter the era of "digitalization". The former state of two-dimensional design is constantly being impacted by three-dimensional and four-dimensional design. Designers are constantly searching for new fields. Due to the support of science, designers' thinking also continues to find inspiration for breakthroughs in other fields [1]. Junior designers are often confused and overwhelmed when designing the relationship between science and design. Therefore, as designers should first have a deeper understanding of science and design.

The intersection and use of science and design can bring a stronger visual impact to the design work. It also brings more possibilities of interaction between human and machine, and gives the design connotation and contemporary value. Therefore, science is one of the important factors to consider when designing products. This paper proposes a product innovation idea based on the relationship between science and design.

The paper is structured as follows. First, the relevant literature on the relationship between science and design is summarized. Based on this, a design idea based on a scientific perspective is proposed for designers. Finally, an application of this idea is carried out.

2   Literature Review

2.1   Definition

Academia has not developed a unified understanding of either science or design.

Regarding the definition of design, Morris Asimow proposed, "Design is a high-risk decision-making process under conditions of uncertainty [2]". Wojciech Gasparski states, "Design is an activity that aims to improve reality [3]". In Christopher Jones' opinion, "Design is about making man-made objects change [4]". Bruce Archer believes that "Design is an activity that seeks to solve a problem for a target [5]". Herbert Simon sees design in this way: "What design is concerned with is the discovery and careful construction of alternatives [6]". Klaus Krippendorff asserts, "Design is a conscious creation of form for human needs [7]". Rigomant believes that "design is a social mediation activity [8]". Rosman and George argue that "design is a purposeful human activity that uses cognitive processes to transform human needs and intentions into materialized entities". Zeng Yong emphasized that "design is the process of simultaneously producing artificial objects and their behavioral systems [9]".

Based on the key words extracted from these perspectives, the following key words can be used to describe the view of design: "decision making", "activity", "change," "solving activity", "discovery and construction", "form creation", "mediation activity", "transformation", and "emergent process".

The definitions of design can be broadly classified into five categories based on key words:

a. Design is an activity about decisions and choices.
b. Design is a problem solving activity.
c. Design is a creative activity.
d. Design is the activity of transforming nature into artifacts [10].
e. Design is a mental activity that creates a desired situation from existing reality [11].

Regarding the definition of science, Wikipedia describes it this way: "Science, a systematic system of knowledge that constructs knowledge about the universe in a testable explanatory and predictive manner [12]". In the Dictionary is explained this way: "Science refers to the system of knowledge that reflects the nature and laws of various phenomena in the real world using categories, theorems, laws and other forms of thinking [13]". The president of the Chinese Academy of Sciences, writing in the first issue of Science and Technology Tide in 1998, pointed out that "the essence of science is to constantly create new knowledge and pursue new truths [14]".

Science is the body of knowledge by which humans understand nature, society, and their own physiology, psychology, and thinking. This human intellectual pursuit is usually characterized by rationality. From a lexical point of view, "science" as a noun can be interpreted as an intelligent act to better understand the world, leading to a novel, significant, and well-founded norm; "science" as a verb can be seen as performing an intelligent act.

2.2 Differences and Connections

The distinction and connection between art and science was highly summarized by the 19th century French scientist Claude Bernard in the first person singular and plural: "Art is I, science is we".

Design is a designer's creative activity based on available materials and manipulable tools. Under the role of thinking, the creative activity is carried out by digesting the existing scientific and technological civilization. Design is both art and science. It is a cross-discipline of science, technology and art [15].

Both science and design are essentially exploratory activities, a process of continuous innovation and solution seeking.

2.3 Development and Application

With the progress of modern technology and civilization, it makes the relationship between science and design closer and closer.

Science and design have been used in China since the Western Han Dynasty. The Western Han Dynasty's Changxin Palace Lamp is in line with modern "ergonomics" and "human-centered" design concepts. It uses a rainbow tube to absorb the smoke of the lamp and send it to the lamp base, dissolving it in water. The lamp is 48 cm high, with a scientific structure and appropriate scale, and the light irradiation range is basically suitable for people's eyes when sitting on their knees. The design of the lampshade not only has the function of reflection and concentration of light, but also can adjust the angle and illumination of the light through the opening and closing of the lampshade [16].

The Renaissance is also able to represent well the integration of science and design. During this period, the representative figure was Leonardo da Vinci. He was profoundly thoughtful and knowledgeable. His design practice and the spirit of scientific exploration had a profound impact on later generations [17].

Modern abstractionists, futurists and surrealists advocated the use of various achievements of modern natural sciences, such as relativity and quantum mechanics in their works. Since the 1920s, many new schools and trends of design, structural mechanics, applied mechanics, material science, construction techniques and other revolutionary achievements have emerged. Until the widespread use of computers, new paths were opened for the original practice of design. Modern buildings such as the Brussels Atomium, the Sydney Opera House and the Pompidou Center for Art and Culture are examples of the fusion of science and design.

3   The Interrelationship Between Science and Design

The development of design applies scientific innovation tools and theories to accelerate the effectiveness of product creation, enrich creative inspiration, and achieve innovation in product design. The ultimate goal of both science and design is to better serve humanity [18]. Design and science, as branches of the discipline, belong to the same philosophy. And then with the refinement of the discipline, more and more branches of the discipline are separated from philosophy. Between science and design, they are crossed, related and intergraded, both independent and connected [19]. Therefore, art and science have endless overlap and crossover, and the two are full of dialogue and conflict [20].

3.1   Science Triggers Design Innovation

a. Science has changed the way of thinking about design
Science and design originate together from people's material production practice. Science has created human material civilization, while design has created human spiritual civilization [21]. Science brings more ways of thinking and expression to design forms, and AI artificial intelligence has become popular in recent years. Artificial intelligence-assisted design such as CHATGPT and Midjourney has changed the design thinking and design process of some designers.

b. Science has created more possibilities for design
Science is present throughout Chinese history. The innovation of products, design aspects and product forms are based on a certain scientific basis. The "porcelain" that can symbolize China can well present this in its development process. China's porcelain technology advances, from the original form of a single colorless porcelain type transition to an all-encompassing, regional characteristics and integration of porcelain. In some selection of materials, molding and artistic processing has reached a high level of technology, but

also the crystallization of the level of science and technology at the time. In the gradual development of science on the basis of the development of porcelain design, while ancient China on top of the continuous development of science to have the ancient Silk Road porcelain trend, to have porcelain transported to Western countries to become a symbol of identity of the upper class people in Western countries [22].

In today's high-speed development, science and technology are changing rapidly, 5G technology, 4D printing technology, 4K aerial camera, VR holographic technology and new materials and new energy [23], all provide new ways of presentation and new forms of human-computer interaction for art, creating more possibilities for design.

3.2 Design Pulls Science Forward

The success of the Sonnet chair is a typical example. At the beginning of the industrial revolution, handcrafted products were beautiful, ornate and contained a lot of curves. The industrial revolution swept in, and mechanized production methods righteously replaced the manual production methods. However, the new mechanical tools did not meet the design requirements. To enable mechanized woodworking techniques to produce beautiful curved shapes, German furniture craftsman Michael Thonet invented the steam bent wood process. The new product shape and the affordable selling price achieved the great success of Thonet chair.

When science fails to meet the needs of design, it drives the development of related sciences. It leads to new product opportunities, simplified processing and lower production costs.

3.3 Science and Design Develop Together

Science permeates all stages of product design, and product design continues to reveal the role and connotation of science. First, the tools used in contemporary design activities come from the results of scientific and technological research, such as computer-aided design hardware and software, supporting intelligent devices and their related technologies. Secondly, one of the sources of inspiration for design activities is science. Finally, scientific theory is the theoretical basis for design.

Design and science both in step, coordinated development, to achieve a virtuous cycle of innovation and development. So that the product development and manufacturing business all the way to open up, and constantly generate new human material and spiritual civilization.

4 Design Idea

This section provides designers with an idea for product design that incorporates science. The idea is based on the relationship between science and design.

Design is not just about the appearance of a product, but a comprehensive planning of the product. Designers create products that uniquely satisfy users according to their functional and psychological needs, and in response to the requirements of the times. All this is supported by science and technology, and product design thinks about how to translate the new science and technology into social life. One of the mediums between these is human-computer interaction. The development of science has also brought more options for human-computer interaction.

Human-computer interaction aims to achieve a natural, efficient, and harmonious human-computer relationship, and to study the technology of human, computer, and two-way information exchange between them [24]. With the development of science, some new technologies have enriched the expression of human-computer interaction. However, so far there is no systematic approach for an introductory understanding by junior designers.

In 1932, the American political scientist Lasswell proposed the "5W1H analysis method". This method is widely used in design and is easy to understand. So in this paper, we want to combine this analysis method and propose a design idea that uses the interrelationship between science and design (see Fig. 1). And the "who/when/where-why-what-who" recycling pattern is formed (see Fig. 2).

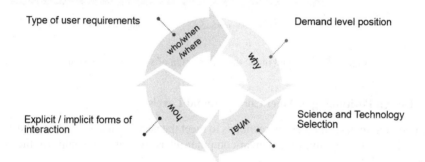

Fig. 1. Circular model based on "5W1H".

4.1 Using Crowd Analysis

Analyzing the psychological and physical characteristics of users, clarifying the environment in which the product is located can help designers find the actual pain points. It can be combined with methods such as empathy map and user journey map as a starting point. Grasp the user needs, product use scenarios, and product usage, and seek the optimal solution to match the needs and functions. Locate the specific functions of the product and clarify the interaction methods.

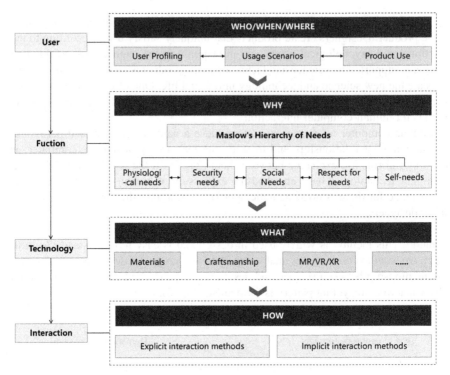

Fig. 2. Design thinking at the intersection of science and design.

4.2 Design Positioning to Meet Core Demand Levels

The core of human-computer interaction is to meet the needs of users. Studying the core needs of users can optimize the human-computer interaction and thus improve the user experience of users.

The American psychologist Maslow proposed the Maslow's Hierarchy of Needs in 1943, which divides human needs into five levels. From low to high: physiological, security, social, respect and self-actualization needs. These five levels develop from low to high. When many needs are not met, it is more urgent to meet the lower level needs. After a certain level of needs is satisfied, people will seek higher levels of satisfaction. The relationship between each level of needs is cross-over [25]. Based on the user needs, product usage scenarios, and product uses in the previous step, the core functions as well as the secondary functions of the product can be initially determined.

4.3 Selecting a Suitable Scientific Vehicle

After determining the design positioning of the product, it is important to choose the appropriate scientific and technological vehicle.

The choice of carrier and product function are closely related. On the one hand, the designer can find the relevant science and technology suitable for the solution according to the product function; on the other hand, the designer can also think out of the box according to the advanced technology to create more avant-garde works. Designers should keep pace with the times and keep up with the development of science. On the basis of the minimum amount of loss, the optimal human-computer interaction experience is achieved.

4.4   The Combined Effect of Explicit and Implicit Interaction Methods

The current interaction process is mostly command-based. Human-computer interaction by the device user through keyboard, mouse, gestures and voice commands is called explicit interaction. Implicit interaction, on the other hand, is defined by Schmidt as invisible interaction [26]. The explicit and implicit interactions are distinguished by two dimensions, device initiative and user attention [27] (see Fig. 3).

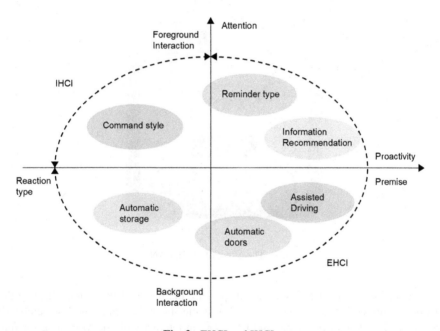

Fig. 3. EHCI and IHCI.

Explicit and implicit interaction methods are interrelated to make the whole human-computer interaction process natural and smooth, while expanding the dimensions of human-computer interaction methods. The design method of using explicit and implicit interaction methods together in the design process can improve the efficiency of human-computer interaction for core functions [28].

5   Application of Ideas

The home growing robot "SHUBAN" is based on the above design idea. It is designed to meet the needs of children and people at home. It uses biodegradable household waste as composting material to meet the needs of growing green vegetables at home. Through MR technology, it can interact with people and visualize the needs of plants (see Fig. 4).

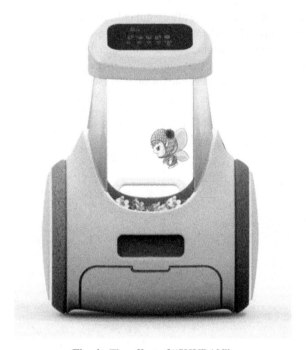

Fig. 4. The effect of "SHUBAN".

The top is a 7-in. LCD screen for displaying the needs of the plant. Through the MR device projection, it can observe the MR genie above the plant. The MR genie will respond to the state of the plant, and the user can interact with the MR genie for fun, increasing the user's sense of interactive experience.

There is a compost bin in the front belly of the robot, in which food waste and delivery boxes can be put to compost. The compost bin can be taken out for cleaning. In addition to this, artificial lighting is used to meet the needs of plants. And provide dark mode, the lights on both sides to give the dark environment to provide a weak light, with a sense of technological intelligence. The rollers can be opened for easy movement. The four hole chambers provided can grow four different plants at the same time, and the open space around allows the plants to grow freely (see Fig. 5).

To reflect the needs of the plant in real time, the interface is designed with cute expressions to interact with the child. The primary interface shows three kinds of expressions under different conditions: normal state (smiling), abnormal state (crying) and feedback state (blinking) to reflect the plant state. When the expression is abnormal state, click

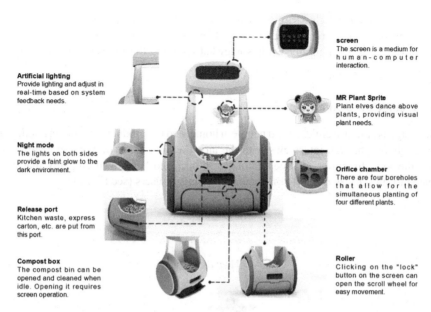

Artificial lighting
Provide lighting and adjust in
real-time based on system
feedback needs.

Night mode
The lights on both sides
provide a faint glow to the
dark environment.

Release port
Kitchen waste, express
carton, etc. are put from
this port.

Compost box
The compost bin can be
opened and cleaned when
idle. Opening it requires
screen operation.

screen
The screen is a medium for
h u m a n - c o m p u t e r
interaction.

MR Plant Sprite
Plant elves dance above
plants, providing visual
plant needs.

Orifice chamber
There are four boreholes
that allow for the
simultaneous planting of
four different plants.

Roller
Clicking on the "lock"
button on the screen can
open the scroll wheel for
easy movement.

Fig. 5. Functional Structure.

to enter the second-level interface to show the cause of plant abnormality (including moisture, humidity, temperature, air, minerals, etc.). Select the abnormal item to click to enter the tertiary interface, which shows the relevant information of the four pore chambers, so that users can make precise adjustment conveniently (see Fig. 6). There is a child lock in the first level interface to prevent children from accidentally opening the compost bin.

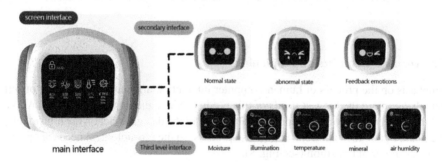

Fig. 6. Display of some user-interface. (Color figure online)

Simple and modern shape, smooth lines and one-piece appearance with a thin blue light band are in line with the home of the future technology. In terms of color scheme, the colorless black, white and gray is used, which is suitable for various home environments and gives a clean and tidy feeling. In terms of material, the white body is flame retardant ABS material, composting and watering parts are made by two-color injection. The blue part is LED ambient light strip, showing a sense of future technology. Four pieces of frosted glass cover are connected in the middle of the product to ensure that the plants are allowed to grow naturally while somewhat reducing the impact of light on users' eyes.

5.1 Using Crowd Analysis

The design is aimed at children and people at home, and the product category is intelligent home robots. Through interviews with the target audience, we drew an empathy map from the four directions of "see", "think", "think" and "do". The empathy map was created to summarize and vote on some pain points of users (see Fig. 7).

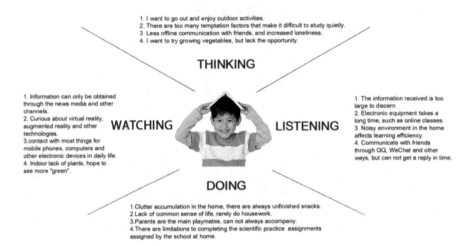

Fig. 7. Empathy map of primary and middle school students living at home.

5.2 Demand Level Design Positioning

Emphasis on the process of human-computer interaction and meeting the value of self-actualization are the biggest needs of this product. Since the target population involves children, safety is also very important. The focus of the design is not on the high yield of the plant, but on the experience of the use process, so the physiological needs are placed in a less important position (see Fig. 8).

5.3 Scientific Carrier

Virtual reality technology is a new type of human-computer interaction developed in recent years, which can immerse people in a computer-generated virtual world. Ting Qiu et al. proposed to apply VR technology to planting design and integrate it into virtual simulation experimental teaching to break the limitations of design teaching and

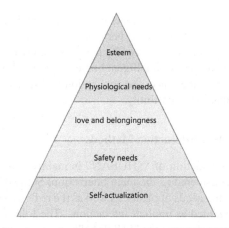

Fig. 8. Analysis of the demand for "SHUBAN".

apply virtual simulation technology to solve traditional teaching challenges [29]. MR technology, as a further development of VR and AR technology, can also be integrated into experimental teaching.

Mixed Reality (MR) is a type of digital perception technology that uses digital means to capture, regenerate, or synthesize various sensory inputs from the external world to achieve an immersive sense of immersion. It is able to establish interaction between the virtual world and the real world, to form a hybrid world in which the virtual and the real interact [30]. As MR technology is widely used, the technology is becoming more and more mature. Currently, MR technology is being explored and used in the fields of education, medical care, games, and sports [31]. Through MR technology, the audience is fully immersed in the virtual space, and some real feelings are induced by the virtual space. These experiences are real existences for human sensory experiences, but these objects are indeed fictional objects, thus blurring the boundary between virtual and reality [32].

Through MR technology, the "SHUBAN" projects the plant genie, and through the detection of soil, the plant genie's demeanor shows the state of the plant. For example, if the plant is short of water, the plant genie will show a thirsty demeanor (see Fig. 9).

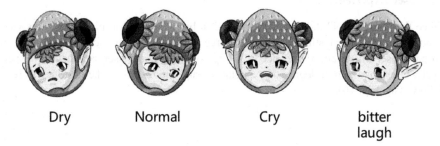

| Dry | Normal | Cry | bitter laugh |

Fig. 9. The different demeanor of plant elves.

Jia Zixi et al. realized the control of inverted pendulum and robotic arm system in a virtual environment based on the virtual experiment system of MR technology [33], and the control of other virtual objects realized by MR technology provides practical experience for the application of MR in intelligent home growing robots. To meet the user's immersive home growing experience, the application of MR technology to intelligent home growing robots has some feasibility.

5.4 Explicit and Implicit Interaction Methods

The human-computer interaction of "SHUBAN" is mainly between the user and the plant sprite, which is considered as the main interaction. Some of the interactions that systematically regulate the needs of plants, as well as the tedious, simple and uninteresting interactions, are regarded as implicit interactions. The following Table 1 gives the explicit and implicit interactions of the "SHUBAN".

Table 1. Explicit and implicit interaction of "SHUBAN".

Explicit Interaction	Implicit Interaction
Robot expression interaction	Automatically turn on night mode at night
Delivery port switch	Real-time light adjustment
Compost bin switch	Automatic locking
Plant Genie	Automatic water storage
Plant Genie Interaction	
Roller switch	

The use of explicit and implicit interactions together in the design process can improve the human-computer interaction of core functions. More able to reflect the characteristics of the product, overly complex interactions may lead to misuse of product features.

5.5 User Experience

Since the "SHUBAN" did not actually land, a brief description plus interviews were conducted in the user testing session. The three aspects of communication were focused on basic user information, user needs, living conditions, and user satisfaction, respectively. Users had a high degree of expectation, and the results of the interviews are as follows (see Fig. 10).

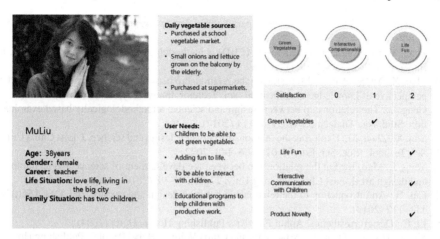

Fig. 10. User testing and scoring table.

6   Conclusion

This paper presents a product innovation design idea based on the interrelationship between science and design. Based on the literature review, this paper first summarizes the definitions of science and design and briefly describes the difference, connection, development, and application between the science and design. Next, the interrelationship between science and design in product design is summarized. Based on this, the design of product innovation ideas is proposed. Finally, a design case is used for validation and evaluation. Applying MR technology in intelligent home growing robots to achieve more interesting, human-machine interactive, and intimate product design. With the development of AI, it also makes the design of some concepts possible.

As demonstrated in this paper, the designer's grasp of science involves many aspects of design research. Considering that the idea is not explicitly targeted, future research can use the idea as a guide for different design themes, already for further exploration. In order to bring inspiration to similar design research in terms of innovative approaches and applied practices.

References

1. Yao, X.: Exploring the relationship between science and technology and design art. Electron. Prod. **245**(20), 186 (2013)
2. Asimow, M.: Introduction to Design. Prentice - Hall, Englewood Cliffs (1962)
3. Gasparski, W.: Praxiological -systemic approach to design studies. Des. Stud. **1**(2) (1979)
4. Jones, C.: Design Methods -The Seed of Human Future. Wiley, New York (1980)
5. Bruce, A.: Systematic method for designers: the praxiological perspective. In: Cross, N. (ed.) Development in Design Methodology. Wiley, Chichester (1984)
6. Simon, H.B.S.S.: Artificial Science. Wuyishan, Translation. The Commercial Press, Beijing (1987)
7. Krippendorff, K.: On the Essential Contexts of Artifacts or on the Proposition That "Design is Making Sense (of Things)". Des. Issues **5**(2) (1989)

8. Liddament, T.: The computationalist paradigm in design research. Des. Stud. **20**(1), 41–56 (1999)
9. Zeng, Y.: Environment - based design (EBD): a methodology for transdisciplinary design. J. Integr. Des. Process Sci. **19**(1) (2015)
10. Mao, X., Yu, S.: A brief discussion on the relationship between design and science: from the perspective of knowledge classification. Sci. Technol. Innov. (22), 32–33 (2018)
11. Geng, L.: The relationship between design and science: a methodologically based examination. Stud. Nat. Dialect. **33**(12), 111–114 (2017)
12. Sun, X., Zhou, M.: Exploring the relationship between design and science. J. East China Univ. Sci. Technol. (Soc. Sci. Ed.) **37**(01), 136–148 (2022)
13. Yang, J., Mao, K.: On the relationship between the development of science and technology and design art. J. East China Jiaotong Univ. **27**(02), 95–98 (2010)
14. Cui, H.: An introduction to the relationship between design and science. Ind. Des. **156**(07), 111–112 (2019)
15. Li, C.: Design Aesthetics. Anhui Fine Arts Publishing House, Hefei (2004)
16. Shi, Z.: History of Chinese Art — Arts and Crafts Volume. Hebei People's Publishing House, Shijiazhuang (2006)
17. People's Education Publishing House, Institute of Curriculum and Teaching Materials, Research and Development Center for Art Curriculum and Teaching Materials, Shanghai Book and Painting Press, ed. Compulsory Education Textbooks for Teachers Teaching Book Art Grade 6 on (2019 printing), pp. 93–94. People's Education Publishing House, April 2014
18. Fan, Q.: The mutually reinforcing relationship between science and technology and art and design. Chin. Handicraft **172**(02), 88–89 (2021)
19. Guo, Y.: Applying science and technology to achieve product design innovation. J. Hangzhou Univ. Electron. Sci. Technol. (Soc. Sci. Ed.) **13**(03), 53–57 (2017)
20. Cheng, Y., Yin, F.: Research on the interrelationship between art and science in the perspective of sustainable development. Coast. Enterp. Technol. **207**(02), 44–49 (2022)
21. She, X.: On the influence of science on the development of art and design. Modern Bus. Ind. **25**(16), 82–83 (2013)
22. Wang, R.: A brief discussion on the mutually promoting relationship between science and technology and art and design. In: CPC Shenyang Municipal Committee, Shenyang Municipal People's Government, Asia-Pacific Academy of Materials Science . Proceedings of the 15th Annual Scientific Conference of Shenyang (Economic, Management and Social Sciences). CPC Shenyang Municipal Committee, Shenyang Municipal People's Government, Asia Pacific Academy of Materials Science: Shenyang Science and Technology Association, pp. 347–349 (2018)
23. Wang, L.: "The Carnival of Reason": Digital Technology Intervention in Art and its Aesthetic Experience. Guangzhou Academy of Fine Arts (2017)
24. Shan, M.: Human-Computer Interaction Design, pp. 1–5. Electronic Industry Press, Beijing (2016)
25. Peng, Z.: General Psychology, pp. 329–330. Beijing Normal University Publishing Group, Beijing (2003)
26. Schmidt, A.: Implicit human computer interaction through context. Pers. Technol. **4**(2/3), 191–199 (2000)
27. Wang, W., Huang, X., Zhao, J., Shen, Y.: Implicit human-computer interaction. Inf. Control **43**(01), 101–109 (2014)
28. Bai, Y., Zhang, J.: Research on wearable water rescue product design strategies from the perspective of human-computer interaction. Design **35**(23), 154–157 (2022)
29. Qiu, T., Chen, Z.: Research on the application of VR technology in planting design —— take the virtual simulation experiment teaching of seasonal phase change of plant landscape as an example. For. Sci. Technol. Inf. (04), 1–6 (2022)

30. Hao, Y.: A new mode of human-computer interaction, VR/AR/MR industry began to form. New Ind. **08**, 65–70 (2016). https://doi.org/10.19335/j.cnki.2095-6649.2016.08.009
31. Peng, L., Luo, P.: New media technology is changing and enhancing news media —— based on VR technology, AR technology and MR technology investigation. J. Southwest Univ. Natl. (Humanit. Soc. Sci. Ed.) **10**, 153–157 (2016)
32. Lin, J.: Application of MR technology in fine art design. New Technol. New Prod. China **21**, 36–38 (2021). https://doi.org/10.13612/j.cnki.cntp.2021.21.012
33. Jia, Z., Wang, S., Hao, Y., Wu, Y.: The application of MR technology in the practical teaching of robot engineering specialty. Exper. Technol. Manag. (09), 139–142 (2020). https://doi.org/10.16791/j.cnki.sjg.2020.09.032

The Choice of a Persona: An Analysis of Why Stakeholders Choose a Given Persona for a Design Task

Joni Salminen[1]([✉]), Sercan Şengün[2], João M. Santos[3], Soon-gyo Jung[4], Lene Nielsen[5], and Bernard Jansen[4]

[1] School of Marketing and Communication, University of Vaasa, Vaasa, Finland
jonisalm@uwasa.fi
[2] College of Fine Arts, Illinois State University, Normal, IL, USA
[3] Instituto Universitário de Lisboa (ISCTE-IUL), Lisbon, Portugal
[4] Qatar Computing Research Institute, Hamad Bin Khalifa University, Doha, Qatar
[5] IT University of Copenhagen, Copenhagen, Denmark

Abstract. Although personas have been applied for two decades, not much is known about why a designer chooses a specific persona for a given design task. This question matters because if designers prefer one persona over another, then the needs and attributes of that persona would be favored in the design process, resulting in possible "blind spots" and bias in regards to other personas. To explore reasons and behaviors associated with the choice of a persona, we conduct an on-site user study with 37 participants in a workplace setting focused on a social media content creation task. Our findings show that factors affecting the choice of persona include age similarity between the persona and the designer, persona's looks, how many users the persona represents, time spent browsing the persona information, and whether the persona is (a)typical relative to other personas. Under different persona sets, these factors were correlated with the probability of a persona being chosen for a design task, and also supported by a qualitative analysis of the think-aloud records where the participants explained their persona choice. The findings provide implications for developing interaction techniques that support users' varying information needs and persona selection strategies, including recommenders that would increase the match between the designers' information needs and the available personas.

Keywords: Personas · User choice · User study · Human factors

1 Introduction

Personas are 'customer segments with a face,' i.e., fictitious people that represent key customer segments [31]. Therefore, personas inform stakeholders (i.e., designers, marketing managers, software developers, etc.) about end-user aims, interests, and actions through depicting central user characteristics [14]. Personas embody behaviors and traits – such as pain points, needs, and wants –

M. Kurosu et al. (Eds.): HCII 2023, LNCS 14054, pp. 288–310, 2023.
https://doi.org/10.1007/978-3-031-48038-6_18

of end-users that designers seek to address. Personas were originally devised to address the prejudices and self-serving biases of designers, who may create systems that relate to their own interests without clear guidance on who the user is [11]. Representing customers as personas intends to minimize reliance on personal viewpoints when trying to understand end-users' experiences, perceptions, and mental processes [31].

Cooper [7] identifies persona creation as a powerful tool for communication and interaction design. This is because personas represent real people by outlining goals and preferences that are directly extracted from the experiences of real end-users. Nielsen [30] highlights that personas can be understood as a means of communicating customer data by focusing on field observations rather than preconceived ideas, thus improving customer understanding and leading to higher customer-centricity. In the industry, personas are well-established, and they have been broadly applied in software engineering, human-computer interaction (HCI), health informatics, journalism, cybersecurity/privacy, video games, marketing, and other domains [4,7,9,16,25,30]. To support these efforts, several variants of personas have been developed, such as design personas, marketing personas, buyer personas, segment personas, patient personas, cybersecurity/privacy personas, player personas, and so on. For example, companies such as Spotify[1] and Microsoft[2] use personas to enhance their understanding of users and customers. The applicability of the persona method is thus broad and personas remain topical in industry and research.

Nevertheless, how stakeholders engage with personas is not well understood. *What makes a persona interesting? Why do users focus on one persona over another? Why do users select a specific persona for their task?* These are some of the open questions that motivate our research.

Stakeholders are people that use personas to make decisions about users or customers. Typically, after persona creation, these stakeholders are presented with several personas, referred to as a 'persona set' or a 'cast of personas' [30]. According to our experience from empirical persona user studies, for a given design task, the users tend to browse the available personas and then focus on one persona at a time for their task. Sometimes different users may choose the same persona, but often they choose different personas. The intriguing question is: *Why?* The answer may enhance the theoretical understanding of the mechanisms of how personas are used in practice. Answers can also inform persona design on what kind of personas to develop, as well as contribute to theory development regarding interaction between personas and their users. Overall, understanding persona choice can inform the HCI community on three vital aspects:

1. **Creation of personas** – empirically analyzing users' persona choice gives an idea of what information users pay attention to in the persona profile, which has direct implications for persona design.

---

[1] https://spotify.design/article/the-story-of-spotify-personas.

[2] https://techcommunity.microsoft.com/t5/driving-adoption/driving-user-adoption-user-personas-and-user-journey-maps/m-p/82058.

2. **Use of personas** – gives an idea of the users' voiced reasoning of who fits the task they are going to do and why, which can enhance theoretical understanding of how people relate to personas and actually use them for design.
3. **Theory of personas** – through understanding persona choice, we can take steps towards generating a broader theory for persona–user interaction, which the HCI literature is currently missing.

Persona choice matters because—similar to the theory of selective attention [23]—the choice of whom to design dictates everything that follows! So, the selection mechanism is of interest - it deals with the designer contemplating, "I think this persona is worthwhile, I should focus on it." But why that persona and why not the next one? Contrary to this being a trivial matter, it is actually a fundamental matter for persona use. In turn, persona use dictates whether personas are valuable and for whom. Whose interests are product designers promoting?

The bottom line – to use a persona for decision making, you need to first choose one. We could, in some settings, argue that designers can choose and consider the interests of many personas, but from an experimental standpoint, the most straightforward way to study this is to ask them focus on one persona.

Even though persona choice is an interesting and important topic that can shed light on the interaction between personas and marketing stakeholders, there is little work on this topic. The consequence from this lack of attention is that users' strategies, behaviors, and given rationales of choosing one persona over another are poorly understood. Not much is known about the process of the users forming a connection with a specific persona, and what human factors contribute to such connections. So, there is a lack of understanding as to why a user chooses a certain persona over another when carrying out a design task, forming the research gap that our study addresses. We empirically investigate the choice of personas, formulating hypotheses and having professional users conduct tasks with different sets of personas in workplace setting. Our overarching research question (RQ) is: *Why do stakeholders choose a certain persona for a marketing task?* We investigate three aspects of this choice process:

RQ1: What characteristics of (a) the persona and (b) the stakeholder explain the stakeholders' persona choice? We address this question through quantitative analysis.
RQ2: What interaction aspects, including (a) persona presentation in the user interface (UI) and (b) stakeholders' interaction with personas (i.e., dwell time, frequency of visits), explain stakeholders' persona choice? We address this question through quantitative analysis.
RQ3: What strategies do stakeholders apply for their persona choice? We address this question through qualitative analysis.

To address these questions, we conduct a mixed-method study, using quantitative and qualitative methods. We carry out an empirical user study using an interactive persona system deployed in a large non-profit organization. *Interactive persona system* refers to a Web-based system that allows users to browse personas and their information freely using mouse navigation and interaction techniques, such as selection of persona, scrolling the information, viewing data distributions, and so on [18]. The study applies two persona sets: one with less diversity, and another with more diversity, in terms of age, gender, and locations of personas. This is achieved using a data-driven persona system to generate these two sets. Data-driven persona generation refers to using algorithms and statistic techniques for automatic or semi-automatic segmentation and enrichment of digital user data [34]. We recruit thirty-seven participants from this organization, who each choose a persona for a design task (designing online content for the freely-chosen persona). We test six hypotheses that potentially explain the participants' choice of personas. Our results inform persona design by offering guidance on what factors matter for persona choice, as well as shedding light on users' reasoning and experiences when employing a persona for design tasks.

2 Literature Review

2.1 Cross-Disciplinary Perspectives to Persona Choice

Personas are fictitious people characterizing core or target customer or user groups [7]. A persona has a name, picture, and written description – it is an alternative to nameless, faceless group of people [18]. Personas are said to enhance the consideration of customer needs among design teams and other professionals engaged in customer-centric decision making [26]. They group similar customers under one archetype, facilitating the understanding of customers' needs and wants [30]. While it may not be practical to consider hundreds or thousands of individual customers when making business decisions, considering a core set of personas is manageable [17]. This concept of manageability is pervasive in persona theory, and can be generalized as follows: *There is a lot of information about customers. That information is summarized into a set of personas through a process of segmentation and personification. Then, among this persona set, stakeholders learn from one or more personas and make actionable decisions.*

Previous research in multiple fields presents potential reasons for stakeholders' focus on a given persona for a marketing task. Particularly relevant fields include HCI, information science (IS), and social psychology (SP). Their views can complement each other to form a more holistic picture of how stakeholders interact and engage with personas. In particular, HCI research highlights the importance of professionals' empathy for personas and the underlying customer base for accomplishing user-centered design goals. The psychological study of person perception (i.e., how people form impressions of others) can be extended to personas, even though personas are fictive in nature [30]. HCI and IS tend to speak of people as "users," whereas in SP, the notion of humans is closer to "individuals." Central in the psychological view of personas is the concept of person perception, which refers to the general tendency to form impressions of other people, which is a facet that also affects how stakeholders perceive personas [3]. From the IS field, we gain foundational insights on how stakeholders process information to support their decision making [38].

3 Hypothesis Development for RQ2 and RQ3

3.1 Hypotheses About Persona and User Characteristics

H1: Users Are More Likely to Choose Personas that are Similar to the User. In social psychology, evidence points out that similarity with another person is associated with a positive attitude towards that person [27]. This is referred to as *homophily* [20], defined as the "tendency of individuals to associate and bond with similar others" [28]. Here, we measure similarity in terms of demographic matching between all participant-persona pairs (cf. [40]). We focus on two traits: gender (H1a: Users are more likely to choose a persona from their own gender) and age (H1b: Users are more likely to choose a persona with an age similar to their own age). Initially, we also wanted to include the country for this analysis, but the personas did not have enough geographic variation to make this test possible.

H2: Users Are More Likely to Choose Attractive Personas. According to the *"what is beautiful is good"* effect, individuals perceive attractive people as having more desirable interpersonal traits. This results into higher willingness to form social bonds with these people relative to less attractive individuals. This concept is also known as the "physical attractiveness" bias, and it originated from a study by Dion et al. [8]. In the case of personas, we surmise that more attractive pictures increases the persona's probability of being chosen, so that the personas are chosen because they appear as more physically attractive than other personas.

H3: Users Are More Likely to Choose Personas that are Different from Others. The observed *salience* of an item is the state or quality by which it stands out from its neighbors [15]. The generated personas are all slightly different, but we label those are distinctly different from others as outliers. We then test if these outlier personas are more or less likely to be chosen by the participants. It is expected that, due to these personas being different, they are treated differently than other personas. Here, we classify a persona as an outlier based on their age, gender, nationality, and audience size relative to the entire persona set, with audience size referring to how many people the persona represents (see the method section for details).

H4: Users Are More Likely to Choose Personas with a High Segment Representation. The effect of *popularity*, arising from childhood where children learn that popularity is a desirable quality [22], drives social behavior from an early age. According to this notion, individuals are more willing to associate themselves with individuals that they perceive as popular or important than with individuals that lack these qualities [32]. In our case, the participants may presume that a persona with a large segment size is more popular or represents a larger group of people, and therefore should be chosen. The number of people the persona represents may be a predominant characteristic motivating the choice of a persona. This is because the user may presuppose that by choosing a persona that represents a large group of people, they are able to reach more people with their message because of the target's large audience representation. In other words, this is a form of marketing logic [21], which may be relevant considering the type of task employed in the experiment (see the method section).

3.2   Hypotheses About System Features and User Behavior

H5: Users Are More Likely to Choose Personas that Appear either (a) Higher or (b) Higher and Lower in the Order of Presentation. In his work dating to 1885, Ebbinghaus [10] observed a relationship between recall and serial position, subsequently becoming a major benchmark for future studies. In his work of word list learning, Ebbinghaus proposed a U-shaped curve of recall, with the first and last items in a list being best remembered, referred to as primacy effect and recency effect, respectively.

In general, order effects refer to differences in individuals' responses that result from the order (e.g., first, second, third) in which the experimental materials are presented to them [39]. In the interactive persona system deployed in the current study, the personas are displayed in a user interface sorted by their representativeness of the data. We test two order effects: the *primacy effect* and the *serial-position effect*. The primacy effect is the tendency to remember the first piece of information better than information presented later on [33]. The personas are presented in a listing, so this effect suggests personas first in the listing are more likely to be chosen. According to this idea, a persona is chosen because participants see it sooner than the other personas. The participants either interpret the first seen information as more important, or simply remember it better than the subsequent information [33]. In turn, serial-position effect is the tendency of a person to recall the first and last items in a series best, and the middle items worst [29]. This effect suggests personas higher and lower in the listing are more likely to be chosen because, similarly to the primacy effect, these personas are more memorable due to their order of presentation.

H6: Users Are More Likely to Choose Personas They Engage Most with Based on (a) Dwell Time and (b) Number of Visits. The use of an interactive persona system allows us to measure user interaction (engagement) with the personas, which is an important aspect when personas are integrated into tools or systems that can be supervised [12].

From this idea, we surmise that the personas that are chosen are most often visited or viewed for a longer duration than other personas. The motivation for this hypothesis is given by the *uncertainty reduction theory* [5], which states that individuals reduce uncertainty about others by gaining information about them. We expect that the users engage more with the personas they end up choosing relative to other personas. According to this idea, users spend time viewing the personas' information, developing a preference for the personas they visit more often (or spend more time with), leading to positive affirmation and choice. Therefore, we surmise that more visits and higher dwell times for a persona increase its probability of being chosen. The difference of uncertainty reduction and mere-exposure effect [41] – which could also be seen as a relevant rationale for this hypothesis – is that the latter deals with how much a user would be exposed to the persona is that in our research design, the participants were actively deciding the number and duration of persona visits, rather than being passively exposed to them. Therefore, we presume that more visits for a given persona took place because the participant was interested in that persona and wanted to learn more, which is compatible with the premise of uncertainty reduction.

4 Methodology

4.1 Research Site and Participants

Our data collection site was a major non-profit organization that advances important programs in education, research, and public health. We chose this organization because of their past experience of working with personas. The organization uses personas (a) to better understand their online audience, and (b) for strategic planning of online content design, which involves crafting communication policies and content to serve the various stakeholder groups of the organization. In total, there were 37 participants, of which 10 (27%) were females. The average age of the participants was 32.9 years (SD = 6.9). The participants held a variety of job positions within the organization, including data analysts, engineers, software developers, researchers, editors, social media managers, copywriters, project managers, and content specialists. The participant pool thus represents the myriad of positions dealing with creating end-user experiences in large organizations, involving people with varied backgrounds and expertise. The participants' earlier experience of personas was varied, including most having conceptual experience (i.e., knows what personas are but has not used them previously) (71%, n = 26), a little less than third (27%, n = 10) having some practical experience (has applied personas before, but not often), and one (3%, n = 1) having extensive experience (has frequently used personas in their job). Each participant was explained the foundational concept of personas regardless of their level of previous experience. Furthermore, it was clarified that the personas they were about to see were based on their organization's actual YouTube end-user data, i.e., that they were data-driven.

4.2 Persona Creation and Interactive Persona System

We generated the personas using a data-driven persona methodology reported and validated in previous work [1,2]. Several other persona experiments have applied this methodology [35–37], as it affords a standardized way for generating personas from real end-user data, enables users to interact with the personas, and records the interactions users have with personas in the system logs. The data-driven personas were automatically generated from the focal organization's YouTube end-user statistics using an algorithmic process and a system that has been validated by previous research [1, 2, 19]. The data for the persona creation comprised 1,473,275 view counts on 125 videos thru December 31, 2019 that were retrieved automatically via the YouTube Analytics API[3]. This data was automatically organized in the form of an interaction matrix, and decomposed using non-negative matrix factorization [24]. Then, the system created the personas by automatically incorporating demographically tagged name, picture, and other information from a database. As the underlying analytics platform current defines only two genders, that is the number we used in this research, deferring other gender identities for future work.

The personas were provided to the participants using an interactive persona system, giving users the option to freely browse the personas and their information. The personas were shown to the participants using the interactive persona system, available at https://persona.qcri.org. The participants could freely interact with the generated personas, including switching between the personas, scrolling their information, learning about information definitions, reading the quotes, and so on. The persona information contained a (1) name, (2) demographics (age, gender, country), (3) picture, (4) text description, (5) sociographics (job, marital status, education), (6) sentiment, (7) topics of interest, (8) quotes, (9) most viewed content, and (10) audience size – i.e., the number of people the persona represents. For the experiment, two sets of personas were generated, as explained in the following section.

4.3   Experiment Design

In the experiment, each user went through two sessions of first using the interactive persona system and then carrying out the design task (also referred to as work task scenario). Because each user used the system twice with a different set of personas, the study design corresponds to within-subjects experiment – which is beneficial for mitigating the impact of individual user behaviors on the results. For both sessions, the participant was presented with a work task scenario (WTS) before being shown the system:

> *"Your task is to promote the [organization] as a workplace to a specific persona. A persona is a fictitious person that describes a real user segment. The personas you will see are created from the real audience data from [organization]'s YouTube channel. They represent [the organization]'s audience segments in YouTube."*

In the WTS, participants engaged with the interactive persona system to review personas and select the persona for which they were creating a YouTube video. This can be considered as a content design task in social media management, i.e., designing content for a specific target group. The organization

---

[3] https://developers.google.com/youtube/analytics.

suggested using this task because they perceived it natural for their intended use of personas. Thus, the task reflects a real use case of personas in an organization. For the within-subjects design, we used the persona generation system to automatically generate two persona sets of different number of personas. As a common practice, a persona set contains 3–7 personas [6]. We created such a set (**PS1** that contained 5 personas) first. However, due to the nature of our research question, we also needed a larger persona set to better capture variation among the persona attributes. Therefore, we created another set (**PS2**) that contained 15 personas and had a higher degree of demographic diversity than the **PS1**. Both sets were automatically generated by the persona system from the same data collected from YouTube Analytics that represented the audience population watching the videos in the organization's YouTube channel. As we wanted the personas to remain data-driven, no other manipulations to the personas were made, apart from varying the number of personas generated, which afforded different personas for both sessions. Personas are illustrated in Fig. 1 and Fig. 2. The persona profiles with full information are shown in the Supplementary Material[4].

(a) Jafar	(b) Ghada	(c) Bassam	(d) Faisal	(e) Osamah

Fig. 1. Pictures of the personas in PS1. Jafar (a) and Bassam (c) were chosen the most often.

(a) Naif	(b) Rami	(c) Sami	(d) Rajab	(e) Imran
(f) Cambell	(g) Jameela	(h) Maryam	(i) Michael	(j) Faleh
(k) Nada	(l) Alanood	(m) Huda	(n) Noura	(o) Fatima

Fig. 2. Pictures of the personas in PS2. All personas, except Sami (c) and Alanood (l), were chosen at least once. Imran (e) was chosen more often than the other personas.

---

4 https://www.dropbox.com/sh/gtuopopbqwgxjbw/AABPBK8KByeX2rvo3uOTsGNda?dl=0.

We counterbalanced the order of presentation, so that each participant was randomly assigned to either first seeing the **PS1** and then the **PS2**, or *vice versa*. For this, we manually created two different experimental sequences – in Sequence 1 the participant first saw the **PS1** and then the **PS2**; in Sequence 2, the order is the opposite. The purpose of this is simply to avoid the results from being biased by all the participants first seeing the set with a less diverse set of personas and then the more diverse set of personas. Instead, half will the see less diverse set first and the other half will see the more diverse set first. During the experiment, this was controlled by logging the user into a correct sequence and keeping record of which participant was allocated to which sequence.

4.4   Data Collection and Pre-processing

We gathered two main types of data: (1) system logs recorded the participants' engagement with the personas (the duration and number of visiting each persona), and (2) survey data was collected after task completion to collect user characteristics and their persona choices. After using the persona system, the participants selected a specific persona for their task. For statistical analysis, the data was structured so that each observation represents a participant session and a persona. For each such combination, two outcomes are possible – either the persona is chosen, or it is not. A 'Choice' variable was created, assuming a value of 1, if the participant chose the persona, or a 0, if the participant did not choose the persona. This was used as the dependent variable. The independent variables were:

- **Age delta** – the absolute difference between the persona and the participant's age for that combination;
- **Same Gender** – 1 if the participant and the persona are of the same gender;
- **Attractiveness** – a rating of attractiveness which was ascribed to the persona by an independent sample;
- **Outlier** – 1 if the persona is classified as an outlier;
- **Audience size** – indicates how many people are similar to the persona (according to data from Facebook Marketing API). The log of this variable was used to address its skewed distribution;
- **Order** – the relative presentation order of the persona (lower numbers indicating a higher position of the presentation order, i.e. 1 is the first, 2 is the second, etc.);
- **Visits** – the number of times the participant visited the persona's page; and
- **Dwell time** – the combined duration, in seconds, of all the participant's visits to the persona's page.

To isolate the effect of pictures, we recruited an independent sample of 50 people via the Prolific[5] survey platform to rate the attractiveness of the personas' facial pictures. The participants rated each picture using a Likert scale (1: Not at

---

[5] https://prolific.ac.

all – 5: Very much). Based on the responses, we assigned a mean attractiveness score for each persona. To address H6a, we calculated the timestamp differences between persona visits in the system log data to get the duration each persona was perused. We then compared that number with the ratio of each persona being chosen for the design task. From the log data, we also computed the number of visits (H6b) for each of persona-participant pair.

To test the outlier effect, we classified seven personas as outliers based on the following criteria. Three were in the **PS1** (Ghada because of gender; Faisal because of age; and Osamah because of country), and four were in the **PS2** (Cambell because of country, Michael because of country, Nada because of age (young), and Alanood because of age (elderly)).

To test the order effects, we computed the probability of a given persona being chosen, and correlated that probability with the persona's order using Spearman's correlation coefficient (ρ).

5 Exploratory Data Analysis

For the **PS1**, users' persona choices are strongly centered to two personas (see Fig. 4). Together, Jafar and Bassam are chosen more than half of the time (59%, n=22). Osamah was chosen only once (3%). The tendency to select only a couple of personas did not appear in the **PS2**, but the choices were more evenly distributed. To quantify the variability of users' persona choices, we computed the *relative standard deviation (RSD)*, a standardized measure of variability of a distribution (in this case, the probabilities of each persona being chosen) (Fig. 3).

The values – obtained by dividing standard deviation of the probability distribution by its mean – indicate that the choice variation is higher for the **PS2** (RSD = 0.837) than for the **PS1** (RSD = 0.695). Therefore, more personas appear to increase the variability of users' persona choices. In the **PS1**, all personas were chosen at least once. In the **PS2**, 13 personas (86.7%) were chosen at least once. This indicates that increasing the number of personas results in users collectively making use of more personas – otherwise, there would be a stronger tendency of choosing just a few personas even with the **PS2**. The tendency of the users to make use of more personas is illustrated in Fig. 4a.

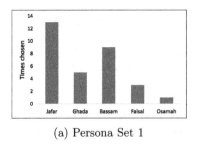

(a) Persona Set 1

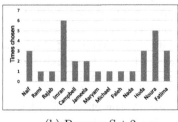

(b) Persona Set 2

Fig. 3. The number of times a persona was chosen in the two sets (x axis follows the order of personas shown in the system listing). Visually, the choices in the **PS1** seem to center around two personas, whereas in the **PS2** they are more evenly distributed.

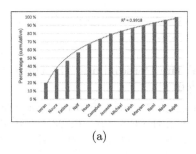
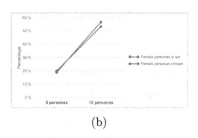

(a)   (b)

Fig. 4. (a) Cumulative percentage of selected personas in the PS2. The dotted line describes the logarithmic function that is well matching the data ($R^2 = 0.99$), indicating a declining (but consistent) increase in participants' tendency to select different personas. This means more personas become a part of the set of chosen personas, but at a decreasing rate. **(b)** The ratio of female personas (i.e., the share of female personas in the generated persona set) and the share of participants choosing a female persona are almost perfectly correlated, which implies that the demographic attributes in the persona set strongly influence users' choice of a persona.

We also contemplated that the gender of the persona would be an influential factor in the choice because, in the **PS1**, the most popular personas (Jafar and Bassam) are both male. However, the choices in the **PS2** refute this idea, since there women are actually chosen more often (56.7% of the time) than men (43.3%). In fact, it appears that the gender ratio of personas shown to the user affects the gender ratio of their chosen personas (see Fig. 4b). To test this effect, we conducted a chi-square test of independence for the likelihood of selecting a specific gender between the two persona sets. This association is statistically significant, such that increasing the number of personas increased the likelihood of selecting a female persona, X^2 (1, N = 74) = 11.26, p = .001.

Interestingly, more than half of the participants (59%, n = 22) chose a persona with a different gender in the second task. Out of those that changed, the vast majority (82%, n = 18) shifted from Male to Female persona. The remaining 18% (n = 4) changed from Female to Male persona. Thus, participants are 4.5 times more likely to first choose a Male persona and then Female persona than *vice versa*. These results imply that the consecutive use of different persona sets increases the diversity of the users' choice of personas.

Overall, the findings indicate an association between diversity – achieved by increasing the number of personas shown to users – and the users' persona choices. In terms of gender, the diversity of personas chosen mimics the diversity of personas shown, which is illustrated in Fig. 4b.

6   RQ1 and RQ2: Hypothesis Testing

The hypotheses were tested using a logistic regression due to the binary outcome variable (apart from H5 that was tested using Spearman's correlation). Three regressions were conducted; one for the **PS1**, another for the **PS2**, and a third using the combined sets. We report the unstandardized coefficients (B), p-values, and odd ratios (OR) with the 95% confidence intervals (CI).

6.1 RQ1: What Characteristics of (a) the Persona and (b) the User Explain the Users' Persona Choice?

H1a: Users Are More Likely to Choose a Persona from Their Own Gender. There was no evidence of this effect in the **PS1**, $B = 0.123$, $p = 0.806$, OR $= 1.131$ [95% CI 0.422 - 3.024]; the **PS2**, $B = 0.144$, $p = 0.806$, OR $= 1.131$ [95% CI 0.423 - 3.024]; or the combined sets $B = 0.229$, $p = 0.727$, OR $= 1.154$ [95% CI 0.515 - 2.588]. Therefore, *H1a is not supported*: there is no evidence that users are more likely to choose a persona from their own gender.

H1b: Users Are More Likely to Choose a Persona with an Age Similar to Their Own Age. Age delta was found to have a significant effect for the **PS1**, $B = -0.121$, $p < 0.05$, OR $= 0.886$ [95% CI 0.803 - 0.976]; and also in the combined sets, $B = -0.067$, $p < 0.05$, OR $= 0.934$ [95% CI 0.889 - 0.982]. Each year of difference, in either direction, between the participant and the persona, reduces the likelihood of that persona being chosen. No evidence of this effect was found for the **PS2**, $B = -0.025$, $p = 0.431$, OR $= 0.974$ [95% CI 0.915 - 1.038]. Therefore, *H1b is partially supported: for the **PS1**, users were more likely to choose a persona with an age similar to their own age.*

H2: Users Are More Likely to Choose Attractive Personas. No evidence of the 'what is beautiful is good' effect was found for the **PS1**, $B = 3.736$, $p = 0.141$, OR $= 41.946$ [95% CI 0.289 - 6067.582]; or the combined sets, $B = 0.162$, $p = 0.547$, OR $= 1.175$ [95% CI 0.693 - 1.992]. However, there is evidence of this occurring for the **PS2**, $B = 1.026$, $p < 0.05$, OR $= 2.789$ [95% CI 1.083 - 7.180]. Therefore, *H2 is partially supported: for the **PS2**, users are more likely to choose attractive personas.*

H3: Users Are More Likely to Choose Personas that Are Different from Others. We found evidence of an outlier effect for the **PS1**, $B = -1.718$, $p < 0.01$, OR $= 0.179$ [95% CI 0.053 - 0.607]; and the **PS2**, $B = -2.261$, $p < 0.05$, OR $= 0.104$ [95% CI 0.016 - 0.660]. The effect was not statistically significant in the combined sets, despite the result being very close to significance, $B = -0.638$, $p = 0.072$, OR $= 0.528$ [95% CI 0.264 - 1.057]. Moreover, the detected effect *decreases* the persona's chance of being chosen, rather than increasing it (we will interpret this finding in the discussion). Therefore, *H3 is not supported: in both sets, personas that are different from others are less likely to be chosen.*

H4: Users Are More Likely to Choose Personas with a Higher Segment Representation. Higher audience representation was found to not influence the odds of a persona being chosen in the **PS1**, $B = -0.707$, $p = 0.187$, OR $= 0.493$ [95% CI 0.172 - 1.410]; or combined sets, $B = 0.017$, $p = 0.697$, OR $= 1.017$ [95% CI 0.846 - 1.222]. However, there was evidence of this occurring in the **PS2**, $B = 0.373$, $p < 0.05$, OR $= 1.451$ [95% CI 1.050 - 2.005]. Therefore, *H4 is partially supported: in the PS2, users were more likely to choose personas with a higher segment representation.*

6.2 RQ2: What Interaction Aspects, Including (a) Persona Presentation and (b) Users' Interaction with Personas Explain Users' Persona Choice?

H5: Users Are More Likely to Choose Personas that Appear either (a) Higher or (b) Higher and Lower in the Order of Presentation. In the **PS1**, there is a very strong correlation between order and the probability of a persona being chosen ($\rho = -0.900$, p < 0.05). Indeed, the persona which was first in order had a 41.93% probability of being chosen, while the second most likely persona to be chosen – with a 29.03% probability – was third in order. All others had even lower probabilities, the smallest of which was the last in order. This correlation was no longer present in the **PS2** ($\rho = 0.174$, p $= 0.534$), and likewise also absent in the combined sets ($\rho = -0.192$, p $= 0.418$). We also tested the quadratic and cubic fits for the **PS2**, but both fits were non-significant (Quadratic, p $= 0.509$; Cubic, p $= 0.476$). Therefore, *H5a is partially supported: for the **PS1**, personas appearing higher in the listing are more likely to be chosen. However, H5b is <u>not</u> supported: there is no evidence that personas appearing higher and lower in the listing are more likely to be chosen.* Fig. 5 illustrates the order effects.

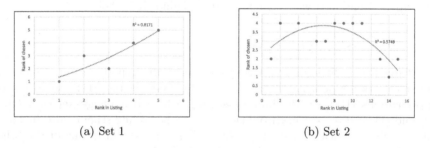

(a) Set 1   (b) Set 2

Fig. 5. Correlations between the ranking of persona being chosen (y axis) and ranking of the persona in system's listing (x axis). **(a)** shows close resemblance with the expected primacy effect. The inverse U-shaped curve in **(b)** is compatible with Ebbinghaus's U-shaped curve, where the first and last items in a list are best remembered. (Note that the curve is inverse here as lower position in y-axis implies higher probability of being chosen.) Yet, this effect is not statistically significant.

H6: Users Are More Likely to Choose Personas that (a) They Spend More Time Engaging with or (b) View More Frequently. For H6a, in the **PS1**, the longer a user spends on the persona's page, the greater the probability of that persona being chosen, $B = 0.010$, p < 0.05; OR $= 1.009$ [95% CI 1.001 - 1.018]. For the **PS2**, no significant effects were detected for dwell time, $B = 0.002$; p $= 0.067$, OR $= 1.002$ [95% CI 0.999 - 1.004]. For the combined sets, dwell time is also significant, $B = 0.003$, p < 0.05, OR $= 1.003$ [95% CI 1.000 - 1.005]. Therefore, *H6a is partially supported: for the **PS1** and the combined* *persona sets, users were more likely to choose personas they spend more time with.*

For H6b, no evidence was found in the **PS1**, $B = -0.062$, $p = 0.588$, $OR = 0.939$ [95% CI 0.750 - 1.177]; or the **PS2**, $B = 0.087$, $p = 0.412$, $OR = 1.090$ [95% CI 0.886 - 1.341]. However, in the combined sets, the number of times the participant visited the persona increased the likelihood of that persona being chosen. Each visit increases the odds of that persona being chosen by roughly 1.2 times, $B = 0.164$, $p < 0.05$, $OR = 1.178$ [95% CI 1.039 - 1.335]. Therefore, *H6b is partially supported: for the combined persona set, users were more likely to choose personas they frequently view in the persona system.*

7   RQ3: What Strategies Do Users Apply for Their Persona Choice?

To explore the reasons given by the participants for their choice of a persona, we qualitatively coded their responses to the open-ended question: "Why did you choose this persona?". For this analysis, we combined the responses of the **PS1** and the **PS2** and analyzed them collectively. The analysis was done by categorizing each response according to the type of information or rationale the participant mentioned was a driving factor behind their choice.

7.1   Hypothesized Strategies

We defined a coding scheme based on the study hypotheses, and included five strategies for persona choice: (a) **similarity-seeking** (H1), (b) **looks or appearances** (H2), (c) **deviance-seeking** (H3), (d) **average-seeking** (H3), (e), and (f) **audience maximization** (H4). The coding scheme also included "other" which indicates a strategy that was not expressed in any of the other choices. In these cases, the coders were asked to write a note describing the strategy.

Two of the researchers coded the open answers independently for these strategies. The two researchers then discussed in order to reconcile their views on the disagreed instances ($n = 36$). Through this discussion, final labels were assigned to the disagreed instances, which meant that the two researchers now fully agreed on the coded instances. On two instances, it was agreed that both coders were correct, so both labels were assigned to the instances – *"He seemed distinctive in terms of age and I can identify more with him. He was also single."* (Participant B22) [similarity & deviance-seeking] and *"Because of the falcon (unique and interesting)"* (B01) [looks or appearances & deviance-seeking].

Table 1 shows the coding results. Out of the predefined strategies, the most common was similarity-seeking (n=11, 16.9%). Reasoning based on demographic similarity was made based on gender and age – e.g., *"Female and she is close to my age"* (A15) – but not country. While similarity was mentioned in terms of demographics seven times, it was also mentioned in terms of interests six times – e.g., *"I feel I share [with] him the interest in volunteering and giving to the community"* (A02). Two cases had both types of similarity – e.g., *"Most similar to me in age and interest"* (A04). This indicates that, when forming connections with personas, participants are not only seeking for demographic similarity, but also for interest-based similarity.

Table 1. Seven strategies for persona selection. Sorted from most to least common. N = 68 instances.

Strategy	The user chooses the persona based on...	Frequency (%)
Fit-seeking	...the compatibility with the task; compares personas with an ideal profile	29 (42.6%)
Similarity-seeking	...similarity in terms of interests, background, or demographics	11 (16.2%)
Deviance-seeking	...something different that caught their attention	9 (13.2%)
Audience maximization	...the audience representation	8 (11.8%)
Looks or appearances	...appearances (i.e., the picture)	6 (8.8%)
Diversity-seeking	...increasing gender diversity in their sequential choices (e.g., first chooses a male, then a female persona)	3 (4.4%)
Average-seeking	...the persona being typical or representative of the persona set	2 (2.9%)

All of the predefined strategies appeared in the open answers, lending support for the hypotheses. Strategies for similarity (esp. age), audience maximization and deviance-seeking support the hypotheses. However, even though the participants referred to looks or appearances, we did not find any case where the participant mentions that the persona looks good or attractive. Instead, the persona's looks were referred to as "authentic" (A10), "friendly" (B03), "smiling and happy" (B07), and "formal and [appropriate]" (B20). Thus, the visual information participants evoke deals more with aptitude and personality than attractiveness. This conclusion in supported by the fact that the most frequently selected persona among the **PS1** is Jafar (chosen 35% of the time, n = 13), then Bassam (24%, n = 9). If we consider only the 84% (n = 31) of the participants that were able to name a persona, then the combined share of Jafar or Bassam goes up to 71% – 42% and 29%, respectively. Therefore, Jafar and Bassam were particularly selectable. Figure 1 shows that these personas appear as young, dynamic, and positive, which could contribute to their choice.

Furthermore, **average-seeking** refers to choosing the persona because it represents the group of personas – that is, is typical or representative of the personas being shown. Two participants (3.1%) expressed this strategy (e.g., *"Personal interests similar to the average, he feels positive in social media, his occupation is popular, the videos he watched were related to [the organization], his age is representative to the biggest group."* (B08)).

7.2 Strategies Emerging from the Qualitative Analysis

In addition to the predefined strategies, the coding led to the discovery of two new strategies. These strategies were identified inductively, i.e., through the analysis of the participants' responses. Conceptually, these did not match any of the expected strategies. Out of these, (6) **diversity-seeking** refers to choosing a persona with a different gender for the second task. Three participants (4.6% of the coded instances) made an explicit note of this (*"Trying to advertise [the organization's] content and [the organization] as a workplace to a more gender balanced audience"* (A01)). This strategy can be seen as an effect of the sequential nature of the study: the participants had to choose two personas, so some of them considered that it would be justified to pick personas with different genders. This behavior was not especially encouraged by the researchers, but instead if reflects the general awareness of gender diversity among the participants.

Finally, (7) **fit-seeking** focused on the compatibility between the persona and the task. After reconciling the coding, fit emerged as the most prevalent category (n = 28, 43.1% of total instances). The responses in the fit category indicated that several participants already had an ideal profile in their minds before interacting with the personas (*"I was looking for a middle age local female persona."* (A02); *"young, midway between western and Arabic culture, so both open and traditional as I see [the organization]"* (B04)) and were comparing personas against this ideal profile. The discussions among the two coders also clarified the conceptual boundaries of fit. Three aspects of fit were particularly striking: cultural, ideal target, and intersectional fit. *Cultural fit* implies that the participant focuses on the match between the organization's culture and the participant. *Ideal segment identification* implies that the participant has a predefined sense of the ideal persona for the task, defined typically by age, gender, or interests. *Intersectional fit* implies that the participant focuses on several features simultaneously, not highlighting one dominant reason for their choice – e.g., *"[I chose this persona] because of his age range, his positive sentiments, his interest in sports, startup and research which are key functional areas of [the organization] and his persona range of 299,300"* (B17).

Even though there may be some conceptual overlap between these subcategories, it became clear that what we termed as "fit" was a major driver in how the users approached the persona selection. For example, Nada appeared as a professionally promising person with the right interests for the task, as well as having cultural fit with the organization: *"As a young aspiring woman, she would make a perfect candidate as an employee or a higher education student."* (B12).

8   Discussion

8.1   Implications for Persona Theory

The findings revealed interesting insights about the use of personas. As mentioned in the beginning of this work, the reasons for applying personas in the design process is to help overcome the problem of self-referential design [30]. This generally requires that the persona description (a) can enable the persona user to have empathy for the persona, and (b) that the persona user has the ability to be empathetic. For the first point, taking a further look at the similarity seeking

(*"I feel I share him the interest in volunteering and giving to the community"* (A02)) shows that the description enables the user to have empathy and perceive the persona profile as a realistic replacement of real users.

On the other hand, the fact that the persona's similarity to one-self was mentioned on several occasions in participants' voiced reasoning implies that self-referential information does play some role in persona use. This is also supported by the significant findings regarding age match between the persona and the user, indicating that personas from the same age group are more likely to be chosen. As such, it appears that *persona users are not completely free from using self-referential information in their designs – users not only compare a persona to other personas, but also to their own attributes.* This finding highlights the role of social and human factors in persona use.

The appearances of the persona seem to influence the choice, but not necessarily in the terms of the persona being "beautiful" or attractive, even though evidence for this was found in the **PS1**. More commonly, the appearances of the persona seem to be intertwined with other factors, such as similarity – the persona looking like "me" or "my kind of person". Possibly, other traits in the pictures such as youth and dynamism may play a more important role, as these serve as information that relates to task. Overall, *physical attractiveness does not increase the persona's likelihood of being chosen for the task.*

The fact that outlier personas are *less* likely to be chosen suggests that going for average personas is typical behavior. As most users seem to choose majority personas, *marginalized groups may require extra support (e.g., visual saliency, higher rank of presentation) to increase their chances of being chosen for design tasks by users.* A corollary is that increasing the demographic diversity of the persona set shown to users seems to increase the diversity of the personas chosen by the users, which could be seen beneficial for inclusive design [13].

The persona's audience size also seems to matter, in that some users justify their decisions based on it. This may result from the nature of the task: a YouTube content creation task implies the goal of reaching a large audience. Other task types should be tested to understand persona choice in a variety of settings. Therefore, the observed popularity effect might in fact represent another facet of the fit theory, i.e., the idea that the persona is predominantly chosen based on its compatibility for the task, rather than its external qualities, such as demographics or attractiveness.

The primacy effect was only significant for the **PS1**, where there was a strong linear relationship. Thus, *the order of presentation and the layout, in this case the persona listing, seems to have an impact especially on the smaller number of personas, where the faster overview makes the persona user pick the top persona instead of one that serves the task best.*

In terms of users' engagement with the persona profile increasing the persona's chance of being selected, the results indicate that engagement with a specific persona profile does not predict that the persona will be chosen, but, out of the tested interaction metrics, *dwell time is a stronger predictor for persona choice than the number of times the persona was visited.*

8.2   Design Implications

The design implications from this work are as follows.

First, interactive persona systems afford flexibility for users to find personas that match a wide range of strategies for a given task. As users can choose and browse personas that fit with their choice criteria for completing tasks, they can ultimately find the personas deemed appropriate for the task at hand. Therefore, *persona developers should consider presenting the personas via digital media, such as Web browsers, using functionality that enables browsing, searching, and filtering based on persona attributes (e.g., demographics, audience size).*

Second, the fact that the increase in the proportions of the shown and chosen female personas are almost perfectly correlated implies that users' choices are influenced by gender proportions in the persona set. If persona developers show more female personas, more female personas are chosen for the design task. Therefore, *when the overall goal is to increase the persona user's knowledge of the demographic diversity of the end-user base, it is advisable to show personas in balanced demographic proportions.*

Third, the fact that personas' order can affect how they are used and chosen implies that persona systems should give tools for persona developers to change the order of personas when this is considered important. For example, minority groups could be prioritized to increase their visual saliency in the UI. *The choice of directing users' attention towards default personas versus letting them discover personas freely remains an important design choice for interactive persona systems.*

8.3   Limitations and Future Work Avenues

The results imply that either the diversity or the number of personas affects users' persona choice, but our analysis does not disentangle these two explanations. Some users explicitly mentioned the number of personas when using the system (e.g., "(...) if you have like fewer number of personas, you will have maybe more diverse kind of group and segments, and as you increase the number of personas, you know, if your [data] has like more fine-grained groups, that might do the same [...] just because you're increasing, then you're creating things that are kind of similar." (B19)). Even though we leave the detailed analysis for future work, our exploratory findings imply that, as diversity and the number of personas are strongly correlated, persona creators can increase the number and diversity of personas in order to target more inclusive design outcomes, as designers choosing more diverse personas would logically result in consideration for the needs of more diverse groups of people (all else being equal).

Using a data-driven persona creation methodology can be considered both as a strength and as a weakness. It is a strength because by using authentic personas that we researchers did not manipulate gives the users an authentic purpose as opposed to us purposefully making choices regarding the personas' gender, age, or any other attribute. On the other hand, by not making such choices, we lose the control over these factors; so the results are exploratory rather than definitive. We opted for the data-driven approach because we wanted to keep the personas realistic for the participants, so that personas actually represent the YouTube viewers. Not using data-driven personas and claiming that the personas were based on real data would have been deceptive.

In terms of research design, the study design was not optimal for testing the order effects. Ideally, we would need to present the order randomly to a number of different participants and see if the probabilities of the personas remain similar regardless of position. These limitations originate, on the one hand, from the limited sample size (it is difficult to recruit enough participants to satisfy sample size requirements for complex experimental designs) and, on the other hand, from the use of the data-driven persona system that by default shows the personas in a specific order for all users. Future studies should more rigorously test the order effects associated with persona presentation.

Our coding of persona information does not necessarily correspond with the participants' understanding of the information. For example, we did not encode the persona with a falcon in the picture as an outlier (see Fig. 1d), but this was nonetheless observed as an outlier by one of the participants because falcons have a particular meaning in the persona's country. Because such tacit cultural nuances can be easily overlooked by persona developers when choosing persona information, validation of the personas for cultural sensibilities would be advisable, although it is likely impossible to perfectly control the subjective interpretation of personas by the participants.

A particularly interesting aspect is the role of the algorithm – when generating more personas, the persona set becomes more varied. This can be interpreted by the mechanism by which increasing the number of personas allows for more "demographic slots" to be filled. This interpretation encourages future studies with persona sets containing more personas. The conventional rationale of keeping persona sets small, typically within the range of 3–7 [6], is that a small number of personas is cognitively more manageable (e.g., considering printing out 100 persona profiles in paper sheets – presenting them to end users in an efficient way would be difficult if not impossible). However, given the search and filtering functions of an interactive persona system, the cognitive burden can be decreased, thus enabling a host of future studies with a higher number (and a higher degree of demographic diversity) of personas.

9   Conclusion

Exploratory support explaining business professionals' persona choice was found for age similarity, persona appearances, number of people the persona represents, dwell time with the persona, and whether or not the persona is an outlier. The qualitative analysis revealed that participants applied seven different strategies for persona selection: similarity-seeking, looks or appearances, deviance-seeking, diversity-seeking, average-seeking, fit-seeking, and audience maximization. The process of choosing personas appears to be influenced by the diversity of the personas available to the user. Persona choice and related interaction between stakeholders and personas requires more empirical research.

References

1. An, J., Kwak, H., Jung, S.G., Salminen, J., Jansen, B.J.: Customer segmentation using online platforms: isolating behavioral and demographic segments for persona creation via aggregated user data. Soc. Netw. Anal. Mining **8**(1) (2018). https://doi.org/10.1007/s13278-018-0531-0. https://www.readcube.com/articles/10.1007/s13278-018-0531-0
2. An, J., Kwak, H., Salminen, J., Jung, S.G., Jansen, B.J.: Imaginary people representing real numbers: generating personas from online social media data. ACM Trans. Web (TWEB) **12**(3) (2018)
3. Anvari, F., Richards, D., Hitchens, M., Babar, M.A., Tran, H.M.T., Busch, P.: An empirical investigation of the influence of persona with personality traits on conceptual design. J. Syst. Softw. **134**, 324–339 (2017). https://doi.org/10.1016/j.jss.2017.09.020. http://www.sciencedirect.com/science/article/pii/S0164121217302078
4. Atzeni, A., Cameroni, C., Faily, S., Lyle, J., Flechais, I.: Here's Johnny: a methodology for developing attacker personas. In: 2011 Sixth International Conference on Availability, Reliability and Security, Vienna, Austria, pp. 722–727 (2011). https://doi.org/10.1109/ARES.2011.115
5. Berger, C.R., Calabrese, R.J.: Some explorations in initial interaction and beyond: toward a developmental theory of interpersonal communication. Hum. Commun. Res. **1**(2), 99–112 (1974)
6. Blomquist, A., Arvola, M.: Personas in action: ethnography in an interaction design team. In: Proceedings of the Second Nordic Conference on Human-Computer Interaction, Aarhus, Denmark, pp. 197–200. ACM (2002). http://dl.acm.org/citation.cfm?id=572044
7. Cooper, A.: The Inmates Are Running the Asylum: Why High Tech Products Drive Us Crazy and How to Restore the Sanity, 2nd edn. Pearson Higher Education (2004)
8. Dion, K., Berscheid, E., Walster, E.: What is beautiful is good. J. Pers. Soc. Psychol. **24**(3), 285 (1972)
9. Duda, S.: Personas—who owns them. In: von Gizycki, V., Elias, C.A. (eds.) Omnichannel Branding, pp. 173–191. Springer, Wiesbaden (2018). https://doi.org/10.1007/978-3-658-21450-0_8
10. Ebbinghaus, H.: Memory: a contribution to experimental psychology. Ann. Neurosci. **20**(4), 155 (2013)
11. Faily, S., Flechais, I.: Persona cases: a technique for grounding personas. In: Proceedings of the SIGCHI Conference on Human Factors in Computing Systems, pp. 2267–2270 (2011)
12. Faily, S., Lyle, J.: Guidelines for integrating personas into software engineering tools. In: Proceedings of the 5th ACM SIGCHI Symposium on Engineering Interactive Computing Systems - EICS 2013, London, United Kingdom, p. 69. ACM Press (2013). https://doi.org/10.1145/2494603.2480318. http://dl.acm.org/citation.cfm?doid=2494603.2480318
13. Goodman-Deane, J., Waller, S., Demin, D., González-de Heredia, A., Bradley, M., Clarkson, J.P.: Evaluating Inclusivity using Quantitative Personas (2018). https://doi.org/10.21606/drs.2018.400. https://www.dropbox.com/sh/cbj04ez206dexrd/AADKHi9uwwDXvpwndnSWEAk1a?dl=0&preview=Goodman-Deane+Waller+Demin+Gonz%C3%A1lez-de-Heredia+Bradley+Clarkson+400.pdf

14. Grudin, J.: Why personas work: the psychological evidence. In: Pruitt, J., Adlin, T. (eds.) The Persona Lifecycle, pp. 642–663. Elsevier (2006). https://doi.org/10.1016/B978-012566251-2/50013-7. https://linkinghub.elsevier.com/retrieve/pii/B9780125662512500137

15. Hamilton, D.L., Fallot, R.D.: Information salience as a weighting factor in impression formation. J. Pers. Soc. Psychol. **30**(4), 444–448 (1974). https://doi.org/10.1037/h0037033

16. Holmgard, C., Green, M.C., Liapis, A., Togelius, J.: Automated playtesting with procedural personas with evolved heuristics. IEEE Trans. Games **11**(4), 352–362 (2018). https://doi.org/10.1109/TG.2018.2808198

17. Jansen, B.J., Jung, S.G., Salminen, J.: Creating manageable persona sets from large user populations. In: Extended Abstracts of the 2019 CHI Conference on Human Factors in Computing Systems, Glasgow, United Kingdom, pp. 1–6. ACM (2019). https://doi.org/10.1145/3290607.3313006

18. Jansen, B.J., Salminen, J.O., Jung, S.G.: Data-driven personas for enhanced user understanding: combining empathy with rationality for better insights to analytics. Data Inf. Manag. **4**(1), 1–17 (2020). https://doi.org/10.2478/dim-2020-0005. https://content.sciendo.com/view/journals/dim/4/1/article-p1.xml

19. Jung, S.G., Salminen, J., Kwak, H., An, J., Jansen, B.J.: Automatic persona generation (APG): a rationale and demonstration. In: Proceedings of the 2018 Conference on Human Information Interaction & Retrieval, New Brunswick, NJ, USA, pp. 321–324. ACM (2018). https://doi.org/10.1145/3176349.3176893

20. Kandel, D.B.: Homophily, selection, and socialization in adolescent friendships. Am. J. Sociol. **84**(2), 427–436 (1978)

21. Kotler, P., Levy, S.J.: Broadening the concept of marketing. J. Mark. **33**(1), 10–15 (1969)

22. LaFontana, K.M., Cillessen, A.H.: Children's perceptions of popular and unpopular peers: a multimethod assessment. Dev. Psychol. **38**(5), 635 (2002)

23. Lavie, N., Hirst, A., De Fockert, J.W., Viding, E.: Load theory of selective attention and cognitive control. J. Exp. Psychol. General **133**(3), 339 (2004)

24. Lee, D.D., Seung, S.H.: Learning the parts of objects by non-negative matrix factorization. Nature **401**(6755), 788–791 (1999)

25. LeRouge, C., Ma, J., Sneha, S., Tolle, K.: User profiles and personas in the design and development of consumer health technologies. Int. J. Med. Inform. **82**(11), e251–e268 (2013)

26. Long, F.: Real or imaginary: the effectiveness of using personas in product design. In: Proceedings of the Irish Ergonomics Society Annual Conference, vol. 14. Irish Ergonomics Society Dublin (2009)

27. Lydon, J.E., Jamieson, D.W., Zanna, M.P.: Interpersonal similarity and the social and intellectual dimensions of first impressions. Soc. Cogn. **6**(4), 269–286 (1988)

28. Murase, Y., Jo, H.H., Török, J., Kertész, J., Kaski, K.: Structural transition in social networks: the role of homophily. Sci. Rep. **9**(1), 4310 (2019). https://doi.org/10.1038/s41598-019-40990-z. https://www.nature.com/articles/s41598-019-40990-z

29. Murdock, B.B., Jr.: The serial position effect of free recall. J. Exp. Psychol. **64**(5), 482–488 (1962). https://doi.org/10.1037/h0045106

30. Nielsen, L.: Personas - User Focused Design, 2nd edn. Springer, New York (2019). https://doi.org/10.1007/978-1-4471-7427-1

31. Nielsen, L., Nielsen, K.S., Stage, J., Billestrup, J.: Going global with personas. In: Kotzé, P., Marsden, G., Lindgaard, G., Wesson, J., Winckler, M. (eds.) INTER-

ACT 2013. LNCS, vol. 8120, pp. 350–357. Springer, Heidelberg (2013). https://doi.org/10.1007/978-3-642-40498-6_27

32. Parkhurst, J.T., Hopmeyer, A.: Sociometric popularity and peer-perceived popularity: two distinct dimensions of peer status. J. Early Adolesc. **18**(2), 125–144 (1998). https://doi.org/10.1177/0272431698018002001

33. Raffel, G.: Two determinants of the effect of primacy. Am. J. Psychol. **48**(4), 654–657 (1936). https://doi.org/10.2307/1416518. https://www.jstor.org/stable/1416518

34. Salminen, J., Guan, K., Jung, S.G., Chowdhury, S.A., Jansen, B.J.: A literature review of quantitative persona creation. In: Proceedings of the ACM Conference of Human Factors in Computing Systems (CHI 2020), Honolulu, Hawaii, USA. ACM (2020)

35. Salminen, J., Jung, S.G., Chowdhury, S.A., Sengün, S., Jansen, B.J.: Personas and analytics: a comparative user study of efficiency and effectiveness for a user identification task. In: Proceedings of the ACM Conference of Human Factors in Computing Systems (CHI 2020), Honolulu, Hawaii, USA. ACM (2020). https://doi.org/10.1145/3313831.3376770

36. Salminen, J., Jung, S.G., Santos, J.M., Jansen, B.J.: Does a smile matter if the person is not real?: the effect of a smile and stock photos on persona perceptions. Int. J. Hum.-Comput. Interact. **36**, 1–23 (2019). https://doi.org/10.1080/10447318.2019.1664068

37. Salminen, J., Santos, J.M., Jung, S.G., Eslami, M., Jansen, B.J.: Persona transparency: analyzing the impact of explanations on perceptions of data-driven personas. Int. J. Hum.-Comput. Interact. **36**, 1–13 (2019). https://doi.org/10.1080/10447318.2019.1688946

38. Singh, V.: Personas and scenarios as a methodology for information sciences. Qual. Quant. Methods Libr. **7**(1), 123–134 (2019). http://qqml-journal.net/index.php/qqml/article/view/462

39. Stewart, R.H.: Effect of continuous responding on the order effect in personality impression formation. J. Pers. Soc. Psychol. **1**(2), 161 (1965)

40. Westphal, J.D., Zajac, E.J.: Who shall govern? CEO/board power, demographic similarity, and new director selection. Adm. Sci. Q. 60–83 (1995)

41. Zajonc, R.B.: Attitudinal effects of mere exposure. J. Pers. Soc. Psychol. **9**(2p2), 1 (1968)

Machine Learning for Gaze-Based Selection: Performance Assessment Without Explicit Labeling

Yulia G. Shevtsova[1,2]([✉]), Anatoly N. Vasilyev[1,3] [ID], and Sergei L. Shishkin[1] [ID]

[1] Moscow State University of Psychology and Education, Moscow, Russia
shevtsova.jg@gmail.com
[2] Moscow Institute for Physics and Technology, Moscow, Russia
[3] M.V. Lomonosov Moscow State University, Moscow, Russia

Abstract. Gaze-based interaction typically requires certain actions to confirm selections, which often makes interaction less convenient. Recently, effective identification of the user's intention to make a gaze-based selection was demonstrated by Isomoto et al. (2022) using machine learning applied to gaze behavior features. However, a certain bias could appear in that study since the participants were requested to report their intentions during the interaction experiment. Here, we applied several classification algorithms (linear discriminant analysis, RBF and linear support vector machines, and random forest) to gaze features characterizing selections made in a freely played gaze-controlled game, in which moves were made by sequences of gaze-based selections and their gaze-based confirmations, without separate reporting the correctness of the selection. Intention to select was successfully predicted by each of the classifiers using features collected before the selection.

Keywords: Gaze-Based Interaction · Selection · Machine Learning

1 Introduction

Gaze interaction is most often based on dwell time (Duchowski 2018; Majaranta et al. 2019). However, dwell time threshold is often exceeded during natural gaze behavior unrelated to selection intent, which leads to frequent false selections (the so-called Midas touch problem, (Jacob 1990)). Means used to solve this problem, such as higher dwell time threshold, confirmation actions (Velichkovsky et al. 1997) etc. typically make interaction significantly less convenient.

A promising extension of the dwell time selection approach could be replacing simple rules like dwell time threshold by machine learning algorithms applied to multiple features that characterize gaze behavior (Murata et al. 2021; Isomoto et al. 2022). With this approach, an impressive improvement was demonstrated in identification of intentional selection compared to traditional methods that used only dwell (Isomoto et al. 2022). However, the results of this study could be biased, because the participants were

© The Author(s), under exclusive license to Springer Nature Switzerland AG 2023
M. Kurosu et al. (Eds.): HCII 2023, LNCS 14054, pp. 311–322, 2023.
https://doi.org/10.1007/978-3-031-48038-6_19

required to report manually if the selection corresponded to their intentions, which was not specific to normal use of gaze interaction technology and could distract them from interaction.

Here, we collected statistics describing gaze behavior and estimated classification performance for a more natural task, where explicit reports about intentions were not required. In our experiment, selections made with 500 ms dwell time threshold had to be confirmed by the participants to lead to actions and could be ignored by them for no cost when not corresponded to intentions, so we assumed that such selections did not trigger avoidance gaze behavior. In offline analysis, we used selection confirmation and some additional rules to label selections as intentional or unintentional. We applied several machine learning algorithms to a number of gaze behavior features extracted from gaze data collected before each selection and estimated how well they can classify selections from participants unseen by them. The modeling confirmed that intentional dwell-based selections can be successfully identified without confirmation, using only gaze features.

2   Methods

We used data recorded in 40 healthy participants who played a gaze-controlled game EyeLines in the study (Ovchinnikova et al. 2021). In this game, a player has to put "balls" of the same color into a straight line on a squared board (see Fig. 1). For this, in each move, they selected a ball (in this case, a square frame appeared around this ball), confirmed their choice at a "confirmatory" position outside the board and then selected a position to which it should be moved. A dispersion-based criterion with 500 ms gaze dwell threshold was used to make each selection. If the confirmatory fixation was not made and, instead, another ball was selected, the previous ball was unselected (the frame around it disappeared). Therefore, incorrect selections did not lead to any actions, thus relieving participants of any concerns about making mistakes.

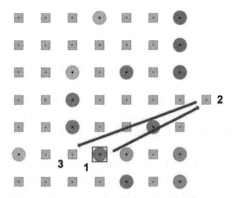

Fig. 1. An example of EyeLines game board, with a sequence of eye dwells constituting a move: 1 – a target ball (the squared frame indicates selection); 2 – the confirmatory position; 3 – a new position (Ovchinnikova et al. 2021). Distance between the centers of each two adjacent cells was seen at ~1.56°.

The goal of the study (Ovchinnikova et al. 2021) was to classify the intended and unintended selections using the magnetoencephalography (MEG) data co-registered with the eye tracker data, but the eye tracker data were not analyzed in detail and the gaze features were not used for classification. In contrast, here we did not use the MEG data and focused on gaze features alone.

Gaze data collected prior to each ball selection were analyzed offline. Raw labeling of ball selection was provided by the fixations on the confirmatory position or the absence of such confirmation. To further rectify the resulting sets of intentional and unintentional selections, we applied several additional rules. In particular, selections not confirmed by a saccade to the confirmation position starting later than 600 ms from the selection feedback were excluded from the analysis, because slow confirmation could be indicative of late decision making, i.e., some of such selections could be originally unintentional. On the other hand, selections which were not confirmed could be the result of eye-tracking mistakes and not necessarily be unintentional (in case the participant wanted to select one ball, but another one standing nearby was selected instead). To prevent such situations, unconfirmed ball selections were excluded if the participant's next move was selection of an adjacent ball and this selection was confirmed.

The number of both types of selections varied depending on the individual style of playing and gaze behavior. In 14 participants the number of selections in at least one of the two sets were lower than 100. After excluding these participants, 26 participants remained for further analysis. From each of them, 100 intentional and unintentional selections were randomly chosen for further analysis and classification performance.

We characterized gaze behavior prior to each selection with two sets of features (Table 1). The first set consisted of three features related to the saccade that preceded gaze dwell on the ball. The second set consisted of several types of features describing gaze micro-behavior during the dwell on the ball.

The distance to the center of the selected ball was computed in 10 non-overlapping windows. Four other types of features were computed in overlapping windows of varying length, in an attempt to follow the presumably increasing importance of these features closer to the upcoming selection feedback (see Table 1 for details). The first fixation refers to the fixation detected by the EyeLink algorithm which was closest to the start of gaze dwell delay. The dispersion of coordinates is calculated separately for X and Y coordinates as the difference between their maximum and minimum values within this interval. Microsaccades in this context refer to the saccades that are detected during the dwell.

To estimate how well the intentional selections can be identified using statistical classifiers, each selection was characterized by a vector comprising 67 features, derived from pre-selection data. The participants were randomly divided into training ($N = 20$) and testing ($N = 6$) sets. Feature standardization was performed using the mean and standard deviation calculated from the training set.

Classification was run using Linear Discriminant Analysis (LDA), Support Vector Machines (SVM) with radial basis function kernel (RBF SVM), Linear SVM and Random Forest. Hyperparameters were optimized on the train set data according to ROC AUC obtained in 5-fold cross-validation, using random search (Bergstra and Bengio 2012) implemented in RandomizedSearchCV tool.

Table 1. Gaze behavior features used for classification of intentional and unintentional selections.

Type	Feature description	
Saccade before dwell	Peak velocity	
	Average velocity	
	Amplitude	
	Duration	
Dwell	Variance of coordinate x	
	Variance of coordinate y	
	Duration of the first fixation	
	Distance to the center of selected ball	× 10 windows 0–50, 50–100, … 450–500 ms
	Dispersion of coordinate x	× 10 windows 0–500, 50–500, … 450–500 ms
	Dispersion of coordinate y	× 10 windows 0–500, 50–500, … 450–500 ms
	Gaze path length	× 10 windows 0–500, 50–500, … 450–500 ms
	Count of microsaccades	× 10 windows 0–500, 50–500, … 450–500 ms
	Total amplitude of microsaccades	× 10 windows 0–500, 50–500, … 450–500 ms

For all classification-related computations, the scikit-learn package (https://github.com/scikit-learn/scikit-learn) was utilized.

3   Results

3.1   Features

Visual inspection of the distributions of the gaze feature values shows that each feature alone could not enable effective classification, as the distributions were highly overlapping for all features. However, the distributions remain interesting to study.

The histograms of coordinate variance (Fig. 2) and coordinate dispersion (Fig. 3) demonstrate that during intentional gaze dwells, micro eye movements occur within a smaller range compared to spontaneous dwells. The most significant differences are observed within the first 100 ms.

For the gaze path (Fig. 4, left), minimal differences were observed, whereas for the deviation from the center of the object (Fig. 4, right), intentional gaze dwells exhibit smaller deviations compared to spontaneous dwells. This distinction is particularly pronounced within the last 100 ms of the dwell time.

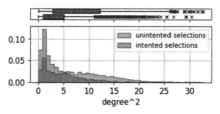

Fig. 2. Mean value of variances of x and y coordinates. Distributions of the values for intended (red) and unintended (blue) selections.

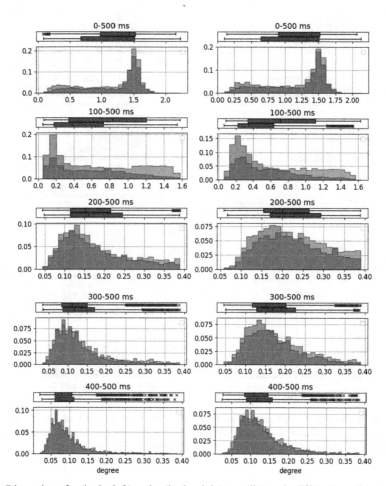

Fig. 3. Dispersion of x (in the left) and y (in the right) coordinates in different overlapping time intervals. Distributions of the values for intended (red) and unintended (blue) selections.

Figure 5 illustrates the distribution of duration values for the first fixation. Since in many cases this measure exceeded 500 ms, we rounded all larger values to 500 ms to facilitate the subsequent use of the classifier models in online mode.

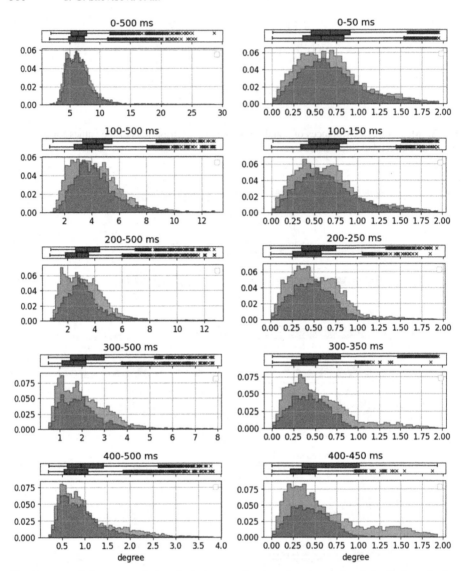

Fig. 4. In the left: gaze path length during overlapping time intervals of dwell time. In the right: distance to the center of selected ball during non-overlapping time intervals of dwell time. Distributions of the values for intended (red) and unintended (blue) selections.

During intentional and spontaneous gaze dwells, different numbers of microsaccades are observed, as can be seen in the histograms of the count and total amplitude of microsaccades during gaze dwell time (Fig. 6).

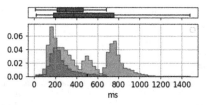

Fig. 5. Duration of the first fixation. Distributions of the values for intended (red) and unintended (blue) selections. The black vertical line shows the moment of dwell detection (500 ms)

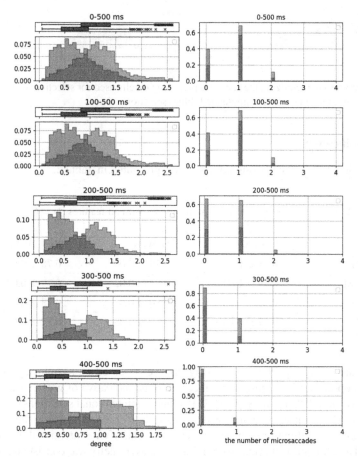

Fig. 6. In the left: total amplitude of microsaccades during overlapping time intervals of dwell time. The 0 values were excluded for better visualization. In the right: the number of microsaccades during overlapping time intervals of dwell time. Distributions of the values for intended (red) and unintended (blue) selections.

Figure 7 displays the characteristics of the preceding saccade, where no significant differences are observed between intentional and spontaneous gaze dwells.

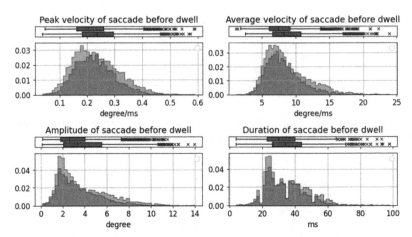

Fig. 7. Features characterizing the saccades preceding dwells used for selection: distributions of the values for intended (red) and unintended (blue) selections.

3.2 Classification

Classification performance using all features is presented in Table 2.

Table 2. Classification performance on the test set with all features (N = 6), M ± SD.

	accuracy	f1-score	ROC AUC
RBF SVM	0.78 ± 0.03	0.79 ± 0.06	0.78 ± 0.03
Linear SVM	0.79 ± 0.03	0.81 ± 0.02	0.79 ± 0.03
LDA	0.78 ± 0.03	0.80 ± 0.03	0.78 ± 0.03
Random Forest	0.77 ± 0.03	0.79 ± 0.03	0.77 ± 0.03

After analyzing the ROC curves (Fig. 8), we observed an asymmetry in the true positive proportion (TPP). Such asymmetry may be indicative of greater variability in the negative class (Bhattacharya et al. 2019) (here, unintentional selections). In fact, the number of false positive outcomes was typically 2–3 times higher than the number of false negatives, resulting in higher accuracy when classifying intentional events (0.86) compared to unintentional events (0.69). This TPP asymmetry was consistent among the top ten highest-scored subjects (accuracy for intentional selection: 0.94 ± 0.04; for unintentional selections: 0.77 ± 0.08) as well as the bottom ten lowest-scored subjects (0.78 ± 0.12 and 0.64 ± 0.11, respectively). (All accuracy values reported in this paragraph were obtained using the RBF SVM classifier).

We also assessed classifier performance using a limited set of features. To select them, we employed a Random Forest model. We evaluated the classification performance of the Random Forest model using different numbers of features, gradually removing the features which were less significant for the model. The accuracy of the classification

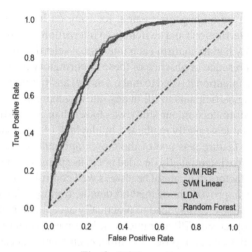

Fig. 8. ROC curves

remained stable when using only the top 20 most significant features instead of the full set of 67 features but dropped when the feature set was further reduced. Finally, we selected three highly significant features with relatively low correlation between them (Pearson correlation coefficient <0.7), namely, total amplitude of microsaccades during 200–500 ms time interval, y coordinate dispersion during 250–500 ms time interval, distance to the center of the selected ball during 450–500 ms time interval. Classification results using only these three features are presented in Table 3.

Table 3. Classification performance on the test set with three features (N = 6), M ± SD.

	accuracy	f1-score	ROC AUC
RBF SVM	0.74 ± 0.03	0.77 ± 0.03	0.74 ± 0.03
Linear SVM	0.74 ± 0.03	0.78 ± 0.03	0.74 ± 0.03
LDA	0.74 ± 0.03	0.77 ± 0.02	0.74 ± 0.03
Random Forest	0.75 ± 0.03	0.77 ± 0.03	0.75 ± 0.03

4 Discussion

In this study, we identified an intention to select a screen object during gaze-based interaction with a 500 ms gaze dwell time threshold by machine learning algorithms, which were applied to features obtained from the eye tracker data before selection. Interaction in our experiment was made as natural as possible, resembling a normal use of a gaze-based interface. Unlike in the experiment (Isomoto et al. 2022), the experimental paradigm used here did not force the participants to pay attention to their intentions. Our participants freely played an engaging game, focusing on it during game intervals of 5 min each without interruptions and switching to interaction means other than gaze. To make moves, they only had to confirm each intentional selection by an additional gaze-dwell. Based on the presence or absence of these confirmatory actions, we were able to label the selections as intentional (used to make a move) and unintentional (spontaneous) without requesting the participants to fill in any questionnaires.

Classification performance in our study was lower than in the study (Isomoto et al. 2022). This could be at least partly explained by the lack of pupil size data among our features, because this feature was one of the most important in the feature set used in (Isomoto et al. 2022). We intentionally decided not to use pupil size due to its well-known dependence on many factors that cannot be always well controlled in practical situations. We hope that further improvement of method details, training on larger datasets, fine-tuning on individual data, etc. may lead to practically acceptable performance.

Considering the observed TPP asymmetry, it becomes evident that achieving high specificity in online classification poses a significant challenge, necessitating the implementation of a robust deselection solution. However, it is worth noting that this particular challenge, albeit substantial, is preferable in comparison to a scenario characterized by low sensitivity (TNP asymmetry) within the same application context.

Not all features that we calculated were valuable for classification performance. For example, characteristics of saccade before dwell showed no difference for intentional and unintentional selections. This can be explained by the specificity of our experiment in which objects on which fixations were typically made (balls) could be located both far and close to each other.

One peculiarity of gaze behavior during intentional dwells could be the expectation of a black border around the ball, which served as the indication of a selection. This expectation could affect some features. In particular, during intentional selections participants usually directed their gaze closer to the center of the ball. Such behavior was especially clear during the last 100 ms, because in spontaneous dwells participants have started to move the gaze to the next ball by that time.

Likely also due to the expectation of the selection feedback, first fixation duration for many intentional dwells was 700–800 ms, which meant that gaze stayed on the ball for an additional 200–300 ms after the dwell was detected. Such prolonged fixations are rare in the natural gaze behavior associated with vision. Therefore, the dwells are clearly distinguishable in these ranges of values. However, we used only features describing gaze behavior before dwell detection, because we plan to use them in real-time mode in the future work. To correctly model a real-time application, we had to set a value of this feature to 500 ms when it was longer. For the same reason, when the first fixation duration appeared in the range of 500–600 ms it was shortened to 500 ms too, so it also lost its significance for the classification.

According to the number and total amplitude of microsaccades, a lower number of uncontrolled eye movements was observed during intentional dwells. Also, the dispersion and variance of coordinates show that gaze was located, on average, in a smaller area around the ball center when there was an intention to select the ball. However, such a behavior could also be associated with an increased level of attention, which can be observed not only during intentional selection but also in many other scenarios. In a future study, we plan to test whether we could still discriminate intentional selection from spontaneous prolonged gaze dwells in a situation when visual attention is high.

On the other hand, detection of inattentive states could probably help to exclude unintentional selections. One interesting way to improve performance may be enriching the feature set with the eye vergence data, as they were shown to label inattentive states very effectively (Huang et al. 2019), although this approach would require good binocular data.

Although our experiment paradigm enabled good immersion into gaze interaction, the need to confirm each selection still could alter gaze behavior. It is therefore very important to explore gaze behavior in real-time intention classification experiments without such confirmation, which we are going to start soon. It is also important to test intention identification algorithms using wider sets of real-life tasks. Finally, testing the approach with simpler, affordable eye trackers will be necessary to assess the practical value of the approach in the near future.

Acknowledgement. This research was funded by the Russian Science Foundation, grant 22-19-00528.

References

Bergstra, J., Bengio, Y.: Random search for hyper-parameter optimization. J. Mach. Learn. Res. **13**, 281–305 (2012)

Bhattacharya, B., Hughes, G.: On shape properties of the receiver operating characteristic curve. Statist. Probab. Lett. **103**, 73–79 (2015)

Duchowski, A.T.: Gaze-based interaction: a 30 year retrospective. Comput. Graph. **73**, 59–69 (2018). https://doi.org/10.1016/j.cag.2018.04.002

Huang, M.X., Li, J., Ngai, G., Leong, H.V., Bulling, A.: Moment-to-moment detection of internal thought during video viewing from eye vergence behavior. In: Proceedings of the 27th ACM International Conference on Multimedia, pp. 2254–2262. Association for Computing Machinery, New York (2019). https://doi.org/10.1145/3343031.3350573

Isomoto, T., Yamanaka, S., Shizuki, B.: Dwell selection with ML-based intent prediction using only gaze data. In: Proceedings of the ACM on Interactive, Mobile, Wearable and Ubiquitous Technologies, vol. 6, pp. 1–21 (2022). https://doi.org/10.1145/3550301

Jacob, R.J.K.: What you look at is what you get: eye movement-based interaction techniques. In: Proceedings of the SIGCHI Conference on Human Factors in Computing Systems, pp. 11–18. Association for Computing Machinery, New York (1990). https://doi.org/10.1145/97243.97246

Majaranta, P., Räihä, KJ., Hyrskykari, A., Špakov, O.: Eye movements and human-computer interaction. In: Klein, C., Ettinger, U. (eds.) Eye Movement Research. Studies in Neuroscience, Psychology and Behavioral Economics, pp. 971–1015. Springer, Cham (2019). https://doi.org/10.1007/978-3-030-20085-5_23

Murata, A., Doi, T., Kageyama, K., Karwowski, W.: Development of an eye-gaze input system with high speed and accuracy through target prediction based on homing eye movements. IEEE Access, 22688–22697 (2021). https://doi.org/10.1109/ACCESS.2021.3055514

Ovchinnikova, A.O., Vasilyev, A.N., Zubarev, I.P., Kozyrskiy, B.L., Shishkin, S.L.: MEG-based detection of voluntary eye fixations used to control a computer. Front. Neurosci. **15**, 619591 (2021). https://doi.org/10.3389/fnins.2021.619591

Velichkovsky, B., Sprenger, A., Unema, P.: Towards gaze-mediated interaction: collecting solutions of the "Midas touch problem". In: Howard, S., Hammond, J., Lindgaard, G. (eds.) Human-Computer Interaction INTERACT '97. IFIPAICT, pp. 509–516. Springer, Boston (1997). https://doi.org/10.1007/978-0-387-35175-9_77

The Effect of Pseudo-Haptic Feedback on Weight Perception of Virtual Objects on the Computer Side

Yan Wang and Fan Qian[✉]

Department of Art Design and Media, East China University of Science and Technology,
Shanghai 200237, China
1184657217@qq.com

Abstract. In this paper, we investigate the effect of mouse cursor visibility on pseudo-haptic weight perception on the computer side through a static control display ratio (C/D ratio) method and construct a pseudo-haptic weight perception prediction model for it under mouse interaction mode. Unlike the traditional dynamic C/D ratio approach, the static C/D ratio approach used in this paper can also evoke the same pseudo-haptic weight perception of the user. Also, the final results show that hiding the cursor image of the input device in the display can reduce the effect of the difference between object displacement and cursor displacement on the pseudo-haptic perception. To a certain extent, it is demonstrated that the pseudo-haptic weight perception can be induced by fatigue through hand work as opposed to the pseudo-haptic perception by visual illusion. The model provides interaction designers with some design references to enhance the immersive experience of users in the process of using computers.

Keywords: Human-computer Interaction · Pseudo-haptic · User Experience

1 Introduction

The human-computer interaction interface is the medium of information transfer and exchange between the user and the computer system, which mutually converts the human "language" and the form of information inside the computer system to realize the communication between the human and the computer [1]. The human-computer interface has gradually evolved from command-line and graphical user interfaces to natural user interfaces [2]. In a natural user interface, people can communicate with the computer in the most natural way (e.g., voice, motion gestures, etc.) with two-way interactivity [3]. However, the current design homogeneity of HCI modalities largely limits the development of natural interaction between users and computer systems, making it difficult to enhance user experience. In the past interface design, the functional interfaces of human-computer interaction are mostly focused on the visual and auditory sensory modalities, and rarely involve haptic-related experiences [4].

Haptics, is an important tool for people to know and understand the world. People perform various exploration and manipulation tasks in the real world through the sense of touch [5]. People's skin is richly distributed with tactile receptors and various nerve endings, through which external information can be transmitted to the central nervous system, thus allowing people to acquire tactile perception [6]. People can identify the material properties (temperature, softness, density, etc.), appearance characteristics (texture sense, viscosity, graininess, etc.), spatial characteristics (shape, volume, contour, etc.), etc. of an object through the tactile senses. Compared with other senses, touch allows the most direct physical contact between people and objective objects. At the same time, these tactile experiences allow people to generate emotions such as happiness, surprise, and fear [7]. If multi-sensory information such as touch, vision, and hearing are incorporated into the natural interaction interface, the user experience can be greatly improved.

In recent years, with the development of haptic interaction technology, it has gradually been integrated into natural interaction interface design in a new interaction way. In existing research, there are two main types of haptic feedback methods [8]: the first type is to obtain haptic perception directly by means of physical stimulation, and these haptic feedback devices include wearable, handheld, and grounded; the second type is to use multisensory illusions to obtain a virtual pseudo-haptic experience. Although the first type of method can obtain real haptic perception, but these haptic feedback devices have some unavoidable problems. In terms of usability, the devices are clumsy, difficult to operate, and poorly portable; in terms of cost, they are more difficult to develop and manufacture as their hardware devices are more expensive [9–13]. However, the second type of method can alleviate these problems to a large extent. Therefore, more and more scholars have started to research the field of pseudo-haptic sensing.

2 Related Work

The pseudo-tactile feedback technique, first proposed by Lécuyer et al. is a technique that does not rely on real tactile feedback but is based on the integration of information from multisensory channels to obtain tactile perception [12, 14]. Multisensory illusion is a cross-channel illusion phenomenon that is mainly triggered by stimulation of one or more channels to produce perception in another channel [15]. Thus, pseudo-haptic feedback can be described as a perceptual illusion in nature. When the speed of image movement in the display device does not match the speed of movement in the input device, people will have an illusory haptic perception [16]. That is, when the user believes that the visual image in the display device moves with his or her own body, the change in the movement of the visual image can be perceived as a change in the force or object friction felt in the subject's hand, thus causing a pseudo-haptic perception by the user. That is, a dynamically changing control/display ratio (C/D) is used to simulate the sense of touch.

It has been shown in existing studies that one can simulate the perception of haptic dimensions such as weight [17–19], roughness [20, 21], and hardness [22–24] of an object by flexibly changing the visual display of the virtual object in the display interface using pseudo-haptic feedback techniques. In terms of the weight perception dimension, Dominjon et al. [25] in their psychophysical experiments had users lift a ball simulated by a phantom and asked them to perceive its weight. It was eventually found that when the displacement of the visual feedback was greater than the actual input displacement of the user, the user could perceive the object as lighter than its weight in the real world. Samad et al. [19] applied a similar approach in virtual space and found in their experiments that a reference mass of 185 g could be adjusted to ± 5 g under conditions that induced a 5–10 cm difference in hand displacement. Rietzler et al. [26] visualized the position offset gap between the real hand position and the virtual hand position in their study as a way to give the user weight cue. When the user lifts heavier objects, it results in a larger offset gap. Their results suggest that users can associate the weight properties of objects with the visual stimuli designed in the experiment and see them as part of the virtual world. Yu and Bowman [27] in their study changed the weight perception of the object by the user by scaling the rotational motion. As the rotation angle becomes smaller, the weight perception of the object will be heavier and conversely weaker. Their experimental results show that controlling this method has more than an 80% probability of making the user perceive the object as heavier than the object without using this method. In terms of the roughness of the object, it is also a weight perception in a sense. In their study, Narumi et al. [28] had subjects slide the background image on a touch screen and gave them a sense of friction by varying the ratio between the displacement of the subject's finger movement and the scrolling displacement of the background image on the screen. The final results showed that the user could obtain the sense of friction when the displacement ratio was less than 1. Hashimoto et al. [29] used the same method in their study and investigated the effect of this method on the memory task.

From previous research, we can find that the pseudo-haptic feedback technique of changing the control display ratio (C/D ratio) can allow users to perceive the weight of virtual objects. As a computer is one of the interactive devices we use every day, continuously improving the haptic experience on the computer side (allowing people to feel the weight of virtual objects in the interface when controlling them with the mouse) can largely enhance the immersive experience of user interaction. However, when the sense of difference between visual information and the proprioceptive information is strong, it can affect the user's pseudo-haptic perception [30]. Lécuyer has shown in his study that hiding the user's hand (equivalent to hiding the input device displacement) and keeping the hand away from the visual feedback in the display is effective in guiding the user to generate pseudo-haptic perception [31]. Therefore, we believe that the visibility of the mouse cursor during computer-side interactions may also affect the degree of pseudo-haptic weight perception by the user.

In summary, in this paper we will investigate the effect of different C/D ratios and mouse cursor visibility in the screen on the user's pseudo-tactile weight perception during computer-side interaction.

3   Tactile Perception Method

In the previous studies by scholars, most of them set the parameter of control display ratio (C/D) to allow the user to obtain the weight perception of the object when grasping or moving the virtual object, that is, to change the ratio α between the moving displacement D of the input device and the visual displacement D' in the display device. The control display ratio is a unitless parameter that maps the movement in the input device to the movement of the visual image in the display [32]. Thus, the value of the C/D ratio can be used to describe the degree of sensitivity of the input device [33]. When α is equal to 1, the displacement speed of the input device is exactly the same as the visual displacement speed in the display. When α is less than 1, the visual movement speed in the display is slower than that of the input device, the movement distance becomes smaller, and the user feels the weight of the virtual object becomes heavier. When α is greater than 1, the visual image in the display moves proportionally faster and farther than that of the input device, so the user feels the weight of the virtual object becomes lighter. However, in the existing research, scholars have different understandings of the "control display ratio". Some scholars consider the control-display ratio as the output gain of the input (e.g., [19]), i.e., the visual displacement of the display is smaller than the displacement of the input device when the C/D ratio is less than 1. However, some other scholars consider the C/D ratio as part of the control and display process (e.g., [34]), i.e., the visual displacement of the display is greater than the displacement of the input device when the C/D ratio is less than 1. In this paper, we adopt the first understanding that when the C/D ratio is less than 1, the visual movement speed is smaller than the input movement speed, and the user feels that the virtual object in the display device is heavier.

The research method in this paper differs from the traditional dynamic C/D ratio method in that it focuses on the static C/D ratio method. The pseudo-haptic approach of dynamic C/D ratio is mainly based on changing the C/D ratio so that the user feels a sudden "anomalous mapping" of the corresponding visual image on the display when using the input device, thus creating a pseudo-haptic perception. However, Narumi et al. [35] kept the C/D ratio constant for each subject during the sliding background image in their study, and eventually they found that as the control display ratio was gradually reduced, the user gradually felt stronger friction in the touch screen. Therefore, the study in this paper also draws on this method to allow users to feel pseudo-haptic weight perception in the computer-side interface by means of the static C/D ratio.

In order to realize the functions related to the experimental design, we have developed an application in Unity 2021.3.16f1c1 software using C# language. In this application, we can set the C/D ratio of the square at will, so that the user can feel the different weight sensation during dragging the square along the track by the mouse. Also, in this program we set the visual visibility of the mouse in the display according to different situations. During the development of the program, we found that the setting of the C/D ratio was related to the unit conversion between coordinates (3D spatial coordinates and screen coordinates) in the software Unity. Also, we found that the change of screen resolution caused the change of unit conversion rate in Unity. The application is mainly run on a Dell Precision 7720 laptop with a screen resolution of 1920×1080, so the unit conversion rate between the corresponding object's 3D coordinates in Unity and the screen coordinates is 90.7. Theoretically, when the C/D ratio is 1, the displacement of the input device should be equal to the visual displacement, but we do not take the displacement of the mouse (input device) moving in the real world as the input displacement, but keep the daily habit of people using the mouse. We regard the movement of the mouse cursor as the "input displacement" and the movement of the cube in the visual interface as the "visual displacement". Therefore, in this study, we define the standard C/D ratio as 1 when the distance of mouse cursor movement is equal to the distance of cube movement.

4 Experiment

We allowed the user to perceive the weight of the object in the interactive interface by means of the mouse operation by randomly changing the static control display ratio of the object (the object C/D ratio was constant during each trial of the operation). It was assumed that when the object C/D ratio was less than 1 and the mouse cursor was not visible, the user could feel the weight of the virtual object in the interactive interface more.

4.1 Participants

There were 8 participants (age: {M = 24.25, SD = 0.24}, 5 females, 3 males), all subjects were used to manipulating objects with their right hand and they were not depressed, anxious, or extremely fatigued. The study materials and procedures of the experiment were started after obtaining approval from the Bioethics Committee of East China University of Science and Technology. And we all obtained informed consent from the participants before the formal experiment started.

4.2 Experimental Equipment

The main experimental device in this experiment was a Dell Precision 7720 computer equipped with a wireless Bluetooth mouse with a sensitivity of 1000 dpi for operation.

4.3 Procedure

The overall flow of the experiment is shown in Fig. 1. Before the experiment began, we would briefly introduce the purpose and the process of the whole experiment to the subjects. Then, all subjects were randomly divided into two groups A and B by drawing lots, with four people in each group. Group A conducted the mouse cursor invisibility test first, followed by the mouse cursor visibility test; Group B conducted the mouse cursor visibility test first, followed by the mouse cursor invisibility test. In order to avoid the influence of different external environments on the experimental results, both groups were tested in the same environment.

As shown in Fig. 2, the interface design was the same for each experiment. In order to avoid the influence of brightness, color and other attributes on the perceived weight of the virtual object, the two squares appearing in the interface were identical in appearance, but the control display ratio (C/D ratio) parameters were set differently. One cube had a constant C/D ratio set to 1 and was the standard cube (which was not known to the subjects as a reference during the experiment); another cube had a random C/D ratio parameter of one of the nine parameters (0.48, 0.58, 0.69, 0.83, 1.00, 1.20, 1.44, 1.73, 2.08). In this case, these nine C/D ratio parameters were set in the form of an equiprobable series, so as to theoretically achieve the same perceived difference brought to the subjects by each rising C/D level. At the same time, each C/D ratio level appeared four times during the experiment. Thus, 36 trials (9 C/D ratios × 4) were performed for each subject in both the visible and invisible mouse experiments. This experiment

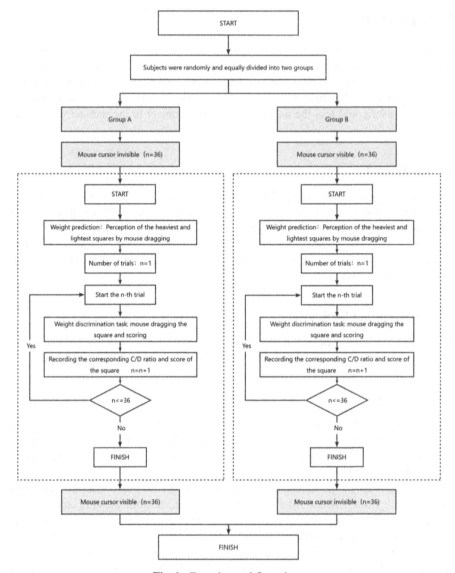

Fig. 1. Experimental flow chart.

used a within-group design in which each participant was subjected to two experiments (mouse visibility experiment and mouse invisibility experiment), so that a total of 72 trials were performed for each participant.

Before the start of each experiment, subjects were required to perform a weight perception pre-experiment, which served as a reference for the subsequent scoring process. In this process, subjects could perform weight perception by dragging the heaviest square and the lightest square with the mouse, and both the heaviest and lightest squares individually corresponded to the two extremes of the score (10 and −10 points).

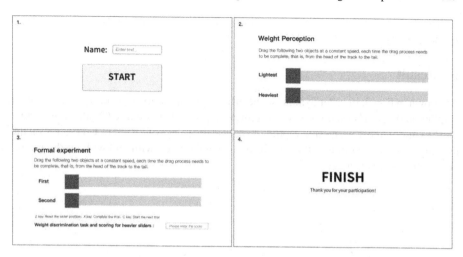

Fig. 2. Experimental interface design.

Once the formal experiment began, the main task of the subjects was to identify the weight of the two squares in the interface and to choose the heavier one for scoring its degree of weight perception. Scores can only be rounded to the nearest whole number, ranging from −10 to 10 points, and also including 0 points. When the first square was heavier than the second square, the score was negative; when the second square was heavier than the first square, the score was positive. For example, if the first cube was significantly heavier than the second cube, the score could be −10; when the first cube was a little heavier than the second cube, the score could be −2; if the subject felt that the two cubes weighed the same, the score could be 0. In the experiment where the mouse cursor was visible, we would set the cursor to be visible throughout; in the experiment where the mouse cursor was not visible, we would set the mouse cursor image in the interface to be invisible when the subject started to drag the square, and the mouse cursor would be visible again after the square dragging was finished. In the process of dragging the cube to identify the weight, there were several points to note: first, each time the cube dragging process should be complete, and must be dragged from the head to the end of the track, without stopping in the middle; second, the speed of the subject dragging the cube should be kept as uniform as possible, and could not suddenly accelerate or decelerate in the middle; third, in order to accurately perceive the weight of the cube, the subject could drag the cube several times for weight perception, but the dragging direction was fixed, could only drag the cube from left to right; fourth, in the course of the experiment, we could press the "Z" key to restore the cube to the initial position of the track with one key. When you finished the current trial, you could press "X" to end it, then the square would disappear. When you clicked "C", it meant to start the next trial and the square would appear again.

During the whole experiment, the number of trials would not be reminded in the experiment interface, and when the experiment was completely finished, the interface would automatically tell the subjects in the form of a pop-up window. At the same time, in order to avoid the effect of fatigue on the experimental results, the subjects could rest for 30 s for every 9 trials completed.

5 Result

As shown in Fig. 3, in order to analyse the effect of mouse cursor visibility in a computer display on the user's pseudo-tactile weight perception at different C/D ratios, this paper used a simple linear regression model to analyse the effect of different C/D ratios on the degree of user perception of the weight of a virtual object, with and without the mouse cursor visible, respectively.

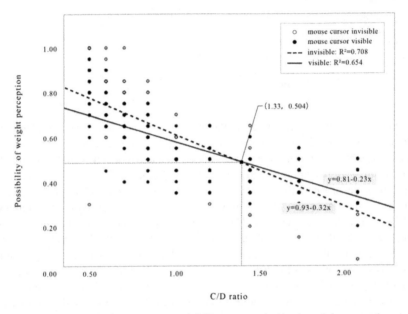

Fig. 3. The effect of mouse cursor visibility on pseudo-haptic weight perception.

Firstly, in the case of the interactions where the mouse cursor was visible, the simple linear regression results showed a linear relationship between the control display ratio and the user's degree of pseudo-haptic weight perception. We first judged visually that a linear relationship existed between the two factors by plotting scatter plots, and then verified that the experimental data met the characteristics of equal variance and normality of residuals by drawing standard residual scatter plots, bar charts with normal curves and P-P plots. At the same time, three outliers were removed to improve the accuracy of the data, and the final regression equation obtained was Eq. (1). When the mouse cursor was visible, the different C/D ratios had a statistically significant effect on the degree of pseudo-tactile weight perception, $F(1,283) = 534.30$ ($p < 0.001$). The control display ratio explained 65.4% of the variance in the degree of pseudo-tactile weight perception of the user, which had a larger effect (adjusted $R^2 = 65.3\%$).

$$y = 0.81 - 0.23x \tag{1}$$

Secondly, in the case of mouse cursor-hidden interactions, the simple linear regression results also showed a linear relationship between the control display ratio and the user's degree of pseudo-haptic weight perception. The linearity of the relationship between the two factors was first determined visually by plotting scatter plots, and then verified by drawing standard residual scatter plots, bar charts with normal curves and P-P plots to show that the experimental data were characterised by equal variance and normality of residuals. Also, to improve the accuracy of the data, one outlier was removed and the final regression equation obtained was Eq. (2). Statistical results showed that when the mouse cursor was not visible, different C/D ratios had a statistically significant effect on the degree of pseudo-haptic weight perception, $F(1,285) = 689.75$ (p < 0.001). The control display ratio explained 70.8% of the variance in the degree of user pseudo-haptic weight perception and the effect was greater (adjusted $R^2 = 70.7\%$).

$$y = 0.93 - 0.32x \qquad (2)$$

Finally, by grouping the fit functions of the scatter plots we can find that the linear functions when the mouse cursor is visible and invisible intersect at the point (1.33, 0.504). This means that in both cases, when the C/D ratio is 1.33, the user has the same level of pseudo-tactile weight perception (i.e. 50.4%). When the C/D ratio is less than 1.33, the degree of the weight perception with the cursor invisible is higher than the degree of the weight perception with the cursor visible.

6   Discussion

Firstly, from the overall results of the experiment, in addition to the traditional dynamic C/D ratio approach, we can find that the static C/D ratio approach can also induce a pseudo-tactile weight perception on the computer side of the user. Yuki Ban et al. [36] and Takuji Narumi et al. [28] used a similar approach in their study to elicit pseudo-haptic weight perception during the interaction of the user with the touch screen. The traditional dynamic C/D ratio approach focuses on visually inducing a haptic illusion for the user by changing the C/D ratio so that the user suddenly feels an 'abnormal mapping' of the corresponding visual image on the display. The static C/D ratio approach is based on both visual and mechanical work to induce a pseudo-tactile weight perception. Its principle is that a smaller C/D ratio allows the user to move a larger distance through the input device but only produces a smaller visual displacement, which in this case causes the user to feel tired during the dragging of the cube, thus creating a pseudo-tactile weight perception of the cube.

Secondly, from the grouped scatter plots we can visualize that the smaller the C/D ratio, the higher the degree of pseudo-haptic weight perception generated by the user in the case where the mouse cursor is invisible compared to the case where the mouse cursor is visible. This is likely due to the fact that the immersive experience is greater when the mouse cursor is invisible, and the user can feel the weight of the cube more immersive by not seeing the cursor shift while dragging the cube. However, when the mouse cursor is visible, the difference between mouse movement and cube movement is obvious to the user, so it is difficult for the user to perceive the pseudo-tactile weight perception of the cube. When the C/D ratio is larger, the degree of pseudo-touch weight perception by the user is higher with the mouse cursor visible than with the mouse cursor invisible. However, the difference in the degree of weight perception between the two cases was smaller when the C/D ratio was larger compared to when the C/D ratio was smaller. This may be due to the fact that when C/D is larger, a smaller input displacement can cause a larger visual displacement and subjects can easily drag the cube from the head of the track to the tail during the experiment, so that they do not have time to perceive the weight of the cube yet. It also shows that larger C/D ratios (C/D greater than 1) are more difficult to elicit pseudo-tactile weight perception from the user.

7   Conclusion

Firstly, the main contribution of this paper is to demonstrate that hiding the mouse cursor during user interaction is more likely to elicit pseudo-tactile weight perception, and to construct a predictive model for pseudo-tactile weight perception on the computer side. The model can predict the user's weight perception of virtual objects in the computer-side interface. Therefore, the model can be used as a design reference for interaction design, and to a certain extent, it can help interaction designers to design interface interactions so as to enhance the immersive experience of users during computer interactions.

Second, the research method in this paper is different from the traditional method that the static C/D ratio method used in this paper can also cause the pseudo-haptic weight perception of the user. In other words, when the mouse cursor is not visible, setting the C/D ratio of the object smaller (C/D ratio close to 0) and keeping the parameters of its C/D ratio setting constant can cause a stronger pseudo-tactile weight perception of the virtual object.

However, the research in this paper still has a large limitation. Although the prediction model constructed in this paper can predict the corresponding user pseudo-tactile weight perception according to different C/D ratios, the weight perception in this model has no real physical meaning in the real world. In the future, we can continue to investigate and upgrade this pseudo-tactile weight perception prediction model to correspond the weight of virtual objects in the interface to the weight of objects in the real world, thus further enhancing the immersive experience of user interaction.

References

1. Ting, Z.: Research on the application of human-computer interaction interface design in product usability. Packag. Eng. **35**(20), 63–66 (2014)
2. Yongliang, P.: Naturalistic trends in human-computer interaction interface design. ZHUANG-SHI **06**, 130–131 (2008)
3. Zichen, Z.: A Study of Natural Interaction Interface Design from the Perspective of Boosting Theory. Southeastern University (2021)
4. Xiaona, M., Qianqian, T., Yihan, L., Xukun, S.: Research on building haptic experience of intelligent design based on multimodal haptic and pseudo-haptic feedback. ZHUANGSHI **09**, 28–33 (2022)
5. Lederman, S.J., Klatzky, R.L.: Haptic perception: a tutorial. Atten. Percept. Psychophys. **71**(7), 1439–1459 (2009)

6. Sathian, K.: Analysis of haptic information in the cerebral cortex. J. Neurophysiol. **116**(4), 1795–1806 (2016)
7. Si, C., Jianpeng, Z., Zhengchun, P., Jianning, D.: From sense of touch to tactile intelligence: thoughts from the 2021 Nobel prize in physiology or medicine. Chin. Sci. Bull. **67**(06), 561–566 (2022)
8. Peng, D.: Research on Force Haptic Modeling and Reproduction Methods for Mobile Terminals. Southeastern University (2016)
9. Bosman, I.D.V.: Using Binaural Audio for Inducing Intersensory Illusions to Create Illusory Tactile Feedback in Virtual Reality. University of Pretoria (2018)
10. Culbertson, H., Schorr, S.B., Okamura, A.M.: Haptics: the present and future of artificial touch sensation. Ann. Rev. Control Robot. Autonom. Syst. **1**, 385–409 (2018)
11. Ujitoko, Y., Ban, Y., Hirota, K.: Modulating fine roughness perception of vibrotactile textured surface using pseudo-haptic effect. IEEE Trans. Visual Comput. Graph. **25**(5), 1981–1990 (2019)
12. Ujitoko, Y., Ban, Y., Hirota, K.: Presenting static friction sensation at stick-slip transition using pseudo-haptic effect. In: 2019 IEEE World Haptics Conference (WHC), pp. 181–186. IEEE (2019)
13. Wang, D., Ohnishi, K., Xu, W.: Multimodal haptic display for virtual reality: a survey. IEEE Trans. Industr. Electron. **67**(1), 610–623 (2019)
14. Kang, N., Lee, S.: A meta-analysis of recent studies on haptic feedback enhancement in immersive-augmented reality. In: Proceedings of the 4th International Conference on Virtual Reality, pp. 3–9 (2018)
15. Bizley, J.K., Shinn-Cunningham, B.G., Lee, A.K.: Nothing is irrelevant in a noisy world: sensory illusions reveal obligatory within-and across-modality integration. J. Neurosci. **32**(39), 13402–13410 (2012)
16. Lécuyer, A., Coquillart, S., Kheddar, A., Richard, P., Coiffet, P.: Pseudo-haptic feedback: can isometric input devices simulate force feedback?. In: Proceedings IEEE Virtual Reality 2000 (Cat. No. 00CB37048), pp. 83–90. IEEE (2000)
17. Bi, W., Newport, J., Xiao, B.: Interaction between static visual cues and force-feedback on the perception of mass of virtual objects. In: Proceedings of the 15th ACM Symposium on Applied Perception, pp. 1–5 (2018)
18. Hirao, Y., Takala, T.M., Lécuyer, A.: Comparing motion-based versus controller-based pseudo-haptic weight sensations in VR. In: 2020 IEEE Conference on Virtual Reality and 3D User Interfaces Abstracts and Workshops (VRW), pp. 305–310. IEEE (2020)
19. Samad, M., Gatti, E., Hermes, A., Benko, H., Parise, C.: Pseudo-haptic weight: changing the perceived weight of virtual objects by manipulating control-display ratio. In: Proceedings of the 2019 CHI Conference on Human Factors in Computing Systems, pp. 1–13 (2019)
20. Ota, Y., Ujitoko, Y., Ban, Y., Sakurai, S., Hirota, K.: Surface roughness judgment during finger exploration is changeable by visual oscillations. In: Nisky, I., Hartcher-O'Brien, J., Wiertlewski, M., Smeets, J. (eds.) EuroHaptics 2020. LNCS, vol. 12272, pp. 33–41. Springer, Cham (2020). https://doi.org/10.1007/978-3-030-58147-3_4
21. Sato, Y., Hiraki, T., Tanabe, N., Matsukura, H., Iwai, D., Sato, K.: Modifying texture perception with pseudo-haptic feedback for a projected virtual hand interface. IEEE Access **8**, 120473–120488 (2020)
22. Kawabe, T.: Mid-air action contributes to pseudo-haptic stiffness effects. IEEE Trans. Haptics **13**(1), 18–24 (2019)
23. Li, M., et al.: Evaluation of pseudo-haptic interactions with soft objects in virtual environments. PLoS ONE **11**(6), e0157681 (2016)
24. Matsumoto, D., et al.: An immersive visuo-haptic VR environment with pseudo-haptic effects on perceived stiffness. In: Hasegawa, S., Konyo, M., Kyung, K., Nojima, T., Kajimoto, H.

(eds.) AsiaHaptics 2016. LNEE, vol. 432, pp. 281–285. Springer, Singapore (2018). https://doi.org/10.1007/978-981-10-4157-0_48

25. Ujitoko, Y., Ban, Y.: Survey of pseudo-haptics: Haptic feedback design and application proposals. IEEE Trans. Haptics **14**(4), 699–711 (2021)
26. Rietzler, M., Geiselhart, F., Gugenheimer, J., Rukzio, E.: Breaking the tracking: enabling weight perception using perceivable tracking offsets. In: Proceedings of the 2018 CHI Conference on Human Factors in Computing Systems, pp. 1–12 (2018)
27. Yu, R., Bowman, D.A.: Pseudo-haptic display of mass and mass distribution during object rotation in virtual reality. IEEE Trans. Visual Comput. Graph. **26**(5), 2094–2103 (2020)
28. Narumi, T., Ujitoko, Y., Ban, Y., Tanikawa, T., Hirota, K., Hirose, M.: Resistive swipe: visuo-haptic interaction during swipe gestures to scroll background images on touch interfaces. In: 2017 IEEE World Haptics Conference (WHC), pp. 334–339. IEEE (2017)
29. Hashimoto, T., Narumi, T., Nagao, R., Tanikawa, T., Hirose, M.: Effect of pseudo-haptic feedback on touchscreens on visual memory during image browsing. In: Prattichizzo, D., Shinoda, H., Tan, H.Z., Ruffaldi, E., Frisoli, A. (eds.) EuroHaptics 2018. LNCS, vol. 10894, pp. 551–563. Springer, Cham (2018). https://doi.org/10.1007/978-3-319-93399-3_47
30. Pusch, A., Lécuyer, A.: Pseudo-haptics: from the theoretical foundations to practical system design guidelines. In: Proceedings of the 13th International Conference on Multimodal Interfaces, pp. 57–64 (2011)
31. Lécuyer, A.: Simulating haptic feedback using vision: a survey of research and applications of pseudo-haptic feedback. Presence Teleoperators Virtual Environ. **18**(1), 39–53 (2009)
32. Blanch, R., Guiard, Y., Beaudouin-Lafon, M.: Semantic pointing: improving target acquisition with control-display ratio adaptation. In: Proceedings of the SIGCHI Conference on Human Factors in Computing Systems, pp. 519–526 (2004)
33. Ahlström, D., Hitz, M., Leitner, G.: An evaluation of sticky and force enhanced targets in multi target situations. In: Proceedings of the 4th Nordic Conference on Human-Computer Interaction: Changing Roles, pp. 58–67 (2006)
34. Lécuyer, A., Burkhardt, J.M., Etienne, L.: Feeling bumps and holes without a haptic interface: the perception of pseudo-haptic textures. In: Proceedings of the SIGCHI Conference on Human Factors in Computing Systems, pp. 239–246 (2004)
35. Ban, Y., Kajinami, T., Narumi, T., Tanikawa, T., Hirose, M.: Modifying an identified curved surface shape using pseudo-haptic effect. In: 2012 IEEE Haptics Symposium (HAPTICS), pp. 211–216. IEEE (2012)
36. Ban, Y., Ujitoko, Y.: Enhancing the pseudo-haptic effect on the touch panel using the virtual string. In: 2018 IEEE Haptics Symposium (HAPTICS), pp. 278–283. IEEE (2018)

Gesture Mediated Timbre-Led Design based Music Interface for Socio-musical Interaction

Azeema Yaseen[✉][ID], Sutirtha Chakraborty[ID], and Joseph Timoney[ID]

Maynooth University, Maynooth, Ireland
{azeema.yaseen.2020,sutirtha.chakraborty.2019}@mumail.ie,
joseph.timoney@mu.ie

Abstract. Third-wave HCI broadens technology from traditional settings to everyday life. This wave has also influenced the internet of musical things (IoMusT) and ubiquitous music (ubimus), and these fields are inspired by the idea of including everyday things to act as musical things and become part of the push for ubiquitous computing for musical activities. This multiplies the possibilities in which musical interactions can occur and thus allows participants with various levels of musical experience to engage in musical activities. The interface design that not only supports musical activities but also delivers the experience of the musical activity is a challenging task for IoMusT. This paper presents a gesture-based timbre-led musical interface designed for casual musical activities. Earlier studies with this interface have shown the social aspect of interpersonal interactions in a musical activity. As music has a social role when individuals are connected in a musical activity, it is vital to understand the patterns of these interpersonal interactions. Here, we present a qualitative study that explores this social bond and how individuals perceive their own abilities and participation during such activities. The individual and dyadic musical interactions were structured into two steps and the results are explained to discuss the dimensions of this interaction.

Keywords: Gestures · Musical interfaces and interaction · Timbre · Social interaction

1 Introduction

Music-based interventions are applied to the fields of well-being and healthcare for their communicative abilities. Music is a noteworthy medium for sharing emotions [20] and a creative space for exploring the pattern of one's personal identity [6]. The emergence of ubiquitous technology in music could be capable of delivering digital musical interfaces for socially shared meaningful interactions. These new computer-based musical interfaces have facilitated new ways of music-based interactions but the study of these interfaces to explore the socially interactive nature of music and technology has not been focused on as of yet.

M. Kurosu et al. (Eds.): HCII 2023, LNCS 14054, pp. 335–347, 2023.
https://doi.org/10.1007/978-3-031-48038-6_21

The proposed design of a gesture-mediated virtual music interface is based on the concepts of the Internet of musical things (IoMusT) and ubiquitous music (ubimus). The designed interface will allow users to interact with sonic resources represented as color-supported visual tokens. The interface elements will support 1) whole-body tracking 2) visual tokens for sonic resources 3) control over those sonic resources and 4) an individual/cooperative musical interaction. The interface design does not follow the "instrumental" way of mapping sounds, instead, it is timbre-driven.

Visual tokens (colors) and gestures would be common channels of communication when amateurs or non-musicians are not able to describe rhythmic patterns and audio characteristics. In our study, the dyadic musical interaction is informed by the idea of multidisciplinary studies associated with music and well-being. Music is a social stimulus and creativity-supported interactions can support social interactions. It would be important to study how differently skilled participants synchronize and how their mutual interaction supports the synchronization goal at the core of any musical interaction. The interface aims to support musical interaction as a process that stimulates users to participate in a musical manner but also functions as a platform for social interaction as well. A user study that includes measuring the musical and social aspects of the interaction is reported. The musical experience of the users, the number of used sonic resources, and familiarity with fellow participants are the main control variables.

2 Related Fields and Concepts

2.1 Internet of Musical Things (IoMusT) and Ubiquitous Music (ubimus)

IoMusT has been inspired by the conventional Internet of Things (IoT) with the extension of its concepts and infrastructure to the field of music. Musical things refer to the local or remote connectivity between musical or associated and linked physical or virtual objects. These things must have the ability to sense, actuate, process and exchange musical information within the IoMusT network. This is an emerging field, first referenced by [4]. [19] explains its concepts, ecosystem, and proposed applications in the area of networked music, music education, and music e-learning. From the technological perspective, ubiquitous technologies (Laptops, notebooks, smartphones, tablets, wearable devices, and sensors) can be the components of the IoMusT ecosystem. The use of these technologies in the field of music might not be recent but the proposed frameworks of distributed connectivity are opening up many opportunities including creativity-centered musical interactions, which have been gaining popularity over the last decade. A dedicated and major contribution in this area is the emerging field of ubimus, which was historically established before IoMusT. IoMusT additionally provides visual and haptic experiences other than the sonic distribution of materials as well.

Ubiquitous music is a field of research that intersects areas including sound and music computing, human-computer interfaces, creativity studies, and music education, to propose, explore, establish, and accept ideas for creative music practices [7]. It refers to the music-related activities not solely diffused among the musician's community but includes amateurs and non-musicians as essential stakeholders connected locally or at remote locations [18]. The work presented by [11] proposed the definition of ubimus as ubiquitous systems of human agents and material resources that afford musical activities through creativity-supported tools. Apart from the nature of participating agents, this community strives to propose, design, and conduct user studies for non-traditional musical interactions with applications to areas other than the music itself, such as social interaction, health, and well-being [10]. It expands the possibilities of musical interactions and these could be assigned dimensions based on: i) the context of interaction ii) who is the subject (agents), and iii) what type of activity is being performed. Ubimus promotes the idea of sonic resources, their availability, and distribution among a larger community.

IoMusT and ubimus are interrelated and support music technology and interaction in non-traditional or multi-domain scenarios. The multidisciplinary nature of these fields involves components that could be integrated to design applications in diverse disciplines.

2.2 Color-Timbre

Using colors as an interaction metaphor is derived from the conceptualized relationship between color and music, which is not new. This might have originated from the observation of a neurological condition called Synaesthesia [12]. For example, in some synesthetes, music can trigger colorful shapes. Different timbral-colors classification will be based on the systematic color visualization method [8]. The different timbre classes will enable users to choose from multiple Sonic resources. The cross-domain mappings allow the division of the cognitive load into visual and auditory interactions for amateur-centered musical activities. Many color-music metaphors would lean on complex mappings for music elements that mediate the relationship between the users' interactions and the resulting sound. An example of this interactivity is in [9] where the color-music relationship was experimented with to symbolize sound and explore the educational value of this analogy.

2.3 Human Computer Interaction (HCI) and Ubiquitous Computing (Ubicomp) in Music

Ubiquitous computing is a subpart of HCI for technologies where users interact with environments, systems, or screens. To design embedded interactions through ubicomp research, HCI studies are helping to understand the users and their behaviors regarding technology and its everyday use. Ubicomp and HCI have significantly contributed to the field of music [5]. The interdisciplinary efforts from the ubimus group and IoMusT community have led to new patterns of sonic/musical interactions with computing devices. Interaction, customization, flexibility, and accessibility are the key features that separate ubiquitous music-making systems from traditional ones. Two dedicated conferences on interaction with sound/ music are Audio Mostly [1] and the Ubiquitous Music annual symposium [3]. Interaction is a conceptually rich phenomenon including the modality that offers a certain type of interaction (e.g. gesture, audio, textual), the context in which it occurs, the environment, the target audience, and the platforms offering that interaction. HCI research methods shed light on the use of ubicomp in general, and they can be adapted to study the interactions offered by ubiquitous music-making systems.

This research is an attempt towards the expanded design and study of a gesture-mediated musical interface (Mid-air Timbre) using Mediapipe Pose [2], suitable for casual musical interactions. The deployed design is a timbre-informed approach rather than using instrument-specific stimulations. One of the core objectives of ubimus research is the design of ecosystems that are "inclusive" and support open participation in musical activities. Within this context, measuring user experience (UX) and study of opportunities offered by these systems play a significant role.

2.4   Gestures, Music, and Technology

Gestures are natural and intuitive. Gestures as interaction modality for music making add physicality to the making process and add embodiment to the overall process. This ubiquitous gestural technology would render the music-making experience to be more engaging and expressive in either individual or cooperative musical activities. Gesture-based music generation has been covered by many studies. In [16] gestures are defined to control different sound parameters (e.g. pitch, octave, and loudness) based on the instruments chosen by the user in the system. An interface with a data glove was used in [15] to perform live music. These studies for gesture-based musical interactions have adopted mapping from traditional instruments. In these studies, gesture-sound mappings have used terms and audio control parameters as they are in a traditional instrument. This instrumental approach to design, even though the interaction mode is natural, discourages amateurs to participate in everyday music-based creativity.

The "ubiquity of music technology" is the increasing presence and accessibility of technology in passive or active musical activities. On the other hand, "Ubiquitous computing for music " is the integration of computing devices and systems into music creation, distribution, and consumption. This includes using computers, smartphones, sensors, wearables, and other computing devices to create new musical instruments and interfaces. Ubicomp for music would open new patterns of creating and experiencing music that is seamlessly integrated into our daily lives. Ubimus also includes HCI for user-centered interfaces and activities where "users" refer to differently-skilled people in a musical activity.

The gesture-mediated musical interface is a timbre-informed design rather than an instrument-specific design approach. Designing new interfaces that take advantage of digital technology can provide new forms of expression and creativity that are not possible with traditional instruments. If the new interfaces require a set of technical knowledge and abilities as required for traditional instruments, they might not fit well within a larger community. Our timbre-led approach emphasizes interaction with sound with minimal technical configurations and formal music knowledge. we tried to use sounds without associating them with an instrument. We found out in our precious study When users listen to a specific instrument, they try to apply traditional metaphors instead of exploring new forms of interactions [21]. The study for this interface aims to collect data about user experiences and their own reflection regarding participation using the current design. This would help us to develop our own reflections on the current design and how we can build interactions that would support technology support socially rich musical interactions.

3 Social Interaction Embedded in Musical Interaction

Music-based interventions have a positive influence on social interaction that leads to improved communication abilities [7]. Rhythmic interactions connect humans to cooperate and move together with the music. Rhythm also facilitates group interactions in terms of how different people talk and think about it based on their personal identities and cultural values. [13]. The social role of music is linked to synchronization when interpersonal communication coordinates actions and vice versa. How certain humans take actions and what affects the quality of this social bond is important to study when designing musical interfaces that support beyond music too. How musicians synchronize and communicate, those patterns could be different than how amateurs achieve these actions. More has been done to create musical interfaces than to explore their role in music-based interventions. The idea of studying social aspects through our gesture-based interface comes from our previous data collected during the experiment for [21]. We have selected amateurs as our target audience. Studying interactions on ubiquitous-music-making systems from their viewpoint would support the design of musical activities (using ubiquitous devices) that are inclusive.

In this work, a vision-based gesture recognition system is employed using Mediapipe Pose to enable the development of a natural HCI (human-computer Interaction) to capture and interpret real-world gestures. These gestures are performed mid-air, meaning that there is no physical reference that tracks and analyses what it sees. When a specific gesture is recognized, sound event triggers. "Timbre" in the title is referred to the gestural mode of interaction with different types of sounds. The gestures must be analyzed to extract their musical intention. Gesture-based can interfaces can support full-body interactions but this interface only used gesture-sound mapping for arm movements and upper half body to align the interface elements according to the user's position in the real space. The elements are scaled based on how far or close a user is from the display screen. To calculate the distance, the coordinates of the head position are recalculated in every frame.

4   The Interface

The current design of the interface includes: 1) whole-body tracking 2) visual tokens for sonic resources 3) control over sonic resources (changing colors) 4), and two modes (4- Timbre and 6-Timbre) of musical interaction. Colors associated with sounds in these modes are shown in Fig. 1 (a) and (b). The available set of timbres in the current design includes clap, hi-hat, kick, snare, cymbal, and short bass. Full body tracking is adaptive to the human position. It has a walk-and-play mode too. When the interface is launched, the user could listen to sounds by clicking on the colors given by default in the design (Fig. 2 (a)). The two black buttons on the top right in part (a) of Fig. 2 give user option to listen to the sound and see the visual tokens before the camera stream starts. If they want to change the color of tokens, the color-customization option is available (Fig. 2 (b)). Figure 3 (a) shows an individual participant interacting with the gestural interface. The dyadic session included 2 participants that played together during the musical activity as can be seen in Fig. 3 (a).

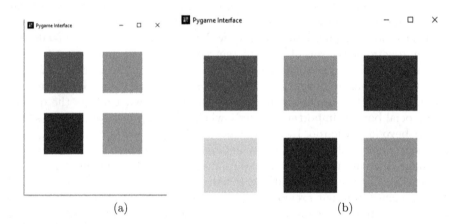

(a)   (b)

Fig. 1. a) 4- Timbre mode. b) 6- Timbre mode.

4.1   Timbre-Led Design

"Timbre" in the interface is referred to the gestural mode of interaction with different types of sounds. Timbre is a tonal quality of sound that ensure that a sound can be perceived differently and this is how we differentiate between instruments and vocals for example. Each timbre is represented as a colored visual token. At this phase of design, the colors-timbre mapping is random and the user can customize the color for any timbre. The strategical mapping from [8] could be a solution to an instrumental way of exploring color-pitch associations. In the current design, the 4-Timbre mode gives users 4 different timbres to create a musical pattern. In the 6- Timbre mode, 4 timbres remain the same but 2 different timbres are included. The participants were asked to interact with both until they choose one of them for their musical pattern. Further study is required to incorporate such mappings as metaphorical representations for ubiquitous musical interfaces that are more inclusive.

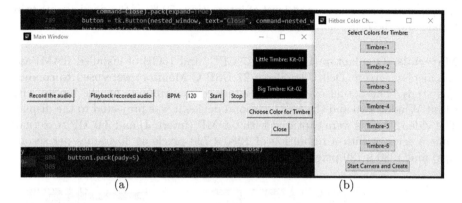

Fig. 2. a) The main interface. b) Color change mode.

4.2 Limitations

The interface can introduce more video and audio lags based on the lighting conditions and the processing resources. The materials used for our study are mentioned in the later section and the interface performed well with a significantly low latency rate. The interface is suitable for rhythmic phrases that are, 60 to 125 BPM (for the simple sequences) or 60 to 90 BPM (for the complex ones), the current interface only supports two modes (4- Timbre and 6-Timbre)

5 Individual and Dyadic Musical Interactions: Materials, Method, and Results

Dyadic Musical interaction refers to the social interaction between two individuals, such as two musicians, or a client-therapist during a musical activity. This term and type of interaction is mostly studied in music-based therapeutic sessions [17]. We have selected dyadic sessions for the study because they are less complex than co-payer sessions where many users are engaged in an activity. The main objective of the study was to explore and understand the patterns of interactions among interconnected participants during a musical activity. The impact of the number of participants on the level of interaction in this activity is not in the scope of the proposed research. Before dyadic interaction, individual participation provides data to compare the patterns of interest in two modes of music activity (individual/ dyadic).

5.1   The User Study and Participants

For the study, our primary goal was to focus on dyadic interaction, we collected
data about both that are individual interactions, (n = 6), and (dyadic) amateur-
amateur interaction features (n = 3) providing qualitative results regarding experience, mode preferences, and level of interaction. 50 % of the participants were
female and the other half were male.

Materials. One laptop (Intel Core i7 CPU, and 16GB of installed RAM) and
one display screen (Dell UltraSharp 27 USB-C Monitor) were used to conduct
this study. The actual event of the interface was running on the laptop with
64-bit Windows 10 and the for the second device it was projected to the display.
The video streams were captured with 0.9 MP (internal) and 3.0 MP (external)
camera sensors with a resolution of 1280 × 720 pixels at 30 frames per second
(fps) and 1080 × 720 pixels at 30 fps.

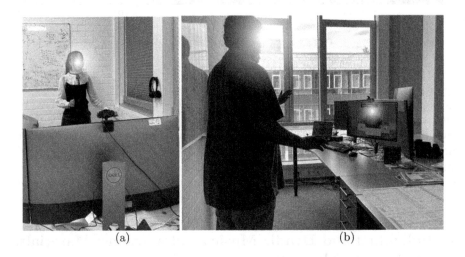

Fig. 3. a) Individual interaction. b) Dyadic interaction.

Methods. The structure of the study was formal but the results (sounds) produced by participants were based on free and random interaction with the interface. In the first step, participants were informed about the design without mentioning the study goal explicitly. It was chosen to keep the results unbiased so
that we could find the aspects of dyadic musical interaction that might have
been left unexplored by the participants otherwise. Each participant was given
5 to 10 min to interact with the interface (4 timbre mode and 6 timbre mode).
After this, both participants were asked to interact at the same time and they
should be able to reflect on the process of creating a sound pattern together.
The maximum recorded time for the overall study session was not more than
30 min. Their responses were recorded through an online survey once the study
was finished.

5.2   Results

The qualitative study was conducted to explore the interface mainly for dyadic musical interactions. The data was collected about their choice of mode and their reflection on how they interacted within the session. To better differentiate the impact of group interactions and explore the presence of social aspects as embodied part of the experience in the later session we organized the study in two steps. In the first step, every individual was given some time to explore the interface. Once they interacted with both 4- Timbre and 6-Timbre modes, they were engaged in the dyadic session. The first step helps the participants to select their preferred mode when playing with their fellow participants. Overall, the big timbre mode was preferred because it gave participants more options to create something truly musical. This free musical activity-based study helped us to explore the dimensions of the experience in a more flexible way. The control variables were the time and skill level of participants. All of them were amateurs and had no experience using any computer-based tool for a music or sound-based activity.

Individual Interaction. In the individual session (fig 3 (a)), 33 % of the participants enjoyed the experience and 67%)were more interested to achieve a particular music pattern. This can be considered as two dimensions of the same interaction. The first represents the informal engagements during such an interaction and the other is about being more focused on a musical goal that a participant has made. Followed by these dimensions of interaction, all the participants were asked to reflect on their final product (a music pattern). 33%) of them created something simple, and 33% were stuck and needed help to contribute to the session. The sound lag was mentioned by 17% and the same percentage considered it simple and pleasant with no data about latency.

Levels of Interaction in Dyadic Session. While a dyadic interaction can take many forms as it proceeds in time, these forms can be explored to categorize them as different levels of interaction. A dyadic session during the study is presented in Fig 3 (b). The participants were asked to reflect on their own and their fellow participants. Half of the participants were able to create something simple and synchronize, but the latency was clearly present. The other half did not report any level of synchronization and could not play any pattern. During the session, they described their participation differently. The first form was verbal communication (20%)) when they exchanged ideas to play a beat and synchronize. The colors were their shared medium to refer to different timbres on the display. As a second form of interaction, the participants observed (40%)) their fellows listen to their pattern and synchronize later. 10% of responses indicate the level of engagement when certain participants considered themselves to be more involved than their fellow players. For the last option, the data showed that participants did not meet the level of cooperation as their fellow participants did. These forms can be summarised as verbal communication, observation and following, more socially engaged, and less participation. The reason they felt less engaged was because they were stuck and needed help. 50% of the participants asked their fellow players to assist them to make progress while the rest of them did not mention the reason for less interaction.

The Differences. In computer-based music-making tools, audio latency can affect the product (a music pattern here), and in group interactions, synchronization would be compromised too. During this study, the participants recorded their experience with delay but also mentioned what they could achieve in the presence of it. Due to this delay, they used slow movements to better control their hand movements and sound events. The delay was not caused by the network but video lags and false positives during gesture recognition were challenging problems. The responses for the individual interactions tended towards using moderate movements for 50%) of the total participants. The second highest was fast (33%)) followed by 17%) of the participants who preferred slow hand movements, and these were mostly selected by the participants that had no experience with any musical activity at all. It shows that as previous experiences can help us to build new knowledge, these could also affect how a certain task is perceived. These responses changed for the dyadic interaction as they were not only creating a pattern but also trying to cooperate with the other participants. Slow movements were mostly preferred for better synchronization as indicated by 50%) of total responses. 33%)) of choices were recorded for fast movements and 17%)was the least selected option for this question.

When the participants were asked about their preferred mode of interaction considering this interface as a medium, only one person responded to state dyadic interaction. To give the interaction a meaningful title, they were asked to describe the overall experience from one of these four states: a) confusion, b) enjoyment, c) expressiveness, or d) challenging. Even though the preferred choice was individual interaction, participants felt more expressive in dyadic sessions. If participants enjoyed more as individuals and were more focused, then in the dyadic session the music was not what only mattered. They reflected on their level of interaction and tried to express themselves. Music and mood are interconnected and mood can be a factor to help individuals express themselves [14]. In the context of our study, expressiveness refers to the part of the session where participants tried to achieve a certain mood in their musical patterns such as calmness, happiness, or sadness. Without any formal musical knowledge, participants did not have any experience of achieving certain moods but they tried to categorize their musical patterns as "slow beat", or "fast beat" sounds. For example, one of them used a low-pitched timbre mostly to create the pattern and the selection was intentional. Words like "slow", "fast", and " shooting" sound were used by the participants to describe the mood of the music. For the dyadic interactions, the experience was enjoyed by 17%) of them, the same percentage of participants were more interested in expressing their music preference, and the highest (66%)) number of participants were trying to cooperate with their fellow to synchronize and create a musical pattern. The last point indicates that if the objective of the dyadic interaction is understood by the users, they try to achieve something in the group not as an individual. However, in what stages they cooperate and how they achieve those stages is not covered in this data, but these patterns of interactions could inform the level of support that an interface must incorporate for group interactions. Another interesting fact that we extracted from the recorded data is that the participants don't need to know each other well to enjoy the socially rich aspects of music. Instead, the groups who were familiar with each other relatively less preferred to engage in group interaction. It indicated that music creation can be an individual choice to enjoy and not always requires a group participant to experience its significant communicative nature. The dyadic session was preferred by the participants who did not know the other participants in their group.

5.3   Discussion

Gesture-based musical interactions can be a significant addition to the music-making tools that are not necessarily complex but more ubiquitous and inclusive. The proposals on the scope of new musical interfaces and musical things that can participate in the IoMusT network support the idea of considering everyday devices as musical things. The inclusion of projects based on ubiquitous computing that are designed and deployed to support creative music-making activities is a sustainable part of ubimus research as well. Based on these we proposed the design of a gesture-based interface that allows the creation of a music pattern or any sound that is meaningful to an individual.

The result of the study shows the diversity in the communicative and social aspects of musical interactions. While it can be a significant medium to connect unknown individuals, the same can not be true for others. Based on our study, some participants enjoyed and created patterns in the individual session. This is because of the freedom and flexibility to create their musical patterns before they engage in a group activity. Another factor informed by the study is available support for an activity. For an amateur-amateur musical interaction, some people were more experimental, and they managed to create something on their own. The data also showed that interfaces for similar interactions need to be designed for more than as a medium. Intermediate support was required in dyadic interactions and participants mentioned this as they "did not know how to start". From the latency point of view, the synchronization was compromised but half of them enjoyed the experience and expressed themselves more during the dyadic session. We did not collect the data on participants' performances. The study was more about amateurs and their free improvisation. But the observation during this study showed that even with limited formal vocabulary from the domain of music, verbal communication helped the interaction to reach some level of synchronization.

6   Conclusion

In this era of digital technologies, many of the available tools have been designed to be socially blended and have proved their significance in many aspects of our daily lives. The camera-based techniques for gesture recognition are promising solutions for many ubiquitous technology-based interventions. These techniques are very much used in social applications (e.g., Facebook, Instagram, and games). In the field what is of music and technology, these techniques have been recently introduced that provide new ways of music making. But how do these music-making tools blend into our daily lives and how ubiquitous are they if they are not covered in most of the studies? ubiquitous technology in music is different than ubiquitous music technology. This paper is an initial effort to understand the aspects of the ubiquity of technology in music making and what is associated with the music itself and how these could be leveraged by new interfaces. The presented results are based on data collected through a survey but it was not enough to do a statistical analysis. Also, we did not predetermine any aspect of the interaction to measure specifically. So, the discussed facts are more exploratory than to prove a research outcome or a hypothetical statement. The social and communicative opacity of music as given by the literature, the patterns of interaction, and factors that are influenced by or influence these patterns remain unexplored. An investigation in this direction could facilitate the design of interactions that are not just product-focused but also incorporate the factors involved in the process as well. This would be our further goal towards the design of interfaces that support beyond just musical purpose behaviors such as resilience and well-being.

References

1. AM 2022: Proceedings of the 17th International Audio Mostly Conference. Association for Computing Machinery, New York, NY, USA (2022)
2. Bazarevsky, V., Grishchenko, I., Raveendran, K., Zhu, T., Zhang, F., Grundmann, M.: BlazePose: on-device real-time body pose tracking. arXiv preprint arXiv:2006.10204 (2020)
3. Bernardes, G., Magalhães, E., Messina, M., Keller, D., Davies, M.E.: Proceedings of the 11th Workshop on Ubiquitous Music (UbiMus 2021) (2021)
4. Borgia, E.: The internet of things vision: key features, applications and open issues. Comput. Commun. **54**, 1–31 (2014)
5. Chamberlain, A., Hazzard, A., Kelly, E., Bødker, M., Kallionpää, M.: From AI, creativity and music to IoT, HCI, musical instrument design and audio interaction: a journey in sound. Pers. Ubiquit. Comput. **25**, 617–620 (2021)
6. Gunn, J., Hall, M.M.: Stick it in your ear: the psychodynamics of iPod enjoyment. Commun. Critical/Cult. Stud. **5**(2), 135–157 (2008)
7. Harwood, J.: Music and intergroup relations: exacerbating conflict and building harmony through music. Rev. Commun. Res. **5**, 1–34 (2017)
8. Hu, G.: Art of musical color: a synesthesia-based mechanism of color art. Color. Res. Appl. **45**(5), 862–870 (2020)

9. Keelan, C.: The pedagogical applications of associating color with music in entry level undergraduate aural skills (2015)
10. Keller, D., Lazzarini, V., Pimenta, M.S.: Ubiquitous music. Springer, Cham (2014). https://doi.org/10.1007/978-3-319-11152-0
11. Keller, D., Schiavoni, F., Lazzarini, V.: Ubiquitous music: perspectives and challenges. J. New Music Res. **48**(4), 309–315 (2019)
12. Küssner, M.B., Orlandatou, K.: Sound-colour synaesthesia and music-induced visual mental imagery. Music and Mental Imagery (2022)
13. Lesaffre, M., Maes, P.J., Leman, M.: The Routledge companion to embodied music interaction. Taylor & Francis (2017)
14. Micallef Grimaud, A., Eerola, T.: An interactive approach to emotional expression through musical cues. Music Sci. **5**, 20592043211061744 (2022)
15. Mitchell, T.J., Madgwick, S., Heap, I.: Musical interaction with hand posture and orientation: a toolbox of gestural control mechanisms (2012)
16. Shang, K., Wang, Z.: A music performance method based on visual gesture recognition. In: 2022 China Automation Congress (CAC), pp. 2624–2631. IEEE (2022)
17. Smetana, M., Stepniczka, I., Bishop, L.: COME_IN: a qualitative framework for content, meanings and intersubjectivity in free dyadic improvisations. Nord. J. Music. Ther. **32**(2), 157–178 (2023)
18. Stolfi, A., Costalonga, L., Messina, M., Keller, D., Aliel, L.: Proceedings of the 10th Workshop on Ubiquitous Music (UbiMus 2020) (2020)
19. Turchet, L., Fischione, C., Essl, G., Keller, D., Barthet, M.: Internet of musical things: vision and challenges. IEEE Access **6**, 61994–62017 (2018)
20. Vanhatalo, S., Liedes, H., Pennanen, K.: Nature ambience in a lunch restaurant has the potential to evoke positive emotions, reduce stress, and support healthy food choices and sustainable behavior: a field experiment among finnish customers. Foods **11**(7), 964 (2022)
21. Yaseen, A., Chakraborty, S., Timoney, J.: A cooperative and interactive gesture-based drumming interface with application to the internet of musical things. In: Stephanidis, C., Antona, M., Ntoa, S. (eds.) HCI International 2022 Posters. HCII 2022. Communications in Computer and Information Science, vol 1581. Springer, Cham (2022). https://doi.org/10.1007/978-3-031-06388-6_12

Cognitive Engineering and Augmented Cognition

A Helping Hand: Benefits of Primary Task Haptic Augmentation on Secondary Visuospatial Task Performance

Charlotte Collins[✉], James Blundell, John Huddlestone, and Don Harris

Coventry University, Coventry CV1 5FB, UK
{aa8764,ac7045,ab4919,ab3693}@Coventry.ac.uk

Abstract. The quality of pilot decision making remains a significant determinant of recent aviation incidents and accidents. With the development of haptic stick inputs pilots have additional sensory cues to aid in the decision making process. Limited experimental research has investigated the impact of directional haptic cues, delivered via side stick devices, on user performance and subjective workload. The current experiment examines the performance and workload benefits granted by augmenting a visual dual-task with haptic information in a sample of eleven participants. The current visual dual-task experiment consisted of 1) a primary manual error cancellation tracking task and 2) a secondary visuospatial memory N-back task. The haptic implementation in the current study involved the provision of corrective directional "nudges" on the tracking task, conditionally delivered when participants breached a prescribed error margin.

The primary finding was that haptic feedback on the tracking task improved visuospatial memory performance on the secondary N-back task. Importantly, no increase in workload was reported in tandem with the observed visuospatial memory enhancement offered by the haptic cues. Future research should review the impacts of randomizing the signal speed as seen in turbulence situations and changes to peripheral ranges with performance of eye time on task.

Keywords: haptics · active stick · dual-task performance · workload

1 Introduction

Developments of automation have alleviated some of the workload pilots encounter when operating an aircraft. 'Error proof' or fully automated aircraft are currently still not in use, thus requiring pilots to remain engaged in making the best decisions (Orasanu, 2017). To this end, haptic inputs have been proposed as a human-machine interaction approach to conveying system state information to pilots to aid in pilot decision making process. From initial investigations of haptic input types there are limited experimental published works that identify improvement in user performance and subjective workload using directional cue types. The works show mainly investigation into the use of resistive force feedback guidance cues. Including stick centering to aid with path following (Alaimo et al., 2010; de Stigter et al., 2007; Olivari et al., 2012; Repperger et al., 1997; Schutte

© The Author(s), under exclusive license to Springer Nature Switzerland AG 2023
M. Kurosu et al. (Eds.): HCII 2023, LNCS 14054, pp. 351–362, 2023.
https://doi.org/10.1007/978-3-031-48038-6_22

et al., 2012), control and using inverted resistive force cues (Lam et al., 2004) to help aid in obstacle avoidance pushing the stick away from the obstacle. In the above studies, the effect of providing haptic task revealed mixed workload results, however some findings have shown an improvement in task performance associated with haptic information. For instance, using stick centering for a path following tasks, De Stigter et al (2007) identified a reduction in subjective workload with an increase in physical workload. This was coupled with an increase in task performance and cognitive capability to perform a secondary task. From both studies the haptic cueing can be reviewed in its first principle state as a lateral and longitudinal stick tracking movement task. The increased physical workload (Lam et al., 2004) is not an ideal effect which is seen when using high resistive forces to push the user to the desired direction. This is especially important if the use of this type of force feedback is required for an extended period of flight time. Research is needed to determine if directional force feedback cues could be used to aid in a tracking task and review if a physical workload can be maintained. In addition, de Stigter et al. (2007) states having a secondary task that is suitable to participant's ability level is critical and must be managed within the trial.

Research into side stick haptics delivered vibrotactile cues, another form of haptic information, this has demonstrated how cueing users with a "shaker signal" can be valuable source of stall warning information (Ellerbroek et al, 2016). Findings have identified that primary task performance improves with a non-directional vibrotactile cue and stick centering shift, however, these evaluations did not show any clear indications of subjective workload changes.

In the current study the benefits of a haptic directional force feedback cue, implemented alongside stick centering, are examined in a human-in-the-loop experiment. Haptic aiding will be added to the primary task. The study involved non-pilots completing a task that reviewed the impacts of haptic feedback upon two simultaneously completed visual tasks (i.e., a visual/visual dual-task). A cognitive task capable of manipulating task load to emphasize the potential secondary performance related benefits of the haptic implementation. Trials were designed to evaluate the performance, workload, and interface usability benefits of haptic directional cues. Quantitative (e.g., participant performance data, post-trial scale data) and qualitative data (post-study questionnaire) collection methods were employed in the current evaluation.

2　Methods

2.1　Participants

Eleven non-pilot aeronautical staff/students from the Coventry University participated in the study. Participants average age was 32 years (SD = 15.01). All participants had flown a desktop aircraft simulator with an average of 4.95 years (SD = 5.75), during a normal operating time would spend 1.45 h using a simulator (SD = 2.31). From the eighteen participants there were seventeen males and one female. The experiment was approved by the Coventry University Ethics Committee and was in line with ethics guidelines as per the British Psychological Society.

2.2 Materials

A PC was running MATLAB (The MathWorks Inc, 2021) script that was created for the trials. The PC was a HP Z4 G4 workstation Operating Windows 10 Pro 64 with an Intel Core i7 9800X Processor, 32 GB (2 × 16 GB) Memory and 512 GB SSD Hard Drive. Each participant was positioned with a gaming keyboard located on the left and the side stick (Microsoft Sidewinder) located on the right. The screen used for the participant was 1920 × 1080p Full HD screen with a 590 mm (width) × 332 mm (height). Participants were seated of 825 mm from the screen – producing a 46 screen pixels per visual angle (VA). Overall, this produced an overall viewing area of 40.85 (width) × 23 (height) degrees VA within the 1920 × 1080p screen.

Psychophysics Toolbox extensions (Brainard, 1997) was used to draw the visuals to the screen. The software maintained the visual and stick guidance cues logging at 60 Hz and allowed for the retrieval of relevant stick position and keyboard inputs for subsequent performance analyses.

The two continuous tasks were presented simultaneously. Each task was offset from the screen centre by 12 degrees of VA. Thus, tasks were spatially separated by 24 degrees of VA, remaining within participants near peripheral vision range (± 30 degrees of VA). The display area of each task was confined to an 8 (width) × 8 (height) degrees of VA area.

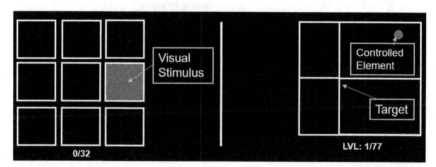

Fig. 1. Tracking (primary) task and Visual N-back (secondary) task presented on the right- and left-hand side of the screen, respectively.

2D Tracking (Primary) Task. On the right-hand side of the screen the 2D tracking task was presented (see Error! Reference source not found.). This task served as the primary task, where participants were required to maintain the active stick controlled green dot on the moving target cross hair position. The duration of the task was set by the number of N-back trials, hence was 5-min. The dot and cross hair target positions were confined in the 8 × 8 VA task space. A non-harmonic wave frequency was used to define the 2D movement signal of the tracking cross hair. This was preferred to a typical sine wave defined movement trajectory, as non-harmonic wave frequencies reduce the predictability of a signal (Drop et al., 2016b; Scheer et al., 2014). The movement signal of the target cross hair was defined by combining the signals of 10 non-harmonic waves using Eq. 1 and 2.

$$S = A \sin(\omega * P(t + \varphi)) \tag{1}$$

$$WaveSignal = S_1 + S_2 + S_3 + S_4 + S_5 + S_6 + S_7 + S_8 + S_9 + S_{10} \qquad (2)$$

The difficulty of the tracking task was manipulated asymmetrically using a staircase method. Whereby the target's default movement speed was set to 0.3 degrees of visual angle (VAdeg)/sec, which was incremented at a rate of 0.3 VAdeg/sec if the participant was able to maintain the controlled green dot within a proximity of 1.5 degrees of VA from the tracking target for 3 s. The difficulty of the task was lowered whenever the proximity of the controlled green dot exceeded the 1.5 VA radius proximity of the tracking target for 1 s. The difficulty of the 2D tracking task was limited to a speed of 3 VAdeg/sec.

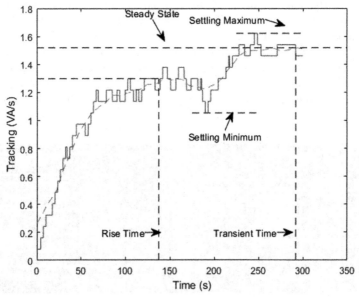

Fig. 2. Tracking step response with annotations of Rise Time (RiT), Transient Time (TT), Settling Minimum (Min), Settling Maximum (Max) and Steady State (SS)

Performance variables were taken from the tracking task which included the maximum difficulty (Settling Maximum, (Max)), Settling Minimum (Min) which was the minimum drop in performance, the steady state (SS), and the time taken to reach the initial (Rise Time, (RiT)) and maximum level of tracking (Transient Time, (TT)). The rise time (RiT) was calculated using the step-response characteristics of participants' staircase performance on the tracking task using the stepinfo function in MATLAB (Fig. 2). RiT here was defined as the time taken for tracking performance to rise from 10% to 90% of the highest difficulty level achieved to the level of SS achieved presents how these different metrics summarized the tracking performance of one of the participants. Only SS is considered in the analysis.

Haptic Characteristics. Force feedback was delivered through a Microsoft sidewinder side stick with stick centering. The haptic nudge cue and force profiles are demonstrated in Error! Reference source not found. Stick centering force size was limited to allow for a comfortable force profile to be applied, with a low increase in physical force required to control the stick. There were no shifting forces, and a small dead band is given within the stick centering force profile.

The directional nudge was designed to both alert the participant to tracking task deviation and to provide corrective directional guidance. The cue used a discrete signal that produced a force in the direction of the preferred stick movement to reduce error between the controlled dot and the target cross hair. A nudge was activated if the deviation of the stick from the target was greater than 1 degree of visual Angle (VA). The nudge force cue was delivered as a X and Y directional tangential force. This was dependent on the x and y distance away from the target so that the user could perceive a directional cue (Fig. 3).

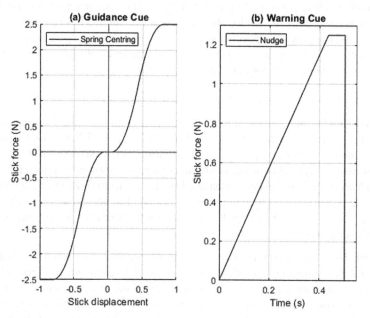

Fig. 3. Stick force feedback: (a) stick centering force (b) directional nudge cue force

2-Back Task (Secondary) Task. A 2-back version of a visuospatial N-back task required participants to store and continuously update visuospatial information in the working memory. The 2-back task was presented on the left-hand side of the screen (see Fig. 1) and consisted of a 3 × 3 grid (each square - 2.5 × 2.5 VA), where target grid locations were illuminated grey for 500 ms. An inter-stimulus-interval of 2500 ms was used producing a duration of 3 s per N-back trial (Kane et al., 2007). The task consisted of 100 2-back trials and lasted for five minutes. A third of the total trials (32 trials) were randomly assigned as 2-back targets, trials where the cued grid location matched the cued grid location from 2 trials ago.

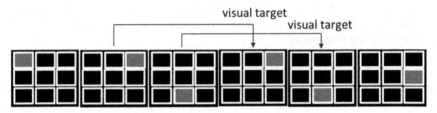

Fig. 4. Example of a 2-back condition

Correct responses were defined as instances where participants pressed the spacebar when a visual stimulus grid location was presented (see Fig. 4). Incorrect responses were classified where participants pressed the space bar when a non-target grid location position was presented (i.e., a false alarm). Misses were defined as instances where the participant did not press the spacebar when a target was shown. On each run an N-back score was calculated by subtracting the combined frequency of incorrect responses and misses from the number of correct responses (see Eq. 3).

$$Nback\ Score\ =\ Correct\ Reponse - (IncorrectReponses + Misses) \qquad (3)$$

Post-Trial Workload Questionnaire. Participants completed the NASA Task Load Index (TLX) questionnaire (Hart & Staveland, 1988). The TLX is a long-established scale designed to capture subjective workload ratings across six workload dimensions: mental demand, physical demand, temporal demand, performance, effort, and frustration. Each workload dimension is measured on a scale from 0–20 (Hart, 2006), where higher ratings represent higher subjective workload. The abridged non weighted approach was chosen due to the inconclusive evidence that dimension weighting improves the TLX's sensitivity (Hart, 2006).

Post-Study Usability Questionnaire. Participants completed a 10-min questionnaire at the end of the experiment to provide feedback on the different haptic elements. The questionnaires began with the high-level consideration of the effectiveness the cue modalities (visual alone, haptic alone, and multimodal) in supporting participants with the task. Questions then proceeded to a more specific, low-level review of the functional and physical qualities of the different side stick features. This structured approach was chosen to maximize the level of formative feedback that was achievable within the short time frame. The participants' data was then grouped by stick preference, calibration and application acceptance. A summary of the difference is opinions and thoughts were reviewed and summarized.

Scenario and Procedure. The scenario for the current trials were non-specific so that the application of the cue type can be reviewed without the application of effects to review a 2D tracking task using a haptic stick.

The trial lasted approximately 1.5–2 h. Participants began the trial by receiving a verbal and visual presentation briefing to introduce them to the 2-back and haptic interface features. This was followed by a practice session that allowed the participants to familiarize themselves with the layout and the 2-back task. All participants completed three single tasks: 2-back, task tracking task (no haptics) and task tracking task (with haptics). Practice trials were then followed by six dual task trials to evaluate experimental factor: Haptic Nudges presence (2 levels: on/off). The single tasks involved blanking one task and kept the visual angle offset of the task during the trial. After each trial, participants completed the NASA-TLX. At the end of the experiment the participants took part in a debrief questionnaire to obtain insights into the usability benefits of the different haptic features.

Data Analysis. Performance and NASA-TLX workload data were analyzed with a series of general linear mixed effects models (GLMMs) using the MATLAB Statistical Toolbox. To examine the effects of the tracking task haptic directional cues on dual-task performance and workload the data were fitted using a fixed factor for Nudge (2 levels: Nudges On, Nudges off). In addition, change in dual-task performance and workload over the 3 dual-task runs was achieved using a continuous fixed effect called Run. GLMMs are a powerful statistical method that allows the analysis of multiple observations from each participant without violating the critical statistical assumption of independence. For repeated measures designs, the use of common ANOVA methods which average across individual participant observations, are discouraged in favour of these more robust GLMM methods (Graziotin et al., 2015; Gueorguieva & Krystal, 2004; Laird & Ware, 1982; Winter & Grawunder, 2012).

In the current analysis, we used maximal random effects structures that included random participant intercepts and slopes for all fixed effects that were included in the models. In this paper, we checked the significance (alpha = 0.05) of fixed effects by calculating p-values obtained by likelihood ratio tests. Visual inspection of residual plots was used to ensure no obvious deviations from homoscedasticity or normality.

3 Results

3.1 Tracking Performance

Steady state (SS) performance differences on the primary tracking task between trials with and without nudge cues were minimal; SS difference between conditions 0.05 VAdeg/sec. In addition, SS was relatively stable across the 3 runs. This was supported by the lack of significant ($p > 0.05$) main effect and interactions including *Nudge*.

3.2 N-Back Performance

N-back Score, the frequency of correct response minus errors, is presented in Fig. 5. Overall, the presence of the haptics increased participant scores by a mean of 1.29. Though there was considerable variability seen between the participants. Across the input mode and runs, participants scored the highest during the third run with the haptics (mean /SD = 15.82/7.18). Similar deviations were observed during run 2 with the haptics (mean/SD = 13.40/9.71). Across runs, as expected, scores were lower at the start compared to the second and third runs where learning has taken place. The GLMM analysis for N-back score revealed a significant interaction between Run and Haptics ($p < 0.05$), but no main effects for *Nudge* ($p = 0.24$) or *Run* (p = 0.67). The interaction represented a 3.31 mean increase (CI: 0.01 - 6.64) in N-back score for each run with the haptics.

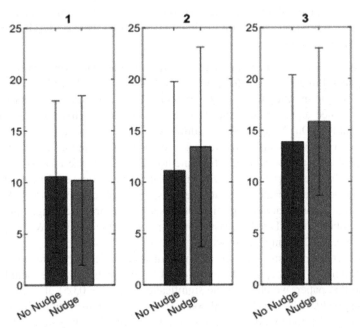

Fig. 5. N-back score grouped by trial and presence of the haptic nudges. Score standard deviations are shown as error bars.

3.3 Subjective Workload (NASA-TLX) Performance

Overall, there was little difference between subjective workload rating on the TLX between when nudges were present or absent (mean TLX difference = 0.55 points). The GLMM analysis found no significant main effects or interactions for *Nudge* or *Run*.

3.4 Post Study Usability

Participant views were collected in a short questionnaire, which have been analyzed and grouped by stick preference, calibration, and application acceptance.

Stick Preference. A participant struggled at the start to set up the stick comfortably but did achieve this during the task. Two participants struggled to get used to the nudges but felt they got better with time. Two participants mentioned that they found the nudges distracting and prompted them to look at the tracking task. Four participants found the nudges helpful and useful information. One participant struggled with feeling the nudge forces on the stick and only felt the nudge on a few small occasions all other participants could feel the transition between the stick centering and the nudge cue.

Calibration. One participant mentioned that they found during the dual task they were overshooting the target because of the nudges and impacted their performance on the 2-back task. "When tracking I was travelling towards the force it was overshooting. My brain sent a signal to my hand, but nudges caused overshoot. Nudges draw my attention away from 2-back task which caused me to lose track of the order."

One participant mentioned the dead band in the stick centering as distracting. Three participants found the nudges were too strong, one participant found it useful in the dual task but not in the single task when focused on the tracking task. Six participants were happy with the size of the nudges.

The nudges were seen to be useful for seven participants and the stick centering was also helpful one participant mentioned the ergonomic shape of the stick as useful.

Four participants thought it would be useful to calibrate the haptics, five participants were happy with the current configuration and did not want to change anything and one was unsure.

Application Acceptance. Four participants preferred a haptic stick than the usual aircraft controls. Three thought that haptics would be as beneficial as regular yoke or side stick. Two mentioned that with experience the nudge cues would be useful. Participants mentioned priority layering, risk based hierarchical cues that could be used in several phased of flight conditions, user calibration of the size of stick force, training is required and timing between cues are needed to prevent misinterpreting the stick forces.

4   Discussion

In the current study, benefits of side stick force feedback nudge cues were evaluated in a human-in-the-loop trial. Eleven non-pilot participants completed a dual-task experimental that required the completion of two simultaneously presented visual tasks: a primary 2D manual tracking task and a secondary visual-spatial 2-back memory task. The benefits of haptic guidance within the context of a dual-task paradigm were explored by augmenting the primary manual control task with directional force feedback guidance, delivered via the haptic side stick, on half of dual task trials. Enhanced visuospatial memory efficiency was expressed as improved performance in the absence of a corresponding self-reported workload increase.

Research findings investigating force feedback (i.e. stick stiffness) and vibrotactile (i.e. stick shaker) cues (Ellerbroek et al., 2016) have indicated that task performance improves with a non-directional cue, without an increase in subjective workload which supports the study's findings using directional cues. Stick centering cues have been shown to reduce primary task error and secondary task decision time, and primary task workload (de Stigter et al., 2007) which was not seen in this study.

A possible explanation for the current and previous research findings can be found within Wicken's Multiple Resource Theory (MRT) (Wickens, 2002, 2008). MRT describes the human brain as having several semi-independent cognitive resources that serve different sensory modalities (e.g., visual, audio, or haptic), and that tasks requiring the use of different resources can often be effectively performed together. Conversely, where two visual tasks are performed simultaneously, as in the current study, the tasks will be in competition with one another for the same resource and will produce interference. Hence, by augmenting one of these tasks with haptic information it is possible the degree of interference between tasks can be reduced. Specifically, participants' required allocation of visual attention to the target tracking task is reduced in the instance where haptic augmentation is provided. Allowing further visual attention resources to be allocated to the visuospatial 2-back task. Some research suggests that the haptic senses may be a further independent information processing resource that can be used in parallel to the auditory and visual channels (e.g., Sklar and Sarter, 1999; Ho, Tan and Spence, 2005).

User-feedback in the current study revealed that participants perceived haptic inputs through an active stick to be helpful. This is corroborated by a range of applied haptic studies where pilots have reported haptic feedback to be beneficial (Ellerbroek et al., 2016b; van Baelen et al., 2021), even in the absence of any objective benefit (Blundell et al., 2020, van Baelen et al., 2019). However, some participants remarked that the nudge force cue was distracting and needed time to learn to be effective. They also suggested a suitable training period being given. Some participants found the stick forces too large or too small and calibration to the pilots preferred force should be reviewed in future studies.

5   Conclusions

Overall, the findings of the study underline the benefits of adopting a human-centered design approach from early in the design process of complex aviation systems. Results from the study highlight that the haptic augmentation of a manual visual task will likely improve efficiency of a second visuospatial task, when the two tasks are conducted in concert. This consideration will be taken forwards with future applications and experiments. These include increasing the spatial separation between the primary and secondary tasks for mid and far peripheral ranges measuring visual time on task and impacts of turbulent conditions. Specifically, incorporating the end user in the design process results in the development of systems with improved acceptance and should be reviewed and taken forwards with pilots within application-based experiments.

Acknowledgements. This paper is based on work performed in the Open Flight Deck project, which has received funding from the ATI Programme, a joint government and industry investment to maintain and grow the UK's competitive position in civil aerospace design and manufacture. The programme, delivered through a partnership between the Aerospace Technology Institute (ATI), Department for Business, Energy & Industrial Strategy (BEIS) and Innovate UK, addresses technology, capability and supply chain challenges.

References

Alaimo, S.M.C., Pollini, L., Bresciani, J.P., Bülthoff, H.H.: A comparison of direct and indirect haptic aiding for remotely piloted vehicles. Proc. - IEEE Int. Workshop Robot Hum. Interact. Commun. **506–512** (2010). https://doi.org/10.1109/ROMAN.2010.5598647

Blundell, J., et al.: Low-visibility commercial ground operations: an objective and subjective evaluation of a multimodal display. Aeronaut. J. **127**(1310), 581–603 (2023). https://doi.org/10.1017/aer.2022.81

Brainard, D.H.: The Psychophysics Toolbox. Spatial Vision 10 (1997)

de Stigter, S., Mulder, M., van Paassen, M.M.: Design and evaluation of a haptic flight director. J. Guid. Control. Dyn. **30**(1), 35–46 (2007). https://doi.org/10.2514/1.20593

Drop, F.M., de Vries, R., Mulder, M., Bülthoff, H.H.: The predictability of a target signal affects manual feedforward control. IFAC-PapersOnLine **49**(19), 177–182 (2016). https://doi.org/10.1016/J.IFACOL.2016.10.482

Ellerbroek, J., Martin, M.J.M.R., Lombaerts, T., van Paassen, M.M., Mulder, M.: Design and evaluation of a flight envelope protection haptic feedback system. IFAC-PapersOnLine **49**(19), 171–176 (2016). https://doi.org/10.1016/j.ifacol.2016.10.481

Graziotin, D., Wang, X., Abrahamsson, P.: Do feelings matter? on the correlation of affects and the self-assessed productivity in software engineering. J. Softw.: Evol. Process **27**(7), 467–487 (2015). https://doi.org/10.1002/smr.1673

Gueorguieva, R., Krystal, J.H.: Move over ANOVA: progress in analyzing repeated-measures data and its reflection in papers published in the archives of general psychiatry. Arch. Gen. Psych. **61**(3), 310–317 (2004). https://doi.org/10.1001/archpsyc.61.3.310

Hart, S.G.: NASA-TASK LOAD INDEX (NASA-TLX). Years Later. **20**, 904–908 (2006)

Hart, S.G., Staveland, L.E.: Development of NASA-TLX (Task Load Index): results of empirical and theoretical research sandra. Adv. Psychol. **52**(Human Mental Workload), 139–183 (1988)

Ho, C., Tan, H.Z., Spence, C.: Using spatial vibrotactile cues to direct visual attention in driving scenes. Transp. Res. F: Traffic Psychol. Behav. **8**(6), 397–412 (2005). https://doi.org/10.1016/j.trf.2005.05.002

Kane, M.J., Conway, A.R.A., Miura, T.K., Colflesh, G.J.H.: Working memory, attention control, and the N-back task: a question of construct validity. J. Exp. Psychol. Learn. Mem. Cogn. **33**(3), 615–622 (2007). https://doi.org/10.1037/0278-7393.33.3.615

Laird, N.M., Ware, J.H.: Random-effects models for longitudinal data. Biometrics **38**(4), 963–974 (1982). https://doi.org/10.2307/2529876

Lam, T.M., Boschloo, H.W., Mulder, M., van Paassen, M.M., van der Helm, F.C.T.: Effect of haptic feedback in a trajectory following task with an unmanned aerial vehicle. Conf. Proc. - IEEE Int. Conf. Syst. Man Cybern. **3**, 2500–2506 (2004). https://doi.org/10.1109/ICSMC.2004.1400705

Olivari, M., Nieuwenhuizen, F.M., Venrooij, J., Bülthoff, H. H., Pollini, L.: Multi-loop pilot behaviour identification in response to simultaneous visual and haptic stimuli. In: AIAA Modeling and Simulation Technologies Conference 2012, August, 1–23 (2012). https://doi.org/10.2514/6.2012-4795

Orasanu, J.M.: Decision-making in the Cockpit. In: Harris, D., Harris, D., Li, W.-C. (eds.) Decision Making in Aviation, pp. 103–138. Routledge (2017). https://doi.org/10.4324/9781315095080-6

Repperger, D.W., Haas, M.W., Brickman, B.J., Hettinger, L.J., Lu, L., Roe, M.M.: Design of a haptic interface as a pilot's assistant in a high turbulance task environment. Perceptual Motor Skills **85**, 1139–1154 (1997)

Schutte, P., Goodrich, K., Williams, R.: Towards an Improved Pilot-Vehicle Interface for Highly Automated Aircraft : Evaluation of the Haptic Flight Control System. In: Advances in Human

Aspects of Aviation (Advances in Human Factors and Ergonomics Series), pp. 2524–2533 (2012)

Sklar, A.E., Sarter, N.B.: Good vibrations: tactile feedback in support of attention allocation and human-automation coordination in event-driven domains. Hum. Factors **41**(4), 543–552 (1999). https://doi.org/10.1518/001872099779656716

The MathWorks Inc. (2021). *MATLAB* (MATLAB 2021b)

van Baelen, D., Ellerbroek, J., van Paassen, M.M.R., Mulder, M.: Evaluation of a haptic feedback system for flight envelope protection. In: AIAA Scitech 2019 Forum (2019). https://doi.org/10.2514/6.2019-0367

van Baelen, D., van Paassen, M.M., Ellerbroek, J., Abbink, D.A., Mulder, M.: Flying by feeling: communicating flight envelope protection through haptic feedback. Int. J. Human-Comput. Interact. **00**(00), 1–11 (2021). https://doi.org/10.1080/10447318.2021.1890489

Wickens, C.D.: Multiple resources and performance prediction. Theor. Issues Ergon. Sci. **3**(2), 159–177 (2002). https://doi.org/10.1080/14639220210123806

Wickens, C.D.: Multiple resources and mental workload. Hum. Factors **50**(3), 449–455 (2008). https://doi.org/10.1518/001872008X288394

Winter, B., Grawunder, S.: The phonetic profile of Korean formal and informal speech registers. J. Phon. **40**, 808–815 (2012). https://doi.org/10.1016/j.wocn.2010.11.010

Re-designing the Interaction of Day-to-Day Applications to Support Sustained Attention Level

Naile Hacioglu[1]([✉]), Maria Chiara Leva[2], and Hyowon Lee[1,3]

[1] School of Computing, Dublin City University, Glasnevin, Dublin 9, Ireland
naile.hacioglu2@mail.dcu.ie
[2] School of Food Science and Environmental Health, Technological University Dublin, Grangegorman, Dublin, Ireland
[3] Insight Centre for Data Analytics, Dublin City University, Glasnevin, Dublin 9, Ireland

Abstract. Digital distractions in decreasing people's attentional abilities have become a subject of increasing concern and scrutiny in recent years. Based on the existing literature regarding the negative impact of technology on attention, this paper examines various solutions, encompassing mostly reactive strategies. It also questions the prevailing design practices prioritising learnability and efficiency and proposes a shift towards designing interactions that minimise distractions and promote sustained attention while emphasising the negative consequences of distraction-prone interactions on users' attentional resources. As a proactive solution, we present a novel interaction strategy called "Attention mode," which selectively reduces distractions when using apps. We developed three prototypes that consistently incorporate this strategy, each used in a different application on a different device: a news website on a desktop, an e-book reading app on a tablet, and a video-watching app on a smartphone. We conducted usability testing with 13 participants to evaluate this design feature and address the implications of these in the interaction design knowledge and practice today. By advocating for considering users' attentional abilities in design, this work contributes to the field of Human-Computer Interaction (HCI) and calls for a balance between cognitive well-being and traditional usability criteria.

Keywords: Sustained Attention · Cognition · User Interface Design · Usability · Digital Technology · Smart Devices · Distraction · Task Switching · Notifications

1 Introduction

In recent years, there has been considerable interest and concern surrounding the influence of digital technology on human cognition. Numerous studies have documented detrimental effects on various cognitive abilities, including memory, decision-making, and problem-solving skills. Among these, attention has emerged as the most extensively studied area concerning the adverse impact of smart devices and digital applications. People's deteriorated attentional abilities are no longer only in the form of personal

© The Author(s), under exclusive license to Springer Nature Switzerland AG 2023
M. Kurosu et al. (Eds.): HCII 2023, LNCS 14054, pp. 363–377, 2023.
https://doi.org/10.1007/978-3-031-48038-6_23

anecdotes shared in friendly conversations, as increasing scientific evidence in academic studies and experimental results have appeared for the past 15 years or so [1, 2]. Trends that contribute to speeding up the worrying phenomenon of reduced attention span include shorter durations of media content on TV and the content presented on popular social media apps such as TikTok, YouTube Shorts and Instagram.

In particular, the interactions provided in today's computing systems that facilitate the consumption of media contents and those supporting other daily tasks seem to have been specifically designed to aggravate the situation: web user interfaces are filled with elements diverting the user's attention away from the main task of the page (a myriad of navigational elements such as menu bars, short-cut buttons and other non-content-related information, notwithstanding the commercial advertisements embedded as part of business model); "related" items frequently shown on informational and e-commerce systems almost as *de facto* standard; operating systems supporting easy switching amongst multiple applications; constant email/message notifications, to name but a few. Cognitive scientists have already established that frequent multitasking reduces the user's cognitive resources while at a task, consequently making the person more susceptible to distractions [1, 3].

Commonly-used interactions provided in day-to-day websites and applications on their smartphones, tablets and desktop/laptop computers today have been designed to support a broad umbrella concept of "usability" where typically a few criteria such as learnability (designing it to be easy to learn how to use for the first-time users) and efficiency (designing it to require less user effort or time) are prioritised as the main aim of the design and all subsequent success measures based on achieving these criteria. Alongside these criteria, there is an abundant quantity of design knowledge and guidelines in the form of influential academic textbooks [4, 5], as well as heuristics, checklists, and design tips available today, accumulated and refined over the past few decades as the results of on-going theoretical discourses, experiments, and trial-and-error iterations on the market.

If the distraction-prone interactions we use today result from learnability- and efficiency-focused design practice, can we re-design these interactions that consider the negative consequences on the users' attentional abilities now that we are aware of the problem? Available literature in this area is mostly about confirming the negative impacts on our attention (e.g. [6–8]), and existing solution ideas are almost exclusively either more disciplines on the side of the user, such as pre-commitment [2] and self-regulation [1, Chapter 13] or reactive strategies such as automatic blocking of app usage or batching of notifications. Few proactive design proposals are available where considering such impacts on cognition is an integral part of interaction design, other than tentative design ideas that gamify conventional apps to reduce the potentially harmful effects of over-relying on daily technologies [9].

In this context, we propose a design solution that aims to minimise such negative impacts on attention by helping easily control major factors that will make the user more prone to distractions directly available on the user interface of the application currently used. This approach can help users turn off potential distractions from the tasks more readily, thus remaining focused on them, and reduce cognitive load to improve sustained attention, ultimately expected to improve their overall experience. We share the insights gained through the design process, usability testing sessions with 13 participants using three prototype mock-ups that implement this idea, and the analysis of feedback and reflection on in what ways the usability/design knowledge, such as well-established usability criteria and design principles might be augmented or extended to help the designers take this issue into account when designing.

2 Disruptive Behaviours Related to Digital Technology Usage

2.1 Effects of Digital Technology Use on Attention

Table 1 summarizes a body of evidence from the literature regarding the detrimental effects of digital technology on our attentional processes, despite some reported benefits in some cases. Various behaviours related to technology usage can disrupt our attentional systems and executive control in the short and long term. For instance, adolescents who frequently engage with technology are at a higher risk of developing symptoms associated with ADHD due to multitasking and repetitive shifts in attention [6]. Ophir et al. [7] found that individuals who engage in extensive media multitasking exhibit decreased voluntary attention allocation performance when faced with distractions.

Extended internet and social media use can potentially deteriorate the executive attention network, which is responsible for executive functions such as inhibitory control and willpower [10, 11]. The continuous bombardment of notifications intervenes with inhibitory control and aggravates the situation further. Habitual social media use makes it harder for people to control their social media use even when they have other primary tasks [12–14]. However, digital technologies do not only adversely affect attentional systems: regularly playing video games enhances and improves visual, divided, and sustained attention in some cases [14, 15].

2.2 Exploring Existing Solutions and Their Limitations

The scientific literature available today predominantly mentions digital media's negative (and occasionally positive) effects on cognition as their conclusions of the study. Only a few of the authors move on to suggest any possible solutions to these effects. Those who do advise solutions require serious commitment and dedication from the end-user side, as observed in the last two columns in Table 1, as cognitive training/CBT and behavioural intervention (such as pre-commitment and self-constraints in digital technology usage that require a great deal of discipline and efforts).

Pre-commitment to Limit Digital Technology Use. Findings from the literature suggest that time away from screen-based media improves attention [22]. One study mentions that Intel Corporation implemented "quiet time", where employees took time off from electronic communication during designated periods to minimise distractions to mitigate this problem [14].

Popular culture has also become aware of smartphones' cognitive costs [23]. News articles and books mention individuals replacing their smartphones with basic mobile phones with limited functionality to increase productivity and eliminate distractions [2, 24]. There are also software programs that block the internet for designated periods and

Table 1. Key papers referring attention and executive control effects of digital technology and solution type proposed or hinted if any [32].

Study	Effect on Attention	Proposed (or Hinted) Solutions	
		Cognitive Training or CBT[1]	Behavioural Intervention
Barasch et al., 2017 [16]	↑[2]		
Cardoso-Leite et al., 2021 [17]	↓		
Davis, 2001 [10]	↓	✓	
Du et al., 2019 [12]	↓		
Freytag et al., 2020 [13]	↓		
Green and Bavelier, 2003 [15]	↑	✓	
Madore and Wagner, 2019 [3]	↓		
Madore et al., 2020 [18]	↓		
Misra and Stokols, 2012 [14]	↓		✓
Ophir et al., 2019 [7]	↓		
Rosen et al., 2012 [8]	↓		✓
Rosser et al., 2007 [19]	↑	✓	
Schacter, 2022 [20]	↓ ↑		
Small et al., 2020 [6]	↓ ↑	✓	
Uncapher & Wagner, 2018 [21]	↓		
Throuvala et al., 2020 [22]	↓	✓	✓

web browser extensions that remove irrelevant contents such as notifications, newsfeeds, and advertisements [25–27].

Cognitive Training. Some studies found that specific behavioural interventions such as internet searching might reduce cognitive decline in older adults [19]. This practice could be termed cognitive training since users must complete search tasks in different sittings over a period. For example, Cogmed offers five weeks of digital cognitive training programmes to improve their clients' attention and working memory [28].

---

[1] Cognitive Behavioural Therapy.

[2] "↑" icon refers to improvement in attention and executive control whereas "↓" refers to deterioration.

Cognitive-behavioural therapy investigates cognitive distortions and replaces problematic internet use with healthy behaviours [17], using various methods such as recording internet use, keeping individuals away from the Internet for a period and having them observe the change in their cognitive skills.

Most of the suggested solutions summarised above see the technologies and people's interactivity with them as given and try to reduce the negative consequences during or after using technology instead of re-thinking how the technology could be designed differently in the first place to result in fewer such consequences. Considering the attention issue from the start when developing the technology will be a more holistic solution, though very little is known about applying design knowledge to support this.

3   Design Approach for Sustained Attention

3.1   Design Strategy and Approach

We developed the "Attention Mode" concept that effectively tackles distractions in diverse contexts. Triggered by clicking, dragging, tapping, or swiping depending on the platform's supported modality, the mode supports the reduction/removal of potential media distractions. This feature bears a resemblance to the "Focus" [29] and "Downtime" [30] functionalities found on smart devices, which aim to reduce distractions. However, unlike these existing features that require multiple steps scattered across various locations and only address specific distractions, the Attention Mode collectively eliminates designated media distractions with a single action. In this sense, the mode is perhaps more analogous to "airplane mode" of a typical smartphone which, when turned on, will collectively turn off all functions related to mobile/wi-fi usage scattered around in different parts of the settings and options. Furthermore, we intend to seamlessly integrate this mode into the user interface of applications, allowing users to trigger it more effortlessly while engaging in tasks.

3.2   Attention Mode Button

Interaction Strategy. The Attention Mode button simplifies user interaction by presenting a button strategically placed within the user interface. Upon interaction, this button instantly reveals a set of sub-options that can be selected (see Fig. 1a). When the button is pressed, users can choose between one or two different modes, depending on the application, platform, and device. These modes exclude various distractions (refer to Fig. 1b and 1c). Furthermore, in some instances, the interface provides customisation options in the settings menu, as depicted in Fig. 2a. In this settings menu, users can change pre-set default values for Attention Mode Level 1 (Fig. 2b). Customisation options allow users to personalise the mode to their liking (i.e., what distractions should constitute as Level 1 and 2 thus be blocked when it is activated). In contrast, the pre-set default values provide users with a convenient starting point for users who may not want to customise the mode.

Once a level is selected, the mode is activated instantly and can be turned off without requiring confirmation. A concise explanation of the Attention Mode is provided within

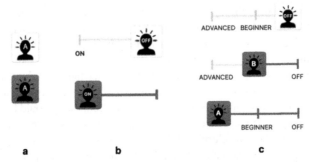

Fig. 1. Attention Mode can be turned off and levels can be selected by using Attention Button. **a** Attention Button. **b, c** Attention Mode level options (appears when pressed).

the Options window for first-time users. If users do not want to see it, they can press the "up" arrow for the window to collapse and hide the explanation and settings. They can display them again by pressing the "down" button. The Options disappear when the close icon or an area outside the window is clicked or tapped. Once it disappears, users can still see the status of Attention Mode on the UI as a single button.

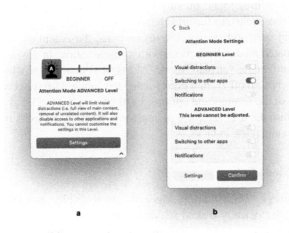

Fig. 2. Attention Mode options can be customised in settings menu when relevant for a specific application or platform. Levels can be selected by using Attention Button. (a) Settings button (b) Setting options where all attention-related features are grouped into Level 1 and 2.

While turning on/off with different option sets is not novel, we are gathering a few design choices to enable an interaction that is particularly suitable for our purpose. In summary:

- It collects options otherwise scattered around into one location for access, thus a single button press to activate/deactivate.

- Information about distractions and usage is given to help users raise awareness of digital distractions.
- The user can select one of the levels of attention, each representing a higher-level set of options as needed.
- The widget-level interaction mechanism can be designed slightly differently to suit different applications on different platforms.

We developed three different user interfaces each for three interaction devices: a news website on a desktop, an e-book reader app on a tablet, and a video-streaming app on a smartphone. This diverse set of media was to test how the overarching concept of the Attention Mode strategy could be consistently applied to the three commonly used interaction platforms and what aspects each might require some design customisation due to the unique affordances of each medium.

Prototype 1: News Website on Desktop. This prototype is designed to demonstrate a desktop environment with minimum distractions when the user's primary task is to read an online newspaper article. Distractions such as recommended articles, website advertisements, browser settings, desktop view, and other open applications on the computer are considered irrelevant to the article itself. To eliminate these distractions and allow users to focus solely on reading the article, Attention Mode can be activated (refer to Fig. 3).

Here, the Attention Button should be present in the top-right corner of every page. The purpose of the button is to provide a consistent function across all pages, while the specific function may vary slightly depending on the page.

In this example, customization is available for Attention Mode at the Beginner Level, while the Advanced Level cannot be personalized. The Advanced Level entails the elimination of all distractions, including irrelevant visual content, email, and messaging notifications, and switching to other applications to prevent media multitasking. It is crucial to note that activating the Attention Button on any page will have a global effect on all other site pages ensuring the user's preferences and selected settings are consistently saved and applied throughout the site. Users can allocate their attention more effectively by eliminating visual distractions that may prompt task switching and blocking external notifications during tasks [7]. Helping users focus on their primary task, in turn, reduces the occurrence of attention lapses [18] as the opportunities for multitasking behaviour decrease.

Prototype 2: E-book Application on Tablet. Designing an interface for e-book reading on a tablet requires different considerations than designing for news sites or other browsing activities on a desktop. While both activities involve reading, the reading experience for an e-book is typically longer and requires more sustained focus.

Since consistent media multitasking reduces sustained attention ability in the long term [3, 18], it is essential to design an interface that encourages users to stay focused for extended periods by preventing them from switching to other applications [1]. Therefore, the user can set a target duration on Attention Mode to stay in the reading task (Fig. 4), where the user cannot switch to other applications until the specified time is up. Since the app has no visual distraction (tablet apps typically occupy the whole screen visually),

Fig. 3. (a) Attention Mode options are displayed when Attention Button is clicked on with general information. (b) Attention Mode maximised the main content and removes irrelevant visual distraction when set to level 1.

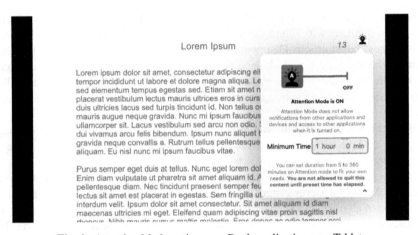

Fig. 4. Attention Mode options on eBook application on a Tablet.

only ON-level multitasking and notifications are prevented, unlike the desktop example above.

Prototype 3: Video Streaming Application on Smartphone. Implementing Attention Mode in this video-watching app was to augment a full-screen button typically featured on many video players by blocking notifications and other distractions, easily selectable in one go. Located at the bottom-right corner of the video player panel, the user can turn the mode on to maximise the video as in the classic full-screen feature. Additionally, notifications are silenced, switching to other applications is prevented, and buttons like the share, comment and "more videos" buttons are removed, as these options might encourage multitasking at the ON level, thus increasing the user's susceptibility to further distraction (Fig. 5).

The three designs were implemented in Sketch prototyping tool, to be used for the usability testing reported in the next section.

a   b

Fig. 5. In Attention Mode ON level, video occupies the whole screen, notifications are turned off, switching to other applications are not allowed, and several video features are removed.

4 Usability Testing and Evaluation

4.1 Participants

Thirteen participants (n = 13) from diverse cultural backgrounds (2 French, 2 Indian, 1 Italian, 1 Brazilian, 1 Spanish, 1 Moroccan, 1 Colombian, 1 Chinese, 1 Kazakh, 1 Russian) took part in the study. The sample consisted of seven females and six males, ages 25 to 35 (mean age = 28.5 years). The participants were recruited through events organised by third-level institutions in Ireland. All participants provided informed consent prior to participating in the study. The study protocol was approved by the Ethics Review Commission of the Dublin City University.

It is important to acknowledge that the sample size is relatively small, which may limit the generalizability of the results. Nonetheless, efforts were made to include participants from various nationalities and genders within the available pool of participants.

4.2 Study Design

Prototype Development and Feedback Iterations. The development of the prototypes involved a series of iterations in the Sketch prototyping tool. Initially, three different prototypes were created, and these prototypes were refined through four iterative cycles. After each iteration, improvements and modifications were made based on the feedback. Following the third iteration, a preliminary feedback session was conducted with five experts from the technology and design fields. These experts provided valuable insights and suggestions for further refinement of the prototypes, reported elsewhere [32].

Usability Testing Sessions. Prior to the study, participants were provided with plain language statements and informed consent forms, which they were required to read and understand. After reviewing the materials, participants signed the consent form, indicating their willingness to participate in the study.

The usability testing sessions were conducted individually, each lasting approximately 15 min. Before the testing began, the context of the study was briefly explained to the participants verbally. Participants were then instructed to interact with each of the three prototypes. Using the Sketch environment, the news website app was accessed on a MacBook Air M2 2022, the e-book app on a 5th Generation 12.9-inch iPad Pro, and the video streaming app on an iPhone 11.

After using each prototype, participants were asked to complete the printed System Usability Scale (SUS), a validated questionnaire designed to assess the usability of a system. Additionally, participants were encouraged to provide their thoughts and feedback on their experiences with each prototype. They were provided with space to write down their comments and suggestions on the SUS form.

Data Analysis. The collected data, including the SUS scores and participant feedback, were analysed to assess the usability of the prototypes and identify areas for further improvement. The SUS scores were aggregated and analysed using descriptive statistics. The qualitative feedback provided by participants was examined to identify recurring themes and patterns.

Participant privacy and confidentiality were ensured throughout the study. Data were anonymized and stored securely, and personal identifiers were removed during analysis and reporting.

4.3   Results and Evaluation

Table 2 shows the mean and standard deviation values of the SUS scores for each prototype, providing an overview of the usability assessment. The SUS scores for all prototypes exceeded 80, falling within the "excellent" range [31]. This indicates that participants found the prototypes to be highly usable.

Among the three prototypes, the Attention mode feature on the video streaming app on the smartphone (Prototype 3) received the highest SUS score of 86.34, indicating a high level of usability. On the other hand, the same feature on the e-book app (Prototype 2) obtained the lowest score of 80.97, suggesting slightly lower usability compared to the other prototypes. The participants' preference was more varied for Prototype 2 compared to the other prototypes. This finding suggests that participants had mixed opinions and preferences regarding the usability of the e-book app.

Interestingly, despite Prototype 3 having the highest SUS score, participants were more inclined to use this feature when integrated into a news website on a desktop environment (Prototype 1), evidenced by the higher scores for Question 1 (S1), as seen in Table 3. These results suggest that while Prototype 3 performed well in terms of overall usability, Prototype 1 seemed to have an advantage regarding initial user preference. Further analysis and qualitative feedback could help provide deeper insights into the specific features or aspects that influenced participants' preferences and perceptions of usability.

Overall, the SUS scores indicate that all three prototypes were well-received and demonstrated high usability. The variations in scores and participant preferences provide insights for refining and optimising the prototypes in future iterations.

Together with SUS scores, the participants' comments provide valuable insights into the strengths and weaknesses of each prototype, as well as recommendations for potential improvements.

Prototype 1 received positive feedback from participants, who recognised the value of the concept and expressed willingness to recommend it to others. However, participants also highlighted the need for a tutorial to aid new users in navigating the prototype. The recommendation to include a tutorial aligns with the suggestion for customisation

Table 2. Overall SUS score chart for each prototype.

	Prototype 1	Prototype 2	Prototype 3
Mean Value	83.65385	80.96154	86.34615
Standard Deviation	13.60206	24.14234	14.3111

Table 3. Number of participants based on the score they reported for each question after using prototypes.

	Prototype 1 News website					Prototype 2 E-book app					Prototype 3 Video streaming app				
	1	*2*	*3*	*4*	*5*	*1*	*2*	*3*	*4*	*5*	*1*	*2*	*3*	*4*	*5*
	1: Strongly Disagree														*5: Strongly Agree*
S1	0	-	1	5	7	1	2	2	5	3	-	2	3	3	5
S2	7	5	1	-	-	11	-	1	1	-	8	2	3	-	-
S3	-	-	2	7	4	1	1	1	1	9	-	-	2	4	7
S4	6	3	3	-	1	9	2	1	-	1	8	2	3	-	-
S5	-	-	3	5	5	-	2	1	4	6	-	1	-	6	6
S6	11	1	1	-	-	9	2	2	-	-	12	-	1	-	-
S7	-	1	2	5	5	1	-	1	4	7	-	-	1	6	6
S8	10	3	-	-	-	9	3	-	1	-	10	1	1	1	-
S9	-	-	3	4	6	1	2	-	4	6	-	-	1	5	7
S10	9	2	1	-	1	8	3	1	-	1	11	1	-	-	-

Statements:
S1. I think that I would like to use this feature frequently.
S2. I found this feature unnecessarily complex.
S3. I thought this feature was easy to use.
S4. I think that I would need assistance to be able to use this feature.
S5. I found the various functions in this feature were well integrated.
S6. I thought there was too much inconsistency in this feature.
S7. I would imagine that most people would learn to use this feature very quickly
S8. I found this feature very cumbersome/awkward to use.
S9. I felt very confident using this feature.
S10. I needed to learn a lot of things before I could get going with this feature.

options, emphasising the importance of providing a user-friendly and personalised experience. The feedback for Prototype 1 also emphasised its suitability for individuals with attention problems or those who engage in extensive web reading. The participants appreciated the UI's simplicity and ease of use when the Attention Mode is on, while providing suggestions for minor improvements such as reducing the size of the icon. There were differing opinions on the customisation of mode levels. One participant expressed interest in the idea of customising the level of distraction settings, while another participant raised concerns about potential confusion for less technologically inclined users. This feedback highlights the importance of considering the balance between customization and simplicity in the design of the Attention Mode.

Prototype 2 received mixed feedback, with some participants finding it helpful for avoiding distractions while reading and recommending it to others. Participants also mentioned the desire for a time display as an additional feature. Those unfamiliar with tablet-based interactions found the UI unintuitive and had difficulty using the prototype independently. Several participants reported they would have liked the flexibility to quit the mode whenever they wanted, even if they had set a target duration. The user having control over the usage (including multitasking) is one of the important design guidelines available today. However, prioritising attention by reducing the cognitive cost of task switching means that this guideline may need to be compromised, raising an issue on how the existing usability criteria could accommodate this.

The integration of the Attention Mode button within the video-streaming application was well-received by participants. However, there were differing opinions regarding the exclusion of certain features, such as the comment section. Participants highlighted the need to balance distraction reduction and retaining desired functionalities. Suggestions were made for including an ad-blocking option that appears when a video is streaming and improvements to the settings' accessibility. One participant liked the minimalist approach with fewer video options which also prevents accidental touches on the screen and unintended interruptions. This feedback suggests that users value simplicity and ease of use in the design of Attention Mode.

Overall, the feedback from the participants indicated that the proposed design approach of Attention Mode was well-received, with participants expressing positive sentiments about the concept of reducing distractions and creating awareness about their digital technology use. Suggestions for additional features, customisation options, and improved accessibility were highlighted.

Building upon the discussion on user feedback and the implications of design choices, it is evident that interactive applications' usability and user experience play a crucial role in shaping attentional processes. However, it is essential to recognise that an overemphasis on efficiency, effectiveness, and learnability in interaction can negatively affect specific attentional processes in the short and long term. Efficiency-oriented applications prioritise saving time and mental effort, which can lead to reduced cognitive engagement. Users may rely less on attentional systems and executive networks when interacting with such applications. Similarly, when learnability is prioritised, users require minimal attention during initial interactions, potentially leading to decreased attention involvement. These patterns of reduced cognitive effort can contribute to degradation in attention skills over time, like how muscles can weaken without regular exercise. Therefore, it is worth noting that prioritising cognitive well-being, including the attention process, may sometimes conflict with efficiency and learnability criteria, highlighting the need for careful consideration and balancing of design goals.

There are limitations of this study, including the small sample size and potential biases in participant selection. Conducting larger-scale user testing with diverse participants would further validate the findings and provide more comprehensive insights.

Additionally, conducting follow-up studies to assess long-term usability and user satisfaction with the prototypes would be beneficial for evaluating their effectiveness and practicality in real-world scenarios.

5   Conclusion

As our time spent on everyday digital applications continues to increase, evidence of negative consequences such as distractions and reduced attention span is also growing. While approaches like blocking, pre-commitment, and creating awareness about digital technology use have been suggested to mitigate these issues, a more proactive stance would be to redesign those applications in such a way as to reduce such effects. This study demonstrates a design approach that prioritises our attentional well-being by minimising digital distractions on everyday digital platforms and the usability of this approach on different applications and devices. As the design of these prototypes prioritised sustained attention rather than other usability criteria, such as learnability or efficiency, some features conflict with conventional design guidelines. For example, our e-book prototype prevented the user from switching to a different app/task, helping save cognitive switching costs for better-focused reading. However, such prevention inevitably takes away control/flexibility from the user. We plan to work on using these conflicting points identified to analyse the implications of the existing usability criteria, principles, and guidelines and discuss how to make sense of designing for sustained attention.

This work contributes to the HCI community by demonstrating how the interaction design could and should start more pro-actively taking into consideration the users' attentional abilities as part of the design and how such a stance might manifest as a factor to be balanced among other conventional usability criteria that have worked so well in creating easy-to-use and efficient interactions. As the impacts of long-term use of our everyday technologies on our cognition are becoming more known, it is important that the interaction design field responds to them by re-considering, re-adjusting, refining, and augmenting our design knowledge, know-how and skill base accordingly and start producing new generations of apps and services for people's cognitive well-being.

Acknowledgement. This work was conducted with the financial support of the SFI Centre for Research Training in Digitally-Enhanced Reality (d-real) under Grant No. 18/CRT/6224 and the SFI Centre Grant No. 12/RC/2289_P2 at Insight the SFI Research Centre for Data Analytics at Dublin City University. For the purpose of Open Access, the author has applied a CC BY public copyright license to any Author Accepted Manuscript version arising from this submission.

References

1. Mark, G.: Attention Span: Finding Focus for a Fulfilling Life, 1st edn. William Collins, London (2023)
2. Hari, J.: Stolen Focus, 1st edn. Bloomsbury Publishing, London (2022)
3. Madore, K.P., Wagner, A.D.: Multicosts of multitasking. Cerebrum **2019**, 04–19 (2019)

4. Shneiderman, B., Plaisant, C., Cohen, M., Jacobs. S., Elmqvist, N., Diakopoulos, N.: Designing the User Interface: Strategies for Effective Human-Computer Interaction, 6th ed. Pearson, England (2016)

5. Rogers, Y., Sharp, H., Preece, J.: Interaction Design: Beyond Human-Computer Interaction, 6th edn. Wiley, USA (2023)

6. Small, G.W., Lee, J., Kaufman, A., et al.: Brain health consequences of digital technology use. Dialogues. Clin. Neurosci. **22**, 179–187 (2020). https://doi.org/10.31887/DCNS.2020.22.2/gsmall

7. Ophir, E., Nass, C., Wagner, A.D.: Cognitive control in media multitaskers. Proc. Natl. Acad. Sci. U.S.A. **106**, 15583–15587 (2009). https://doi.org/10.1073/pnas.0903620106

8. Rosen, L.D., Mark Carrier, L., Cheever, N.A.: Facebook and texting made me do it: media-induced task-switching while studying. Comput. Hum. Behav. **29**, 948–958 (2013). https://doi.org/10.1016/j.chb.2012.12.001

9. Balasubramanian, G., Lee, H., Poon, K., et al.: Towards Establishing Design Principles for Balancing Usability and Maintaining Cognitive Abilities, pp 3–18 (2017)

10. Davis, R.A.: A cognitive–behavioral model of pathological Internet use. Comput. Hum. Behav. **17**, 187–195 (2001). https://doi.org/10.1016/S0747-5632(00)00041-8

11. Goldstein, E.B.: Cognitive Psychology: Connecting Mind, Research, and Everyday Experience, 5th edn. Cengage Learning, Boston, MA (2018)

12. Du, J., Kerkhof, P., van Koningsbruggen, G.M.: Predictors of social media self-control failure: immediate gratifications, habitual checking, ubiquity, and notifications. Cyberpsychol. Behav. Soc. Netw. **22**, 477–485 (2019). https://doi.org/10.1089/cyber.2018.0730

13. Freytag, A., Knop-Huelss, K., Meier, A., et al.: Permanently online—always stressed out? the effects of permanent connectedness on stress experiences. Hum. Commun. Res. **47**, 132–165 (2021). https://doi.org/10.1093/hcr/hqaa014

14. Misra, S., Stokols, D.: Psychological and health outcomes of perceived information overload. Environ. Behav. **44**, 737–759 (2012). https://doi.org/10.1177/0013916511404408

15. Green, C.S., Bavelier, D.: Action video game modifies visual selective attention. Nature **423**, 534–537 (2003)

16. Barasch, A., Diehl, K., Silverman, J., Zauberman, G.: Photographic memory: the effects of volitional photo taking on memory for visual and auditory aspects of an experience. Psychol. Sci. **28**, 1056–1066 (2017). https://doi.org/10.1177/0956797617694868

17. Cardoso-Leite, P., Buchard, A., Tissieres, I., et al.: Media use, attention, mental health and academic performance among 8 to 12 year old children. PLoS ONE **16**, e0259163 (2021). https://doi.org/10.1371/journal.pone.0259163

18. Madore, K.P., Khazenzon, A.M., Backes, C.W., et al.: Memory failure predicted by attention lapsing and media multitasking. Nature **587**, 87–91 (2020). https://doi.org/10.1038/s41586-020-2870-z

19. Rosser, J.C., Lynch, P.J., Cuddihy, L., et al.: The impact of video games on training surgeons in the 21st century. Arch. Surg. **142**, 181–186 (2007). discusssion 186 https://doi.org/10.1001/archsurg.142.2.181

20. Schacter, D.L.: Media, technology, and the sins of memory. Mem. Mind Media **1**, e1 (2022). https://doi.org/10.1017/mem.2021.3

21. Uncapher, M.R., Wagner, A.D.: Minds and brains of media multitaskers: Current findings and future directions. Proc Natl Acad Sci U S A **115**, 9889–9896 (2018). https://doi.org/10.1073/pnas.1611612115

22. Throuvala, M.A., Griffiths, M.D., Rennoldson, M., Kuss, D.J.: Mind over matter: testing the efficacy of an online randomized controlled trial to reduce distraction from smartphone use. Int. J. Environ. Res. Public Health **17**, 4842 (2020). https://doi.org/10.3390/ijerph17134842

23. Ward, A.F., Duke, K., Gneezy, A., Bos, M.W.: Brain drain: the mere presence of one's own smartphone reduces available cognitive capacity. J. Assoc. Consum. Res. **2**, 140–154 (2017). https://doi.org/10.1086/691462

24. Bearne, S.: The people deciding to ditch their smartphones. BBC News (2022)

25. Calkuta. Distraction Free for YouTubeTM. In: Chrome Web Store (2019). https://chrome. google.com/webstore/detail/df-tube-distraction-free/mjdepdfccjgcndkmemponafgioodelna. Accessed 11 Apr 2023

26. Freedom: Internet, App and Website Blocker. In: Freedom. https://freedom.to. Accessed 11 Apr 2023

27. Hill, R.: uBlock Origin. In: Chrome Web Store (2023). https://chrome.google.com/webstore/detail/ublock-origin/cjpalhdlnbpafiamejdnhcphjbkeiagm. Accessed 11 Apr 2023

28. Focus Learn Get things done. In: Cogmed. https://www.cogmed.com/. Accessed 11 Apr 2023

29. Set up a Focus on Mac. In: Apple Support. https://support.apple.com/en-ie/guide/mac-help/mchl613dc43f/mac. Accessed 11 Apr 2023

30. Set up Screen Time for yourself on iPhone. In: Apple Support. https://support.apple.com/en-gb/guide/iphone/iphbfa595995/ios. Accessed 11 Apr 2023

31. Bangor, A., Kortum, P.T., Miller, J.T.: An empirical evaluation of the system usability scale. Int. J. Hum. –Comput. Interact. **24**, 574–594 (2008). https://doi.org/10.1080/104473108022 05776

32. Hacioglu, N., Leva, M.C., Lee, H.: Designing interaction to support sustained attention (Poster). In: 19th International Conference of Technical Committee 13 (Human-Computer Interaction) of IFIP (International Federation for Information Processing), York, U.K., 30 August - 1 September 2023 (2023)

Research on Human Eye Fatigue Coefficient in Target Recognition Tasks

Wanrong Han, Chengqi Xue$^{(\boxtimes)}$, Shoupeng Li, and Xinyue Wang

School of Mechanical Engineering, Southeast University, Nanjing 211189, China
ipd_xcq@seu.edu.cn

Abstract. In massive image recognition tasks, it is worth researching whether human eye fatigue leads to decreased performance or safety accidents. Although excessive task recognition numbers can seriously affect user fatigue and the efficiency of visual recognition tasks, few people can currently determine the numerical relationship between the coefficient of human visual fatigue and time performance. Therefore, this study reflects the changes in the fatigue level of the participants through time performance, analyzes the quantitative relationship between the duration of the task and the recognition time for a unit quantity of images, forms a curve model of the accumulated fatigue level over time, and can further deduce the performance of humans in identifying massive images. Participants were presented with 2,400 remote sensing images in an image recognition task and required to make correct decisions by pressing corresponding keys on a keyboard. The results showed that the aspect ratio of the participants' eyes reached a state of fatigue when it was below the threshold of 0.2, and the reaction time for recognizing a single image increased with time. These findings can quickly and effectively evaluate and define people's mental fatigue state, avoiding working personnel to operate in a state of mental fatigue.

Keywords: Visual Fatigue · Fatigue Threshold · Time Performance · Target Recognition Task

1 Introduction

With the development of modern sensors and image technology, massive amounts of images have been generated. Detecting valuable targets in these images has become an important requirement for information acquisition and processing. Although computer target recognition has made significant progress, computer vision mainly relies on low-level semantic features such as color, shape, and texture to extract image features [1]. As a result, solely relying on computer vision technology leads to poor target detection and significant identification errors in some complex images. To achieve accurate image detection results, human supervision remains crucial. However, with the development of information visualization, the amount of image information that needs to be collected and processed continues to increase, increasing the load on the human-machine-environment system and exacerbating the human-machine space conflict. At

M. Kurosu et al. (Eds.): HCII 2023, LNCS 14054, pp. 378–388, 2023.
https://doi.org/10.1007/978-3-031-48038-6_24

the same time, increasing demands for information response speed lead to increasing mental stress among operators, further accelerating the speed of fatigue. Therefore, measuring people's ability range threshold is essential for effective human-machine division of labor and collaboration, reducing the workload of operators, while leveraging the advantages of the auxiliary system, such as fast, accurate, good repeatability, and no fatigue. This is an important issue to investigate in the human-machine system, and it is significant for its future development.

Currently, many researchers believe that fatigue caused by long-term tasks is the direct cause of a decrease in visual monitoring alertness and performance, but there is no consensus on when fatigue begins to occur [2]. Subjective assessment methods can easily be influenced by personal motives, factors, and experiences, and may not objectively reflect the true state of fatigued individuals. Therefore, in order to accurately reflect changes in the human body during mental fatigue, objective evaluation methods are needed to assess changes in the body during fatigue. Currently, there are three main types of fatigue detection methods widely used for subjects: those based on human physiological parameters [3–5], those based on subject behavior characteristics [6–8], and those based on human face facial features [9–11]. When a person is fatigued, their eyes become difficult to open and will remain closed for longer periods than usual, which is an obvious feature that almost all people show when they are tired. Therefore, analysis of eye fatigue features has strong universality and reliability. Jo J et al. use the eye aspect ratio (EAR) to judge the degree of eye opening [12]. Eye feature points are shown in the Fig. 1:

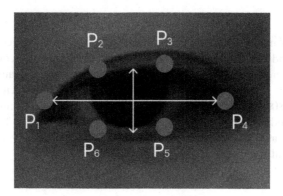

Fig. 1. Eye feature points.

The formula for calculating the value of α (i.e. EAR) is:

$$\alpha = \frac{(D(p2, p6) + D(p3, p5))}{(2 * D(p1, p4))} \tag{1}$$

When a person's eyes are open, α is almost constant, approximately 0.2, whereas when the eyes are closed, α tends towards zero. This is applicable to most people, with only slight individual variations in α values due to uniform scaling and in-plane rotation of the images which are completely invariant. Since human blinking is synchronous between both eyes, the average α value is used for processing. An initial threshold of 0.2 is set. The α value of each frame captured by the camera is assessed and compared with the threshold of 0.2. After multiple comparative tests, this threshold can be used to effectively screen fatigued experimental samples.

Reasonable arrangement of rest breaks is an important means to solve the problem of decreased operational performance caused by fatigue during monitoring and alertness operations. The performance inflection point is often used to judge the fatigue of the subject in the task, and the time at which the inflection point appears is used as the basis for arranging rest for the subjects [13]. Therefore, this article mainly reflects the changes in the fatigue level of the subjects through time performance. Based on this analysis, a quantitative relationship between the duration of the task and the time required to recognize a unit of pictures is established. The EAR algorithm is used to measure the fatigue state of the eyes, obtain the fatigue boundary threshold of the person, and achieve better curve fitting effect, and finally form the derivation equation of the time required for a person to complete a massive recognition task. Therefore, this study aims to determine the fatigue coefficient of human eye recognition of massive pictures in target recognition tasks, and ultimately obtain the time performance fitting formula for human eye recognition. Through human-factor experiments, the visual ability threshold and time performance of humans are determined, laying the foundation for subsequent research on human-machine cooperation.

2   Methodology

2.1   Materials

The experimental material used the FAIR1M dataset [14], with the target categories set to aircraft, ships, and cars. In this experiment, there were 200 pictures containing aircraft targets, 200 pictures containing ship targets, and 200 pictures containing car targets. The total number of non-target and target pictures selected for each target category experiment was 800, with a total of 2400 pictures. Clear and readable images containing aircraft, ships, and cars were selected as the target images from the FAIR1M dataset, and non-target images, i.e. background images that do not contain any of the three target categories, were also selected (see in Table 1).

2.2   Subjects

To determine the sample size, this article used G*Power 3.1.9 software to estimate the number of participants. With an effect size of 0.40, alpha of 0.05, and five levels of the independent variable, a total sample size of 80 is needed to achieve 80% statistical power. This means that at least 16 participants are required for each level of the experiment. Therefore, 20 subjects were enrolled from school of mechanical engineering in Southeast University. Subjects included 10 males and 10 females between the ages of 23 and 26 years (M = 24.54), all of whom were right-handed and had normal vision or corrected vision. Subjects all had basic knowledge of computer operation and were trained to make rational decisions in the experiment. To ensure the normal conduct of the experiment, subjects were required to avoid staying up late on the night before the experiment.

Table 1. Experiment interfaces.

Type	Target	Non-target

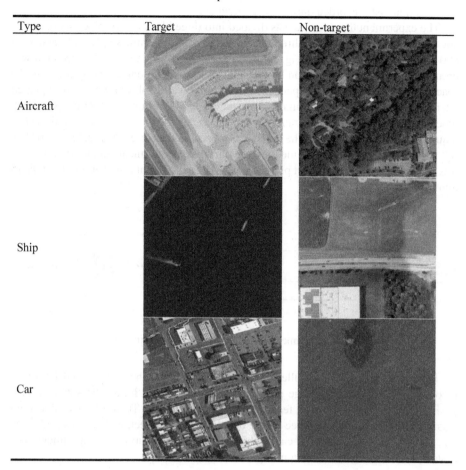

Aircraft

Ship

Car

2.3 Experimental Equipment and Experimental Procedures

The experiment was based on a monotonous visual task, and the data collected included behavioral data and eye movement data. Behavioral data included decision time and accuracy. Eye movement data included blink frequency and eye aspect ratio of the left and right eyes.

Behavioral data was recorded using Eprime 2.0. Subjects were required to complete a task of judging whether multiple targets were threatening in a simulated system, after understanding and familiarizing themselves with the experimental process. Each decision was to judge all targets as quickly and accurately as possible while ensuring accuracy, and reaction time and accuracy of the subjects were recorded. Prior to the experiment, subjects were asked to maintain a distance of 620–660 mm between their eyes and the screen. Subjects were not allowed to drink beverages such as alcohol or caffeine that stimulate brain function during the experiment. Eye changes of the subjects were continuously recorded during the experiment.

The experimental procedure was divided into three blocks, each block recognizing one category of targets, with three categories in total: aircraft, ships, and cars, with 800 pictures per block (see in Fig. 2). Before each block, the target to be detected was prompted, and after confirmation by the subject, the experiment began by pressing the space bar. At the start of the experiment, a red cross was displayed, which disappeared after 500 ms, followed by automatic presentation of 800 remote sensing images. Each time a target image appeared randomly in the center of the screen, the subject was required to press the "q" key if the target was present in the current round, or the "p" key if it was absent. There was no time pressure during the experiment, and the next picture was shown only after the subject pressed a key. The experiment lasted approximately 45 min for each subject.

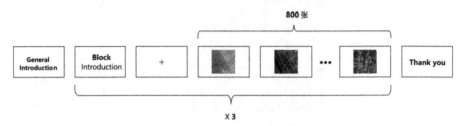

Fig. 2. Experimental flow chart: Decision-making part.

Eye movement data was collected using a camera, and the system used Dlib face recognition and OpenCV image processing technologies to locate the subject's face position information and facial feature position information. Then the EAR algorithm was used to determine the degree of eye opening of the subject, with a threshold set at 0.2, and eye movement data of each subject was recorded during the experiment. The system detection effect is shown in Fig. 3:

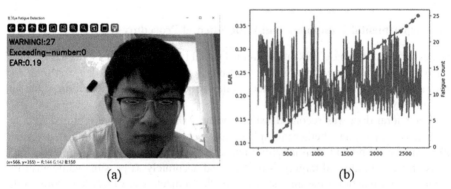

Fig. 3. EAR system detection effect figure. (a) Eye fatigue detection. (b) Relationship fatigue count and task duration.

3   Results

3.1   Behavioral Data

Following the onset of mental fatigue, specific psychological and cognitive functions may undergo disparate degrees of deterioration, often manifested as a decline in accuracy and reaction capacity. Reaction time (RT), being an operable measure, has emerged as a common tool for evaluating mental fatigue. RT is defined as the duration between the onset of a stimulus and the organism's corresponding response, classified as simple or choice reaction time depending on the number of stimuli and responses involved. Research suggests that when mental fatigue sets in, a shift occurs in human cognitive abilities, leading to an extended cognitive reaction time and a reduced level of accuracy, irrespective of whether it pertains to simple or choice reaction time. This reduction in accuracy may be accompanied by an increase in error rates while reacting [15].

Table 2 shows the decision accuracy of the participants at different levels of target types. The calculation method for accuracy is the number of correctly answered interfaces divided by the total number of interfaces at the same level of the target type. The "Type" column represents the target objects that need to be recognized from the three target images listed in Table 1. The "Number" column represents the number of images that have been identified at the current stage. The "All" column represents the average accuracy for all participants at the current level.

Table 2. Correct rate.

Type	Number	All
Aircraft	400	0.937
	800	0.936
Ship	1200	0.898
	1600	0.909
Car	2000	0.905
	2400	0.899

Table 3 shows the decision time of the participants at different levels of target types. The unit of time is milliseconds. The decision time calculation starts from the moment the image is presented on the screen until the keyboard button is pressed to end it. The "Type" column represents the target objects that need to be recognized from the three target images listed in Table 1. The "Number" column represents the number of images that have been identified at the current stage. The "All" column represents the average decision time for all participants at the current level.

Decision efficiency is defined as the ratio of correct rate to decision-making time. As a comprehensive indicator of decision making, the higher the decision efficiency, the better the quality of decision-making. The decision efficiency is calculated by dividing the values in Table 2 by the corresponding values in Table 3, and the data is represented

Table 3. Decision-making time (ms).

Type	Number	All
Aircraft	400	928.288
	800	791.307
Ship	1200	893.470
	1600	905.521
Car	2000	998.254
	2400	981.366

by a line graph as shown in Fig. 4. From the graph, it can be seen that the decision efficiency initially starts to rise, reaching its maximum when there are 800 images, and then gradually decreases.

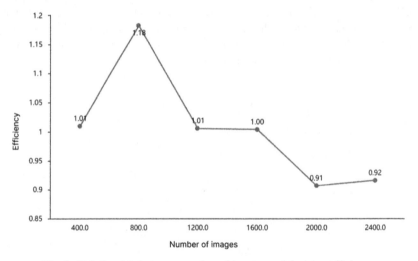

Fig. 4. Relationship between number of images and decision efficiency.

The performance level of the subjects can be reflected by the relationship between the total time the subjects spend identifying images and the average time it takes to identify each image. As shown in Fig. 5, at the beginning of the task, the subjects may not understand the cognitive strategy required for the task and may spend more time understanding the task requirements and finding suitable strategies. Therefore, the performance of the subjects may be relatively poor in the initial few tasks, and the data may be more scattered, but gradually stabilize afterwards. From the figure, it can be seen that the recognition speed of the subjects is fast at first and then slows down during the identification process.

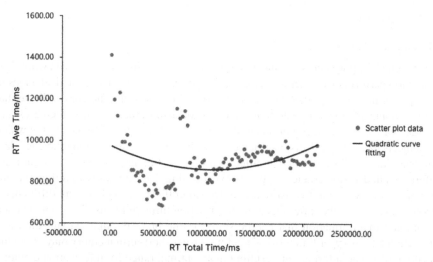

Fig. 5. Relationship between recognition time per image and total task duration.

3.2   Eye Movement Data

The Eye Aspect Ratio (EAR) is a metric calculated using Eq. (1) to assess the fatigue state of participants in a video. Specifically, we measure the absolute difference between the aspect ratio of each frame's eyes and that of the previous frame, and use a threshold to determine whether the participant is experiencing eye fatigue. As depicted in Fig. 6, which indicates an increasing frequency of eye fatigue as task completion time lengthens.

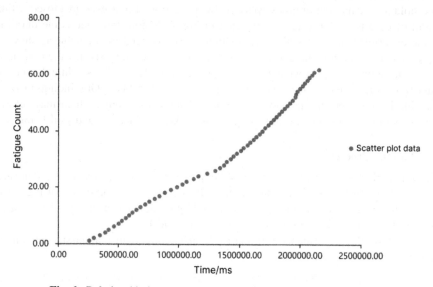

Fig. 6. Relationship between number of fatigue and total task duration.

4   Discussion

4.1   Decision Efficiency

When mental fatigue occurs, the most important manifestation is a decrease in work ability and job performance. Therefore, mental fatigue can be evaluated through changes in work performance. As shown in Fig. 4, the results of decision efficiency indicate that as the amount of image recognition increases, decision efficiency first increases and then decreases. Human recognition ability exists within an optimal range, within which the subjects have higher decision efficiency. Further analysis of decision efficiency data using variance analysis shows that different numbers of images do not show significant differences in decision efficiency ($p > 0.05$), meaning that samples with different numbers of images all exhibit consistency in decision efficiency, without any differences. Studies have shown that after receiving information through the user's visual channel, the amount of information that can be stored in the brain through classification and integration has an upper limit [16]. Therefore, visual short-term memory may affect the reception of visual information, resulting in an optimal range for information quantity. The optimal range of information quantity may be related to the upper and lower limits of the amount of information people receive.

4.2   Decision Load

Fatigue is a complex physiological manifestation of reduced bodily function, which can result from prolonged engagement in the same, overloaded work. Extensive test data have shown that the level of fatigue experienced by subjects can be accurately and effectively reflected through physiological indicators. For this study, we selected EAR as the characteristic parameter for eye fatigue and obtained relevant data by setting the threshold for the number of times eyes close and duration of time eyes are closed within a unit of time to 0.2. The results depicted in Fig. 6 demonstrate that as the duration of the experiment increases, the level of fatigue experienced by the subjects shows a rapid increase. Notably, the density of the scatter plot data suggests that the first stage of fatigue begins to appear when the experiment reaches 1299292 ms, while the second stage of fatigue appears when the experiment reaches 1957528 ms. Our findings provide valuable insights into the physiological underpinnings of fatigue, which may inform strategies for mitigating its negative impact on worker productivity and well-being.

4.3   Fatigue Prediction

Curvilinear regression refers to the method of performing a regression analysis on variables with a non-linear relationship. Using SPSS software, a curve (see in Fig. 5) is fitted to the change in recognition time required by participants as the number of tasks increased, and the basic parameters are shown in Table 4.

Therefore, the performance formula for humans to recognize a massive amount of images can be obtained as follows:

$$RT\ Total = 44544.220 + 812.375 * SubTrial + 0.030 * SubTrial^2 \qquad (2)$$

where RT Total is the recognition time required by participants to complete the task, and SubTrial is the amount of image recognition.

Table 4. Experiment interfaces.

R^2	Adjusted R^2	S.E	AIC
0.032	0.031	193.769	32093.914

5 Conclusions

(1) From the statistical data of reaction time, it can be seen that the reaction time of the participants recognizing a single image increases with time. (2) This system employs machine vision methods to avoid direct physical contact with the subjects, eliminate interference from environmental light sources, improve the applicability of the device environment, and meet monitoring requirements. (3) As the level of fatigue deepens, the participants are unable to concentrate, have a low level of awareness, feel drowsy, and their recognition performance gradually decreases. However, as the identification performance gradually decreases to a certain level of fatigue, the subjects exhibit a phenomenon of resistance to fatigue and will blink rapidly to keep themselves alert. (4) From the experimental results, it can be seen that when the target recognition task exceeds the threshold of human visual ability, the use of computer recognition operations can obviously improve work efficiency, reflecting the maximization of division of labor and collaboration between humans and machines.

Calculating human fatigue and time performance in human-machine collaboration can help us better understand human cognitive load and behavioral performance in human-machine interaction processes. This paper aims to study the relationship between the level of fatigue and time performance of the human eye when recognizing massive images, and lays the foundation for evaluating the fatigue status of human eye recognition tasks by fitting the equation of the time performance curve. Research on the fatigue ability of human eye recognition of massive images will become an important reference standard for guiding user visual target cognitive processing. The data analysis and conclusions of this paper can provide a new and valuable efficiency guide for the field of human-machine collaboration, and evaluate and implement early warning on the human eye fatigue status of various key technical personnel (such as pilots, submarine crew, drivers, etc.), effectively improving operation efficiency in the human-machine collaboration process, which is of great practical significance for reducing accidents caused by human eye fatigue.

Acknowledgement. This work was supported jointly by National Natural Science Foundation of China (No. 72271053, 71871056) Joint fund. And I would like to express my sincere gratitude to the volunteers who participated in the data collection experiment.

References

1. Qu, Y.: Application of the computer vision technology in the image feature extraction. In: Xu, Z., Choo, K.-K.R., Dehghantanha, A., Parizi, R., Hammoudeh, M. (eds.) CSIA 2019. AISC, vol. 928, pp. 351–356. Springer, Cham (2020). https://doi.org/10.1007/978-3-030-15235-2_53

2. Zhang, D., Cheng, W., Yang, H.: Evaluation of workload, arousal, fatigue, and attention on time-series vigilance task. In: Long, S., Dhillon, B.S. (eds.) MMESE 2018. LNEE, vol. 527, pp. 65–69. Springer, Singapore (2019). https://doi.org/10.1007/978-981-13-2481-9_9

3. Svensson, U.: Blink behaviour based drowsiness detection: method development and validation. Statens väg-och transportforskningsinstitut (2004)

4. Papadelis, C., Kourtidou-Papadeli, C., Bamidis, P.D., et al.: Indicators of sleepiness in an ambulatory EEG study of night driving. In: 2006 International Conference of the IEEE Engineering in Medicine and Biology Society, pp. 6201–6204. IEEE (2006). https://doi.org/10.1109/IEMBS.2006.259614

5. Jap, B.T., Lal, S., Fischer, P.: Comparing combinations of EEG activity in train drivers during monotonous driving. Expert Syst. Appl. 38(1), 996–1003 (2011). https://doi.org/10.1016/j.eswa.2010.07.109

6. Fountas, G., Pantangi, S.S., Hulme, K.F., et al.: The effects of driver fatigue, gender, and distracted driving on perceived and observed aggressive driving behavior: a correlated grouped random parameters bivariate probit approach. Anal. Methods Accid. Res. 22, 100091 (2019). https://doi.org/10.1016/j.amar.2019.100091

7. Alkinani, M.H., Khan, W.Z., Arshad, Q.: Detecting human driver inattentive and aggressive driving behavior using deep learning: Recent advances, requirements and open challenges. IEEE Access 8, 105008–105030 (2020). https://doi.org/10.1109/ACCESS.2020.2999829

8. Li, J., Li, H., Umer, W., et al.: Identification and classification of construction equipment operators' mental fatigue using wearable eye-tracking technology. Autom. Constr. 109, 103000 (2020). https://doi.org/10.1016/j.autcon.2019.103000

9. Kim, T., Lee, E.C.: Experimental verification of objective visual fatigue measurement based on accurate pupil detection of infrared eye image and multi-feature analysis. Sensors 20(17), 4814 (2020). https://doi.org/10.3390/s20174814

10. Li, X., Hong, L., Wang, J.C., Liu, X.: Fatigue driving detection model based on multi-feature fusion and semi-supervised active learning. IET Intell. Transp. Syst. 13(9), 1401–1409 (2019). https://doi.org/10.1049/iet-its.2018.5590

11. Chen, X., Sun, Y., Miao, P., et al.: Deep belief network face recognition algorithm based on multi-level texture features. Comput. Appl. Softw 37, 156–163 (2020)

12. Jo, J., Lee, S.J., Park, K.R., et al.: Detecting driver drowsiness using feature-level fusion and user-specific classification. Expert Syst. Appl. 41(4), 1139–1152 (2014). https://doi.org/10.1016/j.eswa.2013.07.108

13. Lin, H.J., Chou, L.W., Chang, K.M., et al.: Visual fatigue estimation by eye tracker with regression analysis. J. Sens. 2022, 1–7 (2022). https://doi.org/10.1155/2022/7642777

14. Sun, X., Wang, P., Yan, Z., et al.: FAIR1M: a benchmark dataset for fine-grained object recognition in high-resolution remote sensing imagery. ISPRS J. Photogrammetry Remote Sens. 184, 116–130 (FEB 2022). https://doi.org/10.1016/j.isprsjprs.2021.12.004

15. Lim, J., Dinges, D.F.: A meta-analysis of the impact of short-term sleep deprivation on cognitive variables. Psychol. Bull. 136(3), 375 (2010). https://doi.org/10.1155/2022/7642777

16. Sörensen, L.K., Boht'e, S.M., Slagter, H.A., et al.: Arousal state affects perceptual decision-making by modulating hierarchical sensory processing in a large-scale visual system model. PLoS Comput. Biol. 18(4), e1009976 (2022). https://doi.org/10.1371/journal.pcbi.1009976

Survey and Analysis on Experience Satisfaction of Remote ATC Tower System User in China

Tingting Lu[1], Zhixuan An[1(✉)], Romano Pagliari[2], Haiming Shen[1], Zheng Yang[3], and Yiyang Zhang[4]

[1] Air Traffic Management College, Civil Aviation University of China, Tianjin 300300, China
14747405753@163.com
[2] Centre for Air Transport Management, Martell House, Cranfield University, Bedfordshire MK43 0TR, UK
[3] Zhejiang General Aviation Industry Development Co., Ltd., Hangzhou 311612, China
[4] College of Arts & Sciences, Embry-Riddle Aeronautical University, Daytona Beach, FL 32114, USA

Abstract. Recently, the application of remote ATC tower technology has solved many problems in the development of civil aviation, such as the blind field of vision in the apron control of large airports, the high operating cost of small and medium-sized transport airports, general airports and helicopter take-off and landing points and brain drain and so on. Therefore, the remote ATC tower system has received more and more attention and has been promoted in more scenarios. The use of remote ATC tower system is a typical process of human-computer interaction, and human-computer interaction is the basis of the study of human factor ergonomics. This paper mainly studies the human factor ergonomics from the perspective of user experience satisfaction. It studies the user experience satisfaction of remote ATC tower system from four dimensions of work efficiency and safety, remote ATC tower system availability, management procedures and environment. It designs the corresponding questionnaire and investigates a total of 95 remote ATC tower controllers in China. After that, SPSS software was used to analyze the questionnaire results. According to the multi-dimensional analysis results, relevant suggestions are put forward for the technology improvement of remote ATC tower system and controller training. The results of this paper not only fill the gaps of research and data in the field of human factor ergonomics of remote ATC tower system in China, but provide an important basis for the improvement and improvement of remote ATC tower system technology.

Keywords: Remote ATC tower · User satisfaction · Questionnaire survey

1 Introduction

Remote ATC tower using the mode of "remote + digital" instead of the traditional "scene + visual" provides airport air traffic control services including approach guidance, scene monitoring, release management and so on. The remote ATC tower technology has solved a lot of problems in the development of civil aviation, such as the blind field of vision in

© The Author(s), under exclusive license to Springer Nature Switzerland AG 2023
M. Kurosu et al. (Eds.): HCII 2023, LNCS 14054, pp. 389–407, 2023.
https://doi.org/10.1007/978-3-031-48038-6_25

the apron control of large airports, the high operating cost of small and medium-sized transport airports, general airports and helicopter landing points and the brain drain, some airport tower control emergency backup and so on. Therefore, the remote ATC tower technology has been paid more and more attention and applied in the world.

At present, the research on remote ATC tower mainly focuses on three aspects, namely operation mode and function introduction, simulation and technology realization, and human factor ergonomics research [1]. In 2010, Papenfuss et al. simulated and evaluated the efficiency of remote ATC tower control at low-density airports by combining eye movement data and questionnaire data [2]. In 2011, Moehlenbrink and other scholars took a controller as the research object and asked the controller to carry out control services in different airports and tested and verified the level of visual perception in two situations [3]. In 2016, Furstenau designed and tested a set of remote ATC tower visual test indicators to test the controller's visual perception level in different situations [4]. In 2019, Arico and other scholars used EEG as a measurement index to measure workload changes under different remote control conditions [5]. In the same year, Liu Jin mainly studied the basic meaning of augmented reality technology and remote tower control, the technical composition of remote ATC tower and the effective application of augmented reality technology in remote ATC tower control, and came to the conclusion that the effective application of augmented reality technology can expand the functional surface and improve the quality of ground tower control system [6]. In 2021, Cheng Qing and other scholars adopted the gradient watershed image segmentation algorithm to optimize the image of airport surveillance video from the two dimensions of operation time and accuracy [7]. In the same year, Liu Yawei and other scholars studied the influence of visual and auditory dual-channel prominence on controllers' situational awareness, providing scientific support for improving the human-computer interaction level of remote virtual tower [1]. In 2022, Xu Bin and other scholars used FMECA reliability analysis method to study the safety and reliability of the remote ATC tower system. Taking the remote ATC tower system configuration guide implemented by Xinjiang Airport in China as an example, they established the functional and mission reliability block diagram, and proposed measures to improve reliability through analysis and verification [8].

In conclusion, the research on remote ATC tower in China mainly focuses on the optimization and simulation of technical systems, lacking research on human factors efficiency indicators [9], and research results on user experience satisfaction of remote ATC tower systems are rare. The research of system user experience satisfaction can directly reflect the effect of human-computer interaction, directly affect the improvement and improvement of remote ATC tower system technology, and is also the premise and basis of human factor ergonomics research. Secondly, China is in the critical stage of the start of remote ATC tower technology different pilot scenarios have been used, and there will be more application requirements in the later stage. The study of system user experience satisfaction is the safety basis to ensure the wide application of this technology. Moreover, the standards for providing remote ATC tower technology in China are not unified at present, and there is a lack of relevant human factors ergonomics research and data. This paper is the first time in China to conduct a system satisfaction survey for all remote ATC tower controllers in China using unified standards and data analysis methods, which is of great significance for the research and development and standard formulation of this technology in China.

Common methods for investigating user experience satisfaction include multi-class ordinal Logit regression model, analytic hierarchy process (AHP) to construct satisfaction evaluation model, questionnaire survey method, Rodski user satisfaction survey method, LibQUAL + TM survey method, Kano model and its method, ICSI-L model and other methods. Among them, the questionnaire survey method can objectively reflect the social reality, save time, manpower and costs, and the survey results are easy to quantify and facilitate data processing and analysis [9, 10]. This paper is based on the SHELL model, which is a tool to analyze the interaction between other elements of the system and people with human factors as the core [11]. At the same time, combined with the research experience of domestic and foreign research on system usage satisfaction, The questionnaire was designed from the four dimensions of work efficiency and safety, remote ATC tower system availability, management procedures and environment. Then, by using SPSS (Statistical Product and Service Solutions) 28.0.1.1 software, the collection, sorting, analysis, inference and statistics of a large number of data can be effectively processed.

2 Method

2.1 Participants

Currently, China's remote ATC tower system is used in six airports (three application scenarios), including China's Harbin Taiping International Airport, Guangzhou Baiyun International Airport, Guiyang Longdongbao International Airport, Xinjiang Narati Airport, Yunnan Lugu Lake Airport and Jiande General Aviation Airport. Among them, Harbin Taiping International Airport, Guangzhou Baiyun International Airport and Guiyang Longdongbao International Airport all provide apron control services; Xinjiang Narati Airport and Yunnan Luguhu Airport mainly provide remote ATC tower command for remote airports with small flight capacity. Jiande General Aviation Airport mainly provides remote ATC tower command services for general airports and heliports with small flight capacity. The participants of this paper are 95 remote ATC tower controllers from all the above-mentioned airports. A total of 95 questionnaires have been issued, 95 questionnaires have been returned, and 95 valid papers have been returned. The effective rate of questionnaires is 100%. The results of questionnaire survey show that the age of remote ATC tower controllers in China is generally distributed between 20 and 40 years old. The reason is that the remote ATC tower system is an emerging technology in China, and every airport tends to select the young backbone when selecting remote ATC tower controllers, because people in this age group have strong ability to accept new things and master new technologies. As stated in the questionnaire, participants are anonymous and have the right to withdraw their data at any time after data collection is complete.

2.2 Data Collection Method

(1) Questionnaire is used to collect data in this paper. The questionnaire starts from four dimensions: work efficiency and safety, remote ATC tower system availability,

management procedures and environment. A total of 39 questions are set, and each question adopts a five-level grading system.

(2) Self-compiled basic information questionnaire: collected demographic data of participants. The content includes 9 parts: age, gender, working scenario, work task, educational background, qualification, work schedule type, in addition to the remote ATC tower system, Whether the unit still retains the traditional tower mode and can be used as backup at any time to replace the remote ATC tower system to ensure operation, and whether the remote ATC tower system of the unit not only guarantees the control services of the airport, but also provides the support services of other airports and landing points.

(3) The remote ATC tower system user experience satisfaction questionnaire is selected as the test tool and its reliability and validity are tested. Reliability analysis and validity analysis aim to measure the consistency of hypothesis variables in the questionnaire in order to determine whether the scale has stability and reliability [12]. Reliability analysis can be divided into four categories: α reliability coefficient, broken half reliability, duplicate reliability and retest reliability. This paper mainly uses α reliability coefficient for reliability analysis. The reliability analysis results of the questionnaire are shown in Table 1. Cronbach's Alpha coefficients of each dimension and the overall questionnaire are 0.854, 0.889, 0.806, 0.895 and 0.937, respectively. Therefore, it can be concluded that the reliability of each dimension of the questionnaire is good and the overall internal consistency of the questionnaire is very high. Therefore, the questionnaire has certain use value.

Table 1. Results of questionnaire reliability analysis

Dimension	Cronbach's Alpha	Number of terms
Work efficiency and safety	0.854	3
Remote ATC tower system availability	0.889	20
Management procedures	0.806	8
Environment	0.895	8
Overall questionnaire	0.937	39

2.3 Data Processing Method

The data are input into Excel, and SPSS 28.0.1.1 software is used for statistical analysis. t test is used to compare the difference of measurement data between the two groups, and analysis of variance is used to compare the difference of measurement data between the two groups and above, and the results is expressed as mean ± standard deviation ($\bar{x} \pm s$). Test level: $\alpha = 0.05$. $P < 0.05$ is considered statistically significant.

3   Results and Discussion

3.1   Characteristic Analysis of Survey Data

A total of 95 remote ATC tower controllers in China are selected as participants. Gender distribution: 82 male controllers and 13 female controllers; Age distribution: 64 people between 20 and 30 years old, 31 people between 30 and 40 years old; Distribution of work scenarios: There are 2 controllers in military-civilian airports, 43 controllers in civil airports, 14 controllers in general airports, and 36 controllers in partial apron control. Task distribution: There are 23 air traffic controllers within the landing routes, and 72 ground traffic controllers in the airport mobile area. Education distribution: 90 people with bachelor's degree, 5 people with master's degree; Qualification distribution: 13 trainee controllers, 44 newly released controllers (working for 3–5 years), 21 mature controllers (working for more than 5 years), 17 control instructors (the old controllers who have supervised trainee controllers); Scheduling: 4 people in administrative class, 47 people in four-shift system, 44 people in business class. In addition, 81 employees in the work unit still retain the traditional tower mode and can be used as backup at any time to replace the remote ATC tower system to ensure operation. The remote ATC tower system in the work unit of 34 employees not only guarantees the control service of the airport, but also provides the security service of other airports and landing points.

3.2   User Experience Satisfaction Analysis of Remote ATC Tower in China

Table 2. Mean scores of each dimension($\bar{x} \pm$ s)

Dimension	N	$\bar{x} \pm$ s
Work efficiency and safety	95	7.36 ± 2.49
Remote ATC tower system availability		51.28 ± 9.33
Management procedures		17.47 ± 4.33
Environment		20.04 ± 5.50
Total score		96.16 ± 17.98

Table 2 shows that the mean scores of 95 remote ATC tower controllers in each dimension are 7.36, 51.28, 17.47, 20.04 and 96.16, respectively.

3.3   Difference Analysis

Analysis Results of Differences in Efficacy Evaluation Scores of Remote ATC Tower Controllers with Different Ages

According to the data in Table 3, there is no significant difference in the overall mean scores of all dimensions of remote ATC tower controllers of different ages($P > 0.05$).

According to the comparison results of the mean values in Fig. 1, it can be seen that the mean scores of remote ATC tower controllers aged 30–40 are higher than those of remote ATC tower controllers aged 20–30 in all dimensions.

Table 3. Analysis results of differences in efficacy evaluation scores of remote ATC tower controllers with different ages($\bar{x} \pm s$)

Dimension	Age	$\bar{x} \pm s$	T	Sig.(two-tailed)
Work efficiency and safety	1	7.17 ± 2.00	−1.048	0.298
	2	7.74 ± 3.29		
Remote ATC tower system availability	1	50.19 ± 8.99	−1.662	0.100
	2	53.55 ± 9.74		
Management procedures	1	17.27 ± 4.33	−0.671	0.504
	2	17.9 ± 4.38		
Environment	1	19.42 ± 5.51	−1.593	0.115
	2	21.32 ± 5.32		
Total score	1	94.05 ± 17.52	−1.660	0.100
	2	100.52 ± 18.40		

Note: "1" indicates controllers aged 20–30; "2" indicates controllers aged 30–40

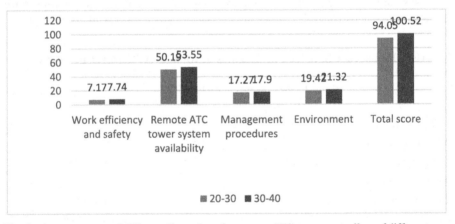

Fig. 1. Average scores of different dimensions for remote ATC tower controllers of different ages

Analysis Results of Differences in Efficacy Evaluation Scores of Remote ATC Tower Controllers with Different Genders

According to the data in Table 4, there is no significant difference in the overall mean scores of all dimensions of remote ATC tower controllers of different genders ($P > 0.05$).

According to the comparison results of the mean values in Fig. 2, it can be seen that the mean values of males are higher than those of females in terms of work efficiency and safety, while the mean values of males are lower than those of females in terms of remote ATC tower system availability, management procedures, environment and total scores.

Table 4. Analysis results of differences in efficacy evaluation scores of remote ATC tower controllers with different genders($\bar{x} \pm$ s)

Dimension	Gender	($\bar{x} \pm$ s)	T	Sig.(two-tailed)
Work efficiency and safety	1	7.4 ± 2.60	0.436	0.664
	2	7.08 ± 1.71		
Remote ATC tower system availability	1	50.71 ± 9.53	−1.525	0.131
	2	54.92 ± 7.22		
Management procedures	1	17.21 ± 4.27	−1.516	0.133
	2	19.15 ± 4.51		
Environment	1	19.67 ± 5.48	−1.670	0.098
	2	22.38 ± 5.22		
Total score	1	94.99 ± 18.06	−1.607	0.112
	2	103.54 ± 16.15		

Note: "1" means male; "2" means female

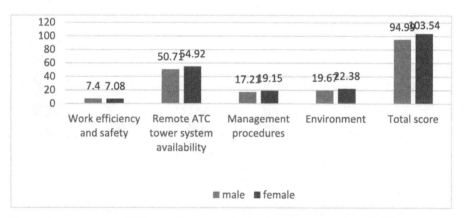

Fig. 2. Average scores of different dimensions for remote tower controllers of different genders

Analysis Results of Differences in Efficacy Evaluation Scores of Remote ATC Tower Controllers with Different Work Tasks

According to the data in Table 5, there are significant differences in the overall mean scores of remote ATC tower controllers with different work tasks in terms of management procedures and environment($P < 0.05$); However, there is no significant difference in work efficiency and safety, remote ATC tower system availability and total score($P > 0.05$).

According to the comparison results of the mean values in Fig. 3, it can be seen that in terms of work efficiency and safety, the mean scores of ground traffic controllers in the

Table 5. Analysis results of differences in efficacy evaluation scores of remote ATC tower controllers with different work tasks($\bar{x} \pm s$)

Dimension	Work task	($\bar{x} \pm s$)	T	Sig.(two-tailed)
Work efficiency and safety	1	7.52 ± 3.50	0.361	0.719
	2	7.31 ± 2.09		
Remote ATC tower system availability	1	51.26 ± 10.60	−0.014	0.989
	2	51.29 ± 8.96		
Management procedures	1	15.13 ± 2.94	−3.115	0.002
	2	18.22 ± 4.45		
Environment	1	17.48 ± 4.33	−2.651	0.009
	2	20.86 ± 5.60		
Total score	1	91.39 ± 18.78	−1.470	0.145
	2	97.68 ± 17.58		

Note: "1" indicates the air traffic controller within the landing route; "2" indicates the ground traffic controller in the airport mobility area

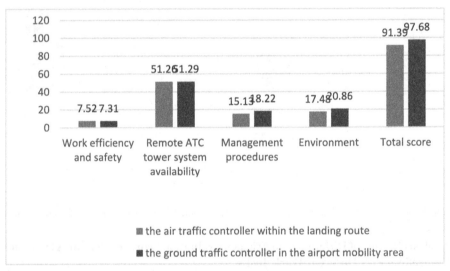

Fig. 3. Average scores of different dimensions for remote ATC tower controllers with different work tasks

airport mobility area are lower than those of air traffic controllers within landing routes; However, in terms of remote ATC tower system availability, management procedures, environment and total scores, the mean score of ground traffic controllers in the airport mobility area is greater than that of air traffic controllers within landing routes.

Analysis Results of Differences in Efficacy Evaluation Scores of Remote ATC Tower Controllers with Educational Backgrounds

According to the data in Table 6, there is no significant difference in the overall average scores of all dimensions of remote ATC tower controllers with different educational backgrounds ($P > 0.05$).

Table 6. Analysis results of differences in efficacy evaluation scores of remote ATC tower controllers with educational backgrounds ($\bar{x} \pm s$)

Dimension	Educational background	($\bar{x} \pm s$)	T	Sig.(two-tailed)
Work efficiency and safety	2	7.39 ± 2.52	0.513	0.609
	3	6.80 ± 1.92		
Remote ATC tower system availability	2	51.37 ± 9.47	0.364	0.717
	3	49.8 ± 6.76		
Management procedures	2	17.43 ± 4.29	-0.383	0.702
	3	18.2 ± 5.63		
Environment	2	20.3 ± 5.51	1.970	0.052
	3	15.4 ± 2.51		
Total score	2	96.49 ± 18.09	0.760	0.449
	3	90.20 ± 16.33		

Note: "2" indicates bachelor's degree; "3" indicates master's degree

According to the comparison results of the mean values in Fig. 4, it can be seen that the mean scores of remote ATC tower controllers with bachelor's degree are higher than those of remote ATC tower controllers with master's degree in terms of work efficiency and safety, remote ATC tower system availability, environment and total scores. In terms of management procedures, the mean score of remote ATC tower controllers with bachelor's degree is lower than that of remote tower controllers with master's degree.

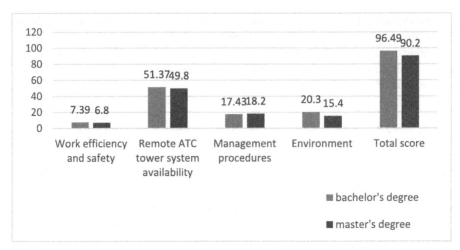

Fig. 4. Average scores of different dimensions of remote ATC tower controllers with different educational backgrounds

The Difference Analysis Results of Remote ATC Tower Controller's Scores on Remote Tower Personnel Evaluation Based on Efficacy Under the Condition that the Unit Retains or Does not Retain the Traditional Tower Mode

According to the data in Table 7, there are significant differences between the work efficiency and safety of remote ATC tower controllers, the availability of remote tower systems, the environment and the overall mean scores of total scores when the traditional tower mode is retained or not($P < 0.05$); There was no significant difference in the management procedures($P > 0.05$).

Table 7. The difference analysis results of remote ATC tower controller's scores on remote tower personnel evaluation based on efficacy under the condition that the unit retains or does not retain the traditional tower mode ($\bar{x} \pm s$)

Dimension	Whether to retain the traditional tower mode	($\bar{x} \pm s$)	T	Sig.(two-tailed)
Work efficiency and safety	1	7.10 ± 2.37	-2.510	0.014
	2	8.86 ± 2.71		
Remote ATC tower system availability	1	50.22 ± 9.27	-2.762	0.007
	2	57.43 ± 7.26		
Management procedures	1	17.16 ± 4.31	-1.712	0.090
	2	19.29 ± 4.12		
Environment	1	19.27 ± 5.19	-3.475	0.001
	2	24.5 ± 5.24		
Total score	1	93.75 ± 17.42	-3.297	0.001
	2	110.07 ± 15.02		

Note: "1" indicates yes; "2" indicates no

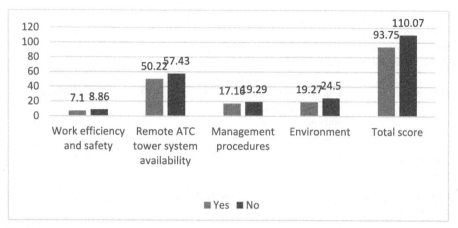

Fig. 5. Average scores of various dimensions of remote ATC tower controllers in the case of whether the traditional tower mode is retained

According to the comparison results of the mean values in Fig. 5, it can be seen that in all dimensions, the mean scores of remote ATC tower controllers in the case that the traditional tower mode is not retained in the unit are greater than those in the case that the traditional tower mode is retained.

Difference Analysis Results of Remote ATC Tower Controller's Assessment Scores of Remote Tower Personnel Based on Efficacy Under the Condition that the Remote ATC Tower System of the Unit not Only Guarantees the Control Service of the Airport but also Provides the Support Service of Other Airports and Landing Points
According to the data in Table 8, there is no significant difference in the overall average scores of all dimensions of the remote ATC tower controller in the case that the remote ATC tower system of the unit guarantees the provision of control services of the airport or does not provide the support services of other airports and landing points($P > 0.05$).

According to the comparison results of the mean values in Fig. 6, it can be seen that in terms of management procedures, environment and total scores, the mean scores of remote ATC tower controllers in the case that our company does not provide support services of other airports and landing points are higher than that of remote ATC tower controllers in the case that our company provides support services of other airports and landing points. In terms of work efficiency and safety as well as the availability of remote ATC tower system, the mean score of remote ATC tower controllers is lower than that of remote ATC tower controllers when the unit does not provide support services of other airports and landing points.

Table 8. Difference analysis results of remote ATC tower controller's assessment scores of remote tower personnel based on efficacy under the condition that the remote ATC tower system of the unit not only guarantees the control service of the airport but also provides the support service of other airports and landing points($\bar{x} \pm s$)

Dimension	Whether to provide security services for other airports and landing points	($\bar{x} \pm s$)	T	Sig.(two-tailed)
Work efficiency and safety	1	7.94 ± 3.13	1.724	0.088
	2	7.03 ± 2.00		
Remote ATC tower system availability	1	51.41 ± 11.30	0.099	0.921
	2	51.21 ± 8.13		
Management procedures	1	16.91 ± 4.26	−0.943	0.348
	2	17.79 ± 4.38		
Environment	1	19.65 ± 5.26	−0.521	0.604
	2	20.26 ± 5.66		
Total score	1	95.91 ± 20.31	−0.099	0.921
	2	96.30 ± 16.72		

Note: "1" indicates yes; "2" indicates no

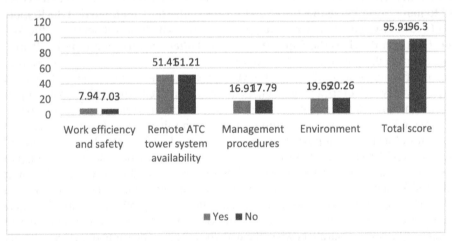

Fig. 6. Average scores of the remote ATC tower controller in each dimension when the remote ATC tower system of the unit not only guarantees the control services of the airport but also provides the support services of other airports and landing points

Analysis Results of Differences in Efficacy Evaluation Scores of Remote ATC Tower Controllers with Different Working Scenarios, Qualifications and Scheduling Types

According to the data in Table 9, there are no significant differences in the overall mean scores of remote ATC tower controllers in work efficiency and safety, remote ATC tower system availability, management procedures, environment and total scores under different working scenarios ($P > 0.05$). There are no significant differences in the overall mean scores of remote ATC tower controllers with different qualifications in work efficiency and safety, remote ATC tower system availability, management procedures, environment and total scores ($P > 0.05$). There are significant differences in the overall mean scores of remote ATC tower controllers working in different scheduling types in terms of management procedures ($P < 0.05$), but there are no significant differences in the overall mean scores in terms of work efficiency and safety, remote ATC tower system availability, environment and total scores ($P > 0.05$).

Table 9. Analysis results of differences in efficacy evaluation scores of remote ATC tower controllers with different working scenarios, qualifications and scheduling types

Dimension	Working scenarios		Qualifications		Scheduling types	
	F	significance	F	significance	F	significance
Work efficiency and safety	2.059	0.111	2.628	0.055	1.512	0.226
Remote ATC tower system availability	2.407	0.072	1.419	0.242	0.844	0.433
Management procedures	0.893	0.448	0.511	0.676	5.725	0.005
Environment	1.239	0.300	2.566	0.059	0.310	0.734
Total score	1.448	0.234	2.086	0.108	1.026	0.363

According to the comparison results of the mean values in Fig. 7, it can be seen that the mean scores of remote ATC tower controllers working in some apron control scenarios in terms of management procedures and environment are higher than those of remote ATC tower controllers working in other scenarios. The average scores of remote ATC tower controllers working in general airport scenarios in terms of work efficiency and safety, remote ATC tower system availability and total scores are higher than those of remote ATC tower controllers working in other scenarios.

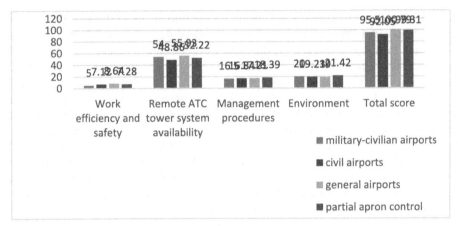

Fig. 7. Average scores of different dimensions of remote ATC tower controllers under different work scenarios

According to the comparison results of the mean values in Fig. 8, it can be seen that the average scores of newly released remote ATC tower controllers (working 3–5 years) on work efficiency and safety, remote ATC tower system availability and total scores are higher than those of other qualified remote ATC tower controllers; The mean scores of control instructors(the old controllers who have supervised trainee controllers)on management procedures are higher than the mean scores of remote ATC tower controllers with other qualifications; The mean environmental scores of mature remote ATC tower controllers(more than 5 years of experience)are higher than the mean scores of remote ATC tower controllers with other qualifications.

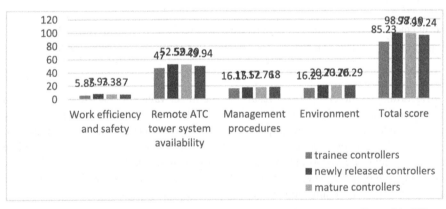

Fig. 8. Average scores of different dimensions of remote ATC tower controllers with different qualifications

According to the comparison results of the mean values in Fig. 9, it can be seen that the mean scores of remote ATC tower controllers with four-shift system are higher than those of remote ATC tower controllers with other work schedule types in terms of management procedures. The mean scores of remote ATC tower controllers with business class are higher than those of remote ATC tower controllers with other work scheduling types in terms of work efficiency and safety, remote ATC tower system availability, environment and total scores.

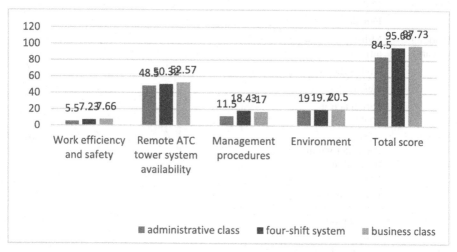

Fig. 9. Average scores of different dimensions for remote ATC tower controllers with different scheduling types

3.4 Satisfaction of Different Types of Remote ATC Tower Controllers in Each Dimension

According to the results in Table 10, relevant remote ATC tower application units should pay attention to the satisfaction of different types of remote ATC tower controllers in various dimensions. For example, focus on the satisfaction of remote ATC tower controllers aged between 20 and 30 years old, under the condition that the unit retains the traditional tower mode, working scenarios in civil airports, trainee, administrative class and four-shift system in terms of work efficiency and safety, remote ATC tower system availability, management procedures and environment, etc. Develop effective measures to improve the remote ATC tower system hardware and software, management and operation procedures and environmental problems, so as to improve the safety and effectiveness of the remote ATC tower system.

Table 10. Satisfaction of Different Types of Remote ATC Tower Controllers in Each Dimension

Dimension		Work efficiency and safety	Remote ATC tower system availability	Management procedures	Environment	Total score
Age	Aged 20–30	✓	✓	✓	✓	✓
	Aged 30–40					
Gender	Male		✓	✓	✓	✓
	Female	✓				
Working scenario	Military-civilian airports	✓		✓	✓	✓
	Civil airports	✓	✓	✓	✓	✓
	General airports			✓	✓	
	Partial apron control	✓				
Work task	Air traffic controller within the landing route		✓	✓	✓	✓
	Ground traffic controller in the airport mobility area	✓				
Educational background	Junior college					
	Bachelor's degree			✓		
	Master's degree	✓	✓		✓	✓
	Others					
Qualification	Trainee controllers	✓	✓	✓	✓	✓
	Newly released controllers					
	Mature controllers					
	Control instructor	✓	✓			✓
Work schedule type	Administrative class	✓	✓	✓	✓	✓
	Four-shift system	✓	✓	✓	✓	✓
	Business class			✓		

(*continued*)

Table 10. (*continued*)

Dimension		Work efficiency and safety	Remote ATC tower system availability	Management procedures	Environment	Total score
Whether to retain the traditional tower mode	Yes	√	√	√	√	√
	No					
Whether to provide security services for other airports and landing points	Yes			√	√	√
	No	√	√			

Note: "√" means that the mean score of a certain type of remote ATC tower controller in a certain dimension is lower than the total mean score, indicating that the satisfaction of this type of controller in this dimension needs to be improved

4 Conclusion

4.1 Research Conclusion

(1) The research results of this paper comprehensively and intuitively reflect the current user satisfaction status of China's remote ATC tower system, and reveal the main factors affecting the user satisfaction of China's remote ATC tower system. After investigation and discussion with remote ATC tower operators, it is concluded that the research results are consistent with the actual operation situation and feeling.

(2) Based on the data analysis of the survey research, China's remote ATC tower technology still has shortcomings and room for improvement in many aspects, such as the number and position of cameras installed in the remote ATC tower system, the capability of monitoring image capture and alarm, the comfort of the control interface and studio, the automatic identification and tracking function of aircraft or objects, the brightness and color of visual images, etc.

(3) In addition to hardware and software systems, human subjective influence can not be ignored. On the basis of the original training of air traffic controllers and based on the research results of this paper, the civil aviation of China should increase the relevant training of remote ATC control controllers. For example, for relatively young remote ATC tower controllers, relevant units should train them on skills related to traditional physical tower and remote ATC tower, so that they can better master the command operating system, so as to improve the user experience satisfaction of the system, so as to improve the level of human-computer interaction, and the safety and efficiency of aviation operation will be correspondingly improved.

4.2 Research Innovation Points

From four dimensions, this paper for the first time conducted a study on the system experience satisfaction of all remote ATC tower users in China. The survey results directly and comprehensively reflect the current experience satisfaction status of remote ATC tower controllers in China, and through in-depth analysis of the data results, the important factors affecting the system experience satisfaction are obtained, so as to put forward suggestions for the improvement of remote ATC tower technology and personnel training in China. In particular, based on the research results of this paper, the data foundation of human factor ergonomics research in China has been established, filling the gap in this field in China, and becoming the basis for the formulation of subsequent relevant standards and relevant research.

4.3 Research Prospect

Because of the advantages of the remote ATC tower system itself, the system has been paid attention to and widely promoted by the aviation industry in the world. In China, in addition to the six airports already using remote ATC tower systems, a number of other airports are currently building remote ATC tower systems. For example, Chengdu Shuangliu Airport and Beijing Daxing International Airport will soon implement remote tower control for part of the apron; Changbaishan Airport equipment has been demonstrated, immediately ready for experimental operation; Fuyun Airport in Xinjiang, Xilinhot Airport in Inner Mongolia, Erenhot Airport, Jinwan Airport in Zhuhai, Yushu Batang Airport, Golmud Airport, Delingha Airport, Huatugou Airport, Guolumachin Airport, Rizhao Shanzihe International Airport in Shandong, Jiuhuashan Airport in Chizhou, Anhui, Shanghai Longhua Airport and other airports are conducting technical demonstration and application. Therefore, in China, with the increasingly prominent safety and efficiency problems of remote ATC tower system, the research on user experience satisfaction and human factor ergonomics of remote ATC tower system will become more and more important. Due to the limitation of time and resources, the research in this paper still has some limitations. For example, the survey method is relatively simple, but with the continuous extensive application of remote ATC tower system in China, and the continuous enrichment of scenarios, cases and data, the authors will continue to follow up the research, further carry out human factor ergonomics assessment, and establish a more systematic and comprehensive evaluation method. It is committed to improving the user experience satisfaction of remote ATC tower system in China and the research level of remote ATC tower system on human factor ergonomics.

Acknowledgements. The authors would like to express special thanks to all the remote ATC tower controllers in China who participated in the questionnaire survey. Their love for their work and serious and responsible attitude have provided valuable suggestions and help for the authors' relevant research.

References

1. Yawei, L.I.U., Guangchun, L.I., Qingmin, S.I., Xinyao, G.U.O.: Influence of visual and auditory dual channel highlighting on situation awareness of remote virtual tower controllers. J. Civil Aviation **5**(3), 45–50 (2021). https://doi.org/10.3969/j.issn.2096-4994.2021.03.009
2. Papenfuss, A., Friedrich, M., Möhlenbrink, C., et al.: Assessing operational validity of remote tower control in high-fidelity tower simulation. IFAC Proc. Vol. **43**(13), 117–122 (2010)
3. Moehlenbrink, C., Papenfuss, A.: ATC-monitoring when one controller operates two airports: research for remote tower centres. In: Proceedings of the Human Factors and Ergonomics Society Annual Meeting, pp. 5576–5580 (2011). https://doi.org/10.1177/1071181311551016
4. Fürstenau, N.: Virtual and Remote Control Tower. Springer International Publishing, Switzerland (2016). https://doi.org/10.1007/978-3-319-28719-5
5. Aricò, P., Reynal, M., Di Flumeri, G., et al.: How neurophysiological measures can be used to enhance the evaluation of remote tower solutions. Front. Hum. Neurosci. **13**, 1–10 (2019)
6. Jin, L.: Application of augmented reality technology in remote tower control. Electron. Test (16), 121–122 (2019). https://doi.org/10.16520/j.cnki.1000-8519.2019.16.054
7. Cheng, Q., Tang, W.-H., Li Y.-D.: Research on remote tower image mosaic technology based on watershed algorithm. Aeronaut. Comput. Tech. **51**(5), 6–9,14 (2021). https://doi.org/10.3969/j.issn.1671-654X
8. Xu, B., Pan, W., Luo, Y., Han, S., Zhong, L.: Failure Mode Effect and Criticality Analysis of Airport Remote Tower System. Ship Electron. Eng. **42**(2), 115–119 (2022). https://doi.org/10.3969/j.issn.1672-9730.2022.02.026
9. Tao, H., Chao, Z.: Remote tower operation evaluation research review. Aerosp. Sci. Technol. **11**, 1 (2022). https://doi.org/10.19452/j.issn1007-5453.2022.11.001
10. Jingjing, Z.: A review of research on questionnaire survey. Heilongjiang Educ. (Theory and Pract.) **10**, 31–32 (2014)
11. Weizhong, Q., Yanfei, T., Xiaofei, W., et al.: Risk identification of intelligent ship at sea test based on SHELL model. Maritime Transp. Manage. **44**(7), 20–22, 33 (2022). https://doi.org/10.3969/j.issn.1000-8799.2022.07.006
12. Delei, L., Xiaojing, W.: The innovative exploration of questionnaire survey method. Res. Pract. Innov. Entrepreneurship **1**(20), 96–98 (2018)

Resilience Strategies of Aviation During COVID-19 – A Bibliographical Review

Chien-Tsung Lu[⊠], Taoran Yin, and Haoruo Fu

School of Aviation and Transportation Technology, Purdue University, 1401 Aviation Driver, West Lafayette, IN 47906, USA

`{ctlu,yin177,fu361}@purdue.edu`

Abstract. The aviation industry has suffered from the COVID-19 pandemic since early 2020. Airlines, airports, and manufacturers reacted to fight against the disease to protect passengers as well as remain sustainable. This study analyzes existing archives and presents plans and strategies implemented by essential actors of the commercial aviation system. Using inductive Meta-Analysis in conjunction with VOSviewer, this study answers three important questions: What were the strategies of resilience enacted by the airline industry during the public health crisis? How did manufacturers remain sustainable during the global pandemic? And What innovations did commercial airports implement to cope with the global pandemic? For airlines, the main strategies include passenger protection, retrenchment, innovation, and long-term management. For manufacturers, the main approaches are expanding business associated with maintenance, repair, and overhaul (MRO) on top of alternative fuel innovations for emission reduction. Finally, airports adopt policies and protocols to screen and protect passengers, share information about infected passengers, and create a contactless airport environment for the prevention and control of pandemic infectious diseases.

Keywords: COVID-19 · MRO · retrenchment · emission reduction · pandemic protocols · VOSviewer

1 Introduction

The aviation industry is one of the most popular modes of international transportation. The United States Federal Aviation Administration (FAA) stated that aerospace and other related industries made up 5.2% of the U.S. gross domestic product (GDP) in 2016 [1]. Based on Bureau of Transportation Statistics (BTS) data, after the COVID-19 pandemic hit at the beginning of 2020, passenger volume dropped to below 400 million passengers, a 62.2% decrease in passenger count and a 68.6% decrease in revenue-passenger-miles (RPM) leading to a net loss of USD$42 billion among US carriers, as of quarter two of the 2021 fiscal year [2, 3]. Despite the exponential increase in air cargo shipping in 2019 during the COVID-19 pandemic outbreak [4], only 4.5 billion passengers traveled on 38.3 million flights traveling around the world [5] regardless of the forecasted flight growth to 10 billion by 2040 [6].

The severe acute respiratory syndrome (SARS) outbreak between 2002 and 2003 resulted in drastic flight reductions. China took aggressive emergency management measures to successfully restore the business scale. The Middle East Respiratory Syndrome (MERS) outbreak between 2012 and 2017 spread to 27 countries, and significantly slowed down the aviation industry [7], where South Korea reported a 12% decline in revenue-passenger-kilometers (RPKs) right after the confirmation of MERS transmission via aircraft [8]. The outbreak of Ebola between 2013 and 2016 infected 28,602 people causing Sierra Leone alone a 13% decline in seat capacity in 2014 [10]. However, these numbers would pale in comparison to the worldwide COVID-19 pandemic [9]. While the aviation industry is gradually recovering from the impact of coronavirus, strategies being successfully developed and deployed shall be known so the aviation industry can learn and prepare for the future public health crisis.

2 Literature Review

2.1 Previous Efforts from the Aviation Industry

The aviation industry is very fragile, as examined by the Ebola and SARS pandemics that struck in the last decade, which sheds light on the criticality of infectious disease prevention programs Joseph Amankwah-Amoah [39] stated how the airlines followed three influential stages in mitigating the evolution of an epidemic into a pandemic, including: 1) recognition stage - disease analysis and policy development; 2) retrenchment stage – reduction of air service to and from high-risk regions, and 3) recovery stage - return to new and normal operations with improved tactics of disease prevention [10].

In tandem, the International Air Transport Association (IATA) (2022) [11], in response to the COVID-19 global health crisis, has created an effective Health Safety Checklist for Air Providers (IHSC) that encapsulates the essential aspects of disease spread prevention. The IHSC suggests systemic approaches for airline operations by providing a new standard of safety protocols and sanitation. The IHSC advocates a communication avenue between passengers and airline from pre-departure to post-arrival, staff training, cleaning, and sanitation process, installation of onboard high-efficiency particulate air (HEPA) filters, embarking and disembarking procedures as well as employee self-awareness working processes [11]. IATA also expresses the adoption of the epic Safety Management System (SMS) to identify health concerns prior to an etiological incident. Following the health SMS (HSMS), IATA suggests a health safety risk management (HSRM) to assess the risk (likelihood and severity) of each hazard imposed by the pandemic [11]. These systems are crucial to identifying failure points in the system for the airline to take advanced action. The robust ideas that HSMS and HSRM bring to the aviation industry yield an effective ability to offer proactive solutions.

Moreover, Suk and Kim [12] give the 2 × 2 matrix describing the varying responses that a health crisis might invoke based upon the dimension of time and the destructive magnitude of the crisis (see Fig. 1).

In the case of COVID-19, many airlines initially moved quadrants from Quadrants I to Quadrants II once the severity of the pandemic starts hitting the industry. Quadrants II is where the industry seeks governmental help when the liquidity of assets is an immense struggle for airlines, airlines receive aid in the form of grants and loans such as the

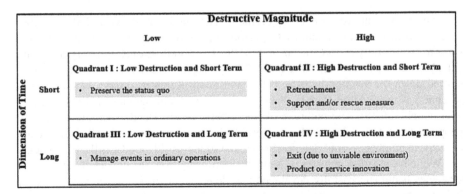

Fig. 1. Quadrants of Risk Matrix.

Coronavirus Aid, Relief, and Economic Security (CARES) Act. Furthermore, airlines begin hunkering down in Quadrant II cutting back on revenue loss such as reducing flights, laying off employees, and other methods. For a longer impact, airlines would move from Quadrant II into Quadrant IV, where airlines consider initiatives to change the business model and continue surviving [12]. Airlines would move from Quadrant IV to Quadrant III maintaining realistic operations while hoping to grow into the new normal [12].

2.2   Challenges and Response of Airports

Airports, serving as the node of daily aviation operations, process passengers and cargo from different countries. As the major country's point of entry for international visitors, airports are undoubtedly the focal point of epidemic prevention. WHO's Article 20 of the International Health Regulation (IHR) indicates airports possess unique characteristics, which require the highest level of sanitation, control, and reporting procedures during pandemics [13]. For instance, Singapore Changi International Airport, Dubai International Airport, and Doha Hamad International Airport, where only international flights, process a large volume of transit traffic would carry significant responsibility to execute epidemic prevention plans. These responsive plans include four intertwined levels: policy, process, technology, and individual levels [14]. For policy and process levels, Changi airport developed the Transit Holding Areas (THA) concept, which requires transit passengers to deboard after arrival and are immediately directed to the transit holding area to avoid cross-contamination. Technological innovations such as no-touch security screening, online check-in system, e-boarding passes, and facial recognition are enacted to interfere with communicable paths [14, 15]. Like the IATA's HSRM, a pandemic threat matrix provides the danger levels of a public health problem as well as corresponding recommendations while the terminal design should have the characteristic of geometrical simplicity and modularity, which allows converting the function of terminal layout for a dynamic emergency demand [16, 17].

2.3   Airports in the Post-public Health Crisis Era

The Airports Council International (ACI) provides a series of experience-based guidelines: operational and managerial recommendations offering new concepts and standards based on the latest technology trend [18]. Abeyratne [19] promulgates systematic general training for airport managers as most do not realize that artificial intelligence (AI) and statistical algorithm can be useful for disease forecast and prevention during a public health crisis. However, the collaborative synergy among airports worldwide regarding information sharing would be imperative while ACI, IATA, and ICAO can be the platform to coordinate the existing data for analysis. During the COVID-19 pandemic, airports are deemed dangerous places due to populated passengers and employees. Establishing safety protocols to ease passengers' fear of aviation is necessary. Some researchers have suggested and enacted safety procedures to create a comfort zone or onboard social distancing against possible infection [19, 20]. The learning curve of rebuilding passengers' confidence in airport safety will take a relatively long time when responding to the COVID-19 pandemic. Even though the development of an ongoing pandemic is unpredictable, archived lessons and experiences would be useful for data analysis and proactive controls.

2.4   Aviation Manufacturers Survivability

During the downturn in the aviation industry in the aftermath of the 2001 terrorist attacks, the purchasing and leasing of aircraft decreased but the aviation parts industry was able to be profitable due to the exponential increase of both C and D checks or overhauls [21]. This can be seen in Boeing's financials which showed a backlog of $377 billion and 535 added net commercial orders and $16 billion in revenue. In 2021, the delay of Air Force One, the failure of the Starliner Launch, and the continued difficulties in getting China to approve the airworthiness of the 737-MAX [22] while Airbus experienced a €62 billion increase in order intake, nearly doubling their 2020 order intake despite 264 orders being canceled resulting in record net income of €4.2 billion for the year [23]. While there will not be a noticeable immediate effect regarding new orders of large aircraft, Boeing earned significant profits from the global market of Maintenance, Repair, and Overhaul (MRO). Besides, a recent trend shows flexibility in layout configuration rather than compactness and efficiency in response to the international passenger reduction due to travel restrictions, flight cancellations, or lockdowns [24, 25]. On the other hand, Airbus has strongly gained the upper hand in the battle between the American and European juggernauts. What Airbus did was the abandonment of practices that led to "Eurosclerosis" ("overly rigid labor markets and overregulation of the economy in favor of established special interests in Europe in the'70s and the '80s") [26]. That said, to recover from COVID-19, European companies came together across national lines, avoided over-regulation, and embraced emergent technologies that Airbus has already been successful.

2.5 Supply Chain during the Pandemic

Another less visible hit by the pandemic is the jet fuel industry. With severe reductions in the use of AvGas and Jet A, major fuel stocks stood at 95% fuel storage capacity resulting in a drop in fuel prices [27]. Economists are worried that COVID-19 might result in unique long-term consumer behavioral changes that could shape the benefit of reducing global CO_2 emissions [28]. The fuel price has been in a promptly changing marketplace. The gruesome fluctuations, currency inflation, and ill workers have impeded the smooth fuel supply chain to be functional, from delayed loading and unloading process to ground transportation congestion. Moreover, the aviation industry typically does not use maritime cargo shipping parts or components due to the nature of time sensitivity as well as the corrosive sea salt. As a result, difficulties in securing space in air cargo have generated an additional financial burden for shippers. Another challenge is the recruitment, retention, and payment of a highly skilled workforce. Businesses must invest heavily in the workforce as competition is fierce [29] while considering cost efficiency, agility, flexibility, and carefully leveraging environmental footprint [30]. The aviation supply chain has been affected substantially related to aviation fuel production, aircraft parts shipment, currency exchange rate, and lack of skilled professionals.

2.6 Global Governance of Pandemics

The aviation industry inevitably inherits the nature of uncertainty and complexity of global governance responding to COVID-19. Both ICAO and WHO establish regulations and recommended practices fighting against global health crises such as ICAO's Article 14 of the Convention on International Civil Aviation [31] and WHO's International Health Regulations (IHRs) [13]. However, Cuinn and Switzerr [32] point out that the global governance of the public health crisis in the aviation industry is highly complex and hard to predict in the past due to the lack of interactions between countries and corresponding laws. Fortunately, the Severe Acute Respiratory Syndrome (SARS) in 2003 demonstrated an opportunity to resolve the conflicts and regulatory gaps between ICAO and WHO in coping with the pandemic. ICAO reviewed and modified existing Standards and Recommended Practices (SARPs) in the Chicago Convention related to passenger and crew health considering global public health issues [31]. Two huge modifications to SARPs include creating a Passenger Locator Form, which helps track passengers who are potentially exposed to infectious diseases during a flight. A Universal Precaution Kit has been introduced on board to help crew members manage possible in-flight infectious disease incidents.

ICAO took a further step to create a "coordinating group" in 2016 under the program Collaborative Arrangement for the Prevention and Management of Public Health Events in Civil Aviation (CAPSCA). Currently, the CAPSCA acts as a linkage between countries of the IHR and the Chicago Convention [32]. Non-governmental organizations, such as International Air Transport Association (IATA) and Airports Council International (ACI), as well as experts and private foundations within the aviation and public health fields, have been actively involved in such programs helping design detailed guidelines and suggestions under the laws and regulations published by ICAO and WHO. The ICAO SARPs have limited effects on stopping the transmission of the contagious virus via air transportation, while a state/country could add uncertainty and barriers interrupting the harmonic collaboration. Lockdowns and strict border controls posted by various countries during the COVID-19 pandemic directly resulted in the massive cancellation and suspension of international flights [14]. Karns et al. [33] pointed out that the vital actors in global governance are generally identified as states, intergovernmental organizations, non-governmental organizations, experts and epistemic communities, networks and partnerships, multinational corporations, and private foundations. With this in mind, global governance of the public health crisis in the aviation industry remains challenging such as protocols and policies between China and U.S.A.

2.7 Research Questions

This study intends to understand three essential segments of the global aviation industry – airlines, manufacturers, and airports, regarding what active defenses have been implemented to fight against the COVID-19 pandemic. The research questions are defined as follows:

1. What were the strategies of resilience enacted by the airline industry during the public health crisis?
2. How did manufacturers remain sustainable during the global pandemic?
3. What innovations did commercial airports implement to cope with the global pandemic?

3   Research Methodology

The authors use a qualitative approach with inductive Meta-Analysis as the methodology to collect and analyze archives in conjunction with the application of VOSviewer for bibliographical visualization [34]. As defined by Timulatk [35], Meta-Analysis is based on existing finished research that provides a more comprehensive analysis and findings regarding the given topic. The trustworthy documentation is reviewed concerning pandemic outbreaks, including 2003 SARS, 2012 MERS, 2013 Ebola, and COVID-19. To avoid trait error, this study purely focuses on existing finished research and cases and has no interference with people. The inter-rater tactic is used to secure the reliability of the result [36]. This study uses criterion validity to measure how the result reflects on present implementation [37].

4   Findings

4.1 Strategies of Resilience Enacted by the Airline Industry

Looking into the myriad of studies, many common thematic areas displayed themselves. This study inductively categorizes four main stages that the airlines go through, those being the P.R.I.M., namely Prevention (P), Retrenchment (R), Innovation (I), and Long-term Management (M), representing the primary strategies of resilience.

Prevention. During the Prevention stage, airlines focused on monitoring and assessing the situation and crisis at hand while closely looking upon governmental guidance and instruction on how to proceed. Especially after governmental instruction, many studies found that airlines began to alter their networks in response to passenger volume change and simultaneously to mitigate the possibility of virus spreading [12, 38–41]. Additionally, airlines implemented new standard operational procedures, in the hope of eliminating the spread of active health threats to crew members and other passengers, including altering boarding and exiting patterns, enhancing cabin cleaning procedures, and crew protective equipment, and elevating cabin hygienic and air-circulation standards [10–12, 39, 40, 42–45].

Retrenchment. Retrenchment is seeking to restructure the financial portfolios of its fleet, through a variety of means such as leasing, bank loan refinancing, initial public offers, etc. The Retrenchment stage can take many forms with the goal of maintaining operations and staying out of financial trouble while preserving a good public image. Through the *Retrenchment* strategy, many airlines acted to survive due to reduced air travel and took reactive actions by removing less profitable flight routes [12, 38, 39, 41, 43, 46, 47], furloughing workers or offering early retirement packages [11, 39, 45], canceling procurement contracts or postponing aircraft deliveries, retiring costly or aged aircraft, grounding less efficient aircraft [39, 48], and liquidating assets via aircraft sales among other methods [12, 42, 46]. Airlines would be patient and attempt to wait out the worst timeframe of the global health crisis and see the resurgence of air travel.

Innovation. The Innovation stage brings to light that airlines attempt to produce revenue in regularly unconventional ways such as reconfiguring aircraft to accommodate greater cargo storage and shipping needs. Many airlines reconfigured their passenger aircraft fully into cargo aircraft or efficiently divided useful aircraft spaces while transporting fewer passengers [12, 38, 42–50]. In addition, airlines continued searching for means to refinance and leverage aircraft and other assets. Some airlines restricted frequent flyer programs allowing for more cashflow [5, 12, 38, 42, 46–48]. Using VOSviewer, the bibliographical clusters are provided below (see Fig. 2) showing Innovation, Crisis Management, Pandemic Control, and Customer are intertwined and closely correlated.

Long-term Management. Lastly, when airlines are facing a lengthened global health crisis, airlines would adopt new procedures, such as requiring face masks, prescreening passengers, distancing passengers, and frequently cleaning cabins, just to name a few in order to stay operational until the full return of normal air travel [10–12, 39–44, 48, 51].

Table 1 shows the Bibliographical Overview of Airline Actions Facing Public Health Crisis.

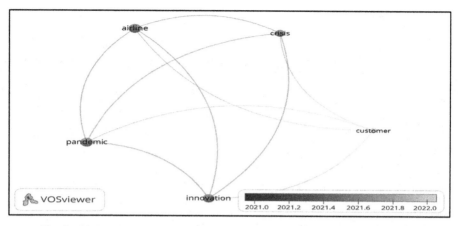

Fig. 2. Airline Resilience Strategies Facing Public Health Crisis via VOSviewer.

4.2   How Did Manufacturers Remain Sustainable During the Global Pandemic?

In contrast to many other parts of the aviation industry discussed above, the aviation parts manufacturing industry did not experience a major recession during the public health emergency. Yet, the aviation supply chain has been impacted greatly. This study analyzes nineteen (19) articles and summarizes them into three thematic categories: Aviation Parts Manufacturing, Jet-A Storage, and Sustainable Fuels. The focus of each article and the corresponding theme are provided in Table 2.

Aviation Parts Manufacturing Industry.   All the big players: Airbus [23], Boeing [22], General Electric (GE) Aviation [52], Bombardier [53], and COMAC [54] experienced growth and profits due to heavy demands in Maintenance, Repair, Overhaul (MRO) services during the pandemic [30]. Both reduction of demand for new aircraft and the sheer size of the backlog of producing aircraft eclipse the number of active aircraft in the market. However, the fact is that many factories did not shut down due to the aviation manufacturing industry being considered essential maintenance work [25]. This has been consistent compared to the case of SARS and Ebola pandemics [26]. One informative aspect during the COVID-19 was that the demand for large aircraft like Boeing B777 and Airbus A380 in the early 2000s shifted to the need for smaller, more efficient aircraft due to the lack of passengers and flight cancellations [21]. The impetus on aviation manufacturers is leaning toward fuel efficiency from smaller jets, rather than relying on large capacity sizes [24].

Jet-A Fuel Storage.   A major problem many people may not be aware of in the aviation industry caused by the pandemic revolves around the usage and storage of aviation fuel [28]. Crude oil is the source of gasoline, kerosene (Jet-A), diesel, asphalt, petroleum, lubricants, and various plastics, which are all produced consistently during the refining process. Whenever gasoline is refined from crude oil, all other products are also created regardless of whether they are in demand or not. With the airline industry experiencing a major downturn between May 2020 and December 2021, the reserves of Jet-A fuel have

Table 1. Overview of Airline Actions Facing Public Health Crisis

Sources	Prevention			Retrench				Innovate		Recovery
	Assessment and Monitoring	Network Alteration	Implement New SOPs	Flight Removal	Lay Off Workers	Retire Aircraft	Liquidate Assets	Refinance	Restructure Aircraft	Manage
Abate et al. (2020)		X		X				X	X	
Albers & Rundshagen (2020)				X		X	X	X	X	
Amankwah-Amoah (2016)		X	X							X
Amankwah-Amoah (2020)	X	X	X	X	X	X				X
Bielecki et al. (2020)	X	X	X							X
Bjelicic (2012)						X	X	X		
Cain & Pascual (2021)								X	X	
Chikodzi et al. (2021)			X				X	X	X	X
Cohen et al. (2016)	X		X	X					X	X
Czerny et al. (2021)				X				X	X	
IATA (2022)			X		X					X
Sources	Prevention			Retrench				Innovate		Recovery
	Assessment and Monitoring	Network Alteration	Implement New SOPs	Flight Removal	Lay Off Workers	Retire Aircraft	Liquidate Assets	Refinance	Restructure Aircraft	Manage
Islam et al. (2021)	X								X	X
Leder & Newman (2005)	X								X	
Mangili & Gendreau (2005)	X		X						X	X
Read et al. (2014)			X							X
Suk & Kim (2021)		X	X	X			X	X	X	X
Thaichon (2021)			X		X				X	X
Tuite et al. (2019)		X		X						X

been almost at capacity causing Jet-A to be sold at a loss to keep up with gasoline production [27]. Yet, through sanctions against Russian oil, imports of crude oil have gone down, which has had two effects on the Jet-A industry: 1) less Jet-A is being produced, and 2) using more fuel around restricted Russian airspace. While most countries have lifted travel restrictions, however, at the time of this study, China, the second largest airline market, continues reinforcing the "Dynamic COVID Zero" strategy and airline "Circuit Breaker" policy. The usage, as well as storage of Jet-A in the long term, stays unpredictable [55].

Sustainable Fuels. Regardless of COVID-19, the aviation industry is tackling the aviation fuel economy and "emissions reduction" challenge by researching alternative, enviro-friendly, or renewable fuels [29]. One way this is being handled is by reducing the aromatics (n-alkanes, iso-alkanes, cyclo-alkanes, and methyl/ethyl components) found in Jet-A fuel specifically consumed by large aircraft. Another way being researched is the

Table 2. Overview of Article Bibliographies

Source	Aviation Manufacturing Performance	Jet-A Fuel Storage	Alternative Sustainable Fuels
Archibugi, 2020	x		
Airbus, 2022	x		
Boeing, 2022	x		
Bombardier, 2022	x		
Bouwer et al., 2021	x		
Collings et al., 2021	x		
COMAC, 2020	x		
Faber et al., 2022 [70]			x
Farooq et al., 2021	x		
GE, 2022	x		
Hosseini, 2022		x	
Nie et al., 2022			x
Paul et al., 2021			x
Santos & Delina, 2021			x
Schneider et al., 2013	x		
Tisdal et al., 2021		x	
Youssef et al., 2020		x	
Yusaf et al., 2022 [71]			x

development of high-energy-density liquid aerospace fluids which are being compiled with new technologies to mimic the hydrocarbon properties of traditional fuels without many of the problematic carcinogens [56]. One exciting potential fuel alternative is hydrogen which is abundant, clean, and produces no carbon emissions, which has the potential to help ease Global Warming. The main argument against hydrogen includes its high price and the fact that mixing hydrogen and fossil fuels creates a slighter thrust [57, 70, 71]. But as seen in the reports from Boeing, Airbus, COMAC, and Bombardier, helping researchers to achieve environmentally friendly fuels has been at the forefront. While the air transportation industry starts to recover from the major pandemic impact, the environment briefly absorbed less quantity of pollutants due to the lack of air travel [57]. Figure 3 below demonstrates three critical bibliographical themes including fuel technology embracing emission reduction during the pandemic time between 2020 and 2021.

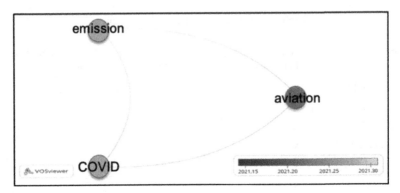

Fig. 3. Fuel Technology Innovation - Emission Reduction

4.3 What Innovations Did Commercial Airports Implement to Cope with the Global Pandemic?

To understand, this study reviews the responsive plans, preparedness, and sustainability plan of twelve airports. Seven airports are identified as reactive-oriented, as the actions were taken after the existence of a new communicable disease. Figure 4 demonstrates essential bibliographical clusters showing intercorrelated connections among three thematic areas, namely Passenger Screening, Cohort Groups, and Information Sharing.

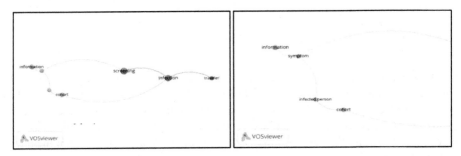

Fig. 4. Airport Thematic Areas – Responses to Pandemics

Temperature Screening and Identification. Six (6) out of twelve (12) airports in this study included temperature screening passengers and staff at airports as one of the procedures against contagious disease spread. It is worth noticing that those six airports are all large in passenger volumes, which means they could be riskier for virus transmission in frequently populated areas. Other airports in this study also mentioned temperature monitoring policies, but it relied more on the passengers/employees to report voluntarily.

Physical Distancing. All twelve airports in this study included physical distancing as a standard procedure to prevent or slow down the transmission of the communicable virus. Some airports have detailed quarantine/isolation plans, including treating passengers and crews according to the public health emergency policy. Some airports require aircraft doors to remain closed, and passengers and crew must remain on board until permission from the national/local public health agencies if a contagious disease is discovered in flight [58, 59]. Airports also establish temporary isolation and quarantine locations/facilities at the airport to take care of infected personnel [59–62]. Other physical distancing methods such as close a portion of the terminal, remove seats at airport restricted areas, and 6 feet/1-m social distancing requirements published by U.S. C.D.C. or equivalent foreign agencies. In conjunction with the required face masks, physical distancing has proven to be the most widely used and the most effective action for an airport to prevent transmission during the pandemic.

Sanitizing and Cleaning. Frequent sanitizing and cleaning the airport facilities, using human beings or robots, is another widely adopted action by airports worldwide. It is believed that frequent sanitizations can significantly reduce the chances of disease transmission happening at the airport, and it is recognized as an essential procedure during the pandemic [18].

Contact Tracing. Only two (2) airports in this study adopted contact tracing as one of their preventive programs facing a public health crisis. One of them is Tulsa International Airport but enforcing it on employees only [63]. Another airport, Kapiti Coast Airport, included it under physical distancing as a response to identifying potentially infected staff after a contagious disease has been discovered post disembarkation [58]. Other airports would provide a passenger's data only if the national/local public health agencies required it.

Information Seeking. Twelve airports would notify corresponding local or national public health agencies to seek professional guidance and instructions when dealing with a communicable disease [58–69]. Some airports have limited information dealing with new contagious diseases. As a result, more detailed guidelines and instructions published by professional agencies and international organizations are much needed for the airport to eliminate the transmission of diseases at the begging. Several international agreements and protocols require airports to notify public health agencies when discovering the existence or tendency of transmission of disease during operations. The World Health Act 1956 is the most common reference listing most infectious diseases and corresponding procedures an airport should take to reduce the possibility of disease spread [58].

Information Dissemination. Airports, except Tulsa International Airport [63] and Phoenix-Mesa Gateway Airport [68], suggest that information communication with the general public is vital and indispensable to minimize the impact on public health. Communication in the early phase of virus transmission is critical to increasing public awareness, so the general public can take protective measures such as Personal Protective Equipment (PPE) accordingly. Transparent information communication during the pandemic can help rebuild public confidence to travel, which is vital for the industry's recovery from a public health crisis [64]. Airports can also restate information gathered from international or national health agencies to help disseminate essential information.

New Technology. Two airports responded that the implementation of new technology would help contain disease transmission listed in their emergency response programs (ERPs). Understandably, an ERP can only reactionarily adopt the latest technology at the airport. But both airports mentioned that the new touchless technology such as biometrics and advanced kiosks could largely eliminate personal contact and thus reduce the risk of virus transmission [62, 64].

Target Procedure. Target procedure means the specific procedure that will only apply to a certain type of virus outbreak based on the virus's unique characteristics. In this study, eight airports have target procedures or similar equivalent actions in response to the contagious disease. The most common target procedure is the checklist. Airport authorities tailor-make checklists for a particular type of virus with support from international/national organizations to help quickly identify the spreading tendency and reduce the risk of transmission [59, 61–66, 68]. A bibliographical overview of the airports' actions is provided in Table 3.

Table 3. Overview of Airports' Actions Facing Public Health Crisis

Responsive Plan

Airport Name	Information Seeking	Information Dissemination	Screening & Identification	Physical Distancing	Sanitizing & Cleaning	Contact Tracing	New Technology	Target Procedures
Melbourne International Airport	x	x	x	x	x		x	x
Minneapolis-Saint Paul International Airport	x	x	x	x	x			x
Pensacola International Airport	x	x	x	x	x			
Philadelphia International Airport	x	x	x	x	x			x
Seattle-Tacoma International Airport	x	x		x	x		x	x
St. Pete-Clearwater International Airport	x	x		x	x			
Tulsa International Airport, NZ	x			x	x	x		x

Preventive Plan

Kapiti Coast Airport, NZ	x	x		x	x	x		
Fairbanks International Airport	x	x		x				
Tokyo Narita International Airport, Japan	x	x	x	x	x			x

(*continued*)

Table 3. (*continued*)

Responsive Plan								
Airport Name	Information Seeking	Information Dissemination	Screening & Identification	Physical Distancing	Sanitizing & Cleaning	Contact Tracing	New Technology	Target Procedures
Phoenix-Mesa Gateway Airport	x		x	x	x			x
Wichita Dwight D. Eisenhower National Airport	x	x		x	x			x

5 Conclusion

The aviation industry is extremely vulnerable to a global health crisis. This study delivers a holistic review for airlines, airports, and manufacturing/MRO industries to prepare for the ongoing and future communicable diseases. This study finds that airlines conduct four main stages, prevention, retrenching, innovation, and recovery, of operations during the public health crisis while expecting a full recovery. For the aviation manufacturing industry, the pandemic did not have a significant impact compared to that of both airline or airport industries due to the increased opportunities to perform MRO and optimized reconfigurations of airplanes for cargo services. Airlines are focusing on the efficiency of smaller aircraft with more environmentally friendly and sustainable operational features. Moreover, the balance point between aviation fuel usage and storage remains unpredictable; in particular when the Russia-Ukraine war continues to develop while China's airline market stays largely intangible.

This study also unveils that airports follow suggested guidelines published by WHO, IATA, and U.S. C.D.C. to construct their preventative and emergency response plans. Information sharing and transparent communication with the flying public can primarily help create public awareness and significantly reduce the risk of communicable diseases at the beginning stage. Other practices such as screening and identification, face masks and physical distancing, and sanitizing and cleaning programs are the top-used practices by airports and are proven relatively effective by the practitioners.

5.1 Future Study

There is no air cargo service provider included in this study. A future study on air cargo may be performed to fill the gaps. By the time of this study, China has imposed most strict pandemic policies against public health crises such as "Dynamic COVID Zero," "Stay-at-Home," "Circuit Breaker" protocols. A future Case Study of the post-COVID pandemic achievement in China compared to other leading aviation countries like the U.S.A and Europe Union countries would be researchable.

References

1. Federal Aviation Administration [FAA]. The Economic Impact of Civil Aviation on the US Economy (2020). https://www.faa.gov/sites/faa/files/about/plans_reports/2020_jan_eco nomic_impact_report.pdf

2. Bureau of Transportation Statistics. U.S. Airlines Show First Profit Since COVID-19 in 2nd Quarter 2021 (2021). https://www.bts.gov/newsroom/us-airlines-show-first-profit-COVID-19-2nd-quarter-2021

3. Bureau of Transportation Statistics. Passengers: All Airlines - All Airports (2021). https://www.transtats.bts.gov/Data_Elements.aspx?Qn6n=G

4. International Air Transportation Association. What Types of Cargo are Transported by Air? (2021). https://www.iata.org/en/publications/newsletters/iata-knowledge-hub/what-types-of-cargo-are-transported-by-air/#:~:text=Where%20to%20find%20more%20information,jobs%20are%20always%20in%20demand

5. International Air Transportation Association [IATA]. Air passenger market analysis (2019). https://www.iata.org/en/iata-repository/publications/economic-reports/air-passenger-monthly---dec-2019/

6. International Civil Aviation Organization [ICAO]. Annual report 2019 (2019). https://www.icao.int/annual-report-2019/Pages/default.aspx

7. Baldwin, G.: The future of Canada's transportation system: Has Canada learned from its experiences with outbreaks such as SARS, Ebola, H1N1 and MERS? In: Proceedings of 53rd Annual Conference. Canadian Transportation (2018). Research Forum. https://ctrf.ca/wp-content/uploads/2018/06/CTRF_2018_Baldwin_7_2.pdf

8. International Air Transportation Association. IATA Economics' Chart of the Week: What can we learn from past pandemic episodes? 24, January 2020. https://www.iata.org/en/iata-repository/publications/economic-reports/what-can-we-learn-from-past-pandemic-episodes/

9. WHO. Weekly epidemiological update on COVID-19 - 1 February 2022 (2022). https://www.who.int/publications/m/item/weekly-epidemiological-update-on-COVID-19---1-february-2022

10. Amankwah-Amoah, J.: Ebola and global airline business: an integrated framework of companies' responses to adverse environmental shock. Thunderbird Int. Bus. Rev. **58**(5), 385–397 (2016). https://doi.org/10.1002/tie.21789

11. International Air Transport Association. IATA Health Safety Checklist for Air Operators, 4th ed. (2022)

12. Suk, M., Kim, W.: COVID-19 and the airline industry: crisis management and resilience. Tourism Rev. **76**(4), 984–998 (2021). https://doi.org/10.1108/TR-07-2020-0348

13. World Health Organization [WHO]. International health regulations (2005) Third Edition. Geneva: World Health Organization (2016). https://www.who.int/publications/i/item/9789241580496

14. Arora, M., Tuchen, S., Nazemi, M., Blessing, L.: Airport pandemic response: an assessment of impacts and strategies after one year with COVID-19. Trans. Res. Interdiscip. Perspect. **11**, 100449 (2021). https://doi.org/10.1016/j.trip.2021.100449

15. Berry, L.L., Danaher, T.S., Aksoy, L., Keiningham, T.L.: Service safety in the pandemic age. J. Serv. Res. JSR **23**(4), 391–395 (2020). https://doi.org/10.1177/1094670520944608

16. Shuchi, S., Drogemuller, R., Buys, L.: Flexibility in airport terminals: identification of design factors. J. Airport Manag. **12**(1), 90–108 (2017)

17. Štimac, I., Pivac, J., Bračić, M., Drljača, M.: The impact of COVID-19 pandemic on the future airport passenger terminals design. Int. J. Traffic Transp. Eng. **11**(1), 129–142. (2021). http://ijtte.com/uploads/2021-01-18/b2dd2cfa-f626-cc75ijtte.2021.11(1).08.pdf

18. Airports Council International. Airport Operational Practice: Examples for Managing COVID-19. ACI World (2020). https://store.aci.aero/wp-content/uploads/2020/04/Airport-Operational-Practice-Examples-for-Managing-COVID19.pdf

19. Abeyratne, R.: Training the airport manager in a post-COVID-19 world. J. Airport Manag. **14**(4), 1–9. (2020). https://content.ebscohost.com/ContentServer.asp?T=P&P=AN&K=146323385&S=R&D=a9h&EbscoContent=dGJyMNXb4kSeqLY40dvuOLCmsEqep7dSsqy4S66WxWXS&ContentCustomer=dGJyMO7r8Hzz27mF39%2FsU%2BPe7Yvy

20. Tuchen, S., Arora, M., Blessing, L.: Airport user experience unpacked: conceptualizing its potential in the face of COVID-19. J. Air Transp. Manag. **89**, 101919 (2020). https://doi.org/10.1016/j.jairtraman.2020.101919

21. Schneider, S., Spieth, P., Clauss, T.: Business model innovation in the aviation industry. Int. J. Prod. Dev. **12, 18**(3–4), 286–310 (2013). https://doi.org/10.1504/IJPD.2013.055010

22. Boeing. Boeing Reports Fourth-Quarter Results, Quarterly Reports Q4 (2022). https://investors.boeing.com/investors/investor-news/press-release-details/2022/Boeing-Reports-Fourth-Quarter-Results/default.aspx

23. Airbus. Airbus reports strong Full-Year (FY) 2021 results, EN Press Release Airbus FY 2021 Q4 (2022). https://www.airbus.com/en/newsroom/press-releases/2022-02-airbus-reports-strong-full-year-fy-2021-results

24. Bouwer J., Saxon S., Wittkamp, N.: Back to the future? Airline sector poised for change post-COVID-19. McKinsey & Company (2021). https://www.mckinsey.com/industries/travel-logistics-and-infrastructure/our-insights/back-to-the-future-airline-sector-poised-for-change-post-COVID-19

25. Collings, D., Corbet, S., Hou, Y.G., Hu, Y., Larkin, C., Oxley, L.: The effects of negative reputational contagion on international airlines: the case of the Boeing 737-MAX disasters. Int. Rev. Fin. Anal. **80** (2022). https://doi.org/10.1016/j.irfa.2022.102048

26. Archibugi, D.: Post-pandemic reconstruction: airbus can serve as an investment model for Europe. LSE Bus. Rev. (2020). http://eprints.lse.ac.uk/104769/1/businessreview_2020_05_16_post_pandemic_reconstruction_airbus_can.pdf

27. Tisdall, L., Zhang, Y., Zhang, A.: COVID-19 impacts on general aviation–comparative experiences, governmental responses and policy imperatives. Transp. Policy **110**, 273–280 (2021). https://doi.org/10.1016/j.tranpol.2021.06.009

28. Youssef, A. B., Zeqiri, A., Dedaj, B.: Short and long run effects of COVID-19 on the hospitality industry and the potential effects on jet fuel markets. IAEE Energy Forum 121–124 (2020)

29. Paul, S.K., Chowdhury, P., Moktadir, M.A., Lau, K.H.: Supply chain recovery challenges in the wake of the COVID-19 pandemic. J. Bus. Res. **136**, 316–329 (2021). https://doi.org/10.1016/j.jbusres.2021.07.056

30. Farooq, M.U., Hussain, A., Masood, T., Habib, M.S.: Supply chain operations management in pandemics: a state-of-the-art review inspired by COVID-19. Sustainability (Basel, Switzerland) **13**(5), 2504 (2021). https://doi.org/10.3390/su13052504

31. International Civil Aviation Organization. Protection of Health of Passengers and Crews and Prevention of the Spread of Communicable Disease Through International Travel, Res A35–12 (2004). https://www.icao.int/Security/COVID-19/ReferenceMaterial/Assembly%20Resolution%20A35-12.pdf

32. Cuinn, G.O., Switzerr, S.: Ebola and the airplane – securing mobility through regime interactions and legal adaptation. Leiden J. Int. Law **32**(1), 71–89 (2019). https://doi.org/10.1017/S0922156518000547

33. Karns, M.P., Mingst, K.A., Stiles, K. W.: International organizations: the politics and processes of global governance, 3rd edn. Lynne Rienner Publishers, Inc. (2015)

34. Martínez-López, F.J., Merigó, J.M., Valenzuela-Fernández, L., Nicolás, C.: Fifty years of the European journal of marketing: a bibliometric analysis. Eur. J. Mark. **52**(1/2), 439–468 (2018). https://doi.org/10.1016/j.jiph.2017.12.011

35. Timulatk, L.: Meta-analysis of qualitative studies: a tool for reviewing qualitative research findings in psychotherapy. Psychother. Res. **19**(4–5), 591–600 (2009). https://doi.org/10.1080/10503300802477989

36. Schwarz-Shea, P., Yanow, D.: Interpretive Research Design. Routledge (2013). https://learning.oreilly.com/library/view/interpretive-researchdesign/9780415878081/

37. Salkind, N.: Exploring Research, 9th edn. Pearson Education Limited (2018). https://www.pearson.com/us/higher-education/program/Salkind-Exploring-Research-Books-a-la-Carte-9th-Edition/PGM2481416.html

38. Abate, M., Christidis, P., Purwanto, A.J.: Government support to airlines in the aftermath of the COVID-19 pandemic. J. Air Transp. Manag. 89 (2020). https://doi.org/10.1016/j.jairtraman.2020.101931

39. Amankwah-Amoah, J.: Note: Mayday, Mayday, Mayday! Responding to environmental shocks: Insights on global airlines' responses to COVID-19. Transp. Res. Part E: Logist. Trans. Rev. 143 (2020). https://doi.org/10.1016/j.tre.2020.102098

40. Bielecki, M., et al.: Air travel and COVID-19 prevention in the pandemic and peri-pandemic period: a narrative review. Travel Med. Infect. Disease 38 (2020). https://doi.org/10.1016/j.tmaid.2020.101939

41. Tuite, A.R., Watts, A.G., Khan, K., Bogoch, I.I.: Ebola virus outbreak in North Kivu and Ituri provinces, Democratic Republic of Congo, and the potential for further transmission through commercial air travel. J. Travel Med. 26(7) (2019). https://doi.org/10.1093/jtm/taz063

42. Chikodzi, D., Dube, K., Nhamo, G.: COVID-19 pandemic and prospects for recovery of the global aviation industry. J. Air Transp. Manag. 92 (2021). https://doi.org/10.1016/j.jairtraman.2021.102022

43. Cohen, N.J., et al.: Travel and border health measures to prevent international spread of ebola. Supplements 65(3), 57–63 (2016). https://www.cdc.gov/mmwr/volumes/65/su/su6503a9.htm

44. Mangili, A., Gendreau, M.A.: Transmission of infectious diseases during commercial air travel. Lancet 365(9463), 989–996 (2005). https://doi.org/10.1016/S0140-6736(05)71089-8

45. Thaichon, P.: COVID in the aviation industry: crisis management, its decisions and outcomes. In: Ratten, V., Thaichon, P. (eds.) COVID-19, Technology and Marketing. Palgrave Macmillan, Singapore (2021). https://doi.org/10.1007/978-981-16-1442-2_2

46. Albers, S., Rundshagen, V.: European airlines' strategic responses to the COVID-19 pandemic. J. Air Transp. Manag. 87 (2020). https://doi.org/10.1016/j.jairtraman.2020.101863

47. Czerny, A.I., Fu, X., Lei, Z., Oum, T.: HPost-pandemic aviation market recovery: experience and lessons from China. J. Air Transp. Manag. 90 (2021). https://doi.org/10.1016/j.jairtraman.2020.101971

48. Bjelicic, B.: Financing airlines in the wake of the financial markets crisis. J. Air Transp. Manag. 21, 10–16 (2012). https://doi.org/10.1016/j.jairtraman.2011.12.012

49. Leder, K., Newman, D.: Respiratory infections during air travel. Intern. Med. J. 35(1), 50–55 (2005). https://doi.org/10.1111/j.1445-5994.2004.00696.x

50. Cain, L.N., Pascual, M.E.: Loyalty programs: the vital safety feature for airlines to survive COVID-19. Int. Hospital. Rev. (2021). https://doi.org/10.1108/IHR-03-2021-0017

51. Read, J.M., Diggle, P.J., Chirombo, J., Solomon, T., Baylis, M.: Effectiveness for screening for Ebola at airports. Lancet 385(9962), 23–24 (2015). https://doi.org/10.1016/S0140-6736(14)61894-8

52. General Electric (GE). GE Announces Fourth Quarter and Full Year 20201 Results (2022). https://www.ge.com/news/press-releases/ge-announces-fourth-quarter-and-full-year-2021-results

53. Bombardier. Annual Information Form 2021. Bombardier Financial Reports (2022). https://bombardier.com/system/files/financial-reports/2022-02/Bombardier-2021-Financial-Report-en.pdf

54. COMAC. COMAC Market Forecast 2020–2039 (2020). http://www.comac.cc/fujian/2020-2039nianbao_en.pdf

55. Hosseini, S.E.: Transition away from fossil fuels toward renewables: lessons from Russia-Ukraine crisis. Future Energy 1(1) (2022). https://orcid.org/0000-0002-0907-9427

56. Nie, J., Jia, T., Pan, L., Zhang, X., Zou, J.J.: Development of high-energy-density liquid aerospace fuel: a perspective. Trans. Tianjin Univ. **28**(1), 1–5 (2022). https://link.springer. com/article/https://doi.org/10.1007/s12209-021-00302-x
57. Santos, K., Delina, L.: Soaring sustainably: promoting the uptake of sustainable aviation fuels during and post-pandemic. Energy Res. Soc. Sci. **77**, 102074 (2021). https://doi.org/10.1016/j.erss.2021.102074
58. Kapiti Coast Airport. Airport Emergency Plan (AEP) (2019). https://www.kapiticoastairport. co.nz/media/pdfs/Kapiti-Coast-Airport-Holdings-Ltd_Exposition_Airport-Emergency-Plan. pdf
59. Wichita Airport Authority. Wichita National Airport Procedures for responding to infectious disease situations and pandemic plan (2015). https://www.flywichita.com/wp-content/upl oads/2018/02/No.15-PROCEDURES-FOR-RESPONDING-TO-INFECTIOUS-DISEASE-SITUATIONS.pdf
60. Fairbanks International Airport. Fairbanks Airport Emergency Plan (2019). http://dot.alaska. gov/faiiap/pdfs/FAI_airportemergencyplan.pdf
61. Philadelphia International Airport. PHL COVID-19 Recovery playbook (2020). https://www. phl.org/drupalbin/media/PHL%20COVID19%20Recovery%20Playbook091120.pdf
62. Seattle-Tacoma International Airport - Port of Seattle. FlyHealthy@SEA. A plan for protecting the health of SEA passengers and employees and restoring confidence in air travel (2020). https://www.portseattle.org/sites/default/files/2020-09/FlyHealthy%40SEA_Sep3_S PREADS.pdf
63. Tulsa Airports Improvement Trust. COVID-19 Response Plan (2020). https://www.tulsaairp orts.com/wp-content/uploads/2020/06/TAIT-COVID_19_Response-Plan-Updated-9-2-20. pdf
64. Melbourne International Airport – Australia COVID-Safe Airport Operations (2020). https:// www.melbourneairport.com.au/getmedia/e0e25cc3-74e4-4c87-9375-5e0c04833aae/200 901-Melbourne-Airport-COVID-Safe-Plan-Airport-Operating-Standard-(FINAL).pdf.aspx
65. Minneapolis-St. Paul International Airport. Travel Confidently Playbook: A comprehensive guide for COVID-19 pandemic response and recovery (2021). https://www.mspairport.com/ sites/default/files/2021-01/TravelConfidentlyMSP%20PLAYBOOKv3.pdf
66. Narita International Airport. Measures to Prevent COVID-19 Infection at Narita Airport. Narita Airport News Release 1–17 (2020). https://www.naa.jp/en/20200612-prevent_corona_ en.pdf
67. Pensacola International Airport. COVID-19 Response Plan (2020). http://flypensacola.com/ wp-content/uploads/2020/12/ATR_Plan-102020.pdf
68. Phoenix-Mesa Gateway Airport. Phoenix-Mesa Gateway Airport Pandemic Response Plan (2009). https://airportscouncil.org/wp-content/uploads/2018/08/PMGA_Pandemic_R esponse_Plan_05.28.09.pdf
69. St. Pete-Clearwater International Airport. PIE COVID-19 Action Plan (2020). https:// fly2pie.com/docs/default-source/news/press-releases/2020/pie-COVID-19-updated-action-plan-media-release-6-24-20-with-action-plan.pdf?sfvrsn=c64a53db_0
70. Faber, J., Király, J., Lee, D., Owen, B., O'Leary, A.: Potential for reducing aviation non-CO2 emissions through cleaner jet fuel. CE Delft (2022). https://cedelft.eu/wp-content/uploads/ sites/2/2022/03/CE_Delft_210410_Potential_reducing_aviation_non-CO2_emissions_cle aner_jet_fuel_FINAL.pdf
71. Yusaf, T., et al.: Sustainable aviation—hydrogen is the future. Sustainability **14**(1), 548 (2022). https://www.mdpi.com/2071-1050/14/1/548/pdf

Trends in Machine Learning and Electroencephalogram (EEG): A Review for Undergraduate Researchers

Nathan Koome Murungi[1](✉) ⓘ, Michael Vinh Pham[1] ⓘ, Xufeng Dai[2], and Xiaodong Qu[1] ⓘ

[1] Swarthmore College, Swarthmore 19081, USA
{nmurung1,mpham1,xqu1}@swarthmore.edu
[2] Haverford College, Haverford 19041, USA
xdai1@haverford.edu

Abstract. This paper presents a systematic literature review on Brain-Computer Interfaces (BCIs) in the context of Machine Learning. Our focus is on Electroencephalography (EEG) research, highlighting the latest trends as of 2023. The objective is to provide undergraduate researchers with an accessible overview of the BCI field, covering tasks, algorithms, and datasets. By synthesizing recent findings, our aim is to offer a fundamental understanding of BCI research, identifying promising avenues for future investigations.

Keywords: Machine Learning · Deep Learning · Brain-Computer Interfaces · BCI · Electroencephalography · EEG · Undergrad · Review

1 Introduction

Since the advent of computing, the disparity between human and computer technology has significantly diminished. Starting with early human-computer interfaces like keyboards and microphones, the boundary between humans and computers has been progressively blurred, primarily owing to the emergence and utilization of brain-computer interfaces [34]. In the rapidly advancing field of Brain-Computer Interfaces (BCI), Electroencephalography (EEG) analysis plays a crucial role in establishing a connection between the human brain and Machine Learning (ML) algorithms [5,11,37,40,43–45]. The proliferation of ML algorithms and the increasing availability of EEG data have created exciting opportunities for researchers to explore new approaches to interpreting raw EEG data. However, this progress presents a challenge for newcomers due to the overwhelming volume of research papers and the rapid rate at which they become outdated, making it challenging to navigate the research landscape effectively.

Nathan, Michael, and Xufeng are the first three authors of this paper, and they contributed equally. Professor Xiaodong Qu is the mentor for this research project.

© The Author(s), under exclusive license to Springer Nature Switzerland AG 2023
M. Kurosu et al. (Eds.): HCII 2023, LNCS 14054, pp. 426–443, 2023.
https://doi.org/10.1007/978-3-031-48038-6_27

To tackle this formidable challenge, we present a meticulous examination of the existing literature in the field of Brain-Computer Interfaces (BCI), with a specific focus on the most recent advancements up to 2023. This paper is tailored to cater to undergraduate researchers, serving as a comprehensive overview and guide for those aspiring to conduct research in the Electroencephalography (EEG) domain. By systematically analyzing and organizing the obtained findings, our objective is to facilitate a profound comprehension of the current landscape of BCI research while identifying promising avenues for future investigations.

In addition to providing a comprehensive review, this paper specifically delves into utilizing Transformers, a prominent and rapidly emerging machine learning algorithm, within the realm of BCI research. By focusing on the application of Transformers in this context, we aim to shed light on its significance and impact, offering insights into its potential advantages and limitations. Table 1 lists the acronyms used in this paper.

1.1 Research Questions

Our research aims to address the following questions at the intersection of ML and EEG research:

- What are the most suitable tasks, datasets, and ML algorithms for undergraduate researchers to explore the realms of Machine Learning (ML) and Electroencephalography (EEG)?
- What are the prevailing trends observed within the intersection of ML and EEG in 2023?

Table 1. List of Acronyms

Abbreviation	Definition
ML	Machine Learning
DL	Deep Learning
LSTM	Long Short-Term Memory
CNN	Convolutional Neural Network
DNN	Deep Neural Network
AE	Autoencoder
GAN	Generative Adversarial Network
SVM	Support Vector Machine
RNN	Recurrent Neural Network
ANN	Artificial Neural Network
RF	Random Forest
KNN	K-Nearest Neighbor
DBN	Deep Belief Network
EEG	Electroencephalography
BCI	Brain-Computer Interfaces

By answering the first question, we aim to provide guidance to undergraduate researchers, helping them identify appropriate starting points and resources for their ML and EEG investigations. This will enable a seamless entry into the research domain and facilitate their understanding of fundamental concepts and methodologies.

Regarding the second question, we plan to provide an overview of the current trends within the EEG-ML field, highlighting the latest advancements and emerging research directions as of 2023. Understanding these trends may help undergrad researchers stay informed about cutting-edge developments and identify promising avenues for their investigations.

2   Methods

2.1   Keywords

Preferred Reporting Items for Systematic Reviews and Meta-Analyses (PRISMA) is the systematic review method that was used to identify relevant EEG research papers that use ML methods, as mentioned in [5,43]. This search was conducted in February 2023 within Google Scholar, Paperwithcode, arXiv, and PubMed databases using keywords: (*'Machine Learning' OR 'LSTM' OR 'Deep Learning' OR 'CNN' OR 'RNN' OR 'Classification' OR 'DNN' OR 'Autoencoder' OR 'GAN' OR 'Transformer' AND 'Brain Computer Interface' OR 'Motor Imagery Classification' OR 'seizure' OR 'EEG Review' OR 'Speech' OR 'Emotion' OR 'Parkinson's' OR 'Alzheimer's' OR 'Depression' OR 'Rehabilitation' OR 'Gender Classification' OR 'Stroke' OR 'Person Identification' OR 'Age Classification' OR 'Task classification') AND ('EEG' OR 'Electroencephalography' AND 'Survey' or 'Review'*). Figure 1 visualizes this screening method and shows how the best 76 papers were selected and further narrowed down to the 9 recommended papers for undergraduates, as they are limited in time. Furthermore, with the understanding that undergraduate researchers are limited in time, we also narrowed all the papers we reviewed down to 9 suggested research papers that a new undergraduate researcher should start with and read to get acclimated with the current trends within the field.

The criteria for selecting appropriate papers are as follows:

- **EEG only:** We only look at Electroencephalography (EEG) studies with human subjects to keep type of data consistent.
- **Time:** Due to constantly new discoveries within the Machine Learning field and EEG field, we only included up-to-date literature published in 2020 and after.
- **ML/DL included:** Highly focused on Machine Learning and Deep Learning approaches to EEG processing.
- **Reproducibility:** Papers that include data preprocessing, feature extraction, results, code, and data source.
- **Target Audience:** Comprehensible to undergraduate students majoring or minoring in computer science, interested in the topic of machine learning.

3   Results

3.1   Tasks

In the healthcare field, EEG data can be decoded to understand the underlying and psychological status of affected individuals [2, 39].

From our review, most BCI research has been conducted in the clinical setting, specifically MI, Seizure, and Emotion Detection. As such, and due to their high accuracy, it's recommended that undergraduates start with these tasks. Table 2 shows the most common tasks found for BCI research (with the top 3

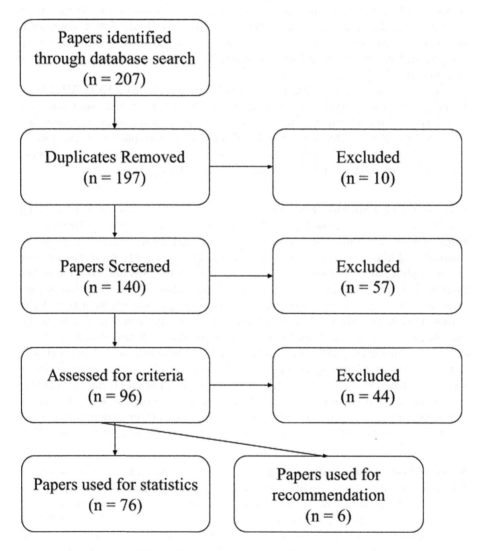

Fig. 1. Selection process for the papers

bolded). Also there are nonclinical tasks, such as [41,55,63] Fig. 2 shows the most common algorithms used for ML. The most common algorithms for Emotion were CNN, RNN, SVM, and KNN. For Seizure, the most commonly used were CNN, RNN, Transformer, and KNN. These top 3 tasks found in our literature review are described below.

Motor Imagery. Motor imagery EEG tasks involve the measurement and analysis of EEG brain activity patterns associated with mentally envisioning particular motor actions. Rehabilitation and assistive technologies can benefit from EEG/ML Motor Imagery by facilitating the development of solutions for individuals with motor and limb impairments via a means of communication from acquired neural activity of the kinesthetic imagination of limbs. [48] Some healthcare systems utilize EEG signals to allow individuals to sense and interact with the physical world by controlling exoskeletons, wheelchairs, and other assistive technologies [2].

Not only can patients with motor disabilities benefit from EEG/ML Motor Imagery, but also everyday users through the development of Brain-Computer Interfaces to control specific motor actions. Current work done in classifying imaginations of the right or left hand and fingers for example could translate to a future where users are able to imagine specific motor actions such as moving a cursor, controlling a robotic arm, or navigating a video game. [2]

Emotion Recognition. Emotion detection EEG/ML tasks entail identifying and classifying patterns of EEG brain activity associated with different emotional states [57]. Emotion is commonly associated with perception, decision-making, and human interaction. As the BCI field continues to grow, the interest in establishing an "emotional" interaction between humans and computers has increased in consumer products such as virtual reality [50]. In addition, a persons mental condition and emotional state can be apparent through their EEG waves. Therefore, emotion detection finds application in mental health contexts, enabling remote assessment and monitoring of patients' emotional states by therapists or counselors which can facilitate timely interventions and support and better treatment. Emotion recognition is the leading scientific problem in Affective Computing, which is how computer systems recognize and comprehend emotional information for natural human-computer interactions. With better Affective Computing, AI chatbots and voice assistants can better understand human users' emotions providing more personalized and empathetic interactions. [25]

Seizure Detection. Epileptic seizures are chronic neurological diseases that can substantially impact the lifestyle of an affected individual. For some patients, there could be hundreds of seizures a day, which greatly affects their brain. They are sudden abnormalities in the brain's electrical activities, which is manifested as excessive discharge of the neuronal network in the cerebral cortex [1]. Accurate and timely detection for seizures can greatly help improve the livelihood of many

Table 2. Task Breakdown for Non-Review Papers

Task	Paper Count
Motor Imagery	**19**
Seizure	**12**
Emotion	**12**
Parkinson's	3
Gender/Age	2
Depression	2
Stroke	1
Person Identification	1
Inner Speech	1
Dementia	1
Lie Detection	1

affected individuals by preemptively describing seizure risk which can allow an individual to seek medical expertise. For studies that highlight seizure detection, EEG signals are recorded during the phases of a seizure: prodromal, early ictal, ictal, and postictal as well as seizure free periods. In addition, the control class consisted of non-epileptic subjects.

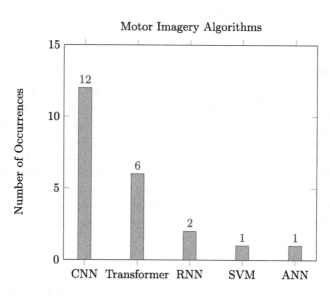

Fig. 2. Breakdown of Algorithms used for Motor Imagery Classification

Table 3. Algorithm Breakdown for Non-Review Papers

Algorithm	Paper Count
CNN	20
RNN	13
Transformer	5
SVM	4
KNN	4
ANN	4
RF	3
AE	2

3.2 Algorithms

Compared with review papers in previous years [5,9,38,43,61,62], many of the algorithm findings were the same such as CNN dominating as the most frequently used in BCI research. But there were also interesting trends with Transformers and DBN. Transformers, a new ML algorithm, replace RNNs with sequential data because they have a self-attention mechanism that allows them to process input sequences of varying lengths and extract relevant information from them [56]. DBN also makes this list as an algorithm that has fallen out of trend. Despite making up a sizeable portion of earlier BCI research and review, rarely any research, we came across used DBN. Table 3 shows the most common algorithms found for BCI research.

3.3 Datasets

The datasets used in the studies vary based on the task that the study focuses on, and the most used are BCI Competition Dataset IV for validating signal processing and classification method; DEAP for analyzing human affect states; SEED, a various use EEG dataset; and EEGEyeNet, and Eye-tracking Dataset and Benchmark for Eye Movement Prediction. Other available datasets include 'Thinking out loud,' an EEG-based BCI dataset for inner speech recognition, 'Feeling Emotions,' and EEG Brainwave Dataset for emotion recognition. The datasets cover a wide range of topics for BCI research and are accessible to undergraduate students.

4 Discussion

We identified the most recent trend in Machine learning BCI research based on the papers we reviewed. We presented our recommendations for the top three tasks, algorithms, datasets, and review papers for undergraduate researchers.

It is clear that transformers are becoming more and more utilized in the last year to classify EEG data. Transformers have traditionally been used in natural

Table 4. Dataset Breakdown for Non-Review Papers

Dataset	Task	Year	Cited
DEAP [21]	Emotion	2011	3439
BCI Competition IV [53]	MI	2012	783
Dreamer [20]	Emotion	2016	517
SEED [10]	Emotion	2013	358
Bonn [24]	Seizure	2013	316
CHB-MIT [36]	Seizure	2021	21
EEGEyeNet [19]	MI	2021	16

language processing (NLP) due to their ability to handle long-range dependencies [51]. Therefore, transformers can be efficient with the recognition of EEG data, a set of time series signals. However, transformers are commonly paired with algorithms such as CNNs, RNNs, or DBNs. We further expand our analysis by exploring a range of scholarly articles that employ analogous time-series data [3,4,6,7,17,18,26,28–30,32,33,35,46,52,58–60,64].

4.1 Guide of Techniques Required for Research

In order for an undergraduate research to be successful in their research, knowledge of some techniques is required. These techniques include an understanding of a computer programming language such as Python and various tools and packages.

Tools and Packages. Fluency in Python is extremely beneficial for replicating the works mentioned in this paper effectively. Its readability, position as the de facto language for ML, and extensive community support make it an excellent choice for beginners in the EEG-ML field. NumPy and Pandas are useful ML libraries for numerical operations and data manipulation, making them convenient for tasks such as data preprocessing and exploration for EEG data. Overwhelmingly, the aforementioned works employed the Python library Scikit Learn to train classical ML algorithms such as Random Forests and SVMs. Deeper machine learning algorithms such as CNNs and Transformers had split usage between the PyTorch and Tensorflow/Keras Python libraries. Amazon Web Services (AWS), a cloud computing solution, offers services such as Sage-Maker which offers a complete ML development environment and EC2, an elastic virtual server service, which enables the ability to launch and oversee virtual machine instances to run ML code.

In summary, Python is quite mandatory for understanding EEG-ML source code; Although not mandatory, familiarity and being comfortable using Numpy, Pandas, Sci-kit Learn, PyTorch or Tensorflow/Keras, are advantageous in further enhancing the replication process. Finally, AWS or other cloud computing services are nice tools to have especially when working with large EEG datasets.

Table 5. Recommended Papers to Start Research

Recommended Paper Title	Paper
Deep learning-based electroencephalography analysis: a systematic review	[43]
Deep learning for electroencephalogram (EEG) classification tasks: a review	[5]
Fear of the CURE: A Beginner's Guide to Overcoming Barriers in Creating a Course-Based Undergraduate Research Experience	[12]

Recommended Courses. It is optional to enroll in a college course to learn Python. Many universities such as Stanford, Cornell, and MIT provide free online courses that are very efficient in their programming methods. Reading Python's online documentation is an alternative to gaining a proficiency of Python and its syntax. Researchers lacking ML knowledge can also use online courses to gain an understanding of the topic. Based on our own undergraduate research experience, we recommend that undergraduate computer science researchers watch Stanford CS 229 and CS 230 lectures online.

In addition, researchers should be comfortable utilizing NumPy, Pandas, Sci-kit Learn, PyTorch, and Tensorflow/Keras libraries. We recommend that researchers read each library's documentation which outlines the capabilities of each method in the libraries. These documentations can be found for free online.

Recommended Papers. In addition to completing courses to understand the techniques and packages needed to get started in BCI machine learning research, we recommended that undergraduates read the papers outlined in Table 5.

4.2 Algorithms

Frameworks for Recommended Algorithms. CNNs are widely used in computer vision and image classifications. In [27], they discuss a novel network that combines CNNs, SAE, and DNN to convert EEG time series data into 2D images for good emotion classification. Once the EEG data is transformed into 2D images, features extracted from the original EEG data are sent to the CNN. The model includes many pooling layers and one output layer. After pooling, data is subsampled into images with smaller sizes. The weights and filters are learned through back-propagation. [27]

SVMs are a very useful supervised machine learning algorithm. It works by separating the dataset into two sections. This sectioning of the data can either be linear or nonlinear. Linear sectioning includes a discriminant hyperplane, while nonlinear separation includes a kernel function. Though computational complexity is low for this algorithm, its performance is heavily dictated by the kernel function. [45]

Transformers are a trending algorithm for EEG classification. A transformer network is a neural network that is based on a self-attention mechanism. The network consists of encoders and decoders. Each encoder has two sub-layers, a multi-head self-attention mechanism, and a position-wise connected forward feeding network. There is a residual connection around the sub-layers, which is followed by a normalization layer. [47]

Table 6. Recommended Tasks

Task	Recommended Paper	Paper Count
Motor Imagery	[23]	6
Seizure	[42]	5
Emotion	[54]	1

Table 7. Recommended Algorithms

Algorithm	Recommended Paper
CNN	[27]
SVM	[45]
Transformer	[47]

Table 8. Combination of Algorithms with Transformers

Algorithm	Dataset	Paper
CNN + Transformer	SEED	[13]
DNN + Transformer	TUEG	[22]
S3T	BCI Competition IV	[49]

Recommended Tasks. The tasks in Table 6 are recommended for undergraduate researchers to include in their studies because they are extensively researched and have ML high accuracy. The paper count column counts the number of papers that include the use of transformers.

As shown in Table 6, transformers can be used on a majority of Brain-Computer Interface tasks, but are most commonly used for Motor Imagery, Emotion Recognition, and Seizure Detection.

Recommended Algorithms. The algorithms in Table 7 are recommended. CNN is the most prominent; SVM is low in computation cost, high in accuracy, and easy to understand. Transformers are trending in BCI research, and have high accuracy and parallelization.

Forms of Transformers. According to our finds, transformers are commonly accompanied with other algorithms or are utilized in different forms. Table 8 outlines some of the forms of transformers used from the papers found.

For several emotion recognition tasks, transformers were combined with CNNs. CNNs are fed the input DE features and extract complete information for multi-frequency data with a depthwise convolution layer, which is then fed to a transformer model [13].

A combination of DNNs and Transformers was for a Motor Imagery task. DNNs were used for pre-training, while transformers were used as the classification algorithm. [22].

S3T is a Spatial-Temporal Tiny Transformer used for Motor Imagery tasks due to its ability to capture spatial and temporal features. S3T requires an attention mechanism to transform the data into a highly distinguishing representation. The model consists of a spatial filter, spatial transformation, temporal transformation, and a classifier. [49]

4.3   Datasets

Dataset Users. Each dataset utilizes different subjects with the goal to be classified for different tasks. The goal of the BCI Competition datasets is to validate signal processing and classification methods for Brain-Computer Interfaces (BCIs). Each data set consists of single-trials of spontaneous brain activity, one part labeled (calibration or training data) and another part unlabeled (evaluation or test data), and a performance measure. The goal is to infer labels (or their probabilities) for the evaluation data sets from calibration data that maximize the performance measure for the true (but to the competitors unknown) labels of the evaluation data.

The DEAP dataset is a multimodal dataset for the analysis of human affective states. The EEG and peripheral physiological signals of 32 participants were recorded as each watched 40 one-minute long excerpts of music videos. Participants rated each video in terms of the levels of arousal, valence, like/dislike, dominance and familiarity.

The SEED dataset contains subjects' EEG signals when they were watching films clips. The film clips are carefully selected so as to induce different types of emotion, which are positive, negative, and neutral ones.

The STEW dataset consists of raw EEG data from 48 subjects who participated in a multitasking workload experiment utilizing the SIMKAP multitasking test. The subjects' brain activity at rest was also recorded before the test and is included as well.

Recommended Datasets. Table 9 overviews a recommended dataset based on the aforementioned recommended tasks in Table 4.

Dataset Breakdown for Transformers. From the papers found that utilize transformers, Table 10 shows the breakdown of the datasets that were used. The other category is a combination of privately collected datasets or uncommon individual sets. DEAP and SEED are available to the public.

Table 9. Dataset Recommendations

Task	Recommended Dataset
Motor Imagery	EEGEyeNet
Emotion Recognition	DEAP
Seizure Detection	Bonn

Table 10. Dataset breakdown for Transformer Algorithm

Dataset	Paper Count
DEAP	5
SEED	2
Other	8

Table 11. Individual Papers

Paper	Algorithm	Task
[47]	Transformer	Age/Gender
[14]	RF	Parkinson's
[27]	CNN/AE	Emotion

Table 12. Review Papers

Paper	Algorithm	Task
[44]	ML	BCI
[15]	DL	BCI
[16]	ML	Emotion

4.4   Papers

Paper Recommendation for Undergraduate Researchers. We recommend 3 individual research papers in Table 11 and 3 review papers in Table 12 to any new researcher to get acclimated with trends in BCI research.

There is limited available literature where EEG data has been used for gender and age classification. The recommended paper for Age/Gender classification gives a firm overview of the task as well as the algorithm. The paper discusses how a transformer network was used for raw EEG data classification. The utilization of Transformers in the classification aided in the achievement of start-of-the-art accuracy for both gender and age. [47] Similarly, the other two papers give a firm overview of their respective tasks, as well as a clear insight into the framework and architecture of the algorithm.

Each of the papers highlighted in Table 12 gives a strong overview of either Machine Learning or Deep learning for their respective tasks. We recommend

Table 13. Recommended Transformer Papers

Paper	Task	Dataset(s)
[51]	Motor Imagery	HysioNet
[31]	Emotion Recognition	DEAP/SEED
[8]	Seizure Detection	CHB-MIT

that undergraduate researchers read these papers and get an even stronger understanding of the BCI research landscape.

Paper Recommendation for Undergraduate BCI Research Using Transformers. We recommended 3 individual research papers in Table 13. Each paper has a different task and dataset. Each paper clearly explains its algorithms framework, methodologies, and results.

4.5   Challenges

One challenge encountered in utilizing ML algorithms for EEG task classifications is their limited robustness. Often, these algorithms are trained on data obtained from a single individual or a small group of individuals. Consequently, when tested on data from a different individual who was not part of the training set, ML algorithms tend to exhibit subpar performance, requiring additional calibration and fine-tuning. To address this issue, a potential solution lies in employing data augmentation techniques, such as Generative Adversarial Networks (GANs). GANs can generate synthetic EEG data, augmenting the existing dataset and enhancing the generality and robustness of the models.

The practical utilization of brain waves for real-world task classifications poses another challenge. Primarily, EEG data collection predominantly occurs in controlled environments, which fails to capture the authentic real-world conditions and factors that impact brain waves, including sensory stimuli and varying levels of concentration. Consequently, ML algorithms often exhibit underperformance when tested in real-world scenarios compared to their performance on laboratory test data. It is imperative to undertake a comprehensive evaluation and understanding of these factors during the design phase to effectively integrate Brain-Computer Interfaces (BCIs) into real-world applications within authentic environments.

4.6   Future Work

The utilization of transformers in classification models for BCI research has demonstrated promising improvements in accuracy across a range of tasks, rendering them applicable in the BCI and medical fields. Subsequent studies can delve deeper into the analysis and exploration of transformers, expanding upon the groundwork established by this paper, with the aim of enhancing their performance by potentially mitigating computational requirements while further improving accuracy. Similar avenues for improvement exist for other algorithms, such as Recurrent Neural Networks (RNNs) and Convolutional Neural Networks (CNNs).

In future research, it is imperative to investigate and identify algorithms that exhibit the highest accuracy for specific tasks while also considering their computational efficiency. This will provide clarity on which algorithms are the most optimal in terms of both accuracy and computational requirements for each task, thus enabling informed decisions in selecting the most suitable algorithms for specific BCI applications.

5 Conclusion

In this paper, we have presented a comprehensive overview of essential tasks, algorithms, and datasets that serve as foundational components for undergraduate researchers embarking on EEG-based Brain-Computer Interface (BCI) research using machine learning (ML).

Based on our extensive analysis, we recommend focusing on prominent tasks such as Motor Imagery, Seizure Detection, and Emotion Classification. These tasks offer a wealth of available datasets and exhibit high accuracy classification rates. To assist researchers in getting started, we have identified specific datasets that align with each task, providing valuable resources to facilitate their investigations.

Furthermore, we suggest the incorporation of popular algorithms such as Convolutional Neural Networks (CNNs), Support Vector Machines (SVMs), and Transformers. These algorithms have consistently demonstrated remarkable accuracy in EEG classification tasks, making them reliable choices for further exploration. Specifically, we have highlighted the growing trend of Transformers in EEG-based BCI research, providing an overview of the most common task-dataset-algorithm combinations associated with this emerging approach.

By following our recommendations, undergraduate researchers can establish a solid foundation in the field, enabling them to confidently contribute to the rapidly evolving landscape of BCI research. We believe that this systematic overview and the suggested starting points will empower newcomers, facilitating their exploration of novel techniques and inspiring their contributions to advancements in BCI research.

As the field continues to progress, it is crucial to stay abreast of the latest developments and embrace new opportunities for innovation. We hope that this paper serves as a valuable resource, guiding researchers towards exciting avenues and inspiring future discoveries in the dynamic realm of EEG-based Brain-Computer Interfaces.

References

1. Ahmad, I., et al.: EEG-based epileptic seizure detection via machine/deep learning approaches: a systematic review. Comput. Intell. Neurosci. **2022**, 6486570 (2022)
2. Altaheri, H., et al.: Deep learning techniques for classification of electroencephalogram (eeg) motor imagery (mi) signals: a review. Neural Comput. Appl. **35**, 1–42 (2021)
3. Basaklar, T., Tuncel, Y., An, S., Ogras, U.: Wearable devices and low-power design for smart health applications: challenges and opportunities. In: 2021 IEEE/ACM International Symposium on Low Power Electronics and Design (ISLPED), p. 1. IEEE (2021)
4. Chen, L., et al.: Data-driven detection of subtype-specific differentially expressed genes. Sci. Rep. **11**(1), 332 (2021)
5. Craik, A., He, Y., Contreras-Vidal, J.L.: Deep learning for electroencephalogram (eeg) classification tasks: a review. J. Neural Eng. **16**(3), 031001 (2019)
6. Deb, R., An, S., Bhat, G., Shill, H., Ogras, U.Y.: A systematic survey of research trends in technology usage for Parkinson's disease. Sensors **22**(15), 5491 (2022)
7. Deb, R., Bhat, G., An, S., Shill, H., Ogras, U.Y.: Trends in technology usage for Parkinson's disease assessment: a systematic review. MedRxiv (2021). https://doi.org/10.1101/2021.02.01.21250939
8. Deng, Z., Li, C., Song, R., Liu, X., Qian, R., Chen, X.: EEG-based seizure prediction via hybrid vision transformer and data uncertainty learning. Eng. Appl. Artif. Intell. **123**, 106401 (2023)
9. Dou, G., Zhou, Z., Qu, X.: Time majority voting, a PC-based EEG classifier for non-expert users. In: Kurosu, M., et al. (eds.) HCI International 2022 – Late Breaking Papers. Multimodality in Advanced Interaction Environments. HCII 2022. LNCS, vol. 13519. Springer, Cham (2022). https://doi.org/10.1007/978-3-031-17618-0_29
10. Duan, R.N., Zhu, J.Y., Lu, B.L.: Differential entropy feature for EEG-based emotion classification. In: 2013 6th International IEEE/EMBS Conference on Neural Engineering (NER), pp. 81–84 (2013). https://doi.org/10.1109/NER.2013.6695876
11. Gong, S., Xing, K., Cichocki, A., Li, J.: Deep learning in EEG: advance of the last ten-year critical period. IEEE Trans. Cogn. Develop. Syst. **14**(2), 348–365 (2021)
12. Govindan, B., Pickett, S., Riggs, B.: Fear of the cure: a beginner's guide to overcoming barriers in creating a course-based undergraduate research experience. J. Microbiol. Biol. Educ. **21**(2), 50 (2020)
13. Guo, J.Y., et al.: A transformer based neural network for emotion recognition and visualizations of crucial EEG channels. Phys. A Statist. Mech. Appl. **603**, 127700 (2022)
14. Hassin-Baer, S., et al.: Identification of an early-stage Parkinson's disease Neuromarker using event-related potentials, brain network analytics and machine-learning. PLoS ONE **17**(1), e0261947 (2022)
15. Hossain, K.M., Islam, M., Hossain, S., Nijholt, A., Ahad, M.A.R., et al.: Status of deep learning for EEG-based brain-computer interface applications. UMBC Student Collection (2023)
16. Houssein, E.H., Hammad, A., Ali, A.A.: Human emotion recognition from EEG-based brain-computer interface using machine learning: a comprehensive review. Neural Comput. Appl. **34**(15), 12527–12557 (2022)
17. Huang, D., Tang, Y., Qin, R.: An evaluation of planetScope images for 3D reconstruction and change detection-experimental validations with case studies. GISci. Remote Sens. **59**(1), 744–761 (2022)

18. Jiang, C., et al.: Deep denoising of raw biomedical knowledge graph from COVID-19 literature, Litcovid, and Pubtator: framework development and validation. J. Med. Internet Res. **24**(7), e38584 (2022)

19. Kastrati, A., et al.: EEGEyeNet: a simultaneous electroencephalography and eye-tracking dataset and benchmark for eye movement prediction. In: Thirty-fifth Conference on Neural Information Processing Systems Datasets and Benchmarks Track (Round 1) (2021). https://openreview.net/forum?id=Nc2uduhU9qa

20. Katsigiannis, S., Ramzan, N.: Dreamer: a database for emotion recognition through EEG and ECG signals from wireless low-cost off-the-shelf devices. IEEE J. Biomed. Health Inform. **22**(1), 98–107 (2018). https://doi.org/10.1109/JBHI.2017.2688239

21. Koelstra, S., et al.: DEAP: a database for emotion analysis; using physiological signals. IEEE Trans. Affect. Comput. **3**(1), 18–31 (2012). https://doi.org/10.1109/T-AFFC.2011.15

22. Kostas, D., Aroca-Ouellette, S., Rudzicz, F.: BENDR: using transformers and a contrastive self-supervised learning task to learn from massive amounts of EEG data. Front. Hum. Neurosci. **15**, 653659 (2021)

23. Li, F., He, F., Wang, F., Zhang, D., Xia, Y., Li, X.: A novel simplified convolutional neural network classification algorithm of motor imagery EEG signals based on deep learning. Appl. Sci. **10**(5), 1605 (2020)

24. Li, S., Zhou, W., Yuan, Q., Geng, S., Cai, D.: Feature extraction and recognition of ictal EEG using EMD and SVM. Comput. Biol. Med. **43**(7), 807–816 (2013)

25. Li, X., et al.: EEG based emotion recognition: a tutorial and review. ACM Comput. Surv. **55**(4), 1–57 (2022)

26. Liu, C., Li, H., Xu, J., Gao, W., Shen, X., Miao, S.: Applying convolutional neural network to predict soil erosion: a case study of coastal areas. Int. J. Environ. Res. Public Health **20**(3), 2513 (2023)

27. Liu, J., Wu, G., Luo, Y., Qiu, S., Yang, S., Li, W., Bi, Y.: EEG-based emotion classification using a deep neural network and sparse autoencoder. PubMed, pp. 1–42 (2020)

28. Lu, Y., Wang, H., Wei, W.: Machine learning for synthetic data generation: a review. arXiv preprint arXiv:2302.04062 (2023)

29. Lu, Y., et al.: COT: an efficient and accurate method for detecting marker genes among many subtypes. Bioinform. Adv. **2**(1), vbac037 (2022)

30. Luo, X., Ma, X., Munden, M., Wu, Y.J., Jiang, Y.: A multisource data approach for estimating vehicle queue length at metered on-ramps. J. Transp. Eng. Part A: Syst. **148**(2), 04021117 (2022)

31. Luo, Y., et al.: EEG-based emotion classification using spiking neural networks. IEEE Access **8**, 46007–46016 (2020)

32. Ma, X.: Traffic performance evaluation using statistical and machine learning methods, Ph. D. thesis, The University of Arizona (2022)

33. Ma, X., Karimpour, A., Wu, Y.J.: Statistical evaluation of data requirement for ramp metering performance assessment. Transp. Res. Part A: Policy Pract. **141**, 248–261 (2020)

34. Padfield, N., Zabalza, J., Zhao, H., Masero, V., Ren, J.: EEG-based brain-computer interfaces using motor-imagery: techniques and challenges. Sensors **19**(6), 1423 (2019)

35. Peng, X., Bhattacharya, T., Mao, J., Cao, T., Jiang, C., Qin, X.: Energy-efficient management of data centers using a renewable-aware scheduler. In: 2022 IEEE International Conference on Networking, Architecture and Storage (NAS), pp. 1–8. IEEE (2022)

36. Prasanna, J., Subathra, M., Mohammed, M.A., Damaševičius, R., Sairamya, N.J., George, S.T.: Automated epileptic seizure detection in pediatric subjects of CHB-MIT EEG database-a survey. J. Personal. Med. **11**(10), 1028 (2021)

37. Qu, X., Hickey, T.J.: EEG4Home: a human-in-the-loop machine learning model for EEG-based BCI. In: Schmorrow, D.D., Fidopiastis, C.M. (eds.) Augmented Cognition. HCII 2022. LNCS, vol. 13310. Springer, Cham (2022). https://doi.org/10.1007/978-3-031-05457-0_14

38. Qu, X., Liu, P., Li, Z., Hickey, T.: Multi-class time continuity voting for EEG classification. In: Frasson, C., Bamidis, P., Vlamos, P. (eds.) BFAL 2020. LNCS (LNAI), vol. 12462, pp. 24–33. Springer, Cham (2020). https://doi.org/10.1007/978-3-030-60735-7_3

39. Qu, X., Liukasemsarn, S., Tu, J., Higgins, A., Hickey, T.J., Hall, M.H.: Identifying clinically and functionally distinct groups among healthy controls and first episode psychosis patients by clustering on EEG patterns. Front. Psych. **11**, 541659 (2020)

40. Qu, X., Mei, Q., Liu, P., Hickey, T.: Using EEG to distinguish between writing and typing for the same cognitive task. In: Frasson, C., Bamidis, P., Vlamos, P. (eds.) BFAL 2020. LNCS (LNAI), vol. 12462, pp. 66–74. Springer, Cham (2020). https://doi.org/10.1007/978-3-030-60735-7_7

41. Qu, X., Sun, Y., Sekuler, R., Hickey, T.: EEG markers of stem learning. In: 2018 IEEE Frontiers in Education Conference (FIE), pp. 1–9. IEEE (2018)

42. Qureshi, M.B., Afzaal, M., Qureshi, M.S., Fayaz, M.: Machine learning-based EEG signals classification model for epileptic seizure detection. Multimedia Tools Appl. **80**, 17849–17877 (2021)

43. Roy, Y., Banville, H., Albuquerque, I., Gramfort, A., Falk, T.H., Faubert, J.: Deep learning-based electroencephalography analysis: a systematic review. J. Neural Eng. **16**(5), 051001 (2019)

44. Saeidi, M., et al.: Neural decoding of EEG signals with machine learning: a systematic review. Brain Sci. **11**(11), 1525 (2021)

45. Sha'abani, M.N.A.H., Fuad, N., Jamal, N., Ismail, M.F.: kNN and SVM classification for EEG: a review. In: Kasruddin Nasir, A.N., et al. (eds.) InECCE2019. LNEE, vol. 632, pp. 555–565. Springer, Singapore (2020). https://doi.org/10.1007/978-981-15-2317-5_47

46. Shen, X., Sun, Y., Zhang, Y., Najmabadi, M.: Semi-supervised intent discovery with contrastive learning. In: Proceedings of the 3rd Workshop on Natural Language Processing for Conversational AI, pp. 120–129 (2021)

47. Siddhad, G., Gupta, A., Dogra, D.P., Roy, P.P.: Efficacy of transformer networks for classification of raw EEG data. arXiv preprint arXiv:2202.05170 (2022)

48. Singh, A., Hussain, A.A., Lal, S., Guesgen, H.W.: A comprehensive review on critical issues and possible solutions of motor imagery based electroencephalography brain-computer interface. Sensors **21**(6), 2173 (2021)

49. Song, Y., Jia, X., Yang, L., Xie, L.: Transformer-based spatial-temporal feature learning for EEG decoding. arXiv preprint arXiv:2106.11170 (2021)

50. Suhaimi, N.S., Mountstephens, J., Teo, J., et al.: EEG-based emotion recognition: a state-of-the-art review of current trends and opportunities. Comput. Intell. Neurosci. **2020**, 8875426 (2020)

51. Sun, J., Xie, J., Zhou, H.: EEG classification with transformer-based models. In: 2021 IEEE 3rd Global Conference on Life Sciences and Technologies (LifeTech), pp. 92–93. IEEE (2021)

52. Tang, Y., Song, S., Gui, S., Chao, W., Cheng, C., Qin, R.: Active and low-cost hyperspectral imaging for the spectral analysis of a low-light environment. Sensors **23**(3), 1437 (2023)

53. Tangermann, M., et al.: Review of the BCI competition IV. Frontiers Neurosci. **6**, 55 (2012)

54. Wang, J., Wang, M.: Review of the emotional feature extraction and classification using EEG signals. Cogn. Robot. **1**, 29–40 (2021)

55. Wang, R., Qu, X.: EEG Daydreaming, a machine learning approach to detect daydreaming activities. In: Schmorrow, D.D., Fidopiastis, C.M. (eds.) Augmented Cognition. HCII 2022. LNCS, vol. 13310. Springer, Cham (2022). https://doi.org/10.1007/978-3-031-05457-0_17

56. Yi, L., Qu, X.: Attention-based CNN capturing EEG recording's average voltage and local change. In: Degen, H., Ntoa, S. (eds.) Artificial Intelligence in HCI. HCII 2022. LNCS, vol. 13336. Springer, Cham (2022). https://doi.org/10.1007/978-3-031-05643-7_29

57. Zhang, S., Zhao, Z., Guan, C.: Multimodal continuous emotion recognition: a technical report for ABAW5. In: Proceedings of the IEEE/CVF Conference on Computer Vision and Pattern Recognition, pp. 5763–5768 (2023)

58. Zhang, Y., et al.: Biotic homogenization increases with human intervention: implications for mangrove wetland restoration. Ecography **2022**(4), 5835 (2022)

59. Zhang, Z., et al.: Implementation and performance evaluation of in-vehicle highway back-of-queue alerting system using the driving simulator. In: 2021 IEEE International Intelligent Transportation Systems Conference (ITSC), pp. 1753–1759. IEEE (2021)

60. Zhang, Z., Tian, R., Sherony, R., Domeyer, J., Ding, Z.: Attention-based interrelation modeling for explainable automated driving. IEEE Trans. Intell. Vehicles **8**, 1564–1573 (2022)

61. Zhao, Z., Chopra, K., Zeng, Z., Li, X.: Sea-Net: squeeze-and-excitation attention net for diabetic retinopathy grading. In: 2020 IEEE International Conference on Image Processing (ICIP), pp. 2496–2500. IEEE (2020)

62. Zhao, Z., et al.: BiRA-Net: bilinear attention net for diabetic retinopathy grading. In: 2019 IEEE International Conference on Image Processing (ICIP), pp. 1385–1389. IEEE (2019)

63. Zhou, Z., Dou, G., Qu, X.: BrainActivity1: a framework of EEG data collection and machine learning analysis for college students. In: Stephanidis, C., Antona, M., Ntoa, S., Salvendy, G. (eds.) HCI International 2022 – Late Breaking Posters. HCII 2022. Communications in Computer and Information Science, vol. 1654. Springer, Cham (2022). https://doi.org/10.1007/978-3-031-19679-9_16

64. Zong, N., et al.: Beta: a comprehensive benchmark for computational drug-target prediction. Brief. Bioinform. **23**(4), bbac199 (2022)

A Study on Workload Assessment and Usability of Wind-Aware User Interface for Small Unmanned Aircraft System Remote Operations

Asma Tabassum$^{(\boxtimes)}$, He Bai , and Nicoletta Fala

Oklahoma State University, Stillwater, OK 74075, USA
{asma.tabassum,he.bai,nfala}@okstate.edu

Abstract. This study evaluates pilots' cognitive workload and situational awareness during remote small unmanned aircraft system operations in different wind conditions. To complement the urban air mobility concept that envisions safe, sustainable, and accessible air transportation, we conduct multiple experiments in a realistic wind-aware simulator-user interface pipeline. Experiments are performed with basic and wind-aware displays in several wind conditions to assess how complex wind fields impact pilots' cognitive resources. Post-hoc analysis reveals that providing pilots with real-time wind information improves situational awareness while decreasing cognitive workload.

Keywords: Wind-aware simulation · Pilot-in-the-loop experiment · Cognitive workload · Situational awareness

1 Introduction

The idea of urban air mobility (UAM) encompasses air transportation within and above a city, as well as a subset of advanced air mobility [1], which aspires to produce a safe, secure, and efficient air traffic operation. With the aggressive integration of unmanned aircraft system (UAS) into the National Airspace System, more than 250 prototypes of vertical take-off and landing (VTOL), electric, and autonomous aircraft are being designed and tested [1]. Even with all the growing attention and a global expected growth of 13.8% by 2025 [2], the designs for UAS and large-scale integration are being challenged by environmental uncertainties [3]. One of these critical environmental hurdles is turbulent wind, especially in urban settings. Around 52 percent of respondents (out of 1702 people) express an increased level of fear and concern while flying in the turbulent wind in UAM [1]. For aerospace applications, control design for a standalone

The work is supported by the U.S. National Science Foundation (NSF) under award number 1925147.

airborne system itself demands more scrutiny and requires guaranteed operability in a dynamic environment. This becomes more challenging for UAS remote control operations, where the pilot cannot analyze the dynamic environment onboard. Due to sensory isolation caused by the Ground Control Station (GCS) being located on the ground, the UAS pilot is deprived of possible vestibular and onboard visual senses. However, the UAS pilot must acquire and interpret the equivalent level of awareness and information (as of a crewed aircraft) through sensors and interfaces regardless of autonomous or manual operation. On top of that, challenges imposed by uncertainties degrade UAS operation and navigation tasks. Therefore, compensating for the reduced situational awareness (SA) is a major challenge in UAS GCS User Interface (UI) design. Situational awareness refers to the operator's internal model of the surrounding world around them at any time. Addressing drawbacks of reduced SA in UAS is not straightforward as it relates to including additional information, layouts, and audio-visual inputs into the UI. As a consequence, UAS UI design incurs major pitfalls such as

- misidentification of operational information during the design phase [4],
- addition of irrelevant information leading to additional cognitive processing [5]
- inaccurate representation of information leading to inadequate/incorrect responses of the operator [6].

Thus, poor display design and poor information presentation increase task overhead and significantly impact mission quality and operator performance.

Modern UI designs have focused on user-centric designs [7] which emphasize a user's needs and application requirements. UAS UI design through research, simulation, and usability testing could potentially satisfy users' needs and design standards [8]. While the research effort in the interaction between human pilot and autopilot in crewed aircraft is more mature, less attention has been expended to investigate interaction strategies associated with remote UAS pilot and onboard command and control [9]. An initial design guide for interface design that involves viewpoint design, control level design, and autonomy level design is illustrated by FAA [10]. In [11], the author recommends an iterative task analysis throughout the design process to better understand key task components, user needs, and the user's mental representation of the displayed information. The necessity of the assessment of the pilot's cognitive states with autonomy is reported in [12]. Other studies [13,14] also discuss the design criteria for the sUAS interface. In our previous work [15], we adopt a user-centered design methodology to develop a wind-aware UI and simulation pipeline for small UAS (sUAS). We identify information components and derive specific display designs based on a focus group study with subject matter experts (SME). Our subject matter experts are four pilots, and three of them have FAR 107 certifications. One of the biggest concerns of SMEs is the lack of wind velocity information in the current off-the-shelf displays. They also mention that operators mostly rely on local wind predictions and do not have access to wind information through the GCS UI during flight. Based on experts' suggestions, we implement a design that overlays wind information into the QGroundcontrol UI to accommodate a wind-aware framework throughout small UAS missions.

Literature indicates that about 69% of the UAS mishaps (damage or loss of platform) are caused by human factors [16]. In this work, we aim to address the rising operational and navigational challenges that turbulent wind imposes on human pilots and investigate how wind-aware UI may reduce a remote pilot's subjective cognitive load and improve situational awareness. We expect that given that a human pilot has adequate knowledge (training) of the system and tasks, including real-time information on wind will assist accurate perception of the vehicle and environment, reduce cognitive load, and enhance the piloting interaction experience. Toward this end, we evaluate the usability of wind-aware UI and assess the cognitive workload of the participants while flying with the UI. Usability refers to the quality of a UI that is easy to learn, has effective use, and is enjoyable from the user's perspective [17].

The main goal of our design is to improve situational awareness through the easy and effective use of wind-aware UI. We test usability by evaluating the improvement in situational awareness while reducing cognitive workload. We use a fully manual mode for the experiment. This mode does not support stable hover or station keeping in the presence of disturbance, i.e., the pilot must keep it stable using manual input. Manual modes are specifically used during search and rescue operations or to capture pictures of particular objects [2]. While relatively stable manual control or GPS-guided control options are available in off-the-shelf platforms, the rationale behind choosing this mode is twofold. First, this mode allows us to let the pilot experience the wind as is so that we can capture relatively accurate cognitive exhaustion that the wind imposes on the pilot. We use pilots' cognitive data in our subjective analysis. Second, this mode is expected to apprehend how individual flight experiences cause different performances. These effects are expected to be captured by flight record data, e.g., states and input, and will be assessed for objective analysis in subsequent studies. Based on the subjective interpretation of participants, this study aims to answer the following three questions:

- Does wind significantly increase the workload for remote pilots?
- Does wind-aware UI alleviate pilots' cognitive loading?
- Does wind-aware UI improve subjective situational awareness?

Based on our research questions, we deduce three hypotheses and test them with the experimental data. The rest of the paper is organized as follows. The simulator, mission, and experimental procedures are illustrated in Sect. 2. We briefly review evaluation methodology in Sect. 3. The finding of our experiments and hypotheses testing are provided in Sect. 4. We discuss our result and future work in Sect. 5.

2   Experiment Design and Procedure

2.1   Wind-Aware Simulator-UI

The wind-aware simulator is built upon three open-source software codebases; 1) AirSim [18], 2) PX4 [19] and 3) QGroundControl (QGC) station[1]. These platforms have been selected based on AirSim's capability to conduct software-in-the-loop (SITL) with PX4 and QGC. We use a PlayStation controller to integrate human pilot inputs into the system. While the original implementation of AirSim only allows global wind, we integrate an additional module to the core physics engine to handle local wind. Local wind changes based on the position of the quadcopter and simulation time. We also update the quadcopter dynamics to capture the effect of time-varying wind. The PX4 flight stack is modified to allow the transfer of local wind velocities to the QGroundControl station through the MAVLink communication protocol. PX4 communicates state observations to QGC for the pilot's interpretation. We use QML to develop wind widgets that display the local wind velocity in a variety of ways. An example of wind widgets is provided in Fig. 1. Each interface conveys the velocity both numerically and graphically with the graphical implementation varying. Figure 1a uses a compass-style display, where the horizontal velocity of the wind is represented as an arrow conveying the wind's direction and magnitude. An alternative display is shown in Fig. 1b with the planar velocity split into north and east vector components. Both displays show vertical wind with another arrow beside the compass. A third implementation is shown in Fig. 1c, where the direction is conveyed using a compass, similar to Fig. 1a. The magnitude is displayed on a green-yellow-red gradient beneath the compass. The final design refers to Fig. 1d, similar to the third display with wind direction placed in the outer dial and indicates the relative direction of the wind with respect to the vehicle.

(a) Compass-based heading (planer direction) with a vertical wind component.

(b) Component-wise display (north-east velocity split) with vertical wind component.

(c) Gradients-based display with vehicle heading and wind direction in compass.

(d) Gradients-based display with vehicle heading and wind direction in the outer dial.

Fig. 1. Wind velocity module in wind-aware UI: pilot can choose preferred display from the drop-down menu.

---

[1] http://qgroundcontrol.com/.

The displays are designed based on our SME's suggestions. During the experiment, we let the pilot choose their preferred display and let them scale the utility of each display on a 5-point Likert scale [20] shown in Table 1. A Likert scale allows an individual to express how much they agree or disagree with a particular statement. This enables us to gather feedback from the user which is a important part of user-centric design validation. We plot the voting scale of 11 participants in terms of population percent in Fig. 2. The outer gradient display that shows the wind direction with respect to vehicle heading received higher ratings than all other displays.

Table 1. Likert scale for feedback to wind display design.

Scale	Meaning
Unacceptable	functionality is not sufficient to meet mission needs
Marginal	functionality sufficient to meet mission needs, but with at least one deficiency.
Acceptable	functionality is sufficient to meet mission needs
Superior	functionality is sufficient to meet mission needs and exceeds at least one desired parameter
Outstanding	functionality exceeds all mission needs

2.2   Mission Design

The experiment is carried out in the simulator with the capacity of first-person view (FPV) through the camera. An upper screen shows a video feed of the simulated scenario and a lower screen shows the wind-aware UI. This imitates the real flight setup scenario since the operator usually holds a screen with a controller in hand and looks up at the flight environment (head-down display). Figure 3 shows the experimental setup with the controller. Experiments include conducting a mission in five different environment conditions and UI combinations. The experimental design matrix is provided in Table 2.

Table 2. Experimental design matrix.

Experiment	Wind condition	display
NW	No wind	No wind
CW	Constant wind	No display
TW	Turbulent wind	No display
CWD	Constant wind	With display
TWD	Turbulent wind	With display

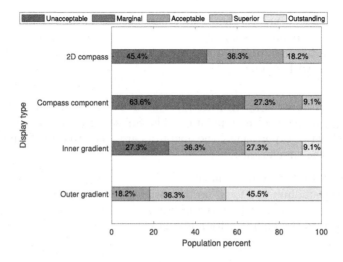

Fig. 2. Likert plots showing survey on users' perspectives of different displays. Outer gradient where the wind can be interpreted relative to the vehicle position received the most positive vote. 9 out of 11 participants selected outer gradient for experiments.

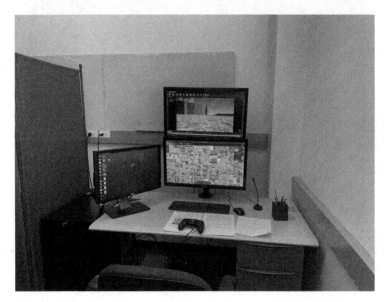

Fig. 3. Experimental setup: upper screen shows the environment and the lower screen shows the ground control station. Participants are also required to use the mouse and the joystick.

Training. The participants are provided with a training session to help them understand the setup and tools available to them. This includes understanding and interpretation of wind displays as well. Different wind displays are explained from pictures and a video. The flight in simulations is fully manual and collision avoidance capability is not available. During training, participants also go through controller manipulation and are allowed as much as time they need to be comfortable with setups.

Main Experiment. Experiments start after the participants feel confident about setups and control manipulation. The full set of experiments runs about 2 h. For each set of experiments, the operators are asked to achieve the following objectives in the simulations:

– Take off and take manual control,
– Survey the stadium and focus on the assigned picture as steadily as possible. The whole environment is shown in Fig. 4,
– Come back to the home position and land.

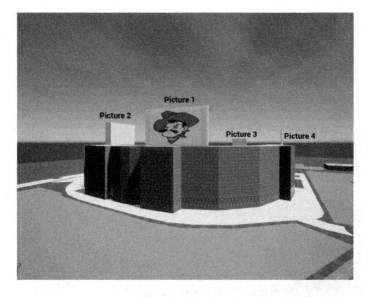

Fig. 4. Mission: Go around the Boone Pickens Stadium and focus on the pictures at four different places.

Participants. As of June 18, a total of 11 participants with varying flight experience, as shown in Fig. 5, have participated in the experiment. Our recruitment and experiments are still ongoing. The participants are recruited via email distribution list and snowball method with emails. The emails are circulated to the Mechanical and Aerospace Engineering, Electrical and Computer Engineering graduate students, and the College of Education and Human Sciences: Aviation students at Oklahoma State University. The experiment is approved by the

Institutional Review Board (IRB) at Oklahoma State University. All participants were compensated with a gift card.

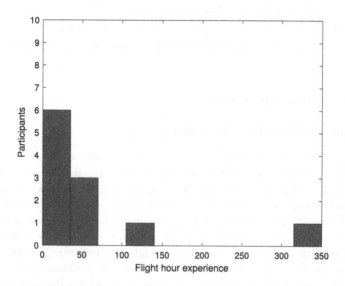

Fig. 5. A histogram plot showing participants' flight experience. The mean and standard deviation of flight experience between participants are $M(11) = 61.54, SD(11) = 103.54$, respectively.

Measurements. Pre-experiment and logistic training surveys are conducted prior to starting the experiment. In the pre-experiment survey, we gather the flight experience data of the participants. The logistic survey questionnaire provided in Table 3 is used to analyze the operator's understanding of the setup and display. After the experiments, operators are given Subjective Work Assessment Technique (SWAT) [21] questionnaires for each set of experiments, a post-experiment survey, and a generic survey. The post-experiment survey consists of queries related to situational awareness assessment and wind information utility. In the generic survey, the operator can provide feedback on the various features developed in this program and on how to improve them to better fit their needs in remotely piloting a UAS during windy conditions. Along with the surveys from the participants, state and control input data are collected through the PX4 log file, and image data are automatically stored in the computer.

Table 3. Logistic questionnaires.

Questions
Are you able to interpret all the displays provided in the interface?
Which display serves best to understand the wind information?
Please identify the wind magnitude and direction of your chosen display

3   Assessment Methods

3.1   Cognitive Workload Assessment

Workload assessment is a critical part of the study while designing a new interface or integrating layers of information into the interface. In our context, we evaluate mental workload since our working environments impose more cognitive demands upon operators than physical demands. In highly dynamic environments with a multidimensional task load, an uncertain environment increases the operator's workload [22]. In many situations, operators may have to increase and exhaust cognitive resources to maintain a high performance [23]. Several tools are used in the literature [24] to measure and assess workload. Some tools are considered intrusive [23] that require operator interaction with designated tools. These tools may further increase the workload on top of the actual workload. Non-intrusive measurement tools have been widely used and accepted. In this measurement, operators are required to fill up the questionnaire at the end of the experiment sessions. Since the answers to the questionnaire are based on the operators' perceptions, these are called subjective assessments. Among several subjective assessment ratings, NASA-TLX [25], Subjective Workload Assessment Technique (SWAT) [23], and Bedford Scale [26] are frequently used in aerospace applications [27]. NASA-TLX and SWAT are both multi-dimensional methods: NASA-TLX comprises six subjective factors whereas SWAT comprises only three factors. Originally, SWAT has two phases. The first phase starts with sorting 27 cards with various combinations of workload, according to the individual perception of subjective cognitive loading in high to low order. A scale is then developed using the sorting order. The cognitive load is measured based on the questionnaire and developed scale. Bedford scale follows a flow pattern of questions, where answering to some question "*yes*" prompts another question and "*no*" ends the questionnaire. Although NASA-TLX and SWAT both incorporate a scaling procedure by obtaining the results from a number of individuals factor, we have chosen SWAT (see Table 4) since it is based on a minimal scaling method while still producing meaningful results in relevant applications [28]. The modified SWAT is adopted where the pre-sorting and scaling steps are skipped and the workload score is calculated based on the raw scores of the participants with Principal Component Analysis (PCA) [29].

Table 4. Subjective Workload Assessment Technique (SWAT) questionnaire.

Load	Scale and meaning
Time load	• Often have spare time - 1
	• Occasionally have spare time - 2
	• Almost never have spare time - 3
Mental effort load	• Very little conscious mental effort or concentration required - 1
	• Moderate conscious mental effort required - 2
	• Extensive mental effort and concentration are necessary - 3
Psychological stress load	• Little confusion, risk, frustration, or anxiety exists and can be easily accommodated - 1
	• Moderate stress due to confusion, frustration, or anxiety noticeably adds to the workload - 2
	• High to very intense stress due to confusion, frustration, or anxiety - 3

3.2 Situational Awareness Assessment

Endsley [30] defines situation awareness (SA) as being comprised of three components: 1) the perception of the elements in the environment within a volume of time and space (L1), 2) the comprehension of their meaning (L2), and 3) the projection of their status in the near future (L3). SA is critical for successful decision-making, especially in the aerospace domain [31]. Each of these levels may comprise specific situation awareness such as mission awareness, spatial awareness, and time awareness [32]. While effectively measuring SA poses considerable challenges due to its multivariate nature, it provides valuable information with higher subjective sensitivity. In the literature, three main methods had been utilized to measure and quantify SA. First, the explicit methods directly measure SA by assessing the features of participants' mental models concurrently with the tasks. One of the most sought methods is SAGAT (Situational Awareness and Global Assessment Technique) [33], which is developed based on *freeze technique*. In this assessment, the tasks are halted and assessment questionnaires are presented to the participants. While explicit methods are well accepted in the aviation domain, particularly in Air Traffic Control [34,35], for safety-critical operations such as piloting airborne vehicles, obstructing or freezing tasks may not be an appropriate option. The second method is the implicit method that assesses situational awareness by inferring another intermediate variable. One common variable is task performance (TP) [36,37], which can be formulated based on mission accomplishments. Predefined performance metrics may also be used. Despite being the minimal invasive assessment technique, this method may falsely tie poor performance with poor SA, as performance may vary for a variety of reasons, especially on the experience of the operator. The third method called the subjective method uses the participant's own judgment. The method is based on the principle that the participants know better. The assessment is conducted post-tasks and creates no obstruction during the experimental procedure. Due to the nature of self-assessment, this technique provides greater accuracy in understanding user-centric designs. Since we use an already established popular UI as our base display, we formulate SA questionnaires based on mission criteria. We follow the third method and adapt the Post Assessment of Situational Assessment (PASA) [32] structure while setting up the questions and the 5-point rating scale and assigning the level of SA with each question (provided in Table 5).

Table 5. Post-experiment survey for subjective situational awareness assessment with response type and associated SA level.

Questions	Basic/wind-aware	Answer/ rating	Level
Were you able to know exactly where the quadcopter's position was at all times?	Both	Rating	L1
Were you able to identify building structures easily?	Both	Answer	L1
Were you able to keep track of time?	Both	Rating	L2
Does display help you understand wind throughout the mission?	Wind-aware	Answer	L2
How often do you use wind information to make decisions i.e. change control? Please rank for constant and turbulent wind separately	Wind-aware	Rating	L3
Was it easy to follow the mission goal with the wind-aware display? Please rank for constant and turbulent wind separately	Wind-aware	Rating	L3
Were you able to change the course of action because you felt more confident with the wind-aware display than with a basic display?	Wind-aware	Rating	L3

4   Result Analysis

To study the usability of the wind-aware display we formulate the following null hypotheses.

Null Hypothesis 1. ($H1_0$): *There is no significant difference between cognitive load in different wind conditions.*

Null Hypothesis 2. ($H2_0$): *There is no significant difference between cognitive load in different display conditions.*

Null Hypothesis 3. ($H3_0$): *There is no significant difference between situational awareness in different display conditions.*

To assess the hypothesis we adopt a one-way ANOVA analysis with 95% confidence interval setting. The cognitive workload is calculated from the raw scores provided by the participants. We skip the time-consuming sorting card stage and utilize PCA instead. The PCA scores are used to deduce the total cognitive load which is then normalized to achieve a workload value spanning from 0 to 100. The overall cognitive workload is illustrated in Fig. 6a and the mean workload is shown in Fig. 6b.

Both plots imply the fact that the complexity of wind increases participants' cognitive workload. With ANOVA analysis, we see a statistically significant difference in workload ($p - value = 3.67 \times 10^{-11} < 0.05$) in different wind conditions (see Fig. 7a). A summary of the cognitive workload analysis and hypotheses results are provided in Table 6. The F-statistics for hypothesis 1, $F(2, 11) = 59.43$ signify how large the variance between workloads are in the different wind. We also observe that providing the participants with the wind information alleviates the cognitive workload significantly ($p - value < 0.05$) in both constant and turbulent wind conditions (refer to Figs. 7b and 7c). ($H2_0$).

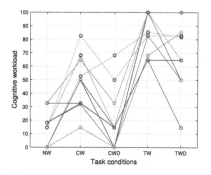

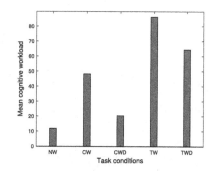

(a) Cognitive workload of participants ($N = 11$).

(b) Mean cognitive workload for each task condition.

Fig. 6. Cognitive workload: (a) shows individual workload and (b) shows mean workload for each task condition. Both figures indicate that with display the cognitive workload tends to decrease in both constant and turbulent task conditions.

Table 6. Descriptive statistics of ANOVA analysis of cognitive workload for $N = 11$ participants.

Hypothesis	F-value	p-value	Decision
$H1_0$: No wind	59.43	3.67×10^{-11}	Reject
$H2_0$: Constant wind	10.05	0.0048	Reject
$H2_0$: Turbulent wind	6.8	0.00168	Reject

We next evaluate the null hypothesis 3 ($H3_0$) for situational awareness. To do that, we first add up the answer and ratings provided by the participants post-experiments. The questionnaires are categorized into both basic and wind-aware displays (see Table 5). The score is normalized on a scale of 1. The subjective situational awareness scores for each participant is shown in Fig. 8. While most participants feel the acquired SA is the same for constant and turbulent wind, a few participants rated SA differently for constant and turbulent wind conditions, which is visible in Fig. 8. Table 7 shows the ANOVA statistics for the post-assessment of situational awareness questionnaires, where we include the F and p values. The ANOVA analysis shows that wind information significantly improves subjective situational awareness in both constant ($p - value = 0.0056 < 0.05$) and turbulent wind situations ($p - value = 0.0064 < 0.05$). The box plots in Fig. 9 visualizes the impacts of the wind information in improving situational awareness. The F values are very close for constant wind ($F(1, 11) = 9.62$) and turbulent wind ($F(1, 11) = 9.26$) with the constant wind case being slightly higher. This is because the participants who reported different SA for constant and turbulent wind indicated higher SA acquired during constant wind operations except for participant $P11$. Some of the SA questionnaires are based on if participants were able to utilize wind information for decision-making. A few

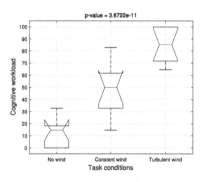

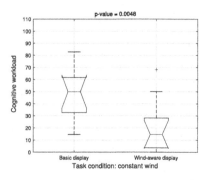

(a) Cognitive workload in the different wind conditions without display.

(b) Cognitive workload in the constant wind with different display conditions.

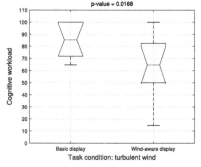

(c) Cognitive workload in the turbulent wind with different display conditions.

Fig. 7. Illustration of ANOVA results in box-plot. The red line represents the median of the data, and the starting, and ending of the notch represent the first and third quartiles of the data. Here, (a) clearly outlines the variability of the workload between wind conditions. In plots (b) and (c) we also distinctly notice the difference in workload data spans. (Color figure online)

Table 7. Descriptive statistics of ANOVA analysis of subjective situational awareness for $N = 11$ participants.

Hypothesis	F value	p-value	Decision
$H3_0$: Constant wind	9.62	0.0056	Reject
$H3_0$: Turbulent wind	9.26	0.0064	Reject

participants expressed that due to the higher cognitive loading on quadcopter control during turbulent operations, oftentimes they were unable to make use of wind information provided at a desired level, which could be the reason that we see a lower SA acquired in the turbulent case than in the constant case.

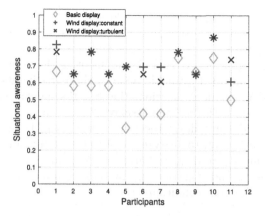

Fig. 8. Subjective situational awareness score for each participant in different wind conditions. Some participants feel wind-aware display improved SA equally during constant and turbulent wind conditions which is depicted by overlapping red and blue points. (Color figure online)

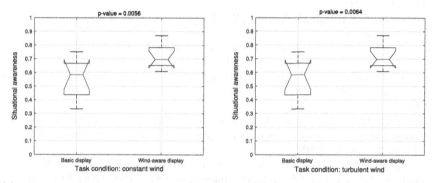

(a) Subjective situational awareness in the constant wind with different display conditions.

(b) Subjective situational awareness in the turbulent wind with different display conditions.

Fig. 9. Illustration of ANOVA results in box-plot. It should be noted that the data spans for constant and turbulent wind look similar from the box plots (a) and (b), as most of the participants rated SA the same for both constant and turbulent wind.

5 Discussion and Future Work

The preliminary post-hoc analysis exclusively focuses on understanding subjective perspectives. Although the sample size is small, consistent outcomes are noticed while analyzing the results in varying sample sizes starting from $N = 6$. Hence, we expect a similar outcome as we continue experiments with more participants. Participants were also asked what they liked or disliked about the experiment. The most positive remark is that the wind display makes them more confident. It is also noted that the pilots benefited more from the direction than the magnitude. In real time while there is turbulence during taking pictures, most of the pilots use wind direction while projecting the outcome of their decision, not the magnitude. All participants mention they would take assistance from autonomous control if available. One of the participants, who frequently operates some sUAS missions mentions that the first-person view helped carry out the mission along with the wind display.

The current study provides subjective or user insights using a wind-aware display. It is also important to analyze the objective or mission-specific improvement with the wind-aware display. Future work includes analysis of flight and image data to understand objective improvement and measure the performance of the pilot under different conditions.

References

1. Reiche, C., Cohen, A.P., Fernando, C.: An initial assessment of the potential weather barriers of urban air mobility. IEEE Trans. Intell. Transp. Syst. **22**(9), 6018–6027 (2021)
2. Rebensky, S., Carroll, M., Bennett, W., Xueyu, H.: Impact of heads-up displays on small unmanned aircraft system operator situation awareness and performance: a simulated study. Int. J. Hum.-Comput. Interact. **38**(5), 419–431 (2022)
3. Black, T.: Ups CEO says wind and rain are holding back delivery drones (2022). https://www.bloomberg.com/news/articles/2022-01-11/ups-ceo-says-wind-and-rain-are-holding-back-delivery-dronesxj4y7vzkg. Accessed 30 Sept 2022
4. Vincenzi, D.A., Terwilliger, B.A., Ison, D.C.: Unmanned aerial system (UAS) human-machine interfaces: new paradigms in command and control. Procedia Manuf. **3**, 920–927 (2015)
5. Tvaryanas, A.P., Thompson, W.T.: Recurrent error pathways in HFACS data: analysis of 95 mishaps with remotely piloted aircraft. Aviat. Space Environ. Med. **79**(5), 525–532 (2008)
6. Hobbs, A.: Unmanned aircraft systems. In: Human Factors in Aviation, pp. 505–531. Elsevier (2010)
7. Chammas, A., Quaresma, M., Mont'Alvão, C.: A closer look on the user centred design. Procedia Manuf. **3**, 5397–5404 (2015)
8. Haritos, T.: A study of human-machine interface (HMI) learnability for unmanned aircraft systems command and control. Ph.D. thesis, Nova Southeastern University (2017)
9. Terwilliger, B.A., Ison, D.C., Vincenzi, D.A., Liu, D.: Advancement and application of unmanned aerial system human-machine-interface (HMI) technology. In: Yamamoto, S. (ed.) HIMI 2014. LNCS, vol. 8522, pp. 273–283. Springer, Cham (2014). https://doi.org/10.1007/978-3-319-07863-2_27
10. Williams, K.W.: An assessment of pilot control interfaces for unmanned aircraft. Technical report, Federal Aviation Administration Oklahoma City ok Civil Aeromedical Inst (2007)
11. Maybury, M.T.: Usable advanced visual interfaces in aviation. In: Proceedings of the International Working Conference on Advanced Visual Interfaces, pp. 2–3 (2012)

12. Jimenez, C., Faerevaag, C.L., Jentsch, F.: User interface design recommendations for small unmanned aircraft systems (SUAS). Int. J. Aviat. Aeronaut. Aerosp. **3**(2), 5 (2016)

13. Vinot, J.-L., Letondal, C., Pauchet, S., Chatty, S.: Could tangibility improve the safety of touch-based interaction? Exploring a new physical design space for pilot-system interfaces. In: Proceedings of the International Conference on Human-Computer Interaction in Aerospace, pp. 1–8 (2016)

14. Monk, K., Shively, R.J., Fern, L., Rorie, R.C.: Effects of display location and information level on UAS pilot assessments of a detect and avoid system. In: Proceedings of the Human Factors and Ergonomics Society Annual Meeting, vol. 59, pp. 50–54. SAGE Publications, Los Angeles (2015)

15. Tabassum, A., DeSantis, M., Bai, H., Fala, N.: Preliminary design of wind-aware sUAS simulation pipeline for urban air mobility. In: AIAA Aviation 2022 Forum, p. 3872 (2022)

16. Waraich, Q.R., Mazzuchi, T.A., Sarkani, S., Rico, D.F.: Minimizing human factors mishaps in unmanned aircraft systems. Ergon. Des. **21**(1), 25–32 (2013)

17. Preece, J., Sharp, H., Rogers, Y.: Interaction Design: Beyond Human-Computer Interaction. Wiley, Hoboken (2015)

18. Shah, S., Dey, D., Lovett, C., Kapoor, A.: AirSim: high-fidelity visual and physical simulation for autonomous vehicles. In: Hutter, M., Siegwart, R. (eds.) Field and Service Robotics. SPAR, vol. 5, pp. 621–635. Springer, Cham (2018). https://doi.org/10.1007/978-3-319-67361-5_40

19. Meier, L., Honegger, D., Pollefeys, M.: PX4: a node-based multithreaded open source robotics framework for deeply embedded platforms. In: 2015 IEEE International Conference on Robotics and Automation (ICRA), pp. 6235–6240. IEEE (2015)

20. Joshi, A., Kale, S., Chandel, S., Pal, D.K.: Likert scale: explored and explained. Br. J. Appl. Sci. Technol. **7**(4), 396 (2015)

21. Potter, S.S., Bressler, J.R.: Subjective workload assessment technique (swat): a user's guide. Technical report, Systems Research Labs Inc, Dayton, OH (1989)

22. Hooey, B.L., Kaber, D.B., Adams, J.A., Fong, T.W., Gore, B.F.: The underpinnings of workload in unmanned vehicle systems. IEEE Trans. Hum.-Mach. Syst. **48**(5), 452–467 (2017)

23. Reid, G.B., Nygren, T.E.: The subjective workload assessment technique: a scaling procedure for measuring mental workload. In: Advances in Psychology, vol. 52, pp. 185–218. Elsevier (1988)

24. Young, M.S., Brookhuis, K.A., Wickens, C.D., Hancock, P.A.: State of science: mental workload in ergonomics. Ergonomics **58**(1), 1–17 (2015)

25. Hart, S.G., Staveland, L.E.: Development of NASA-TLX (task load index): results of empirical and theoretical research. In: Advances in Psychology, vol. 52, pp. 139–183. Elsevier (1988)

26. Roscoe, A.H., Ellis, G.A.: A subjective rating scale for assessing pilot workload in flight: a decade of practical use. Technical report, Royal Aerospace Establishment Farnborough (United Kingdom) (1990)

27. Jennings, S., Craig, G., Carignan, S., Ellis, K., Qinetiq, D.T.: Evaluating control activity as a measure of workload in flight test. In: Proceedings of the Human Factors and Ergonomics Society Annual Meeting, vol. 49, pp. 64–67. SAGE Publications, Los Angeles (2005)

28. Zak, Y., Parmet, Y., Oron-Gilad, T.: Subjective workload assessment technique (SWAT) in real time: affordable methodology to continuously assess human oper-

ators' workload. In: 2020 IEEE International Conference on Systems, Man, and Cybernetics (SMC), pp. 2687–2694. IEEE (2020)

29. Senders, J.W.: Axiomatic models of workload. In: Moray, N. (ed.) Mental Workload: Its Theory and Measurement, pp. 263–267. Springer, Boston (1979). https://doi.org/10.1007/978-1-4757-0884-4_15

30. Endsley, M.R.: Design and evaluation for situation awareness enhancement. In: Proceedings of the Human Factors Society annual meeting, vol. 32, pp. 97–101. Sage Publications, Los Angeles (1988)

31. Gibb, R.W., Olson, W.: Classification of air force aviation accidents: mishap trends and prevention. Int. J. Aviat. Psychol. 18(4), 305–325 (2008)

32. Gatsoulis, Y., Virk, G.S., Dehghani-Sanij, A.A.: On the measurement of situation awareness for effective human-robot interaction in teleoperated systems. J. Cogn. Eng. Decis. Mak. 4(1), 69–98 (2010)

33. Stanton, N.A., Hedge, A., Brookhuis, K., Salas, E., Hendrick, H.W.: Situation awareness measurement and the situation awareness global assessment technique. In: Handbook of Human Factors and Ergonomics Methods, pp. 445–453. CRC Press (2004)

34. Endsley, M.R., Rodgers, M.D.: Situation awareness information requirements analysis for EN route air traffic control. In: Proceedings of the Human Factors and Ergonomics Society Annual Meeting, vol. 38, pp. 71–75. Sage Publications, Los Angeles (1994)

35. Kaber, D.B., Perry, C.M., Segall, N., McClernon, C.K., Prinzel III, L.J.: Situation awareness implications of adaptive automation for information processing in an air traffic control-related task. Int. J. Ind. Ergon. 36(5), 447–462 (2006)

36. Neal, A., Griffin, M., Paterson, J., Bordia, P.: Human factors issues: performance management transition to a CNS. ATM Environment (1998)

37. Muniz, E., Stout, R., Bowers, C., Salas, E.: A methodology for measuring team situational awareness: situational awareness linked indicators adapted to novel tasks (SALIANT). NATO human factors and medicine panel on collaborative crew performance in complex systems, Edinburgh, North Atlantic Treaties Organisation, Neuilly-sur-Seine, pp. 20–24 (1998)

Influence of Movement Speed and Interaction Instructions on Subjective Assessments, Performance and Psychophysiological Reactions During Human-Robot Interaction

Verena Wagner-Hartl[(✉)] [iD], Solveig Nakladal, Tobias Koch, Dzenan Babajic,
Sergei Mazur, and Jonas Birkle

Faculty Industrial Technologies, Furtwangen University, Campus Tuttlingen, Kronenstraße 16,
78532 Tuttlingen, Germany
verena.wagner-hartl@hs-furtwangen.de

Abstract. Information technology is advancing rapidly, and with it, robots. Nowadays, the interaction between robots and humans changes e.g., from the execution of simple movements towards a new level where they can perform different work-related aspects almost completely independently. Therefore, especially in production, the prevention of negative emotions is important. Consequently, attention should not only be focused on the physical safety of workers but also on their acceptance, fears and biases. An experimental study focuses on the impact of two different interaction instruction variants, with and without direct human-robot interaction, on acceptance, trust, performance and participants' psychophysiological (ECG and EDA) reactions during human-robot interaction with an industrial robot (Horst600, fruitcore robotics GmbH). Furthermore, the movement speed of the robot was variated (five levels) within a simple handover task. Overall, 14 men and 5 women participated in the study. They were randomly assigned to the two different instruction variants. On the one hand, the results indicate significant differences regarding the movement speed levels and interestingly, on the other hand, the results did not show significant effects regarding the investigated instructions. To sum it up, the results of the study should help to understand how people perceive a physical interaction with an industrial robot.

Keywords: Human-Robot Interaction · Multidimensional Approach · Psychophysiology

1 Introduction

Information technology is advancing rapidly, and with it, robots [1, 2]. Market research [3] assumes that there will be a steady global growth in the field of robotics in the coming years. The continuing growth is expected to vary by region. Especially Asia is predicted to continue to be the region with the highest robot volume, followed by Europe and North America. Nowadays, robots are not only present in the industrial context anymore

[4], robots are also increasingly being used in commercial and private environments [5]. Additionally the number of scenarios where the contact between humans and robots is part of the everyday life is increasing, whereas the interaction between robots and humans changes. One reason of this is the fact that the complexity of a robot's motion changes from the execution of simple movements towards a new level where they can perform different work-related aspects almost completely independently. Even, cultural differences do exist regarding the requirements to optimize human-robot interaction [6].

Following Pott and Dietz [5] the current development in robotics is driven by the innovations achieved in research. Nowadays, robots can be used more flexibly thanks to newly developed sensors, algorithms for image processing and increased automation. Increasing digitalization and the ability to obtain and process data from various sources enable robots to be used successfully in a wide variety of tasks. As a result, human-robot collaboration is becoming an essential success factor for Industry 4.0, with robots bringing accuracy, endurance and physical strength to production. Also, the COVID-19 pandemic increased the need for technologies which have the possibility to support humans [7]. Therefore, it is important to focus on a good interaction between both parts, the humans and the robots. To enable a good and productive human-robot interaction, especially the prevention of negative emotions, like fear and anxiety is important.

Human-robot interaction can be applied in many areas, such as manufacturing, logistics, medicine, or the service sector (e.g., care for the elderly people) [4, 8, 9]. Especially in production, where productivity and flexibility continue to increase, collaboration between humans and robots is becoming more and more important. Following Weber et al. [10] robots should no longer act purely as "tools" but also become members of a team in which they complement humans for example with their strengths. It is crucial for the success of these cooperations that robots have the ability to record and process complex environmental information and learn to react to them appropriately. Furthermore, as mentioned before, they must be accepted and trusted by humans. Especially trust seems to be a dominant factor for a positive collaboration between humans and robots [11]. Here, the overall performance of the robot seems to have a crucial influence. Other important factors reported by the authors are speed, acceleration, the physical appearance, and the size of the robot.

1.1 Safety and Interaction Instructions

Instructions are an integral part of the professional world and are legally enshrined, for example in Germany, in the German Occupational Safety and Health Act [12]. According to this legislation, employers are obliged to provide their employees with comprehensive and accurate information about potential hazards, safety precautions, and health protection measures. In the context of occupational safety, initial instructions are particularly relevant as they sensitize employees to potential dangers and promote awareness of safety-conscious behavior [13]. This allows individuals who work in potentially risky workplaces to adequately respond to hazards.

Various studies suggest that safety instructions that include practical demonstrations of tasks should be performed because they are more effective than purely verbal instructions [14]. Especially with regard to human-robot interaction, observing specific work steps can build expectations that have the potential to positively influence interaction behavior [15]. This should help to familiarize with the robot and supports safer behavior.

Moreover, the use of video instructions offers numerous advantages like the visual representation of safety behaviors and sources of danger. Furthermore, they can facilitate dealing with new technologies and tools. In relation to human-robot interaction, it was shown that video instructions that depict such interactions can increase acceptance and readiness for dealing with robots [14].

1.2 Movement Speed

Previous studies have shown that different aspects can have an influence on humans while interacting with a robot [11, 16, 17]. One of the most important aspects is the speed of a robots' movement. Or et al. [18] demonstrated that the robots' movement speed influences the perception of industrial robots and, consequently, affects their perceived safety. Furthermore, Thiemermann [16] showed that the increase in movement speed in the range of 1000 mm/s to 2000 mm/s was subjectively indistinguishable for humans. Also, it seems that at very high speeds, humans' visual perception cannot make distinctions anymore. Following Arai et al. [17], speeds above 500 mm/s, can result in high mental workload for participants. The authors also emphasize the importance of using psychophysiological measures to measure mental strain during human-robot interaction. This is also supported by other research groups for research regarding human-system interaction in general (e.g., [19, 20]) as well as for human-robot interaction in particular (e.g., [21, 22]). Therefore, it should be considered, that psychological processes (cognitive, social or emotional) are in general accompanied by physiological responses [23]. These are relatively easy to measure using non-invasive measurement techniques. For activation/arousal as well as emotional responses, parameters of the autonomic nervous system (ANS) are widely used [24]. Especially, cardiovascular (ECG) and electrodermal activity (EDA) are commonly used because they can be integrated into a participants' task without restricting them much [23, 25] and they can provide insights into otherwise invisible processes like the emotional experience during a human-robot interaction or other emotional and mental processes [26].

1.3 Aim of the Study

As presented before, when designing a collaborative workplace, attention should not only be focused on the physical safety of workers but also on their acceptance, fears and biases. Here, the way in which the work instruction is conducted could have a relevant impact. Therefore, the aim of the presented experimental study was to focus on the impact of two different interaction instruction variants, with and without direct human-robot interaction, on acceptance, trust, performance and participants' psychophysiological reactions during human-robot interaction. A simple handover task with an industrial robot (Horst600, fruitcore robotics GmbH) was chosen for the collaboration. Furthermore, following the first results regarding the importance of the robots' movement speed [16, 17, 21], five different movement speed variants resp. levels of movement speed and their impact on the different dependent variables should be analyzed.

2 Method

2.1 Sample

Overall, 14 men and 5 women ($N = 19$) aged between 19 and 27 years ($M = 22.42$, $SD = 1.98$) participated in the experimental study. The participants were randomly assigned to the two different instruction variants: Eleven participants participated in the instruction group without, eight in the instruction group with direct human-robot interaction. Age and gender were statistically equally distributed in the two groups (age: $t(17) = .08, p = .934$; gender: $\chi^2(1) = .17, p = .677$). Prior to the experimental study, a preliminary online questionnaire was used to evenly group the participants among the groups of the independent variable "interaction instruction" regarding their affinity for technology (measured with the TA-EG [27]) and previous experience with robots.

2.2 Study Design, Materials and Measures

A multidimensional approach that combines subjective assessments, objective performance parameters as well as objective psychophysiological parameters of cardiovascular (ECG) and electrodermal (EDA) activity was used to measure emotions and the acceptance during human-robot interaction with an industrial robot (Horst600, fruitcore robotics GmbH).

A 2 × 5 mixed-methods study design (see Table 1) was chosen for the study, incorporating and extending the design from a former study of our research group (see Birkle et al. [21] for more details). The used independent variables are the movement speed of the robot (S1–S5) and the type of instruction (with or without interaction) given regarding the interaction before the start of the procedure. The independent variables are described in more detail below.

Table 1. Study design

		Movement speed of the robot				
		S1	S2	S3	S4	S5
Introduction	with interaction					
	without interaction					

Movement Speed. The movement speed of the robot represents the repeated-measures factor (independent variable 1, IV1). It was scaled using five different levels: The lowest chosen speed (S1) corresponds to 40% of the maximum possible movement speed of the robot. For the following four levels of the variable, the speed of the robot was increased by 15% of the maximum speed in each case. This results in 55% (S2), 70% (S3), 85% (S4) and 100% (S5). The distance between the participants and the robot was kept consistent over the five interaction tasks.

Interaction Instructions. Two videos were recorded for the dichotomous independent variable "interaction instruction" (independent variable 2, IV2). The videos which were shown to the participants before the start of the procedure, comprise the instruction into the study and into the interaction (task) that should be performed with the robot. Two different versions of the video resp. interaction instruction were used: One with and one without interaction. In the "instruction without interaction" variant, the description of the interaction task took place only verbally, while in the "instruction with interaction" variant, the actual interaction with the robot was also shown visually. Figure 1 shows excerpts from the two videos at the same point in time, each using the example of

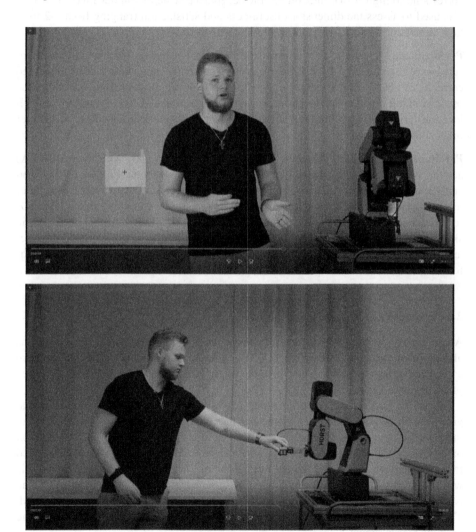

Fig. 1. Excerpts from the two instruction videos at the same point in time. The variant "Instruction without interaction" is shown in the top figure. The variant "Instruction with interaction" is shown in the bottom figure.

the handover task. The spoken text was always identical in both videos and was only expanded by snippets of the interactions in the second case.

Subjective Assessments. The subjective assessment was performed in blocks after each measurement (a total of five times, repeated measurement), by using the following questionnaires. First, the three dimensions valence, arousal and dominance of the self-assessment-manikin by Bradley and Lang [28] (analyzed values ranging from 1–5; higher values correspond to a higher expression) were used. Subsequently, perceived trust was assessed using a 13-items questionnaire ([29, 30]; five-point rating scales; high values correspond to high trust). In addition, the acceptance scale of van der Laan et al. [31] was used to assess the dimensions usefulness and satisfaction (ranging from −2 to 2; high values correspond to high usefulness or satisfaction).

Performance Measures. In addition to the subjective measures, two performance measures were also collected. First, it was observed whether the interaction task was executed correctly or not (0 = incorrect, 1 = correct). Furthermore, it was recorded whether the participant left the intended location during the interaction task (0 = remained, 1 = left location during the task). Both performance measures were collected by the experimenter in dichotomous form.

Psychophysiological Parameters. Cardiovascular (ECG) and electrodermal (EDA) activity were measured using the EcgMove 4 [32] respectively the EdaMove 4 [33] and analyzed using the software DataAnalyzer [34] from movisens. The analyzed parameters were: Heart rate (HR) in beats per minute and heart rate variability (HRV RMSSD) for cardiovascular activity; skin conductance level (SCL), amplitude of non-specific skin conductance responses (NS.SCR amp), frequency of non-specific skin conductance responses (NS.SCR freq) and mean sum amplitude (NS.SCR amp/NS.SCR freq) for the electrodermal activity.

2.3 Procedure

As previously mentioned regarding the study design, the experimental procedure was also based on the study of Birkle et al. [21]. Limitations presented by the authors were considered as far as possible. The procedure was confirmed by the local ethics committee of Furtwangen University.

After the participants were informed and welcomed, the respective instructional video was shown (see Sect. 2.2 - Interaction instructions). Participants then filled out an informed consent and generated the participants' code to enable the pseudonymization of their data. The measurement devices to measure ECG and EDA were then applied to the participants' body and a brief verification of their function was performed. This was followed by a five-minute baseline measurement (see Fig. 2a), during which the participants were asked to look at a fixation cross at a distance of 1.8 m while seated. The participants were asked to sit still and to think about as little as possible during the baseline measurement.

Afterwards, the interaction tasks with the industrial robot took place in iterative form. In the beginning of each task, the participant stood on a marked area on the floor, which was marked at a distance of 1 m from the industrial robot [35]. At the start of the task, the robot picked up one of five wooden cubes with an edge length of 4 cm and handed it over to the participant. The participant was then asked to leave the marked location and take the cube from the robot (see Fig. 2b). Afterwards, the participants task was to return to the initial (marked) location.

Three of the five cubes were marked with an "X"-symbol. A visual inspection was now to be performed by the participants at the adjacent table. Therefore, they had to check the cube for the presence of the small "X"-symbol on the cube. The result of this visual inspection was documented in the study booklet and also represents the first performance measure (correct execution of the task; see also Sect. 2.2). After completion of the inspection, participants had to return the cube to the robot. Then, the participants had to take a step back to the marked starting point again. The task was completed by the robot returning the cube to its starting position. The order in which the dice were presented was permuted. The subjective evaluation was conducted afterwards, at the

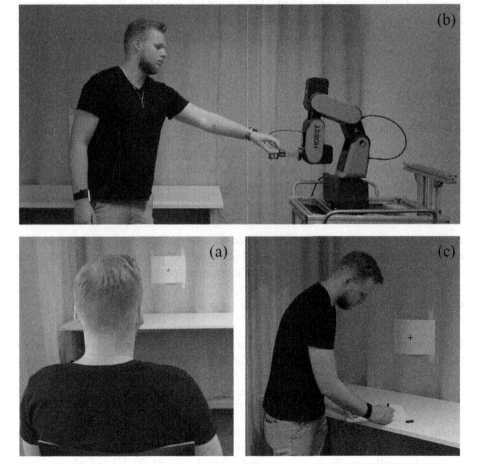

Fig. 2. Procedure of the study with the three main parts: baseline measurement/rest phase (a), interaction task (b) and subjective assessment (c).

end of each of the five tasks (see Sect. 2.2 - Subjective assessments; Fig. 2c). This was followed by a rest measurement with a duration of three minutes.

This whole procedure was repeated for each of the movement speeds, a total of five times. The movement speed levels were presented in ascending order to allow the participants to slowly cope to faster speed levels. The study could be interrupted at any point if the participants felt uncomfortable. At the end of the study the measuring devices were removed from the participants. Finally, there was the possibility to ask open questions.

2.4 Data Analyses

Psychophysiological data were first analyzed using the software DataAnalyzer from movisens [34] and afterwards baseline corrected (see also Sect. 2.3). The statistical data analyses were conducted using SPSS 28 for Windows. ANOVAS with repeated measures, Cochran's Q test, χ^2-tests, Friedman tests and Mann-Whitney u-tests were chosen as statistical procedure and the analyses were based on a significance level of 5%. For multiple testing, error type 1 was adjusted using the Bonferroni-Holm procedure [36] for each effect.

3 Results

3.1 Subjective Assessments

Valence. The mean valence [28] of the different measurement times were assessed from 4.50 to 4.61. An ANOVA with repeated measures revealed no significant effects of movement speed, $F_{GG}(2.06, 32.90) = .31$, $p = .739$, $\eta^2_{part.} = .019$, interaction instruction, $F(1, 16) = .07$, $p = .791$, $\eta^2_{part.} = .005$, nor the interaction of movement speed x interaction instruction, $F_{GG}(2.06, 32.90) = 1.24$, $p = .302$, $\eta^2_{part.} = .072$.

Arousal. The mean subjectively perceived arousal [28] of the different measurement times ranged from 1.53 to 1.74. Following the results of an ANOVA with repeated measures no significant effects of movement speed, $F(4, 14) = .46$, $p = .767$, $\eta^2_{part.} = .115$, interaction instruction, $F(1, 17) = 2.42$, $p = .138$, $\eta^2_{part.} = .125$, and the interaction movement speed x interaction instruction, $F(4, 14) = .96$, $p = .458$, $\eta^2_{part.} = .216$, can be shown.

Dominance. Regarding the mean dominance [28], the different measurement times were assessed from 4.11 to 4.21. Results of an ANOVA with repeated measures revealed no significant effects of movement speed, $F(2, 16) = 1.23$, $p = .318$, $\eta^2_{part.} = .134$, interaction instruction, $F(1, 17) = .71$, $p = .412$, $\eta^2_{part.} = .040$, nor the interaction of movement speed x interaction instruction, $F(2, 16) = .75$, $p = .488$, $\eta^2_{part.} = .086$.

Trust. Overall, the subjectively perceived mean trust [29, 30] was assessed from 4.34 to 4.54 for the different measurement times. An ANOVA with repeated measures showed no significant effects of movement speed, $F_{GG}(1.84, 31.21) = 1.62$, $p = .215$, $\eta^2_{part.} = .087$, interaction instruction, $F(1, 17) = .06$, $p = .818$, $\eta^2_{part.} = .003$, and the interaction of movement speed x interaction instruction, $F_{GG}(1,84, 31.21) = .16$, $p = .834$, $\eta^2_{part.} = .009$.

Usefulness. The subjectively perceived mean usefulness [31] ranged from .63 to 1.13 for the different measurement times. Following the results of an ANOVA with repeated measures, a significant effect of movement speed, $F_{GG}(1.70, 28.91) = 3.76, p = .042,$ $\eta^2_{part.} = .181$ can be shown (see Fig. 3). Both, interaction instruction, $F(1, 17) < .001,$ $p = .983, \eta^2_{part.} < .001$, and the interaction of movement speed x interaction instruction, $F_{GG}(1.70, 28.91) = .47, p = .600, \eta^2_{part.} = .027$, did not reach the level of significance.

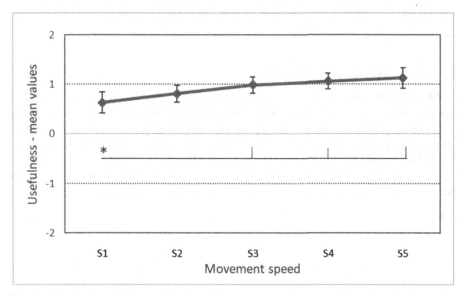

Fig. 3. Perceived usefulness of the different movement speed levels of the robot. *Note.* I ... standard error of mean, * ... $p < .050$

Post-hoc analyses showed that the slowest movement speed level (40% of maximum speed of the used robot) was assessed as significantly less useful than the three fastest variants S3, S4 and S5 (all $p < .050$).

Satisfaction. Overall, the subjectively perceived mean satisfaction [31] for the different measurement times were assessed from .83 to 1.15. The results of an ANOVA with repeated measures indicate no significant effects of movement speed, $F_{GG}(2.08, 35.32) = 2.31, p = .113, \eta^2_{part.} = .119$, interaction instruction, $F(1, 17) = .02, p = .903, \eta^2_{part.} = .001$, and the interaction of movement speed x interaction instruction, $F_{GG}(2.08, 35.32) = .16, p = .861, \eta^2_{part.} = .009$.

3.2 Performance

Correct Execution. Overall, with two exceptions, on each for the movement speed level S1 and for S2, the task was performed correctly by all participants. So, following the results of Cochran's Q test, the participants did perform statistically equally well regarding the different movement speeds, $Q(4) = 3.00, p = .558$. Furthermore, no significant differences could be shown for the performance of the two interaction instruction groups (S1: $\chi^2(1) = .03, p = .870$, S2: $\chi^2(1) < .001, p = 1.000$).

Localization. In summary, with one exceptions for the movement speed level S2, the participants did not left there intended location during the interaction task. The results of a Cochran's Q test indicate that the participants did perform statistically equally during the different movement speed levels, $Q(4) = 4.00, p = .406$. Furthermore, no significant differences could be shown for the performance of the two interaction instruction groups (S2: $\chi^2(1) < .001, p = 1.000$).

3.3 Psychophysiological Parameters

Cardiovascular Activity (ECG). Following the results of a Friedman test, a significant effect of movement speed can be shown for the heart rate (HR), $\chi^2(4, N = 8) = 21.80$, $p < .001$. Post-tests revealed that the heart rate of the participants was significantly lower while performing a task with the slowest movement speed S1 than the three fastest movement speeds (S3: $p = .002$, S4: $p = .011$, S5: $p < .001$). Additionally, the second slowest movement speed S2 lead to significantly less high heart rate responses than the fastest movement speed S5 ($p = .007$). Boxplots are presented in Fig. 4.

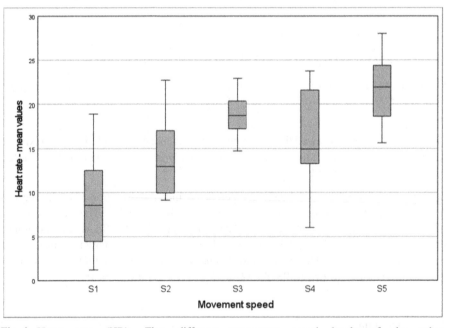

Fig. 4. Heart rate (HR): Five different movement speed levels of the robot. *Note.* Baseline-corrected values.

Results of Mann-Whitney u-tests showed that the interaction instruction groups did not differ significantly regarding their heart rate responses during the different tasks (all

$p > .05$; error type 1 was adjusted using the Bonferroni-Holm [36] procedure for each effect; $N = 15–17$).

Regarding the heart rate variability (HRV RMSSD), the results of a Friedman test, indicate no significant effect of movement speed regarding HRV (RMSSD), $\chi^2(4, N = 8) = 8.70, p = .069$. Following the results of Mann-Whitney u-tests (error type 1 was adjusted using the Bonferroni-Holm [36] procedure for each effect) the interaction instruction groups did not differ significantly regarding their HRV (RMSSD) during the different tasks (all $p > .05; N = 15–17$).

Electrodermal Activity (EDA). Following the results of a Friedman test, a significant effect of movement speed can be shown for the skin conductance level (SCL), $\chi^2(4, N = 9) = 13.69, p = .008$. Post-tests showed that the SCL was significantly lower while performing a task with the slowest movement speed S1 than the two fastest movement speeds (S4: $p = .003$, S5: $p = .001$). Additionally, a tendency towards significance was shown for movement speed level S3. SCL was significant lower during task-performance of S1 than of S3 ($p = .053$). Boxplots are presented in Fig. 5.

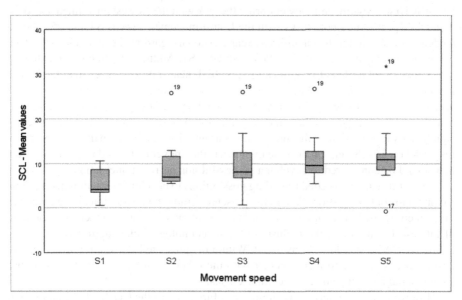

Fig. 5. Skin conductance level (SCL): Five different movement speed levels of the robot. *Note.* Baseline-corrected values.

The results of the statistical analyses of all other researched parameters of the electrodermal activity did not reach the level of significance.

4   Discussion

As presented in the literature review, when designing a collaborative workplace, attention should not only be focused on the physical safety of workers but also on their acceptance, fears and biases. The presented experimental study was designed to examine the effect of two different interaction instruction variants, with and without direct human-robot interaction, on acceptance, trust, performance and participants' psychophysiological reactions during human-robot interaction. Furthermore, the effect of five different movement speed levels of an industrial robot (Horst600, fruitcore robotics GmbH [35]) were analyzed performing a simple handover task in cooperation with the robot.

On the one side, the results show that the two investigated instruction groups did not differ significantly regarding the different dependent variables (subjective assessments, performance parameters and psychophysiological parameters). On the other side, a significant effect of movement speed can be shown regarding the perceived usefulness of the robot. The slowest movement speed level (40% of maximum speed of the used robot) was assessed as significantly less useful than the three fastest variants.

This is also supported by the results of the psychophysiological reactions of the participants. The psychophysiological responses of the participants point (partly) in the same direction. The heart rate of the participants was significantly lower while performing a task with the slowest movement speed S1 than performing a task with the three fastest movement speeds S3, S4 and S5. In addition participants' skin conductance level (SCL) was significantly lower during the task with the slowest movement speed S1 than while performing both tasks with the fastest movement speeds S4 and S5. Also, a tendency towards a significant difference can be shown regarding the SCL during the task using movement speed level S3 and the task with S1. Additionally, the second slowest movement speed S2 lead to significantly less high heart rate responses than the fastest movement speed S5. Following the results, tasks performed with slower movement speed levels seem to be significantly less demanding and less emotional arousing than faster movement speeds. At the same time, the slowest movement speed was assessed as significantly less useful than the three fastest variants. The results are in line with previous research [11, 16–18] and support the hypothesis that movement speed is a crucial factor that should be considered to develop a successful human-robot interaction.

Further research is needed regarding possibilities to develop interaction instructions for human-robot interaction. Within the presented study the instructions were given via video recordings. In the future, e.g., instructions in presence or via video call could be of interest. Furthermore, the inclusion of new technologies like augmented or virtual reality (AR, VR) should be considered. Within the presented study, a relatively simple handover task was performed together with the robot. From our point of view, future studies should also include more complex tasks.

However, the study has some limitations. First, due to the COVID19-situation and its restrictions during the development of the experimental study, the overall sample size was relatively small. Unfortunately, there were some missing data, especially in the psychophysiological measurements due to technical problems e.g., recordings, robots grab-performance during the tasks. Therefore, the sample with complete data for all measurement times was somewhat small. The study included eight participants with complete data regarding cardiovascular activity and nine participants with complete data regarding electrodermal activity. Regarding the single measurement times the sample sizes ranges from 15–17 participants with analyzable recordings. Non-parametric analyses were performed to take the small sample size into account. Nonetheless, the results can show first indications regarding the importance to include a multidimensional approach combining subjective and objective measures into the research of human robot inter-action. Especially, psychophysiological parameters which under normal circumstances are not under active resp. willingness control of the participants [24] can provide a sub-stantial value for research including emotional and activation/arousal parameters of the autonomic nervous system (ANS). Furthermore, they are measurable using non-invasive measurement techniques [23].

To sum it up, the results of the study should help to understand how people perceive a physical interaction with an industrial robot. Therefore, the study can provide first indications, especially regarding movement speed.

Author's Statement. The authors state no conflict of interest. Informed consent has been obtained from all individuals included in this study. The research has been approved by the ethics' committee of Furtwangen University. The authors would like to thank all participants that participated in the study as well as Peter Anders and Katharina Gleichauf for their support.

References

1. Soori, M., Arezoo, B., Dastres, R.: Artificial intelligence, machine learning and deep learning in advanced robotics, a review. Cogn. Robot. **3**, 54–70 (2023). https://doi.org/10.1016/j.cogr.2023.04.001

2. Ajoudani, A., Zanchettin, A.M., Ivaldi, S., Albu-Schäffer, A., Kosuge, K., Khatib, O.: Progress and prospects of the human–robot collaboration. Auton. Robot. **42**, 957–975 (2018)

3. Statista. Volume of robotics market worldwide from 2016 to 2027, by region (in thou-sands) [Graph]. In: Statista. https://www.statista.com/forecasts/1388113/global-robotics-volume-by-region (2022)

4. Lai, R., Lin, W., Wu, Y.: Review of research on the key technologies, application fields and development trends of intelligent robots. In: Chen, Z., Mendes, A., Yan, Y., Chen, S. (eds.) ICIRA 2018. LNCS (LNAI), vol. 10985, pp. 449–458. Springer, Cham (2018). https://doi.org/10.1007/978-3-319-97589-4_38

5. Pott, A., Dietz, T.: Industrielle Robotersysteme [Industrial robot systems]. Springer, Wies-baden (2019). https://doi.org/10.1007/978-3-658-25345-5

6. Gasteiger, N., Hellou, M., Ahn, H.S.: Factors for personalization and localization to optimize human-robot interaction: a literature review. Int. J. Soc. Robot. **15**, 689–701 (2023). https://doi.org/10.1007/s12369-021-00811-8

7. Chandra, M., Kumar, K., Thakur, P., Chattopadhyaya, S.: Digital technologies, healthcare and Covid 19: insights from developing and emerging nations. Heal. Technol. **12**, 547–568 (2022). https://doi.org/10.1007/s12553-022-00650-1

8. Sheridan, T.B.: Human-robot interaction: status and challenges. Hum. Factors **58**(4), 525–532 (2016)

9. Heyer, C.: Human-robot interaction and future industrial robotics applications. In: IEEE Xplore: The 2010 IEEE/RSJ International Conference on Intelligent Robots and Systems, pp. 4749–4754 (2010)

10. Weber, M.A., Schüth, N.J., Stowasser, S: Qualifizierungsbedarfe für die mensch-roboter-kollaboration [Qualification Needs for Human-Robot Collaboration.]. Zeitschrift Für Wirtschaftlichen Fabrikbetrieb [Journal For Economical Factory Operation] **113**(10), 619–622 (2018)

11. Hancock, P.A., Billings, D.R., Schaefer, K.E., Chen, J.Y.C., de Visser, E.J., Parasuraman, R.: A meta-analysis of factors affecting trust in human-robot interaction. Hum. Factors **53**, 517–527 (2011)

12. Arbeitsschutzgesetz – ArbSchG. Gesetz über die Durchführung von Maßnahmen des Arbeitsschutzes zur Verbesserung der Sicherheit und des Gesundheitsschutzes der Beschäftigten bei der Arbeit. Bundesministerium der Justiz, Deutschland [Occupational Safety Act - ArbSchG. Law on the implementation of occupational health and safety measures to improve the safety and health of employees at work. Federal Ministry of Justice, Germany] (2023)

13. Konradt, U., Vibrans, O., König, C.-D., Hertel, G.: Wirksamkeit und Akzeptanz eines Videos zur Erstunterweisung in Arbeitssicherheit [Effectiveness and acceptability of an initial occupational safety instruction video]. A&O **46**(2), 78–83 (2002)

14. Chien, S.-E., Yu, C.-J., Lai, Y.-Y., Liu, J.-C., Fu, L.-C., Yeh, S.-L.: Can older adults' acceptance toward robots be enhanced by observational learning? In: Rau, P.-L. (ed.) HCII 2020. LNCS, vol. 12192, pp. 564–576. Springer, Cham (2020). https://doi.org/10.1007/978-3-030-49788-0_43

15. Eigenstetter, M., Sen, S., Kremer, L.: Kurzfristige Beanspruchungen, Akzeptanz und Sicherheit im Umgang mit einem kollaborierenden Roboter: die Rolle der Vorhersehbarkeit [Short-term stresses, acceptance, and safety when using a collaborative robot: the role of predictability]. In: GfA, Dortmund (Hrsg.): Frühjahrskongress 2020, pp. 1–7, GfA, Berlin (2020)

16. Thiemermann, S.: Direkte Mensch-Roboter-Kooperation in der Kleinteilemontage mit einem SCARA-Roboter [Direct human-robot cooperation in small parts assembly with a SCARA robot], Germany, Stuttgart (2005)

17. Arai, T., Kato, R., Fujita, M.: Assessment of operator stress induced by robot collaboration in assembly. CIRP Ann. **59**, 5–8 (2010)

18. Or, C.K.L., Duffy, V.G., Cheung, C.C.: Perception of safe robot idle time in virtual reality and real industrial environments. Ergonomics **39**(5), 807–812 (2009)

19. Boucsein, W., Backs, R.W.: Engineering psychophysiology as a discipline: historical and theoretical aspects. In: Backs, R.W., Boucsein, W. (eds.) Engineering Psychophysiology: Issues and Applications, pp. 3–30. CRC Press, Boca Raton (2000)

20. Dawson, M.E., Schell, A.M., Filion, D.L.: The electrodermal system. In: Cacioppo, J.T., Tassinary, L.G., Berntson, G.G., (eds.), Handbook of Psychophysiology (Fourth Edition), pp. 217–243. Cambridge University Press (2017)

21. Birkle, J., Vogel, A., Wagner-Hartl, V.: Impact of distance and movement speed on the acceptance of human-robot interaction – method and first evaluation. In: Stephanidis, C., et al. (Eds.): HCII 2022, CCIS 1655, pp. 483–490, Springer, Cham (2022). https://doi.org/10.1007/978-3-031-19682-9_61

22. Bethel, C.L., Salomon, K., Murphy, R.R., Burke, J.L.: Survey of psychophysiology measurements applied to human-robot interaction. In: 16th IEEE International Conference on Robot & Human Interactive Communication, Korea, Jeju (2007)

23. Boucsein, W.: Psychophysiologische Methoden in der Ingenieurspsychologie [Psychophysiological methods in Engineering Psychology]. In: Zimolong, B., Konradt, U., (eds.), Sonderdruck aus Enzyklopädie der Psychologie: Themenbereich D Praxisgebiete: Serie III Wirtschafts-, Organisations- und Arbeitspsychologie. Band 2: Ingenieurspsychologie [Offprint from Encyclopedia of Psychology: Subject Area D Practice Areas: Series III Business, organizational, and industrial psychology. Volume 2: Engineering Psychology], pp. 317–358. Göttingen: Hogrefe (2006)

24. Boucsein, W., Backs, R.W.: The psychophysiology of emotion, arousal, and personality: methods and models. In: Duffy, V.G. (ed.), Handbook of Digital Human Modeling. Research for Applied Ergonomics and Human Factors Engineering, pp. 35-1–35-18. CRC Press, Boca Raton (2009)

25. Fahr, A., Hofer, M.: Psychophysiologische Messmethoden [Psychophysiological measurement methods]. In: Möhring, W., Schlütz, D. (eds.) Handbuch standardisierte Erhebungsverfahren in der Kommunikationswissenschaft [Handbook of standardized survey procedures in communication science], pp. 347–365. Springer, Wiesbaden (2013)

26. Gramann, K., Schandry, R.: Psychophysiologie: körperliche indikatoren psychischen geschehens [Psychophysiology: Physical indicators of mental events]. Beltz (2009)

27. Karrer, K., Glaser, C., Clemens, C., Bruder, C.: Technikaffinität erfassen – der Fragebogen TA-EG [Measuring affinity for technology - the TA-EG questionnaire]. In: Lichtenstein, A., Stößel, C., Clemens, C., (eds.), Der Mensch im Mittelpunkt technischer Systeme. 8. Berliner Werkstatt Mensch-Maschine-Systeme [Humans at the center of technical systems. 8th Berlin Human-Machine Systems Workshop], pp. 196–201. VDI Verlag. (2009)

28. Bradley, M.M., Lang, P.J.: Measuring emotion: the self-assessment manikin and the semantic differential. J. Behav. Ther. Exp. Psychiatry 25(1), 49–59 (1994)

29. Gleichauf, K., Schmid, R.: Akzeptanz und Vertrauen in die MenschRoboter-Interaktion anhand unterschiedlicher Szenarien [Acceptance and trust in human-robot interaction based on different scenarios] (unpublished project work, supervised by Wagner-Hartl, V.). Furtwangen University (2022)

30. Wagner-Hartl, V., Schmid, R., Gleichauf, K.: The influence of task complexity on acceptance and trust in human-robot interaction - gender and age differences. In: Paletta, L., Ayaz, H., (eds.), Cognitive computing and internet of things 43, pp. 118–126. AHFE International (2022)

31. Van Der Laan, J.D., Heino, A., De Waard, D.: A simple procedure for the assessment of acceptance of advanced transport telematics. Transp. Res. Part C: Emerg. Technol. 5(1), 1–10 (1997)

32. movisens GmbH. EcgMove 4 | movisens Docs (2022)

33. movisens GmbH. EdaMove 4 | movisens Docs (2022)

34. movisens GmbH: DataAnalyzer (2022)

35. fruitcore robotics GmbH: The industrial robot HORST600. https://fruitcore-robotics.com/horst600/ (2022)

36. Holm, S.: A simple sequentially rejective multiple test procedure. Scand. J. Stat. 6, 65–70 (1979)

Exploring the Challenges and Mitigations Associated with Operating Multi-variant Aircraft

Benjamin Whitworth[(✉)] [ID] and Rebecca Grant [ID]

Human Systems Integration Group, Faculty of Engineering, Environment and Computing, Coventry University, Coventry, UK
whitworb@uni.coventry.ac.uk

Abstract. Within some aircraft types, there are different variants that a pilot is permitted to fly on a single type rating. Previous research has investigated multi-variant flying on specific fleets, supporting the notion that differences should be proactively considered. Regulation describes the level of training pilots receive and this is based upon how different the variants are from one other. Recently, this training entered the spotlight, due to the tragic Boeing 737-Max accidents. This research further explored the human factors challenges and mitigations associated with multi-variant flying.

Twenty-eight pilots including Captains and First Officers with recent multi-variant operational experience at multiple airlines, were interviewed using a semi-structured technique. A rich and detailed data set was subsequently analysed using a thematic method, with themes identified and examined.

Whilst participants commented positively regarding multi-variant flying in the example used, the challenges of this were also highlighted and these differed from airline to airline, varying significantly as a result of fleet complexity, age, and commonality. Challenges were identified in terms of differences both within and between variants, information recall, navigation of variant information in manuals, and scheduling on multiple variants within the same day.

How variant challenges were routinely managed, from an individual and organisational perspective were described, with documentation, briefings and training raised, but often variable and in some cases lacking in key areas. Differences were identified between those who perceived receiving adequate training, and those who had not, as well as those operating within simple or complex fleets. A simple approach to identifying and comprehending differences was identified.

The results call for further research to explore the appropriateness of current regulation, considering fleet size, variability and fit, alongside industry recommendations. These include the provision of industry developed improved differences documentation and differences training, simulation replicating the fleet, and line training for all variants.

Keywords: Multi-variant flying · Human Factors · Pilot · Training

© The Author(s), under exclusive license to Springer Nature Switzerland AG 2023
M. Kurosu et al. (Eds.): HCII 2023, LNCS 14054, pp. 476–490, 2023.
https://doi.org/10.1007/978-3-031-48038-6_30

1 Introduction

Within some aircraft types, there are different variants that a pilot is permitted to fly on a single type rating. The Airbus A320 and Boeing 737 families offer examples and variants may differ in size, capabilities and equipment fits. Research into the potential human factors issues of multi-variant flying is limited. Lyall and Wickens [1] reviewed the concept of mixed-fleet flying, and despite observing only minimal issues, they did support the concept that differences be proactively considered. One method for doing this utilizes Endsley's [2:14] situational awareness (SA) paradigm within briefings; sharing mental models "generate a set of expectancies" about how equipment/systems might behave, despite occasionally being inaccurate [3]. This model first considers perception, where threats are noted with little or no understanding, followed by comprehension where threats are identified with potential impact considered. Finally, projection – which involves considering how the threat impact may impact future events, with 'what if' scenarios agreed.

The Japanese Transport Safety Board (JTSB) [4:3] investigated a Boeing 737–700 incident where a pilot "erroneously operated the rudder trim", instead of the door control, resulting in the aircraft entering an unusual attitude. The rudder trim control was similar to the door control of the previous variant the pilot had operated, a Boeing 737–500, and it is likely "the similarities between the switches" contributed to the event [4:4]. This may have been too subtle to notice, resulting in a "visual awareness" failure [5:529]. Generally, people are overly confident regarding their ability to notice small changes, despite the opposite being true [6] and attentional failures may prevent "changes in objects or the presence of an unexpected object" being noticed [7:36]. A study by Lyall [8] compared two 737 variants, discovering that pilots hand flew one variant more on tours that included both variants, compared to a tour with just one – perhaps implying that pilots guard against skill-fade by exposing themselves to the variant characteristics. Lyall [8] also recommended not operating different variants within the same day.

In 2016, an ATR-600 descended below a safe altitude on approach, involving a Captain with just 61 h on the -600 variant [9]. The -600 is recognized as simply a "commercial designation", but findings cited lack of experience on this variant as a contributory factor [9:6]. Soo, Mavin and Roth [10] explored systems and cognition within ATR aircraft, identifying that even for experienced pilots', threats exist. When information is "meaningful", it is "more easily transferred and stored" into long-term memory [11:32] and the episodic memory is used to recall past experiences [7]. Effective recall, and decision making takes time, but "when under time pressure, decision makers may only consider limited options" [12: 272] potentially considering just the first, degrading "the quality of novice decision makers" more so than experienced ones [3:146]. Rasmussen [13:258] describes cognitive performance as skill, rule, and knowledge-based; the expert generally using "skill-based behaviour", moving between levels depending upon task complexity [3], thus the potential role of experience. Distributed cognition, described as a "hybrid approach" related to "all aspects of cognition", from a "cognitive, social and organisation perspective" [14:1], may also influence variant comprehension.

The International Federation of Airline Pilots Association (IFALPA) [16, 2] suggests pilots "receive sufficient additional training" on all variants, clearly highlighting "operational and technical differences". Pilots desire greater "systems knowledge" [16:571] and given "skills cannot be improved without practice" [17:40], the importance of training is noted. Since a task can be difficult when trained poorly, but simple when trained well [18], the significance of appropriate training is highlighted.

2 Regulation

Orlady and Barnes [19:1869] suggests the "industry considers workload for new aircraft designs" but can often "ignore the impact" of incremental changes "made to modify the aircraft or its systems". After the Boeing 737-Max accidents, the process which determines what 'differences training' pilots require was in the spotlight [20]. Operational suitability data enables "types in a series to be compared for training and operational purposes" and may have pushed the intent of the regulation beyond "intended boundaries" [20:1]. Differences training should be carried out when "operating another variant of an aeroplane of the same type" [21:85] with the level of 'difference' determining the training requirement (Table 1).

Table 1. EASA [21:85] differences training requirement.

Level	Example	Training requirement
A	No influence on flight characteristics, procedures, presentation, or operation	Self-instruction via documentation
B	No influence on flight characteristics but influences procedures and possible difference in presentation/operation	Computer based training (CBT), system training, or information
C	Influence on flight characteristics, procedures, and differences in presentation/operation	Special instructor training, selected training, or special training programme
D	Influence on flight characteristics, procedures, and differences in presentation/operation	Special training within simulator/aircraft

Braune [22:1459] identified two core issues with multi-variant flying: negative transfer (potential error) and lack of adequate training (potential mitigation), calling for further research. Simulator fidelity influences training effectivity but "the degree of fidelity necessary to achieve maximal transfer of training" is the challenge with negative training occurring when there is a mismatch between the training system and the task [23:61].

This research aimed to explore the human factors challenges and mitigations associated with multi-variant flying, using the Airbus A320 family as a common example of such operations.

3   Method

Given limited previous research and the need to seek rich end-user views, an exploratory qualitative semi-structured interviewing approach was used, based on IATA's pilot competencies (Table 2), academic literature and the researcher's industry flying experience as guiding frameworks.

Table 2. IATA Pilot competencies [24:3].

Application of knowledge	Application of procedures	Communication
Aeroplane flight path management; manual	Aeroplane flight path management; automatic	Leadership & Teamwork
Problem solving and decision making	Situational awareness and management of information	Workload management

Topic areas and exemplar questions were reviewed for appropriateness and face validity by a subject matter expert, and a small-scale pilot was undertaken.

Recent Airbus piloting experience was used as a criterion of participation. Non-probability, quota sampling was chosen to ensure rank representation. Participants from a range of airlines were also actively recruited.

The interviews were conducted over video conferencing (Microsoft Teams) and recorded, giving the benefits of face-to-face interaction and engagement, irrelevant of geographical location.

After participant demographics, the variants operated were identified, alongside what participants believed the human factors related challenges to be, alongside individual and airline mitigations. Throughout each interview, different question approaches were used where appropriate, in line with Brinkmann and Kvale [25]. Care was taken not to lead participants into predictable responses or result in socially desirable answers by keeping questions open and raising the themes as areas for discussion.

Interviews were conducted between March and May 2021. The interview duration ranged from 45–90 min, dependent on individual participants.

The research complied with the British Psychological Society [26] guidelines and university ethical approval for the study was obtained (Fig. 1).

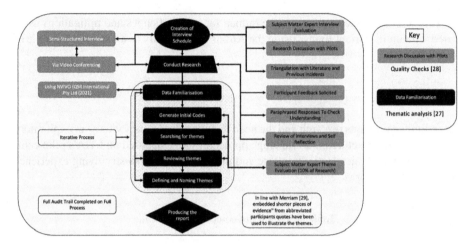

Fig. 1. Data collection and analysis process

An iterative thematic analysis process, utilizing Braun and Clarke's suggested stages [27] and numerous qualitative data and analysis trustworthiness checks [28] were undertaken. The result was two high level themes - challenges and mitigations, each with multiple sub-themes, which are outlined with embedded shorter "pieces of evidence" from abbreviated participant quotes (shown within inverted commas) to illustrate the themes [29:254].

4   Results and Discussion

4.1   Participants

Twenty-eight participants (14 Captains and 14 First Officers) from 11 airlines across five different regions were interviewed. In terms of average total flight experience, Captains had 11778.57 h (SD = 4590.15) and 22.71 years of service (SD = 9.67). First officers (FOs) had 3058.57 h (SD = 2487.44), with 7.18 years of service (SD = 7.11). In terms of average Airbus experience Captains presented with 5078.57 h (SD = 3473.73) and 9.04 years of service (SD = 6.58) with First Officers presenting with 2158.57 h (SD = 1623.85) and 4.46 years of service (SD = 3.07).

All participants had flown three or more variants except for one who had operated two.

4.2   The Challenges

Participants generally described the Airbus positively, describing commonality as advantageous despite identifying multiple challenges. These varied from airline to airline, with fleets varying significantly in terms of complexity, age, and commonality.

Differences. The first challenge identified by most participants were variant differences. It became apparent that there were more than just differences **between** variants, differences **within** variants presented significantly, too. "It's not just as easy as turning up and getting into an aircraft and flying it", described one Captain. The differences described were more commonly related to some variants than others.

Within airlines that included variants with different equipment fits, participants described more challenges than those operating within consistently presented, and in some cases, newer fleets. The depth of complexity was described more by Captains than FOs, possibly a result of experience and exposure to technical knowledge through training/checking – a feature noted throughout.

One Captain suggested differences add "challenge" and "workload", another using "trial and error" to learn. One described "familiarity", and the ability to perform tasks "without any cognitive effort", as useful, despite over familiarity occasionally being "your own worst enemy", indicating that cognitive processes must continuously adapt, with the risk being things getting "missed". Differences were sometimes referred to as "out of sight, out of mind" since some do not present regularly within the daily operation, especially within non-normal scenarios. Another suggested their community "paid lip service" to differences comprehension, due to operational pressure, or a lack of/unable to access knowledge. Pilots may consider differences as obvious, and if believed to be "known", may not be highlighted effectively [17:140], in a similar vein to the JTSB [4] investigation implying that cockpits that present in this manner, may generate issues.

"Every subgroup has different fits, layouts and configurations", one Captain described, another stated "multiple sub-fleets", with "multiple differences across multiple systems" existed. One FO described the cockpit/cabin fit, varied "massively", and another proposed the biggest challenge was understanding what equipment exists, what the aircraft can do, and what "is going to help". One Captain suggested pilots routinely use fit to try and identify other characteristics; "if your aircraft has square LCD screens", then it has other equipment, for example. Non-standardized equipment increases long-term memory loading, preventing the development of "simple schemas" [3:118].

However, one FO described Airbus flying as "pretty common", with a Captain offering that their aircraft were "pretty standard". Promoting a "well organized", and "semantically associated with other information" approach reduces memory loading [3:118]. Furthermore, these participants described procedures and limitations as "aligned", stating they were "lucky" to access such a common fleet, suggesting it may be an exception that pilots operate consistently presented aircraft.

Non-normal Events. While exploring non-normal events, the sample was mixed regarding whether variants have an appreciable impact, potentially the result of participant experience/knowledge. It was noted that simulation representing *all* variants, was not routinely available.

In "some older aircraft", one Captain described a "commercial electrical switch" that did not exist, potentially having a "massive impact" within a smoke scenario. This wasn't understood until many years had passed, with the implications of intricate, subtle differences not always obvious, resulting in situations potentially "more difficult" to manage, with pilots "unaware of the serious implications".

During engine-out operations, one Captain noted that the amount of rudder-trim required varied, with cockpit scales presenting differently between variants; unlikely to be well known, and potentially affecting those who prefer to memorize and 'fly by numbers', increasing memory demand [3]. Also, multiple participants shared concerns regarding engine-out operations in one particular variant; an FO confirming one cannot see how it "works in the simulator", since they are not available, highlighting the importance of appropriate training including simulation for multi-variant operations.

However, three participants suggested that despite differences existing, non-normal events "shouldn't be a problem". However, these pilots operated within simple and consistent fleets, and generally had less experience than other participants. Generally, pilots were complimentary of the Airbus non-normal philosophy.

Manuals. Participants revealed that manuals include useful, detailed information, but were not easy to navigate quickly. Although information for the aircraft they were on at the time was available, one cannot easily compare variants, and the equipment fit within.

An observation was that pilots generally referred to variants when discussing equipment or functionality. Conversely, manuals use manufacturer serial number (MSN) or registration, inferring a mismatch between design and requirement, potentially impacting top-down memory processing [3]. An FO described a curious situation during an open-book exam, with a question that related to a specific variant. However, to locate the information, they first had to pick a registration that matched that variant before they could locate the required information. It was not possible to search by variant, impacting how quickly information could be obtained and the criticality of the documentation. Furthermore, a poorly organized, non-standardized manual is likely to negatively influence recall [3] and attentional failures may make it additionally challenging to notice absent or changes between variants [7] something people are poor at [6], highlighting the importance of the usability and organization of the documentation.

Within manuals, a Captain suggested it was easy to misidentify variants and one must be careful to look at "the specific airframe". Information is "scattered" around, suggested one FO, adding when pilots seek information, there are multiple layers to pass through, adding for "quick reference, they are not really appropriate". Another described multiple caveats existing within text, adding potential confusion. Furthermore, a Captain outlined a procedure that directed one in multiple, MSN dependent directions, concluding that it was easy to both mis-identify the MSN, and mis-apply the wrong drill.

Participants suggested it would be simpler if comparisons were made "between the different types", rather than by MSN/registration, suggesting an ideal strategy would involve identifying a baseline aircraft, and referring differences to that. Ensuring key information on variants is easily accessible, clear, and presented in a format that aligns with the user's information requirements is highlighted.

Information Recall. Limitations and gross-error checks were explored to understand if pilots can easily recall operationally useful, variant-dependent information. Participants generally reported finding this challenging, with experience assisting. Reflecting upon previous types, some commented that recall was a cognitively more challenging process due to the array of differences. Interestingly, most believed that incorrectly presented performance data would be identified.

An FO explained that "crosswind and tailwind limitations" varied, contrasting Lyall and Wickens [1], recommendation that limitations be aligned for simplicity, influencing memory loading [3]. Many admitted recalling incorrect information, suggesting a summary document would be useful. As with other documentation, this would need to be presented in an unambiguous manner that aligned with the user's requirements.

Captains "routinely" checked "facts and figures", describing knowledge as "not as good as it should be", tending "not to remember numbers anymore", favoring looking information up. This improves memory retrieval [3], potentially an experience-based strategy, occasionally hampered by manual structure, as described. Knowledge is "built up over time", offered one Captain, and some suggested it would "be easier to have just one aircraft", with one set of numbers. However, some FOs described it as "not that difficult", potentially lacking the experience/cognitive considerations exhibited by Captains.

Interestingly, participants generally believed they would notice "immediately" if they were presented with incorrect performance data, although Levin et al. [6] caution that people are overconfident in this regard.

Scheduling. All participants recalled routinely flying different variants within the same day, if their airline required it, opposing the recommendation by Lyall [6], and was described as an additional threat. "Whatever comes your way you have to fly it", revealed one Captain and operating from different bases with different variant fits, resulted in pilots being caught out "all the time", according to another.

Some participants described moving between variants with different equipment fits as challenging having potential to affect information retrieval from long-term memory [3]. Failing to discuss "some of the things that the aircraft is going to do" in a certain situation, may trigger a "what's it doing now" moment, suggesting the importance of effective and applicable briefings.

4.3 The Mitigations

The research now explores mitigations that pilots *and* airlines routinely use to manage the identified challenges/differences.

Experience. Generally, participants described multi-variant flying as simpler with increased experience, reflecting the AAIU [9] investigation citing reduced experience as a contributory factor and lack of familiarity has potential to move an "expert" back to novice, "analytical knowledge-based" [3:152] performance [13].

Participants suggested differences became more obvious and they "became more aware" over time. However, the challenge never "washes out fully", described one FO; an advantage because even with "experience", threats still exist, and one may become "blasé". Through "experience", one develops "rules" promoting easier movement between knowledge levels [13:258], especially within novel situations [3].

Some proposed that airlines "could do better" with respect to differences training, despite a Captain suggesting new pilots generally possess a good knowledge of "critical safety differences". However, some FOs suggested their initial training was challenging because they routinely operated multiple variants, but simulator training was on one variant, so lacked practical experience across all variants. Some Captains revealed that when "new", it "is a challenge".

Some suggested experience helped bridge the gap between differences comprehension, and how they should be managed, despite challenges existing even for experienced pilots [10].

Identification of Variants. Cockpits were described as virtually identical, with Airbus doing a "really good job" despite being easy environments to "get confused", or "brush off the differences" within. One Captain commented that it can be "obvious" to some, which variant one is in, but "not immediately obvious to others" and subtle differences increase the chances of a "visual awareness" failure [5:529]. Simple strategies were described to identify variants/characteristics, including simply looking around, and piecing all the "little clues" together. This commences in the crew room, described one FO, particularly if there are route/mission capability considerations, developing a "mental idea of what to expect".

Errors were described as more common when pilots had recently spent time within different variants, and participants described it being easy to notice differences when they were obvious, and harder when they were subtle, especially when not specifically directed to look for them, reflecting Jensen et al. [5] and JTSB [4] observations.

Since cockpits are virtually identical, one FO offered that "if you were to just walk into the cockpit", one might not be able to identify the variant, especially if arriving in the dark, via an airbridge. Another added that during briefings, they "include the aircraft registration", describing a "common alphabet". Using the registration to trigger an association was a commonly described technique, despite incorporating an additional, associative cognitive step, potentially increasing the risk of mis-association, alongside increased workload [19].

Participants often described "looking around", initially "out of the terminal window", to identify "what it's got". A Captain habitually does this because it is a "physical reminder" of the aircraft, and when asked if it would be useful if there was a reminder of the variant within the cockpit, they stated "absolutely". Many agreed; something "simple in front of each pilot" stating the variant, could be "useful" since "recognition-prompted recall" is better than pure memory recall [11:32]. When encountering high workload/stressful situations, the potential for type reversion exists, described a Captain, therefore a physical reminder could be "effective". Those from the one airline that does incorporate a placard "memory aid" [3:118] within some cockpits, "right in front of your eyes" described it as beneficial. Another described heuristic involved printing "a piece of paper" and writing the variant on it, promoting effective memory recall [3].

Conversely, some participants described easily identifying variants, especially with obvious differences such as screen age as an example. The importance of a simple and quick means of identifying aircraft variant is relevant across all multi-variant operations.

Briefings and Briefing Documentation. "Accurate, shared SA is critical for effective team operations" [2:198] and briefings enhance SA, promoting the consideration of differences, as recommended by Lyall and Wickens [1]. Participants routinely highlight variants within briefings, and some airlines provide additional briefing materials.

Contrasting the advice of Lyall [8], participants who moved between variants, described "time pressures" that should not be underestimated, resulting in pilots not "fully aware" of "key differences", affecting their ability to perceive, *and* understand them. When time-limited, decision makers may only entertain limited options [12], affecting those with less experience more [3]. Changing variants increases workload, is "tiring", and negatively influences capacity, generating enhanced error opportunities according to some; a threat identified by Braune [22]. Although briefing differences "adds time", some suggested one should "make time", or even delay the departure for, added one FO. "Categorically no" was one FO's response when asked whether they had enough time, described as "the main threat", by one Captain. They suggested that everything "in the manual can never be achieved in the time frame that's available", therefore comprehension must "happen at home". However, an FO praised their airline, suggesting "there is specific emphasis and time allocated", and were routinely encouraged to discuss "key differences", relevant since time pressures restrict information processing, degrading performance [3]. The alternative, staying on the same variant, was described as "a lot easier to manage", and those who did this, did not cite time pressures as a concern, reaffirming Lyall's [8] recommendations. The importance of adequate time for briefings is highlighted for all multi-variant aircraft types.

When airlines provided briefing documentation, a form of memory aid, these were described as beneficial, recommended for infrequently performed tasks [3]. One Captain suggested their document was "useful", containing relevant threats that one might have "to encounter". One FO suggested it helped "adapt your briefing accordingly", striking the balance between content and useability. However, the presentation could be "confusing", as columns could "merge", rendering it easy to "read the wrong column", potentially referencing a different equipment fit; something a Captain recalled doing. One Captain described a "tendency to skip over" these documents, giving them a "quick run through", and another proposed that differences are not "absorbed as well as they should be". Whilst these documents explain that differences exist, they do not provide strategies with how to mitigate them, something which is left to the pilots.

"It would be better if we had access to one document" outlining "key safety critical differences", suggested one Captain, and some reported sourcing information themselves, since their "company did not provide them" with anything. Many proposed a more bespoke approach: one Captain suggesting a variant specific document. Documents generally describe fit on a particular MSN. However, one Captain, whose airline operates a relatively new/standardized fleet, commented that their document took a different approach, describing equipment that *was not* present. Using new aircraft as a baseline, older aircraft listed equipment which *did not* feature. A simpler process described one FO, since "most of our fits are the same", potentially not an option for more complex fleets. Conversely, one FO suggested each aircraft was different from something, but as their airline lacked reference to a baseline aircraft, this relied on pilots having similar mental models. A potential challenge when moving between aircraft, increasing the reliance on briefings. Ideally, a common fit would exist, or alternatively, a document that allowed easy comparison of equipment between variants they were most familiar with/or had just operated would apply to all aircraft types with multiple variants. Shared SA within teams, "involves accurate and timely sharing of system and environmental information that affects both team members" [2:201], promoting expectation and understanding of systems [3]; trickier when under time pressure, and when using potentially misleading documentation.

Differences Training. After the Boeing 737-Max accidents, differences training was a focus [20]. Differences training is both recommended [8, 15] and regulated [21]. However, both the reality *and* perception of variant differences differed. As fleet variability increased, the call for additional training and preparation for all multi-variant operations also increased.

Participants described provided materials including iBook's, PDF documents, exams (level A/B requirements – Table 1), and in rare cases, dedicated training in the simulator/the line was provided (level C/D requirements - Table 1). This suggests operators perceive the differences/challenges differently or can simply offer an additional standard of training when they have any multi-variant operations.

One Captain was surprised "the manufacturer doesn't produce their own training programme", suggesting "each airline has to reinvent the wheel", however the regulations [21] requires airlines to establish and develop the training. This process requires airlines to perceive and understand the differences across variants, and there is the potential for information to be missed.

A provided iBook, describing the "main differences", was cited as "comprehensive" by one Captain, despite an FO suggesting it lacked detail. Describing a "small differences PDF", one FO felt it wasn't "complete enough", adding that during initial training, "instructors told us" to "focus on" one variant, whereas in reality, further variant knowledge was required, resulting in pilots filling in gaps themselves: lack of "contextual understanding can lead to misinterpretation and unintended consequences" [16:571]. Another recalled one "hour of differences training" for one variant featuring "a PowerPoint presentation", and another described "a series of presentations and documents", suggesting the training was "a box ticking exercise" on behalf of the regulator; a widely held view amongst those who did not experience dedicated simulator training. The importance of comprehensive differences training across any multi-variant flying was highlighted in the responses. Braune [22:1458] identified that "training did not always prepare pilots well enough", potentially still an issue today.

Simulator Training. Participants described their simulator training, recalling how it helped to prepare them for multi-variant operations. Simulation develops "motor actions", preparing pilots "mentally and physically", despite variants often lacking simulator representation. Furthermore, simulators do not always match aircraft fit, with new features often unavailable, generally viewed as sub-optimal. Effective recall requires "past events" to be available within one's episodic memory [7:274] with lack of familiarity potentially influencing cognitive performance within Rasmussen's [13] expertise taxonomy.

One Captain described only one of two engine types used were replicated by simulation within their airline, another suggested fit varied because training was outsourced, and one airline failed to "replicate any of the aircraft" on the line. Equipment standardization reduces long-term memory load, promoting development of effective "mental models" [3:118], one Captain suggesting it to be "very useful" experiencing training in simulators that represent aircraft in service, increasing the odds of positive training transfer [23]. Orlady and Barnes [19] suggest regulatory guidance is lacking regarding cockpit integration, potentially an issue here.

All participants who experienced simulators that matched their aircraft, were "not aware of any significant concerns", highlighting the crucial role effective and aligned simulator training can have.

Vincenzi et al. [23] warns that negative training may occur if a mismatch between task and training exists, potentially the situation where simulation isn't available for all variants. Training outcomes rely on regulation and airline ability coming together effectively, and Orlady and Barnes [19:1869] note the disconnect between "human factors research, engineering, operational and regulatory members of our aviation community".

Line Training. Within line-training, participants described a lack of structure, operating whatever was allocated, and a pilot's first variant experience could be post training. One Captain suggested this wasn't "reasonable", proposing new pilots undergo specific training on variants, allowing differences to be discussed/experienced. In the pursuit of commonality/lower costs, potentially pilot training needs are not always considered. It is important to develop cognitive routines with practice [17] made difficult if not adequately trained [18].

A Captain, whose airline recently introduced a new variant, recalled a dedicated line-training requirement – the only airline in the sample with such an offering. This was described as "comprehensive and well thought out", and anecdotally, trainees recalled it being useful practicing within a live training environment. A Captain at the same operator explained that although that "no formal syllabus" existed, it was useful to discuss and experience "potential issues". This example highlights the importance of appropriate training across all variants in multi-variant operations.

Individual Heuristics. Finally, some specific, individual mitigation strategies are described. On short final, many participants recalled verbalizing the variant when taking "the autopilot out", to remind themselves of key characteristics. Repetition of key issues improves memory recall [3] and the more frequently this is done, the stronger the link becomes [11]. Interestingly, only one participant recalled doing this before departure, and one FO did this silently. When suggested, one Captain described this as "an excellent idea", stating they would incorporate this into their own operation. Many participants described noting information on paper, with one Captain, adding that if the wind was changing, they would note limitations for easy reference, a simple form of distributed cognition [14]. Interestingly, all participants bar two, suggested variants were not a consideration when it came to hand flying, contrasting Lyall's [8] findings.

Potential limitations regarding the sample size and participants having different operational backgrounds are noted, but these in turn elicited a range of experiences and opened up further research opportunities in an organizational specific context.

4.4 Research Summary Diagrams

Figure 2 shows how the challenges and mitigations identified within this research interact with the human performance theory that has been introduced throughout. The diagram is intended to easily showcase the associations the challenges and mitigations have with the various identified human performance constructs. In all cases, the identified constructs impact the identified challenges and mitigations in different and complex ways. For example, identified differences impact pilot situational awareness and mental models. They have the ability to drive attentional failures, drive memory encoding and recall challenge, requiring cognition to be distributed effectively, requiring effective recall, and depending upon the amount of them, may impact cognitive performance. Variant identification as a mitigation example, has the potential to influence attentional failures, memory encoding and recall, distributed cognition, and again, cognitive performance. In summary, the impact on human performance of the various challenges and mitigations is both challenging and complicated, with the impact often variable depending upon both operational considerations and indeed the associations described in Fig. 2.

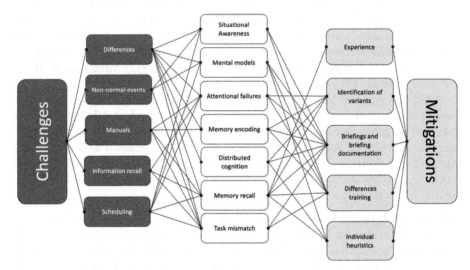

Fig. 2. Human performance interaction diagram

5   Conclusions

The following summarizes the key observations:

1. Participants commented positively regarding the Airbus family, used here as a common example of multi-variant flying. This research was always unlikely to uncover significant problems given successful operations for many years.
2. Differences in multi-variant flying may present as 'minor', but when combined, have the potential to generate other issues.
3. A range of mitigations were observed, and despite pilots routinely mitigating any challenges effectively, these differ across individuals and are not standardized.
4. Simulation is routinely not available for all variants, equipment, and fits.
5. Line-training may not be conducted on all variants.
6. Manuals refer to MSN, and pilots refer to variant. This does not promote quick checking.
7. Experience generally makes differences comprehension/application easier.
8. Variant identification techniques exist, and it is not easy to identify variants from the inside.
9. Briefings generally discuss the variant, although as time pressures exist, more focused documentation is desired.

6   Research and Industry Recommendations

Further research should explore the effectiveness of current regulation, considering the limitations of multi-variant operations, fleet size, complexity, and human performance. Industry recommendations are shown below:

1. Airlines should consider standardizing variant equipment fit and introduce a variant placard within cockpits.
2. Airlines should review the time allocated to pilots to comprehend variant differences.
3. Airlines should incorporate all variants within line training.
4. Simulation should replicate airline fleets.
5. Industry should develop a 'differences section' within manuals, promoting simple, quick comparisons.
6. Dedicated, specific and standardized variant differences training material should be developed by industry.

References

1. Lyall, B., Wickens, C.D.: Mixed fleet flying between two commercial aircraft types: an empirical evaluation of the role of negative transfer. In: Proceedings of the Human Factors and Ergonomics Society Annual Meeting, vol. 49, no. 1, pp. 45-48 (2005).https://doi.org/10.1177/154193120504900111
2. Endsley, M.R., Jones, D.G.: Designing for Situation Awareness: An Approach to User-centred Design, 2nd edn. CRC Press, Boca Raton (2011)
3. Wickens, C., Lee, J., Liu, Y., Gordon-Becker, G.M.: Introduction to Human Factors Engineering, 2nd edition (2013)
4. JTSB, Air Nippon Co, Ltd. Boeing 737–700, JA16AN Nosedive from upset (LOC-I) at an altitude of 41,000ft approx. 69nm East of Kushimoto, Wakayama Prefecture, Japan around 22:49 JST, September 6, 2011, JTSB, Tokyo (2014)
5. Jensen, M., Yao, R., Street, W., Simons, D.: Change blindness and inattentional blindness. Wiley Interdiscipl. Rev. Cogn. Sci. 2(5), 529–546 (2011). https://doi.org/10.1002/wcs.130
6. Levin, D., Momen, N., Drivdahl, S., Simons, D.: Change blindness blindness: the meta-cognitive error of overestimating change-detection ability. Vis. Cogn. 7(1-3), 397–412 (2000).https://doi.org/10.1080/135062800394865
7. Eysenck, M., Keane, M.: Cognitive Psychology: A Student's Handbook, 7th edn. Psychology Press, Hove, Hove (2015)
8. Lyall, E.: The effects of mixed-fleet flying of the boeing 737-200 and −300. In: Proceedings of the Human Factors Society Annual Meeting, vol. 36, no. 1, pp. 35–39 (2000). https://doi.org/10.1177/154193129203600110
9. AAIU, Final report: Serious incident ATR 72–212A, EI-FAW Dublin Airport, Ireland, (2016)
10. Soo, K., Mavin, T., Roth, W.: Mixed fleet flying in commercial aviation: a joint cognitive systems perspective. Cogn. Technol. Work 18, 449–463 (2016)
11. Harris, D.: Human Performance on the Flight Deck, CRC Press, Farnham. http://ebookcentral.proquest.com/lib/coventry/detail.action?docID=740089 (2011)
12. Flin, R., Slaven, G., Stewart, K.: Emergency decision making in the offshore oil and gas industry. Hum. Factors 38, 262–277, (1996)
13. Rasmussen, J.: Skills, rules, and knowledge; signals, signs, and symbols, and other distinctions in human performance models. IEEE Trans. Syst. Man Cybern. 257–266 (1983). https://doi.org/10.1109/TSMC.1983.6313160

14. Rogers, Y.: A Brief Introduction to Distributed Cognition, University of Sussex, Brighton (1997). http://www.id-book.com/downloads/chapter%208%20dcog-brief-intro.pdf
15. IFALPA, Mixed fleet flying (2015). https://ifalpa.org/media.2141.15pos20-mixed-fleet-flying.pdf
16. Orlady, L.: Airline pilots, training, and CRM in today's environment. In: Kanki, B.G., Anca., J., Chidester, T.R, Crew Resource Management 3rd edition, pp. 553–579, Academic Press, London (2019). https://doi.org/10.1016/B978-0-12-812995-1.00021-X
17. CAA, Flight Crew Human Factors Handbook CAP737, CAA, Gatwick (2016)
18. Orlady, C.: Advanced cockpit technology in the real world. In: Proceedings of the Royal Aeronautical Society Conference: Human Factors on Advanced Flight Decks, England (1991). https://www.flightsafety.org/ap/ap_jul91.pdf,
19. Orlady, H., Barnes, R.: A methodology for evaluating the operational suitability of air transport flight deck system enhancements. SAE Trans. J. Aerosp. **106**, 1869–1879 (1997)
20. Learmount, D.: Differences training under scrutiny after 737 Max crashes (2019). https://www.flightglobal.com/analysis/differences-training-under-scrutiny-after-737-max-crashes/132746.article
21. EASA, Subpart FC – Flight Crew (2013). https://www.easa.europa.eu/sites/default/files/dfu/04%20Part-ORO%20%28AMC-GM%29_Amdt2-Supplementary%20document%20to%20ED%20Decision%202013-019-R.pdf
22. Braune, R.: The Common/Same type rating: Human Factors and other issues, SAE technical paper 892229 (1989). https://doi.org/10.4271/892229
23. Vincenzi, D., Mouloua, M., Hancock, P., Wise, J.: Human Factors in Simulation and Training, CRC Press, Boca Raton (2008). https://doi.org/10.1201/9781420072846
24. IATA, Evidence Based Training Implementation Guide (2013). https://www.iata.org/contet assets/c0f61fc821dc4f62bb6441d7abedb076/ebt-implementation-guide.pdf
25. Brinkmann, S., Kvale, S.: Doing Interviews 2nd edition, London, SAGE (2018). https://doi.org/10.4135/9781529716665
26. British Psychological Society, Code of Ethics and Conduct, BPS, Leicester (2018)
27. Braun, V., Clarke, V.: Using thematic analysis in psychology. Qual. Res. Psychol. **3**(2), 77–101 (2006). https://doi.org/10.1191/1478088706qp063oa
28. Lincoln, Y., Guba, E.: Naturalistic Inquiry, Newbury Park, California (1985)
29. Merriam, S.: Qualitative Research: A Guide to Design and Implementation. Wiley, Somerset (2009)

Engineering Psychology in Job Design

Anastasia Wood[✉], Alexander Clark, and Vincent G. Duffy

Purdue University, West Lafayette, IN 47906, USA
`wood231@alumni.purdue.edu`, {`clark660,duffy`}`@purdue.edu`

Abstract. The purpose of this report is to analyze the effects of Engineering Psychology on Job Design. Specifically relating to increasing Occupational Safety. The report uses several different citation and data analysis tools to complete the study. Google Ngram was used in the preliminary data collection phase to predict the trends in topics. MAXQDA, VOSviewer, BibExcel, and Citespace were also utilized in the generation of analyzing the citations and their data. Three articles were analyzed where the safety of the operator was the focus, and the goal was to measure cognitive workload. Most concluded that eye tracking can be used to assess the impact of mental workload on job design, and the findings can help engineers design and implement better working conditions.

Keywords: Engineering Psychology · Job Design · Occupational Safety · VOSviewer · MAXQDA · Citespace

1 Introduction and Background

The field of industrial engineering is very broad and has many applications. Industrial engineers can work in health care, manufacturing, operations, automation, and more. With this, using psychology to help design and implement new processes is vital in order to design with the human in mind. The study of people has been around for thousands of years, so using this valuable information will help engineers do their job even better. Specifically related to job design, it helps to have a holistic approach so the changes or designs being made are curated to the population at hand. *The Handbook of Human Factors* does not have one chapter fully devoted to the topic of engineering psychology, because it can truly apply to all areas of job design.

Engineering psychology is a field of psychology that focuses on the relationship between humans and the products that we use every day. Engineering psychology differs from ergonomics in that engineering psychology does not simply compare two possible designs for a piece of equipment, but also specifies the capacities and limitations of the human who will be in control of the equipment (Fitts 1958). This relation to designing to the abilities of human operators is a direct relation to the topic of job design. Job design refers to the process of organizing and structuring job tasks and activities (Tims & Bakker 2010). This affects how workers can perform tasks and also react to differing situations. Job design can also influence job satisfaction, employee motivation, and work effort (De Cooman et al. 2013).

© The Author(s), under exclusive license to Springer Nature Switzerland AG 2023
M. Kurosu et al. (Eds.): HCII 2023, LNCS 14054, pp. 491–507, 2023.
https://doi.org/10.1007/978-3-031-48038-6_31

A key aspect of job design is the ability to create jobs/tasks that are safe for the worker to complete. This relates job design, and ultimately engineering psychology, to occupational safety. Occupational safety is defined to be the measures taken to ensure the health, safety, and welfare of workers in the workplace. It involves identifying and assessing workplace hazards, implementing controls to prevent or minimize those hazards, and providing training and education to workers to ensure they can work safely (Occupational Safety and Health Administration 2023). The purpose of defining the three terms above [Occupational Safety, Engineering Psychology, and Job Design] is this report will work to show not only their relations to one another but their importance in current research and industry.

The next step before digging deeper into this study is analyzing the trend of articles published related to the topic. Below is the Google Ngram for "Engineering Psychology" where the date range was 1900–2019. It is clear that around 1950 is when the topic really took off and became more popular (Fig. 1).

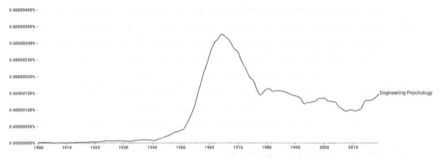

Fig. 1. Google Ngram 1900–2019

To do a deeper analysis, the date range was changed to 1980–2019 and it became clear that there have not been many large changes in the number of publications each year. It has remained pretty steady each year with a small dip around 1995 and 2006 (Fig. 2).

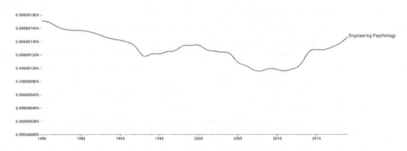

Fig. 2. Google Ngram 1980–2019

While Google Ngram does not go past 2019, it would be interesting to see what the trends are after the COVID-19 Pandemic because it has changed the way people do work and life as a whole. In addition, with the growth of smart devices, there are more ways that Industrial Engineers can apply Psychology knowledge to interface and display design.

Compared to two other topics, the Google Ngram below is highlighting the trend, between Engineering Psychology, Job Design, and Occupational Safety. The range was set to 1950–2019 because that is when Occupational Safety started to trend up. When looking at this, it is clear that Occupational Safety has significantly more publications than the other two topics. This is good information to have leading into further analysis later in the report (Fig. 3).

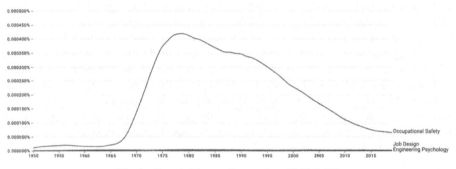

Fig. 3. Google Ngram Comparison 1950–2019

2   Purpose of Study

The study of engineering psychology is important because it helps to improve the safety, efficiency, and usability of products and systems. By understanding how people interact with such items, designers can create products that meet the needs of consumers. A unique aspect of engineering psychology is its focus on the user. Engineering psychology emphasizes human-centered design to ensure that products/systems are designed to accommodate the needs and abilities of their users. This approach improves safety, efficiency, and user satisfaction when using a product (Salvendy 2012).

The Handbook of Human Factors and Ergonomics focuses on a wide array of topics in Job Design. Because Engineering Psychology has applications in many areas, there is not one sole chapter devoted to this topic. While doing the bibliometric analysis, it was clear that eye-tracking is the main way engineering psychology, job design, and occupational safety are tied together. This is talked about in many chapters, but chapter 38 is titled "Usability and User Experience: Design and Evaluation". In this, eye-tracking is introduced, and the uses of it are explained. Not only can engineering psychology be used in job design and designing interfaces, but it can be applied to occupational safety. This can be done by utilizing eye-tracking techniques to see how users most commonly use the platforms and how they carry out their daily jobs (Salvendy pg. 972). Another chapter in the textbook that is relevant to this report is Chapter 55 "Human Factors in Ergonomics and Aviation." Later in this report, aviation applications will be highlighted.

But in this chapter, it is clear that designing the planes to be most easily used when in the air is important. For engineers to do this well, they must understand how and why pilots do things, and this can be done by the use of eye-tracking, engineering psychology, and fundamentals of job design (Salvendy pg. 1460).

When looking at the current literature on the subject, researchers often reference engineering psychology when looking at occupational safety. It is widely known that most safety incidents that occur in the field happen as a result of human error. Thus, by using aspects of engineering psychology, such as user-friendly and adaptable technologies that are replicable, researchers can better understand the variables responsible for human performance (Gunda et al. 2023). This expands on the ideas presented in the previous paragraph by utilizing the aspects of uniqueness for engineering psychology and applying them to a real word problem such as reducing human error.

The purpose of this study is to gain a deeper understanding of how Engineering Psychology can be used to leverage increased occupational safety. In addition, by doing a literature review of articles related to this topic, the hope is to highlight what articles and authors are leading in this industry. Throughout this report, there will be several different data visualizations to highlight popular articles, authors, and topics in this field of study. In addition, these tools will help give an overview of the information these articles yield. Some of the tools that will be used include CiteSpace, MAXQDA, BibExcel, VOSviewer, and more.

3   Research Methodology

Prior to conducting the analysis of engineering psychology, it was important to understand the level of engagement that this topic had with the scientific community. Such research is important for a literature review as the amount of research done and the recent trends of when articles were published for a topic can alter how relevant a review actually is (Zhang et al. 2021).

3.1   Data Collection

A systematic literature review was conducted by looking at the number of articles published between 2010–2023 that included the phrase "engineering psychology" and the word 'safety'. The reasoning for the timeline restraint is to show the relatively recent research. The search terms are used to find all articles that discuss the topic specific to this paper, engineering psychology, and safety is included to allow for more focused results. Within our research into databases, specifying any further would result in little to no articles. The below table shows these search criteria carried out amongst three different databases and the resulting number of articles that were retrieved (Table 1).

From the above table, it appears that ProQuest produced the most amount of search results for the search terms. The data for the search results of Scopus were downloaded in "CSV" format. The data from Web of Science was downloaded as a plain text file. The data from ProQuest could not be downloaded due to the size of the file exceeding the allowed number of articles.

Table 1. Search Results within Databases

Database:	Search Terms:	Number of Articles from 2010-2023:
Scopus	"Engineering Psychology" AND Safety	34
Web of Science	"Engineering Psychology" AND Safety	106
ProQuest	"Engineering Psychology" AND Safety	2,180

3.2 Engagement Measure

Another way to analyze the popularity of a topic is by the use of Vicinitas. It is a Twitter analytics tool that highlights the popularity of a topic. To get an analysis the user needs a Twitter account to log into, then search for the term they are wanting to learn about. The search term used for this report was "Engineering Psychology." First, a Word Cloud was found that reveals keywords that are in tweets containing the words "Engineering Psychology." This is seen in Fig. 4 below.

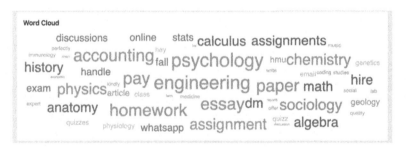

Fig. 4. Vicinitas Word Cloud

Vicinitasalso includes an Engagement Timeline, Post Timeline, Type of Posts, and Types of Rich Media data visualizations. The timeline for these tweets was from April 11, 2023 – April 19, 2023. These graphs and charts show an increasing interest in the topic (Fig. 5).

3.3 Trend Analysis

Using the data gathered from the search results within Scopus the number of articles published per year can be analyzed. This objectively portrays the interest in the subject of Engineering Psychology concerning safety from the scientific community. The trend analysis for the number of articles per year can be seen below (Fig. 6).

It can be seen that there is no rising interest in the area but rather a semi-constant rate of articles being released from year to year. The highest number of articles published

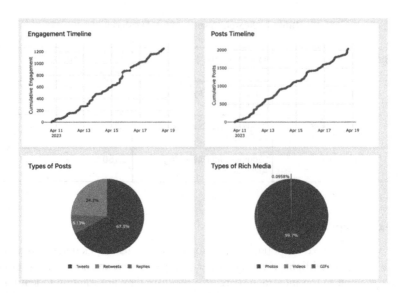

Fig. 5. Vicinitas Engagement

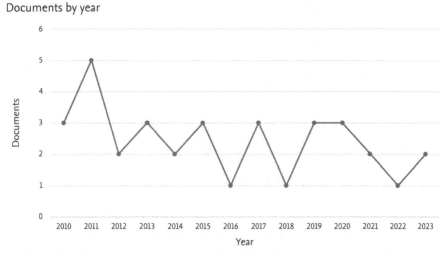

Fig. 6. Trend Analysis via Scopus

related to the subject of engineering psychology and safety was in 2011 with five articles. The gradual decline since then may elude to the lack of interest in the subject from researchers. However, it does show that research continues to take place within the field of engineering psychology.

4 Results

4.1 Co-citation Analysis

Often when researching a topic, finding a common piece of literature that provides foundational information is a key part of understanding a topic. Using a co-citation analysis shows the articles that have been referenced by multiple articles. Using the data exported from Web of Science, sources that had been referenced by articles in the search results at least three times were visualized below (Fig. 7).

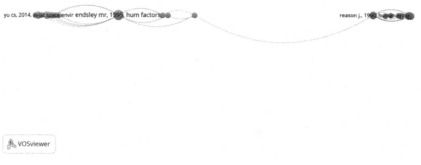

Fig. 7. VOSviewer sources that had been referenced by articles three or more times

Of the almost 2,300 cited references, 29 sources met the above criteria. Out of these 29 sources, seven of them weren't connected to any cluster and were thus scraped. This left 22 references forming the three clusters you see above. As can be seen in the figure, there are three different clusters of references. The blue cluster is related to both clusters, however, is more closely related to the green cluster. From these clusters, eight sources were picked at random to be reviewed in the discussion section of the paper (Table 2).

Table 2. Eight Sources of Focus

Diehl A. (2009). *Human performance and systems safety considerations in aviation mishaps*
Parasuraman R. (1997). *Humans and automation: Use, misuse, disuse, abuse*
Endsley M. (1995). *Toward a theory of situation awareness in Dynamic Systems*
Rayner K. (1998). *Eye movements in reading and information processing: 20 years of research*
Li, W.C., Braithwaite, G., & Yu, C. (1970, January 1). *The investigation of pilots' eye scan patterns on the flight deck during an air-to-surface task*
Wickens, C. D. (2013). Engineering psychology and human performance
Kuo, F.-Y., Hsu, C.-W., & Day, R.-F. (2009, June 22). *An exploratory study of cognitive effort involved in decision under framing-an application of the eye-tracking technology*
Stanton, N. A., Salmon, P. M., Rafferty, L. A., Walker, G. H., Baber, C., & Jenkins, D. P. (2017). Human factors methods: A practical guide for engineering and design

4.2 Co-occurrence Analysis

A co-occurrence analysis is used to determine the relatedness of items based on the number of documents in which they occur together. The importance of using co-occurrence analysis here is to understand the footprint of engineering psychology in reference to other subjects. Using the Web of Science.txt file, a co-occurrence analysis was conducted. This analysis can be visualized in the figure below (Fig. 8).

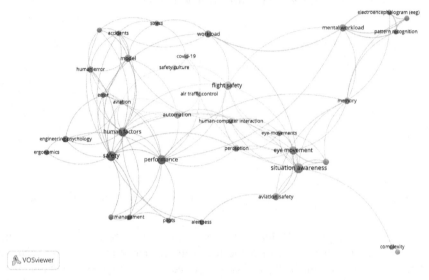

Fig. 8. Important Keywords in Articles

The figure above shows keywords that are used in different articles and displays the connections of these different keywords. Articles were selected to be a part of this cluster given they had three or more keywords shared with a different article. The specific keywords present in the cluster can be found in the figure below. This paper's topic keywords are engineering psychology, occupational safety, and job design. Aspects of these keywords are present in the figure above. Thus, providing a basis for the importance of the connection between the keywords present in this paper (Fig. 9).

4.3 Content Analysis using MAXQDA

Later in the Discussion section of this paper, three articles will be analyzed. There we will discuss its main findings and how they relate to the topics in this paper. The three articles were downloaded into MAXQDA, and from that, a Word Cloud of important repeated terms is created. This helps readers see what the main topics are in those three articles. This can also be done for all of the articles in the References section if wanted, but we stuck to the three main articles. This helped us get a summary of the topics that are discussed before reading all of them. In Fig. 10, you will see the Word Cloud.

Verify selected keywords

Selected	Keyword	Occurrences	Total link strength
☑	safety	10	23
☑	human factors	9	17
☑	eye movement	7	16
☑	situation awareness	10	16
☑	performance	9	15
☑	mental workload	6	14
☑	model	5	12
☑	flight safety	7	11
☑	accidents	3	10
☑	automation	6	10
☑	electroencephalogram (eeg)	3	10
☑	pattern recognition	3	10
☑	signal processing	3	10
☑	aviation	3	9
☑	memory	4	9
☑	attention distribution	4	8
☑	eye-movements	3	8
☑	human error	4	8
☑	human reliability	3	8
☑	perception	4	8
☑	aviation safety	5	7
☑	error	3	7
☑	workload	5	7
☑	engineering psychology	4	6
☑	human-computer interaction	3	6
☑	management	3	6
☑	stress	3	5
☑	air traffic control	3	4
☑	covid-19	3	4
☑	pilots	3	4
☑	alertness	3	3
☑	safety culture	3	3
☑	usability	3	3
☑	complexity	3	2
☑	ergonomics	3	2
☑	resilience	3	1

Fig. 9. VOSviewer Keyword Frequency

Another analysis that was completed in MAXQDA was a lexical search of three terms: Job Design, Occupational Safety, and Engineering Psychology. Again, the three articles used in this search are the ones focused on in the Discussion. Table 3 shows all the times one of those search items is found in those three articles, and where the item is in the article. This again can also be done for all of the articles but is limited for this report.

4.4 BibExcel Pivot Table

In Harzing, the keywords Engineering Psychology, Job Design, and Occupational Safety were input with the settings of maximum results being 200 with no date constraints. From there, the results were input into BibExcel. BibExcel helps with converting files from Google Scholar, WebofScience, etc. into Excel. This helps the studier be able to visualize

Fig. 10. MAXQDA Word Cloud

Table 3. Lexical Search via MAXQDA

Preview	Document name	Search item
Engineering Psychology	Scan Patterns on the Flight Dec	Engineering Psychology
Engineering Psychology	Scan Patterns on the Flight Dec	Engineering Psychology
11th International Conference on Engineering Psychology and Cognitive	Scan Patterns on the Flight Dec	Engineering Psychology
ontains papers focusing on the thematic area of engineering psychology and co	Scan Patterns on the Flight Dec	engineering psychology
Engineering Psychology and Cognitive Ergonomics	Scan Patterns on the Flight Dec	Engineering Psychology
sharing of knowledge, for job design, mission planning and dynamic (real-time)	Scan Patterns on the Flight Dec	job design
Engineering Psychology &	Scan Patterns on the Flight Dec	Engineering Psychology
Federal Institute for Occupational Safety and Health,	Scan Patterns on the Flight Dec	Occupational Safety
ided lab of the Federal Institute for Occupational Safety and Health and were c	Scan Patterns on the Flight Dec	Occupational Safety
Federal Institute for Occupational Safety and Health, Berlin, Germany	Scan Patterns on the Flight Dec	Occupational Safety
Engineering psychology and human performance.	Scan Patterns on the Flight Dec	Engineering psychology
Engineering Psychology, pp.	Scan Patterns on the Flight Dec	Engineering Psychology
Engineering Psychology and Human Performance, 3rd edn.	Scan Patterns on the Flight Dec	Engineering Psychology
Engineering Psychology and Human Performance, 2nd edn.	Scan Patterns on the Flight Dec	Engineering Psychology
Engineering psychology and human performance (2nd.	d Automation: Use, Misuse, Dis	Engineering psychology
Engineering psychology and human performance (1st ed.	ry of Situation Awareness in Dyn	Engineering psychology
Engineering psychology and human performance (2nd ed.	ry of Situation Awareness in Dyn	Engineering psychology

the bibliometric information. Below in Fig. 11 is a table of leading authors within the searches from Harzing. The table shows how many articles they have published relating to these topics. It is clear that P. Carayon is a leading author.

4.5   CiteSpace Burst Analysis

CiteSpace is a tool that researchers use to visualize patterns within the scientific literature. These patterns can also be analyzed. Using the data collected from the Web of Science database search results, a burst analysis can be conducted. A burst in bibliometric data occurs when there is a sudden increase in the citation of a particular keyword or subject. Essentially, when an area of research becomes suddenly popular, there will be a 'burst'

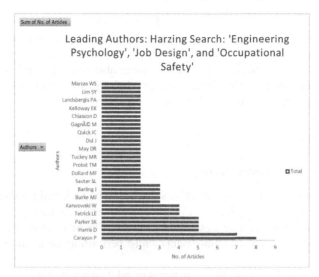

Fig. 11. BibExcel Pivot Chart

in citations about the subject area. Below is the figure that was created using the Web of Science data in CiteSpace (Fig. 12).

Fig. 12. CiteSpace 'Burst' via Web of Science Data

As visualized, the data seems to be spread out with multiple, small clusters present. There is no burst present within the data set provided to CiteSpace. This means that there was no event or extreme increase in interest in the subject of engineering psychology with a focus on safety. This result coincides with the previous findings from the trend analysis, which showed a stagnation of articles published. The limitations of CiteSpace are that the range of years was not the full extent of articles present within the data and that there is a chance the data set provided to CiteSpace could be too small to see the potential changes of interest. The subject might also be too general, as researching a specific method for accessing engineering psychology problems in job design might provide data more inclined to burst behavior.

5 Discussion

5.1 Co-citation Literature Review

In Sect. 4.1, Table 2 shows a list of articles that are to be reviewed for their relation to occupational safety and/or job design in the scope of engineering psychology. In this section, three of the eight references will be analyzed. The first source to be analyzed is Li's (1970) study of pilots' eye movements whilst performing air-to-surface tasks on a flight deck.

The article aimed to track the eye patterns of pilots when performing air-to-surface tasks, which in the case of the article was when an aircraft would attack ground targets. The experiment was conducted within a flight simulator rather than in the field and used an eye-tracking device to record the eye movements of pilots when doing the task. The authors analyzed the data to identify the eye scan patterns and determine whether different tasks affected them. Also evaluated were the effectiveness of cockpit user interfaces and how they influenced eye movement. The results of the study showed that the pilots' eye scan patterns varied depending on the task they were performing. And that the cockpit displays did influence the pilots' eye movement patterns. Thus, it was suggested that the design of the cockpit should take into account the pilots' eye scan patterns to optimize their performance during critical tasks (Li et al. 1970).

This paper is an excellent example of engineering psychology in the real world as these researchers are looking to understand the cognitive process that a pilot endures when completing a task. Their goal was to engineer a more optimal way for pilots to process information when completing critical tasks. We can see that within this article the author discusses that the design of the cockpit has a direct effect on the pilot's ability to perform. Therefore, showcasing the importance of job design when discussing engineering psychology. Occupational safety is also an underlying point of the article. The unspoken goal is for these pilots to complete a task unharmed. This article analyzed the design of the task and the tools used to decrease the odds of incidents occurring to increase the odds of a successful mission. That is directly related to the topic of occupational safety.

The next article is written by Raja Parasuraman (1997) titled "Humans and Automation: Use, Misuse, Disuse, Abuse" which studies the human-automation relationship. This paper is unique in that it provides both pros and cons for the use of automation citing its effects on human performance. Parasuraman argues that automation can be incredibly powerful when used appropriately but can also lead to unintended consequences when used improperly or excessively. This introduces what is defined as the 'ironies of automation', which is the idea that the more efficient and reliable an automated system becomes, the more vulnerable it is to breakdowns and unexpected failures.

The author states that humans need to be aware of their role within the system to prevent incidents. This relates to the idea of job design. Defining an operator's role within the system is a critical element of any job design. Additionally, when personnel is not aware of their role in the system or how it operates, the odds of there being a safety risk increases or in other words occupational safety.

The final article is titled "Toward a Theory of Situational Awareness in Dynamic Systems" (1995). The author, Mica Endsley, presents a theory of situational awareness that tries to explain how humans perceive and process information in complex and dynamic environments. These environments present rapid and unpredictable changes to which an operator must be able to quickly adapt. The article outlines a model of situation awareness that has three levels: perception, comprehension, and projection. It is stressed throughout the article that situational awareness is key to navigating dynamic systems. Several factors can influence situation awareness: workload, stress, training, and the design of the human-machine interface. Endsley argues that understanding these factors is essential for developing effective training programs and designing systems that support situation awareness in dynamic environments. This argument that is provided by Endsley outlines how critical job design for such systems is for the safety and success of the operator. Thus, circling back to the importance of using engineering psychology within job design.

Within all the sources of reference, some commonalities were present. Many of the authors looked at eye movements to track cognitive engagement and/or workload. The experiments were designed using practices of engineering psychology, where the focus would be centered around the operator. Problems of efficiency were answered by accessing the design of the system that the operator interacted with. Each article had a relation to the safety of the user, whether direct or indirect. The motif of the references reviewed was that within the field of engineering psychology, there is an importance placed on utilizing aspects of job design to solve problems centered around the cognitive abilities of an operator. Additionally, many questions that revolve around the optimization of tasks or increasing the success rates of systems also involve the assessment of occupational safety to some degree.

5.2 Reappraisal of Subject

When evaluating the subject, eye-tracking came up a lot as a way to measure mental workload. Thus, this section evaluates articles that use eye-tracking to model the mental workloads of individuals.

The first article for the reappraisal is done by Jiang et al. (2019), who examined the use of eye-tracking to infer mental workload in adaptive educational games. They found that eye-tracking metrics, such as pupil diameter and fixation duration, were sensitive to changes in mental workload and could be used to design better adaptive learning systems. The second article evaluated was written by Wilson and Russell (2003) in which they used eye-tracking as one of several measures to assess mental workload in real-time. They found that such measures, like blink rate, pupil diameter, and fixation duration, could be used to predict changes in mental workload, and that an artificial neural network could be trained to accurately classify mental workload levels based on these measures.

Both articles have significant use of eye-tracking for modeling mental workload However, whilst such a subject is significant on its own, its relevance to the field of engineering psychology is important. By measuring mental workload, eye-tracking can provide valuable information about the cognitive demands of a task or system, which can help engineers design interfaces and workflows that are appropriate for the cognitive abilities and limitations of the user. Furthermore, eye-tracking can also be used to assess the impact of job design on mental workload. For example, an engineer could use eye-tracking to compare the mental workload of workers performing a task under different ergonomic conditions. This data could then be used to reduce mental workload by optimizing the work environment. Thus, the topics selected, while general, are relevant

6 Conclusion

Engineering Psychology is something that has been around for a while and has not gained much popularity in the last few years, staying relatively constant even after the COVID-19 Pandemic. When considering the keywords: Job Design, Engineering Psychology, and Occupational Safety, there is a lot of research. A lot of these topics have a heavy focus on human factors and aviation. There is a very specific and heavy focus on eye-tracking, which can be done in many different areas of focus. Eye-tracking is only improving because of technology, and it can be utilized in different settings making it an appealing option for engineers when trying to improve occupational safety. In addition, eye-tracking has a heavy application to psychology, because it helps highlight how people digest things visually, and psychology can explain why. All of this can help engineers design, test, and implement better systems and automated processes to make occupational safety better. Thus, eye-tracking seems to have great importance in job design, occupational safety, and engineering psychology.

7 Future Work

Throughout this report, there has been a focus on many different areas of Job Design and Occupational Safety. Engineering Psychology can relate to many different industries such as automation, aviation, manufacturing, healthcare, and more. However, as technology is improving it is clear that research will need to follow in that direction as well. The National Science Foundation is part of the US government, and they are responsible for supporting upcoming and current research. On their website, one can find current and upcoming grants to reveal where research is focusing in upcoming years. When visiting their website, a couple of grant proposals were found and pointed to the future being in automation. Figure 13 from the NSF website, shows a project with up to a million USD budget partnering with Amazon. This project is going to consist of a team of ten to twelve people, and the NSF and Amazon are partnering to focus on fairness of research in Artificial Intelligence and Machine Learning. From the NSF website directly they say, "the goal of contributing to trustworthy AI systems that are readily accepted and deployed to tackle grand challenges facing society." Not only can Engineering Psychology help design, train, and equip employees to do their job better, but it can help robots and machine learning predict and aid humans in doing their job better and safer.

It is clear AI is taking over more and more, so this will be a main focus in the future of Engineering Psychology, Occupational Safety, and Job Design as a whole.

Fig. 13. NSF Future Research with Amazon

On a broader scale, the NSF website highlights another area where they are investing their time and money. They are recruiting for research at minority-serving institutions (MSIs). They want to increase the research in STEM-related topics. Because of the increase in technology in the world, opportunities like this are available and will continue to be of importance. Areas, where they want to focus their research that relate to this report, include: cognitive neuroscience, psychology, and other STEM topics (Fig. 14).

Fig. 14. NSF Research with MSIs

References

BibExcel. n.d. https://homepage.univie.ac.at/juan.gorraiz/bibexcel/

CiteSpace. n.d. http://cluster.cis.drexel.edu/~cchen/citespace/

De Cooman, R., Stynen, D., Van den Broeck, A., De Witte, H.: How job characteristics relate to need satisfaction and autonomous motivation: implications for work effort. J. Appl. Soc. Psychol. **43**(6), 1342–1352 (2013). https://onlinelibrary.wiley.com/doi/10.1111/jasp.12143. Accessed 26 Apr 2023

Diehl, A.: Human Performance and Systems Safety Considerations in Aviation Mishaps. Taylor & Francis (2009). Accessed 28 Apr 2023

https://www.tandfonline.com/doi/abs/10.1207/s15327108ijap0102_1

Endsley, M.: Toward a theory of situation awareness in dynamic systems. Sage Journals (1995). Accessed 28 Apr 2023

https://journals.sagepub.com/doi/abs/10.1518/001872095779049543?journalCode=hfsa

Fitts, P.: Engineering psychology|Annual review of psychology. Ann. Rev. (1958). http://www.annualreviews.org/doi/10.1146/annurev.ps.09.020158.001411. Accessed 26 Apr 2023

Gunda, Y.R., Gupta, S., Singh, L.K.: Assessing human performance and human reliability: a review. Scopus (2023). https://www.scopus.com/record/display.uri?eid=2-s2.0-704493 64765&origin=recordpage. Accessed 26 Apr 2023

Jiang, Y., Du, Y., Huang, D., Ren, X.: Using eye tracking to infer mental workload in adaptive educational games. IEEE Trans. Learn. Technol. **12**(4), 452–462 (2019). https://doi.org/10.1109/TLT.2019.2924442

Kuo, F.-Y., Hsu, C.-W., Day, R.-F.: An exploratory study of cognitive effort involved in decision under framing-an application of the eye-tracking technology. Decis. Support Syst. **48**(1), 81–91 (2009). https://www.sciencedirect.com/science/article/abs/pii/S01679236090 01481. Accessed 28 Apr 2023

Lewis, J.: Usability and user experience: design and evaluation In: Handbook of Human Factors and Ergonomics (5th ed.). edited by John Wiley & Sons, Inc

Li, W.C., Braithwaite, G., Yu, C.: The investigation of pilots' eye scan patterns on the flight deck during an air-to-surface task. SpringerLink (1970). http://link.springer.com/chapter/10.1007/978-3-319-07515-0_33. Accessed 28 Apr 2023

MAXQDA. n.d. https://www.maxqda.com/

Mendeley. n.d. https://www.mendeley.com/

NSF program on Fairness in Artificial Intelligence in collaboration with Amazon. NSF. (n.d.). https://new.nsf.gov/funding/opportunities/nsf-program-fairness-artificial-intelligence. Accessed 30 Apr 2023

Occupational Safety and Health Administration. (n.d.). What is occupational safety and health?. https://www.osha.gov/oshinfo/whatwedo/index.html. Accessed 24 Apr 2023

Parasuraman, R.: Humans and automation: use, misuse, disuse, abuse. Sage Journals (1997). https://journals.sagepub.com/doi/abs/10.1518/001872097778543886

ProQuest. (n.d.). https://www.proquest.com

Rayner, K.: Eye movements in reading and information processing: 20 years of research. Am. Psychol. Assoc. **124**(3), 372 (1998). https://psycnet.apa.org/doiLanding?doi=10.1037%2F0 033-2909.124.3.372. Accessed 28 Apr 2023

Salvendy, G., (Ed.).: Handbook of Human Factors and Ergonomics (4th ed.). Wiley (2012)

Scopus. (n.d.). https://www.scopus.com

Stanton, N.A., Salmon, P.M., Rafferty, L.A., Walker, G.H., Baber, C., Jenkins, D.P.: Human Factors Methods: A Practical Guide for Engineering and Design. Taylor and Francis (2017)

Tims, M., Bakker, A.B.: Job crafting: towards a new model of individual job redesign. SA J. Ind. Psychol. (2010). https://sajip.co.za/index.php/sajip/article/view/841. Accessed 26 Apr 2023

VOSviewer. (n.d.). https://www.vosviewer.com/

Web of Science. (n.d.). https://www-webofscience-com.ezproxy.lib.purdue.edu/wos/woscc/basic-search

Wickens, C.D.: Engineering Psychology and Human Performance. Routledge (2013)

Wilson, G.F., Russell, C.A.: Real-time assessment of mental workload using psychophysiological measures and artificial neural networks. Hum. Fact. J. Hum. Fact. Ergon. Soc. **45**(4), 635–643 (2003). https://doi.org/10.1518/hfes.45.4.635.27250

Zhang, Z., Duffy, V.G., Tian, R.: Trust and automation: a systematic review and bibliometric analysis. In: Stephanidis, C., et al. HCI International 2021 - Late Breaking Papers: Design and User Experience. HCII 2021. Lecture Notes in Computer Science, vol. 13094, pp. 451–464. Springer, Cham (2021). https://doi.org/10.1007/978-3-030-90238-4_32

Applying Touchscreen as Flight Control Inceptor: Investigating the Perceived Workload of Interacting with Sidestick and Touchscreen Inceptors

Jingyi Zhang[1](✉) , Wen-Chin Li[1] , and Wojciech Tomasz Korek[2,3]

[1] Safety and Accident Investigation Centre, SATM, Cranfield University, Cranfield, UK
jingyi.zhang2@cranfield.ac.uk
[2] Dynamics, Simulation and Control Group, SATM, Cranfield University, Cranfield, UK
[3] Faculty of Automatic Control, Electronics and Computer Science, Silesian University of Technology, Gliwice, Poland

Abstract. The widespread application of touchscreen technology brought a huge potential for future flight deck design with advanced human-computer interactive mode. The integrated flight displays that enable touchscreen input have been widely examined and validated in the aviation industry. The current research proposed an innovative surface control inceptor based on the touchscreen to control aircraft attitude in flight operations. Fifty-six participants were invited to a flight simulator experiment using the touchscreen and sidestick to perform landing tasks in the scenarios without turbulence and with turbulence. Participants' heart rate variability (HRV) parameters during flight tasks were collected as biomarkers of mental workload. The two-way repeated measures ANOVA results demonstrated significant interactions of participants' mean R-R interval (RR) and mean heart rate (HR) between inceptor and turbulence. The simple main effect analysis indicated that in the turbulence scenario, participants' mean HR significantly decreased and mean RR increased using the touchscreen controller compared to the sidestick inceptor. Furthermore, the standard deviation of normal to normal R-R intervals (SDNN) was higher while performing landing tasks based on the touchscreen in turbulence and non-turbulence scenarios. These findings revealed significant decreases in workload during landing operations from both mental and physical aspects. The applicability of the touchscreen-based control surface inceptor in flight operations was confirmed. This provided a new vision of the advanced aircraft flight control system and future flight deck design for next-generation aviation operations.

Keywords: Touchscreen · Mental Workload · Heart Rate Variability · Aircraft Control

M. Kurosu et al. (Eds.): HCII 2023, LNCS 14054, pp. 508–519, 2023.
https://doi.org/10.1007/978-3-031-48038-6_32

1   Introduction

Touchscreen technology is rapidly developed and integrated into day-to-day life. The simple tactile interface and direct finger-based input enable a more intuitive human-computer interaction process. It has been demonstrated that the application of touch-screen technology will improve task performance and user satisfaction [1, 2]. To date, touchscreen applications also caught considerable interest in the aviation industry, espe-cially in future flight deck design. The F-35 joint strike fighter and Garmin's G3000 inte-grated avionics system have brought touchscreen technology to flight displays in modern flight decks [3]. Previous research confirmed the effectiveness and advantage of touch-screen input system in aircraft manipulation and flight operation: compared to the voice recognition input, touchscreen controller can significantly decrease task completion time and increase user interface satisfaction in specific tasks including executing checklists, addressing the alert messages, changing altitude, and navigation [4, 5]. Furthermore, the integrated touchscreen display in the modern flight deck is easily configurable to achieve a human-centred design of interface and functionality without physical input devices change [6]. Therefore, the application of the touchscreen in the flight deck has significant benefits in user satisfaction, human performance, and cost efficiency, which motivates increasing evolvement and exploration in the avionic industry.

However, there are still challenges facing the large-scale implementation of touch-screen technology in flight operations. One of the major concerns is unintended touch, which can occur due to undesirable finger-based gesture types and too small target size, leading to increased error rate and task failure [7, 8]. Furthermore, the lack of tac-tile feedback in the touchscreen-based system can be detrimental to human-computer interaction efficiency. Without clear system feedback, operators have to devote addi-tional visual attention to the interactive panel, which can negatively impact attention allocation and situation awareness in multi-task operations [9]. In dynamic operational scenarios, motion and vibration also have a key effect on the usability of the touch-screen controller. Goode et al. [10] suggested that the in-vehicle motion would reduce the system usability of the touchscreen-based battle management system; operators' task performance also decreased and perceived workload increased. Wynne et al. [11] indicated that with a stronger turbulence level in the flight deck, the task completion time, additional interactive actions, and perceived workload of pan operation and num-ber entry task would significantly increase; the rating of touchscreen usability decreased. Moreover, Coutts et al. [12] demonstrated that the touchscreen location of touchscreen could regulate the system usability and task performance. Therefore, the human-centred design optimisation in the user-system interface can be a potential solution to cope with the implementation challenges of the touchscreen controller in the flight deck.

Heart Rate Variability (HRV) is composed of the variations in the interval between successive heartbeats, known as the heartbeat interval (IBIs). The oscillations of healthy hearts enable the cardiovascular system to adapt to any challenges for homeostasis quickly. However, HRV is more than just an index of healthy heart function. It can also reflect the integrative system of the brain for adaptive regulation and provide psychophys-iological information related to cognitive capacity in a complex environment [13]. HRV is closely associated with the functions of the cardiovascular system and automatic ner-vous system for the cognitive process [14]. A previous study has noted that pilots' HRV state is a sensitive measure for detecting gradual changes in task workload and mental effort in flight operations [15]. HRV is also sensitive to varying task demands and complexity, thus, is closely associated with pilots' decision-making, situation awareness, and flight performance [16]. Mansikka et al. [17] also indicated that mean heart inter-beat (R-R) intervals (mean RR), the standard deviation of normal-to-normal R-R intervals (SDNN), and mean heart rate (mean HR) are sensitive to the variations in pilots' mental workload and flight task performance due to different levels of cognitive complexity. The current study aims to investigate the influence of advanced touchscreen controller on mental workload and cognitive performance bio-marked by time-domain HRV indices during flight operation. Therefore, there are three hypotheses to be examined as follows:

H1: There is a significant interaction in participants' mean RR during flight operation between inceptors and turbulence

H2: There is a significant interaction in participants' SDNN during flight operation between inceptors and turbulence

H3: There is a significant interaction in participants' mean HR during flight operation between inceptors and turbulence

2   Method

2.1   Participants

Fifty-six participants (12 females and 44 males) volunteered to join the flight simulator experiment conducted on the Cranfield University/Rolls-Royce Future Systems Simulator (FSS) equipped with both traditional sidestick and advanced touchscreen as control surface inceptors. The age of participants ranged between 21 and 63 years of age (M = 31.95, SD = 10.82), and their flight experience varied from 0 to 9,000 h (M = 1069.95, SD = 2289.02). The collected data was gathered from human subjects; therefore, the research proposal was submitted to the Cranfield University Research Ethics System for ethical approval. As stated in the consent form, participants had the right to terminate the experiment at any time and to withdraw their provided data at any moment even after the data collection.

2.2   Apparatus

Future Systems Simulator. The experiment was run on the Cranfield University/Rolls-Royce FSS with six touchscreen monitors representing a model of the Gulfstream G550 flight deck. The Gulfstream G550 aircraft is a generic long-range business jet with two Rolls-Royce BR 710 engines. The flight deck hardware of the FSS is fully representative functionally and visually based on aerospace standards. The flight scenarios in the current research were landing tasks from 5 miles away straight to runway 15R at Incheon International Airport under clear weather conditions. There were two scenario variants: without and with turbulence. The initial speed was 150 knots, the altitude was 1400 ft, and the heading was 90°. Participants were asked to complete these two landing scenarios using the sidestick (Fig. 1a) and the touchscreen (Fig. 1b) as control input inceptors.

a   b

Fig. 1. Future system simulator with sidestick (1a) and touchscreen (1b) control input inceptors for landing scenarios without and with turbulence

Heart Rate Variability Measurement. Participants' HRV parameters were collected by the Inner Balance device (Fig. 2a), which is a lightweight photoplethysmographic (PPG) sensor with a 125 Hz sample rate and 80 h of battery life. Through the Bluetooth connection with personal mobile devices (IOS or Android), participants' HRV data can be measured during the simulator experiment. Then these HRV parameters can be exported and calculated based on the Kubios software (Fig. 2b). In the current study, three time-domain HRV indices (mean RR, SDNN, and mean HR) were involved in data analysis for investigating the mental workload and cognitive performance with different control input inceptors in landing operations. Mean RR is the heart inter-beat (R-R) intervals; SDNN is the standard deviation of normal-to-normal (NN) R-R intervals; Mean HR is the mean heart rate in beats per minute.

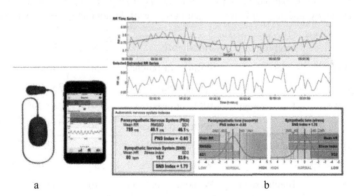

a   b

Fig. 2. Inner Balance device (2a) and Kubios software (2b) for HRV parameters measurement and calculation

2.3   Research Design

Participants were briefed that the experiment would involve wearing an Inner Balance device for HRV measurement. And then they were asked to perform landing tasks without and with turbulence in the FSS using different control input inceptors. The procedures for all participants were as follows: (1) complete the demographic variables, including age, gender, qualifications, and total flight hours (five minutes); (2) complete a briefing regarding the purpose of the study and how to use the sidestick and the touchscreen to perform flight operation (10 min); (3) seat in the future systems simulator to practice sidestick and touchscreen operation (five minutes); (4) perform landing tasks in non-turbulence and turbulence scenarios using the sidestick and the touchscreen inceptors with the real-time HRV parameters measured (10 min); (5) provide feedback on the usability of sidestick and touchscreen inceptors.

3   Results

3.1   Sample Characteristics

During the flight simulator experiment, 56 participants' time-domain HRV parameters including mean RR, SDNN, and mean HR were measured and collected when they performed the landing tasks in normal scenario and turbulence scenario by traditional sidestick and touchscreen control. Two-way repeated measure ANOVA was applied to examine the influence of control inceptors (sidestick vs touchscreen) and flight scenarios (without turbulence vs with turbulence) on participants' time-domain HRV parameters for investigating the fluctuation of cognitive workload during the simulated flight trials. The effect sizes of samples were quantified by partial eta square ($\eta p2$). The descriptive statistics are shown in Table 1.

Table 1. Means and standard deviations of participants' time-domain parameters while performing landing tasks by sidestick and touchscreen in scenarios without and with turbulence

	Inceptor	Turbulence	N	Mean	SD
Mean RR (ms)	Sidestick	Without turbulence	56	746.08	122.70
		With turbulence	56	735.78	118.58
	Touchscreen	Without turbulence	56	747.79	121.35
		With turbulence	56	753.05	115.93
SDNN (ms)	Sidestick	Without turbulence	56	32.30	13.60
		With turbulence	56	32.00	11.57
	Touchscreen	Without turbulence	56	34.40	13.71
		With turbulence	56	35.46	15.05
Mean HR (bpm)	Sidestick	Without turbulence	56	82.72	14.79
		With turbulence	56	83.75	14.38
	Touchscreen	Without turbulence	56	82.52	14.84
		With turbulence	56	81.81	14.71

3.2 Interaction Effects Between Inceptors and Turbulence on Time-domain HRV

The two-way ANOVA results indicated that there is a significant interaction in participants' mean RR between inceptor and turbulence, $F(1, 55) = 9.18$, $p = .004$, $\eta p^2 = 0.143$. Therefore, 'H1: There is a significant interaction in participants' mean RR during flight operation between inceptors and turbulence' was supported. The simple main effect analysis showed that participants' mean RR while performing landing task with the touchscreen inceptor is significantly higher than the traditional sidestick inceptor in turbulence scenario, $F(1, 55) = 7.72$, $p = .007$, $\eta p^2 = 0.123$. Moreover, when using the sidestick to perform landing, participants' mean RR in the turbulence scenario was significantly lower than the normal scenario without turbulence, $F(1, 55) = 7.01$, $p = .011$, $\eta p^2 = 0.113$. However, no interaction effect was found in SDNN between inceptor and turbulence, $p = .267$. Therefore, 'H2: There is a significant interaction in participants' SDNN during flight operation between inceptors and turbulence' was not supported. There was a significant main effect of inceptor on participants' SDNN, $F(1, 55) = 6.50$, $p = .014$, $\eta p^2 = 0.106$. Furthermore, a significant interaction in participants' mean HR between inceptor and turbulence was found, $F(1, 55) = 7.58$, $p = .008$, $\eta p^2 = 0.121$. Therefore, 'H3: There is a significant interaction in participants' mean HR during flight operation between inceptors and turbulence' was supported. The simple main effect analysis showed that participants' mean HR while performing the landing task with the touchscreen inceptor is significantly lower than traditional sidestick inceptor in turbulence scenario, $F(1, 55) = 6.62$, $p = .013$, $\eta p^2 = 0.107$. Moreover, when using the sidestick to perform landing, participants' mean HR in the turbulence scenario was significantly higher than the normal scenario without turbulence, $F(1, 55) = 5.66$, $p = .021$, $\eta p^2 = 0.093$. The details of two-way repeated measure ANOVA results are shown in Table 2.

Table 2. Two-way ANOVA interactions, simple main effects, and main effects on participants' time-domain HRV parameters between inceptor and turbulence

2 × 2 two-way ANOVA		*df* Effect	*df* Error	F	*p*	ηp^2
Mean RR (ms)	Interaction effect 'inceptor × turbulence'	1	55	9.18	.004	0.143
	Simple main effect "inceptor" within					
	Without turbulence	1	55	0.05	.832	0.001
	With turbulence	1	55	7.72	.007**	0.123
	Simple main effects "turbulence" within					
	Sidestick	1	55	7.01	.011*	0.113

(continued)

Table 2. (*continued*)

2 × 2 two-way ANOVA		*df* Effect	*df* Error	F	*p*	η_p^2
	Touchscreen	1	55	2.05	.158	0.036
	Main effect "inceptor"	1	55	2.00	.163	0.035
	Main effect "turbulence"	1	55	0.83	.367	0.015
SDNN (ms)	Interaction effect of "inceptor × turbulence"	1	55	1.26	.267	0.022
	Main effect "inceptor"	1	55	6.50	.014*	0.106
	Main effect "turbulence"	1	55	0.28	.598	0.005
Mean HR (bpm)	Interaction effect 'inceptor × turbulence'	1	55	7.58	.008**	0.121
	Simple main effects "inceptor" within					
	Without turbulence	1	55	0.05	.831	0.001
	With turbulence	1	55	6.62	.013*	0.107
	Simple main effects "turbulence" within					
	Sidestick	1	55	5.66	.021*	0.093
	Touchscreen	1	55	2.50	.119	0.044
	Main effect "inceptor"	1	55	1.81	.184	0.032
	Main effect "turbulence"	1	55	0.26	.610	0.005

4 Discussion

Previous research demonstrated that the mental workload leads to typically decreased mean RR and increased mean HR [18]. The interaction effects on participants' mean RR and mean HR between turbulence and inceptor revealed the applicability of touchscreen and sidestick in different flight scenarios. In the turbulence scenario, participants' mean RR during the landing task by sidestick (M = 735.78, SD = 118.58) is significantly lower than by touchscreen (M = 753.05, SD = 115.93); similarly, mean HR with sidestick control (M = 83.75, SD = 14.38) is higher than touchscreen (M = 81.81, SD = 14.71) in the landing scenario with turbulence. However, similar differences in mean RR and mean HR between two inceptors are not statistically significant in a normal scenario without turbulence, p > .050 (Fig. 3). These findings indicate the touchscreen control input in landing operation causes less mental workload and cognitive stress compared with the traditional sidestick inceptor in the turbulence scenarios. The touchscreen inceptor in the future systems simulator enables a multitouch gesture of dragging the sensor overlaid on the primary flight display (PFD) to control the aircraft attitude of pitch and roll (Fig. 4). Through this interactive mode, flight operation can be performed in a more intuitive way of a "point-where-you-want-to-go" control technique without the additional input device of sidestick. Furthermore, based on the proximity compatibility principle (PCP), the task-relevant information should be rendered close together in perceptual space [19]. In the current research, the centre of the PFD is overlaid with the touchscreen controller. The movements of the control sensor can provide additional information about aircraft attitude without frequent checking and monitoring of navigation display and out-of-window view during flight operation. Therefore, through the reallocation of attention resources, this human-centred design based on PCP can effectively decrease participants' mental workload and improve cognitive performance [20]. Previous research confirmed the advantage of the touchscreen controller in information supply to facilitate situation awareness during flight operation compared to the traditional sidestick [21].

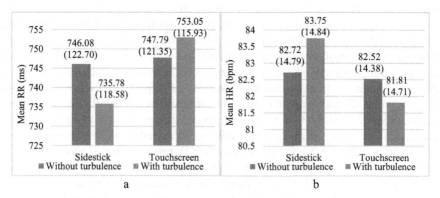

Fig. 3. The interaction effects on participants' mean RR (3a) and mean HR (3b) between control input inceptor and turbulence scenario.

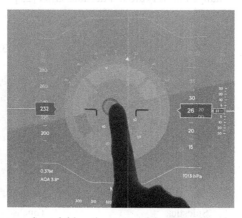

Fig. 4. The touchscreen panel overlaid on the centre of the PFD with a draggable sensor to control aircraft attitude.

SDNN serves as a global indicator of mental workload when the task-relevant physical workload is negligible [22, 23]. That is, SDNN is not only a sensitive measure of psychophysiological variability induced by the cognitive information process and mental workload, but it can also represent physical activities and task loads during complicated operations. In the current study, 'H2: There is a significant interaction in participants' SDNN during flight operation between inceptors and turbulence' is rejected. And the two-way repeated measures ANOVA results demonstrated that participants' SDNN when using the touchscreen (M = 34.93, SD = 14.34) as the inceptor to perform landing operation is significantly higher than sidestick (M = 32.15, SD = 12.57) in both conditions without and with turbulence (Fig. 5). Therefore, it can be concluded that the overall task loads from two sources (mental cognitive process and physical activities demands) when using the touchscreen controllers is significantly lower than the sidestick in a landing operation. In the current experiment, participants need to continuously make force input on the sidestick controller to control the attitude of the aircraft in the landing operation, leading to a higher physical workload and control activity compared to touchscreen operation. Especially in the turbulence scenario, participants' SDNN increased from 32.00ms during sidestick control to 35.46ms for touchscreen control; there is a slighter increase of SDNN from 32.30 to 34.34 in the normal scenario without turbulence (Fig. 5). Moreover, significantly increased mean HR and decreased mean RR when interacting with sidestick with turbulence were found (Fig. 3), revealing higher physical demand and mental workload in a so-called "pilot-induced oscillations" scenario [24]. Robinson and Brewer [2] indicated that in cognitive tasks, the touchscreen operational mode has benefits on cognitive performance and task workload including both mental and physical aspects. Furthermore, in flight operation, the tablet touchscreen-based human-machine interface (HMI) can significantly decrease pilots' workload and improve user interface satisfaction in runway change and reroute to alternate tasks [25].

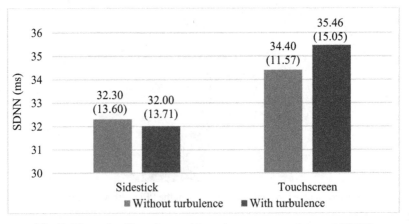

Fig. 5. The main effect of control input inceptor on participants' SDNN

5 Conclusion

The widespread evolution and application of touchscreen technology in day-to-day life provide huge potential for implementation in the future flight deck as an integrated interactive display and control surface inceptor. The current study investigated the psychophysiological state through HRV measures while performing the landing operation with the touchscreen controller and sidestick inceptor. Simulated turbulence during flight operation was also considered in the applicability of different control input modes of touchscreen and sidestick. The data analysis results indicated that the touchscreen controller can significantly reduce the mental and physical workload in landing tasks, especially in the turbulence scenario. Furthermore, the insignificant difference in the mean RR and mean HR between the sidestick and touchscreen in the scenario without disturbance suggested that both controllers are similarly demanding in the flight operation. These findings further explore the practicability and effectiveness of the touchscreen controller in aircraft attitude control and demonstrate the advantages in decreasing both mental workload and physical workload in landing scenarios even with turbulence. A new vision of the integrated aircraft flight control system in the future flight deck is also provided for next-generation aviation operations.

Acknowledgements. This research is co-financed by the European Union through the European Social Fund (grant number POWR.03.02.00–00-I029). The authors would like to thank the FSS Team in Cranfield, especially Mudassir Lone, for his generous support during the project's development, and Rolls-Royce, particularly Peter Beecroft, for approving the research to be carried out in the Future Systems Simulator.

References

1. Rogers, W.A., Fisk, A.D., McLaughlin, A.C., Pak, R.: Touch a screen or turn a knob: choosing the best device for the job. Hum. Factors **47**(2), 271–288 (2005). https://doi.org/10.1518/001 8720054679452
2. Robinson, S.J., Brewer, G.: Performance on the traditional and the touchscreen, tablet versions of the Corsi block and the tower of Hanoi tasks. Comput. Hum. Behav. **60**, 29–34 (2016). https://doi.org/10.1016/j.chb.2016.02.047
3. Kaminani, S.: Human computer interaction issues with touchscreen interfaces in the flight deck. In: 2011 IEEE/AIAA 30th Digital Avionics Systems Conference, pp. 6B4–1. IEEE (2011). https://doi.org/10.1109/DASC.2011.6096098
4. Jones, D.R.: Three input concepts for flight crew interaction with information presented on a large-screen electronic cockpit display (No. NASA TM-4173). National Aeronautics and Space Administration, Washington, DC (1990). https://ntrs.nasa.gov/api/citations/199 00009078/downloads/19900009078.pdf
5. Noyes, J.M., Starr, A.F.: A comparison of speech input and touchscreen for executing checklists in an avionics application. Int. J. Aviat. Psychol. **17**(3), 299–315 (2007). https://doi.org/10.1080/10508410701462761
6. Dodd, S., Lancaster, J., Miranda, A., Grothe, S., DeMers, B., Rogers, B.: Touchscreens on the flight deck: the impact of touch target size, spacing, touch technology and turbulence on pilot performance. In: Proceedings of the Human Factors and Ergonomics Society Annual Meeting, vol. 58, no. 1, pp. 6–10. Sage CA: Los Angeles, CA: SAGE Publications (2014). https://doi.org/10.1177/1541931214581002

7. Jeong, H., Liu, Y.: Effects of touchscreen gesture's type and direction on finger-touch input performance and subjective ratings. Ergonomics **60**(11), 1528–1539 (2017). https://doi.org/10.1080/00140139.2017.1313457

8. Grahn, H., Kujala, T.: Impacts of touchscreen size, user interface design, and subtask boundaries on in-car task's visual demand and driver distraction. Int. J. Hum. Comput. Stud. **142**, 102467 (2020). https://doi.org/10.1016/j.ijhcs.2020.102467

9. Yatani, K., Truong, K.N.: SemFeel: a user interface with semantic tactile feedback for mobile touch-screen devices. In Proceedings of the 22nd Annual ACM Symposium on User Interface Software and Technology, pp. 111–120 (2009). https://doi.org/10.1145/1622176.1622198

10. Goode, N., Lenné, M.G., Salmon, P.: The impact of on-road motion on BMS touchscreen device operation. Ergonomics **55**(9), 986–996 (2012). https://doi.org/10.1080/00140139.2012.685496

11. Wynne, R.A., Parnell, K.J., Smith, M.A., Plant, K.L., Stanton, N.A.: Can't touch this: hammer time on touchscreen task performance variability under simulated turbulent flight conditions. Int. J. Hum.-Comput. Interact. **37**(7), 666–679 (2021). https://doi.org/10.1080/10447318.2021.1890492

12. Coutts, L.V., et al.: Future technology on the flight deck: assessing the use of touchscreens in vibration environments. Ergonomics **62**(2), 286–304 (2019). https://doi.org/10.1080/00140139.2018.1552013

13. Thayer, J.F., Åhs, F., Fredrikson, M., Sollers, J.J., Wager, T.D.: A meta-analysis of heart rate variability and neuroimaging studies: implications for heart rate variability as a marker of stress and health. Neurosci. Biobehav. Rev. **36**(2), 747–756 (2012). https://doi.org/10.1016/j.neubiorev.2011.11.009

14. Forte, G., Favieri, F., Casagrande, M.: Heart rate variability and cognitive function: a systematic review. Front. Neurosci. **13**, 710 (2019). https://doi.org/10.3389/fnins.2019.00710

15. De Rivecourt, M., Kuperus, M.N., Post, W.J., Mulder, L.J.M.: Cardiovascular and eye activity measures as indices for momentary changes in mental effort during simulated flight. Ergonomics **51**(9), 1295–1319 (2008). https://doi.org/10.1080/00140130802120267

16. Sirevaag, E.J., Kramer, A.F., Reisweber, C.D.W.M., Strayer, D.L., Grenell, J.F.: Assessment of pilot performance and mental workload in rotary wing aircraft. Ergonomics **36**(9), 1121-1140(1993). https://doi.org/10.1080/00140139308967983

17. Mansikka, H., Simola, P., Virtanen, K., Harris, D., Oksama, L.: Fighter pilots' heart rate, heart rate variation and performance during instrument approaches. Ergonomics **59**(10), 1344–1352 (2016). https://doi.org/10.1080/00140139.2015.1136699

18. Delliaux, S., Delaforge, A., Deharo, J.C., Chaumet, G.: Mental workload alters heart rate variability, lowering non-linear dynamics. Front. Physiol. **10**, 565 (2019). https://doi.org/10.3389/fphys.2019.00565

19. Wickens, C.D., Carswell, C.M.: The proximity compatibility principle: Its psychological foundation and relevance to display design. Hum. Factors **37**(3), 473–494 (1995). https://doi.org/10.1518/001872095779049408

20. Hancock, P.A., Scallen, S.F.: The performance and workload effects of task re-location during automation. Displays **17**(2), 61–68 (1997). https://doi.org/10.1016/0003-6870(95)00029-C

21. Li, W.C., Wang, Y., Korek, W.T.: To be or not to be? assessment on using touchscreen as inceptor in flight operation. Transp. Res. Procedia **66**, 117–124 (2022). https://doi.org/10.1016/j.trpro.2022.12.013

22. DiDomenico, A., Nussbaum, M.A.: Effects of different physical workload parameters on mental workload and performance. Int. J. Ind. Ergon. **41**(3), 255–260 (2011). https://doi.org/10.1016/j.ergon.2011.01.008

23. Tarkiainen, T.H., et al.: Stability over time of short-term heart rate variability. Clin. Auton. Res. **15**, 394–399 (2005). https://doi.org/10.1007/s10286-005-0302-7

24. McRuer, D.T.: Pilot-Induced Oscillations and Human Dynamic Behavior. NASA Contractor Report 4683 (1995). https://ntrs.nasa.gov/citations/19960020960
25. Rouwhorst, W., et al.: Use of touchscreen display applications for aircraft flight control. In: 2017 IEEE/AIAA 36th Digital Avionics Systems Conference (DASC), pp. 1–10. IEEE (2017). https://doi.org/10.1109/DASC.2017.8102060

Cultural Issues in Design

Cultural Issues in Design

Sustainability in Banana Tree Romanticism in the Economic Cycle of Rural Community through Cultural Creative Design

Erik Armayuda[1]([✉]) [iD], Bayyinah Nurrul Haq[2] [iD], Damar Rangga Putra[1], and Ratih Mahardika[1] [iD]

[1] Visual Communication Design, Trilogi University, Kalibata, South Jakarta, Indonesia
{armayuda,damar.rangga,ratihmahardika}@trilogi.ac.id
[2] Industrial Design, Trilogi University, Kalibata, South Jakarta, Indonesia
bayyinah.nh@trilogi.ac.id

Abstract. The idea of sustainability has become an interesting topic of discussion in recent decades. Not only because of limited resources, but also the increasing of industrial business awareness of the future life. The concept of sustainable living itself has existed since traditional village life. It slowly decreases and weakened by the entry of industrial products into remote villages with plastic material which is ends up as environmental pollution, considering that waste management in villages is not as good as in some big cities. This amplifies the urgent of circular production which produce the product needs by local using source from its environment. This process require a deep understanding of the culture and the resource to be connected as cultural creative product. In addition, the product should not only functional for local but also have a potential in global market, especially creative industry Dealing with creative industries, designer already been involved into several villages in order to produce attractive commodities in the global market. These products unfortunately become commodities that only benefit a few people, not the local people as the source of the inspiration. Commercialization of cultural products on the one hand can help cultural actors known very well, but on the other hand with traditional systems, this idea does not have a very positive impact on residents, especially in the economic field. Using a model from ritual to form, the author tries to classify the villagers' rituals and formulate cultural products that can be made using materials around them. Thus, the results of these products expected to be useful for local and meaningful for the global market. Using a descriptive analytic method, the author tries to formulate a model for creating local products with global value which is expected to be a model that can be applied to the idea of sustainability in villages, especially in Indonesia.

Keywords: Creative product · Sustainability · Ritual to form · Banana tree · circular economy

M. Kurosu et al. (Eds.): HCII 2023, LNCS 14054, pp. 523–535, 2023.
https://doi.org/10.1007/978-3-031-48038-6_33

1 Introduction

Before the industrialization of daily products in harmful material, the village had their respective follow-up systems, by processing its daily needs from the surrounding resources. The excessive use of energy causes increasingly serious negative environmental impacts, including climate change, which needs to be resolved immediately [1]. Advances in technology and daily product packaging, from production to distribution offer a long-impact practical value. After the industrial revolution, intentions of chasing economic growth caused the blooming of mass production and machine manufacture [2]. This mass production targeting not only people in city but also in rural area. Technological advances make it easier but weaken humans. All needs that are based on the ability to manage natural resources are now not inherited because of the challenges of different times. Ironically, this makes several villages that used to be independent (because they can growth and harvest their own needs), to have dependence on products and facilities distributed from remote industrial cities. These advances provide local population awareness of products that they have never imagined need it. In other words, they get the distribution of products that they do not need, but with certain advertising and marketing strategies the products are present like a part of life that must be present where not infrequently the material of these products is made of industrial materials that are wasteful after use. This study provides an alternative proposal in the practice of sustainability in design by utilizing existing resources as the main raw material in its manufacture. This idea is intended to promote circular production cycles with creative products that are beneficial for local residents and mean to the global market.

Regarding local resources as the material potential, in the west java, especially Cianjur Region, there is a village called Cihea. In this village there are plenty of banana tree which is one of the main commodities for local people. The variety of the banana tree is the one who can growth the leaf faster than the other kind, and that is why the fruit itself is not good to consume but that is not a problem since the local only harvest the leaf for economic purposes. This process of harvesting banana leaf is a daily activity which can be seen almost in every house along the way of the main road. Basically, every people just have to collect the banana leaf, bundle it, and leave it in the side of the road or in front of the house, there will be a pick-up car (local people call it "leaf car") which will collect all of the bundle then distribute it collectively to the capital city of Jakarta. Then the owner of the leaf will be paid for how many bundles they can provide that day.

Behind the process of harvesting banana leaf, there is tons of banana leaf branch abandoned in every corner of banana tree field or even in the side of the main street. This is a potential economic loss. If there is a way to utilize it into another purpose that would be another chance to make another profit from it. From this part this case will become the question of the study, how to utilize the local potential into creative product which is functional for the local and potential for global.

The study about banana shown that in 2017 Indonesian Central Bureau of Statistics record that production of banana fruit reaches 8 741 147.00 tons. According to Wijaya (2014) in Iskandar et.al (2018) the production of banana plants reaches 30% of the total production of Indonesian fruit crops. The development of banana production in West Java over the past five years (2017–2021) has increased significantly [3]. Banana tree is a fruit plants that grow spread in Indonesian territory. For people of West Java banana plant inherit and already becomes part of the culture (Fig. 1).

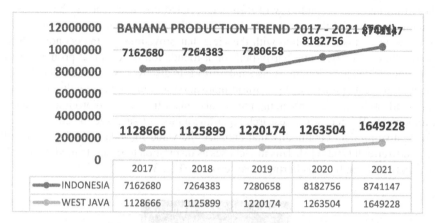

	2017	2018	2019	2020	2021
INDONESIA	7162680	7264383	7280658	8182756	8741147
WEST JAVA	1128666	1125899	1220174	1263504	1649228

Fig. 1. Banana Production trend (2017–2021)

The knowledge of the use of bananas in everyday life is related to the life cycle from birth to death. Almost all parts of the banana tree are used to meet the needs of food, packaging, medicinal plants or herbs, animal feed, to ritual needs. Like Indonesians in rural areas generally plant banana trees in the form of swidden (*ladang* or *huma*), homegardens (*pekarangan*), gardens (*kebon*) and mixgardens (kebon campuran) [4].

According to Iskandar et.al (2018) local knowledge related to banana plants is related to the banana cultivation cycle concerning seed preparation, soil preparation, planting, maintenance, harvesting, and post-harvest treatment. The benefits of banana plants apart from for household purposes also can be a source of additional income [4]. All parts of the banana plant have economic value, parts of the leaves, tree trunks can be sold directly to collectors or use the services of a banana leaf handyman who comes to your house or garden and harvests banana leaves who come regularly or upon call as promised. Banana leaves are generally sold (Fig. 2).

Fig. 2. Banana stalk midrib waste

Through the idea of the idea "from the ritual to the form of" the author tries to connect these two things by observing the daily lives of the residents of Cihea Village, as a daily ritual to record the needs of any product that is relevant to their daily rituals. Then from the data the author will formulate related products that can be created by utilizing the material that can be obtained from the most commodities in the village, a banana tree. This idea in line with the view that provisions for the economic health and wealth of society, while partly built on a foundation of technical proficiency and technological development, must also make efforts to discover excellence and innovative potential in local cultures, using cultural innovation to communicate cultural richness, shaping lifestyle choices, enhancing industrial competitiveness, and promoting regional development [2] There was a research regarding a model to analyze the cultural wealth into creative product commodity that enhance the value for today market generate by Lin and Kreifeldt (2021) [5]. This model uses as inspiration to generate model regarding the ritual and form by considering local resource (Fig. 3).

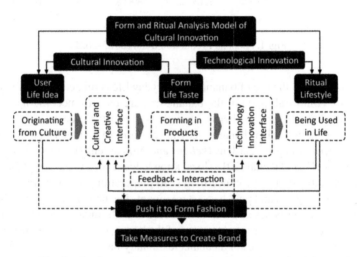

Fig. 3. The form and ritual model of cultural Innovation [5]

It is from all these processes that the idea of movement from an industrial idealist process shifts to products from a more realistic and natural lifestyle.

Along with this paper, the authors understand things that are commonly known and have been researched by other researchers, including the potential and process of formulating cultural creative products through a three-layer cultural approach, in which a product can be created based on the characteristics of a good area of adaptation. Existing form (outer), habits and additions of usability features (behavioural), to symbolic things related to certain meanings and values (spiritual). Meanwhile, in the context of processing banana stems, there are two materials that can be formulated from the processing of banana stems, namely paper material and cloth material. These two materials will become the basis for the development of creative cultural products. Of the two things that are known, the author takes a gap in designing cultural creative products that are carried out in areas that do not have certain cultural characteristics so that the output of this paper is expected to be used as a reference in formulating commodity products that have local nuances even though they do not depart from a specific characteristic. Certain culture.

So that this paper is expected to provide relevant implications both from an academic and policy perspective. From an academic standpoint, this paper can be used as a reference in anthropological studies of a region to formulate products that are unique to that region. Meanwhile, from a policy standpoint, the idea of formulating typical commodity products is expected to become a practical method that can be applied to any area, whether the area has certain cultural characteristics, or an area that does not have certain cultural characteristics, such as an urban area consisting of various cultural mix.

2 Theoretical Framework

2.1 Cultural and Ritual

Koentjaraningrat differentiates cultures into three categories: systems of ideas, systems of activity, and products in the form of artifacts, which are understand as ideas that underlie the patterns of behavior and beliefs of certain groups (ideas), activities, or behaviors that characterize certain cultural groups (activities), and cultural objects that are distinctive and inherent in related culture groups (artifacts) [6]. Liliweri, on the other hand, defines culture as the live view of a group of people in the form of behaviors, beliefs, values, and symbols they receive unconsciously that are all inherited through the process of communication from one generation to the next [7]. From these two perspectives, the study concludes that culture is not a single unique object owned by one group that does not exist in another group, but rather a way of life for a group of humans as a response to their surroundings (Fig. 4).

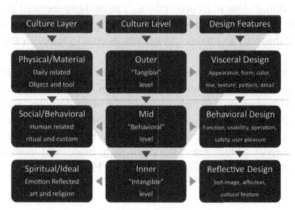

Fig. 4. The Form and Ritual Analysis Model of Cultural Innovation. (Redraw from [8]. Copyright 2001 Lin and Kreif

The other way to select the activity we could explore into creative product is using three level of culture. Lin et.al from their paper shows the three level of culture regarding the tangible level which is material or physical, behavioral level related with custom and ritual, and intangible level which is cover the spiritual and emotional aspect. These two approaches are proposed in order to accommodate different community characters, because not all people in a certain area have a distinctive culture as a source of inspiration, and supporting material so that apart from culture, researchers can use the approach of daily activities which can even be formulated from urban communities.

Cihea Village is in the Cianjur Regency of West Java Province, Indonesia. The village is situated in the northern region of Cianjur and is bounded to the north by Karawang Regency, to the west by Mekarsari Village, to the east by Cimahi Village, and to the east by Sukaluyu District.

The village of Cihea is geographically located in a plain at an elevation of 50–100 m above sea level. The village receives a fair amount of rain throughout the year, with average temperatures ranging from 22 to 27 °C. Cihea Village has and unique topology of hills with rivers flowing between them, providing fertility to the soil. This is one of the reasons why farming and gardening are important sources of income for the country's citizens. Banana trees are a natural wealth that is also a source of income for its residents, but this commodity has not been fully explored beyond the leaves.

Cambridge online dictionary identify ritual as a way of doing something in which the same actions are done in the same way every time. In this context it could be define as the daily living Cihea people as farmer and villager. The routine activities of the lives of Cihea residents are the basis for formulating daily products that will be explored using materials in surround, especially banana trees, into products that are locally useful and globally meaningful.

2.2 Cultural Creative Design

The idea of cultural creative design basically a generated design in respond of cultural expression with adding value to its original one. The design generated may carry a noble mission in preserving culture in today business by bridging the gap between the original, traditional (old fashioned) and today market which tend to focus on the looks, feeling, and value.

In those ways the generated product in this paper is not the product generated by the author. Since this paper attempts to generated pilot model, the product chosen as example is the finished product already create by the other designer. This will help us to validate the idea that those products are possible to generate from the particular material, especially banana tree. In the context of "Ritual to Form" the product is generated from particular daily activity (which may include of man, made, and method) into creative product that locally useful and globally meaningful (Fig. 5).

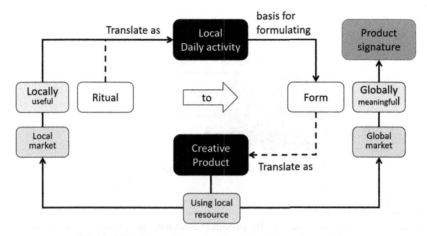

Fig. 5. The Process in generating cultural creative product

A. Sustainability.

The basic idea of sustainability in simple ways could be sign as circular economy that can apply by local living system. While the same time the product use to sell in global may have different treatment. In this case the role of the creative industry is important. Not only as a container for display and marketing of finished products. But also as a system that involves local resources, empowers citizens, and most importantly, has a positive impact on local residents. Especially by utilizing local resources, so that the production cycle is expected to minimize pollution with ideas from nature for local residents and return to nature properly.

The ability to meet the local needs and its material potential to fulfil it becomes the key factor in preventing the waste of the industrial material. Of course we can't sterilize a village from industrial products shipped from cities, but at least with the idea of exploring the materials and materials that are abundant in the region to be used as substitute materials for daily products especially those that are possible to make and have a distinctive value, can be used as an approach to meet the daily needs of the region which simultaneously becomes a unique commodity that is expected to compete in the global market.

B. Ritual.

In the ritual section, designer could identify the daily routine of local people which is typical, has a story to tell, and a value to share. By considering this three that would be a key to enhance the value of final product design which is destined for global. The approach of selecting the activity could use Maslow diagram, and cultural level. Maslow diagram help us to understand the activity and group the activity based on Maslow diagram, either the activity of providing physical needs (related with food, and basic living survival), security and safety needs, social needs, esteem needs, or actualization needs (Fig. 6).

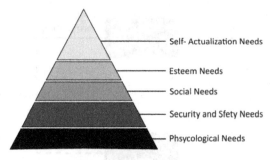

Fig. 6. Maslow Diagram

C. Form.

Form of this context is the creative product result from the process. The consideration aspect in designing final product is the product should be designed using modern referral design which is match with today market. On the other hand, the innovation aspect of designing product could follow pyramid of innovation from Rampino (2016) which focus on aesthetic innovation, utility innovation, meaning innovation or typology innovation.

From those process the model generated by now could be translate as identify daily activities (using Maslow consideration as the basic concept), while process of design innovation use to create creative product (using Rampino baseline innovation). Finally, both of the process should consider to explore local resource in order to establish sustainability idea [9] (Fig. 7).

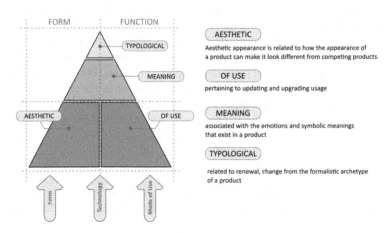

Fig. 7. The Pyramid of Innovation by Rampino [9].

2.3 Sustainability in Banana Leaf Branch Romanticism

The concept of sustainability is currently a source of concern for many research areas. Cambridge online dictionary define sustainability as the quality of causing little or no damage to the environment and therefore able to continue for a long time. Specifically John Elkington emphasize that sustainability encompasses three interrelated aspects: environmental, social and economic. According to John Elkington's triple bottom line, the People, the Planet and Profits are inter-reliant: "society depends on the economy and the economy depends on the global ecosystem, whose health represents the ultimate bottom line." in this context the notion of sustainability define as the way local people living side-by side with its environment which also unleash the potential of global market for economic growth. Adapt by John Elkintons there will be "The local of Cihea village creates economic value which is walk in tune with global market". The statement could be break down as generating the daily product needs from daily activities that produce with local source (banana leaf branch) in order to fulfil local needs by considering global taste.

In other perspective banana tree romanticism is a variable movement which express something is usual in emotional ways. In this case the romanticism from daily product generated from banana tree which is functional for local people and emotional for global market (Fig. 8).

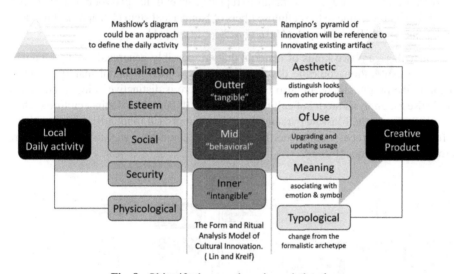

Fig. 8. Objectify the steps by using existing theory.

3   Methodology

In those ways the generated product in this paper is not the product generated by the author. Since this paper attempts to generated pilot model, the product chosen as example is the finished product already create by the other designer. This will help us to validate the idea that those products are possible to generate from the particular material, especially banana tree stalk.

The material itself have material innovation potent, research that explore the banana stalk/midrib waste as a fibre source that uses *pisang kepok* or *Pisang Manggala* describe in three category material exploration.

- Banana leaf stems are processed into composites or pulp to create material in the form of hygroscopic sheet paper [10, 11]. The goal of research on the treatment of banana leaf stem waste is to make the paper whiter by reducing or eliminating lignin levels in the pulp. Chemical processes such as the soda process, sulfate process, and kraft process are currently used to improve the quality of paper sheets [10].
- The researchers use a pulp-composite-cast technique to develop creative products from banana midrib stalk to obtain a three-dimensional shape. Material engineering procedures such as drying - grinding - filtering - baking- the press will generate products with material quality that has a durable material character that is not easily broken but is still hygroscopic, requiring chemical treatments such as coatings [11].
- After the banana leaf is dried, the stalk or midrib is pressed into semi-finished fibers. Furthermore, when mixed with other fibers and resin, a composite material with a plywood-like character is produced. Another potential exploration for banana leaf stalk is material for eyeglass frames to replace conventional plywood materials [12]. This potential is due to the cellulose fibers of banana leaf stem [12] approaching 40% for the type of Pisang kepok (*Musa paradicecae sp*) [11].

Since there are two kinds of material that are possibly generated from the banana stalk, the exploration could be developed from these two potential materials. While defining the product there are also two ways, if there is distinctive culture, a designer could use the analysis model of cultural innovation. If there is no distinct culture such as an urban region, the Maslow pyramid could be an approach to identify typical activity. After all of the process, the model from Rampino could be a way to create signature product commodities (Fig. 9).

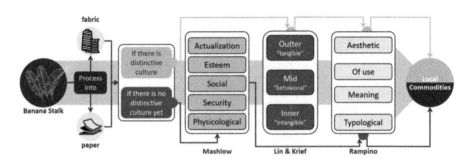

Fig. 9. Objectify the steps by using existing theory.

We can conclude three core keywords are offered by this paper, the typical of a particular area translated into a source of inspiration in the form of "rituals" or typical activities that are carried out repeatedly. Then "form" as a commodity product that is generated from the uniqueness of the region, and "sustainability" is the key to recognizing the potential of the region and bringing it together with the needs of designing creative cultural products (Fig. 10).

Fig. 10. The model of generating creative product locally useful globally meaningful

4 Conclusions

Since this paper attempts to generate pilot model, the product chosen as example is the finished product already create by the other designers or makers. This will help us to validate the idea that those product are possible to generate from the particular material, especially banana tree. From the study above we can conclude that in order to ground the notion of sustainability in rural area in the same hand participate in global creative industry. An attempt could be done by formulating "ritual" into "form". The ritual can be translate as daily routine activity which can be approach by two ways, maslow and cultural level to adjust the condition of the field (Fig. 11).

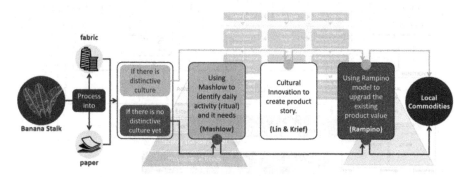

Fig. 11. The model of generating creative product locally useful globally meaningful

If the community inherits particular culture we can use the cultural level model as an approach to identify the proper "ritual" that can be generated later as a basic idea. But if the community does not possess any cultural wealth as we saw in some areas people in a rural area just live by its conventional ways that do not represent typical cultural, we can use the Mashlow diagram as an approach to identify the needs or an idea from its "ritual" to generate an idea in order to create a useful creative product but still meaningful for the global.

From those process the list of the ritual which already gather is connected with the product that equip their "ritual". This kind of product we can take from the existing one or create base on the ritual list. Either the existing and the generated product is design using pyramid of innovation from Rampino in order to create the adding value. So at least it has a story behind to tell as a meaning value for global market. Nevertheless the author expect that this model from this paper could be trigger an advance discussion to help particular community to uplift their economical situation in the same way to foster sustainability awareness.

Both sides of model, either generating product from "ritual" list and innovating product to create a "form" has to be in line with the notion of sustainability. In that ways this process will provide the meaning to the final product automatically. Finally this paper may not be able to shown the product result since this is the step of validating the idea to generate creative product based on "ritual to form" model which can be seen as the picture below (Fig. 12).

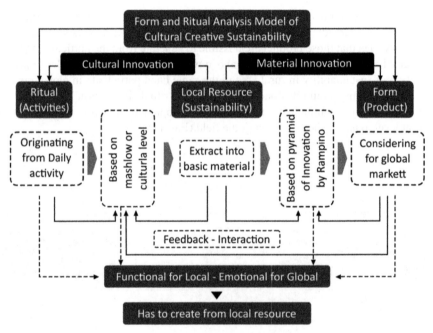

Fig. 12. The analysis framework of generating creative product which is locally useful and globally meaningful, retrieve from [8] and redrawn for this study.

Regarding the condition of Indonesia country which possess cultural wealth this paper expected to be useful in the future cultural exploration especially in design field. Because design should not only a knowledge to deal with commercial aspect, but also the strategy to brighten the society.

References

1. Streimikiene, D., Svagzdiene, B., Jasinskas, E., Simanavicius, A.: Sustainable tourism development and competitiveness: the systematic literature review. Sustain. Dev. **29**(1), 259–271 (2021). https://econpapers.repec.org/RePEc:wly:sustdv:v:29:y:2021:i:1:p:259-271
2. Chiang, I.Y., Lin, P.H., Kreifeldt, J.G., Lin, R.: From theory to practice: an adaptive development of design education. Educ. Sci. (Basel) **11**(11), (2021). https://doi.org/10.3390/educsc i11110673. "bps-file"
3. Iskandar, J., Kusmoro, J., Mubarokah, M., Partasasmita, R.: Ethnobotany of banana plants (Musa x paradisiaca) of Palintang Hamlet, Cipanjalu Village, Bandung, West Java, Indonesia. Biodiversitas **19**(6), 2059–2072 (2018). https://doi.org/10.13057/biodiv/d190611
4. Hsu, C.-H.: Transformation model for cultural creative product design. Doctoral Dissertation, National Taiwan University of Arts (2014)
5. Pengantar antropologi/Koentjaraningrat | OPAC Perpustakaan Nasional RI. https://opac.per pusnas.go.id/DetailOpac.aspx?id=566808. Accessed 06 Mar 2023
6. Liliweri: Gatra-Gatra Komunikasi Antarbudaya Pustaka Pelajar (2001). https://pustakape lajar.co.id/buku/gatra-gatra-komunikasi-antarbudaya/. Accessed 07 Mar 2023
7. Lin, R., Kreifeldt, J.G.: Ergonomics in wearable computer design. Int. J. Ind. Ergon. **27**, 259–269 (2001)
8. Rampino, L.: The innovation pyramid : a categorization of the innovation phenomenon in the product design. Int. J. Des. **5**(1), 3–16 (2016)
9. Bahri, S.: Pembuatan Pulp dari Batang Pisang. Jurnal Teknologi Kimia Unimal **4**(2), 36 (2017). https://doi.org/10.29103/jtku.v4i2.72
10. Rufaidah, R., Kurniawan, O., Setiawardhana, D.R.: Eksplorasi Pelepah Pohon Pisang Untuk Dijadikan Produk Interior. Jurnal IKRA-ITH Humaniora **5**(1), 232–241 (2021)
11. Kustiyani, F., Wijayanti, S.S.W., Sukmawati, P.D., Wrihatno, A., Shafardan, Y.S., Setyaningsih, E.: Potensi Limbah Serat Kayu dari Pelepah Pisang Kering sebagai Bahan Baku Pembuatan Frame Kacamata. Prosiding SNPBS (Seminar Nasional Pendidikan Biologi dan Saintek) Ke-4, pp. 340–342 (2019). http://hdl.handle.net/11617/11337

The Constraints of Global Design Systems on Local User Experience Design

Zhifang Du[1(✉)] and Yong Xiao[2]

[1] R203, Building 37, Long Hu Chang Cheng Yuan Zhu, Miyun District, Beijing, China
zhifang.du@qq.com
[2] Faculty of Humanities and Arts, Macau University of Science and Technology, Macau, China

Abstract. A design system is a 'single source of truth' that combines all components that are utilized by teams to design and develop products. A UI frameworks for digital platform innovation and iteration. For global company's design system iteration process, English will be used to build the framework earlier. When this framework need translate into another language, like Chinese, and local designer to follow this set of designs without any adoption, launch of their digital product through various collaboration with developers, they often power a product that is completely different. It cannot meet the global design system standards, nor can it meet the needs of the user in the domestic market. This kind of thing happens a lot in the past decent years for those global enterprise's digital products in china markets. It harms their businesses in the country. It also make the digital platform functional down for the china markets. We often blame its the constraints of global design system's fault. it does not matching on local user experience, specifically not only refers to the looking and feel's differences, but also it cannot serve the domestic market functionally without the localization transformation of many local engineers. Continuing this direction requires the design system to be aware that it needs to absorb design assets from different markets, while designers from different markets should fully utilize their project experience to supplement the management of this enterprise level design system.

Keywords: Design System · UX Localization · User Experience Design · Chinese typography · Local Culture · Color Language · Customer Experience

1 Introduction

A design system elements include brand principles, specific color palettes, icon libraries, coding guidelines, shared beliefs and working practices. Excepting a bunch of code snippets and a collection of graphic elements. There are also design components, specifications and how to use them. Whats important, they also including UX writing and guidelines for design principles. A design system management is an ongoing effort to further increase the documentation depth our system.

M. Kurosu et al. (Eds.): HCII 2023, LNCS 14054, pp. 536–551, 2023.
https://doi.org/10.1007/978-3-031-48038-6_34

2   Unified User Experience That Drives Customer Success

2.1   Design System is About Building a Unified and Consistent User Experience

As we increasingly move into a world of omnichannel solutions, as clients increasingly expect to interact with brands at a growing range of physical and digital touch points, embracing a unified customer experience strategy could help to drive productivity, profit and process improvements at every turn [1]. Customer success allows users to develop every aspect of customer experience individually through experience design, content management, knowledge sharing tools and more. A unified customer experience ensures that every experience reflects a single brand identity, no matter which channel the customer chooses – whether that is self-service, the phone, social media, etc. The customer should enjoy an experience that contains the same messaging and elicits a similar emotional response through every channel. That the key elements for driving customer success.

Importance of Design Systems: Single Source of Truth
There is no doubt design system is helping for unified our customer experience via so many direction thoughts. Summary the advantages for the design systems, but also need know that there is also disadvantage of design system might could have.

Clear the Clutter
Design systems introduces a shared vocabulary and common functionalities and creates a set of guidelines on how to incorporate these in UX/UI design. This means that even if different teams are working on a product, they know what to base their designs on [2].

Single Source of Truth
A design system evolves with the company and the projects it embarks on and can be easily modified depending on the varying requirements of an organization. It allows the centralization of all elements of the design system onto a single canvas. You can maintain a single workspace for style guides, icon libraries, graphic assets, and sample wireframes with embedded links for coding and editorial guidelines. These workspaces are easily shareable among team members where they can collaborate in real-time on adding updates and comments.

Cost-Effective and Time-Saving
When a design system is in place, there is less room for confusion. It makes the production cycle faster and more efficient as the designs are more accurate with high-fidelity wireframes. Moreover, when products are made according to a design system, maintenance becomes easy and less time-consuming.

Consistency
With a design system, every element of the product is ensured to project a consistent user experience from well-defined and learned behaviors. A design system ensures that a uniform consistency is maintained across the board when it comes to any part of the design process.

Identify Principles and Shared Values
It is also important to include design principles under this category as they are the guidelines that direct teams to achieve the true purpose of the product. For instance, rather than designing different components of the product in different styles, the teams can stick to a simpler and minimalist design that is user-friendly. In addition, databases and information sources also come under this component to promote accessibility.

Determine Brand Identity
Brand identity plays an important role in maintaining consistency across all products. Your brand identity is how you want your brand to be perceived among its target audience. This includes the color palettes and fonts used, logos and the visual language with which your products or services are marketed.

Have a Set of Editorial Guidelines
Editorial guidelines should include information on the voice of tone for the language used, specific words that need to be highlighted across all products, and marketing materials and standard guidelines on capitalization and punctuation. These ensure that all company communications convey a set of messages that are consistent with the brand identity.

Create a Pattern Library
The pattern library is one of the most important components of the design system. The pattern library consists of standard guidelines for UIs, reference documents, and page template styles. Patterns are essentially instructions on using the standard components in a manner that maintains consistency and cohesion throughout the pages or UIs. This should include technical documents on the guidelines to be followed when designing interfaces, in accordance with the principles and brand identity.

Document Coding Standards
Code is the brain of every application or webpage. It controls the functionality of the product. Hence, it is prudent that teams working on different components of the application follow the same principles when developing them.

Create Products that Win.
How successful your product is, primarily depends on user experience and how the audience perceives it. This is why design systems are important to create products that win users. As they bring order into the clutter, they begin narrating the story of your brand and driving the true purpose of your product. This allows users to navigate through the application seamlessly and find exactly what they are looking for.

2.2 Design System Management Support Team Communication and Collaboration

The user experience design of multinational enterprise needs to unifying the user interface and interaction design via design pattern and design assets library. Design is hard work and focusing on solving user and customer problems is the crux of that work. Design patterns is a tool that keeps that focus whilst eliminating some of the hard work then it's clearly save designers from having to reinvent the wheel in their design efforts and allow them to keep focus on solving problems instead.

Design System Management: Save Designers from Having to Reinvent the Wheel in their Design Efforts and Allow Them to Keep Focus on Solving Problems Instead.
A style guide is a part of the design system
Most design systems start as style guides, usually PDF, that designer use to design components and UIs. A style guide will contain information such as the type of fonts and colors to use in addition to editorial practices. Usage, dos and don'ts, etc. Those above assists is storage on your design system with your component library and documentation so everything is in one place. But design system is what's more than this.

UI design patterns are reusable/recurring components which designers use to solve common problems in user interface design
A design pattern is simply a reusable idea, design or code structure that has already been optimized for the purpose it is intended for. It is a very common approach in software design and development and in more visual design approaches too. Design patterns let you save time and money since you can copy and adapt them into your design instead of reinventing the wheel for every new interface. They also facilitate faster prototyping and user familiarity. However, you should use them carefully. The wrong choices can prove costly. Component examples are most helpful for developers because they're interactive and include code snippets. This is important because it allows engineers to see exactly how the component is supposed to work.

Documentation is the core of every design system
The documentation provides users with principles and guidelines to design products, including brand guidelines, design principles, copy guidelines, design system governance, design and code best practices, design system accessibility, resources, tools etc.

UX principle is the tried and tested guideline on how to create simple, accessible, and pleasurable designs and user interfaces
UX principles help designers make decisions about how to organize and emphasize visual cues, draw attention, and address users' needs as simply as possible. These principles provide a framework that helps direct designers' thinking and against which they can lean when in doubt. Set design strategy and principles to guide design work for new projects based on a deep understanding of user needs, business goals and technical limitations.

Design system tools' adoption while making it easier to scale and maintain
With so many design system management tools options on the markets. It makes the communication and collaboration among designers, products owners, developers more easy and also improves the design system's buildup speed. Whether you are starting from scratch or you have an existing design system. You can using design system tools to store code snippets in popular front-end frameworks. Your design system tool must provide a good user experience like version control friendly due versioning is crucial feature every design system must have. Version control creates a new file for every design system release so that teams can switch between versions. It allows teams to update to the latest design system release when they're ready preventing interruptions to workflows.

It also allows teams to work on the same file simultaneously, tracking changes over time, informs teams of what's in each release [3].

3 User Experience Design Localization Could be the Most Crucial Step in Getting Your App to Succeed in the Global Marketplace

3.1 Adapting User Experience to Local Expectations

Things are like this, global enterprise have a product on US, after years of hard work and ongoing pivoting, product runs well, and when it launch their app in China. Even it already juggling 4 (or 40) languages, like Spanish, Russia, Philip. China version trying to keep up with versions and rules and cultural norms. It somehow kept above water with organized chaos or just simple chaos. But things apparently to be known this won't scale. Perhaps enterprise doing localization for a while. It have a system in place so nothing gets lost along the way. Tasks are delivered on time. Translations are technically correct. But feedbacks and comments all makes the products on China feels the results are somewhat generic. As we know, for a global enterprise, users around the world use your products are not all speaking the same language. People from different cultures and languages will not be able to understand your products if your product have not been localized. These are common questions for global companies that use a process called localization or international.

Before UX Localization: It's Important to Plan how to Cater to International Users from the Very Beginning, Long Before Localization Begins.
The internationalization of user experience, also called cross-cultural UX design, is about laying the groundwork for the app or website to meet global users' needs and expectations. These are many things that international UX design takes into consideration. It involves more than just making sure that the core functions of your app work across different languages and regions, but also involves combining usability, UI, and localization best practices. For usability, a cross-cultural design could mean letting the user choose which language they want to use instead of imposing a language based on the user's geographic location. (see Fig. 1); For UI, it could mean allowing users to change their own preferences (e.g. to turn on dark mode, to arrange elements as a list or a grid, etc.).(see Fig. 2); For localization, a cross-cultural UX design could mean allowing the local currency symbol to be displayed next to the price, not leaving untranslated text in images, and supporting local payment methods. (See Fig. 3).

Fig. 1. How to change the language on your iPhone.

Fig. 2. WeChat releases version 7.0.12 with Dark Mode [4]

Fig. 3. Easy transactions with Citi Mobile app - Tech News, Reviews and Gaming Tips [5]

3.2 Identifying Non-textual UI Elements for Localization

Giving users the feeling of comfort, familiarity, and ease of use in whichever corner of the globe they may be is what helps the world's most popular apps. Hence, Localization need adapting any product to a specific country or region. The skill of adapting UX for different markets, is all about adaptation. It's not just about translating content into different languages, it's also about considering a user's cultural context and how that might impact their experience of a product. This process is about crafting cross-cultural products with international UX in mind from the start of the development. Fitting your app's content to the cultural tastes and usage habits of the target market rather than performing a word-for-word translation. Adapting the user interface to the different space requirements of each language; Verifying the cultural appropriateness of graphics, visuals, colors, and icons; and adapting your app's UX to what's expected locally. Tailoring the experience for international users according to regional norms, expectations, thought processes, and language.

The Most Common Non-Textual Elements: Fitting Your App's Content to the Cultural Tastes and Usage Habits of the Target Market Rather than Performing a Word-for-Word Translation.
Providing exceptional user experience when launching an app in a new market will inevitably require that culturally relevant elements are localized. Before that happens, however, first you need to identify them. Images depicting people, animals, symbols, places, and objects that are culturally relevant in the target market; The color palette

used in the UI, to avoid the negative connotations of certain colors in some markets; The layout, visual hierarchy, and information architecture; Animation and video used in onboarding screens and tutorials; Awards and badges displayed on the app's store information page, to make them locally relevant; The use of white space; Call-to-action buttons; Font size; The internal and external links on the app's website, to avoid sending international users down the wrong path, etc. Even strategic considerations such as the payment methods available at checkout and the frequency at which international users will be prompted to make in-app purchases will need localization considerations. This is devising a well-thought-out localization strategy early on in the app's development process is critical to a successful international user experience [6].

Considering language length and font sizes
Foreign language equivalents of texts in your own language will tend to be either shorter or longer. In some cases, the difference can be dramatic. For example, the word "user" in English is usually translated to "Benutzer" in German (twice as many characters) and "utilisateur" in French (almost three times as many characters). Trying to squeeze all these extra letters into a space tailor-made for the shortest version will cause problems with display and layout, usability. Most all english sentence translate into Chinese, the font sizes is 1.2 larger visually(see Fig. 4). And therefore UX Minimum font sizes that work (just) with languages like English may make other more complex language characters unreadable. Most Chinese length are shorten a lot because 1 character means 2–3 english words commonly(see Fig. 5). It might have so many white space on the interface. Additionally, line height used for English or similar Western languages may be too small for Chinese and other languages needing greater line heights. Whatever the font size or line height, the characters for any localized language must be readable. This may mean increasing minimum values for all language versions or possibly using different layout criteria for different locales.

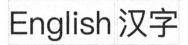

Fig. 4. Chinese characters are smaller than English words visually at the same font size.

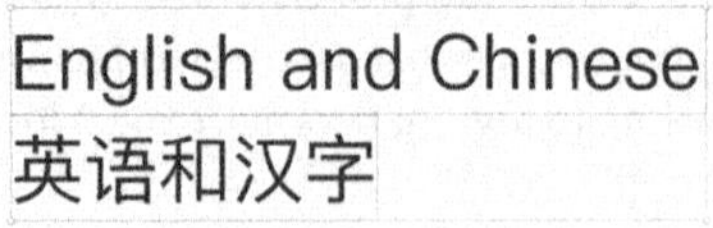

English and Chinese
英语和汉字

Fig. 5. Chinese sentence length is shorten than English commonly.

Using double-length pre- or pseudo-localization to find problems
Word length problems caused by volume expansion as in the English/German/French example above can be detected by making a double-length version of separated text strings and displaying this double-length version. Text overruns will be much more

obvious. However, for app localizations that lead to volume contraction (English to Chinese, for example), the services of a native speaker with an eye for layout may be indispensable to identify where too much blank space is being generated and where fields, buttons, or layouts may need to be modified. (See Fig. 6).

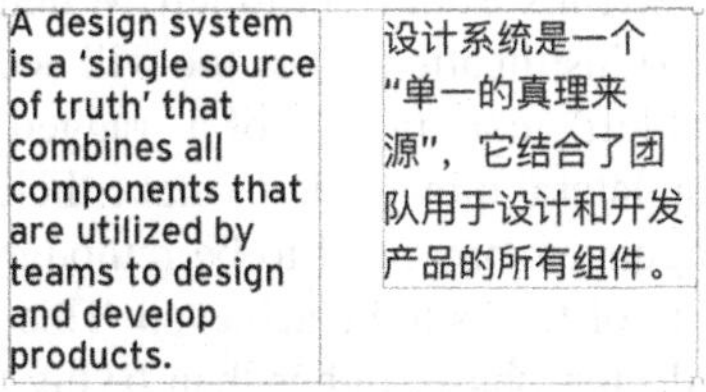

A design system is a 'single source of truth' that combines all components that are utilized by teams to design and develop products.	设计系统是一个"单一的真理来源"，它结合了团队用于设计和开发产品的所有组件。

Fig. 6. Too much blank space is being generated when English to Chinese layout need to be modified apparently.

Handling app localization UX issues caused by layouts
A localized version of an app can lead to unsightly changes in layout, even when automatic adjustment is used, which like Auto Layout in iOS, A layout that is lined up nicely in the default language may become distorted as it struggles to display foreign language equivalents. Efforts to standardize on one set of dimensions for a language with medium space requirements may not work either, especially when volume expansion and contraction can double or halve text lengths, respectively. The best solution or compromise may be different in each case. It's likely you will only recover a reasonable UI and UX that works for different localizations by trying different options and getting a native speaker's input. (See Fig. 7).

Fig. 7. English vs Chinese App Layout Design on same functional page.

Supporting right-to-left and left-to-right languages
Right to left (RTL) languages such as Arabic and Hebrew (See Fig. 8) not only change the direction of text compared to English, for instance, but they also change notions of

time and sequences of actions. RTL native language speakers may therefore expect to see a "trash can" on the left of the screen, rather than the right because thay's where they naturally end up before taking final action to throw something away.

Similarly, "next" and "back" buttons will logically be on the left and the right, respectively, instead of on the right and the left, as in English language screens (See Fig. 9). In RTL displays, time runs from right to left. Watch out also for icons used to indicate functions such as text justification. They too will need to read from right to left, for example, with a "ragged left" icon, instead of a "ragged right" one. App interfaces that are highly dependent on lateral movement to make their logic and user experience work properly for LTR languages may need to be rethought and redesigned for RTL languages if the same quality of UX is to be achieved. This is yet another aspect that's best handled in the initial design phase, rather than trying to change an existing app. Sometimes you will not have the choice. However, if you are in the fortunate position of starting to design a new app, you can take these aspects into account, according to the different localizations you think you will require. You can also avoid the issue by using a vertical navigation design from the start, which obviates the need to start either from the left or the right [7].

Fig. 8. English vs Chinese vs Arabic layout on graphic design.

Fig. 9. English vs Arabic layout on graphic design. Buttons are on opposite place.

Color culture has completely different meanings in different countries
Normally, the green color, in Asian cultures represents new life, but in many South American and latin cultures is associated with death. But Things are more complicated about color green in Chinese culture, which is because the green hat represents infidelity or being cuckolded. This association with unfaithfulness dates back to the Ming Dynasty and has persisted in Chinese popular culture. The phrase "wearing a green hat" is a euphemism for a man whose wife is cheating on him [8].

The drawing shows me
at a glance what would
be spread over ten pages
in a book

Ivan Turgenev

PICTUREQUOTES.com

Fig. 10. Sentence from Ivan S. Turgenev's Fathers and Sons (1862) [9]

More than this, for most global investor might understand green indicates the stock is trading higher than the previous day's close. Red indicates the stock is trading lower than the previous day's close. In the A-share market, red indicates an increase in stock prices, green indicates a decrease in stock prices, which is known as "red up and green down", while in Hong Kong and European and American stock markets, it is the opposite of "green up and red down". However, most domestic stock trading software, in order to avoid confusion among users, will uniformly use red to represent rising and green to represent falling. At the same time, stocks that fall will be distinguished by a minus sign "-", such as "−1%". (See Fig. 10).

4   Global Design System Should Be Compatible with Local User Experience Habits in Different National Markets

4.1   Design with Internationalization in Mind

In the very beginning of the design process, ask yourself which of your international audiences really want this product UX to be localized. If the answer is "no" for a particular market, you can skip the entire process and still succeed in that locale. In these cases, some attention to marketing localization might be much more valuable.

Not every product needs to be localized even if there are localized versions available. Certain products perform better in their original languages anyway, such as video games and software tools for scientists as well. Scientists often operate in the lingua franca of English regardless of which other languages they speak. It would be a complete waste of money to localize a scientific app when the English version would perform just as well and be accepted as a universal standard.

Internationalization Should be a Top Priority During the Design Phase.
If our design system is only responsible for domestic market users, we do not need to

consider local language issues. But if multinational companies launch design systems to unify the global user experience, they should face challenges and maladaptation from other markets, different language countries, and markets with different cultural backgrounds. Internationalization should be a top priority during the design phrase. Therefore, when developing a set of design system needed by multinational enterprises, in order not to harm the user experience of other markets, designers should be familiar with and constantly update and iterate the design system. To embracing international agreement and localization special treatment as well.

Focus on Visual And Media: Adapt Layout to Text Requirements. Convert Units of Measure, Currency, Dates Format, Phone Numbers and Other App Localization Consideration.
"The drawing shows me at one glance what might be spread over ten pages in a book" (See Fig. 11).

Fig. 11. Interface of Chinese bank's local mutual fund's detail page. Red color with " +" for rising or incomes means. (Color figure online)

Icons, pictures, and media, in general, can convey a message in a very quick and effective way notwithstanding the different languages spoken by our target audience but they can also cause misunderstanding! For example, a nine-pointed star could look great for a business logo but it can be problematic when adopted in Persia because it has a religious significance for the Bahá'í Faith, a religion founded in the 19th-century. Some objects, animals, and gestures can bring a wide range of different meanings. They may differ between different cultures in often quite significant ways. The layout must be able to accommodate a string that change length in translation: based on a general rule, a designer must plan for an average of 35% text expansion.

Considering Americans to get used to the 24-h-clock way of stating the time. You might generalize those time display format on your design system. UX strategy be driven by user research over assumptions. It's a matter of usability and it's essential to make sure to maintain the integrity of saved data when a product or service expects user input.

When most people look into the process of UX localization, they're already past the point of fulfilling this best practice. As we know now, it's absolutely critical to include in this list. Even before a company is slated for global growth, it's always a good idea to design the user interface with an international audience in mind. Developers don't often think about design choices from a non-native speaker's perspective, but they should. It results in having to disambiguate more than you might normally do, but that leads to a clearer interface in English and an easier translation process later on.

Best practices to ensure a truly cross-cultural user experience
Ensuring support for local currencies, units, dates, time, and address formats; Choosing the appropriate decimal and thousand separators; Using Unicode UTF-8 encoding to support international text and symbols; Setting the right time zone for each market; Formatting calendars correctly (in some cultures, the week starts on Monday, in others it starts on Sunday); Ensuring that international phone numbers are formatted correctly; Considering the prevalent hardware and operating system in the target market and adjusting the UI accordingly. Name & Date & Address (See Fig. 12, 13) is different display format among Chinese and English customer information display screen. Uniting them visually, but with correct understanding the logic behind. It will need support from designer and developer together efforts to archiving it.

Forms for user input. Some cultures often offer two fields for users to enter their names: given name and family name. Elsewhere, like in Spain, there are two fields for the family name because people use both their father's and mother's surnames. In China, the family name is display at the first place. Not like english display at the last.

Fig. 12. Name: First Name + Middle Name + Last Name(Family Name) VS Family Name + First Name; Date: DDMMYY VS YYMMDD

Fig. 13. Address: Room + Street + District + City + Country VS Country + City + District + Street + Room;

In visual design, aesthetics is important but when talking about localization there's much more beyond it. Designers must consider that a small nuance that recalls some cultural value can change the way visual content is processed by one's mind. Symbols, icons, and colors. Research shows that implementing culturally preferred design elements can positively influence usability. Taking color culture as example. You can hardly see green cars in china roads. Please avoiding using green car photo on marketing promotion even you supporting green painting. This could apply to choices as seemingly small as colors. For example, in far Eastern countries like China, the color red is often used to suggest good luck (unlike Western countries, where people may be more likely to interpret it as a sign of danger). A company that picked up on this was Uber: They understood that Chinese consumers could be lured by the color red, so they made their app's car icons red in China (See Fig. 14).

Fig. 14. Screenshots of Uber application, interface drivers in New York, China, and India at the beginning of 2016 [10].

Digital innovation comes from within
Steve Krug wrote his book "Don't Make Me Think"[11]. Among some of his pithy suggestions. Firstly, don't make people think. People typically don't want to have to puzzle over apps to get what they want out of them. Secondly, Apps should explain themselves at a glance—from the first screen onwards. Thirdly, Don't waste people's time. Keep the text short and sweet, and minimize distances over layouts and through menus. Fourthly, The back button is good. If people guess, don't penalize them. Let them back out again easily.

Information architecture and navigation structure. Different cultures mean different ways of getting around apps. In fact, empirical studies show differences in task completion rates across cultures depending on the use of deep vs broad page navigation structures. Heat maps also show that some cultures focus on textual menu items while others scan the whole page before engaging with it.

Taking the Chinese ID card number as example. if you understanding the ID card number represent the information of City code + District + Date of Birth + Number of your ID [12]. You can easy grab more information on you system. Like when you have this customers ID, you can identify his date of birth automatically without any extra inputs when you do your KYC process. (See Fig. 15)There is no other format of ID card number, so co-work with you engineer for the more user friendly interaction on that.

4.2 UX Writing with Localization

Internationalization is an investment in localization. If internationalization is done well, localization will be more straightforward and less costly because you won't need to rework any aspects of your app to make it fit for a different market.

Importance of Considering Future Localization During UX Writing Derives from a Tenet that Holds True for All Globalized Products.
When UX writing is done with global audiences in mind, achieving a consistent international user experience gets easier. To make your international UX writing work localization-friendly, thinking about removing colloquial language from your English

Fig. 15. Chinese ID card Format is: City code 1234 + Date of Birth: YYYYMMDD + your ID card: 123X.

text; Ditch idioms and phrases that don't translate well or at all across languages; Write unambiguous text to prevent users '(and translators') confusion; Standardize the terminology used throughout the app; Avoid homonyms; Rely on term bases and glossaries; Write short and concise user interface copy; A/B test your UX writing to validate the international results.

Research key terms in your target languages, maintain clear records of your key terminology and build your vocabulary library

There are multiple ways to instruct a user to "tap" or "click" within a user interface. Every command in the user interface is important. Users need a consistent experience that helps them intuit what each command means and where it will eventually lead. Make sure that your app interface uses the same tried-and-true terms that are used in other apps in that target language. Do your research or test to discover what those terms might be (See Fig. 16), and establish standards for the rest of the terminology that will be incorporated into the interface. Ensure they're being used consistently by translators throughout the localization process.

Fig. 16. User test of Button "Next" for Chinese characters on the page when user onboarding success and need moving to the dashboard after.

Provide context for your translators [13]. Avoid or account for cleverness, Protect variables and placeholders, Capture all of your user interface content.

In order to produce high-quality content, translators need context. They need to know where these phrases will live in the UI and how they will look in a live environment. It's also helpful for developers to include metadata in their UI content files so translators can be aware of maximum character restrictions and other real estate issues. If you provide a translator with this context upfront, they can usually come up with a creative way of meeting those requirements.

Think carefully about the variables and placeholders that exist in the English version of your user interface. If those placeholders appear within a phrase, you need to ensure that they're tagged and protected. if you're intent on keeping the puns, be sure to supply translators with a clear definition of what each phrase literally means in the metadata associated with each string. Most developers don't realize the full extent of localizable content in their UI. Strings in a code repository are standard, obvious choices for localization. But just because you provide a date doesn't mean the date itself is recognizable to a foreign audience. That phrase involves an English abbreviation and an American date order and, therefore, should be localized as well. In order to create a smoother user experience, make a diligent sweep of your UI and ensure you're capturing all types of localizable content.

5   Promote Localization in Your Own Company

Another goal of digital product design is improving user engagement. When users encounter a digital product that feels familiar and relevant to their culture and language, they are more likely to engage with it. Create a user experience that feels personalized and relevant to the user, even if they are in a different part of the world. This can improve user engagement and satisfaction, ultimately leading to better learning outcomes for all users.

5.1   Integrating Localization into the Product Lifecycle Process at Early Stages with Localization Platform, We Can Optimize User Experience and Improve Business Results.

An app localization platform allows localization professionals to use a web-based interface to manage all tasks within the localization workflow including creating teams, projects, and tasks; Pulling strings from the source code of your app into the localization platform; Assigning team members for translation and review of said strings; Importing the translated strings back into your source code; Putting it all together and compiling localized builds of your app or website; Centralizing the efforts of developers, designers, marketing managers, and executives by letting them work collaboratively in the same workspace; Generating automatic user interface screenshots that serve as context for translators and reviewers; Checking for linguistic consistency across projects; Automating tasks and workflows to save time.

Designing a system should promote user experience localization in one's own company while highly summarizing. The system needs to be continuously developed and optimized to incorporate local UX design assets into its upgrade and evolution. Raise awareness of the importance of localization and the value it will give to your users and business. Know where your users are from and consider issues such as language, cultural sensitivity, currency, date formats, gender, and local etiquette. Attribute resources to localization and involve them in your work after the wireframe step and before UX implementation, so they can raise red flags in early stages such issues as the length of certain languages or the direction of writing.

Ensuring Usability in Every Market: Continuously Develop and Optimize Design Assets and Integrate Local Customer Experience Heritage into Global Design Systems.

Ensuring usability test in every market. User testing is an essential component of UX design, and it becomes even more critical when designing for a global audience. User testing involves gathering feedback from users to identify pain points, areas for improvement, and opportunities to enhance the user experience. Businesses can conduct user testing in different regions to gather insights and feedback from local users. By doing so, they can identify design elements and content that work well in one region but may need to be adjusted for another. This approach helps ensure that UX design is tailored to the needs and preferences of local audiences, resulting in a better user experience overall.

References

1. Steinberg, S.: How can businesses benefit from a unified customer experience?. Verizon. https://www.verizon.com/
2. Hansani, B.: The Complete Guide to Design Systems. Creately. https://creately.com/
3. UXPin.: https://www.uxpin.com/studio/blog/7-great-design-system-management-tools/. Accessed 12 Apr 2022
4. Grigorian, G..: Wechat release version 7.0.12 with dark mode. www.pandaily.com. Accessed 23 Mar 2020
5. Aguspina, R.: Easy transactions with Citi Mobile app. www.hungrygeeks.com.ph/. Accessed 20 Oct 2018
6. Phrase,: UX Localization: How to adapt user experience for international users. www.phrase.com. Accessed 3 Apr 2023
7. Karl-Bridge-Mrcrosoft, QuinnRadich.: Adjust layout and fonts, and support RTL. Microsoft, Technical documentation, www.learn.microsoft.com. Accessed 24 June 2021
8. Vic-Liu: Why Chinese don't wear green hat?. www.letschinese.com/. Accessed 06 June 2023
9. Ivan, S.: Turgenev.: Fathers and Sons (1862)
10. ITzone via Uber.: Uber engineering tech stack, part1: platform. https://itzone.com.vn/en/article/advanced-uber-engineering-tech-stack-part-i-platform/. Accessed 30 July 2016
11. Krug, S.: Don't make me think (2000)
12. Slater, M.: China ID Card - An Introduction. www.chinacheckup.com/. Accessed 31 Oct 2018
13. Austin, R.: How to share the right context with translators. Localize. https://localizejs.com/articles/translation-context-why-it-matters/. Accessed 23 June 2023

From Useful Art to Service Design. Encouraging Migrants' Creative Thinking Through Translocal Services for Social Innovation

António Gorgel Pinto[1]([✉]) [iD] and Paula Reaes Pinto[2] [iD]

[1] UNIDCOM-IADE/Universidade Europeia, Lisbon, Portugal
`antonio.gorgel@universidadeeuropeia.pt`
[2] CHAIA/University of Évora, Évora, Portugal
`pmrp@uevora.pt`

Abstract. Exploring the areas of *arte útil* (useful art) and service design for social innovation, the research focuses on an art and design hybrid practice that can be understood as transdisciplinary. The social art projects and social design services pointed out as case studies aim to give practical and significant answers to the lack of support given by governmental entities, developing innovative experimental solutions that may contribute to the sociocultural sustainability and inclusion of migrant communities and citizens living in urban areas. The Immigrant Movement International, the Conflict Kitchen, and the Shifting Ground case studies have in common a systematized practice that seeks to enhance social, cultural, and political issues through a creative process to stimulate critical thinking in the new culture where the migrants aim to be integrated. Regarding the Shifting Ground, a common denominator is the relational and dialogical aesthetics crossing all the project iterations, the migrant citizens' participation in ceramic workshops to encourage creative thinking, the production of ceramic sculptures later presented to the community at large in an exhibition-celebration, and the maintenance of an online archive to strengthen community bonds. The practice in question is also contextualized by Bell Hooks' *Eating the Other: Desire and Resistance*, and Rancière's *critical art* concept, to better understand the kind of relationship that may enhance interaction with migrant citizens when developing art and design services for social innovation.

Keywords: Useful Art · Service Design · Social Innovation · Digital Archive

1 *Arte Útil*

The concept of *Arte Útil*, created by Bruguera alongside the development of socially engaged art projects, is based on using a medium according to a particular social and political problem and on "the direct implementation of art in people's lives" [1]. According to Bruguera, *Arte Útil* aims at applying art to society, addressing the gap between knowledgeable audiences and the general public, along with the historical divergence between the language of avant-garde art and the rhetoric of urgent politics [2].

Bruguera highlights the meaning of *útil* in Spanish, which, like in French, Italian, or Portuguese, has a different connotation in the English word useful. Useful derives from *usare*, which means "make use of, profit by, take advantage of, enjoy, apply, consume," while *útil* derives from the Latin word *utilis*, whose significance is related to something "useful, beneficial, profitable." Although from *útil* to useful seems that the idea of benefit is less evident, both Latin expressions have a common origin in the word *uti*, which means "make use of, profit by, take advantage of" [3].

Bruguera's social art practice represents a new paradigm in the visual arts, as she was one of the first artists to develop work over long periods. According to Rinaldo Meschini [4], these examples of socially engaged art are intended both to study and create a common platform for discussing issues related to the theme of migration and to generate a commitment to reality through social and political work.

Among the criteria established by Bruguera to characterize a work of art as useful are issues that are specific to the contemporary art field and others that can be considered transdisciplinary. In this context stands out the importance of a project being time-specific and an answer to urgent needs; being implemented and working in a real situation with tangible results for the benefit of participants, using aesthetics as a system for social transformation, among others [5]. The time-specific issue is part of Bruguera's methodology, which relates to the political context when the artwork unfolds or is materialized. Thus, the object of art exists while certain political circumstances are taking place, becoming a document of a particular political period as soon as those circumstances end [6].

Arte Útil is a social art form that works as a "socially consistent (artistic) material" that reveals itself to the viewer, being more perceptible by a wider public, unlike other artistic possibilities that are difficult to understand. According to Bruguera, this useful dimension is "the key to solve this barrier of communication and interest by the non-informed/non-initiated audience in contemporary art." In addition, the political specificity of *Arte Útil* aims not to turn all participants into artists but that all artists should be aware of their powerful tools to be responsible citizens. Within the Immigrant Movement International project, Bruguera stresses that her role is that of an initiator rather than an artist or author of a social, cultural, and artistic initiative, which she intends to develop in a participatory manner, incorporating everyone's creativity and become the common property of the community in question [5].

The development of relational and dialogical aesthetics is an aspect intensely explored by Bruguera, whose projects delve into several forms of interaction with the Other and the respective inclusion for participation in the programmed artistic initiatives. Among the relationship methods implemented, such as the creation of associations and workshops, among other forms of collaboration, Bruguera uses dialogue to create bonds of understanding and potentiate synergies. Another particularity is the relevance that these collaborative dynamics assume in the projects' communication, in which the collaborative processes are instrumentalized to enable the reproduction of the social contexts in question.

Relational art, which aims to create interactions between the observer and the social context, is associated with the advent of modern art, namely through the aesthetic, cultural, and political movements that have emerged since then. This artistic practice represents a social emphasis, where social relations that stimulate communication between participants are explored to generate spaces for free thought [7].

1.1 Immigrant Movement International

Immigrant Movement International, IM International, or IMI[1], were the terms given to a local organization dealing with legal and political immigration issues, whose aim was to set itself up as "an alternative to the mainstream position in the tradition and legacy of civic movements in the history of political advancement." According to the IMI's statement, it is a creative and educational community focused on developing sustainability systems and alternative economies based on a culture of cooperation; a collective that acknowledges the role of (im)migrants in the progress of society; a lab for developing "artivist tactics" and innovative methods for communication to the larger community; a platform where empirical knowledge is combined with creativity through *Arte Útil* [5].

IMI existed between 2010 and 2015 in the Corona neighborhood of Queens, New York, with the support of the non-profit organization Creative Time and the Queens Museum of Art. In the initial phase, Bruguera lived in a local flat, sharing living quarters with other residents, and ran a community support center for recently arrived immigrants. This space, located in a shop in the multi-ethnic neighborhood of Corona, was characterized as a hybrid conceptual art space in addition to a social support center [1].

Among the social support provided stands out the legal advice, multimedia classes, English, Spanish, Aztec dance and philosophy, and Ecuadorian dance. Always present was also the objective of disseminating the concept of *Arte Útil* in society, focusing on the problem of the precarious living conditions of immigrants. Also noteworthy was Bruguera's ethnographic performative approach in the interviews with emigrants in the metro about their life experiences in the USA [1, 5].

The IMI initiative is characterized as a long-term project that functions for Bruguera as an experimental platform for developing the *Arte Útil* concept. In the artist's view, creating art objects based solely on the problematization of social inequality is no longer sufficient. Bruguera experiments with a new status for the artist, merging the creative agency with strong political activism, which becomes a "yardstick of an art which wants to define itself as useful" [4].

One of the IMI's characteristics is that it establishes a direct interaction with social and political organizations to call attention to the perception, recognition, and representation immigrants have in society. To this end, Bruguera experiments with a strategy for defining models of social organization, highlighting the global problem of immigration and bringing it to public discussion, as well as creating significant conditions for immigrants in search of their own identity through difference and a voice with which they can assume their knowledge and demands [2].

---

[1] http://immigrant-movement.us/wordpress/.

A peculiarity of this social artwork is that Bruguera avoids producing a specific object of representation to value the whole interaction process in the IMI project. However, it is possible to identify a set of media whose aim is to document all the actions produced and inform the different audiences, such as creating and maintaining a website, blog, and social networks, from which greater visibility is given to the initiative [2].

2 Designing Services for Social Innovation

The goal of service design for social innovation is to create and establish situations that result from social innovation cases. This allows services to align with the reality where they are offered since they are founded on relationships developed between all social agents in the community, including local culture and know-how [8].

Services are mainly human-centered, relational, and social entities. They are also cyclical and with a degree of unpredictability since interactions develop over time with no certainty that specific outcomes will be achieved in a predefined manner. When a person engages with a service through a touchpoint, a service interaction takes place. The touchpoints are the tangible representation of services and include the objects that facilitate concrete interactions, playing a crucial role in making relationships smoother, increasingly effective, and more meaningful. Thus, services are physical as they are attached to or backed by an artifact of certain nature. Also relevant is the fact that services may be provided through person-to-person interactions, through multiple relational situations, by means of appropriate digital interfaces, or even through hybrid touchpoints that combine different means [9].

Manzini [10] refers that a common aspect between these modes of design is that they adopt "processes in which what has to be designed are hybrid, dynamic artifacts where products, services, and communication are systemized and presented as a whole."

Designing services for social innovation is also significant in terms of place-making, which is a notion that merges both the perspectives of specialists focused on problem-solving and those who are more concerned about the production and communication of meaning. It is a specific activity related to certain places, in which approaches with different scales take place, which in turn are interconnected in a global logic. In this field, the relationship of agents with local institutions and citizens to enhance the development of specific projects is a recurrent practice. This type of partnership and intervention is particularly paradigmatic for the design discipline since there was no great concern with the place in the tradition of profit-based industrial design.

The advantage of social innovation resulting from the understanding and interaction between designers and other social innovation creatives, makers, and stakeholders is twofold: on the one hand, it is a collaboration for the implementation of ideas to solve societal needs, and on the other hand, it is a demonstration of the will and capacity to act through different synergies. Therefore, all kinds of civil associations, communities, families, and other social groups are significant partners that can actively collaborate with experts to experiment and systematize different approaches. The need to entrench this logic of social performance and citizenship stems from the fact that most governmental measures are ineffective in solving some recurrent problems and overcoming "the conventional polarities of private versus public, local versus global, consumer versus producer, need versus wish." Contrary to the tendency towards contrast, social innovation proposes a dilution between these principles [10].

According to a social innovation art and design practice focused on generating subjectivity, we find authors who use their knowledge to create new products, services, or communication objects. At the same time, there are multiple innovative possibilities streamlined by activist makers seeking to influence cultural attitudes and behaviors, professional artists and designers acting as place makers for local communities, and creative industries working in networks as open services.

Such as in the practice of *Arte Útil*, one of the central aspects of service design for social innovation is the relational dimension, where the service beneficiaries are perceived as relational beings rather than as users or clients. The relational approach is based on the notion of being open to others, allowing interpersonal interaction, which is the raw material for services that might happen. The relational qualities that are established between individuals substantially influence how smoothly the relational service operates. Contrary to other types of services developed around a predetermined interaction between clients and service providers, relational services are better compared to a relationship between guests and service hosts. A more open and unpredictable interaction that encourages the participation of all users taking part in the social innovation service [11].

Art and design services strategically disseminate innovative forms of action and understanding throughout communities to empower and scale social innovation. Empowerment is a key mechanism by which participants develop the capacity to gather resources to accomplish a desired objective. This process depends on the empowerment subjects' "access to resources and the capacity and willingness to mobilize resources to achieve a goal" [12]. In this context, Avelino et al. highlight the importance of getting the willingness, such as referred to above in a citation by Manzini [10], which depends on a set of psychological dimensions, namely relatedness, autonomy, competence, impact, meaning, and resilience. Relatedness is about a sense of community and belonging to a social group, as well as obtaining recognition from it; autonomy refers to the capacity to make decisions for oneself and to behave in accordance with one's ideals and identity; competence refers to acquiring skills and an awareness of one's own efficacy through action; impact is the confidence that is possible to take actions that make the difference; meaning is related with the development of collective identity; resilience is connected with the psychological and behavioral strategies that allow the maintenance of a motivation to pursue goals and to take further steps [12].

This notion of empowerment is relevant to understand how the protagonists of social innovation art and design can feel stronger and more confident in the context of translocal networks, which are a combination of local and transnational synergies. These translocal systems of interconnections focused on transformative social innovation operate on both local and global scales. The different dimensions of empowerment in local services are better suited for specific development, while in the translocal networking they are disseminated in an expanded field of potential synergies. In this context, combining specific local action with translocal diffusion is particularly empowering [12].

2.1 Conflict Kitchen

Pittsburgh's Conflict Kitchen[2], Pennsylvania, USA, is an example of a translocal service for social innovation. The restaurant was open from 2010 to 2017 and was created by the lead artists Jon Rubin and Dawn Welenski, together with the graphic designer Brett Yasko and the culinary director Robert Sayre. As collaborators, the project counted on Afghan, Black and African American, Cuban, Haudenosaunee, Iranian, North Korean, Palestinian, and Venezuelan communities in Pittsburgh and their worldwide diasporas, who contributed with their heritage through stories, opinions, recipes, and creative guidance. The Conflict Kitchen served food from every country with which the United States had a conflict, from Afghanistan to North Korea. It was open seven days a week, changing its visual identity in response to different geopolitical developments [13].

Publications, performances, conversations, and several other activities to increase public awareness around cultural and political issues at stake in different world geographies, such as printing interviews with locals in the reverse of food containers, were held in the restaurant, which received new iterations according to the themes in question. Among the most uncommon actions of the Conflict Kitchen: customers were invited to have lunch with a citizen of the featured country in a series called *The Foreigner*; for those who couldn't visit the restaurant in person, there were synchronous international public dinner parties and cooking classes, held in several time zones; research activities based on food experience and culture worldwide to enhance the economic and social networks where the participants were part; books, such as one with conversations featuring Palestinian youngsters and a North Korean cookbook with annotation [13].

The objects that were designed to support the project activities have an impactful influence on community re-identification patterns. The expression and emotive character of the Conflict Kitchen visuals, such as the facade and the wrappers, allowed the customer participants to envision and perform different ways to put into question the conventional narratives about Pittsburgh's multicultural reality and the US international affairs. This is related to the concept of *agonism* [14, 15], which is a paradigm that, in this kind of design, enhances the quality of dissent rather than avoiding it, allowing the construction of multiple identities that represent the emergency and vulnerability of contemporary social structures and simultaneously anticipate possible alternatives. *Agonism* is a kind of antagonism, but contrary to the incompatibility of opposing adversaries or enemies who share no conceptual ground, it enables a space where opponents can negotiate the construction of a mutual understanding. Pushing the Conflict Kitchen service users to reconsider societal conventions led to the rise of a citizenry that recognizes and values differences [16].

Conflict Kitchen's actions were not intended to represent a single perspective or judgment but rather to dismantle existing prejudice systems and collective beliefs by highlighting their unfairness and oppression. Despite the social and political purpose of the restaurant, the many activities did not contain specific political orientations or procedures to follow but rather aimed to establish an uncensored context to allow meaningful dialogue and broaden the discussion around the country's international affairs and

---

[2] https://www.conflictkitchen.org.

politics of immigration with the direct involvement of the communities in question. However, the diversity of thoughts generated points of common interest and identification that enabled the creation of a public [16].

3 Intercultural Dialogue

Central to the relational and dialogical aesthetics, as developed in the Immigrant Movement International and the Conflict Kitchen, is the way it occurs the interaction with the Other and their involvement for cooperation in the proposed community projects.

In the essay *Eating the Other: Desire and Resistance*, Bell Hooks [17] points out how nonwhite cultures are often commodified, which is a tendency that has become dominant in Western societies since the mid-twentieth century, such as is well known in the sphere of food culture and business, but also in the visual arts and design fields. Following Hooks' understanding, it is possible to acknowledge that nonwhite cultures are usually contextualized within a white and paternalist narrative through which certain cultural phenomena are appropriated. In commodifying another culture, the object or service is taken out of context and transformed into something easy to consume. On the contrary, consuming the Other's culture should not be the focus, but understanding and appreciating it as a complex human manifestation with common aspects and differences.

This understanding of racism establishes relationships with the Other as an object of play and exotic experimentation without considering the human sameness that should prevail in intercultural interactions. Hooks [17] states that this transformation of racism, from something related to the idea of the nonwhite as something the white culture used to deny, repudiate, and fear to something they obsessively wish to appropriate and enjoy, is related to a colonial past when western countries used to conquer territories to change them according to their principles of civilization. In Western culture, colonialist longing involves reenacting and ritualizing the colonial power, where conquering adventures work as narratives and imaginary of dominance and desire for the nonwhite. The attitude facing the Other is basically the same as it was in the Middle Ages in terms of dealing with the other culture solely for the white benefit, without caring for mutual respect and intercultural dialogue.

Understanding how curiosity for the nonwhite is manifested, experienced, and enhanced through diversity and the significant difference depends upon a sensitive human behavior that might suggest if those potentially transformative feelings and emotions are reciprocal and ever realized. A relationship that may enhance interaction with otherness must start from "one's self vulnerable to the seduction of difference" to interact closely with those who have a different culture, and it should be a mutual choice and negotiation to allow "cultural appreciation" to the detriment of "cultural appropriation" [17].

Seeking the fairest and most impacting ways to inform our "political choices and affiliations," where a desire for interaction with those who are different, have another culture or are labeled as Other, is a human behavior that should be followed when the situation is not regarded as biased, or politically subjected to bad principles [18]. Regarding art and design for social innovation, and particularly when collaborating with migrants and refugees, it is possible to consider it within a sphere of critical art. According to Rancière [18], this is a territory between art and politics. The main aim of critical art is to stimulate the observers' awareness of the existence of control systems aimed at transforming them into conscious actors concerning the evolution of the world. Thus, critical art practices, situated between art and non-art forms, have developed an activity based on the articulation between different discourses, thus being able to communicate doubly. In the case of the representation or self-representation of otherness, recognizing how "the desire for pleasure" shapes our politics and our awareness of diversity allows the citizens who observe to grasp "how desire disrupts, subverts, and makes resistance possible" [17].

4 Shifting Ground

The Shifting Ground is an art and design service for social innovation that started in 2019 in the city of Cedar Rapids, Iowa, USA and continued in Lisbon, Portugal, with two other iterations. In Lisbon, the project was held in 2021 and 2022 and will return to Iowa in the fall of 2023. The main motivation that boosted the project is the times we are living in nowadays, marked by intolerance and social injustice regarding immigration policies, which most probably will grow with the human and environmental crises we are experiencing, such as climate change and war, among others, that force people to migrate and seek a new place with fair conditions to live and expect a better future. With this in mind, a group of artists/designers, namely Jane Gilmor, António Gorgel Pinto, and Paula Reaes Pinto have been experimenting a community-based service for migrants and refugees focused on encouraging creative thinking and ceramic sculpture as survival strategies. In the course of the different editions, the Shifting Ground service already involved immigrants from Mexico, Honduras, Indonesia, Angola, Mozambique, and Sao Tome and Principe, as well as immigrants and refugees from Burundi and the Democratic Republic of Congo.

The interaction with these citizens and the way to establish empathy with the group is established through a game titled MOT (acronym of memory, object, talent), which represents a strategy to allow the participants continuous input in a fluid and customized approach and also as a way of encouraging more spontaneous participation (see Fig. 1). In order to stimulate self-representation, the MOT game arises as a means of generating a creative relationship between the service users, newcomers to a nation, and the host community.

Throughout the Shifting Ground three iterations, different nuances of the MOT have been experimented. In the first workshop sessions, the participants were asked to share through the MOT a personal narrative, a meaningful object, and what they regarded to be their major aptitude. It was also stated that these three issues should be somehow related. In the last Shifting Ground in Lisbon, the life story that was asked focused on memories related to food experiences and knowledge. Every person has a connection to food, some of which are good, while others can be negative. Nevertheless, all experiences are related to impacting feelings and emotions that we aim to explore further through participatory sculpture (see Fig. 2).

The remaining steps were common to all the service iterations, namely the conversation around each participant's MOT, where they shared their personal experiences. The

Fig. 1. Shifting Ground Workshop, participant writing her MOT (memory, object, talent), Cedar Rapids, Iowa, US, 2019.

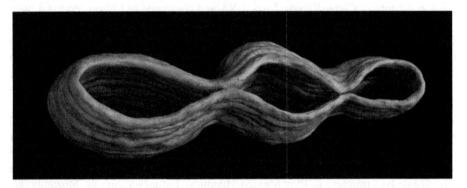

Fig. 2. Shifting Ground ceramic sculpture, Florence Nshimirimana Taylor, 2019.

relational approach reveals itself very significant because, through personal memories, objects, and willingness, the interaction is expanded to other topics of self-representation. This process of conceptualization is followed by an individual exploration of possible forms with clay, from small to large-scale ceramic sculptures. In a collaborative engagement, permanent feedback from peers and artists is maintained. The artists' contribution in this phase is mainly as facilitators, intervening whenever necessary and attempting to increase the participants' initiative while giving technical or conceptual assistance when necessary. The goal is always to create a set of ceramic sculptures to allow the organization of a final show to the community at large, which happens a few days after the workshop while the bonds of friendship are still fresh between everyone involved in the service (see Fig. 3).

The exhibit-celebration has been counting on the presence of participants and artists, their friends and family, local artists, researchers, and stakeholders. This last gathering was emphasized by the immigrants and refugees involved, along with everyone else there during the activity, who agreed that such a demonstration clearly recognized immigrant culture and cooperation across local communities, especially by showcasing their innermost resourceful qualities.

Fig. 3. Shifting Ground Exhibit/Celebration, Cherry Center Space, Cedar Rapids, Iowa, US, 2019.

4.1 Digital Repository of Sculptures

The Shifting Ground translocal system is also supported by a website[3] where networking is seen as a vehicle to expand potential synergies. Besides happening in specific places such as Iowa and Lisbon the art and design service for social innovation has a digital presence. It is a dynamic touch point that facilitates meaningful and interactive experiences with users and participants. Through interactive communication, the Shifting Ground website creates an archive where users and participants feel heard, engaged, and valued. In this context, the service prioritizes a user-centric approach, through which the touch point becomes crucial for building lasting relationships in an increasingly intercultural digital world.

This form of archive, in the words of Miessen [19], generates "a set of spatial and content structures, which produce new works on the basis of the archived material." Within the Shifting Ground website, the idea is to build an archive focused on the act of gathering experiences, and as a type of knowledge that comes from the interaction between all the project participants. The archive in question is supported by an empathetic strategy based on dialogue, and the recounting of life stories represented through ceramic sculptures to engage participants and stimulate the creative process. This is done by using a performative structure and a hybrid and intermedia approach. As a result, this practice serves as a tool for fostering social and cultural sustainability. The collection of movies that depicts the entire procedure and, in particular, the created art objects within the workshops, represents each culture. Because it is founded on an archiving procedure, the digital repository of sculptures is therefore both a process and part of the creative work.

Wolfgang Ernst, in his book titled *Digital Memory and the Archive* [20], explores the impact of digital technologies on memory and archiving practices, discussing how digital platforms generate new forms of cultural memory and transform the traditional notions of archiving. Ernst highlights the transformative power of digital memory and its implications for our understanding of history, culture, and technology. Digital technologies have fundamentally transformed our relationship with memory, leading to a

---

[3] http://shifting-ground.org.

shift from the archive as a stable entity to the archive as a dynamic and processual system. In this context, the archive is not merely a storage space but an active agent in the construction and reconstruction of cultural memory.

Such as Foucault [21] compares the archive study to the practice of learning about the past through its material remains left behind by a specific historical period and culture, Ernst explores the notion of the archive as an archaeological site. In this context, the Shifting Ground digital platform works as an archaeological site where users can uncover and analyze layers of subjective information and memories of past activities. It is a dynamic engagement with digital materials documenting concrete actions of service for social innovation, uncovering hidden histories and alternative narratives.

5   Final Considerations

Designing services for social innovation, such as the Immigrant Movement International, the Conflict Kitchen, and the Shifting Ground, is strongly based on relational and dialogical aesthetics to enhance interactions with the involved participant users. Using dialogue as a central medium to create social and cultural bonds of understanding potentiates synergies allowing further development of the provided service to the community.

Also common to the three projects is the fact of being inserted in translocal networks, combining local and transnational sociocultural characteristics, which define the implemented collaborative platforms involving artists, designers, and other social innovation creatives, makers, and stakeholders for societal transformation and empowerment. This is a key mechanism through which the migrant participants are encouraged to gather the motivation they need to complete their desired objectives.

Creating a sense of community and belonging to a social group, where the socially integrated citizens recognize the importance of welcoming the newcomers to the community and accepting the different ideals and identities as powerful cultural resources, is a way to legitimize collective identity and reinforce social and cultural resilience.

References

1. Gerrity, J.: Visiting Artist Profiles: Tania Bruguera (2011). http://www.artpractical.com/col umn/tania_bruguera/. Accessed 21 Jan 2017
2. Olascoaga, S.: Staging: experiments in social configuration. In: Olascoaga, S., Rabinow, P., Shirazi, S., Tedone, G. (eds.) Foreclosed. Between Crisis and Possibility, pp. 93–105. The Whitney Museum of American Art, New York (2012)
3. Online Etymology Dictionary. https://www.etymonline.com. Accessed 13 June 2023
4. Rinaldo Meschini, E.: Arte Útil Parte 1. Una Teorizzazione Pratica (2013). http://luxflux.net/ arte-util-parte-1-una-teorizzazione-pratica/. Accessed 29 Jan 2017
5. Immigrant Movement International. http://immigrant-movement.us/wordpress/. Accessed 04 Feb 2017
6. Bruguera, T.: Tania Bruguera. http://www.taniabruguera.com/cms/. Accessed 21 Jan 2017
7. Bourriaud, N.: Relational aesthetics. In: Bishop, C. (ed.) Participation: Documents of Contemporary Art, pp. 160–171. Whitechapel: The MIT Press, London (2006)

8. Joly, M., Cipolla, C.: Service design for social innovation: creating services from social innovation cases. In: Fernandes, A.A., Natal Jorge, R.M., Patrício, L., Medeiros, A. (eds.) 3rd International Conference on Integration of Design, Engineering & Management for Innovation, Porto, 4–6 Sept (2013)

9. Penin, L.: An Introduction to Service Design: Designing the Invisible. Bloomsbury Publishing (2018)

10. Manzini, E.: Design, When Everybody Designs. An Introduction to Design for Social Innovation. The MIT Press, Cambridge (2015)

11. Cipolla, C.: Relational services and conviviality. In: Miettinen, S. (ed.) Designing Services with Innovative Methods, pp. 232–243. TAIK Publications/University of Art and Design Helsinki, Helsinki (2009). https://www.researchgate.net/publication/294732271_Relational_services_and_conviviality. Accessed 13 June 2023

12. Avelino, F., Dumitru, A., Cipolla, C., Kunze, I., Wittmayer, J.: Translocal empowerment in transformative social innovation networks. Eur. Plan. Stud. **28**(5), 955–977 (2020). https://doi.org/10.1080/09654313.2019.1578339

13. Smith, C.E.: Designing Peace. Building a Better Future Now. Cooper Hewwitt (2022)

14. Mouffe, C.: The Democratic Paradox. Verso Books (2009)

15. Disalvo, C.: Adversarial Design. The MIT Press, Massachusetts (2012)

16. Uribe del Águila, V.: The agonistic design of conflict kitchen. In: Traganou, J. (ed.) Design and Political Dissent: Spaces, Visuals, Materialities, pp. 187–201. Routledge (2021). https://doi.org/10.4324/9781351187992

17. Hooks, B.: Eating the other: desire and resistance. In: Black Looks: Race and Representation, pp. 21–40. Routledge (2015)

18. Rancière, J.: Problems and transformations in critical art. In: Bishop, C. (ed.) Participation: Documents of Contemporary Art, pp. 83–93. Whitechapel: The MIT Press, London (2006)

19. Miessen, M., Chateigné, Y.: Introduction: productive spaces of conflict. In: Chateigné, Fuchtjohann, D., Hoth, J., Miessen, M., Schmid, L. (eds.) The Archive as a Productive Space of Conflict, pp. 9–28. Sternberg Press (2016)

20. Ernst, W.: Digital Memory and the Archive. University of Minnesota Press (2012)

21. Foucault, M.: The Archaeology of Knowledge and the Discourse of Language. Pantheon Books (1972)

Human Languages in HCI: Beyond User Interface Localization

Diego Moreira da Rosa[1](✉) ⓘ, Leandro Soares Guedes[2]ⓘ, Monica Landoni[2]ⓘ,
and Milene Silveira[1]ⓘ

[1] Pontifícia Universidade Católica Do Rio Grande Do Sul, Porto Alegre, RS, Brazil
diego.rosa81@edu.pucrs.br, milene.silveira@pucrs.br
[2] Università della Svizzera italiana, Lugano, TI, Switzerland
{leandro.soares.guedes,monica.landoni}@usi.ch

Abstract. This paper investigates the role of language in interaction design and computer-mediated communication. It starts by distinguishing between *human languages* and *computer languages*. Human language, as the primary code used in text and voice-based communication, is critical in the majority of communication processes. We also analyze two methods of computer-mediated communication. First, interaction design based on semiotic engineering is investigated; followed by user-to-user computer-mediated communication. This paper provides insights into the design of user interfaces, cross-cultural communication, and social media by discussing the complexities of language in human-computer interaction and computer-mediated communication. The findings highlight the significance of language as the main component of effective communication involving humans and computers in various contexts.

Keywords: Language · Multilingualism · Communication Models · Computer-mediated Communication · Human-computer interaction

1 Introduction

Adapting software systems to international users has been a key issue for the software industry since the emergence of personal computers by the end of the '70 s. For many years, the processes of software internationalization (i18n) and localization (L10n) were the focus of development teams to attend the demands of users in many different countries [6]. Until the popularization of the Internet, most communication occurred between the system and the user, and once the software was installed and configured, a single language was used throughout this interaction. By the turn of the millennium, the emergence of Web 2.0, combined with a wider access to technology and Internet connection in developing countries, radically impacted how computer systems were designed and used [16]. Beyond the system-to-user communication, it is the computer-mediated user-to-user communication that gains importance as users from all over the world start

M. Kurosu et al. (Eds.): HCII 2023, LNCS 14054, pp. 564–574, 2023.
https://doi.org/10.1007/978-3-031-48038-6_36

interacting through social platforms. All these events have taken the multilingualism of human-computer interaction (HCI) to a higher level adding extra challenges to the software globalization process (g11n) [6].

In general, the number of languages or locales supported by a certain application or website was a good indicator of the level of globalization of the system [20,22]. Having a system localized to many different languages guarantees broader access to users from different countries. This can be seen as the multilingualism of the interface, aimed at dealing with the language diversity of the user base. In the context of the social web, in which users are not only consumers but also creators of content, the multilingualism of the individual gains importance, i.e., designers should take into consideration that every user has a linguistic background, may present some degree of bi- or multilingualism, and will have their own language preferences. To address these nuances, researchers in the field of HCI need to expand their focus beyond interface localization and adopt a broader perspective encompassing the multiple forms of multilingualism in interaction design.

This paper aims to provide a theoretical review of human languages within the context of HCI, establishing a foundation for future research within a comprehensive conceptual framework. The presented model of communication explores its relation to HCI, with particular emphasis on the role of human language in message encoding and decoding. Drawing upon theories of semiotic engineering, computer-mediated communication, and other relevant disciplines, we elucidate the diverse forms of communication that occur in HCI, supporting our analysis with real-world application examples. Finally, we discuss how designers, systems, and users negotiate language and engage in various forms of communication.

2 Methodology

To analyze the roles of human language in the many forms of communication involved in HCI, we adopted a three-step methodology as described below:

- **Review of definitions and types of language:** bibliographic research on the definition of language and the classification of the many types of language. Identify the definitions and types that are most relevant to the study of human-computer interaction.
- **Review basic models of communication:** revisit theories of communication and apply them in the context of HCI. Establish basic terminology and analyze the role of human language as the main code in the communication process.
- **Analysis of language use in the many forms of computer-mediated communication:** identify the many forms of communication in HCI and analyze how language is negotiated and used for message en-/decoding in each of them. Through exploratory research, present examples of current user interfaces to illustrate different scenarios.

3   Definition and Types of Languages

Communication and language are intricate concepts that have been extensively studied in fields such as Communication, Semiotics, and Linguistics. The definition and description of language can vary depending on the context and the specific interests or requirements of the study. Lyons suggests that most definitions view language as a system of symbols designed for communication among groups of human beings within a particular community [14]. Languages convey not only ideas but also express emotions, desires, identity, art and poetry [9,11,17,21]. Furthermore, languages can take various forms, including spoken, written, and hand symbols that belong to a convention system. This work focuses on written languages and their usage in human-computer interaction.

It is important to note that human language differs from communication systems used by other animals, such as whale vocalizations. Additionally, language is not the sole code employed in human communication and HCI. Nonverbal communication, such as body language, plays a significant role in human interaction [7], and iconography is essential in user interface design [3].

In the realm of computer science, a wide range of *computer languages* exists, which are formal languages used to communicate with computers. Among them, *programming languages* are employed to communicate instructions to machines, typically computers. In the field of Information Technology, the term *natural language* or *human language* is sometimes used to refer to a language employed in human communication, distinguishing it from various forms of computer languages (hence terms like *natural language processing*). Notwithstanding, some artificially constructed languages, such as Esperanto and Interlingua, effectively facilitate human communication and do not fit strictly within the definition of *natural language*.

In the domain of Human-Computer Interaction, professionals may use the terms *interface language* (referring to the language used by the system interface) and *user language(s)* (referring to the language(s) preferred or spoken by the user). In this study, the term *human language* is employed to denote language in its traditional definition as a system of human communication. This choice helps to avoid ambiguity with other types of language utilized in the field of Computing and its subareas.

4   A Model of Communication

When exploring language use within the context of HCI, it is valuable to establish a model of communication. Over the years, numerous models have been proposed, highlighting the multifaceted aspects of human communication [15]. Generally, a simple linear model that incorporates fundamental concepts is suitable for describing many forms of computer-mediated communication. Figure 1 depicts a straightforward model of communication based on the works of Shannon [19], Jakobson [12], and Schramm [18].

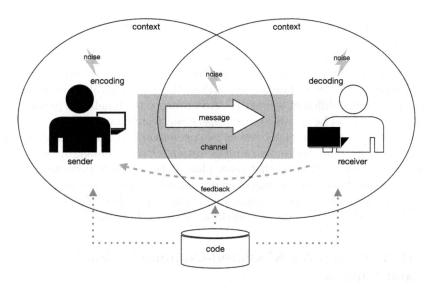

Fig. 1. Model of communication based on Shannon-Weaver's and Schramm's models.

This model incorporates essential elements that aid in describing the communication process and establishing a shared terminology:

1. **The sender**, also referred to as the *source*, is the individual who formulates, encodes, and transmits the message to the receiver.
2. **The receiver**, or *destination*, receives, decodes, and responds to the message sent by the sender.
3. **The message** comprises various types of signs (verbal, written, gestural, etc.) that convey information.
4. **Encoding** is the process of converting the message into a signal that can be transmitted through a channel.
5. **The communication channel** represents the medium, whether physical or logical, that enables the transfer of the message from the sender to the receiver.
6. **Decoding** is the process of translating the signal back into the message (the reverse of encoding).
7. **Feedback** is the response or reaction of the sender to the received message.
8. **The code** refers to any form of sign system, including human languages, utilized for encoding/decoding the message.
9. **The context** encompasses all the circumstances of the communication, including environmental, social, and personal aspects of each individual involved in the process.
10. **Noise** represents any influence on effective communication that has the potential to interfere with the interpretation of the message. Various types of noise can affect the communication channel (environmental) or the encoding/decoding process (psychological, semantic, etc.).

In the presented model, messages are encoded and decoded using a code, which is a sign system based on social convention. In text and voice-based communication, human languages serve as the primary code employed by the interlocutors. Therefore, language plays a key role in most communication processes.

Within the domain of human interaction, there are several types of communication, each in a different context [1]. According to the number of participants, communication can be classified in *intrapersonal* (communication with oneself), *interpersonal* (communication between two persons or in a small intimate group), *group communication*, and *mass communication*. *Organizational communication* describes the communication that takes place in larger, more permanent groups and contributes to the functioning of an organization. Finally, *computer-mediated communication* is the type of human communication that relies on electronic devices and software systems as a medium or channel of communication.

5   HCI, Computer Mediated-Communication, and Language

In the context of HCI, two forms of computer-mediated communication deserve a deeper analysis. The first one is the interaction design process, as described by semiotic engineering. The second one is the communication between users of social media. These two models present particularities regarding language usage in the communication process. In this work, we aim not to analyze the specifics of every existing communication model but to explore basic models that help understand the role of language in HCI.

5.1   Designer-to-User Communication (interaction Design)

De Souza originally proposed Semiotic Engineering as a semiotic approach to the design of user interface languages [4]. According to semiotic engineering, HCI can be viewed as a computer-mediated communication process between designers and users at interaction time [5] (see Fig. 2). In this process, the system itself is the message sent from designers to users. The system's user interface acts as the agent of the designer in communication and is capable of sending and receiving other messages. In other words, systems are metacommunication artifacts that should be engineered according to explicit semiotic principles [4].

The designer relies on a set of sign systems to design the user interface. These systems include the human language(s) in which the text and verbal-based signs of the interface will be produced. Other sign systems include iconography, color symbolism, and UI conventions. These sign systems must be totally or at least partially shared between the design team and the user for the metamessage to be understood. In cases the user base is expected to be representative of many different cultures, with considerably different mindsets, the user interface may have to be adapted in a process known as cross-cultural design.

In this type of designer-user communication, the interface language (the main language to be used at interaction time) is usually chosen by the user from a

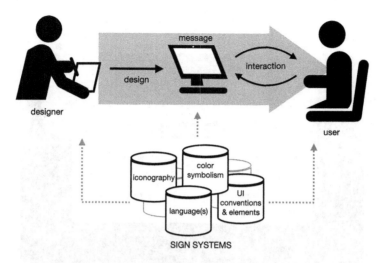

Fig. 2. Interaction design process viewed as designer-user communication according to semiotic engineering.

predefined set of languages or locales. In general, a locale is a combination of language and region/country and defines the linguistic preferences of the user interface. The process of adapting a software interface to different languages and regional peculiarities (including the *translation* of text strings) is called *localization* [6]. In order to operationalize the localization of software systems without the need of severe code changes, design teams adopt the *internationalization* design strategy.

Clearly, the selection of languages that the design team offers to the users is part of the metamessage. The website of Decathlon Switzerland[1] for example, is localized in German and French but lacks localized versions in the other two official languages of the country: Italian and Romansh (see Fig. 3). It would be as if the designer said to the user:

> "I understand that these are the languages that you might be interested in. In case you belong to the Italian- or Romansh-speaking communities of Switzerland, I assume that you can at least understand one of these two languages. Now you can select one of them and continue with your interaction."

Restricting the interface options to only two languages usually means that all associated services (account management, customer support, etc.) will be available only in those languages. Even though around 15% percent of the Swiss population will not have access to the retailer services in their native language, other aspects must also be considered, such as the elevated costs of the localization of an e-commerce platform.

---

[1] Sporting goods retailer: https://www.decathlon.ch/de/splashpage/.

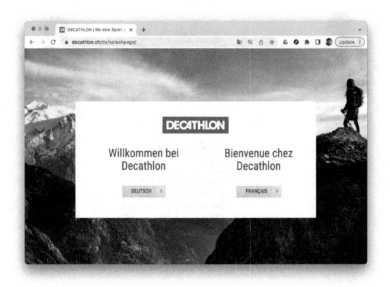

Fig. 3. Language selection page of Decathlon Switzerland website.

5.2   User-to-user Computer-Mediated Communication

In addition to the designer-user communication described in the previous section, HCI design also impacts all forms of user-to-user computer-mediated communication. Figure 4 shows a model for many-to-many communication typical of social media environments. This model is based on the model of intercultural communication proposed by Haworth and Savage [8] and the model for hypermedia marketing proposed by Hoffman and Novak [10]. One-to-one and one-to-many interpersonal communication can be seen as a special cases of this model.

The diagram in Fig. 4 presents eight users from four different countries interacting through a social platform. The platform can be a social network, an online forum, an interactive e-commerce website, or any other form of Web 2.0 application. The multiple countries emphasize the multicultural characteristic of many of these systems. A certain number of languages is attributed to each user representing both the multilingualism of the individuals (who may have skills in one, two, or more languages), and the multilingualism of countries (which are home to individuals with a variety of language skills). The observed increase in language diversity intensifies the challenges of the interaction design process.

Users communicate by posting user-generated content to the platform, which acts as a repository and/or distributor of these content units. The content generated by users can be a post on a social network, a message in a forum, a product review in e-commerce, etc. In this model, user-generated content is equivalent to the message in the traditional model of communication. The social platform, in turn, is the communication channel through which messages are propagated.

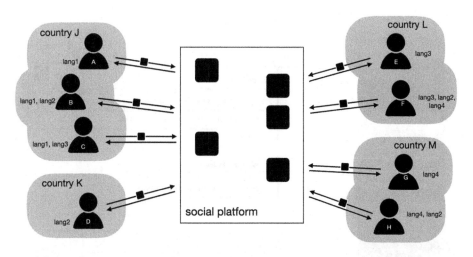

Fig. 4. Intercultural communication through social media (based on Haworth's and Hoffman's works).

Multiculturalism is the first aspect to be observed in the heterogeneous environment of a social media platform. In order to maintain a cordial relationship between members from many different cultures and nationalities, most of these systems publish a set of rules or guidelines that should be followed by every member (e.g., Facebook Community Standards[2], Reddit Content Policy[3], Booking.com Reviews Guidelines[4], etc.). These guidelines are then enforced by the companies' staff and by other members of the online community through abuse reporting.

Multilingualism is also remarkable in social platforms. The level of multilingual support will depend on many aspects of the system design. Some systems may limit the available languages that users can choose due to software/technical constraints. In online forums, it is common to find communities determining which is the language of choice for a certain group/topic of discussion [2]. Multilingual users can also vary the language of messages and posts according to the context [13]. Some systems offer features that facilitate access to multilingual content, such as content filtering by language and automatic machine translation.

Figure 5 shows the user reviews page of an accommodation listing on Booking.com. The image highlights various language-related aspects of the interface. The language settings in the top right corner indicate that the device is configured for English (EN tag). On the left side of the interface, the Booking website itself has been switched to Italian using its configuration options (IT tag). The user reviews are displayed in their original languages. In the given example, one

---

[2] https://transparency.fb.com/policies/community-standards/.

[3] https://www.redditinc.com/policies/content-policy.

[4] https://www.booking.com/reviews_guidelines.html.

Fig. 5. International user reviews on a hotel page of Booking.com website (accessed in Jun 2023).

review is shown in German (DE tag), while another review is in Spanish (ES tag). Notably, the Booking website permits hotel managers to respond to user reviews. These responses can be composed in different languages based on the specific situation. An English response is provided for a German review (EN tag in the center). Additionally, the system offers several features to assist users in dealing with multilingual content. An automatic translation feature allows users to translate other users' reviews. Furthermore, a language filter allows users to sort and visualize reviews based on their preferred language. Nonetheless, it is important to note that the automatic translation feature is not available for hotel management responses.

Booking.com is an exemplary platform in terms of multilingual support, as it offers localized interfaces in 45 languages. This allows a significant portion of the global population to access the platform in their native language. Furthermore, the platform actively encourages the display of international user-generated content. Notable features include facilitating users' access to multilingual content and providing tools to effectively manage and filter such content.

6   Conclusion

This theoretical review provides valuable insights for Human-Computer Interaction researchers interested in exploring language use in interactive system design.

By establishing a common terminology through a communication model, it lays the foundation for discussions on language and HCI. The model's components, such as sender, receiver, message, encoding, decoding, channel, feedback, code, context, and noise, are instrumental in understanding and defining communication in two key contexts: designer-user metacommunication during interaction design (as described by Semiotic Engineering), and user-to-user communication on social media platforms. In the latter context, the review emphasizes the significance of multiculturalism and multilingualism in contemporary systems.

The globalization of information and communication technologies increased the levels of multiculturalism and multilingualism in software usage. Offering localized interfaces is still an important task that guarantees access to digital systems for many users. Nonetheless, design teams now have bigger challenges that go beyond software localization, such as proposing solutions for the presentation and navigation of multilingual user-generated content.

References

1. Adler, R.B., Rodman, G.R., Sévigny, A.: Understanding Human Communication, vol. 10. Oxford University Press, Oxford (2006)
2. Birnie-Smith, J.R.: Ethnic identity and language choice across online forums. Int. J. Multiling. **13**(2), 165–183 (2016)
3. Blankenberger, S., Hahn, K.: Effects of icon design on human-computer interaction. Int. J. Man Mach. Stud. **35**(3), 363–377 (1991)
4. De Souza, C.S.: The semiotic engineering of user interface languages. Int. J. Man Mach. Stud. **39**(5), 753–773 (1993)
5. De Souza, C.S.: The semiotic engineering of human-computer interaction. MIT press (2005)
6. Esselink, B.: A practical guide to localization, vol. 4. John Benjamins Publishing (2000)
7. Fast, J.: Body language, vol. 82348. Simon and Schuster (1970)
8. Haworth, D.A., Savage, G.T.: A channel-ratio model of intercultural communication: The trains won't sell, fix them please. J. Business Commun. (1973) **26**(3), 231–254 (1989)
9. Hébert, L., Tabler, J.: The functions of language. In: An Introduction to Applied Semiotics, pp. 232–240. Routledge (2019)
10. Hoffman, D.L., Novak, T.P.: Marketing in hypermedia computer-mediated environments: Conceptual foundations. J. Mark. **60**(3), 50–68 (1996)
11. Huffaker, D.A., Calvert, S.L.: Gender, identity, and language use in teenage blogs. J. Comput.-Mediated Commun. **10**(2), JCMC10211 (2005)
12. Jakobson, R.: Linguistics and poetics. In: Style in language, pp. 350–377. MA: MIT Press (1960)
13. Karusala, N., Vishwanath, A., Vashistha, A., Kumar, S., Kumar, N.: "only if you use English you will get to more things:" Using smartphones to navigate multilingualism. In: Proceedings of the 2018 CHI Conference on Human Factors in Computing Systems, pp. 1–14 (2018)
14. Lyons, J.: Language and linguistics. Cambridge University Press (1981)
15. Narula, U.: Communication models. Atlantic Publishers and Dist (2006)
16. O'Reilly, T.: What is web 2.0. "O'Reilly Media, Inc." (2009)

17. Sapir, E.: An introduction to the study of speech. Language 1 (1921)
18. Schram, W.E.: The process and effects of mass communication. University of Illinois Press (1954)
19. Shannon, C.E.: A mathematical theory of communication. Bell Syst. Tech. J. **27**(3), 379–423 (1948)
20. Singh, N., Boughton, P.D.: Measuring website globalization: a cross-sectional country and industry level analysis. J. Website Promot. **1**(3), 3–20 (2005)
21. Waugh, L.R.: The poetic function and the nature of language. Verbal art, verbal sign, verbal time, pp. 143–68 (1985)
22. Yunker, J.: Have we reached "peak" language? (2023). https://globalbydesign.com/2023/03/02/have-we-reached-peak-language/. Accessed Apr 2023

Technology Experience: Postsecondary Education Exploration by Non-native English-Speaking Immigrant Parents

Emmanuel K. Saka[✉]

Experiential Design, Belmont University, 1900 Belmont Boulevard, Nashville, TN 37075, USA
emmanuel.saka@belmont.edu

Abstract. The availability and advancement of technology continue to shape the American educational landscape. This makes the exploration of postsecondary education options accessible to all users seeking information about postsecondary education, including non-native English-speaking parents. Despite the acculturation issues faced by immigrants, technology has become an effective tool that enables them to navigate and get accustomed to their new milieu. Amidst the advancement and positive attitude to technology, there is sparse research on how the environment, behavior, and personal factors influence the use of technology by non-native English-Speaking immigrant parents to explore postsecondary education options for their children's success. The goal of this phenomenological study was to identify how the environmental, behavioral, and personal factors influence the use of technology by non-native English-speaking immigrant parents in Iowa, United States to support their children toward postsecondary education. Three main themes emerged after careful analysis of the descriptive data from the semi-structured interviews and demographic survey. The findings show that the interdependent nature of the environmental, personal, and behavioral factors contributes to the perceived usefulness and ease of use which influence the attitude of immigrant parents to use technology to access educational information to support the attainment of postsecondary education for their children. The outcome of this study contributed to the development of a Technology-Mediated Community-Level model. This model allows postsecondary education institutions to collaborate with local organizations to structure educational information in a simplified format accessible to users in their respective native languages via technology.

Keywords: Cross-Cultural design · Human-Computer Interaction · User engagement

1 Introduction

Postsecondary education in today's advanced technology-driven world provides opportunities and "critical avenues for social mobility and economic success in the United States" [1]. Being educated beyond high school is no longer a symbol of luxurious status; instead, it is a hub for innovation and creative thinking [2]. The United States'

M. Kurosu et al. (Eds.): HCII 2023, LNCS 14054, pp. 575–584, 2023.
https://doi.org/10.1007/978-3-031-48038-6_37

long-term economic health depends on innovation and creativity [3]. Given the extent to which postsecondary education is important to an individual and society, much attention is required to ensure the full cultivation of the benefits associated with continuing education past high school.

Over the past two decades, enrollment in postsecondary education within the United States has increased dramatically. According to the U.S. Department of Education, and the National Center for Education Statistics (2018), from 2000 to 2015, postsecondary education – undergraduate enrollment increased by 30%, a jump from 13.2 million to 17 million students. The U.S. Department of Education projects enrollment to increase to 19.3 million students by 2026 [4, 5]. Enrollment in U. S. postsecondary institutions will increase by 15%, with the largest increase coming from underrepresented populations, including students from immigrant families [6].

The advancement and demand for technology continues to shape the American educational landscape [7] and makes the exploration of postsecondary education options accessible to all users. End-users, including non-native English-speaking immigrant parents living in the United States, can utilize the opportunity of technology integration, as adapted by several postsecondary education institutions, to support their children's educational success. The adaptation and use of technology by immigrant parents is dependent on several factors such as the economy, environment, and personal behavior of the end user. Understanding users' motivation, especially users with diverse cultural and educational background experiences outside the American culture and educational system, is important to foster an effective use of technology in this case, within the context of education. Technology in this study refers to information technology.

The goal of this phenomenological study is to identify how the environmental, behavioral, and personal factors influence the use of technology by non-native English-speaking immigrant parents in Iowa, United States to effectively support their children toward postsecondary education. Studying and establishing an in-depth understanding of these experiences is immensely important to an immigrant nation such as the United States. Furthermore, this study will enable stakeholders such as postsecondary educational institutions, support programs, and designers to gain an in-depth understanding of the immigrant population and through technology disseminate educational information from a cross-cultural perspective.

2   Background of the Study

Students from immigrant families constitute a higher percentage of the growing population of students within the U.S. educational system. The integration of technology into education presents non-native English-speaking immigrant parents with opportunities to explore postsecondary education as a tool to help their children become productive citizens of their chosen country.

Fortunately, the most recent groups of immigrants to the U.S. have already exposure and experience with technology usage. Research surrounding the experiences of non-native English-Speaking immigrant parents and the influence of the environment, behavior, and personal factors on technology usage is deficient. Culturally, non-native born immigrant parents deem it as an obligation to support their children for postsecondary education due to the value it offers them and the society. These developments indicate the importance of research into individual experiences with technology, especially for non-native English-speaking immigrant parents, and how the environment, behavior, and personal factors influence how they utilize technology to explore postsecondary education options for their children.

Most research about humans' experiences with technology within education is focused on students' learning experiences, teachers' experiences with educational technology, and users' psychological experiences [8]. However, social development (constructivism) theory argues that the construction of knowledge and meaning is based on experiences embedded within social interaction [9]. According to Vygotsky's social constructivism theory, parental involvement in a child's education is critical since the parent serves as the More Knowledgeable Other (MKO). The parent within the context of MKO is assumed to have a better understanding and higher ability level than the child. Involving parents via sharing educational information significantly contributes to the academic development of students [10]. This study is vital because it helps to ascertain the essence of the lived experiences of non-native English-speaking immigrant parents regarding how the environmental, behavioral, and personal factors influence how they utilize technology to support their children toward postsecondary education.

2.1 Parental Involvement through Technology

Technology has contributed to bridge the gap in collaboration and communication between parents and schools. It has become a significant approach to foster student performance and engagement. Some studies have demonstrated the impact of technology on parental involvement in different contextual frameworks [11, 12, 13].

To investigate the effective use of technology for communication between elementary school teachers and parents, she indicated that some teachers face problems when communicating with parents via the internet [14]. It was revealed in the study that most teachers were not interested in involving parents by using technology that parents perceived to be helpful due to work, personal schedule, and accessibility issues. This continues to be an issue due to the lack of understanding about the means through which information technology can be effectively used to engage parents [15].

Most research about immigrant parental involvement through technology is focused on early literacy development, digital divide and at the K-12 education level [16]. There is not enough research to provide insights regarding the involvement of immigrant parents on how they use technology to gather information to help support their children navigate and explore information for postsecondary education.

2.2 Motivation to use Technology

As posited by Maslow [17], motivation is based on hierarchy of human needs. Low hierarchical needs (physiological needs) must be satisfied before an individual can be motivated to fulfil higher needs (self-actualization).

For instance, the need to utilize technology by immigrant parents to access information for their child's education can be categorized as low-mid to higher hierarchy needs. Their initial motivation to utilize technology upon arrival in the United States is to help them acculturate to the American culture. Immigrant parents migrates to the United States with a prior technology experience, but their motivation to use technology for education in terms of motivation is a secondary need.

Also, the perceived usefulness and perceived ease of use of a particular technology reflects the attitude of users toward that technology [18]. Several research on motivation and acceptance to use technology has shown that both the perceived usefulness and ease of use significantly influence users' attitude toward technology use and the behavioral intention to use technology [19, 20, 21]. The perceived usefulness, perceived ease of use, subjective norms, and quality of work life of the user significantly determines user's behavioral intention towards technology [22]. Also, the subjective norm and behavioral intention stems from the user's cultural values. The neutrality of culture as one of the main factors/variables of the model has been criticized by researchers. The cultural and social context determines how individuals or groups behave toward technology. Other studies also argue that traditions and values differ across cultures and as a result, the perception and attitude to acceptance and use technology would be different among users with diverse cultural values and background experience [23, 24].

2.3 English as a Second Language in America

44% of foreign-born individuals who settled in the United States in 2000 or later were identified to be proficient in English. However, 13% did not speak English at all. 15% of the 41 million foreign-born in America spoke only English as a first language at home [25]. Despite the common trait of migration to the United States among immigrants, those with higher educational attainment (college degree or above) are proficient in the English language (71%). Only 12% among immigrants with less educational attainment i.e., high school diplomas were identified to be highly proficient in English, 67% proficient in English, 40% proficient and 27% could not at all speak English [26].

There is a bad perception of some native-born Americans about individuals that decides to continue to speak their native language. Such perceptions have contributed to the disparity in policies governing how immigrants learn English and a suggestion for the U.S. Congress to maintain bilingualism to sustain language heritage among immigrants [27].

3 Methodology

A phenomenological research methodology was used to help obtain an in-depth narrative and meaning of the importance and truth about the shared lived experience of non-native English-Speaking immigrant parents technology use in supporting their children toward postsecondary education [28, 29].

Albert Bandura's Social-Cognitive Theory (1986) and Davis's Technology Acceptance Model (1989) were used as the theoretical framework for the study. Unlike quantitative research that disintegrates a phenomenon to examine its components, a qualitative approach prioritizes understanding the meaning of an experience and how all parts of a phenomenon work together [30]. Cilesiz [8] highly encourages the use of phenomenological inquiry for studies that seek to understand users' experience with technology within the context of education.

Participants consisted of seven (7) non-native English-speaking immigrant parents living in Iowa, U.S. who had children either currently enrolled or who have recently graduated with a form of postsecondary degree. A purposeful sampling method was used to select participants for the study. In qualitative research, the purposeful sampling method is used to strategically select individuals with a shared experience to collect specific information about a phenomenon [31, 32]. Participants were recruited through emails to local immigrant organizations, recommendations, and word of mouth.

The criteria for selecting participants for the study was based on the following:

1. Immigrants to the United States – must be born in a different country outside the United States (foreign-born).
2. Speak a different language other than English as a native language and the country of birth must have other native languages different from the English language. Participants from countries where English was the official language but not the native language were allowed to participate in the study.
3. Migrated to the United States with a prior educational experience outside the United States educational system.
4. Lived in the United States and Iowa for at least 5 years.
5. Fluent in English.
6. Must be at least 40 years of age and with a child(ren) either enrolled or graduated (less than a year) from a postsecondary educational institution in the United States.
7. Own and use technology toward their child(ren)'s postsecondary education.

A brief demographics survey questionnaire, a semi-structured open-ended interview questions, follow-up conversations and a reflective journal were used to collect data. The nature and expectations of the study were explained to all participants and a verbal consent was used to obtain participants' consent for participation in this study. Participants were informed about the confidentiality of the study and their rights. Each participant was assigned a pseudonym different from their legal name to maintain privacy and security of identity. Carefully, each recorded interview was transcribed and a rigorous data analysis using open and focused coding to establish meaning from the collected data and to determine common themes or shared experience(s) was conducted. The modified Van Kaam methodology, suggested by Moustakas [29], was used to analyze the data. After a careful analysis of the date from the seventh interview, the point of saturation was achieved because no new additional information was emerging. At the point of saturation, the inclusion of extra participants to the study would not add any valuable information to the study [33, 34].

4   Results

After careful review and analysis of documents including the reflective journal and transcribed interviews three themes emerged to reflect the goal of the study:

1. Parental perception about postsecondary education and technology usage for educational purposes;
2. Community engagement experience: School district and access to technology and college prep programs; and

3. Self-value and motivation to support their children's education.

There were seven (7) participants consisting of three (3) males and four (4) females in this study: Makena, Ana, Martin, Mary, Joseph, Olivia, and Dennis. 57% (4) of the participants have been living in the U. S. between 11–20 years and the other 43% (3) have been living in the U. S. for over 20 years. They migrated from Africa, South America, Asia, and the Caribbean. 43% (3) of the participants had a doctoral degree, 29% (2) had a bachelor's degree, 14% (1) had a master's degree and 14% (1) graduated from high school. 100% (7) of the participants indicated that they preferred to use their smartphones the most to access information because of convenience, accessibility and for communication purposes. However, all the participants preferred to use a laptop to access information to support their Childrens' education. They perceived the laptop to be useful and easy to use over the smartphone. Even though the smartphone was convenient to use, it was challenging to use it to access, navigate and comprehend information. The small screen size did not allow them to open multiple pages to compare vital information.

Culturally, most of the participants in this study valued face-to-face interaction with a resourced person to access information about education for their children over inter-action via technological platforms. The findings showed that the participants shared different meanings about why they valued face-to-face interaction. However, it was identified that, the participants prior to a face- to-face consultation with an academic resourced person, would use their laptops to access information and establish meaning from the information through the interaction with the resourced person. This helped them to experience and express emotions during the in-person interactions for fear of been perceived as naive. Also, they expressed concern about how communication over the phone always generated issues due to differences in accent. Even though most of the participants were highly educated and proficient in English, they indicated that their prior education experience outside the United States and native language presented some challenges in accessing and comprehending postsecondary education information for their children. It was noted that the different terminologies or jargons used across most post-secondary education/institutions websites made it difficult for them to infer the meaning for comprehensions.

5   Discussion

The three main themes that emerged from this study confirmed the validity of Bandura's SCT triadic reciprocal determinism. However, it does not represent the experience of all non-native English-speaking immigrant parents living in the United States.

The findings show that the personal, behavioral, and environmental factors did not operate in isolation from each other. As illustrated through the responses to the inter-views, participants shared how their immediate environment and experiences shaped their behavior to use technology toward their child's education. Learning occurs because of an individual's or a group's bidirectional interaction with the environment, personal and behavior factors [35]. The change or development in behavior of a person is not constructed by just a stimulus-observation, instead, it is a construct of multiple stimuli based on self-efficacy that constitute production of the response [35].

5.1 Parental Perception about Postsecondary Education and Technology Usage for Educational Purposes

One significant finding from this study was that most of the participants in the study were highly educated. Their motivation to attain a bachelor's degree or higher was influenced by their extended family background. As a result, they were motivated to inculcate in their children the discipline and culture of attaining higher education past high school as a continuation of the family legacy. They perceived postsecondary education as an avenue to integrate into their host culture as responsible members capable of contributing to the development of the host culture.

Due to collectivist cultural background of the participants, postsecondary education was a catalyst to help minimize their marginalized status enabling them to take up influential leadership positions of service in the workplace and within the community. These factors and technology experience from work enabled them to develop the motivation and confidence to use technology to support their children's education. Their attitude and perceived usefulness of technology for education was based on social trust from their immediate environment [36].

5.2 Community Engagement Experience: School District and Academic Support Groups

The second theme emerged from the influence of the environment in which the participants lived. Some of the participants resided in affluent communities where the school district was well resourced regarding educational technology usage for student learning and parental engagement. As a result, the parents were motivated to use technology to support their children's education and development. This was the same for the participants that homeschooled their children(s). Interestingly, the participants from school districts with college prep programs were less motivated to use technology to help their children. The support received from the college prep program catered for the need to independently use technology to support their child's education. The highlighted phenomenon is that because of the perceived relevance of postsecondary education by the participants they were motivated to use any avenue possible including the use of technology for the exploration of postsecondary education for their children.

5.3 Self-value and Motivation to Support their Children's Education

The findings showed that all the participants migrated to the United States with prior educational experience different from the American educational system. Also, the participants did not grow up using technology. Rather, through the acculturation process, they developed an attitude to use technology. Significantly, it was identified that the participants heavily depended on their immediate cultural/immigrant support groups or a significant other with prior experience as a motivation to use technology to support their children's education. Since they received help from others, they expressed the motivational need to support other immigrant parents to the use of technology.

It is important to note that the identified themes are not independent of each other but rather interdependent of each other. The participants' perceived understanding and importance of postsecondary education together with technology contributed to their ability to learn through modeling and observation. The findings show that the interdependent nature of the environmental, personal, and behavioral factors contributes to the perceived usefulness and ease of use of technology. Therefore, influencing the attitude of immigrant parents to use technology to access educational information to support the attainment of postsecondary education for their children.

6 Conclusion

The need for a user-centered design requires holistic integration of shared experiences to facilitate a cross-cultural HCI (Human Computer Interaction) design and evaluation [37]. This helps to establish contextual framework to ascertain usability issues embedded in culturally influenced conditions [38]. As technology advances, access to information expands and America continues to be the leading destination for immigrants. It is important for educational institutions to use a social capital approach to establish a framework for community-level engagement with immigrants and local communities/organizations. This would help to create more inclusive and effective educational opportunities and experiences for all students.

Social capital uses available structures such as networks, norms and trust between individuals, organizations/society to foster cooperation for mutual benefits [39]. Several studies have shown that the integration of social capital together with TAM, due to social trust ensures a positive attitude and acceptance to use technology [36].

This study contributes to the field of cross-cultural HCI design by suggesting a technology mediated community-level engagement model. The Model helps to create a space that allows educational institutions to collaborate with local immigrant communities and individuals. The goal is to make vital educational information accessible to non- native English-speaking immigrant parents seeking to use technology to support their children for postsecondary education, in their respective native language. This approach could help foster a holistic educational experience for students from immigrant families by eliminating the extra cognitive stress they experience due to lack of parental support in navigating through what so often seems a complex system when accessing information and meaning in the United States K-20 education system.

References

1. Juarez, C.: The Obstacles Unauthorized Students Face in Postsecondary Education." Center for American Progress, http://www.americanprogress.org/article/obstacles-unauthorized-stu dents-face-postsecondary-education, Accessed 12 Dec 2022
2. Robinson, K.: Out of Our Minds: Learning to Be Creative. 3rd edn. Capstone, MN (2017)
3. Wagner, T.: Calling all innovators. Educational Leadership. College, Careers, Citizenship **69**(7), 66–69 (2012)
4. Staklis, S., Horn, L.: New Americans in postsecondary education: a profile of immigrant and second-generation American undergraduates. National Center for Education Statistics, Institute of Education Sciences, US Department of Education. https://nces.ed.gov/pubs2012/ 2012213.pdf. Accessed 12 Dec 2022

5. McFarland, J., et al.: The Condition of Education 2017. NCES 2017–144. National Center for Education Statistics (2017)
6. Hussar, W.J., Bailey, T.M.: Projections of Education Statistics to 2025. NCES 2017–019. National Center for Education Statistics (2017)
7. Rossitto, C., Bogdan, C., Severinson-Eklundh, K.: Understanding constellations of technologies in use in a collaborative nomadic setting. Comput. Support. Coop. Work (CSCW) **23**(2), 137–161 (2014)
8. Cilesiz, S.: A phenomenological approach to experiences with technology: Current state, promise, and future directions for research. Educ. Technol. Res. Develop. **59**(4), 487–510 (2010). https://doi.org/10.1007/s11423-010-9173-2
9. Vygotsky, L.S.: Mind in society: The development of higher psychological processes. Harvard University Press, Massachusetts (1978)
10. Epstein, J.L.: Homework practices, achievements, and behaviors of elementary school students. Center of research on elementary and middle schools report no 26. Baltimore, MD: Johns Hopkins University (1988)
11. Tour, E.: Supporting primary school children's learning in digital spaces at home: migrant parents' perspectives and practices. Child. Soc. **33**(6), 587–601 (2019)
12. Blau, I., Hameiri, M.: (2017). Ubiquitous mobile educational data management by teachers, students, and parents: does technology change school-family communication and parental involvement? Educ. Inform. **22**(3) 1231–1247 (2017)
13. Papadakis, S., Zaranis, N., Kalogiannakis, M.: Parental involvement and attitudes towards young Greek children's mobile usage. Int. J. Child-Comput. Interact. **22**, 100144 (2019)
14. Olmstead, C.: Using technology to increase parent involvement in schools. TechTrends **57**(6), 28–37 (2013). https://doi.org/10.1007/s11528-013-0699-0
15. Patrikakou, E.N.: Parent involvement, technology, and media: now what? Sch. Commun. J. **26**(2), 9–24 (2016)
16. Choi, J., Lee, H.J., Sajjad, F., Lee, H.: The influence of national culture on the attitude towards mobile recommender systems. Technol. Forecast. Soc. Chang. **86**, 65–79 (2014)
17. Maslow, A.: Motivation and personality. New York, NY: Harper (1954)
18. Davis, D.: Perceived usefulness, perceived ease of use, and user acceptance of information technology. MIS Q. **13**(3), 319 (1989). https://doi.org/10.2307/249008
19. Hussain, A., Mkpojiogu, E. O., Yusof, M. M.: Perceived usefulness, perceived ease of use, and perceived enjoyment as drivers for the user acceptance of interactive mobile maps. In: AIP Conference Proceedings (Vol. 1761, No. 1, p. 020051). AIP Publishing LLC. (2016)
20. Chirchir, L.K., Aruasa, W.K., Chebon, S.K.: Perceived usefulness and ease of use as mediators of the effect of health information systems on user's performance. Europ. J. Comput. Sci. Inform. Technol. **7**(1), 22–37 (2019)
21. Yan, D.W., Zhang, X.Y., Su, Q.: The willingness to use mobile libraries in colleges: cognitive lock-in. In: 5th Annual International Conference on Management, Economics and Social Development. Atlantis Press (2019)
22. Tarhini, A., Hone, K., Liu, X., Tarhini, T.: Examining the moderating effect of individual-level cultural values on users' acceptance of E-learning in developing countries: a structural equation modeling of an extended technology acceptance model. Interact. Learn. Environ. **25**(3), 306–328 (2017)
23. Lee, S.G., Trimi, S., Kim, C.: The impact of cultural differences on technology adoption. J. World Bus. **48**(1), 20–29 (2013)
24. Al-Jumeily, D., Hussain, A.: The impact of cultural factors on technology acceptance: a technology acceptance model across eastern and western cultures. Int. J. Enhanced Res. Educ. Develop. **2**(4), 37–62 (2014)

25. US Census Bureau. Close to Half of New Immigrants Report High English-Speaking Ability. https://www.census.gov/newsroom/press-releases/2014/cb14-105.html Accessed 20 Mar 2020

26. Hill, L.: English Proficiency of Immigrants. https://www.ppic.org/publication/english-proficiency-of-immigrants/ Accessed 20 Mar 2020

27. Tse, L.: Why don't they learn English? Separating fact from fallacy in the US language debate. Teachers College Press, New York (2001)

28. Moerer-Urdahl, T., Creswell, J.W.: Using transcendental phenomenology to explore the "ripple effect" in a leadership mentoring program. Int J Qual Methods 3(2), 19–35 (2004)

29. Moustakas, C.: Phenomenological research methods. Thousand Oaks, CA: SAGE (1994)

30. Merriam, S. B.: Case study research in education: A qualitative approach. Jossey-Bass (1988)

31. Glesne, C.: Becoming qualitative researchers: An introduction, 3rd edn. Pearson Education, Inc, Boston, MA (2006)

32. Palinkas, L.A., Horwitz, S.M., Green, C.A., Wisdom, J.P., Duan, N., Hoagwood, K.E.: Purposeful sampling for qualitative data collection and analysis in mixed method implementation research. Adm. Policy Mental Health Mental Health Serv. Res. 42, 533–544 (2013)

33. Dukes, S.: Phenomenological methodology in the human sciences. J. Relig. Health 23, 197–203 (1984)

34. O'Reilly, M., Parker, N.: 'Unsatisfactory saturation': a critical exploration of the notion of saturated sample sizes in qualitative research. Qual. Res. 13, 190–197 (2012)

35. Bandura, A.: Swimming against the mainstream: the early years from chilly tributary to transformative mainstream. Behav. Res. Ther. 42, 613–630 (2004)

36. Grzegorczyk, M.: The role of culture-moderated social capital in technology transfer–insights from Asia and America. Technol. Forecast. Soc. Chang. 143, 132–141 (2019)

37. Winschiers-Theophilus, H.:, ", The art of cross-cultural design for usability, .", Universal Access in Human-Computer Interaction. Addressing Diversity: 5th International Conference, UAHCI 2009, Held as Part of HCI International 2009, San Diego, CA, USA, July 19–24: Proceedings, Part I 5, p. 2009. Springer, Berlin Heidelberg (2009)

38. Bourges-Waldegg, P., Stephen, S.: Meaning, the central issue in cross-cultural HCI design. Interact. Comput. 9(3), 287–309 (1998)

39. Putnam, D.: Social capital and public affairs. Bull. Am. Acad. Arts Sci. 47 5–19 (1994)

Research on the Performance of Participatory Communication on the Effectiveness of Attention Economy on SNS: Analysis Based on the Case of "Xiaohongshu"

Wenhao Shen[✉], Zhiqin Zhao, and Helin Li

Beihang University, Beijing, China
shenwenhao@buaa.edu.cn

Abstract. The rapid development of social networking platforms has led to an important shift in the way information is disseminated, and this shift has profoundly influenced the path of transforming the economic efficacy of the platforms. This study focuses on the impact of the results of participatory communication on the acceptance of commercial information, as well as the impact of the interactive participation mode of platform interface labels on the action decision of public participation in information re-dissemination. Taking the "Xiaohongshu" community, a Chinese SNS with a good business model, as an example, this study selects original content and forwarded content in the technology section and compares them to show that the content produced by the public through the platform significantly affects the attention of re-published content and reflects a higher willingness to consume it. Taking the platform's hot content as the target, the analysis of this study concludes that, in terms of ease of use of interface labels, the use of interactive labels with a general level of engagement significantly increases the motivation of users to participate in redistribution of that content, while the originality of the content is not significantly associated with mass participation in redistribution. The "production-consumption" or "audience labor" theory may provide a behaviorally motivated explanation for the algorithmic black box of platform tweeting, and further mechanism research is needed.

Keywords: platform economy · participatory communication · attention economy · efficiency transformation · production-consumption

1 Introduction

With the development of platform economy, the promotion mode of the traditional market has shifted from visible advertising to user-focused interaction mechanism, and the communication of commercial information has gradually transformed from B to C to C to C. In this process, the market participant and the visibility of business information have been transformed. With the active interaction of users, once invisible consumers as simple audiences come to the front of commercial information, produce information

© The Author(s), under exclusive license to Springer Nature Switzerland AG 2023
M. Kurosu et al. (Eds.): HCII 2023, LNCS 14054, pp. 585–603, 2023.
https://doi.org/10.1007/978-3-031-48038-6_38

content itself, and participate in the communication of information together. The once explicit, visible commercial promotion settles into the masses. Through the participatory communication of transformed commercial information, the accumulation of platform interaction is promoted, and the audience's acceptance of information is further changed, thus affecting the economic efficiency.

Among them, the more prominent shift mode is the combination of social networks services and platform e-commerce. Social network itself is a typical form of network community, such as Facebook, Twitter, YouTube, Weibo, etc., which carries the function of interest exchange and life sharing. Through online communities, people transcend the limitations of time and space, building meaningful relationships while seeking support by similar experiences.

With social network services (SNS) playing an increasingly important role in people's online lives, especially with the rise of flow economy, commodity sellers have entered SNS in various ways, in addition to maintaining existing B to C e-commerce platforms (such as Taobao and JD.com in China), promoting the effective communication of perceived information such as product availability and ease of use through the interweaving of explicit and implicit promotion, striving to convert attention on SNS into their economic efficiency.

In China, Xiaohongshu is a more active SNS, which is a social platform with the theme of sharing and discovering lifestyle, and is known as "the most understanding SNS for young people". Users can share their daily life, shopping experiences, travel experiences, beauty, skin care, fitness and other content on the platform, and communicate with other users through interactive ways such as touching the labels of like and comments. On the basis of the online community, Xiaohongshu continues to develop the functions of its platform e-commerce that users can buy goods shared by other users, and can also buy goods of official cooperative brands on the platform.

Nowadays, Xiaohongshu has become one of the most popular social e-commerce platforms in China, with 70 million users in 2017, 90 million in 2018, and more than 300 million in 2019. By 2022, Xiaohongshu has not mentioned the number of users, because the monthly active users alone have exceeded 200 million, and the creators who are really sharing notes in the community have also exceeded 50 million.

At present, the promotion of e-commerce on SNS focuses more on the invisible communication mode of user interaction. Previous studies have focused on the economic efficiency of interactive behaviors such as live broadcasting, while less attention has been paid to the use of interface labels and their results on SNS.

The use of interface labels on SNS is the intermediary and its result of human-computer-human interaction. In the study of participatory interaction behavior on SNS, many scholars have paid attention to the use of human-computer interaction interface and users' feedback. However, the influence of labels presented as the result of the previous round of human-computer interaction in the new round of interaction behavior is ignored. The phenomenon behind is the effect of user engagement behavior on "attention".

Therefore, this study will focus on the descriptive analysis of the effect of label use on users' attention on SNS. We attend to explain that what kind of participatory behavior will promote the communication of commerce information; and how the information engaged by "human-computer-human" interaction gives an impact on the economic efficiency of attention promoted by commercial information.

2 Literature Review and Research Hypothesis

SNS is not only the virtual practice field connecting social individuals which is realized by computer and internet technology, but also the main way for media platforms to obtain economic benefits in the era of digital capital. It first assumes the social relationship role of "virtual community" and plays the basic function of interpersonal communication. The platform economy, on the other hand, leverages "value-creating interactions between external suppliers and customers… Information, goods and services, and money are the core interactions of the platform economy. "[1] Previous development communication theories have suggested that a lack of public involvement is one of the reasons why some business decisions fail. People's active involvement in projects can make them relevant, effective and sustainable. [2] This kind of communication is essentially the process of sharing information among the participants, dispelling the distinction between the sender and the receiver (provider and audience), marking the liberation of the traditional concept of "audience", replacing "send" or "provide" with "communication" or "interaction", and reinterpreting the role of mass media. The operation of small media in the network community and the application of grassroots communication means, different from the persuasion in the traditional diffusion mode, emphasize the cultural identity and other social attributes of the participants in the community. Its democratic nature will enhance the exchange of information, so it has stronger effectiveness in the communication effect [3].

In participatory communication, all stakeholders generate analysis and problem-solving solutions through dynamic interactions, including dialogue. Thus, communication has changed from a pure information exchange channel to an empowerment tool, and stakeholders play an active and positive role in the decision-making process [4] This positive effect is highlighted in that the gratuitously collaborative creation and communication mode such as UGC (user generated content), citizen news, and peer producers. It will gain a higher social reputation and more social attention [5] That is, the higher the degree of public participation in the communication of content, will attract more user attention. Therefore, hypothesis 1 is proposed in this study:

H1: Participatory communication positively affects the attention of SNS users.

On the interface of XiaoHongshu, the main way for users to participate in the communication is to click and use interface labels such as "like", "comment" and "forward". The user's attention is represented by the numbers under these labels. That is to say, when users browse a piece of published content, they can see others' attitude toward the content, and then they can selectively make their own feedback on the content, assigning a value to the label, and indicating their attitude and willingness on the SNS. The number under the label shows the opinion of the platform network democracy, and also affects the perceptual judgment of later users on the usability, ease of use and trust of the content. [6] Users' perceptual judgment of information in a social context will shift trust into a connected business context, thus affecting users' commercial intention on the platform. [7] In traditional e-commerce platforms, sales can directly indicate the user's commercial intention, while in the business behavior of SNS, the commercial intention of online public opinion is more reflected in the attention flow and interface participatory text discourse [8]. Therefore, hypothesis two is proposed:

H2: Participatory communication positively affects the commercial intention of platform users.

The interactive types of participatory communication are divided into general participation and deep participation according to the degree. Different degrees of participation have different effects on the efficiency of the attention economy. Simple actions such as browsing do not bring about commercial intention, while deeply engaged forms of interaction are directly related to social commerce intention [9]. In the current use of the labels, the basic operation of "Like" needs only one step, which belongs to the type of general participation; "Forward" can lead to external links and it requires at least two steps and belongs to the medium participation type. "Comment" (or "reply to comment") requires subjective content to be typed under the content, which is a deep engagement type. Since there are few studies in the previous literature on the classification of behaviors and the consequences of behaviors in this study case, this study tries to explore the following hypotheses:

H3: Different degrees of participation have different effects on communication results.

Based on the above assumptions, a research model of the influence of participatory communication on the economic efficiency of attention in the platform economy is proposed. The theoretical model is shown in Fig. 1.

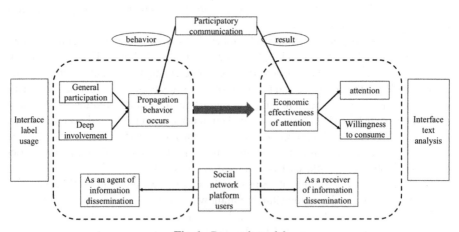

Fig. 1. Research model

3   Research Design and Method

3.1   Variable Selection

The Impact Indicators of the Results of Participatory Communication on the Effectiveness of Attention Economic

The various types of notes published on Xiaohongshu can be divided into original content and forwarded content according to audience participation or not. Original notes are close to the information source and are not re-edited by others in the interface display, which is considered to be of high reliability, timeliness and high perceived content value in traditional research [10]. However, from the perspective of participatory communication, forwarding other people's notes has been screened by "human-computer-human" and is a product of interactive behavior, containing other people's democratic opinions, which marking significance for examining the behavioral results of participatory communication. Therefore, in terms of the selection of published content, this study takes the original contents on Xiaohongshu and the forwarded contents as the control group.

In terms of the economic efficiency of the behavior results, this study takes two dimensions in account: "attention" and "consumption intention". Based on the text under the various labels on the SNS interface, we declare one type of text which shows the number of how many people click the labels "Like", "Comment", and "Forward", indicate the attention of the content, that is, the flow heat; Another type of text is the content in the "Comments", which is crawled according to the keywords that reflect the consumption intention, including "buy", "link", "want", "address", "orange software", "shop", "search" and "find", indicating the consumption intention caused by the content, and its intensity is calculated according to the frequency of occurrence in the study.

The Impact Indicators of Users' Participation on Communication Behavior Decision-Making

According to the complexity of user interface operation, this study takes the usage of "Like" label as the behavioral representation of general degree participation, and "Comment" as the behavioral representation of deep degree participation.

Based on the two basic participation mode, the use of "Forward" label is selected as a representation of the propagation behavior of the published content.

By analyzing the relationship between "Likes" and "Forward" and the one between "Comment" and "Forward", this study attempts to establish the correlation between behaviors with different degrees of participation level and users' spontaneous decision-making behavior of communication (propagation), in response to hypothesis 3.

3.2 Data Collection and Analysis Method

During the period from January 8, 2023 to January 20, 2023, the shopping sharing module of Xiaohongshu (v.7.91.0.f7914f8) is selected as the research scope:

With "Xiaomi Technology" and "Huawei Technology" as the categories, and hot keywords as the coding content, we collected the original note content and forwarded note content, as a total of 500 pages. The number of "Like", "Comment" and "Forward" in the interface of original note content and forwarded note content under the same code were counted respectively; By the way of text extraction, the number of articles containing consumption intention in the "Comment" text is calculated.

A total of 100 pages of hot topic content are selected, that is, the top three forwarded content, the top three commented content and the top three liked content of the whole platform. The number of "Like", "Comment" and "Forward" under these contents interface is counted to analyze the relationship between the three labels' usage. In this study, Eviews11 is used for data analysis.

4 Data Analysis Conclusion

4.1 Descriptive Statistical Analysis on the Impact of Different Participation Modes to Economic Effectiveness

According to the platform diversion recommendation method, under the flow permission allocation rules of Xiaohongshu, the published content will have 200–500 initial views after the first recommendation by the algorithm. Thereafter, under general circumstances, if the content can reach more than 5,000 plays (views), more than 100 likes and more than 10 comments within 1 h of publication, the platform algorithm will make more recommendations.

From Table 1 and Table 2, as long as the likes data of the posted content is above 100, the platform will carry out multiple rounds of recommendation (background propagation). From the shopping sharing contents of the two selected cell phone technology brands:

On the "Like" data, the original notes of "China Huawei" and the forwarded notes received the most attention, reaching 380,000 and 91,000 times;

In the "Forward" data, the highest number of entries coded as "shiny Xiaomi" in the original notes was 26,000, and the highest number of entries coded as "Huawei brand" in the forwarded notes was 26,000. The highest number of forward, 31,000, was for "Huawei Brand";

Table 1. Descriptive statistics of original notes of Xiaomi Technology and Huawei Technology

	category	code	like	comment	forward	consumption intention
Content basic attribute	Xiaomi Technology	Who is Xiaomi?	146	33	33	11
		Xiaomi mobile phone	65000	39	12000	9
		Xiaomi 10S	10000	73	3887	18
		Xiaomi you don't know about	36000	1076	7511	433
		Shiny Xiaomi	110000	1286	26000	419
		Xiaomi TV	8435	75	2128	21
	Huawei Technology	Huawei Technology	26000	729	6568	563
		Huawei mobile phone	19000	420	1273	311
		Huawei brand	44000	1326	13000	894
		Huawei TV	28000	292	17000	215
		Huawei Mate40	34000	803	12000	711
		Huawei of China	380000	616	19000	487
		Kirin chip	73000	678	16000	18

On "Comment", the entry with the code "Huawei brand" in the original notes received 1,326 data, and the entry with the code "Xiaomi TV" in the forwarded notes received 1,419 data. The highest number of comments was 1419.

In the publishing interface of original notes and forwarded notes, the highest coded content in the comment text of ordinary users reflecting the consumption intention is "Huawei brand".

This suggests that, with the exception of the use of the "Like" label, forwarded notes receives more attention than original notes under the high propagation outcome entries. This finding partially supports Hypothesis 1, but the exceptions regarding the use of the " Like " label need to be further analyzed in conjunction with the classification of the ease of use of the interface label.

Table 2. Highest descriptive statistics of forwarded notes by Xiaomi Technology and Huawei Technology

	category	code	like	comment	forward	consumption intention
Content basic attribute	Xiaomi Technology	Who is Xiaomi?	4626	130	899	57
		Xiaomi mobile phone	15000	361	5667	73
		Xiaomi 10S	700	117	260	109
		Xiaomi you don't know about	1878	86	690	214
		Shiny Xiaomi	5653	97	3824	33
		Xiaomi TV	19000	1419	9306	349
	Huawei Technology	Huawei Technology	3954	678	1271	511
		Huawei mobile phone	27000	843	6535	675
		Huawei brand	56000	813	31000	463
		Huawei TV	12000	319	4146	237
		Huawei Mate40	24000	556	10000	339
		Huawei of China	91000	1056	24000	581
		Kirin chip	1404	42	591	3

The relationship between the number of comments reflecting consumption intention and the overall number of comments, likes, and forwards in the comment text was analyzed using Eviews11, and the results are as follows:

Table 3. Analysis of the relationship between "Like", "Comment" and "Forward" in the original note interface of "Xiaomi Technology" and "Huawei Technology" and consumption intention in the comment text

	like	comment	forward	Consumption intention
like	1.00(0.00)			
comment	0.200(0.513)	1.00(0.00)		
forward	0.565(0.044)	0.552(0.05)	1.00(0.00)	
consumption intention	0.212(0.487)	0.797(0.000)	0.312(0.300)	1.00

As shown in Table 3, the results of the univariate linear regression analysis of "Like", "Comment", " Forward" and "consumption intention" in the original content interface of "Xiaomi Technology" and "Huawei Technology" categories show that "Like" and "Forward" are related to "consumption intention". The results of the one-way linear regression analysis of " like", "comment", "forward" and consumption intention data in the text of comments show that "like" and "forward" do not show a significant relationship with consumption intention. This means that the number of users with consumption intention does not increase or decrease as the number of likes or forwards increases or decreases.

Table 4. Analysis of the relationship between "like", "comment", "forward" in the interface of forwarded notes under "Xiaomi Technology" and "Huawei Technology" and consumption intention in the comment text

	like	comment	forward	consumption intention
like	1.00(0.00)			
comment	0.632(0.021)	1.00(0.00)		
forward	0.900(0.000)	0.609(0.027)	1.00(0.00)	
consumption intention	0.639(0.019)	0.769(0.002)	0.552(0.050)	1.00

As can be seen from Table 4, there is a significant positive relationship between all four of the likes, comments, forwards and consumption intentions of the average user in terms of the use of interface labels under the forwarded notes content. That is, ordinary users have higher perceived trust in content processed, approved, and disseminated by others, and show higher willingness to consume. As the consumption intention increases, the use of other labels also increases. This finding significantly supports hypothesis two, that the results of participatory communication positively influence the consumption intention of the new reading audience, shown here by the higher acceptance of users who retweet others' note content than original note content.

4.2 Descriptive Statistical Analysis of the Influence of Different Participation Levels on Communication Behavior Decision-Making

Table 5. Descriptive statistics of label usage in different notes

index	Content topic	Publisher of works	Number of likes	Number of forwarding	Number of comments
Top three forward	other	Piggy girls love digging for treasure	305507	307004	422
	Beauty care	One pepper	285384	215009	1262
	Mother and child care	The evaluation library of Yuanbao mother	170213	125007	832
Top three comment	other	Slum girl	108170	6380	9727
	delicious food	I'm ZI Xiao Jing	25397	13447	9085
	delicious food	Senior evaluation	71197	19238	8994
Top three like	message	Xiaoyi doesn't like drawing	510030	29044	2014
	Hobbies and interests	One bowl is full	451123	105032	6027
	live	Yu Shuxin Esther	331049	21274	8390

The correlation analysis of the above data is as follows (Table 5):

Table 6. Correlation analysis of likes, comments and forwards

	like	comment	forward
like	1.00(0.00)		
comment	0.561(0.00)	1.00(0.00)	
forward	0.381(0.00)	0.046(0.305)	1.00(0.00)

From Table 6, it can be seen that in the correlation analysis between likes, comments and forwards, $p = 0.00$ for likes and comments, and $p = 0.00$ for likes and forwards, indicating that there is a positive correlation between likes and comments and likes and forwards, i.e., indicating that the more likes data, the more comments and forwards data will increase accordingly; while p = 0.305 for forwards and comments, > 0.05, therefore, indicating that there is no significant correlation between the two, i.e., forwarding does not increase or decrease correspondingly to the increase or decrease of comment data.

The analysis of variance for the above data is as follows:

Table 7. Orthogonal distribution test

Variable name	median	average value	Standard deviation	skewness	kurtosis	S-W test	K-S test
like	35809	54144.33	53275.277	3.943	21.376	0.566(0.000)	0.274(0.000)
forward	9103	15724.34	23302.761	6.192	60.974	0.534(0.000)	0.256(0.000)
comment	514.5	988.86	1365.1	3.649	16.854	0.6(0.000)	0.242(0.000)

Note: ***, ** and * represent significance levels of 1%, 5% and 10% respectively

The above Table 7 shows the results of descriptive statistics and normality tests for the quantitative variables likes, forwards and comments, including median and mean, which are used to test the normality of the data. There are usually two tests for normal distribution, one is the Shapiro-Wilk test, which is applied to small sample data (sample size $\leq$ 5000), and the other is the Kolmogorov-Smirnov test, which is applied to large sample data (sample size > 5000). If it presents significance (P < 0.05), it means that the original hypothesis is rejected (the data meets the normal distribution) and the data does not satisfy the normal distribution, and vice versa. It is usually difficult to meet the test in realistic research situations. If the absolute value of its sample kurtosis is less than 10 and the absolute value of skewness is less than 3, combined with the histogram of normal distribution, PP chart or QQ chart can be described as basically meeting the normal distribution (Fig. 2).

The results of the mean analysis of the values of each variable on likes resulted in a p-value of $0.008 \leq 0.05$, therefore the statistical result is significant, indicating that there is a significant difference between the note classifications with different contents on likes; the results of the mean analysis on forwards resulted in a p-value of 0.204 > 0.05, therefore the statistical result is not significant, indicating that there is no significant difference between the note classifications with different notes on forwards; the results of the mean analysis on comments resulted in a p-value of 0.878 > 0.05, so the statistical result is not significant, indicating that there is no significant difference between different note classifications on comments (Tables 8, 9 and 10).

Table 8. Analysis of variance results

Variable name	Variable value	Sample size	average value	Standard deviation	F	P
like	Mother and child care	40	58566.35	53119.713	1.907	0.008***
	Hobbies and interests	33	59338.606	78479.642		
	other	61	69004.262	67986.446		
	live	32	76569.25	75205.644		
	delicious food	86	48644.349	36832.387		
	message	3	190523.667	276769.707		
	Home decoration	20	51626.5	48227.194		
	Beauty care	28	56063.679	57604.605		
	Science and technology Internet	27	45289.63	35618.269		
	Film and television comprehensive	23	45902.217	25905.473		
	Beauty makeup	43	46361.163	28011.986		
	Means of transportation	1	42167	0.000		
	Cute pet	33	50513.212	30214.859		
	Health maintenance	11	31981.636	5272.07		
	Health regimen	9	35935.889	9572.403		
	workplace	8	46394.25	21547.275		
	Dress up	20	39763.3	29669.782		
	Popularization of science	2	27029.5	2.121		
	education	3	57347	44023.01		
	Shoe bag fashion play	8	36075.25	20436.937		
	Exercise and fitness	4	43111.75	17350.957		
	Emotions and signs	3	46730	11963.144		

(*continued*)

Table 8. (*continued*)

Variable name	Variable value	Sample size	average value	Standard deviation	F	P
	marriage	2	52189.5	28137.9		
	total	500	54144.33	53275.277		
forward	Mother and child care	40	22739.9	26922.044	1.246	0.204
	Hobbies and interests	33	18282.182	25608.187		
	other	61	19101.82	40935.798		
	live	32	9821.875	10232.824		
	delicious food	86	12893.907	14330.56		
	message	3	18332.667	10210.621		
	Home decoration	20	16918.85	15876.823		
	Beauty care	28	26841.929	43184.112		
	Science and technology Internet	27	10040.778	8536.061		
	Film and television comprehensive	23	10347.957	12056.754		
	Beauty makeup	43	15745.814	15362.86		
	Means of transportation	1	13040	0.000		
	Cute pet	33	12570.242	12648.346		
	Health maintenance	11	15857.273	14470.627		
	Photography and shooting	9	15619.222	15618.089		
	workplace	8	29832.5	20573.515		
	Dress up	20	7432.8	5544.147		
	Popularization of science	2	1503	140.007		
	education	3	18873	10019.251		
	Shoe bag fashion play	8	10721	10815.779		

(*continued*)

Table 8. (*continued*)

Variable name	Variable value	Sample size	average value	Standard deviation	F	P
	Exercise and fitness	4	28751	23222.719		
	Emotions and signs	3	4899.667	4512.591		
	marriage	2	12239.5	316.077		
	total	500	15724.34	23302.761		
comment	Mother and child care	40	911.575	1149.757	0.66	0.878
	Hobbies and interests	33	1091	1345.592		
	other	61	1188.656	1678.869		
	live	32	1253.062	1537.127		
	delicious food	86	1098.593	1636.556		
	message	3	1366.667	1100.495		
	Home decoration	20	688.05	616.415		
	Beauty care	28	609.036	515.956		
	Science and technology Internet	27	1038.778	1478.416		
	Film and television comprehensive	23	971.913	1142.292		
	Beauty makeup	43	723.395	749.109		
	Means of transportation	1	885	0.000		
	Cute pet	33	976.394	1011.459		
	health regimen	11	947.091	1601.791		
	Photography and shooting	9	646.111	676.66		
	workplace	8	555.625	416.031		
	Dress up	20	1369.8	2272.603		
	Popularization of science	2	98.5	45.962		
	education	3	316.667	280.963		

(*continued*)

Table 8. (*continued*)

Variable name	Variable value	Sample size	average value	Standard deviation	F	P
	Shoe bag fashion play	8	981.375	2020.77		
	Exercise and fitness	4	529.75	357.285		
	Emotions and signs	3	685.667	571.238		
	marriage	2	2052	2402.749		
	total	500	988.86	1365.1		

Note: ***, ** and * represent significance levels of 1%, 5% and 10% respectively

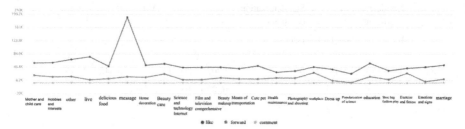

Fig. 2. Graph of ANOVA results

Table 9. Quantitative Analysis of Effectiveness Table

Analysis item	Difference between groups	Total deviation	Partial Eta squared (Partial η^2)	Cohen's f number
like	114502973648.49	1416289324320.55	0.081	0.297
forward	14723292678.545	270966327682.2	0.054	0.24
comment	27486173.461	929885748.2	0.03	0.175

The results of the quantitative analysis of effects showed that the Eta-square (η^2 value) based on likes was 0.081, indicating that 8.1% of the variation in the data was due to differences between groups. Cohen's f value was 0.297, indicating a moderate degree of variation in the quantitative effects of the data.

The results of the effect quantification analysis showed an Eta-square (η^2 value) of 0.054 based on forwarding, indicating that 5.4% of the variation in the data was derived from differences between groups. The Cohen's f value was 0.24, indicating that the degree of variation in the effect quantification of the data was a small degree of variation.

The results of the quantitative analysis of effects showed that based on the comments, the Eta-square (η^2 value) was 0.03, indicating that 3.0% of the variation in the data was from differences between groups. The Cohen's f value was 0.175, indicating that the degree of variation in the quantification of effects of the data was a small degree of variation.

Data regression analysis of labels used under different note content.

Table 10. Regression analysis

Linear regression analysis results n = 500									
	Nonnormalized coefficient		Standardization coefficient	t	P	VIF	R^2	Adjust R^2	F
	B	Standard error	Beta						
constant	3976.313	1241.972	0	3.202	0.001	-	0.348	0.345	F = 132.446, P = 0.000
like	0.278	0.017	0.636	16.226	0.000	1.169			
comment	-3.343	0.669	-0.196	-5	0.000	1.169			

Dependent variable: forward

Note: ***, ** and * represent significance levels of 1%, 5% and 10% respectively

From the analysis of the results of the F-test, it can be obtained that the significance P-value is 0.000 and the level presents significance, rejecting the original hypothesis that the regression coefficient is 0. For the performance of variable co-linearity, VIF is all less than 10, so the model has no problem of multiple co-linearity and the model is well constructed. The equation of the model is as follows (Fig. 3):

y = 3976.313 + 0.278* Likes - 3.343* Comments.

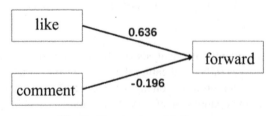

Fig. 3. Structural model diagram

From the above analysis, it can be seen that the general interactive behavior of "like" can positively influence the platform users as content producers to forward the content they are browsing and sharing, i.e., when an ordinary user is the initiator of the behavior, when he "likes" the content he is browsing, it will increase the possibility of the user to forward the content, i.e., it will influence the behavior decision of secondary dissemination of the content; while the interactive behavior of "comment", which is a deep involvement, negatively influences the occurrence of the forwarding behavior, i.e., when a user comments on the content he is browsing, it will cause the user to reduce the possibility of the decision of secondary dissemination of the content he is browsing.

Second, from the correlation analysis, comments do not show significant correlation to forwards, i.e., it shows that there is no correlation between comments and forwarding by ordinary users, which also confirms with the results obtained from the aforementioned regression analysis.

Furthermore, according to the data statistics under the same attribute, ordinary users do not care whether the content is original or not when they read the content shared by shopping, but only like, comment and forward accordingly according to their interest in the content, i.e., the originality of the content of the notes has no significant relationship with the behavior decision of ordinary users as the initiator of communication for secondary communication.

This leads to the conclusion based on hypothesis three: the interaction behavior of general level involvement positively influences the behavioral decision of the information audience to secondary communication as an active agent; the interaction behavior of deep level involvement negatively influences this behavioral decision; the originality of the content is not significantly correlated with the behavioral decision of the information audience to secondary communication.

5   Conclusion

5.1   Key Findings and Contributions

In the context of the development of platform economy, this study attempts to explore the performance of the impact of the change in the communication mode of commercial information on the attention economy. The study divides commercial information communication methods on social network platforms into traditional communication methods and participatory communication methods. The former focuses on one-way, linear communication paths such as B to C point-to-point; while the latter attaches importance to user participation, including the attention and democratic opinions of information audiences, making them participate in the process of information reproduction and re-dissemination.

This study takes the shopping sharing content of the SNS Xiaohongshu as the object, and divides the shopping sharing content into content attributes with a low level of participation (originality in posting notes) and content attributes with a high level of mass participation (forwarding the content of others' notes) from the perspective of information sources, and compares the data indications under various types of labels on the pages of both. The degree of attention received is used as the flow heat indicator of this content, and the frequency of consumption intention keywords in the comment text is used as the effectiveness conversion indicator of this commercial content. It is thus concluded that:

Commercial information sources with a higher level of mass engagement receive more flow heat and perform better in the effectiveness conversion of their attention economy.

This study also classifies the specific behavioral patterns of participatory communication into general and deep engagement based on the use of interface labels in SNS, and examines how different levels of engagement with visible information in platform interaction behaviors affect users' decision-making behavior to make secondary communication. General participation behavior positively influences users to make specific decisions for secondary communication, while deep participation does not. The originality of the information source does not have a significant correlation on users' decision-making behavior for secondary communication.

On the other hand, it also shows that the ease of use of the interface will increase the audience's active participation in information transmission as a self-communicator, rather than just the trust of the content, which is important in traditional communication methods.

5.2   Implications and Further Discussion

In the era of social media, which places more and more emphasis on user experience, the traditional point-to-point communication method is gradually losing its effectiveness. The interactive behaviors of users in social networking platforms have contributed to the formation of new communication methods and greatly increased the economic benefits of information dissemination.

Based on the findings of this study, the development of the platform economy, with the goal of further improving effectiveness conversion, should pay attention to the paths and methods of mass participation in communication, especially to the perceived ease of use of platform interface labels and message credibility acceptance by ordinary users of SNS as audiences. This study will also continue to refine the relationship between interface label ease of use and communication action decisions in order to establish specific factors in terms of platform users' participation in communication behaviors and transformation of platform attention indications.

In addition, this study sheds great light on the production-consumption theory [11] (or audience labor theory) [12] when focusing on the identity transformation of platform users, i.e., as information receivers (acceptance of mass participation in communication outcomes) and as information producers (participation in mass communication behaviors). The theory argues for the involvement of SNS in participatory communication behaviors and promotion results from a motivational perspective, and takes advantage of the high credibility of the masses to the content of participatory communication results to further strengthen the promotion logic of the algorithm with a view to obtaining higher economic benefits of the platform.

In the case of this study, the rules of the Xiaohongshu indicate that the platform will give the original content provider a share of the promotion revenue if the original content publisher's promotion brings economic benefits within the platform site; while there is no relevant share of promotion revenue for the economic benefits brought by the forwarded content publishers. Ordinary users participate in the dissemination of commercial information, as long as the attention of the forwarded content (such as the number of likes, comments, forwards number) has always existed in increments, the platform will obtain the attention of economic revenue increasing accordingly, while not having to pay revenue share to the publisher. In this process, the publishers who edit the content to participate in the production, as well as the ordinary users who use the hashtag to participate in the interaction of the page are creating commercial value for the platform for free.

This theoretical hypothesis attempts to reveal the behavioral motivations behind the black box of platform algorithms, but there is a lack of research on the mechanism between audience behavior and actors' psychological motivation of "participatory communication". This study will continue to explore this aspect.

Fund Sources. This Work is Supported by Beijing Social Science Foundation Project (Youth Program, no. 22ZXC007)

References

1. Parker, G.G., Van Alstyne, M.W. and Choudary, S.P.: Platform Revolution: How Networked Markets Are Transforming the Economy—and How to Make Them Work for You. Illustrated Edition. W. W. Norton & Company (2016)
2. Chitnis, K.: The duality of development: recasting participatory communication for development-using structuration theory. Investig. Desarrollo. **13**(2), 228–429 (2005)
3. Seivaes, J., Jacobson, T.L., White, S.A.: Participatory Communication for Social Change. Sage Publications Thousand Oaks (1996)
4. Mefelopulos, P.: Theory and Practice of Participatory Communication. The case of the FAO Project (2003)
5. Peng, D.: Communities, scenes, emotions: group participation and e-commerce development in short video platforms. J. Res. **1**, 86–124 (2022)
6. Mcknight, D.H., Choudhury, V., Kacmar, C.: Developing and validating trust measures for e-commerce: an integrative typology. Inf. Syst. Res. **13**(3), 334–359 (2002)
7. Baozhou, L., Fan, W., Zhou, M.: Social presence, trust, and social commerce purchase intention: an empirical research. Comput. Hum. Behav. **56**, 225–237 (2016)
8. Hajli, M.N.: The role of social support on relationship quality and social commerce. Technol. Forecast. Soc. Change **87**, 17–27 (2014)
9. Hornga, S.M., Wu, C.H.: How behaviors on social network sites and online social capital influence social commerce intentions. Inform. Manage. **57** (2020)
10. Grazioli, S., Jarvenpaa, S.L.: Perils of internet fraud: an empirical investigation of deception and trust with experienced internet consumers. IEEE Trans. Syst. Man, Cybern. -Part A: Syst. Humans **30**(4), 395–410 (2000)
11. Hughes, K.: 'Work/place' media: locating laboring audiences. Media Cult. Soc. **36**(5), 644–660 (2014)
12. Caraway, B.: Audience labor in the new media environment: a Marxian revisiting of the audience commodity. Media Cult. Soc. **33**(5), 693–708 (2011)

Designing a Pinyin-Based Keyboard Based on the Frequency of Pinyin of Chinese Characters

Chunyan Wang[1]([✉]), Xiaojun Yuan[2], and Xiaoxin Xiao[3]

[1] Xiangqingmei Co., Ltd, Hangzhou 31000, Zhejiang, China
ahwangchunyan@126.com
[2] University at Albany, State University of New York, Albany, NY 12222, USA
xyuan@albany.edu
[3] Longcheng High School, Shenzhen 518100, Guangdong, China

Abstract. The existing Chinese Pinyin keyboard does not accurately reflect the features of Pinyin. By investigating the frequency of Pinyin letters, we have designed a keyboard layout that incorporates all the distinctive elements of Pinyin, including Chinese special two-letter initials, two- or three-letter finals, and tones. Firstly, we propose dividing the letter area of the keyboard into two parts, with initials on the left and finals on the right, arranged according to their spelling order. Secondly, we list the high-frequency or core letters in the middle, with the less-frequency or assisted letters scattered around them in a fan-like pattern. Thirdly, we group letters with the same root together, allowing for easy extension on desktops and convenient folding on laptops and virtual screens. The arrangement of tone keys, based on the size of keyboards, is flexible. With this layout, the most frequently-used Pinyin can be typed within 2 to 3 keystrokes.

Keywords: Pinyin-based Keyboard · Pinyin · frequency · initials and finals

1 Introduction

It has been pointed out that after analyzing 16 language versions of Apple Magic keyboard, it was found that all languages except ZH (Chinese) have their respective language letters protected on the keyboard [1]. Moreover, out of 5,075 keyboards available in China, only 4 of them are Chinese keyboards [1]. This lack of convenience for Chinese users and insufficient protection of Chinese culture are not beneficial [1].

To analyze letters of pinyin, Xiru Ermu Zi (1626) [2] (short for Xiru) is a valuable book to refer to. It is recorded as a famous Latin-Chinese and Chinese-Latin dictionary. It says that I (《易》) (including yin and yang symbols), drawn by Fuxi (an ancient Chinese leader), was treated as "the root of Chinese characters" [2]. "Ming Dynasty (about 1300s-1600s) was the mother country of all characters in the world" [2]. So Xiru uses *yin* and *yang* theories to divide the pronunciations into two parts: those sounded by themselves are self-sounds (finals), those, only be sounded with others are co-sounds (initials) [2]. In 1950s, many of the Latin symbols of Chinese characters in this book were adopted

M. Kurosu et al. (Eds.): HCII 2023, LNCS 14054, pp. 604–618, 2023.
https://doi.org/10.1007/978-3-031-48038-6_39

directly by modern Chinese pinyin [3]. Therefore, we apply the yin and yang theories in pinyin letter groups.

In this paper, pinyin is firstly separated as initials (*yang*) and finals (*yin*). Second, initials are mainly voiced (*yang*) and voiceless (*yin*). Third, finals are generally "i" (*yang*) and "a" (*yin*) centered.

2 Frequency of Initials and Finals

We will first list the frequency of initials and finals based on 4 levels of Chinese characters, then separate them into different groups to cater for different applications.

Three of those data are basic character lists of Chinese curriculum standard for compulsory education required by the Ministry of Education of China [4]. There are 300 basic characters in Level 1 (L1) (page 66–69), 2500 common characters in Level 2 (L2) (page 70–92), and 1000 characters in Level 3 (L3) (page 93–102).

Besides, we have compared the data of 2011 version [5] with that of 2022 version, and found only characters in L1 change. L2 and L3 are rather stable. Since this minor modification of L1 do not influence the design of our pinyin layout, so we focus on 2022 version in this paper.

To make our potential design more flexible, we also analyze 13,180 characters from Xinhua Dictionary of the 12th version [6], which is very popular in China.

The first step is to convert the pinyin for each character. Certain tools, such as Pypinyin, can be helpful in this process. Next, the pinyin is separated into initials, finals, and tones. There are 23 initials, plus 1 zero intial. The zero initial refers to cases where the pinyin actually begins with "a", "o", or "e" finals. These initials cannot be ignored because they may be considered part of the preceding final. For example, let's take the word "Xian". It can be represented as one pinyin with the initial "x" and final "ian", or as two separate pinyin "xi" and "an" to refer to "西安" (the city of Xi'an). To distinguish between these cases, a special apostrophe "'" is arbitrarily used [3]. To clarify this distinction, we label these pinyin as zero initials.

Generally speaking, single-letter initials in Chinese resemble English consonants, but their frequencies differ. Additionally, two-letter initials like "zh," "ch," and "sh" do not exist in English, while "v" does not exist in Mandarin Chinese. Therefore, it is necessary to reorganize the Chinese initials.

2.1 Frequency of Initials

After obtaining the sum of each initial within the four levels, we can calculate their respective percentages within each level. Then, the percentage of the first three levels is averaged as A1 = Round((L1 + L2 + L3)/3,2), two digits are kept; the percentage of four levels is averaged as A2 = Round((L1 + L2 + L3 + L4)/4,2), also two digits are kept. Percentages above 6% are labeled as group 1(G1), those 5% to 6% as G2, 4% to 5% as G3, 3%-4% as G4, 2% to 3% as G5, 1% to 2% as G6. The frequency of initials of A1 and A2 is as follows (see Fig. 1).

From the data, it can be seen that most initials stay in their groups except five ("t, sh, q, s, p"), which only fluctuate within the range of neighboring groups.

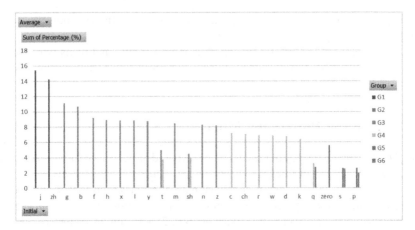

Fig. 1. Frequency of Initials

The high frequently-used initials are "j" and "zh." Currently, we are unable to type "zh" with a single keystroke, instead, we need to input "z" followed by "h". "Z" at the end of G3, however, lags far behind "zh." The same with "sh" in G3 or G4 and "s" in G5 or G6. Letter "s", among the top 3 in English, is not active in Chinese. A more detailed comparison between "zh, ch, sh" and "z, c, s" is shown below (see Fig. 2).

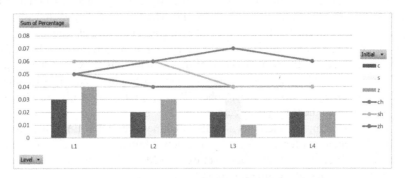

Fig. 2. Percentage of "zh, ch, sh" and "z, c, s"

At first glance, the lines representing the percentages of "zh, ch, sh" are consistently higher than the percentages of "z, c, s" throughout the column. To compare the line and the column with the same color, for example, the green line "zh" and the green column "z", the gap becomes larger from 0.01 to 0.06. If only one of "zh" and "z" could be listed on a Chinese keyboard, "zh" would be more preferable to "z".

Initials "g" and "b" are as active as their English counterparts. Initials "q" and "p", unactive as English "q" and "p", scatter at the corners in Chinese.

An interesting finding is the letter "n". The letter "n" is not particularly prominent when used as an initial in Chinese. However, on an English-based keyboard, the "n" key is often one of the most commonly worn keys. Since English does not have two- or three-letter finals, the letter "n" is frequently borrowed to combine with vowels and/or "g" to form compound finals such as "an," "ang," "en," "eng," "in," "ing," "ong," and others. These compound finals are considered as a single pronunciation.

2.2 Frequency of Finals

Scheme for the Chinese Phonetic Alphabet (《汉语拼音方案》) lays down the rule for technical communication. It prescribes that Chinese finals are 35 + 2 ("er, ê" not in the Final table, but listed as the second and third note): "i, u, ü, a, ia, ua, o, uo, e, ie, üe, ai, uai, ei, uei(ui), ao, iao, ou, iou(iu), an, ian, uan, üan, en, in, uen(un), ün, ang, iang, uang, eng, ing, ueng, ong, iong" [3].

One-Letter Finals

In practice, Pinyin in grade-one Chinese textbook of compulsory education in China reflects the state-of-art of final category [7]. Six one-letter finals (short for 1F) "a, o, e, i, u, ü" are taught first, initials following, then 18 two-or-three finals are learned in groups of three to five.

The letter "ü" (green column) is not an English letter and is not present on an English keyboard. It is not readily available for typing. It is, in fact, more active than "o" (grey column) as a pinyin letter (see Fig. 3).

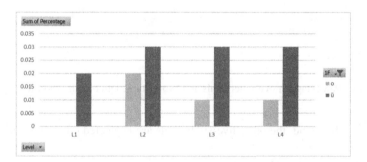

Fig. 3. Percentage of "o" and "ü"

The grey column in level 1 does not appear because the percentage is too small to be shown. It can be seen clear that the lengths of green columns are often twice those of grey columns. The letter "ü" at present can be typed by inserting as a symbol.

Besides, the six finals are not positioned equally (see Fig. 4). Letter "i" (red column) and "u" (yellow column) stands higher than others. Letter "a" (orange column) and "e" (blue column) in the middle. Letter "o" and "ü" lag behind.

One-letter finals are the foundation of Chinese pinyin. The data show that these 6 stand-alone finals out of 37 finals consistently occupy one-third or so in 4 levels (see Fig. 5).

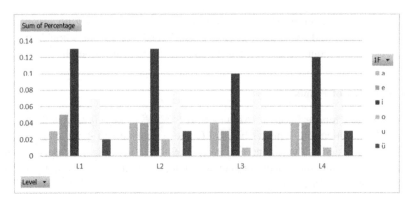

Fig. 4. Percentage of one-letter finals

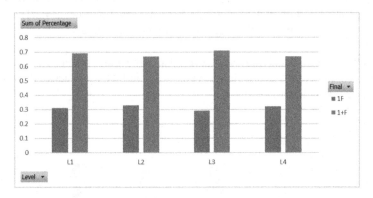

Fig. 5. Percentage of one-letter finals and two-or-three letter finals (short for 1 + F)

On the other hand, the other five-sixth finals are neglected on the present English-based keyboard.

Two-or-Three Letter Finals

The above-mentioned Chinese textbook packages the two-or-three finals based on their endings [7]. Specifically, "ai, ei, ui" share an "-i" ending, "ao, ou, iu" share an "-o" or "-u" ending, "ie, üe, er (not in the Final table)" share an "-e" ending, "an, en, in, un, ün" share an "-n" ending, and "ang, eng, ing, ong" share an "-ng" ending. That means these 18 finals are also regarded as one pronunciation. They can be and should be covered in a ZH keyboard design.

The rest 12 are combined by 1F and 1 + F. Three of the finals from the first level (1F) are selected for further analysis or connection. The highest in frequency "-i-" leads in "ia, iao, ian, iang, iong", second-highest "-u-" leads in "ua, uo, uai, uan, uang, ueng". Only "üan" begins with "-ü-". These combinations will not be included in our future keyboard.

2.3 Tones

Even though pinyin is divided into initials and finals, there is still a problem to solve – homophones. Most homophones can be solved by typing two characters' pinyin as a fixed phrase. Take "ji" as an example, there are 38 characters in L2, 196 characters in L4. If one enters "jiji", there are 29 2-character words for one to choose. Tones are another effective method to decrease the homophones [2]. After all, Chinese is called as a tone language.

There are five tones in pinyin [3], which are indicated by tone marks placed above the finals. Currently, the tone marks can be inserted as symbols [1]. However, the fifth tone is similar to the original finals and there is limited space to display it. Therefore, we aim to include the first four tones on the keyboard for ease of use.

3   Pinyin-Based Chinese keyboard

With 23 initials, 24 finals, and 4 tones, we plan to separate them into three blocks. The initials, left in the pinyin, is in the left part on the keyboard; the finals, in the right part. The tones can be flexible in position depending on the applications.

3.1 Complementary Relationships

To strike a balance between the number of keys and convenience of actions, it is important to examine the relationships between letters. One such relationship is complementary relationships.

Letter "w/u" and "y/i" – Same letters in Complementary Positions
The Scheme prescribes that "u" is replaced with or attached to "w" in the beginning of a pinyin to act as an initial [3]. That means "w" is "u" in different spelling. To save space on the mobile phone, they can be merged into the same key as "w/u." One exception is pinyin "wu", with "w" added to "u". This problem can be resolved by implementing a double-click mechanism.

The letter "i" is replaced with or attached to "y" as an initial [3]. The difference is in that letter "y" is not always equal to "i", however, it is possibly another "ü" in front of "ü". Nevertheless, "i" is never used at that place, so "i" and "y" are also complementary. They can also be on the same key as "y/i." An exception of "yi" can be realized by a double-click mechanism.

Letter "j/zh", "q/ch" and "x/sh" – Different Letters in Complementary Positions
The letters "j" and "zh", "q" and "ch", "x" and "sh" are complementary in that each letter in every pair is followed by different but complementary finals. We group the finals into 6 groups based on their first letter of every final in the following table (Table 1.).

It is clear that the beginning of every final is exactly one of the six one-letter finals. Letters "j, q, x" are followed by "-i" and "-ü" finals. Meanwhile, letters "zh, ch, sh" are followed by "-a, -e, -o, -u" finals except for "zhi", "chi" and "shi". These three are taken as a whole as the letters' pronunciations of "zh", "ch" and "sh" [3]. Certainly, it will

Table 1. Finals following Letters "j/zh", "q/ch", and "x/sh"

	-a	-e	-i	-o	-u	-ü
j			ji, jia, jian, jiang, jiao, jie, jin, jing, jiong, jiu			ju, juan, jue, jun ("ü" is rid of two points following "j", "q" and "x" [3])
zh	zha, zhai, zhan, zhang, zhao	zhe, zhei, zhen, zheng	**zhi**	zhong, zhou	zhu, zhua, zhuai, zhuan, zhuang, zhui, zhun, zhuo	
q			qi, qia, qian, qiang, qiao, qie, qin, qing, qiong, qiu			qu, quan, que, qun
ch	cha, chai, chan, chang, chao	che, chen, cheng	**chi**	chong, chou	chu, chua, chuai, chuan, chuang, chui, chun, chuo	
x			xi, xia, xian, xiang, xiao, xie, xin, xing, xiong, xiu			xu, xuan, xue, xun
sh	sha, shai, shan, shang, shao	she, shei, shen, sheng	**shi**	shou	shu, shua, shuai, shuan, shuang, shui, shun, shuo	

raise new confusion of "ji" and "zhi", both of which cover many common characters. We can set the key "j/zh" followed by "i" defaulted as "j", "zh" is realized by a double-click mechanism.

To pair "j" with "zh", instead of "ch" or "sh", is the result of comparing Chinese dialects. In southern China, many people pronounce "zh" as "j", because there is no "zh" in the dialect. Perhaps these two letters are made by similar parts of tongue. So are "q" and "ch", "x" and "sh".

3.2 Historical Relationships

Pronunciation is constantly changing and influencing each other [8]. Japanese has borrowed traditional Chinese characters to mark the pronunciations of their letters in a matrix known as "Fifty Pronunciation Table" (The Japanese Table) [8]. When Japanese letters were created, they should be sounded the same as the Chinese character they adopted.

The Japanese Table consists of 10-consonant lines and 5-vowel columns. Every letter, ideally, should be sounded as the sum of consonant plus vowel. Chinese sounds, in practice, reflect the dynasties', especially the capitals' real pronunciations. During the last thousands of years, China migrated its capital from Xi'an (in the western part), to Kaifeng (in the eastern part), to Lin'an (in the southern part), to Beijing (in the northern part). The Japanese language often followed similar patterns but not always synchronously. By comparing the original pronunciations with the modern pronunciations of these letters, we can trace many historical changes.

Chinese pinyin is borrowed from Latin letters [3]. The evolution of Latin, in particular, English letter writing systems changing rules can also be helpful.

Letter "h" Gave Birth to "f", "p" and "b"

Japanese "ha-" line shows how "h" gradually changes into other sounds [8]. Japanese "ふ" in "h-" line is the Chinese character "不". To mark the sound /hu/, a combination of line /h/ and column /u/, Japanese "ふ" and Chinese "不" should share the same sound. Today, Japanese "ふ" is read as /fu/, and Chinese "不" is /bu/. Sound /h/, before /u/, gradually evolved into /f/, and then into /b/. Chinese still keeps /hu/ (orange column), but the numbers of characters are smaller than those of /fu/ (blue column) (see Fig. 6).

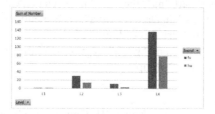

Fig. 6. The percentage of /hu/ and /fu/.

Japanese letters at first are all voiceless sounds. From 1392, Japanese began to use two small dots "ぶbu" as voiced sounds or a small circle "ぷpu" as half-voiced sounds [8]. In Chinese, the only difference of "b" and "p" is aspiration. Letters "h", "f", "b" and "p" are related to each other.

In English, "m" often goes with "b/p". If a word begins with "b/p", the last letter of the suffix is assimilated to "m". For example, "in", "en", "con" is supposed to be "im", "em", and "com" as in "impossible", "empower" and "complete".

Chinese pinyin list "b/p/m/f" as a group [3]. Therefore, we group "b/p/m/f" as "h-" led group.

Letter "r" and "n, l, t, d"

A Chinese character "日" can explain the relationship among "n, r, l". Japanese call their country "にほんNihon". In modern Chinese, "日ri" and "仁ren (Japanese character "に")" are begun with /r/. The traditional /n/, nowadays, gets the value /r/ before /i/. There seems an "r-" line in Japanese alphabet and their roman spellings are "らra, りri, るru, れre, ろro". Actually, the real values of these roman letters are /la, li, lu, le, lo/.

When letter "t" is said quickly and repeatedly, a vibrated /r/ sound will be gradually grasped. Letter "d" is voiced "t". Chinese pinyin list "d/t/n/l" as a group [3]. These five letters constitute "r-" group.

Letter "c" and "k, g, s, z"

Classical Latin "c" has only the value /k/ [9]. In old French, many /k/ sounds drifted to /ts/ and continued to evolve to /s/ [9]. To distinguish the sound, "c" began to represent /s/, (the word "ice" shows that), "k" referred to /k/ [9]. Today, the English letter "c" still has two main values: /s/ is preceding letters "i, e", as in "city, ceiling", while /k/ is preceding "a, o, u", like in "car, cook, cut."

"中国China" was famous as "华夏hua xia" or short for "华hua" for thousands of years. As of 1626, Chinese "华" still kept three pronunciations as "hoa, kua, fu"[10]. Today, only "hua" remains in Putonghua. In translation, the name of a country is usually transcribed literally according to the country's own pronunciation. The other countries, with the help of spelling letter, have recorded the evolution of "hua xia". Japanese lists "华" as "ka, ke, or hana" [11], "夏" as "ka, ge, naci (The first part is "na")" [11]. Once "华ka" and "夏ka" shared the same sound, they maybe differed in tones (without tones in Japanese, we can just guess). Later "华hana" has become China's name and "夏naci" has been a season's name (summer).

With the same second part "na", the first "ha" became "Ci" in Italian "Cina" [12], "Si" in Latin "Sina" [12], "Ki" in Danish "Kina". As is mentioned above, these different spellings "c/s/k" are just the varieties of Latin "c".

Chinese pinyin lists "z/c/s" and "g/k/h" as groups. With letter "h" discussed above, the rest of "z/s/g/k" makes "c-" group.

The Groups of Initials

The 23 initials can be grouped into 4 on a ZH (Chinese) keyboard (Table 2).

Table 2. The groups of initials on a ZH keyboard

Group	Letters
Group 1	c, k, g, s, z
Group 2	j, zh, q, ch, x, sh
Group 3	h, b, p, m, f
Group 4	r, d, t, n, l

The positions of every letter in these groups will be adjusted according to the size of the area of the applications.

3.3 Same Endings

Rhymes (finals with the same endings) are important in traditional Chinese because they are the critical factors to determine the tone of a poem (lyrics) or a play. In the times without recorders or dictionaries, rhymes in poems help to keep valuable ancient pronunciations [13].

Today, Chinese elementary school students still learn finals based on their endings [7]. We can adopt this method and adjust it to accommodate the keyboard layout.

Pinyin as "-i-" Focused

Modern Chinese pinyin typically ends with a vowel ("a," "o," "e," "i," "u," "ü") or a nasal ("n," "ng") (see Fig. 7). The frequencies of 6 endings (except for "-n," and "-i") stay stable in 4 levels. Endings "-n" (golden column) and "-i" (red column) exchange the first place constantly.

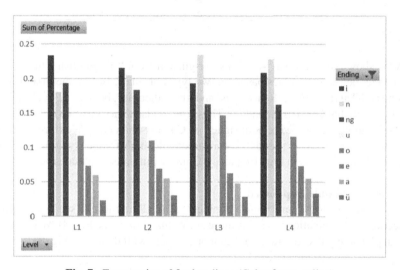

Fig. 7. Frequencies of final endings (Color figure online)

Endings "-n", "-i", "-ng" rank top 3. Letters "-n" (Japanese added "ん" in around 8c [8]) and "-ng" did not append to the vowel when the Japanese letters were created [8]. In the Japanese Table, Chinese word "安an" is Japanese "あa", "良liang" is Japanese " らra".

These two endings "-n" and "-ng" are in fact varieties of "-i" (Table 3). Not only them, but also many initials, like "n," "j," "g," "y," and "m," are evolved from pronunciation /i/. Table 3 lists the components of them based on their historical evolution.

"日 (Japanese "ni")" is the Chinese character to mark Latin letter "j" [10]. "J" first was adopted as a scribal modification of Roman "i" in Latin [14], and then used in English (while "g" in Italian [14]) to symbolize the consonant sound evolved from Roman "i" [14]. Letter "j" is called "long i" in Italian alphabet, and "y" is spelt as "ij" in Dutch alphabet. Compound "ng" was once written as "m" [10], which can be regarded as "nn" together.

Since the dot on the top of the small "i" was not appeared until 11c [15], we can regard "i" without dot as Arabic number "1" (which is also originated from Chinese traditional math [16]) or as I Ching symbol *yang* or "一" [17]. If we set "n" as two "i"'s written horizontally, then "j" is as two "i"'s written vertically. Letter "g", a different spelling of "j", also includes two "i." Letter "y" has three "i." The initial "m-" and ending "-ng" both have 4 "i"'s.

Table 3. Varieties of Letter "i"

	I	II	III	IIII
一 (Chinese No. 1)	i	n (ii)		m (iiii)
二 (Chinese No. 2)		j(ᵢ) g(ᵢ) e(ᵢ)	y(iᵢ)	ng (iiᵢ)

As is shown above, final "-e" is also originated from "-i". English letters "c", and "g" change their sound values based on two types of finals. Before the first group "e," "i," letters "c" and "g" are softened as /s/ and /dʒ/, otherwise, before "a," "o," "u," letters "c" and "g" are hardened as /k/ and /g/. Thus, "-e" is also a modification of "-i". In 1626, final "-e" and initial "g-" were both signed by Chinese character "额e (forehead)" [10].

Two varieties of "i" – "j" and "y" – are among the high-frequency initials. The three ending varieties are also in high frequency. Chinese pinyin is centered around sound /i/.

Pinyin as "a" Mainly Supported
Final "-u" seconds to "-i" and almost doubles "-a" in all four levels (see Fig. 7). But as a connection in combinations, "-a-" is more active than "-u-" (see Fig. 8). With "-an, -ao, -ian, -ang" leading ahead, "-uo, -ou" cannot compete with them (see Fig. 8).

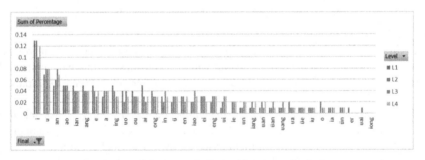

Fig. 8. Frequencies of finals (some lowest-frequency finals do not appear)

The letter "a", not the second highest "u" (Table 4), is chosen to mark "zero" or I Ching *yin* or "- -", because traditional Chinese official language was called "雅ya 言(elegant language)" [18]. The characters "雅" and "鸦crow" were interchangeable for a long time in history [19]. They are names of two kinds of crow. The right parts of "雅" and "鸦crow" reveal that "隹zhui", a small and not completely black crow, is a short-tailed and "鸟niao", a big and completely black crow, is a long-tailed bird [18,

Table 4. Varieties of Letter "a"

	0	1
○ (Chinese zero)	ɑ/o/u/ü	w (uu)

19]. The left parts are the same sound part "牙ya." We know that distinctive "鸦crow" sounds like /ɑ/. "鸦crow" had been respected, as the sacred bird who loaded the Sun (" 日") arising and setting every day, for a long time in China.

Both Chinese and English witness the confusion of "a/o/u" in the spelling or in the pronunciation in their history. "乌wu鸦ya" is shorted for "乌wu" or "鸦ya", but both refer to the same kind of big and black crow. In Chinese, bird's name is usually given by its typical one- or two- syllable sound. That means sound /u/ once took the place of /ɑ/.

As goods spread to other countries, the language associated with those goods also travels along. When Chinese characters "安(now "an")" and "女(now "nü")" were borrowed and changed as Japanese word "あ a め me (rain)", they hitchhiked on Chinese umbrella across Europe and became "om" in Italian "ombrello"[20], "vm" of "vmbella: 伞、雨伞、避雨的伞" in a 1732 dictionary [12], and at last settled as "um" in English "umbrella". These, too, prove that "a, o, v, u, ü, e" share the same root.

A Compromise

On the keyboard, it is important to maintain a balance between high and low frequency finals when condensing them onto a single key. As mentioned above, "y" is added before "-ü" if there is no other initial in pinyin. Therefore, we will place "y/i/ü" in the middle of the keyboard.

The upper group are finals endings of "-ɑ/-e", and the lower groups are ended with "-n", "-ng" and "-w/-u/-o" (Table 5).

Table 5. Groups of finals

Group	Ending	Final
Group 1	ɑ/e	ie, üe, er
Group 2	y/i/ü	ɑi, ei, ui
Group 3	ɑn/g	en/g, in/g, un/ong, ün
Group 4	w/u/o	ɑo, iu, ou

3.4 Pinyin-Based ZH Keyboard of Desktop, Laptop and Mobile

The Pinyin-based ZH keyboards (Table 6., Table 7, and Table 8) are divided into three parts: initials, finals and tones. Pinyin is generally spelt from left to right. To make the keys easy to learn and find, we list the initials on the left (light blue color), finals on the right (orange color) and tones flexible (yellow color).

Table 6. Pinyin-based desktop keyboard design

	1	2	3	4	5	6	7	8	9	10	11
1	1⁻	z	s	g	k	c	α	e	ie	üe	er
2	2′	ch/q	sh	x	zh	**j**	**y/i**	ü	αi	ei	ui
3	3ˇ	b	p	m	f	**h**	**αn/g**	en/g	in/g	un/g	ün
4	4ˋ	d	t	n	l	**r**	**w/u**	o	αo	iu	ou

Desktop Keyboard Design

Desktop keyboard is spacious. Letters are scattered to decrease the homophones. The exceptions of combinations are "ch/q", and "-n" and "-ng" nasal endings. Four lines are designed to make the letters in regular small groups. To realize the order, some of the letters are placed on the now long spacebar, for Chinese do not need space to separate the word [1].

The core of every group is bold (Table 6) to be seen at first glance. They are listed together and in the center of the keyboard to be touched by the most flexible finger, forefingers. The order of the rest of every group is basically arranged as they are in the Scheme [3]. Minor changes are done according to their frequencies (see Fig. 1). In line 1, "z, s" are at the corner, not beside their brother "c," just because "g" and "k" are more popular in typing.

Laptop Keyboard Design

Laptop keyboard is smaller, so 5-column initials are condensed into 3 (Table 7). The voiced and voiceless pairs are grouped together. The voiced one is on the left and set as the default letter. The voiceless one is on the right and can be realized by a double-click.

Table 7. Pinyin-based laptop keyboard design

	1	2	3	4	5	6	7	8	9
1	1⁻	g/k	z/s	c	α	e	ie	üe	er
2	2′	ch/q	sh/x	**zh/j**	**y/i**	ü	αi	ei	ui
3	3ˇ	b/p	m/f	**h**	**αn/g**	en/g	in/g	un/g	ün
4	4ˋ	d/t	n/l	**r**	**w/u**	o	αo	iu	ou

Mobile Keyboard Design

Mobile phone keyboard is focused on nine-key (Table 8, Table 9). Four of them are initials, four are finals, and the tones is on the lower right. It seems crowd of course with so many letters on every key (Table 8). They are designed for the beginners only to help them to be familiar with the letter positions.

Once users become skilled, they can choose to display only the initial consonants in bold (Table 9). The upper line represents the default selection, while the lower line can

Table 8. Pinyin-based Mobile keyboard design (Full)

	1	2	3
1	**g/k** **z**/c/s	α/e ie/üe/er	**w/u**/o **ao**/iu/ou
2	**j**/q/x **zh**/ch/sh	**y/i/ü/** α**i**/ei/ui	a/e/i/u/ü/**n** a/e/i/o/**ng**
3	**h**/b/p/m/f	**r**/d/t/n/l	2ˊ3ˇ4ˋ

Table 9. Pinyin-based Mobile keyboard design (Abridged)

	1	2	3
1	**g** **z**	α/e ie	**w/u** **ao**
2	**j** **zh**	**y/i** α**i**	**an** **ang**
3	**h**	**r**	2ˊ

be accessed through a double-click action. The remaining options are chosen based on the matching of finals with the Chinese word corpus. The first tone is set as the default and does not require a separate key. By touching the tone key (highlighted in yellow), the second tone is activated to distinguish homophones.

4 Conclusion

Our study shows that not only frequencies but also the relationships among the letters should be considered when keyboards are designed. We adopt the methods of I Ching, and point out that two-part pairs (*yin* and *yang*) in a whole exist in many levels. They are helpful to expand and fold letters in a fan-like pattern.

This design still leaves some problems unsolved, such as Zero initials. In the near future, we will test the design and revise it.

References

1. Wang, C., Yuan, X., Xiao, X.: Cultural discourse on keyboards: the selection of alphabets. In: Stephanidis, C., Antona, M., Ntoa, S., Salvendy, G. (eds.) HCI International 2022 – Late Breaking Posters. HCII 2022. CCIS, vol. 1654. Springer, Cham (2022). https://doi.org/10.1007/978-3-031-19679-9_34
2. Trigault, N.: Part 1 of Xiru Ermu Zi (《西儒耳目資》) (E-edition), p19, p35, p44, p157. Peking University, Beijing (1626)
3. Scheme for the Chinese Phonetic Alphabet (《汉语拼音方案》) (1958). http://www.moe.gov.cn/jyb_sjzl/ziliao/A19/195802/t19580201_186000.html, last (Accessed 23 April 2023)

4. Ministry of Education of the People's Republic of China. . Chinese Curriculum Standard for Compulsory Education (2022 Edition) (2022). http://www.gov.cn/zhengce/zhengceku/2022-04/21/5686535/files/6b87c3d3411d45ad9f25f88ee33213b7.pdf, (Accessed 23 May 2023)

5. Ministry of Education of the People's Republic of China. Chinese Curriculum Standard for Compulsory Education (2011 Edition) (2011). http://www.moe.gov.cn/srcsite/A26/s8001/201112/W020220418401378158281.pdf, (Accessed 23 May 2023)

6. Institute of Linguistics: Chinese Academy of Social Sciences: Xinhua Dictionary, 12th edn. Commercial Press, Beijing (2020)

7. Wen, R.M.: Chinese (Grade 1, Part I), pp. 20–50. People's Education Press, Beijing (2020)

8. Zhou, Y.G.: Collections of Zhou Youguang, Volume IV: History of World Words, pp. 48–50, 159–161. Central Compilation & Translation Press, Beijing (2013)

9. Etymonline.com: C https://www.etymonline.com/search?q=c, (Accessed 23 May 2023)

10. Trigault, N.: Part 3 of Xiru Ermu Zi (《西儒耳目資》) (E-edn.), p. 184, pp. 3–4. Peking University, Beijing (1626)

11. Kanji, J.:「常用漢字表, pp. 20–21 (2010).https://www.bunka.go.jp/kokugo_nihongo/sisaku/joho/joho/kijun/naikaku/pdf/joyokanjihyo_20101130.pdf

12. Orazi, Carlo, O.F.M.: 1673–1755 Dictionarium Latino Italico Sinicum Tam vocum, quam Litterarum seu Characterum usualium Sinensium ad usum et commoditatem PP. Missionariorum in hanc Sinicam Missionem noviter adventantium. https://digi.vatlib.it/view/MSS_Vat. estr.or.4, 1732, p 429v, p 502r, (Accessed 7 Sep 2022)

13. Chen, D.: Maoshi Guyin Kao(《毛詩古音考》). Zhonghua Book Company, Beijing (2011)

14. Etymonline.com: J https://www.etymonline.com/search?q=j, (Accessed 23 May 2023)

15. Etymonline.com: I. https://www.etymonline.com/search?q=i, (Accessed 23 May 2023)

16. Lam, L.Y., Ang, T.S.: Fleeting Footsteps: Tracing the Conception of Arithmetic and Algebra in Ancient China (Revised Edition). World Scientific, Singapore (2004)

17. Yang, T.C.: Zhou I (《周易》) 2nd edn. Zhonghua Book Company, Beijing (2022)

18. 雅:https://www.zdic.net/hans/%E9%9B%85, (Accessed 6 June 2023)

19. 鸦:https://www.zdic.net/hans/%E9%B8%A6, (Accessed 6 June 2023)

20. Etymonline.com: umbrella. https://www.etymonline.com/search?q=umbrella, (Accessed 23 May 2023)

Research on the Design and Consumption Intention of Chinese Urban Subway Space Advertisement

Yuxuan Xiao[1] (ID), Yi Liu[2(✉)] (ID), and Zhelu Xu[3] (ID)

[1] Changsha University of Science and Technology (Hunan University), Changsha, China
[2] Hunan University, Changsha, China
530494923@qq.com
[3] Hunan Normal University, Changsha, China

Abstract. As of December 31, 2022, a total of 55 cities in mainland China had opened urban rail transit projects, with a total mileage of 10,291.95 km, of which 8,012.85 km are subways, accounting for 77.85%. With the continuous advancement of rail construction in China's first-tier cities, the value of subway advertising design in the construction of a huge consumer society will continue to be highlighted. This article takes the design of subway advertising as a window to study the commercial and consumption potential of urban subway advertising and focuses on promoting the creativity of space advertising design, broadening the forms of cultural display of subway advertising, further promoting the development of culture and art in each city, and finally improving the soft power of culture, creating a new form of cultural subway construction and operation and a new style of cultural display.

Keywords: Urban subway · Advertising design · Consumption intention

1 Introduction

Subway is a mobile media of both service type and commercial type, which can aggregate various symbols such as text, pictures, video, and sound. It is a living exhibition space embedded in different strata and groups in an all-round way. Among these symbols, the circulation of pictures and text has full visibility and extensive communication, influencing and constructing social life, making the subway one of the effective tools of advertising design in media space. Meanwhile, the quality of the public relations carried by the subway also reflects the level of urban economic development and collective values. Media technology plays a role in the dynamic generation of contemporary urban space and builds the "media city" proposed by the communication scholar McQuail.

In addition to infrastructure, corridor and platform environment, carriage interior environment, station entrance and exit planning, subway space design will selectively integrate urban culture, history culture, art culture, etc., complete the design of the marketing scene with a public curatorial release, achieve a sense of companionship and community, and extend the effective attention range of online advertising flow.

© The Author(s), under exclusive license to Springer Nature Switzerland AG 2023
M. Kurosu et al. (Eds.): HCII 2023, LNCS 14054, pp. 619–634, 2023.
https://doi.org/10.1007/978-3-031-48038-6_40

Although the form of media has made progress from "message paper" to "message screen", the mere acquisition of advertising information through network services cannot significantly improve the willingness to consume. The fragmented time people spend18 waiting for subways and entering and leaving fixed stations has already become an important contact point of commercial value.

According to the "China Cultural Subway Development Report 2021" released in 2022, more than 70% of urban subway operating institutions are not complete in the development planning, cultural manuals, implementation measures and guidance documents of the cultural subway, resulting in some cities with common problems such as the disconnection between subway culture and urban culture, and the lack of public sense of cultural existence. As an important part of the cultural and tourism consumption industry chain "food, accommodation, travel, shopping and entertainment", subway space advertising and cultural construction are urgent and promising. The research findings in this document are as follows:

Advertising attention during subway rides has a positive impact on consumer intention. More than 90% of subway users pay attention to advertisements in subway stations (corridors, platforms, carriages, or tunnels), and more than half of them read the advertisements.

The types of subway advertisements that get users' attention are diversified, which can stimulate 60% of users' desire for shopping and effectively transform it into online and offline consumption. The consumption demand is mainly ticket purchase, involving catering, entertainment, shopping (cultural innovation, clothing), medicine, communication, etc.

Users' trust and awareness of advertisements also have an impact on consumption propensity. Compared with other scene advertisements, a small number of users think subway advertisements are more comprehensive, credible, eye-catching, and good-looking, and they hope to have a deeper understanding of them through different channels.

It is an inevitable trend for the subway economy to develop brand identities in the city. More than 80% of users expect subway advertising to integrate urban culture. In addition to commercial symbols, advertising symbols should also be combined with the unique qualities and contemporary values of the real life of local consumer subjects.

2   Review of the Literature

Most of the current literature on the consumption of urban subway advertising in China focuses on research on advertising design, management and development, visual communication, and cultural image interpretation, with less research on user consumption behavior, as follows:

Research on subway advertising design. Wei Qinghua (2008) noted that subway advertising should improve its effectiveness according to the characteristics of subdivided audiences and travel purposes. Taking the city as an example, Zhao Liyao (2010) analyzed the communication content and effect of subway advertising in Beijing and found that the overall attitude of users was positive, suggesting that subway advertising should form a new media pattern of diversification, interaction, and one-to-one.

Moreover, Li Huilong et al. (2014), based on the investigation and analysis of the Nanjing South subway station, concluded that the design of the subway commercial space should start from the whole and take the design of guide, color, lighting, and cultural characteristics as the focus.

Research on the consumption of subway advertisements. Song Ping et al. (2014) proposed strategies to improve the efficiency of subway advertising resources from the perspective of subway advertising development and operation mode, so as to maximize the commercial value of advertising. Zhang Xueyuan (2021) selects the temporal and spatial characteristics of consumer groups, business types, and consumption behaviors in Guangzhou subway stations and points out that subway space consumption is a kind of passing shopping consumption and a new service paradigm combining transportation and retail.

Research on the mode of analysis of user demand for subway advertising. Fang Xing et al. (2022) constructed a four-dimensional AHCG passenger advertising demand analysis model of "Attribute - Hierarchy - Contact - Guidance" and combined it with the field investigation of the Wuhan subway, found that it had a positive effect on improving the commercial utilization rate of subway advertising space.

Research on the correlation between subway space design and urban culture. Zhang Xiaowei (2019) took the Qingdao subway as an example and pointed out that regional cultural differences contribute to the sustainable cultural development of the artistic design of the public space of the subway. And Zhi Jinyi et al. (2019) summarized three methods of integrating regional culture in the design of station space, such as empathic design, visual metaphor, and narrative spatial design.

Discussion of the application of emotional design in subway design. Previous literature mostly focused on the emotional application of visual design such as exterior modeling, interior decoration, and remaining space of the subway For example, Xu Jing et al. (2017) advocated the integration of emotional design theory into subway interior design in order to pursue good functional experience, visual experience and emotional experience.

3   Method

Through questionnaire survey and data analysis, this research aims to grasp the design characteristics and consumer willingness of urban subway advertising in China, help tap the consumption potential of passengers, and design advertisements suitable for subway advertising release, communication forms and art features, to improve the efficiency of advertising and consumer willingness.

In order to ensure the quality of the questionnaire, the researchers modified the way of questioning and the content of the question after three pilot distribution tests, and finally issued 1,300 questionnaires of "The Impact of Subway Advertising Value". After selecting and deleting illogical and incomplete questionnaires, 1121 questionnaires could be effectively filled in, with an effective questionnaire rate of 86%. Furthermore, the questionnaire investigates the influence of subway advertising information on passenger consumption behavior from the perspective of user consumption intention.

4   Discussion

The research is mainly carried out from the two dimensions of subway advertising design and users' consumption intention, with reference to the three levels of "Emotional Design" theory proposed by American scholar Donald Norman (2012), which are visceral (stimulated by colors and images), behavioral (generated consumption) and reflective (extension of advertising information). This theory aims to achieve design through the satisfaction of visual needs, functional realization, and the interaction of consciousness and emotion, so as to influence users' consumption intention and achieve transformation.

With regard to the research objects, the proportion of male and female respondents is basically equal. While in terms of age, more than half of the respondents are young consumers aged 18–25, and 24.26% are consumers aged 26–40. In terms of educational background, most of the respondents have bachelor's degrees, and nearly half of them have received higher education. Furthermore, nearly half of the consumer groups have a low income of less than 2000 yuan, more than 30% of them have a monthly income of 2000–5000 yuan, and very few of them have a monthly income of 8000 yuan or more. In summary, the respondents to this questionnaire basically fit the consumer portrait in subway advertising. Most of them are young, well educated, have a certain degree of advertising cultural value cognition ability and aesthetic perception, and most of them do not have high income and do not belong to the group with high consumption ability, and will consider more personalized consumption in public scenes.

4.1   Visceral - User Concern and Visual Satisfaction

• Subway Riding Habit.
First, the questionnaire clarified the preference of the respondents for transportation. Apart from walking, the subway became the first choice among eight transportation means, including bicycles, shared tools, electric vehicles, buses, taxis, private cars, and light rail. In terms of frequency of travel, 76.72% of the respondents take the subway 1–3 times a month, while 23.28% take the subway 2–4 times a week at least. As the main link of a city, the metro penetrates deeply into residents' lives, not only linking the cultural and tourism industries between cities, but also connecting the core areas of neighboring cities, helping to form the "one-hour urban life circle" in the sense of urban and inter-city. In addition, the subway's uncongested, high-capacity and regular departure characteristics also make it highly popular (Fig. 1).

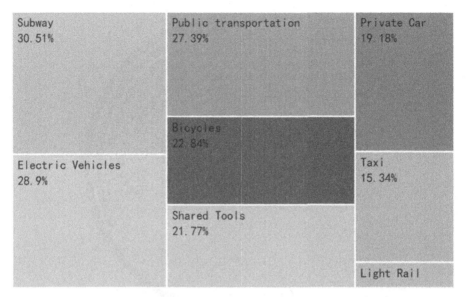

Fig. 1. Transportation options distribution map (Self-Designed Form)

• Subway Advertising and User Attention.

Scene participation is necessarily related to information attention. The visibility of an advertisement is used to measure whether it has a chance of being seen by users. Survey data show that more than 90% of users pay attention to advertisements in the subway station (corridor, platform, carriages, or tunnel), and nearly 30% of users pay attention regularly and actively.

Subway advertising can be divided into high-tech and new media according to the means of delivery. High-tech media include LED display advertising, car TV, and booth PIS. Traditional media include platform light boxes, channel posters, large wall stickers, and escalator side posters. Among them, the "vehicle" purchase advertisement combined with the subway immersive scene has attracted much attention for its features, such as the overall consistency of the picture and a wide range of publicity (Fig. 2).

The questionnaire shows that when taking the subway, users pay more attention to public welfare, culture and tourism, communication, catering, beverage, and city promotion among the 12 forms of advertising. Among them, public service advertisements, a simple conceptual advertisement with simple content, are often accompanied by striking and concise titles and short and profound words, which turn complex into simple in the vast array of advertising pictures and capture nearly 60% of users' attention. The popularity of culture, tourism, catering, urban publicity and other types of advertising points to the visceral level of "emotional design", that is, the use of design directly in line with people's visual and emotional needs, focusing on the visual aesthetic stimulation of color and image. Meanwhile, this is also consistent with the data of the question "How much do you pay attention to subway advertising" in the questionnaire. More than 90% of the users said they were willing to read the advertising content but focused primarily on the title and picture. Although the "message screen", which cannot be wiped away

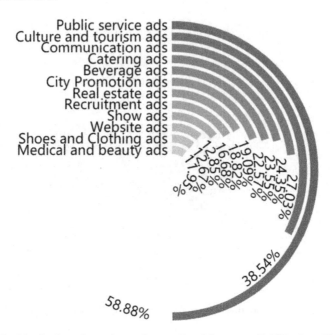

Fig. 2. Distribution of users' attention to advertising types (Self-Designed Form)

by fingertips, can easily win over traditional advertising and outdoor advertising with the "immersive" visual communication brought by color, image and appearance, users spend more time and attention on the event of "catching the subway" in the subway space scene, and the distraction brought by accepting advertisements often takes the second place (Fig. 3).

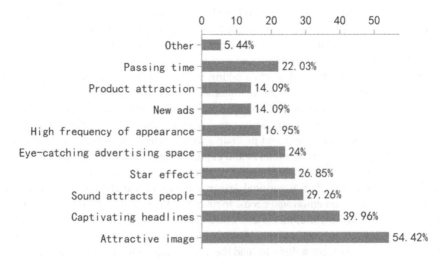

Fig. 3. Distribution of the reasons why users pay attention to advertising (Self-Designed Form)

As for the question "Why do you pay attention to subway advertisements", most users think that the image (54.42%), title (39.96%), sound (29.96%) and other elements are attractive; The star effect of advertising and eye-catching tablets make them willing to stop, and the visibility of media leads to the trend of visiting; Moreover, the time gap of waiting for the bus needs to be filled with relaxing information. It can be seen that the most important thing is the visual impact of subway advertising and the simplification of its connotation. In the subway scene where pedestrians come and go in a hurry, subway advertising is not long enough to reach the hearts of consumers. Using the shortest time, more colorful picture, more resonant title, and more piercing sound to attract the most user attention has become the top priority of subway advertising design.

4.2 Behavioral - User Consumption Intention and Design Usability

• Subway Consumption Habits.

The questionnaire shows that subway advertising can stimulate 70% of users' shopping desires, which can be effectively transformed into online and offline consumption. In terms of total daily average subway consumption, 43.98% of users spend less than 3 yuan per day, 38% of users are willing to spend 3–10 yuan per day, and 13.74% of users are capable of consuming 11–100 yuan per day. Regarding the single consumption caused by subway advertising, apart from the option of zero advertising consumption, 25.96% of the riders choose to spend 11–100 yuan, 22.48% of the riders spend less than 10 yuan, and 10.62% of the 100 riders choose 101–300 yuan. It is worth mentioning that 4.28 percent of passengers are willing to spend more than 300 yuan for a single advertisement. The behavioral level of "Emotional Design" focuses on the realization of product functions. As a form of product materialization, the realization of advertising's functions lies in stimulating and promoting consumption. Therefore, in terms of consumption intention, users can follow the consumption trend in the connection between daily life situations and commercial space, but the realization of subway advertising is clearly less than ideal and still has full market potential.

• User Consumption Content.

The environment created by subway space naturally has the nature of "persuasion". It is an excellent operating space for media technology, which cannot be avoided by the form of swiping the screens. The whole subway travel process can be divided into five scenes in chronological order: before entering the station, after entering the station, during the ride, before leaving the station, and after leaving the station. Each scene is located in the indoor space for a short stay, and there are explicit and invisible experience optimization points worth exploring (Fig. 4).

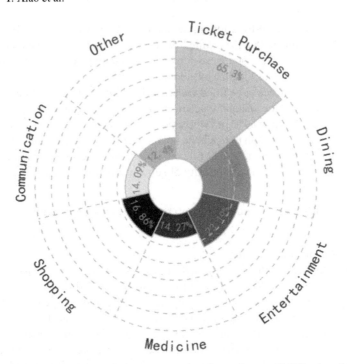

Fig. 4. Distribution of user subway consumption demand types (Self-Designed Form)

The statistics of the questionnaire show that the consumption demand of subway users is mainly ticket purchase (65.3%), catering (28.9%), entertainment (23.19%), shopping (16.86%), medicine (14.27%), communication (14.09%), etc. From the perspective of consumption types, conventional consumption reflects that advertising design focuses on visible things such as clothing, food, housing, and transportation, while ignoring the consumption of invisible things such as positive emotion and negative emotion. The deep involvement of technology helps to bring interaction, service, and experience into the new consumption demands of users.

As a passing shopping consumption, subway advertising should play a service role in the spatial transfer of users and become a psychological and emotional space. Users' consumption behavior can be regarded as participating in the decoding work in the encoding process of "the medium is the message", it is not an excess of energy, but a certain emotional pursuit, so that the nervous and tired soul can be comforted. This positive social resonance is accompanied by the temporary withdrawal of the working situation, and the transformation of advertising attention and consumption can separate users from the noisy environment through space expropriation, which reduces the stimulation of space oppression to a certain extent. In this case, the function, comprehensibility, ease of use, and feeling of subway advertising directly affect the intention of consumption, which should become the focus of media design. The visceral level has stimulated and guided users to read, browse, and make corresponding operational behaviors through visual design elements such as graphics, text, and color, while the behavioral level needs to stimulate users to continuously explore and explore product functions and be willing to integrate into the deep interaction behind advertisements to obtain a more pleasant and humane experience.

4.3 Reflective - User Emotional Needs and Information Extension

The reflective level of "Emotional Design" is more extensive. It relates information, culture, and connotation, is deeply influenced by user memory, knowledge, and experience, and is interwoven with emotional extension, cultural background, and life experience. Maslow's demand theory clarified the five levels of human needs from low level to high level, which are physiological, safety, social, respect, and self-realization. The reflective level points to the highest level. The consumption behavior of users after reading advertisements is a kind of self-realization required by exchanging material and spiritual levels through purchasing.

- **Content Extension Requirements Based on Information Value.**
Users' trust and awareness of advertising information also have an impact on consumption intention. There is no doubt that subway advertising can easily beat traditional advertising, with 62.98% of users agreeing with this. Compared to outdoor advertising, 62.44% of users think that subway advertising is more attractive. In terms of degree of information trust, as a public media platform, the subway has its own brand voice volume, which is easily regarded as the official discourse after certain information screening. Therefore, a small number of users believe that subway advertisements are more comprehensive, credible, brainwashed, eye-catching, and beautiful compared with other scene advertisements. With regard to information awareness, more than 70% of the users said that after watching a short and repeated advertisement, they would get to know it again through different channels. This again shows that subway advertising has a very penetrating communication effect, which can draw attractive brand marks, but it is also a vague mark. Users cannot obtain more extensive information at the moment when they have the strongest purchase intention. In a highly disruptive environment, the more information obstacles there are, the easier it is to interrupt their intention. Just as the more command levels that affect the operation of the application, the easier it is to interrupt the interaction of the interface. Therefore, subway advertising design should take more into account information presentation (Fig. 5).

In fact, most subway advertisements still focus on the presentation of products and ignore the attention to human interaction, which is far away from the real emotional man-machine environment. The results of the questionnaire show that 42% of the users still think subway ads are no different from other ads, and a few users even think that subway ads are worse and less attractive than outdoor ads, and there is room for improvement in media design. In the era of not being satisfied with material sensations, advertising, as a functional carrier of information exchange between people and products, should be given a new "sensory life" by media design. For example, various digital creative technologies such as 3D animation and field modeling should be used to change the communication of advertising from one direction to multiple directions, realize the integration effect of multidimensional space, create a real-life scene of "what you see is what you think" for

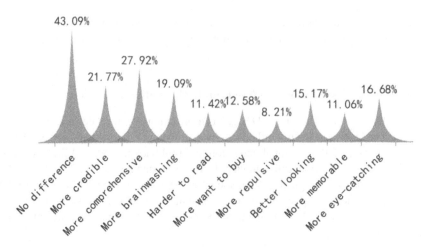

Fig. 5. Subway advertising has more characteristics than other advertising distribution (Self-Designed Form)

users, and make users become new communicators in emotional resonance. Close the distance with the brand.

- **Emotional Needs Based on Urban Identity.**

The consideration of reflective level is an important node in connecting subway advertising with urban culture. 84.92% of users have paid attention to brand image ads for subway lines or city subways and have an impression of it. Although 80.46% of users think it is necessary for subway lines or city subways to establish their own brands. From the perspective of cognition, more than 30% of users think it is very necessary. Cultural moistening is silent, in fact, to help us in the industrial acceleration to obtain a temporary rhythm "deceleration", so as to understand and imagine more continuous cities (Fig. 6).

The research also conducted interviews with the respondents, asking them about the characteristic impression of the subway brand in their past subway ride experience. The interview results involved three aspects. The first was the form of advertising, focusing on public service advertisements and publicity advertisements. The second is the perception of advertising, mainly for the appearance, decoration and the environment of the positive description; and the third is the cultural brand of the city, such as the Changsha local milk tea brand "Sexy Tea". As a "community" of Chinese urbanites, the subway is closely connected with people's living areas and even overlaps a lot. Its advertisements already have a strong urban temperament. The integration of such local brands and subway culture achieves two-way communication and connects with urban temperament.

With the power of this communication platform with a large passenger flow and high reach rate, the media should focus on the creative design of city culture and city brand image, integrate emotion, interaction, and other elements, so as to make the resonance more lasting and complete the transformation from traditional material expression to new wisdom experience. Users' immediate feelings tend to focus on the marketing design in line with the collective view and emotional identification, which can not only avoid the aversion caused by users' passive acceptance of advertisements, but also increase

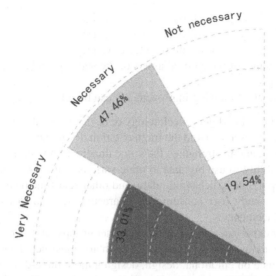

Fig. 6. Subway line construction city branding necessity (Self-Designed Form)

the cultural sense of belonging and the uniqueness of the city. The emotional bond of the passenger community constructed by users can construct self-identity by triggering users' memories and cognition.

5 Conclusion

Transportation, as an economic and cultural phenomenon, can integrate the image of the city. As the economist of urban areas Pascal Maragal argued, "for most people in the world, the future will be marked by cities rather than countries". With the continuous promotion of rail construction in China's first-tier cities, the fit between the expression of subway advertising design and users' emotional demands still needs to be explored. Under the guidance of the new law of advertising communication in the Internet era, advertising design should be more people-oriented and attach importance to the connection of behaviors and emotional experiences with users, so as to open a new situation for traditional physical media in the Internet era.

First of all, compared with traditional advertising, the design of subway carriages with cultural connotation, artistic taste, and social effect has more advantages in consumption transformation. Therefore, it is necessary to maximize its scene advantages and capture users' attention from visual satisfaction.

Secondly, subway space advertising has a bright future in terms of real estate, and users are more positive in their willingness to consume and have more considerable consumption capacity, but the consumption transformation needs to be improved. As a product at the behavioral level, advertising should be the focus of consumer contact research in terms of function, comprehensibility, usability, and feeling.

In addition, the information value of subway advertising needs to be improved. Information trust, awareness, extension, and other aspects should be considered to help users complete information reception, digestion, decomposition, conversion, and purchase.

Finally, in the long run, in addition to placing media design advertising, the construction of self-owned brand cultural advertising of the urban subway is also imperative. It is necessary to excavate the local culture of the city, integrate it into public art, fully activate the potential value of the cultural assets of the subway, and provide some identity positioning for users.

Based on these, the following improvements can be referred to:

(1) Introduce artificial intelligence technology or device to build a smart subway. Technical wonders are used to avoid the fragmentation, formalization, and simplification of visual design, and to strengthen the scene imagination with immersion.
(2) Enhance the ability to use big data to mine various indicators in interactions, such as spatio-temporal data, behavioral data, and other real-time data such as visibility monitoring, to study user consumption characteristics and measure the value of advertising placement.
(3) Based on user experience and specific consumer groups, the concept and evaluation system of the urban subway advertising design are constructed and improved.
(4) Place importance on emotional design, design a more three-dimensional and comprehensive advertising space from the city as a whole, pay attention to the organic integration of the urban cultural brand and commercial transformation, and build identity.

However, there are still some research deficiencies in this paper. First, the sample coverage is not enough to present an exploration of the differences that may exist in the broader user group; Second, this article does not analyze the primary data of subway advertising consumption transformation, which is expected to be discussed in subsequent research.

Appendix

Subway Advertising Value Impact Questionnaire

1. Your gender is [Single-choice]
   A. Male
   B. Female
2. Your age is [Single-choice]
   A. 17 years old or younger
   B. 18–25 years old
   C. 26–40 years old
   D. 41–60 years old
   E. 61 years old or older
3. Your educational background is [Single-choice]
   A. Primary school
   B. Middle school
   C. High school
   D. Specialist
   E. Bachelor's degree

    F. Master and above
4. Your economic income level is [Single-choice]
    A. Below 2000 yuan
    B. 2000–3000 yuan
    C. 3001–5000 yuan
    D. 5001–8000 yuan
    E. 8001–15000 yuan
    F. 15001–30000 yuan
    G. 30001 yuan or more
5. You often choose () for transportation [Multiple--choice]
    A. Walking
    B. Bicycle
    C. Shared tools
    D. Electric car
    E. Public transportation
    F. Taxi
    G. Subway
    H. Private Car
    I. Light rail
6. The frequency of your subway trips is [Single-choice]
    A. 1 time a month or less
    B. 2–3 times a month
    C. 2–4 times a week
    D. 4 times a week or more
7. What is your average daily subway spending? [Single-choice]
    A. 3 yuan and below
    B. 3–10 yuan
    C. 11–100 yuan
    D. 101 yuan and above
8. What are the main aspects of your consumption in the subway space? [Multiple-choice]
    A. Ticket purchase
    B. Dining
    C. Entertainment
    D. Medicine
    E. Shopping (cultural and creative, clothing, etc.)
    F. Communication
    G. Other
9. When you take the subway, do you pay attention to the advertisements inside the station (corridor, platform, inside the car or tunnel)? [Single-choice]
    A. Often
    B. Occasionally
    C. Rarely
    D. Never
10. How much do you care about subway advertisements? [Single-choice]
    A. Look at the headlines and images

     B. Read the content of the ads carefully

     C. Browse in a hurry

     D. Don't look at all

11. Please rank the advertisements in descending order of your concern [Sorting question]

     A. Look at the headline and the picture

     B. Read the content of the advertisement carefully

     C. Browse in a hurry

     D. Never look at them

12. Do you think subway ads are more attractive than traditional media ads? [Single-choice]

     A. Yes

     B. No

13. Compared with outdoor advertisements, are subway advertisements more likely to attract your attention? [Single-choice]

     A. Very attractive

     B. More attractive

     C. Equally attractive

     D. Not as attractive as outdoor

14. Which types of advertisements do you generally pay attention to? [Multiple-choice]

     A. Public service advertisements

     B. Communication advertisements

     C. Cultural and tourism advertisements

     D. Real estate advertisements

     E. Beverage advertisements

     F. Website advertisements

     G. Recruitment advertisements

     H. Food and Beverage advertisements

     I. Medical beauty advertisements

     J. Performance information advertisements

     K. Shoes and clothes advertisements

     L. City promotion advertisements

15. What are the reasons for you to pay attention to subway advertisements? [Multiple-choice]

     A. Attractive picture

     B. Attractive title

     C. Attractive sound

     D. Star effect

     E. Eye-catching advertisement position

     F. High frequency of the same advertisement

     G. New advertisement

     H. Attractive products

     I. Passing time

     J. Other

16. Do the ads you follow in the subway make you want to shop? [Single-choice]

     A. Yes

B. Occasionally

C. Never

17. The consumption you trigger in subway ads is usually [Single-choice

    A. Online consumption

    B. Offline consumption

    C. Both online and offline consumption

    D. Can't cause consumption

18. What is the amount of single consumption you triggered in the subway advertisement [Single-choice]

    A. 0 yuan

    B. 10 yuan and below

    C. 11–100 yuan

    D. 101–300 yuan

    E. 301 yuan and above

19. Do you think the advertisements appearing in subway stations are () compared with those seen elsewhere [multiple-choice]

    A. More credible

    B. More comprehensive

    C. More brainwashing

    D. Uglier

    E. More willing to buy

    F. More revolting

    G. Better looking

    H. More memorable

    I. More eye-catching

    J. No difference

20. Do you learn about new ads appearing in the subway in different ways? [Single-choice]

    A. Yes

    B. Yes, occasionally

    C. No

21. Have you ever paid attention to the advertisements of metro lines or the city metro's own brand image? [Single-choice]

    A. Very impressed

    B. Have an impression

    C. Slightly impressed

    D. Not at all

22. Do you think it is necessary for metro lines or city subways to establish their own brands? [Single-choice]

    A. Yes, very necessary

    B. Yes

    C. No

23. In your riding experience, what are the distinctive subway lines or city subway brand impressions? [Fill-in-the-blank]

References

Qinghua, W.: Research on subway advertising. Market Modernization (05), 106–107 (2008)

Liyao, Z., Yuexian, H.: Survey on the content and effect of subway culture communication in Beijing. Journal of Hunan University of Science and Engineering **31**(06), 218–222 (2010)

Huilong, L., Xiaofeng, S.: On the design of contemporary subway commercial space in the context of consumer society–Nanjing South Subway Station as an example. J. Changzhou Inst. Technol. Soc. Sci. Ed. **32**(04), 43–45 (2014)

Ping, S., Liqi, X., Shi, Q., Qifeng, Y.: Discussion on the development and operation of urban rail transit advertising resources. Railway Transp. Econ. **36**(06), 82–86 (2014)

Xueyuan, Z.: Guangzhou metro station commerce: a study on the characteristics and mechanism of passing shopping consumption. Beijing Planning Review (01), 102–107 (2021)

Xing, F., Yusong, Z., Zhipeng, Z., Boyuan, Z.: The analysis method of subway passengers' advertising demand from the perspective of user experience. Packag. Eng. **43**(18), 178–183 (2022)

Xiaowei, Z.: Research on the cultural sustainability of public art design in Qingdao subway. Packag. Eng. **40**(16), 87–91 (2019)

Jinyi, Z., Qianhui, S., Liuru, B., Zerui, X.: Design reproduction and perceptual experience of regional culture in urban public transportation image. Packag. Eng. **40**(24), 18–26 (2019)

Jing, X., Bingchen, Z., Yanqun, W.: Research on the emotional design of metro interior facilities. Packag. Eng. **38**(16), 168–172 (2017)

Norman, D.A.: Emotional Design. CITIC Press, Beijing of China (2012)

Research on the Current Situation of Yao Embroidery Based on Knowledge Graph and the Aesthetic Characteristics of Its Decorative Patterns

Yinjuan Xu[✉] and Shijun Liu

College of Design, Guangxi Normal University, Guilin 541006, China
j2513497448@163.com

Abstract. Taking Yao's embroidery patterns as the research object, literature research, field investigation and comparative analysis are adopted to analyze their cultural connotation and visual aesthetic characteristics, and it is found that Yao's costume patterns have a pattern system of ethnic cohesion, geometric modeling features and color features that complement the five colors. The in-depth study of the aesthetic characteristics of Yao embroidery patterns has laid the theoretical foundation for the future research and development of Yao tourism cultural and creative products.

Keywords: Yao nationality · Patterns of Yao nationality weaving and embroidered · Aesthetic features

1 Introduction

As an important ethnic force in the Nanling Corridor, most Yao people live deep in the mountains. They practice slash-and-burn farming and have no fixed abode, making their living environment harsh. The low level of productivity and crude means of production greatly restrict the writing and inheritance of Yao culture. "The Record of Rites • Wang System" has recorded that "the South Yue man, engraved Cotoe" [1]. This shows that the Yao people were tattooed in the beginning. Their purpose was not only for body decoration, but also for totem worship. However, with the progress of human beings and the improvement of production level, Yao people have learned to dress up their national ideals, desires, and interests through stitch and thread embroidery, and the "wen" body has been upgraded to the level of "wen" clothing.

2 Research Status of Yao Embroidery Based on Knowledge Graph Discovery

Due to the unique dressing characteristics of Yao costumes, it has attracted the attention of scholars both domestically and internationally. Early scholars, such as Fei Xiaotong, Ling Chunsheng and Takemura Zhuo Er, mainly studied the Yao nationality from the perspective of cultural anthropology. After the 1980s, there began to be more research articles purely from the perspective of clothing and decoration. This article mainly focuses on the literature related to Yao weaving and embroidery published in the CNKI database of China National Knowledge Infrastructure (CNKI) as a sample from 1986 to 2023. Using the keyword "Yao weaving and embroidery", an advanced search was conducted on research literature on Yao weaving and embroidery. A total of 392 articles were obtained, including 4 news reports and 2 conference papers with weaker correlation, to ensure the authority of the data. Finally, 386 articles were obtained. The number of publications on Yao embroidery related literature collected by CNKI can intuitively reflect the progress and importance of this field in the academic community. According to the trend of changes in the number of literature publications (Fig. 1), the research on Yao embroidery in China has gone through three stages: the first stage is the embryonic stage (1986–2008). A total of 36 relevant journal articles were published during this stage, and researchers mainly analyzed and studied from the perspectives of Yao clothing culture, Yao historical changes, and the entire Yao society; The second stage is the mature period (2009–2019), with 227 journal articles published in the past decade, and the annual publication volume has significantly increased compared to the embryonic period; The third stage is the development period (2019–2023), with a total of 123 journal articles published within 5 years, a surge in the number of publications, and reaching its highest value in 2023. Overall, the number of literature on Yao embroidery shows an increasing trend year by year.

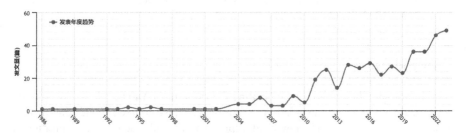

Fig. 1. 1986–2023 Research trend of Yao nationality weaving embroidery research

With the help of Citespace 5.6. R5, the author uses the information visualization analysis method, takes the knowledge map analysis as the main approach, and takes the Yao embroidery as the object to draw a visual map of the dynamic research of Yao embroidery, with a view to revealing the differences in the artistic characteristics of weaving and embroidery among different branches of the Yao people, the development and evolution of many complex relationships, and showing the research progress in the field of Yao embroidery, so as to further discuss the aesthetic characteristics and future development of Yao embroidery patterns.

2.1 Research Hotspot: Keyword Co-Occurrence Analysis

Keyword analysis can explore the status and popularity of Yao clothing and Yao embroidery in the research field. For this purpose, the author selected literature from 1993 to

2023 and divided it by year, extracting the top 30 nodes with higher frequency in each partition to obtain a keyword co-occurrence knowledge graph (Fig. 2). In this graph, each circle represents a keyword node, and the larger the circle, the higher the frequency of occurrence, which means the higher the attention received in the field. In this figure, we can clearly see that the most frequent nodes in the study of Yao clothing are 134 nodes, with a centrality of 0.44. This indicates that Yao clothing is a highly concerned field in literature research. In addition, the keywords that appear more frequently include "Yao", "clothing", "Yao embroidery", "inheritance", and "cultural inheritance". Based on the research topic of this article, we classify and integrate these keywords into two major fields: the study of aesthetic characteristics of Yao clothing patterns and the application research of Yao embroidery. The research in these fields mainly focuses on three aspects: pattern elements, aesthetic features, and innovative design.

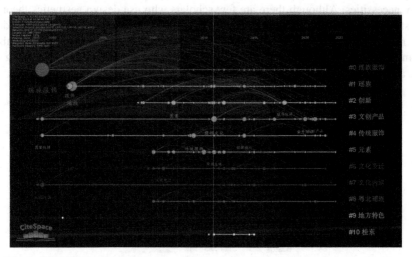

Fig. 2. 1993–2023 Co-present network knowledge graph of Yao weaving embroidery

2.2 Research Trends: Keyword Emergence Analysis

Highlighted vocabulary is a vocabulary that is frequently used at a specific time, and through changes in word frequency, it can determine the forefront and development trends of the discipline. Highlight keywords in Citespace, and the greater the intensity of highlighting, the higher the research popularity during that period. The author analyzed 28 prominent words from 2013 to 2023 in the past 10 years (Fig. 3), and divided the development of Yao embroidery into three stages. The first stage is from 2013 to 2016, with "innovative design", "Yao clothing", "inheritance", and "application" as the main research directions. "Application" is the most prominent keyword in this stage, with a heart rate of 3.75. This indicates that scholars at this stage mainly explore the inheritance, innovation, and application of Yao ethnic patterns. The second stage is from 2017 to 2020, with "aesthetic characteristics", "regional culture", and "applied research" as the research directions for this stage. "applied research" is the keyword with high highlighting intensity in this stage, with a high degree of attention reaching 1.36. This indicates that the main content of this stage is to inherit and apply the Yao embroidery culture, and to inherit the Yao embroidery culture through innovative applications. The changes in the theme words from the first stage to the second stage reflect the shift in research on Yao embroidery culture from basic research to applied research. The third stage is from 2021 to 2023, and the research directions for this stage are "cultural and creative products", "packaging design", and "clothing patterns". In terms of pattern elements, researchers often explore the artistic characteristics of Yao people's weaving and embroidery patterns in terms of their composition, pattern elements, and cultural connotations; In terms of aesthetic characteristics, researchers mainly focus on how to apply the "aesthetic consciousness" of Yao embroidery to modern life; In terms of innovative design, researchers have transformed Yao embroidery patterns into modern clothing or daily necessities. Although there are few scholars who use design aesthetics theory in the study of Yao embroidery, the intervention of design aesthetics theory provides a new research perspective for the contemporary application of Yao embroidery symbols. From the perspective of redesigning and applying cultural symbols, the following will take a holistic view of the aesthetic characteristics of Yao embroidery patterns.

Top 28 Keywords with the Strongest Citation Bursts

Keywords	Year	Strength	Begin	End	2013 - 2023
宗教信仰	2013	0.92	2013	2014	
应用	2014	3.75	2014	2015	
元素	2014	1.04	2014	2017	
八步区	2014	1.02	2014	2015	
发展	2014	1.02	2014	2015	
传统服饰	2014	0.92	2014	2016	
文化内涵	2013	1.51	2015	2017	
广西	2015	1.25	2015	2017	
启示	2015	1.04	2015	2016	
作品欣赏	2015	1.04	2015	2016	
审美价值	2015	0.88	2015	2017	
民俗文化	2016	2.15	2016	2017	
变迁	2013	1.3	2016	2017	
传统文化	2016	0.43	2016	2017	
文化传承	2014	1.39	2018	2019	
传承	2014	1.29	2018	2021	
审美特征	2013	0.61	2018	2019	
民族服饰	2013	1.7	2019	2020	
应用研究	2019	1.36	2019	2020	
地域文化	2019	1.09	2019	2021	
服饰	2013	0.59	2019	2020	
金秀瑶族	2020	2.15	2020	2021	
创新设计	2014	1.18	2020	2021	
创新应用	2020	0.88	2020	2021	
创新	2018	0.36	2020	2021	
文创产品	2021	3.39	2021	2023	
服饰纹样	2018	2.83	2021	2023	
包装设计	2016	0.28	2021	2023	

Fig. 3. 2013–2023 Yao Embroidery Keyword Emergence Network Knowledge Graph

3   The Aesthetic Characteristics of Yao Embroidery Patterns

3.1   A Pattern System that Embodies the Meaning of Ethnic Groups

Through the author's observation, it is found that the costume patterns of the Yao people are relatively highly patterned and symbolized, forming a visual symbol system of their own. Although the Yao branches differ in costume culture, such as clothing styles, they also have some common features, such as weaving techniques and means, which result in the surprising consistency of their patterns and the basic same connotations of their patterns. This may be what Mr. Fei Xiaotong once said: "Each beauty has its own beauty, and beauty shares with each other". What they have in common is that Yao women use unique patterns and symbols to record Yao's history, totems, wars, migrations, natural scenery, customs and activities, emotions, and their yearning for a better life [2]. Thus, a relatively mature symbol system of Yao culture has been established, which is a perfect combination of function and art.

The typical patterns of the Yao ethnic group, as arranged by the author, (Table 1) we can see that Yao patterns mainly include those related to totem worship, those related to nature worship, plant patterns, and geometric patterns. The first type of patterns associated with totemism includes such typical patterns as Pan King seals, three Kings, swastikas, and human figures. The second type of patterns related to nature worship includes dog patterns, fish patterns, spider patterns, bird patterns, and other typical patterns. The third type is plant patterns, such as octagonal patterns and tree text. The fourth type of geometric patterns includes diamond patterns, sawtooth patterns, and other typical patterns. Geometric patterns are not the main patterns in Yao costumes, but they show an overall harmonious charm in pattern composition.

According to the source of inspiration, Yao costume patterns are mostly derived from hunting, farming, religious belief and folk activities. These abstract patterns not only describe the living environment and content of Yao people, but also express their hope for a better life. For example, the "three king pattern" carries the memory of Yao people to their ancestors -- Pan Wang, Tang Wang and Xin Wang. In its "Pan Wang Song · Lianzhou Song", it sings: "The king of Tang was born first, and the king of Tang was born in Lianzhou...... Born the king was born, the king was born without clothes...... Pan Wang was born before he was born, Pan Wang was born in Fujiang [3]."

In the Yao people, there is a special pattern called "Pan Wang Seal" which has the most complex form of expression. Panwang Seal was originally designed to commemorate its ancestor Panhu, but the expression of Panwang Seal and the position of weaving embroidery varied between branches. The most typical examples are Baizuyao from Nandan County, Guangxi and Libo, Guizhou, which embroider the pattern of "Pan Wang Yin" on the visual center of women's backs, commonly known as "back embroidery Dayin" (Fig. 4). However, the position of the "Panwang seal" embroidery of Jinxiu Yao people is different from that of other Yao people. The "Panwang seal" is embroidered in the middle of the headscarf and worn on the top plate (Fig. 5). According to historical records, the ancestor of the Yao people was a dragon dog. Later, he made war achievements and was named "Pan King". He married a little princess and gave birth to six boys and six girls [4]. Panwangyin expresses the worship of its ancestor Panhu. Yao people deliberately visualized the legend about the source of Panhu and reproduced it

Table 1. Typical patterns of Yao nationality weaving and embroidered

Name of pattern	Diagram form	Type of pattern	Name of pattern	Diagram form	Type of pattern
Pan king seal			The dog grain		
Pattern of three Kings		Patterns associated with totemism	fish pattern		Patterns associated with nature worship
Swastika pattern			Spider pattern		
Human shape stripe			Bird patterns		
Star anise pattern		Grain of plant	Diamond shaped pattern		Pattern of geometry
Grain of grain			Saw tooth stripe		

in front of people by means of weaving, which is also a concrete embodiment of ancestor worship and historical tracing. In addition to the "Pan Wang Seal", we also found the "dog tooth pattern" and "dog pattern". Both are symbolic metaphors for this group memory, and in honor of their ancestor, the Dragon Dog.

As a referential form of objects, symbols have the function of generating human nature and shaping human culture. Geometric patterns with cultural symbolism are the carriers for Yao women to express their wishes and ideals based on oral myths, anecdotes, or other ethnic and religious cultures. For example, the "swastika pattern" is originally a Buddhist symbol. In Sanskrit, the Swastika is believed to be the auspicious image on the chest of Sakyamuni, which has the meaning of auspiciousness and longevity.

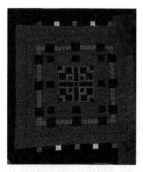

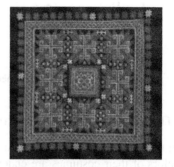

Fig. 4. "King Pan seal" of Baiku Yaoin   **Fig. 5.** "King Pan seal" of JinxiuPanYao
Nandan county, Guangxi

In a word, Yao embroidery patterns are like a system of symbols which can lead people to explore the historical development process of the Yao people, uncover hidden religious and auspicious connotations, as well as the Yao people's understanding of nature and yearning for a better life. Reflecting national history through clothing patterns and spreading them through generations is not only a good way to preserve traditional national culture, but also of great significance for the integration and identity of ethnic groups [5].

3.2 Geometric Modeling Features

Shaping patterns by appearance and meaning are important characteristics of Yao pattern modeling. Yao people use abstract modeling techniques and basic geometric figures, such as the well shape, diamond shape, and cross shape (Fig. 6), to form various things in their living environment and to symbolize certain cultural connotations. This also leads to changes in Yao patterns between similarity and dissimilarity. They choose, process, and beautify images immersed in life, and integrate their simple aesthetic spirit with primitive religious worship. Human pattern, bird pattern, fish pattern, and spider pattern listed in Table 1 are based on the appearance of the object to shape the pattern. They use the form of multiple hybrid expression, the appearance of the object being processed geometrically. The simple exaggeration of four diagonal hooks and a diamond combined to create the spider pattern image. On the basis of these individual patterns, Yao people have derived other rich patterns in different orientations.

In terms of the application of forms, Yao costume patterns pay attention to the characteristics of replacing faces with points and forming images with lines. They also emphasize the changes in the arrangement of the thickness and length of lines, which makes the patterns strongly decorative and contrasting. Influenced by its cross-stitch technique and original waist weaving technique, Yao embroidery has a sense of grain in touch and a "Mosaic" texture in vision. This carefully designed pattern can be described as "applying art according to materials".

Fig. 6. Basic geometric figures constituting patterns

3.3   The color characteristics of Five Colors Complement Each Other

Under the influence of the local ethnic culture and aesthetic concepts of the Yao people, the colors of their costumes are endowed with unusual intrinsic symbolic meanings. It is very appropriate to describe the color characteristics of Yao people's costumes as "seeing the rainbow from a distance and seeing the flowers from a close distance". For the Yao people, who have no written history, color matching also reflects their living conditions and national emotions. Since ancient times, the Yao people have always liked to dress in the five colors of green, yellow, red, white, and black [6]. If one observes carefully, they will find that the colors of Yao people's costumes are a pure five-color combination. With green and black as the base, they are dressed with yellow, red, and white, showing a strong color contrast.

As the old saying goes, "If the colors are colorful, there must be a main color attached to it." Taking Jinxiu Panyao and Longsheng Hongyao as examples (Fig. 7 and 8), warm colors such as orange red and bright yellow are the main colors of their female clothing, accounting for more than 60%, with other colors used as color-matching or base colors. Yao men's dress color is relatively simple, mainly blue and black, with only five colors of heraldry on the corners. As the Yao people are a mountainous nation, hunting is an important economic source. Wearing blue and black has a hidden effect in the jungle and is resistant to dirt, which is helpful for catching prey. Therefore, it makes sense for the Yao people to choose blue and black as the background color for embroidery.

In a word, the colour features of Yao costume patterns also reflect the unique cultural connotations behind the Yao patterns, and reflect the Yao people's simple yet tough aesthetic perception.

Fig. 7. Long Sheng Hongyao.

Fig. 8. Kim Xiu dish Yao

4 Conclusion

Yao clothing is the result of the labor of Yao women. They weave their understanding of life and perception of nature into their clothes with silk threads, weaving them into their belts, which unifies the form and content and expresses the understanding of truth, goodness, and beauty of Yao people. This not only creates an aesthetic form for human society, but also becomes a derivative of Yao people's emotions and life, thus passing the Yao culture from generation to generation.

The research and development of tourism cultural and creative products has become an important component of the economic development of villages in ethnic minority areas, but the homogenization situation it faces greatly restricts the development of the cultural and tourism industry. Only by continuously integrating cultural and creative design with traditional culture and innovating can we develop cultural and creative products that are both national, innovative, and contemporary. The design of Yao cultural and creative products should allow the classic patterns of Yao to be redesigned based on new materials, allowing the products to radiate new vitality and vitality. When creative design collides with traditional culture, it can create the unique charm of national cultural and creative products, which is one of the writing purposes of this article.

References

1. Deng, J., Wancai, P., Ruifu, M.: Yao Embroidery. Guangdong People's Publishing house (2008)
2. Wu, J.F.: Poetic expression of traditional culture in Chinese contemporary design art from "symbol" to "image". Zhejiang Soc. Sci. (11) (2016)

3. Yin, L.: Research on the application of Yao traditional clothing elements in clothing design. Light Ind. Technol. (1), 84–85 (2015)
4. Rong, T.: Guangxi JinxiuDayaoshan Clothing Research. Donghua University (2017)
5. Huang, S., Shijun, L.: Ethnic memory and identity: Interpretation of Hongyao clothing technology and its cultural symbolic meaning, silk. 2020(08), 94–100 (2020)
6. Zhuang, G.: Autonomous Region "Guangxi Yao social history survey editorial group": "Guangxi Yao social history survey (Volume 8)". Nanning: Guangxi Nationalities Publishing House (1984)
7. Yongli, I.: Country, ethnic group and village: A Historical Anthropological Study on the identity construction of Pangu Yao. Guangxi ethnic studies, 2018(4) (2018)

A Study of Interactive Design Based on Local Cultural Creativity in the B&B Space

Chunlan Zeng[1][(⊠)] [iD] and Ganyi Yu[2]

[1] Guilin University, Guilin 541000, China
48681743@qq.com
[2] Guangxi Normal University, Guilin 541000, China

Abstract. B&B is not only a place to eat, stay, rest and entertain, but also a place where users can be inspired to participate more actively in the experience and design through cultural creativity. In interaction systems, behaviour is closely related to context, and the creativity of local vernacular culture becomes more interesting when it takes place in a spatial environment that is suitable for carrying culture and personality through various human behaviours. This paper therefore chooses the B&B as this spatial carrier for research. Local vernacular cultural creativity in a spatial environment can be material or immaterial. This paper focuses on how local cultural and creative design is embedded in the B&B environment and interacts with some of the commercial behaviours, information and media generated by the users, examining the design value and brand value of cultural elements, exploring the dialogue between products, people and materiality, culture and history, to stimulate a deeper value.

Keywords: Interaction Design · Cultural Creativity · Regional Culture · spatial experience

1 Overview

With the development of cultural industries and the emergence of cultural and creative products, the value of regional culture in cultural and creative products has become increasingly important. Regional culture not only enriches the connotation of cultural and creative products, but also has an impact on the appearance, form, use and mode of communication of products. More and more designers, creators and enterprises have begun to pay attention to and invest in the field of cultural and creative products, and have launched a variety of creative products with cultural connotations. The commerciality of the product is always the ultimate goal to be achieved. Therefore, how to consider the commercial effect of local cultural heritage in the design process is the concern of most cultural and creative products. The process of conception, design, production and sale of cultural and creative products can be regarded as the designer's understanding and refinement and creation of culture and its transformation into products. Through the user's contact and understanding of the purchase, a transformation of cultural value is formed, which is a culture-based interaction between designers-objects-users. How to attract users and make them want to buy, the user-centred design concept is particularly important for the sales results of goods.

© The Author(s), under exclusive license to Springer Nature Switzerland AG 2023
M. Kurosu et al. (Eds.): HCII 2023, LNCS 14054, pp. 645–656, 2023.
https://doi.org/10.1007/978-3-031-48038-6_42

The term "B&B" first came from the United Kingdom [1], dating back to around 1960. The development of nationalisation was basically after 2000, and in 2017, the China Tourism Administration officially announced the approval of the "Basic Requirements and Evaluation of Tourism Homestays" industry standard, which was implemented on 1 October 2017. Compared with developed countries in Europe and the United States, China's homestays started later [2]. With economic development and the rise of tourism, the B&B industry everywhere is beginning to take note of the role that local culture can play in promoting the industry. China is a vast country and its customs and traditions vary greatly from place to place, so the establishment of B&Bs in different regions has resulted in a variety of different characteristics due to differences in regional culture. However, no matter how different the style of the B&B may be, it is important to consider the user's needs in the design process, and it is inseparable from the combined effect of the physical and spiritual dimensions.

Designers have always placed a high value on local culture when creating a B&B environment. Many B&Bs attract large numbers of visitors by incorporating distinctive local culture, but the traditional way of operating a B&B is still based on overnight stays and meals, with an emphasis on the quality of accommodation and food.

This paper combines the traditional business model of cultural and creative products with the carrier of the B&B space, studies human behaviour in the B&B space, explores the influence of design empowerment on the cultural creativity of the B&B space, and brings into play the commercialisation of local culture and products to achieve commercial purposes and the promotion of local culture.

2   Characteristics of User-Centred B&B Space Under Regional Cultural Characteristics

The user experience is the basis of the design, and the user behaviour is roughly analysed from the user's point of view, under the interactive influence of the regional culture and the B&B space environmen (see Fig. 1).

Understanding the behavioural characteristics of visitors helps to improve the layout, design and service of the B&B space, and to improve and optimise the interior environment to enhance the user's travel experience. From the user's point of view, tourists have different attitudes towards understanding and accepting regional culture, and we can broadly classify tourists into three categories: the first type of tourists like culture and pay great attention to regional culture. The third type of tourist is not interested in the culture of the region, but focuses on the experience of games, entertainment and accommodation. No matter which category of users they are, they all have their own characteristics. We should start with them and bring into play the thinking of cultural and creative space, allowing users to explore a new model in the traditional consumption process of B&B, allowing them to enter directly or indirectly, actively or passively, into a new consumption model guided by regional culture.

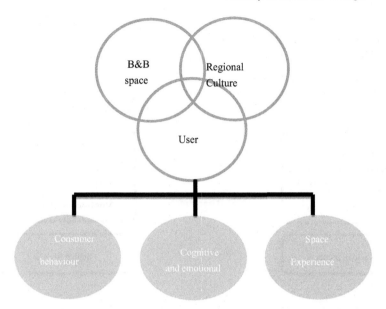

Fig. 1. Behavioural characteristics of users in an interactive relationship

With the innovative design of regional culture, the B&B space will produce new empowering results. Based on the different situations of users, designers can add separate areas for regional cultural experiences or for the sale and display of cultural and creative products to the planning system of the B&B space, so that the B&B space has a complex commercial experience.

Design empowerment under the cultural and creative space mindset is a human-centred design approach, through which the creation and operation of B&Bs by means of design will support and assist the growth and progress of designers and users, thus enabling them to realise their potential and value in a variety of contexts. The interaction between B&B space and regional culture is also a new system reconfiguration brought about by design empowerment. Under its influence, B&B will change from a single residential experience to a space integrated into a commercial open mode, while cultural and creative products will change from a single profit model to a composite commercial experience, and the traditional thinking of selling products will change to the thinking of selling lifestyles (see Fig. 2).

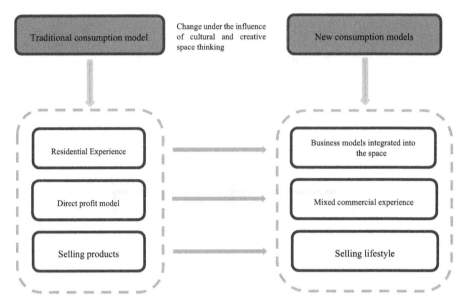

Fig. 2. Before and after cmparison of consumption forms in B&B spaces

2.1 Integration of Business Models into the Space

The integration of business models in space, influenced by the concept of interaction, will raise the integration of space design and business models to a new level.

Branding
The B&B itself is a commercial entity, with a commercial business model, and is branded. From the very beginning of the B&B's design, there must be a sense of branding. The differentiation of its business model, the quality of its services, its communication strategy and the creation of its visual identity are all things that can be done in conjunction with the regional culture, which is more conducive to clarifying the differences between the B&B industry and its own values.

Commercial Layout
The B&B space is set up to display and sell cultural and creative goods, with cultural promotion as the main focus and sales as a complement. If there are no site conditions, objects such as sales links and QR codes can be integrated into the space scene or placed directly in the reception, lounge area or room, places that users can access during the behavioural activities of their stay, and displayed and sold remotely through the online platform.

Spatial Dialogue
Spatial Dialogue is a design philosophy that emphasises the process of designing spaces by considering how to engage with people, nature and the social environment to create more meaningful spaces. When designers design spatial places, it is a mode of spatial

dialogue. The B&B venue is a small complex of food, accommodation, leisure and entertainment, etc. How we can integrate the business opportunities and functional chains of the different spaces throughout is a key consideration for designers in relation to the cultural and creative objects. In the specific practice of spatial dialogue, artistic elements, cultural elements, social elements and natural elements are all commonly used elements. The key lies in the effective integration of cultural elements with other elements, highlighting the regional and cultural characteristics of the whole space, which is an ambience for the user and can be used in any space, such as spatial structure, interface modelling, furnishings, etc., combined with cultural creativity for spatial beautification. The aim of the spatial dialogue is to immerse the user in the ambience of the local culture, to evoke positive emotions and to deepen and enhance the user's impression of the local culture brand.

Internet Experience Space
In the information society, people can experience certain objects or activities through the Internet to get the feeling of experiencing them. The new B&B space can be promoted in conjunction with social media and other online platforms to showcase the aesthetic value of the space place, the regional culture and the state of human activities, which can attract more customers to come and spend money, building word of mouth and brand value. And social media and other online platforms can also generate take-home sales.

Personalized Needs
Personalization is a higher level of demand based on the satisfaction of basic functions to meet the needs of different people, showing great humanistic care and high quality. Whether it is the visual experience, the service experience or the entertainment activities, all can be combined with the regional culture to show a distinctive and individual feel.

2.2 Mixed Commercial Experience

Combining the characteristics and advantages of the B&B space with the commercial needs of the cultural and creative space to create a B&B space with innovative commerciality. By creating an atmosphere of comfort, art and local culture, the commercial attractiveness and selling power of the place is increased and a diversified commercial experience of the B&B space is realised, not only satisfying the users' needs for food and accommodation, but also enhancing the brand and image value of the B&B.

2.3 Selling Lifestyle

Create a specific tourist consumption experience within the B&B space and establish links with the destination, culture and lifestyle to realise the triple value of space, tourism and culture. Specific strategies can be approached in the direction of regional culture, geographical and ecological environment, innovative means, leisure and entertainment, and social exchange.

3   The Significance of Interactive Design of B&B Spaces in the Context of Regional Cultural Characteristics

This paper takes the B&B as a spatial carrier and focuses on how the design of the B&B space can influence the human-spatial-object-cultural elements, choosing the optimal way to achieve the purpose of cultural dissemination and merchandising on the one hand, and improving the comfort and experience of users on the other, improving the accommodation experience and stimulating more consumption potential about the regional culture, thus strengthening the regional cultural heritage and promoting tourism development.

The interaction between the B&B space and the local culture has always been about the 'people'. The name of the B&B, the design concept of the space, the choice of furnishings and the determination of the form are all designed and created by the designer around the user, in the knowledge, understanding and re-creation of the local culture, transforming the abstract local culture into a concrete form. It is user-oriented. Through eating and staying in the B&B, being in the space and using the furnishings, the user is exposed to the local culture and learns about the local cultural connotations. This process can take place through all the user's behavioural activities in the B&B space, such as tableware for eating, food with local characteristics, paper towels for wiping hands, parasols, key rings, etc. All kinds of objects can be designed and created with local culture in mind, expressing specific cultural connotations in addition to meeting basic usage needs and providing a more direct local cultural inculcation for the user. As a place where people and things interact, the B&B space has the advantage of strengthening the cultural heritage of the region and promoting tourism development.

4   Analysis of the Application of Spatial Interaction Design of B&B Under the Characteristics of Regional Culture

The design approach to space tends to have some general paradigms which, in concrete terms, produce specific differences depending on the conditions. The design results of the interaction between people and space and culture, produced under the two conditions of regional cultural identity and B&B space, are unique. This is analysed below in relation to some specific case studies.

4.1   User Research and Demand Analysis

At the heart of interaction design is the user. Through research, we understand the preferences and needs of users and design the interaction experience to meet their needs and behavioural preferences. There are many ways to interact with the local culture and the B&B space, and it is up to the user to decide which approach to take. For example, in relation to the setting of spatial areas, a questionnaire on the preference of regional culture places was collected from some user groups in Guilin, and some data was obtained as a reference. On the question of how to present regional culture in the B&B space, we found through the questionnaire that among the surveyed users, the most approved way is to reflect regional culture in the spatial modelling; independent space to display regional culture and places to experience regional culture are also more approved (see Fig. 3). The results of the survey are a good reference for the design of our spaces.

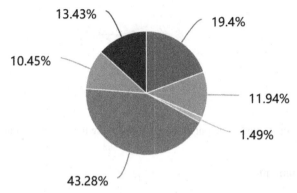

13.43% 19.4%

10.45%

11.94%

1.49%

43.28%

● 独立的空间展示地域文化A separate space to showcase regional culture
● 独立的地域文化体验场所An independent place to experience regional culture
● 借助数字技术直接了解Direct access with digital technology
● 地域文化融入空间造型中Regional culture integrated into spatial form
● 地域文化融入餐饮体验中Regional culture integrated into the dining experience
● 地域文化融入各种用品用具中Regional culture in a variety of products and utensils

Fig. 3. User data analysis table (Source: Questionnaire)

4.2 Spatial Analysis and Planning

The planning of the B&B area is mainly about function, layout and sensible configuration. Planning should take into account the different needs of different groups of people, e.g. children need a play area, young people need an entertainment area, couples need a private area, elderly people need a rest area, etc. Rooms should be designed to meet the needs of different users. The setting of the area for displaying, experiencing and selling regional culture is more conducive to interactive behaviour between the regional culture and the users (see Fig. 4).

The sale of cultural and creative products requires a certain level of popularity and recognition. The establishment of a regional culture exhibition area and a regional culture experience area in the space is to lay a certain foundation for the branding and promotion of cultural and creative products, which is also a direct manifestation of the dissemination of regional culture. In other spaces, although the basic function is not directly related to regional culture, we can still start from the space structure, interface decoration, furnishings and other elements, so that the sense of atmosphere can be substituted into the space, thus realising the interaction of context [3], which is also a concrete expression of the integration of space into the business model.

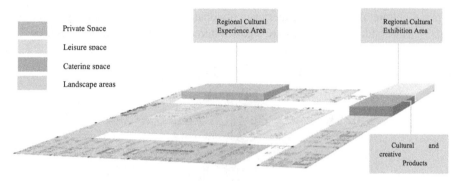

Fig. 4. Spatial layout of the B&B reflecting the regional culture

4.3 Design Elements

The design elements are an important part of the presentation of regional culture, which often includes local history, folklore, geography and geomorphology, human and material products, etc., while the B&B is a platform for communicating and displaying regional culture to the outside world. The design elements are often derived from some figurative objects of the local culture and in the application of the design there will be an extraction of the elements, a transformation of the elements and a concrete application of the elements. These figurative objects are transformed and processed into abstract shapes for better use in spatial structures, interface shapes, furnishings and even the brand logo of the B&B (see Fig. 5).

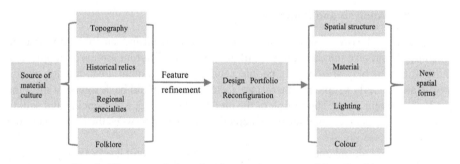

Fig. 5. The extrapolation of regional culture on spatial styling ideas

Through the concrete practice of design, we can see from Table 1 that the elements extracted from the regional culture are transformed and processed through design into an innovative form or shape, decorating the space with the help of different combinations and contrasts of materials and lighting. The space is thus shaped by the local culture and has a certain uniqueness.

Table 1. Regional cultural design practices in B&B spaces

Regional Culture	Extraction of symbols	Space utilisation	Design and Innovation Analysis
			The B&B logo design: Inspired by the unique landscape of the Li River in Guilin, the contour lines of the mountain peaks are extracted and the reflection of the water in the mountains is expressed using a misalignment technique, combined with words to form the pattern.
			Based on the shape of the cultural heritage wind and rain bridge, the shape of the silhouette of the bridge pavilion was extracted, simplified and processed, combined with different materials and displayed on the wall through the relationship of the bottom of the figure.
			The spatial structure of the B&B Book Bar Promenade: the design is inspired by the shape of the cross-section of the promenade space of the Wind and Rain Bridge, which is extracted and simplified, with the same extension repeated in the promenade space.
			The reading area of catering space: the contours of the terraced mountain landscape are translated into a cascading effect on the floor and ceiling.
			The design of the luminaires in the B&B: the shape is inspired by the 'door pin' in traditional architecture, taking the cross-sectional shape of a door pin and retaining the shape of the plexiglass flower.

4.4   Technology Applications

In his book "The Way of the Future", Bill Gates describes the concept of the integration of "human-machine objects" and the application scenarios of the smart home, many of which have already been realised in the future[4]. Smart cities, smart villages and smart homes are the trend of development today. The intelligence of the home is more focused on remote control of various devices, the B&B does not need overly complex control mode, he space can incorporate modern technologies such as online media, digital technology and intelligent control. The most convenient for the customer today would be a mobile application, which can provide services such as booking, payment, room information request and use of the environment by entering the programme through the mobile phone, and even include a travel guide, recommendations for nearby attractions, maps, public transport information, a guide to buying local specialities, etc. Each B&B tailors an exclusive set of interactive programmes and launches the programme during the traveller's stay, perfecting the travel service. The user's accommodation experience and understanding of the surrounding local culture is enhanced. So whether it is management, service, business models or even interaction with local culture, all can be intelligently enhanced with the help of the internet and digital technology.

Compared to the traditional models of regional cultural promotion, online platforms offer a richer and more personalised type, not limited to the traditional space and time frames, and have the advantage of being convenient, real-time, comprehensive and accessible, with the B&B manager or the B&B as a brand maintaining interaction with the user even after the end of the trip.

4.5 Interactive Design

Considering the relationship between people and people, people and things in the B&B space, the purpose of interactive design in the B&B space is to enhance the user experience, increase the interactivity of the space and create a more comfortable and convenient living environment.

The Establishment of Common Areas.
Users can increase interpersonal communication and interaction in B&Bs through common areas such as kitchens, cinemas, study rooms, bars and game rooms. Activities such as exhibitions, lectures, performances and pick-ups on local culture can be organised in B&Bs, helping to create cultural communication between travellers that goes beyond language.

Interactive Installations.
Interactive installations in public areas can be static images, such as graphic patterns of regional cultural atmospheres, photo walls, etc., or dynamic objects, such as music, flowing lights, water features, dynamic electronic devices on screens, etc., that express the cultural atmosphere.

Human-Machine Interaction.
The early human-machine interaction is mainly to meet the service needs of users, but now and even in the future, more attention is paid to the sense of interaction between the environment and the spirit, and regional culture is a very important source object for rendering the environment atmosphere. The immersive, emotional and strong experience characteristics are applied to sensory, action, voice and other interaction methods to help users create an immersive interactive experience, and even more advanced interaction

modes such as AR and VR can be tried [5]. Mobile phones have become an important object that users carry with them today, and are also an important medium for communicating information, whether it is social, learning or entertainment behaviour, and can also achieve interaction with local culture.

4.6 Storytelling

Storytelling is a way of combining design elements and storylines to make spaces more lively and immersive. Spatial ambience, spatial forms, courtyards, furniture, etc. can all be integrated into a storyline with a regional cultural context to enhance the user experience and interactivity. Presenting scenarios and design elements in a storytelling way will make the design more interesting and appealing, open up the possibility of adding a human touch and interest to the product or service, improve the user's sense of experience and experiential effect, and bring new ideas, new directions and new market opportunities for products and sales.

To sum up, the interaction design of the B&B space under the characteristics of the regional culture is based on the user's experience, which can be summarised into three main parts: business behaviour, media innovation and spatial experience, among which there will be some common techniques or paths, but these specific techniques and paths are not completely independent and can interpenetrate each other (see Fig. 6).

Fig. 6. Interaction systems in the context of regional cultural identity

5   Conclusion

The combination of traditional culture and modern technology has contributed greatly to the promotion of local culture and economy, as well as bringing convenience and a sense of spiritual pleasure to the act of living. The study of the interaction of people, objects and space can make a difference under certain conditions. Cultural creativity, which can contribute to economic development, can also transmit and preserve cultural heritage. Compared to traditional hotels, B&Bs are closer to the local environment in terms of architectural design, functional layout and furnishings. Communication and interaction between the user and the housekeeper or owner are more relaxed and casual, which is a better advantage for the dissemination of regional culture. It is also an important task of interaction design for travellers to be able to experience the local culture in their daily food, accommodation and behaviour at the same time, and regional culture is also an indispensable link in promoting tourism consumption: cultural creativity in the B&B space provides new ideas and options for users, in both forms, and should satisfy people's aesthetic, experiential and emotional needs for cultural and creative products on the basis of satisfying functional needs, thus forming a broader and more far-reaching consumption model that is separate from the cultural and creative products themselves.

Funding. Research topics of philosophy and social science planning of Guangxi Zhuang Autonomous Region, "Research on Heritage Protection and Innovation of Ethnic Traditional Villages under the Perspective of "Design Governance (Serial number:21FMZ036).

References

1. Xixiang Ye, F.: Research on the Interior Design of Minshuku Based on Regional Culture. Hunan Institute of Technology, 9–10 (2022)
2. Lina Yan, F., Yi Zhang, S.: Lodging in the People: The Way of B&B Design, 1st edn. Chemical Industry Press, Beijin (2019)
3. Song Huang, F.: Application of interaction design in cultural and creative products. Cult. Ind. **231**(14), 156–158 (2022)
4. Pengyuan Shen, F.: Research on the application of smart home in the design of Huzhou Moganshan Homestay. Huzhou Normal University, 13–15 (2022)
5. Yutong Zhou, F., Jie Liu, S.: Research on interaction design of museums from the perspective of audience experience. J. N. Media Res. **8**(22), 37–40 (2022)

The Influence of Design Aesthetics on the Purchase Intention of AI-Generated Products: Taking Cultural and Creative Products as an Example

Xinrui Zhang and Luo Wang[(✉)]

School of Design, Hunan University, Changsha, China
1426710239@qq.com

Abstract. Artificial intelligence is currently being widely used in product design activities to help companies efficiently produce creative products that meet consumer needs. However, consumers' attitudes towards AI-generated products are still unclear. Therefore, it is of great significance to study how consumers make decisions to purchase such products. In this paper, we examine the relationship between design aesthetics, attitudes toward AI, curiosity, and purchase intentions based on the SOR (Stimulus-Organism-Response) model. We conducted an online questionnaire survey and used partial least squares (PLS) statistics to test the model. The results show that purchase intention is directly and positively affected by both design aesthetics and attitude towards artificial intelligence, and that attitudes toward AI partially mediated the relationship between design aesthetics and purchase intention. Also, curiosity positively moderated the relationship between design aesthetics and attitudes toward AI. In summary, this study can complement research on consumer attitudes towards AI-generated products and help designers and marketers create design norms to improve the competitiveness of their products.

Keywords: AI-generated products · Design aesthetics · Purchase intention · Attitudes toward AI · Curiosity

1 Introduction

In recent years, artificial intelligence technology has developed at a rapid pace, showing a tendency to surpass humans in many professional fields. The performance of AI in the field of creative design, which is traditionally considered to require human intelligence, is also producing breakthroughs. Artificial intelligence is now being widely used in the design activities of various products. Among them, cultural and creative products are products that contain both practicality and culture and are well liked by consumers. Cultural and creative products are consumer products with compound value, and their design requires attention to innovation, culture, and technology. Since, artificial intelligence-based design methods have excellent performance in these aspects [1, 2]. Therefore, this paper takes cultural and creative products as an example to explore the influence mechanism of AI-generated products on purchase intention. The generative design method based on artificial intelligence incorporates artificial intelligence algorithms such as machine learning and deep learning in traditional generative design to achieve a more efficient, fast, and accurate design process. Companies have started to use AI technology to generate creative patterns with cultural elements to assist designers in product development. For example, Microsoft Xiaobing provides an AI design service that can generate many artistic patterns for design quickly. This AI-generated design mode has already provided high-quality customized products for several enterprises. This innovative mode can help companies to rapidly improve their design capabilities and reduce development costs [2], and at the same time, it also helps to meet consumers' diverse and personalized design aesthetic needs and provide innovative consumer experiences [3].

Content generation is an important area of intelligent design, and the application of intelligent content generation methods such as text-generated images [4], style migration [5], and image enhancement [6] can substantially improve the efficiency of design.AI generative design mod has a wide range of applications and has begun to play an important role in the design of graphic visuals [7], clothing [8], architecture [9], industrial products [10], and environmental concepts [11]. Among the studies related to AI-generated cultural creative products, Wang and Alamusi [12] proposed a product design method for watercolor painting cultural creative products based on style migration algorithm. Wang's [13] study used intelligently generated art images to develop design strategies for personalized cultural creative products. Zhang and Romainoor [14], applied GANs and Kmeans generative design approach to develop high-quality cultural heritage creative products and evaluate the finished products. Most of the current studies focus on the algorithmic implementation and design methods of AI generative design, and few studies have explored the impact of generative design models on consumer attitudes from the perspective of consumer behavior. Since, consumer behavior studies are important for the success of new products in the market. Therefore, this paper aims to examine consumers' willingness to purchase AI-generated cultural and creative products to complement the above-mentioned deficiencies.

Previous studies have shown that there is a bias against AI performance in art creation, which can affect their aesthetic evaluation of AI-generated art [15]. This implies a possible market risk for companies to use AI-generated technology to develop creative products. Given that the integration of AI technologies in product design has become an industry trend, there is an urgent need for researchers and companies to understand how generative design will affect consumer behavior. Therefore, it is important to study the determinants that drive consumer purchases.

We specifically study the following two questions to examine consumers' attitudes towards AI-generated products: (1) What are the driving factors for consumers to purchase AI-generated cultural and creative products; (2) What are the mechanisms of action of these factors. With the transformation of the design paradigm, consumers pay more and more attention to the aesthetic attributes of products rather than functional attributes [16]. Under traditional design methods, the impact of design aesthetics on purchase intention has been understood [17]. In this paper we examine the impact of design aesthetics on purchase intentions of generative products. Based on the SOR (Stimulus-Organism-Response) model, we constructed a conceptual model between design aesthetics and purchase intention. This paper examines the positive impact of design aesthetics on purchase intention and excavates the mediating role of attitudes toward AI, as well as the moderating effect of curiosity on the relationship between design aesthetics and attitudes toward artificial intelligence.

Our research will provide theoretical and practical contributions in several ways. In terms of theory, we expand the theoretical research on design aesthetics and supplement the research gap on consumers' attitudes towards generative cultural and creative products. In terms of practice, we have clarified consumers' attitudes through empirical research based on the SOR model. Consumer attitudes toward products can be translated into design information and used to create design specifications. These design specifications can help designers and marketers consider user needs more when formulating strategies for cultural and creative products generated by artificial intelligence, and ultimately enhance the market competitiveness of their products.

This study is organized as follows: In Sect. 2, we provide a literature review, research model and hypotheses. Section 3 introduces our research methods. Section 4 conducts the data analysis and shows the experimental results, and Sect. 5 discusses the results. We then continue with the conclusions and limitations in Sect. 6.

2 Theoretical Background and Hypothesis

2.1 SOR Model

The SOR (Stimulus–Organism–Response) model is a classic psychological and behavioral scientific model proposed by Mechrabian and Russell in 1974 and is often used in research in the field of consumer behavior [18]. The stimulus (S) in the model refers to the external environmental factors that can affect the individual, the organism (O) refers to the internal state of the individual such as attitude, emotion, and cognitive behavior, and the response (R) refers to the behavior of the individual according to the received stimulus and its own state. Emotional expression, cognitive evaluation, behavioral tendency, etc. For how a product succeeds in the market, the SOR model can help analyze and explain the influencing mechanism among factors. The product's external visual stimulation design aesthetics (S) will affect the consumer's psychological process, that is, the attitude towards artificial intelligence (O), and ultimately affect the generation of purchase intention (R). Using the SOR model as the overall theoretical framework of this paper can explain the internal mechanism of design aesthetics on the purchase intention of AI-generated cultural and creative products, better understand the psychological factors that affect consumers' purchase decisions and formulate targeted design and marketing for enterprises Strategies provide guidance. This study puts forward hypotheses with reference to the existing literature, establishes the SOR framework, and explores the impact of various variables on purchase intention.

2.2 Design Aesthetics

Design aesthetics has a crucial role in product design, which influences people's perceptions and behaviors of products through human vision. Studies have shown that design aesthetics can influence the first impression of a product [19], enhance brand evaluation [20], and promote consumer perceived value [21]. In this study design aesthetics is specifically expressed in the aesthetic experience of the product, i.e., the expressiveness and attractiveness of the appearance, the professionalism of the design, and the pleasure the product brings to the consumer. Since design aesthetics is an important factor driving choice behavior [17, 22–24], and previous studies have found significant differences in consumer purchase intentions between products with high and low design aesthetics ratings [25]. Higher design aesthetics of artificially intelligent generative products implies higher purchase intention. Therefore, the hypothesis is proposed:

H1. Design aesthetics positively affects consumers' purchase intentions for AI-generated products.

2.3 Attitudes Towards AI

Attitude is a key factor influencing consumer adoption of technology [26, 27]. Numerous studies have shown that the better consumers' attitudes toward a technology, the higher their acceptance of related technology products [28, 29]. Payne [30] found that consumers' attitudes toward AI had a positive impact on product use behavior. Hong [31] found that acceptance of AI's creative capabilities was necessary for people to positively evaluate AI's artistic performance. In this study, attitudes toward AI were interpreted as the level of acceptance of AI's design capabilities, with higher ratings indicating a higher level of acceptance of their generative designs. Therefore, the more positive consumers' attitudes toward AI's design capabilities the higher their willingness to purchase. Thus, the hypothesis is proposed:

H2. Attitudes towards AI positively influence consumers' purchase intentions for AI-generated products.

Moreover, since the design aesthetics of a product are important for user acceptance of the technology [23, 32]. For example, Hsiao [33] found that design aesthetics positively influenced users' attitudes toward smart watches. Designs with high aesthetic value can demonstrate demonstrated excellent AI idea generation capabilities and can improve consumer attitudes towards smart design. So, hypothesize:

H3. Design aesthetics positively influence individual consumer attitudes toward AI.

2.4 Curiosity

Curiosity reflects the intrinsic desire to acquire new information [34]. This desire is elicited by novel, complex or unclear stimuli that stimulate interest and prompt exploratory behavior to bridge the information-information gap [35–37]. Several studies have been conducted to reveal the impact of curiosity on purchase intention in different consumption scenarios, such as online shopping [38] and cultural consumption [39]. A study by Zhang et al. [3] explored the mediating effect of curiosity on consumers' willingness to pay in the context of intelligent design and found that consumers were more curious about the concept of "artificially intelligent design" than products designed using traditional design methods, which led to an increase in willingness to pay. Curiosity in this study represents consumers' intrinsic interest and novelty triggered by intelligently generated creative products, as well as their desire for AI knowledge. Since acquiring knowledge and satisfying curiosity can be pleasurable [40], when consumers have higher curiosity about AI-generated designs, they can be evoked with higher pleasure by the product's design and accordingly enhance their evaluation of the design aesthetics. This strengthens the role of design aesthetics in making consumers' attitudes towards AI more positive. Therefore, the hypothesis is proposed:

H4. The more curious consumers are, the more pronounced the positive impact of design aesthetics on attitudes toward AI.

Based on the above hypotheses, a research model of the factors influencing AI-generated cultural and creative purchase intention is constructed, as shown in Fig. 1.

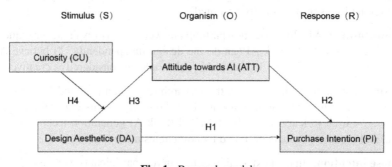

Fig. 1. Research model

3 Methods

3.1 Participants

Three hundred and twenty-eight participants completed the survey, of which those who did not pass the attention check were excluded from further analysis. A final valid complete sample of 216 participants for analysis was generated, of which 60.2% were male and 39.8% were female, with an overall mean age of 29.8 years.

3.2 Procedure

The survey was conducted through Baidu's data crowdsourcing platform with a sample database of over 17,000,000 respondents covering 300 cities in China. At the beginning of the questionnaire, we told participants: "This questionnaire is about your attitude.

The questionnaire will be administered anonymously. All information is guaranteed to be used for academic research purposes only, not for commercial purposes". We then showed and introduced them to a T-shirt of a cultural and creative product generated by artificial intelligence. The experimental stimuli were chosen considering that the garment has good sales in various categories of cultural and creative products [14], as well as the fact that he is the most common clothing product designed by AI [3]. Subsequently, participants were required to answer item and demographic questions related to the variables.

3.3 Measures

To accommodate this study, all measures in this survey were adapted from previous literature. All items were measured on a 7-point Likert scale. The details are described below.

Design Aesthetics. Participants were asked to assess their level of agreement with three measures adapted from Hsiao [26]: 'The overall appearance of this AI-generated product is attractive', 'The colors of this AI-generated product are aesthetically pleasing', and 'This product looks professionally designed'.

Attitudes towards AI. In this section participants were asked to evaluate three questions from Hong et al. [31] "I think AI can do the design independently" "I believe AI can create novel designs" "The work designed by AI should be considered as creative work".

Curiosity. This part is adapted from the research of Litman [36] and Zhang et al.[3]. The items are as follows, "I am curious about how AI designs cultural and creative products," "I want to learn more about AI," "I think AI generation technology makes cultural and creative products designed by companies more innovative ".

Purchase Intention. In the next section of the survey, participants were asked to assess their purchase intention, measured from a study by Li et al. [41]. "I would consider buying this product," "I would tell others about the benefits of this product," and "I would recommend buying this product to friends and relatives."

4   Data Analysis and Results

In this paper, the partial least squares method (PLS) is used to test the structural equation. PLS technology is a structural equation model analysis technology based on principal components, which has no strict requirements on data normality and sample size. Therefore, this paper utilizes the PLS technique in the SmartPLS 4.0 software and follows a two-step process, first analyzing the measurement model and then the structural model.

4.1   Measurement Model

Structural validity was first tested. As shown in Table 1, in this paper, Cronbach's Alpha of all constructs were numerically larger than the threshold value of 0.7, range from 0.717

to 0.825, indicating that the observed variables of the latent variables have sufficient reliability. The values of the composite reliability of the constructs range from 0.841 to 0.895, all of which are much higher than the threshold value of 0.700, indicating that the model has a high internal consistency [42]. The convergent validity of the model was evaluated with reference to the factor loadings of all observed variables and the average variance extracted (AVE). The factor loadings of all items ranged from 0.756 to 0.874, which were higher than the threshold of 0.700. The AVE of each construct ranged from 0.639 to 0.740, which were higher than the threshold of 0.500, indicating that the convergent validity of the model was good [43]. The Fornell-Larcker criterion can be used to test the discriminant validity of the model. The maximum value of the correlation coefficient for all latent variables in this paper is 0.756, which is smaller than the square root of AVE for any of the latent variables (see Table 2), showed that the scale had good discriminative validity [43]. Overall, all aspects of structural validity met all basic requirements. In addition, this paper determined the common method bias by the indicator of variance inflation factors (VIF). The test results showed that the VIF values of each latent variable ranged from 1.041 to 2.077, which was less than the threshold value of 3.000 [44], indicating that the common method bias had no significant impact on the analysis results.

Table 1. The reliability and consistency of the measurement model.

Construct	Item	Loading	α	CR	AVE
Design aesthetics (DA)	DA1	0.871	0.805	0.885	0.720
	DA2	0.847			
	DA3	0.827			
Attitudes towards AI (ATT)	ATT1	0.832	0.770	0.867	0.685
	ATT2	0.802			
	ATT3	0.848			
Curiosity (CU)	CU1	0.756	0.717	0.841	0.639
	CU2	0.814			
	CU3	0.825			
Purchase Intention (PI)	PI1	0.867	0.825	0.895	0.740
	PI2	0.840			
	PI3	0.874			

Table 2. Discriminatory validity of measurement model

Construct	ATT	DA	CU	PI
ATT	**0.828**			
DA	0.673	**0.849**		
CU	0.566	0.631	**0.799**	
PI	0.755	0.676	0.606	**0.860**

Note: DA: Design aesthetics; CU: Curiosity; ATT: Attitude towards AI; PI: Purchase Intention

4.2 Structural Model

In this paper, the significance of each hypothesis is tested by Bootstrapping technique, and the number of repetitive samplings is set to 5000 times. The results of the path test of the model are shown in Table 3 and Fig. 2. The cumulative explained overall variance of the model is 62.2%, indicating that consumers' attitudes toward AI have good explanatory power on their purchase intention. Specifically design aesthetics directly influenced attitudes toward AI ($\beta = 0.583$, $t = 9.081$, $p < 0.001$), and hypothesis 1 was supported. Design aesthetics directly influenced purchase intention ($\beta = 0.0.396$, $t = 4.752$, $p < 0.001$), and hypothesis 2 was supported. Attitude toward AI directly influenced purchase intention ($\beta = 0.549$, $t = 8.951$, $p < 0.001$), and hypothesis 3 was supported.

Table 3. The result of hypothesis testing.

Hypothesis	Path	Coefficient	t value	Supported
H1	DA → PI	0.306***	4.752	Yes
H2	ATT → PI	0.549***	8.951	Yes
H3	DA → ATT	0.583***	9.081	Yes
H4	CU × DA → ATT	0.142*	2.478	Yes

Therefore, an individual's perception of the design aesthetics of things affects his or her attitude, and at the same time, the attitude promotes the individual's behavioral intention. According to the SOR model, stimulus factors need to act on response factors by influencing organismic factors, and to fully understand the mechanism of action between variables, this study also examined whether attitudes toward AI play a mediating role in the effect of design aesthetics on purchase intentions. Based on Hair et al.'s approach [45], it was examined whether attitudes toward AI mediated the effect of design aesthetics on purchase intentions. We calculated the explanation of variance accounted for (VAF) to determine the strength of the indirect effect associated with the total effect, and this VAF value is higher than 20% and lower than 80%, indicating that there is a partial mediating effect. Results show that attitudes toward AI significantly mediates

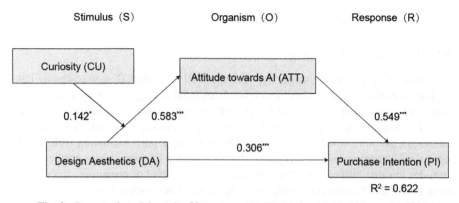

Stimulus (S)   Organism (O)   Response (R)

Fig. 2. Structural model results. **Note:** *p < ψ0.05; **p < ψ0.01; ***p < ψ0.001.

the relationship between design aesthetics and purchase intention, whose VAF value is 55%, exceeding the recommended threshold.

The results of the hypothesis test also indicated that the interaction effect of design aesthetics and curiosity had a significant positive effect on attitudes toward AI ($\beta = 0.142$, $p < 0.05$), therefore, hypothesis 4 was supported and the stronger the curiosity of consumers the more significant the effect of design aesthetics on attitudes toward AI, as shown in Fig. 3.

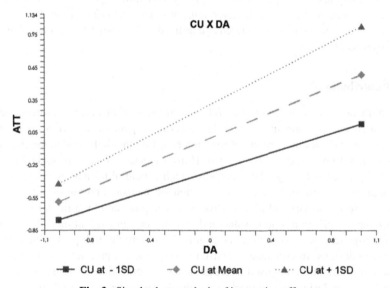

Fig. 3. Simple slope analysis of interaction effects

5   Discussion and Implication

5.1   Discussion of the Results

Experimental results show that our hypotheses are all supported. Design aesthetics has a significant positive impact on attitudes towards artificial intelligence, and purchase intention is directly and positively affected by both design aesthetics and attitudes towards artificial intelligence, and in the relationship between design aesthetics and purchase intentions, attitudes towards artificial intelligence play a part. Mediating Role. At the same time, curiosity positively regulates the relationship between design aesthetics and attitudes towards artificial intelligence. The higher the level of consumer curiosity, the more positively the impact of design aesthetics on attitudes towards AI.

The study comprehensively analyzes the important driving effect of design aesthetics on purchase intention by analyzing direct influence, mediation effect and moderating effect. Specifically, consistent with previous findings [25], higher design aesthetic evaluations imply higher purchase intentions. The better the attitude towards artificial intelligence, the higher the purchase intention. Attitudes towards AI play an important mediating role when a product exhibits good design aesthetics, consumers' attitudes towards AI will improve, which in turn translates into purchase intentions. On this basis, curiosity can further enhance the positive impact of design aesthetics on attitudes towards artificial intelligence, and as curiosity increases, the impact of design aesthetics on attitudes towards artificial intelligence also increases. We speculate that design aesthetics is a way to satisfy and guide people's curiosity by appealing appearance, providing pleasurable experiences, stimulating imagination, and conveying information. Therefore, the curiosity factor can be fully considered and utilized in the design process to enhance the attractiveness of products.

5.2   Contributions

The significance of the research is as follows. In terms of theory, first, we supplement the research gap of consumers' attitudes towards AI-generated cultural and creative products. Second, through empirical research based on the SOR model, the theoretical research on design aesthetics is expanded. Third, we obtained the statistical relationship of the four variables through data analysis, which is helpful for a more comprehensive understanding of consumers' purchase intention mechanism. In terms of practice, in the future, the design of cultural and creative products generated by artificial intelligence will not only focus on aesthetic value and enhance consumers' attitudes towards artificial intelligence, but also enhance consumers' curiosity through packaging and other appearance designs. In conclusion, consumer responses to products can be translated into design information and used to create design specifications. These design specifications can help designers and marketers consider user needs more when formulating strategies for cultural and creative products generated by artificial intelligence, thereby improving the competitiveness of their products.

5.3 Limitations and Future Works

The following limitations of this study may affect the ultimate generalizability of the findings. First, the experiment of this study is only conducted through online questionnaires, and the experimental results may be limited by the online display effect of generative cultural and creative products. Further research can be improved by adding field research or using a set of photos to display products from multiple angles online. Second, the stimuli used in the study are clothing cultural and creative products based on the design of artificial intelligence image generation. In future research, the purchase intention of more types of generative products can be explored to improve the generality of the conclusions.

6 Conclusion

Based on the SOR model, this study comprehensively investigates the influence of design aesthetics, attitude towards artificial intelligence and curiosity on purchase intention. We verify the significant effects of design aesthetics and attitudes towards AI on purchase intention, and AI mediates the relationship between design aesthetics and purchase intention. Furthermore, the study found that curiosity can significantly moderate the relationship between design aesthetics and perceptions of artificial intelligence. Specifically, the higher the curiosity of consumers, the more obvious the impact of design aesthetics on attitudes towards artificial intelligence. We recommend that marketers and designers formulate generative product design strategies based on the findings of this study to improve the competitiveness of corporate products. In addition, we hope that this research work will advance the research on design aesthetics and generative product design to help better understand the influencing mechanism of consumers' purchase of such products.

References

1. Verganti, R., Vendraminelli, L., Iansiti, M.: Innovation and design in the age of artificial intelligence. J. Prod. Innov. Manage **37**, 212–227 (2020)
2. Tang, Y.C., et al.: A review of design intelligence: progress, problems, and challenges. Front. Inform. Technol. Elect. Eng. **20**, 1595–1617 (2019)
3. Zhang, H., Bai, X.F., Ma, Z.G.: Consumer reactions to AI design: exploring consumer willingness to pay for AI-designed products. Psychol. Mark. **39**, 2171–2183 (2022)
4. Xu, T., et al.: AttnGAN: fine-grained text to image generation with attentional generative adversarial networks. In: 31st IEEE/CVF Conference on Computer Vision and Pattern Recognition (CVPR), pp. 1316–1324. IEEE, NEW YORK (2018)
5. Zhu, J.Y., Park, T., Isola, P., Efros, A.A.: Unpaired image-to-image translation using cycle-consistent adversarial networks. In: 16th IEEE International Conference on Computer Vision (ICCV), pp. 2242–2251. IEEE, NEW YORK (2017)
6. Yoon, Y., Jeon, H.G., Yoo, D., Lee, J.Y., Kweon, I.S.: Learning a deep convolutional network for light-field image super-resolution. In: IEEE International Conference on Computer Vision (ICCV), pp. 57–65. IEEE, NEW YORK (2015)
7. Li, G.D., Yang, X.: Smartbanner: intelligent banner design framework that strikes a balance between creative freedom and design rules. Multimed. Tools Appl. **82**(12), 1–15 (2022)

8. Singh, M., Bajpai, U., Vijayarajan, V., Prasath, S.: Generation of fashionable clothes using generative adversarial networks a preliminary feasibility study. Int. J. Cloth. Sci. Technol. **32**, 177–187 (2020)

9. As, I., Pal, S., Basu, P.: Artificial intelligence in architecture: generating conceptual design via deep learning. Int. J. Archit. Comput. **16**, 306–327 (2018)

10. Liu, Z.B., Gao, F., Wang, Y.Z.: A generative adversarial network for AI-aided chair design. In: 2nd IEEE International Conference on Multimedia Information Processing and Retrieval (MIPR), pp. 486–490. IEEE, NEW YORK (2019)

11. Duan, Y.J., Zhang, J.: A novel AI-based visual stimuli generation approach for environment concept design. Comput. Intell. Neurosci. **2022**, 12 (2022)

12. Wang, Q., Alamusi, H.: Design of watercolor cultural and creative products based on style transfer algorithm. Math. Probl. Eng. **2022**, 9 (2022)

13. Wang, Y.: On personalized cultural and creative product design strategy based on AI painting generation. In: 2021 International Conference on Big Data Analytics for Cyber-Physical System in Smart City vol. 102, 1317–1323 (2021)

14. Zhang, B.L., Romainoor, N.H.: Research on artificial intelligence in new year prints: the application of the generated pop art style images on cultural and creative products. Appl. Sci.-Basel **13**, 22 (2023)

15. Chamberlain, R., Mullin, C., Scheerlinck, B., Wagemans, J.: Putting the art in artificial: aesthetic responses to computer-generated art. Psychol. Aesthet. Creat. Arts **12**, 177–192 (2018)

16. Liang, D.: Aesthetic value evaluation for digital cultural and creative products with artificial intelligence. Wirel. Commun. Mob. Comput. **2022**, 10 (2022)

17. Li, Y., Li, J.: The influence of design aesthetics on consumers' purchase intention toward cultural and creative products: evidence from the palace museum in China. Front. Psychol. **13**, 9 (2022)

18. Mehrabian, A., Russell, J.A.: An Approach to Environmental Psychology. The MIT Press (1974)

19. Diefenbach, S., Hassenzahl, M.: The dilemma of the hedonic - Appreciated, but hard to justify. Interact. Comput. **23**, 461–472 (2011)

20. Kreuzbauer, R., Malter, A.J.: Embodied cognition and new product design: changing product form to influence brand categorization. J. Prod. Innov. Manage **22**, 165–176 (2005)

21. Toufani, S., Stanton, J.P., Chikweche, T.: The importance of aesthetics on customers' intentions to purchase smartphones. Mark. Intell. Plan. **35**, 316–338 (2017)

22. Creusen, M.E.H., Schoormans, J.P.L.: The different roles of product appearance in consumer choice. J. Prod. Innov. Manage **22**, 63–81 (2005)

23. Hsiao, K.L., Chen, C.C.: What drives smartwatch purchase intention? Perspectives from hardware, software, design, and value. Telemat. Inform. **35**, 103–113 (2018)

24. Wang, J., Hsu, Y.: Does sustainable perceived value play a key role in the purchase intention driven by product aesthetics? Taking smartwatch as an example. Sustainability **11**, 24 (2019)

25. Shi, A.Q., Huo, F.R., Hou, G.H.: Effects of design aesthetics on the perceived value of a product. Front. Psychol. **12**, 11 (2021)

26. Hsiao, K.L.: Android smartphone adoption and intention to pay for mobile internet Perspectives from software, hardware, design, and value. Libr. Hi Tech **31**, 216–235 (2013)

27. Chawla, D., Joshi, H.: Consumer attitude and intention to adopt mobile wallet in India - an empirical study. Int. J. Bank Mark. **37**, 1590–1618 (2019)

28. Lin, J.S.C., Hsieh, P.L.: The role of technology readiness in customers' perception and adoption of self-service technologies. Int. J. Serv. Ind. Manage. **17**, 497–517 (2006)

29. Liang, Y.L., Lee, S.H., Workman, J.E.: Implementation of artificial intelligence in fashion: are consumers ready? Cloth. Text. Res. J. **38**, 3–18 (2020)

30. Payne, E.M., Peltier, J.W., Barger, V.A.: Mobile banking and AI-enabled mobile banking the differential effects of technological and non-technological factors on digital natives' perceptions and behavior. J. Res. Interact. Mark. **12**, 328–346 (2018)

31. Hong, J.W., Peng, Q.Y., Williams, D.: Are you ready for artificial Mozart and Skrillex? An experiment testing expectancy violation theory and AI music. New Media Soc. **23**, 1920–1935 (2021)

32. Cyr, D., Head, M., Ivanov, A.: Design aesthetics leading to m-loyalty in mobile commerce. Inf. Manage. **43**, 950–963 (2006)

33. Hsiao, K.-L.: What drives smartwatch adoption intention? Comparing apple and non-apple watches. Libr. Hi Tech **35**(1), 186–206 (2017)

34. Hill, K.M., Fombelle, P.W., Sirianni, N.J.: Shopping under the influence of curiosity: how retailers use mystery to drive purchase motivation. J. Bus. Res. **69**, 1028–1034 (2016)

35. Litman, J.A., Collins, R.P., Spielberger, C.D.: The nature and measurement of sensory curiosity. Pers. Individ. Differ. **39**, 1123–1133 (2005)

36. Litman, J.A.: Interest and deprivation factors of epistemic curiosity. Pers. Individ. Differ. **44**, 1585–1595 (2008)

37. Loewenstein, G.: The psychology of curiosity: a review and reinterpretation. J. L. Kellogg Graduate School of Management, Northwestern University; Department of Management, Portland State University, vol. 116, pp. 75–98 (1994)

38. Koo, D.M., Ju, S.H.: The interactional effects of atmospherics and perceptual curiosity on emotions and online shopping intention. Comput. Hum. Behav. **26**, 377–388 (2010)

39. Manolika, M., Baltzis, A.: Curiosity's pleasure? Exploring motives for cultural consumption. Int. J. Nonprofit Volunt. Sect. Mark. **25**, 11 (2020)

40. Perlovsky, L.I., Bonniot-Cabanac, M.-C., Cabanac, M.: Curiosity and pleasure. In: The 2010 International Joint Conference on Neural Networks (IJCNN), pp. 1–3. IEEE, (2010)

41. Li, Z., Shu, S.J., Shao, J., Booth, E., Morrison, A.M.: Innovative or Not? The effects of consumer perceived value on purchase intentions for the palace museum's cultural and creative products. Sustainability **13**, 19 (2021)

42. Bagozzi, R.P., Yi, Y.: On the evaluation of structural equation models. J. Acad. Mark. Sci. **16**, 74–94 (1988)

43. Fornell, C.U.M., Larcker, D.F.: Evaluating structural equation models with unobservable variables and measurement error. Univ. Mich. Northwest. Univ. **18**, 39–50 (1981)

44. Hair, J.F., Risher, J.J., Sarstedt, M., Ringle, C.M.: When to use and how to report the results of PLS-SEM. Eur. Bus. Rev. **31**, 2–24 (2019)

45. Hair Jr., F., Sarstedt, M., Hopkins, L., Kuppelwieser, V.: Partial least squares structural equation modeling (PLS-SEM) an emerging tool in business research. Eur. Bus. Rev. **26**, 106–121 (2014)

Combining Offline with Online: A User Experience Study of Recruitment Platforms for Migrant Workers in China

Hangyu Zhou[1], Fanghao Song[1(✉)], Yulin Wang[1], and Min Hua[2]

[1] School of Mechanical Engineering, Shandong University, Jinan 250061, China
{202114424,202114422}@mail.sdu.edu.cn, songfanghao@sdu.edu.cn
[2] USC-SJTU Institute of Cultural and Creative Industry, Shanghai Jiao Tong University, Shanghai 200241, China
huamin@sjtu.edu.cn

Abstract. The shift from traditional offline labour markets to online recruitment platforms (ORPs) in China has provided employees with more efficient job-searching services. However, the low frequency of use of ORPs by migrant workers, which stands at around 20%, highlights the need to examine factors that influence their engagement. This study aims to address this gap by exploring the factors that affect low engagement on ORPs and proposing a design strategy to enhance user experience. Using Design Research Methodology (DRM), the study conducted a literature review to understand the current labour market and ORP landscape. Furthermore, a field study was conducted in Jinan, China, which involved observations and user interviews to investigate employment behaviours in labour markets and gather insights into user experiences on ORPs. Based on the findings, the OwO design strategy, which combines offline negotiating with online matching and rating, was proposed. To evaluate the design strategy, two service touchpoints, the D-dong Labour mobile app and the D-dong Labour station, were developed before conducting the System Usability Scale (SUS) evaluation. The SUS results indicate that two touchpoints effectively enhanced the user experience. Although the total SUS score (mean = 72.8) of D-dong Labour was at an acceptable grade, the individual items results (SUS01 = 3.87, SUS03 = 4.27, SUS07 = 4.20 and SUS09 = 4.27) revealed high levels of engagement and perceived ease of use among the users. This study contributes to the literature in three ways, i) providing ORPs companies with a general design strategy to improve their product experience, ii) attracting active participation of migrant workers and other workers in the digital transformation of the labour market, and iii) providing public services with decision-making assistance and minimizing the risk of unemployment and market irregularities.

Keywords: User Experience · Online Recruitment Platforms · Migrant Workers · SUS · Service Design

M. Kurosu et al. (Eds.): HCII 2023, LNCS 14054, pp. 670–683, 2023.
https://doi.org/10.1007/978-3-031-48038-6_44

1 Introduction

The labour market in China is transforming from offline to online and from fixed to flexible employment [1], which has implications for the employment behaviour of migrant workers. The gap between urban and rural areas in China has led to a migration of the rural population to urban areas [2]. As a result, rural-to-urban migrant workers have become the most important group in China's flexible employment market. With the emergence of e-commerce, the transactional behaviour between employers and migrant workers is gradually shifting from offline labour markets to online recruitment platforms (ORPs). Compared to traditional labour markets, ORPs have solved the problem of information asymmetry between migrant workers and employers and provided users with efficient job-searching services. However, despite the increasing number of ORPs have been developed, the user experience on these platforms has hardly been explored. Existing platforms focus solely on information matching, such as the type of work and recruitment rules, while ignoring the offline job-seeking habits of migrant workers. It was found that only 20% of migrant workers were able to get going with these platforms. The factors that contribute to low engagement on ORPs need to be explored, and an effective design strategy must be proposed and implemented to improve the user experience on ORPs for migrant workers.

Based on the findings, the study developed a general design strategy, OwO, which combined offline interactions with online interactions to support better user experience on ORPs for migrant workers. To achieve this, a comprehensive user experience study was conducted using the design research methodology (DRM). DRM is widely applied in design research and design practice, and its main process includes Research Clarification (RC), Descriptive Study I (DS-I), Prescriptive Study (PS), and Descriptive Study II (DS-II) [3]. Following the process, the objectives of the study were: 1) to gain a comprehensive understanding of the current labour markets and ORPs in China, 2) to investigate migrant workers' behaviours in labour markets and user experiences with ORPs, 3) to propose a design strategy and establish success criteria for improving user experience, 4) to develop service touchpoints in accordance with the design strategy to enhance user experience and 5) to assess the effectiveness of the two service touchpoints and evaluate the impact of the design strategy on user experience.

2 Methodology

2.1 Review-Based RC

Labour Markets in China
In China, rural-to-urban migration primarily prompts labour markets in large cities, with individuals seeking greater job opportunities and a better quality of life. According to data from the National Bureau of Statistics, the total number of migrant workers in China reached 292.51 million in 2021, reflecting a 2.4% increase compared to the previous year. The growing population of migrant workers has contributed to labour services for urban development and the lives of city residents. However, the interactions between migrant workers and recruiters have led to the emergence of irregular employment in labour

markets [4], where negotiations and employment activities take place. Unfortunately, in China, these irregular activities have brought about various challenges for cities, including traffic congestion and overcrowding on the streets. These phenomena are related to the mismatch of information during the job search and recruitment processes. In 1984, Hall, R.E. et al. [5] proposed the theory of information asymmetry in the labour market. Information asymmetry is a key characteristic of traditional offline labour markets [6], resulting in a mismatch between employers and migrant workers in the recruitment practice [7]. Consequently, while most migrant workers have spontaneously formed offline labour markets, it is not an efficient means of employment for both migrant workers and recruiters.

ORPs in China

With the advent of digital technology, labour markets in China are undergoing a transformation from offline labour markets to ORPs. The digitalization of labour markets has addressed the problem of information asymmetry through online platforms. These ORPs provide job information to both migrant workers and employers through websites or smartphone applications, matching employers' job requirements with workers' practical skills. Current studies on ORPs mainly focus on exploring efficient features such as job matching and hiring decision-making [8]. On these ORPs, migrant workers and other job seekers can upload their CVs, showcasing their work experience and practical skills, and providing specific information to recruiters. Additionally, some researchers have focused on exploring the phenomenon of hiring discrimination on ORPs [9]. They conducted 20 semi-structured interviews specifically with Muslim-American women of colour to gain insights into this issue. However, existing ORPs in China face challenges in engaging migrant workers. Some ORPs aim to serve not only migrant workers but also other users such as undergraduates and unemployed individuals. Some functions of these ORPs do not align with the job-seeking habits of migrant workers, resulting in a high learning curve, which means that it requires a significant amount of time, effort and practice. Additionally, offline labour markets often cater to short-term employment, while ORPs tend to focus on long-term employment with complex application processes. As a result, fewer migrant workers actively utilize ORPs to find jobs. The low engagement of ORPs among migrant workers is evidence of the need to improve the user experience on ORPs for this particular segment.

Research Model

In summary, based on DRM, the user experience study aims to find out the specific reasons for the low engagement of ORPs among migrant workers and develop a design strategy. First, this study conducted comprehensive research in both offline labour markets and ORPs to draw a general design strategy and to establish success criteria. Second, to support the design strategy, the blended service touchpoints that combine offline recruiting with ORPs were developed by using service design tools. Finally, to evaluate the design strategy, the usability test was carried out by using SUS questionnaires. The research model was outlined in Fig. 1 (the solid-line arrows represent the finished works, the dashed-line arrows represent the future work, and the blank arrows link basic means to main outcomes):

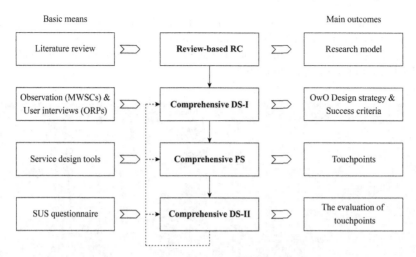

Basic means   Main outcomes

Fig. 1. Research model

2.2 Comprehensive DS-I

In this stage, the study combines observation and user interviews to comprehensively understand migrant workers' job-searching behaviours in Labour Markets and their user experience with ORPs. The field study was conducted in Jinan, China, where migrant workers' service centres (MWSCs) serve as the primary labour markets. Before the observation, extensive urban research was undertaken to gain a thorough understanding of the MWSCs in Jinan. It was observed that these MWSCs were typically located on the outskirts of the city near grade-separated junctions (GSJs). Picture a in Fig. 2 illustrates the four main MWSCs (Huaiyin MWSC, Shizhong MWSC, Jinan central MWSC and Licheng MWSC) marked with filled points, which are situated near four GSJs (Lashan GSJ, Bayi GSJ, Yingxiongshan GSJ and Quanfu GSJ) marked with blank points. A one-day non-involvement observation and a semi-structured interview were conducted at Huaiyin MWSC, which experiences the highest footfall and exhibits typical features. Picture b in Fig. 2 shows the activity square of Huaiyin MWSC.

During the observation, the employment activity at the MWSC was roughly categorized into three stages (Fig. 3): commuting, negotiating, and leaving. In the commuting stage, workers arrived at the square early in the morning around 5:00, had breakfast and a short break, and then waited for employers and other recruiters. In the negotiating stage, recruiters (i.e. employers and citizens) came to the square, searching for workers who matched their job requirements (types of work) from the crowds and negotiating the working time, location, rewards etc. After negotiating, they travelled to the final work location with the selected workers. After 8:00, there was a long-term breaking that those who had not found work engaged in recreational activities while waiting for additional work opportunities or relaxation. In the leaving stage, participants began to leave the square at around 18:00, and some workers went to their final work location for night shifts. Following the observation, the current problems at the MWSC were identified as: 1) low job-searching efficiency and 2) overcrowding on the streets. The low job-searching efficiency resulted from the time-consuming nature and information asymmetry between migrant workers and recruiters. The overcrowding on the streets resulted from the preference that workers gathered around bus stop stations and under the GSJ to wait for job opportunities.

Fig. 2. A. MWSCs and GSJs in Jinan, b. the activity square of Huaiyin MWSC

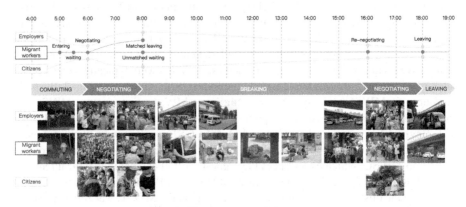

Fig. 3. Employment activity stages

Subsequent user interviews were conducted, focusing on participants' information from three aspects: identity, work and ORPs usage experience. Four researchers, including a presenter, an interviewer, a data recorder, and a photographer, participated in the interview process. After a brief presentation explaining the purpose, nine migrant workers, two employers, and two citizens were individually interviewed for 25 min, answering five to 13 questions. Following the interviews, the frequently used ORPs by migrant workers were categorized into apps with simple functions (such as WeChat) and apps with diverse functions (such as 58 Tongchen and Yupao). It was found that only about 20% of migrant workers were able to effectively use these apps, and they preferred simpler apps. Additionally, most of the applications had not gained the trust of their users.

As a result, the existing ORPs presented low engagement among migrant workers. The possible factors contributing to these issues included the high learning costs associated with ORPs and the offline negotiation habits of migrant workers. In other words, existing ORPs companies have rarely considered offline service touchpoints to improve their product experience.

According to the observation and interviews, three interactions in labour markets (i.e. off-matching, off-negotiating, and off-rating) and three interactions on ORPs (i.e. on-matching, on-negotiating, and on-rating) were defined. First, off-matching contributed to overcrowding and low efficiency, while on-matching was more efficient. Second, compared to on-negotiating by phoning or typing, face-to-face off-negotiating attracted the majority of workers participating. Third, off-rating contributed to recruiters' hiring experience that "memorable profiles" of good workers. In other words, if there were hunting needs, they preferred to choose their familiar and trusted workers in mind. Compared to this empirical experience, digital profiles on ORPs for migrant workers provided recruiters with more objective rating scores of workers.

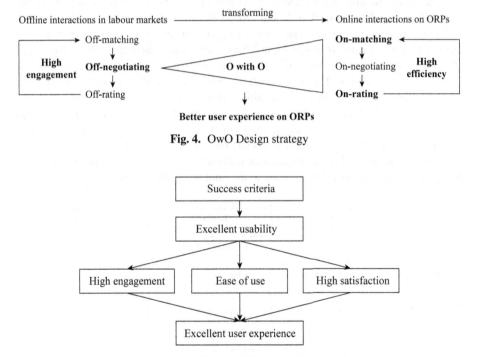

Fig. 4. OwO Design strategy

Fig. 5. Success criteria of ORPs for migrant workers

In summary, it was determined that neither a single offline labour market nor a single online recruitment app could effectively solve the employment problems. The observed issues at the MWSC were low job-searching efficiency and overcrowding on the streets. Additionally, the existing ORPs faced challenges of low engagement and high learning costs for migrant workers. To address these problems, a design strategy, OwO

(Fig. 4) was proposed, which involved combining off-negotiating with on-matching and on-rating. Based on this strategy, a hypothesis was formulated, suggesting that ORPs following the OwO design strategy could enhance the better user experience for both migrant workers and recruiters. To evaluate this hypothesis, the success criteria of ORPs for migrant workers (Fig. 5) were established for the subsequent evaluation in the DS-II phase.

2.3 Comprehensive PS

In this stage, following the OwO design strategy, the two touchpoints, the D-dong labour app and the D-dong labour station were developed. The service blueprints (Fig. 6) consist of three stages: prior-service, in-service, and post-service. In the prior-service phase, users can complete employment activities through the app's three navigation interfaces: Match, Stations and Profile. In the in-service phase, the station provides users with a waiting area for offline negotiation before proceeding to the final work site. In the post-service phase, the app facilitates rating and profiling between workers and recruiters.

The online mobile application (Fig. 7) provides users with three main functions: Recruit/Job search, Recruit Boards and Profile. Based on the user interviews, the work skills obtained by migrant workers were categorized into five types: builder (35%), electrician (20%), handyman (20%), mechanic (15%), and carpenter (10%). The types of work were reflected in the app's recruit boards that provide users with recruiting details about the station. The offline stations (Fig. 8), located at urban transport hubs, provide users with small and recognizable service stations that offer to negotiate and wait for space. The locations of the stations (i.e. on the street, under the GSJ and around the square) were strategically designed to align with the habits of migrant workers. The activity lines show that both workers and recruiters come to the station to check the information on the display screen and then wait on the station benches, and subsequently engage in negotiation before travelling to the final work site together.

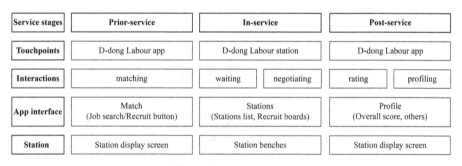

Service stages	Prior-service	In-service		Post-service	
Touchpoints	D-dong Labour app	D-dong Labour station		D-dong Labour app	
Interactions	matching	waiting	negotiating	rating	profiling
App interface	Match (Job search/Recruit button)	Stations (Stations list, Recruit boards)		Profile (Overall score, others)	
Station	Station display screen	Station benches		Station display screen	

Fig. 6. Service blueprints

2.4 Comprehensive DS-II

In this stage, a comprehensive usability evaluation was conducted using the System Usability Scale (SUS) to assess the D-dong Labour touchpoints. Brooke [10] introduced

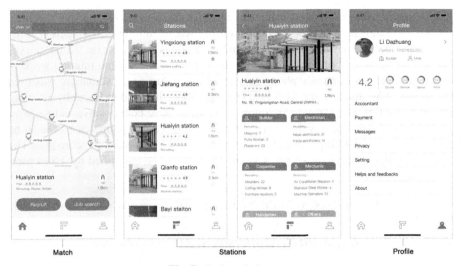

Fig. 7. D-dong Labour app

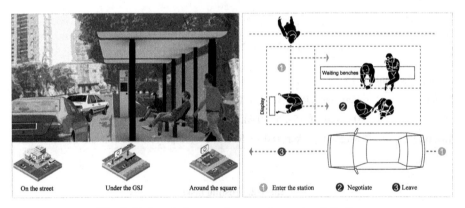

Fig. 8. D-dong Labour station overview and activity lines

the SUS, a ten-item scale subjective assessment of usability in 1996. He mentioned the SUS items (01–10) measure the usability of products, covering effectiveness, efficiency and satisfaction. In addition to this, Alqahtani, F. et al. [11] evaluated the user's engagement with a self-guided mental well-being app by using SUS. Therefore, the success criteria established in the DS-I stage with three measures (i.e. engagement, ease of use and satisfaction) can be roughly assessed by using SUS. To assess the three measures, it was defined that SUS01 corresponded to engagement, SUS03, SUS04 and SUS07 corresponded to ease of use, and SUS08-10 corresponded to satisfaction.

A total of 15 participants (Table 1), including 12 migrant workers and three recruiters, were asked to join the test. The testing tasks are detailed in Table 2, and it is worth noting that the task of offline negotiation at D-dong Labour station was conducted at bus stop stations using scenario simulation. The SUS questionnaire of D-dong Labour consisting of ten items and five-point Likert scales was designed based on the standard SUS. Table 3 presents the English version of the questionnaire, where odd-numbered items (i.e. 01, 03, 05, 07, 09) have positive descriptions and even-numbered items (i.e. 02, 04, 06, 08, 10) have negative descriptions. To ensure the participation of some migrant workers with limited access to mobile phones, a paper-based Chinese questionnaire was used for the test. After the test, the SUS data (n = 15) was computed in Excel by adopting the following Eqs. (1), (2) and (3). Since the 10 items have both positive and negative descriptions, the raw scores that were collected from the five-point scale need to be calculated according to Eqs. (1) and (2) before calculating the total SUS score [12]. The maximum value of the total scores is 40, and it needs to be multiplied by 2.5 to get a percentage scale [10].

$$SUS01/SUS03/SUS05/SUS07/SUS09 = raw\ score - 1 \qquad (1)$$

$$SUS02/SUS04/SUS06/SUS08/SUS10 = 5 - raw\ score \qquad (2)$$

$$Total\ SUS = 2.5(SUS01 + SUS02 + \ldots + SUS10) \qquad (3)$$

Table 1. Participants' demographic information.

Total participants = 15	
Gender	Females (20%), Males (80%)
Age	0–14 (0%), 15–25 (20%), 26–45 (27%), 46–60 (53%), 60–(0%)
Identities	Migrant workers (80%), Recruiters (employers and citizens, 20%)

Table 2. Testing tasks.

Task	Interactions	Touchpoints
Task1	On-matching (click Job search/Recruit, select the station, and navigate to the station)	D-dong Labour app
Task2	Off-negotiating (check station display, wait, negotiate, leave)	D-dong Labour station (scenario simulation)
Task3	On-rating (rate and check profiles)	D-dong Labour app

Table 3. SUS questionnaire of D-dong Labour.

		Strongly Disagree			Strongly agree	
		1	2	3	4	5
01	I think that I would like to use the D-Dong Labour frequently	☐	☐	☐	☐	☐
02	I found the D-Dong Labour unnecessarily complex	☐	☐	☐	☐	☐
03	I thought the D-Dong Labour was easy to use	☐	☐	☐	☐	☐
04	I think that I would need the support of a technical person to be able to use the D-Dong Labour	☐	☐	☐	☐	☐
05	I found the various functions in the D-Dong Labour were well integrated	☐	☐	☐	☐	☐
06	I think there was too much inconsistency in the D-Dong Labour	☐	☐	☐	☐	☐
07	I would imagine that most people would learn to use the D-Dong Labour very quickly	☐	☐	☐	☐	☐
08	I found the D-Dong Labour very awkward to use	☐	☐	☐	☐	☐
09	I felt very confident using the D-Dong Labour	☐	☐	☐	☐	☐
10	I needed to learn a lot of things before I could get going with the D-Dong Labour	☐	☐	☐	☐	☐

3   Results

Figure 9 illustrates the total SUS scores of D-dong Labour among 15 participants, consisting of 12 migrant workers and 3 recruiters, ranging from 62.5 to 90. The mean score for all participants (n = 15) was 72.8, corresponding to Grade B- on the Sauro-Lewis curved grading scale (CGS) [13]. In the empirical evaluation of SUS by Bangor, A. et al. [14], the scores fell within the 2nd quartile and good acceptability ranges. By calculating the mean scores between the two groups, it was found that recruiters (n = 3) gave a higher score of 80, while migrant workers (n = 12) scored 71.

Figure 10 presents the mean values and standard deviation (SD) values of raw scores for the 10 individual items among the 15 participants. Table 4 presents Sauro-Lewis item benchmarks for SUS = 68 (average experience) and SUS = 80 (good experience) [15]. According to the benchmarks, SUS01 achieved a mean score of 3.87, precisely corresponding to a SUS score of 80, thus verifying high engagement. Both SUS03 and SUS07 corresponded to a SUS score of 80, with mean scores of 4.27 and 4.20. However, SUS04 obtained a score of 2.47, which exceeded the upper limit of the target scores. Thus, only SUS03 and SUS07 can verify the ease of use of the touchpoints. SUS09 achieved a score of 4.27, corresponding to a SUS score of 80, while SUS08 and SUS10 obtained scores of 2.00 and 2.40, respectively, exceeding the upper limit of the target score of 80 and 68. As a result, only SUS09 can confirm user satisfaction with the touchpoints.

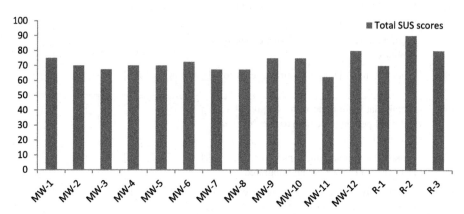

Fig. 9. Total SUS scores from 15 participants

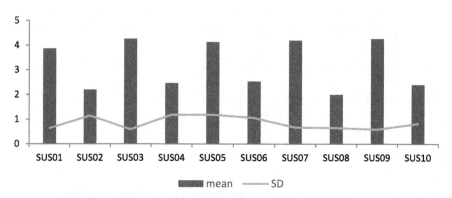

Fig. 10. The mean and SD of raw scores for individual items

Table 4. SUS Item Benchmarks for SUS = 68 and SUS = 80

	lower	Target for SUS = 68	upper	lower	Target for SUS = 80	upper
SUS01	3.30	≥3.39	3.47	3.69	≥3.80	3.90
SUS02	2.42	≤2.44	2.48	1.81	≤1.85	1.89
SUS03	3.64	≥3.67	3.71	4.21	≥4.24	4.28
SUS04	1.80	≤1.85	1.90	1.45	≤1.51	1.57

(*continued*)

Table 4. (*continued*)

	lower	Target for SUS = 68	upper	lower	Target for SUS = 80	upper
SUS05	3.51	≥3.55	3.58	3.92	≥3.96	4.01
SUS06	2.16	≤2.20	2.23	1.73	≤1.77	1.82
SUS07	3.68	≥3.71	3.74	4.15	≥4.19	4.23
SUS08	2.21	≤2.25	2.28	1.61	≤1.66	1.70
SUS09	3.68	≥3.72	3.75	4.21	≥4.25	4.29
SUS10	2.05	≤2.09	2.14	1.59	≤1.64	1.71

4 Discussion

Overall, the results indicate positive feedback for D-dong Labour, indicating that the touchpoints developed based on the OwO design strategy successfully aligned with the success criteria of ORPs and provided migrant workers with a better user experience. Although the total SUS mean score of D-dong Labour did not reach an excellent grade, the individual items' results revealed high levels of engagement and perceived ease of use among the users.

Based on the total SUS results, recruiters generally gave higher scores than migrant workers, indicating a better user experience for recruiters on D-dong Labour touchpoints. One possible reason for this discrepancy is the less well-integrated functions on touchpoints for migrant workers and the limited number of participants in the two groups. In future work, based on in-depth interviews in the second DS-I phase, the functions of D-dong Labour will be redesigned in the second PS phase to better cater to the needs of migrant workers. Additionally, the sample size will be expanded to include 50–70 participants, allowing for a more comprehensive evaluation in the second DS-II phase. This iterative process aims to enhance the user experience and address any existing limitations identified in the study.

Based on the individual SUS item results, D-dong Labour demonstrated close alignment with the success criteria for high engagement, ease of use, and acceptable satisfaction. Specifically, the engagement and ease of use aspects received stronger confirmation compared to user satisfaction. One possible explanation is that the offline negotiation process at the simulated station may contribute to an awkward user experience. Furthermore, during the SUS test, migrant workers were required to complete regulated tasks and adhere to instructions, which may have influenced their overall satisfaction. In future work, the implementation of an actual station in the second PS phase will be explored to provide a more realistic user experience on touchpoints. Additionally, the flexibility of the app test in the second DS-II phase will be taken into consideration. This will allow for a more comprehensive evaluation of the system and address any limitations identified during the study.

5   Conclusions

This study introduces the OwO design strategy, a novel approach to developing recruitment service systems to enhance the user experience. The proposed D-dong labour touchpoints were evaluated for their effectiveness in improving the user experience, as evidenced by high scores in individual items, namely SUS01, SUS03, SUS04, SUS07, and SUS08-SUS10, reflecting a high level of engagement, ease of use, and overall satisfaction. This study addresses the issue of low engagement on ORPs among migrant workers, filling a gap in the existing literature on user experience research for this particular segment. The findings of this study contribute to the field in several ways. Firstly, the proposed OwO design strategy has the potential to enhance product quality for ORP companies and assist public services in making decisions to minimize unemployment risks and market irregularities. Secondly, the developed touchpoints promote active participation from both migrant workers and recruiters in the ongoing digital transformation of labour markets. Finally, the insights gained from the observation in the Huaiyin MWSC of Jinan provide valuable perspectives for future studies in diverse labour markets in other regions. Overall, the study provides insights and inspiration for future work in designing ORPs with improved user experiences for both internal (rural-to-urban) and international (country-to-country) migrant workers.

Funding.   This study was funded by the key project of Shandong University Education Teaching Reform Research [2022Z46]. This information is available upon request.

References

1. Li, L., Mo, Y., Zhou, G.: Platform economy and China's labor market: structural transformation and policy challenges. China Econ. J. **15**, 139–152 (2022). https://doi.org/10.1080/175 38963.2022.2067685
2. Wakabayashi, K.: Migration from rural to urban areas in China. Dev. Econ. **28**, 503–523 (1990). https://doi.org/10.1111/j.1746-1049.1990.tb00195.x
3. Blessing, L.T.M., Chakrabarti, A.: DRM, A Design Research Methodology. Springer, London (2009). https://doi.org/10.1007/978-1-84882-587-1
4. Toksöz, G., Erdoğdu, S., Kaşka, S.: Irregular Labour Migration in Turkey and Situation of Migrant Workers in the Labour Market. International Organization for Migration Ankara (2012)
5. Hall, R.E., Lazear, E.P.: The excess sensitivity of layoffs and quits to demand. J. Law Econ. **2**, 233–257 (1984)
6. Katz, E., Stark, O.: International migration under asymmetric information. Econ. J. **97**, 718 (1987). https://doi.org/10.2307/2232932
7. Adams, J., Greig, M., McQuaid, R.W.: Mismatch unemployment and local labour-market efficiency: the role of employer and vacancy characteristics. Environ. Plan. A **32**, 1841–1856 (2000). https://doi.org/10.1068/a3342
8. Rosoiu, O., Popescu, C.: E-recruiting platforms: features that influence the efficiency of online recruitment systems. IE **20**, 46–55 (2016). https://doi.org/10.12948/issn14531305/20.2.201 6.05
9. Afnan, T., Rabaan, H., Jones, K.M.L., Dombrowski, L.: Asymmetries in online job-seeking: a case study of Muslim-American women. Proc. ACM Hum. Comput. Interact. **5**, 1–29 (2021). https://doi.org/10.1145/3479548

10. Brooke, J.: SUS: a "quick and dirty" usability scale. In: Usability Evaluation in Industry. CRC Press (1996)
11. Alqahtani, F., Alslaity, A., Orji, R.: Usability testing of a gratitude application for promoting mental well-being. In: Kurosu, M. (ed.) Human-Computer Interaction. User Experience and Behavior. pp. 296–312. Springer, Cham (2022). https://doi.org/10.1007/978-3-031-05412-9_21
12. Lewis, J.R.: The system usability scale: past, present, and future. Int. J. Hum. Comput. Interact. **34**, 577–590 (2018). https://doi.org/10.1080/10447318.2018.1455307
13. Sauro, J., Lewis, J.R.: Quantifying the User Experience: Practical Statistics for User Research. Morgan Kaufmann (2016)
14. Bangor, A., Kortum, P.T., Miller, J.T.: An empirical evaluation of the system usability scale. Int. J. Hum. Comput. Interact. **24**, 574–594 (2008). https://doi.org/10.1080/104473108022 05776
15. Lewis, J.R., Sauro, J.: Item benchmarks for the system usability scale. J. Usabil. Stud. **13** (2018)

Author Index

A

An, Zhixuan   389
Armayuda, Erik   523
Avitouv, Nitzan   3

B

Babajic, Dzenan   461
Bækgaard, Per   213
Bai, He   444
Bardram, Jakob E.   213
Birkle, Jonas   461
Blundell, James   351
Brandt, Adam   83

C

Cao, Ying   272
Chakraborty, Sutirtha   335
Chen, Qi   37
Cho, Min Ho   16
Clark, Alexander   491
Colabrese, Silvia   155
Collins, Charlotte   351

D

Dai, Xufeng   426
Dong, Haoyu   37
Du, Le   37
Du, Zhifang   536
Duffy, Vincent G.   16, 491

E

Ebreso, Uko   179

F

Fala, Nicoletta   444
Fann, Shih-Cheng   54
Fisher, Alexander   179
Fu, Haoruo   408
Fussell, Susan R.   142

G

Gong, Rongrong   67
Gorgel Pinto, António   552
Grant, Rebecca   476
Guedes, Leandro Soares   564

H

Hacioglu, Naile   363
Han, Wanrong   378
Harris, Don   351
Hazel, Spencer   83
Hu, Xinhui   101
Hua, Min   67, 670
Huang, Zixuan   272
Huddlestone, John   351

I

Ikeuchi, Kana   126

J

Jansen, Bernard   288
Jung, Soon-gyo   288

K

Kinoe, Yosuke   126
Koch, Tobias   461
Korek, Wojciech Tomasz   508

L

Landoni, Monica   564
Lee, Hyowon   363
Leva, Maria Chiara   363
Li, Helin   585
Li, Shoupeng   378
Li, Wen-Chin   508
Li, Xiaoyan   142
Liao, Yingyu   259
Liu, Shijun   635
Liu, Yi   619

Lu, Chien-Tsung 408
Lu, Tingting 389

M

Mahardika, Ratih 523
Matsuura, Yasuyuki 168
Mazur, Sergei 461
Mele, Maria Laura 155
Millar, Damon 155
Moreira da Rosa, Diego 564
Morreale, Patricia 179
Murungi, Nathan Koome 426

N

Nakane, Kohki 168
Nakayama, Meiho 168
Nakladal, Solveig 461
Nielsen, Lene 288
Nurrul Haq, Bayyinah 523

P

Pagliari, Romano 389
Patel, Pankati 179
Pei, Yuying 194
Persson, Dan Roland 213
Pham, Michael Vinh 426
Porter, Chris 238

Q

Qian, Fan 323
Qin, Qianhang 259
Qiu, Shuwen 272
Qu, Xiaodong 426

R

Rangga Putra, Damar 523
Ravi Kamalraj, Andrew 16
Reaes Pinto, Paula 552

S

Saka, Emmanuel K. 575
Salminen, Joni 288
Santos, João M. 288
Şengün, Sercan 288
Shen, Haiming 389
Shen, Wenhao 585
Shevtsova, Yulia G. 311
Shiozawa, Tomoki 168

Shishkin, Sergei L. 311
Silveira, Milene 564
Skinner, Timothy C. 213
Song, Fanghao 670
Sugie, Rintaro 168

T

Tabassum, Asma 444
Takada, Hiroki 168
Tian, Wenda 259
Timoney, Joseph 335
Twidale, Michael 101

V

Vasilyev, Anatoly N. 311

W

Wagner-Hartl, Verena 461
Wang, Chunyan 604
Wang, Gengyi 259
Wang, Linlin 194
Wang, Luo 657
Wang, Wei 37
Wang, Xinyue 378
Wang, Yan 323
Wang, Yulin 670
Whitworth, Benjamin 476
Wood, Anastasia 491

X

Xiao, Xiaoxin 604
Xiao, Yong 536
Xiao, Yuxuan 619
Xu, Yinjuan 635
Xu, Zhelu 619
Xue, Chengqi 194, 378

Y

Yang, Yijing 37
Yang, Zheng 389
Yaseen, Azeema 335
Yin, Taoran 408
Yoo, Soojeong 213
Yu, Ganyi 645
Yuan, Xiaojun 604

Z

Zammit, Gary 238

Zeng, Chunlan   645
Zhang, Jingyi   508
Zhang, Jun   37
Zhang, Xinrui   657

Zhang, Yiyang   389
Zhao, Zhiqin   585
Zhou, Hangyu   670
Zhou, Youtian   259

Printed in the United States
by Baker & Taylor Publisher Services